THE FEDERAL REPUBLIC OF GERMANY AT
FORTY-FIVE

Also by Peter H. Merkl

AMERICAN DEMOCRACY IN WORLD PERSPECTIVE (*co-author*)
DEVELOPMENTS IN GERMAN POLITICS (*co-editor*)
DEVELOPMENTS IN WEST GERMAN POLITICS (*co-editor*)
ENCOUNTERS WITH THE RADICAL RIGHT (*co-editor*)
THE FEDERAL REPUBLIC AT FORTY (*editor*)
GERMAN FOREIGN POLICIES, WEST AND EAST
GERMAN UNIFICATION IN THE EUROPEAN CONTEXT
GERMANY: Yesterday and Tomorrow
THE MAKING OF A STORMTROOPER
MODERN COMPARATIVE POLITICS
NEW LOCAL CENTERS IN CENTRALIZED STATES (*editor*)
ORIGIN OF THE WEST GERMAN REPUBLIC
THE POLITICS OF ECONOMIC CHANGE IN POSTWAR JAPAN
    AND WEST GERMANY (*co-editor*)
POLITICAL CONTINUITY AND CHANGE
POLITICAL VIOLENCE AND TERROR: Motifs and Motivation
    (*editor*)
POLITICAL VIOLENCE UNDER THE SWASTIKA: 581 Early Nazis
RELIGION AND POLITICS IN THE MODERN WORLD (*co-editor*)
WEST GERMAN FOREIGN POLICY: Dilemmas and Directions
    (*editor*)
WESTERN EUROPEAN PARTY SYSTEMS: Trends and Projects (*editor*)
WHEN PARTIES FAIL: Emerging Alternative Organization (*co-editor*)
WHO WERE THE FASCISTS? Social Roots of European Fascism
    (*co-editor*)

The Federal Republic of Germany at Forty-Five

Union without Unity

Edited by

Peter H. Merkl
Professor Emeritus
Department of Political Science
University of California, Santa Barbara

 NEW YORK UNIVERSITY PRESS
Washington Square, New York

Selection, editorial matter, Introduction and Conclusion
© Peter H. Merkl 1995
Chapters 1–14, 16–22 © New York University Press 1995
Chapter 15 first appeared in *German Politics* (vol. 1, no. 1, 1992,
pp. 13–30) and is reprinted with kind permission.

First published in the U.S.A. in 1995 by
NEW YORK UNIVERSITY PRESS
Washington Square
New York, N.Y. 10003

Library of Congress Cataloging-in-Publication Data
The Federal Republic of Germany at Forty-Five : union without unity /
edited by Peter H. Merkl.
p.   cm.
Includes bibliographical references and index.
ISBN 0–8147–5514–3 — ISBN 0–8147–5515–1 (pbk.)
1. Germany—Politics and government—1990-   2. Germany—Social
conditions—1990-   I. Merkl, Peter H.
JN3972.A58F43 1995
943.087'9—dc20   94–7526
                                                         CIP

Printed in Great Britain

Contents

The Federal Republic of
Germany at forty-five

Contents

Notes on the Contributors

Thomas A. Baylis is Professor of Political Science, University of Texas at San Antonio and past President of GDR Studies Association. His publications include *The Technical Intelligentsia and the East German Elite* (1974), *Governing by Committee: Collegial Leadership in Advanced Societies* (1989), and *The West and Eastern Europe* (1994). Current Research is on elites and political executives in eastern Germany and East Central Europe.

Gerard Braunthal is Professor Emeritus of Political Science at the University of Massachusetts/Amherst and currently regional director/Northeast of the Conference Group on German Politics (CGGP). His publications on Germany include *The German Social Democrats Since 1969: A Party in Power and Opposition* (2nd ed., 1994) and *Political Loyalty and Public Service in West Germany: The 1972 Decree against Radicals and Its Consequences* (1990). His next major study surveys all German political parties, including an analysis of the 1994 elections.

William M. Chandler is Professor of Political Science at McMaster University, Canada. His research and teaching interests are based in European affairs and the comparative study of political parties, public policy and federalism. He has co-authored *Public Policy and Provincial Politics*, and co-edited, *Federalism and the Role of the State* and *Challenges to Federalism: Policy-Making in Canada and West Germany*. Recent research includes publications on party government, the Christian Democrats in Germany, party system change and immigration politics.

Werner J. Feld is a UNO distinguished Professor Emeritus of Political Science, and Director for Comparative Public Policy at the University of New Orleans. He is the author of *American Foreign Policy: Aspirations and Reality* (1984), *Congress and the National Defense* (with John K. Wildgen, 1985), *Arms Control and the Atlantic Community*, and the *Future of the European Security and Defense Policy* (1993). He is currently Adjunct Professor at the Graduate School of International Studies, University of Denver.

ix

Arthur B. Gunlicks is Professor of Political Science at the University of Richmond, Virginia. He is the author of numerous articles and book chapters on German government and politics and the editor of *Comparative Party and Campaign Finance in North America and Western Europe* (1993), co-editor with Rüdiger Voigt of *Föderalismus in der Bewährungsprobe: Die Bundesrepublik Deutschland in den 90er Jahren* (1991), and author of *Local Government in the German Federal System* (1986). His current research focus is on German federalism and political finance.

M. Donald Hancock is Professor of Political Science at Vanderbilt University and Director of its Center for European Studies. He is a specialist in comparative politics, with research interests in the political economy of Germany. Scandinavia, and the European Union and the author of *West Germany: The Politics of Democratic Corporatism* (1989), co-author and co-editor of *Managing Modern Capitalism: Industrial Renewal and Workplace Reform in the United States and Western Europe* (1991), and co-editor of *German Unification: Processes and Outcomes* (1994). He is a member of the European Union's U.S. 'Team Europe', past-chair of the Council for European Studies, immediate past-president of CGGP, and the editor of the CGGP Newsletter.

Arnold J. Heidenheimer is Professor of Political Science at Washington University, St. Louis. He has examined German policies in comparative perspective in books like *Comparative Public Policy: The Politics of Social Choice in Europe and America* (with Hugh Heclo and Carolyn T. Adams, 2nd edn 1983) and *The Development of Welfare States in Europe and America* (with P. Flora, 1981). He is currently engaged in a comparative study of education policy in Germany, Switzerland, and Japan.

Karl H. Kahrs is Professor of Political Science at the California State University, Fullerton. He has written on German politics and U.S.–German relations, for example, a monograph *Der Umbruch in Osteuropa in der Politik und öffentlichen Meinung der USA* (1990), and chapters, such as 'God help us if we lose' in *Children and War* (edited by D. Childs and J. Wharton, 1989). His current research focuses on questions of political economy.

Emil J. Kirchner is Professor in Government and Director of the Center for European Studies at the University of Essex. His publications on Germany are *The Federal Republic of Germany and NATO, 40 Years After* (edited with James Sperling), and *German Perspectives on the Future European Security Policy* (co-edited with Christoph Bluth and James Sperling). He is continuing his research on German foreign and security policy.

Gerald F. Kleinfeld is Professor of History at Arizona State University, Executive Director, German Studies Association, Director, Consortium for Atlantic Studies, Member, Executive Board, *Deutsch-Amerikanischer Arbeitskreis*. He is co-editor of *Yearbook on German-American Relations*, author of various articles on German–American relations and European–American relations, also on German political and social developments, security studies, integration and political economy.

Donald P. Kommers is the Joseph and Elizabeth Robbie Professor of Government and International Studies in the University of Notre Dame. He is also a member of the Notre Dame law faculty where he authored numerous articles and several books dealing with German politics, constitutionalism, and judicial politics, including *Judicial Politics in Germany* (1976) and *The Constitutional Jurisprudence of the Federal Republic of Germany* (1989). His most recent publication, *Germany and the Basic Law* (1993) was co-edited with Paul Kirchhof, Associate Justice of German's Federal Constitutional Court. He is currently preparing a second edition of *Constitutional Jurisprudence* and working on a project entitled 'Constitutional Politics in Germany'.

Gregg O. Kvistad is Associate Professor of Political Science at the University of Denver. His publications on Germany have appeared in *German Politics and Society*, *Comparative Political Studies*, and *West European Politics*. Current research interests include western German party discourse during the unification debate, and citizenship and xenophobia in united Germany.

A. James McAdams is Associate Professor of Government and Faculty Fellow of the Kellogg Institute for International Studies at the University of Notre Dame. He is the author of *Germany Divided: From the Wall to Reunification* and *East Germany and Détente*, as well as co-author of *Rebirth: A History of Europe Since World War II*. He is currently working on the political uses of the past and the transition to democracy.

Andrei S. Markovits is Professor in and Chair of the Board of Politics at the University of California, Santa Cruz. He has published many books, articles and reviews on various aspects of European and German politics, most notably on social democracy, the left, labor, anti-Americanism, and German–Jewish relations. His most recent publications include *The German Left: Red, Green and Beyond* (1993) with Philip Gorski; and *From Bundesrepublik to Deutschland: German Politics after Unification* (1993) co-edited with Michael Huelshoff and Simon Reich. Professor Markovits is also the editor of the journal *German Politics and Society*.

Peter H. Merkl is Professor Emeritus of Political Science at the University of California, Santa Barbara, where he still teaches part-time. A past president of CGGP, he is still active in the International Sociological and Political Science Associations. Recent books are *German Unification in the European Context* (1993), and *Encounters with the Contemporary Radical Right. The Politics of Economic Change in Postwar Japan and West Germany* (with H. Fukui, co-ed., 1993). He is currently engaged in comparative research on political generations and on right-wing extremist movements in Germany, Italy and France.

Joyce Marie Mushaben is Associate Professor of Political Science, Women's Studies, and Research Fellow in the Center for International Studies at the University of Missouri-St. Louis. A former DAAD-Fulbright scholar, Alexander von Humboldt Fellow and Ford Foundation Fellow in GDR studies, her publications focus on peace, feminist, and ecology movements, German national identity and right-wing radicalism. Her book, *The Post-Postwar Generations: Changing Attitudes towards the National Question and NATO in the Federal Republic of Germany, 1949–1989* will appear in late 1994. Two others on *Russia and the New Republics* and *Women and Democratization in Eastern Europe*, are in the pipeline.

Simon Reich is Associate Professor at the Graduate School of Public and International Affairs, University of Pittsburgh, Pennsylvania. He is the author of *The Fruits of Fascism: Postwar Prosperity in Historical Perspective* (1990), and co-editor (with Michael Huelshoff and Andrei Markovits) of *From Bundesrepublik to Deutschland: German Politics After Unification* (1993). He has also published several articles and book chapters on Germany including 'The Latest Stage of the German Question: Pax Germanica in the New Europe', *Arms Control*

December 1991 (with Andrei S. Markovits), 'Modell Deutschland and the New Europe', *Telos*, Fall 1991 (with Andrei S. Markovits) and 'Fascism and the Structure of German Capitalism: The Case of the Automobile Industry' in Volker Berghahn, ed., *German Capitalism in the Twentieth Century* (forthcoming).

Marilyn Rueschemeyer is Professor of Sociology at the Rhode Island School of Design and also holds an appointment at Brown University. Her publications on Germany include *Professional Work and Marriage: An East-West Comparison: The Quality of Life in the GDR* (edited with D. Childs and T. Baylis). Most recently, she edited *Women in the Politics of Post-Communist Eastern Europe*. Rueschemeyer chaired for several years the GDR Study Group at Harvard's Center for European Studies and presently is a Fellow at Harvard's Russian Research Center.

Donald Schoonmaker is Professor of Political Science at Wake Forest University, died May 19, 1993. He wrote sensitively on what political scientists can learn from the arts, as in 'Novelist and Social Scientist: Contrasting Views of Today's West German Political System', *Polity* (Spring 1982), and on the Greens. Recent publications are *The West German Greens: Between Protest and Power* (with Gene Frankland, 1993) and *Preludes and Postludes in English Romanticism* (with John Alford, 1992). He was president-elect of CGGP at the time of his death.

Gordon Smith is Professor Emeritus of Government at the London School of Economics. He is the author of *Politics in Western Europe* (5th edition, 1989) and co-editor of *Developments in German Politics* (1992). He is also co-editor of the two journals: *West European Politics* and *German Politics*.

James Sperling is Associate Professor of Political Science at the University of Akron. His publications on Germany include *Britain and Germany in the New Europe: British and German Perspectives on the Future European Security Policy* (co-edited with Christoph Bluth and Emil J. Kirchner) and *The Federal Republic of Germany and NATO: Forty Years After* (co-edited with Emil J. Kirchner). He has also published several articles on German security and foreign economic policies in *Arms Control, German Politics*, and *West European Politics*. He is currently co-authoring books on the emerging European security order and on weapons technology transfers to the Third World.

Ian Wallace is Professor of German and Head of the School of Modern Languages and International Studies at the University of Bath (England). Founding editor (1979) of the journal *GDR Monitor*. Recent publications include *DDR-Schriftsteller sprechen in der Zeit* (co-edited with Gerd Labroisse); *The German Revolution of 1989* (co-edited with Gert-Joachim Glaessner); and *Berlin*. He is currently preparing a book on Anna Seghers.

Helga A. Welsh is Assistant Professor of Political Science at Wake Forest University. She specializes in European politics and has published in the areas of German history and politics and East European affairs. Recent publications on Germany are *German Unification, Process and Outcomes* (co-edited with M. Donald Hancock) and 'The Divided Past and Difficulties of German Unification' (*German Politics and Society*, Fall 1993). Her current research focuses on political elite changes in times of transitions.

Introduction: Reinventing German National Identity

Peter H. Merkl

'Your book will deal with a very different Federal Republic than any of us could have imagined possible in 1988', as one of the contributors of *The Federal Republic at Forty* (1989), Christian Soe, put it succinctly to me. He was writing under the shadow of the dramatic pictures and headlines of November 1992 – about neo-Nazi and skinhead attacks on foreigners and the massive anti-racist demonstrations that followed – and hoped that Germany would presently overcome that crisis of image and identity. The interval between 1989 and 1994 has indeed brought such extraordinary changes to Germany and Europe as to make the previous 40 years of Cold War existence seem deceptively placid and well-ordered by comparison.

The collapse of communist rule in Eastern Europe, including the East German republic (GDR), the fall of the Berlin Wall and of Soviet control over East Germany in the midst of massive demonstrations against the régime in late 1989 was only the beginning. There followed in short succession the popular turn in the GDR from the goal of a separate, reform communist state (presumably with some democratic trimmings) to an electoral mandate for unification with the old West German Federal Republic[1] (January–March 1990), the Economic and Currency Union (July 1) which to many East German voters was probably a great attraction in contrast to the bankrupt and polluted economy the communists had left behind, and actual political unification (October 3) under a unification Treaty and following the democratic re-establishment of East German *Länder* (states) and their accession to the West German FRG. All through these hectic nine months, the four great powers, the Soviet Union, Great Britain, the United States, and France were meeting with the two German governments in a series of Two-plus-Four conferences to work out agreements to liquidate the remnants of the German occupation status and give united Germany the sovereign autonomy it had not possessed for nearly half a century.[2] The new nation state was then free to choose its allies and to attempt new economic relationships within the processes of European integration – scheduled to intensify with the

1

Maastricht Treaty of 1991 – and with regard to the post-communist countries of Eastern Europe.

A CHANGED INTERNATIONAL CONTEXT

In the context of the sudden death of the Cold War and of the Soviet (or Warsaw Pact) threat which had literally created both the Moscow-aligned GDR and the old FRG with its American, NATO, and European (EC) orientation, this was a major earthquake that could not but affect all notions of German identity, both inside and outside the now unified area. 'There are, of course, those who believe that at the end of the unification process there will simply be the same familiar FRG, extending a bit farther east', one of this volume's authors, Karl Kahrs, wrote to me in a letter, but he doubted it very much. Andrei Markovits and Simon Reich review the external reactions to unified Germany below (Chapter 1) and there can be no mistaking a certain negative tinge in how Germany's European neighbours now view the Germans. Unlike Americans, they fear the sheer size and emerging power of Germany even though public opinion polls on German unification were quite positive in most countries except for Britain, Poland, and some of the smaller countries occupied by German troops in World War Two.[3] Historical memories naturally play a big role in these perceptions, even if they are the synthetic memories of contemporary television and other fiction. So do longstanding popular prejudices as among many Latin nations against the *brutta gente* north of the Alps, or the 'imperial envy' of the Britons against the upstart Germans. The Nicholas Ridley Affair and Prime Minister Margaret Thatcher's secret Chequers Seminar of 1990[4] revealed the deep apprehensions of the Thatcher government about German unification and sovereignty. The Mitterrand government too, in spite of French polls showing popular support for German unification, felt that three decades of good Franco-German relations were put in jeopardy by the collapse of communism and of the GDR, and that a unified Germany with vast economic leverage in newly independent Eastern Europe was at last slipping dangerously out of French control. In this dilemma, French leaders hoped that a 'deepening' of European integration might still put a bridle on united German ambitions, given the degree of past West German commitment to European unification. In a phrase reminiscent of the hope that 'Prussia would dissolve into Germany' of 120 years earlier, the 'Europeanization of Germany' was supposed to contain the dangers of German hegemony in Europe.

If the enlarged size of united Germany was the chief object of European fears, Czechoslovak civil rights leader and president, Vaclav Havel, struck a countervailing note when he said that he felt no anxiety as long as a united Germany would remain as reliably democratic as the old FRG had been. Opposition Labour party leader Shimon Peres of Israel which had maintained a special relationship to the FRG ever since the 1952 compensation agreements, said the same thing, and so did former Labour Prime Minister James Callaghan of Britain. The Eastern Europeans, including successor states of the Soviet Union (particularly the Russian Federation) now looked to unified Germany for massive aid and trade as well as technology transfer. One could even say that suddenly the memory of World War Two conquests by German and Austrian armies appeared to count far less in Eastern and Central Europe than the pre-Nazi and pre-1918 patterns of the Hapsburg and Prussian empires.[5] The collapse of Soviet and communist might, particularly recreated the old cultural and geopolitical bonds of Hapsburg, but this time pitting Germany and Austria in rivalry against each other, the latter now politically more popular, but the former clearly in an economically hegemonial position. It was eerie to see something like the pre-1914 and pre-1939 situations restored in the East,[6] strategic situations that had led to the 30 years of all-out world wars, 1914–1945. Nevertheless, there was no fear of a German military resurgence among East European countries which welcomed German aid and investment. Even Poland soon counted a 60 per cent German share among its foreign investments and obtained German forgiveness of much of its foreign debt, and this despite some initial friction over recognition of the Oder-Neisse border and Polish concessions to the German minority in Poland.[7] Fortunately, the large German minorities that had lived all over Eastern Europe before 1939 had mostly been expelled to the rest of Germany in 1944–47, some 15 million of them, thereby removing the incentive for pan-German expansion that runs like a red thread from the pre-1914 pan-German aspirations to Hitler's brutal campaign to regain the lost Hapsburg and Prussian Eastern territories – and add to them a great deal more.[8] By today, little is left of the German irredentist diaspora in Eastern Europe, especially since the collapse of communist regimes has also permitted ethnic Germans left in Romania, Russia, and elsewhere to opt for immigration to Germany as *Aussiedler* (emigrants).

The most extreme visions of the identity of a united Germany were raised by the writer Conor Cruise O'Brien who in *The Times* (October 31, 1989) predicted the rise of 'a Fourth *Reich*' that might 'rehabilitate racial theories' and erect a Hitler monument in every town. In November 1989, Israeli Likud Prime Minister Yitzak Shamir also expressed the fear on American television that 'a strong and united Germany might again try to annihilate the Jewish people'. He was echoed by former Defence Minister, Ariel Sharon, who said, 'we must not forget what the Germans did to us when they were united'. Neither one explained exactly how the unification of West and East Germany – particularly without Austria or any of the old German minority areas of the East, such as the Sudetenland or the Polish Oder-Neisse area – might lead to such horrendous outcomes. The Jewish World Congress, meeting in 1990 in Berlin at the site of the infamous Wannsee Conference which 50 years earlier had planned the 'final solution to the Jewish question', the holocaust of European Jews, also took a rather guarded view of German unification. Other Israeli and Jewish spokespersons, as mentioned earlier, took a less alarmist view, such as the German-Israeli historian Michael Wolffsohn who, in his book *No Need to Fear Germany* (*Keine Angst vor Deutschland*) argued that the German division had been the result of 'rivalries of power politics and ideology' and not of a moral judgment against the Germans, and that there was no logical connection between Auschwitz and German unification.

GERMAN ATTITUDES TOWARDS UNIFICATION

The German themselves were far from united in their reactions to the sudden prospect of unification even though they had supported it, four out of five, over four decades of West German polls. Studies of East German opinion have also pinpointed a strong early commitment to unification – certainly until the seventies when the GDR government emphatically moved to create an East German national identity, and probably even beyond that – long before the East German demonstrators switched from the slogan 'We are the people' to 'We are *one* people' in November–December 1989. However, polls of West Germans and East Germans also featured a 'reality test' in which the respondents were asked whether or how soon they actually expected German unification to come about. By 1968, only 13 per cent of West Germans and, by 1987, only 3 per cent anticipated that it would happen in the foreseeable future[9] and this undoubtedly encouraged the Brandt government in 1969–71 to embark on its policies of détente (*Ostpolitik*) with the governments of the Soviet Union, Poland, and Czechoslovakia.

When the Wall came down in 1989, it took the East Germans only a few months to rally to the cause of German unification. As their commitment to a 'socialist alternative' faded, advocates of unification with West Germany rose from 48 per cent (November 1989), to 79 per cent by the end of January and 84 per cent by February and March of 1990. The West Germans, by comparison, were far more lukewarm on this issue. After initial enthusiasm about the collapse of the Wall, their support level of 70–75 per cent began to leave a sizeable minority of 25–30 per cent indifferent or opposed to what had been supposed to be the national desideratum of the century (East Germans by then supported it more than 9 to 1). West German reservations ranged from a lack of national pride and identification, especially among the young, to resentment of having to pay higher taxes or forgoing the environmental agenda dear to the opposition parties of the old FRG.[10] Far from the raving nationalist euphoria predicted by Conor Cruise O'Brien, many younger West Germans found the East Germans no closer to their hearts than, say, the French or the Italians. They regarded the exuberant emotions of some older Germans with considerable suspicion and the financial burdens of unity as an outrageous imposition upon their own prosperity.[11] They looked on the Ossis (East Germans), who wanted to be welcomed as long-lost brothers, merely as distant cousins, and the more distant, the better.

Given this dissensus and the astronomical cost to West Germans of rehabilitating the East German economy, a deep post-unification malaise set in on both sides of what used to be the Iron Curtain through the middle of Germany. Wessis (West Germans) and Ossis learned to dislike each other, and the latter began to retreat into a pervasive nostalgia about the bad old times of the GDR, a *Trotzidentität* (Jens Reich), or 'identity of spite'. They simply did not want to hear any more about all that was said to be wrong with their economy, their environment, their working morale. What could be worse, indeed, than to listen to an arrogant *Besserwessi*[12] telling them that they just did not know how to work hard. By mid–1992, in fact, a Committee for Justice was formed for East Germany by two prominent East German politicians, Gregor Gysi (PDS) and Peter Michael Diestel (DSU), to defend the interests of East Germans against West German discrimination and exploitation. Well-known writers like Stefan Heym and other notables joined the group. The West Germans had their own route of escapism, betraying their own confusion about the consequences of the larger role of a united Germany in the world. Under the gathering storm clouds of the Gulf War, they responded to a survey of how they envisioned Germany in the year 2000: 40 per cent said 'like Switzerland' and another 27 'like Sweden', both prosperous and neutral small countries, far from the path of international confrontations.[13]

The gathering of the international strike force against Saddam Hussein, in mid-January 1991, triggered a massive wave of peace demonstrations, mostly by very young West Germans who seemingly put to rest any international apprehensions of a militarily aggressive Germany. Caught between the pacifists in parliament and in the streets and the demands of Germany's Western allies, the Kohl government chose to hide behind constitutional barriers – there was considerable controversy whether the Basic Law indeed prohibited Germany from sending troops to the Gulf – and contributed only money and token forces to the UN operation. The public debates over these issues, among other things, painfully split the entire German Left between pacifists and pro-Israeli interventionists. It also revealed the shocking extent to which parts of German industry had helped Saddam Hussein to arm his troops with weapons of mass destruction, including poison gas, that might have been employed against Israel.[14] Even though the debate over whether, or under what circumstances, a united Germany should participate in international peace enforcement actions has continued with varying results, the pronounced pacifism of the German public on this occasion clearly constitutes a major post-unification element of German identity.

Questions about the united country's sense of identity can also be answered with reference to public opinion polls about national pride and self-perception over the years. The Euro-Barometer, for example, asked West Germans in 1970 whether they felt 'very proud to be German' and received a positive response from only 38 per cent of the respondents, as compared to 66 per cent of French, 56 per cent of Britons, and 62 per cent of Italian respondents, with an EC average of 55 per cent. Another 33 per cent of West Germans were 'rather proud' (EC average 27 per cent); 23 per cent of West Germans were 'not very' or 'not at all proud' (EC average 13 per cent). During the peace demonstrations of the early eighties, the percentage of the not proud West Germans even climbed to 33 per cent, mirroring specially their 'postindustrial' attitudes and a low, historically-determined self-image.

Did the low level of national self-esteem change as a result of the longed-for unification, as some observers suggested? We can take the 1970 level of 71 per cent 'very' and 'rather proud' as our point of departure – in the turbulent eighties only 17–20 per cent expressed great and 47–53 per cent some pride – and note the recorded rise of West

German 'satisfaction with our democracy' between mid–1989 and mid–1990 from 73 per cent to 85 per cent in response to the failed communist system of the GDR.[15] Such satisfaction is not quite the same as national pride, but in any case, the level of 'very' and 'rather satisfied' promptly dropped to 78 per cent in 1991 and 65 per cent in 1992 (52 per cent and 48 per cent, respectively, in East Germany). For 1990 and 1991, there are also polls on national pride: In 1990, West Germans still have 70 per cent positive (as in 1989), although the per cent 'not proud' has risen from 10 per cent (1989) to 13 per cent. 79 per cent of East Germans, in spite of 40 years of communist indoctrination, pronounced themselves proud to be German. In 1991, the West German per cent 'proud to be German' had dropped to 65 per cent (16 per cent 'not proud') and those in East Germany to 70 per cent and 11 per cent not.[16] As compared to other Europeans, not to mention the flag-waving patriotism of Great Britain and the United States, this is hardly evidence for a revival of German nationalism.

A DIFFERENT EAST GERMAN IDENTITY

There still remains the question whether, perhaps, a virulent German nationalism has found a new home in the former GDR where higher levels of national identification and pride have indeed been reported. Is it possible that, after 40 years in the 'internationalist' communist deep freeze – when East Germans were neither properly re-educated about the failings of national socialism nor permitted to take any pride in their national identity – aggressive nationalism might rise again like a ghost from the crypts of the Third *Reich*.[17] In spite of some misleading impressions (see Chapter 23), this conclusion is quite wrong, even perverse. East German identity should be described instead as a sense of disorientation, of a great void in the values that governed their lives until 1990, a sense of marginality by the side of their well-ordered and prosperous West German cousins. Something died in the East, the faith in an alternative 'socialist' Germany better than the militaristic, exploitative Germany of history and, presumably, of Bonn under the thumbs of NATO and American capitalism. Instead of semifeudal and nationalist German history the communist founders and élites identified with the 16th century peasant wars, with the radical democratic tradition of 1848, the Paris Commune of 1879, Third World liberation movements and, of course, an idealised vision of twentieth century communist movements and states. And even though their early enthusiasm of the fifties faded into 'realistic socialism' (*real existierender Sozialismus*), that is bureaucratic authoritarianism, party rule, bosses, and corruption, their great propaganda machine kept on going and spreading the message in schools and public life – effective in spite of Stasi surveillance and repression – right up to the great disillusionment of 1989–90.[18]

It is not easy to describe the collapse of all the values learned in school and in public ceremonies – even by the sceptical, inward-turning Ossis of the eighties – in the midst of the dénouement of the communist economy which may take a decade to rebuild and adjust to the world market. Learning the depths of the failure of the proud industrial machine must have been as hard for the East Germans as, in 1918, for patriotic Germans to learn of the sudden collapse of their proud army after they had been lied to for so long by their generals and governors. The Ossis too reacted by looking beyond reason for scapegoats, in this case the West German 'takeover', manipulations of Western capitalists and politicians, or their own 'bloc parties' which had so quickly been co-opted by their West German equivalents. We do have polls on how the belief in 'socialism' (really communism) shrank from an adherence of three fourths of respondents in early December of 1989 to only half by the March 1990 elections to the *Volkskammer*. We can guess at its subsequent near-demise and transmutation into a nostalgia for a fraternal, friendly and egalitarian society rather than the dog-eat-dog world of market competition. Psychologists like Hans-Joachim Maaz have described the forms of the eventual East German rejection of the competitive individualism of the West. There is a new (or renewed) emphasis on group solidarity over individual assertiveness of achievement, on friendship, security, and simplicity, and a rejection of money as the measure of all things. It sounds like the emotional residue of the failed socialist alternative.

As many as one third of the Ossis of 1991 admitted to pollsters that they 'often', and another one third that they 'sometimes' still thought of the good old times in the GDR, without going into any details about their daydreams.[19] In place of the old Berlin Wall that painfully kept people apart who wanted to be with each other, there is now a new 'inner wall', particularly in East German minds, and along with seething resentments towards West German carpet-baggers and Wessis that are believed to be so. In 1991, 11 per cent of East Germans felt their country had been 'overwhelmed and taken over by West Germany'. They suddenly rediscovered the charms of their own landscape, their own local products – long spurned for West German imports – and their own people. But they have also agonised about being too Wessified already and being *westgeil* (too ready to be embraced by the West). It will be a long time until they overcome these agonies of a wounded mind.

Many of these differences between Eastern and Western identity are hard to measure but there are others that can be pinned down. Aside from their understandably greater concern about the high level of unemployment and lower wages and pensions, Ossis differed in other ways too. They were far more emphatic in their support for Berlin over Bonn as the future capital – over 90 per cent of East Germans wanted Berlin whereas a majority of West Germans preferred Bonn. Ossis under 40, and especially under 30 years of age also showed their greater level of prejudice towards foreigners early: in mid-1990 already, around 70 per cent of these cohorts expressed their opposition to granting local suffrage to foreign residents, about the same as all age cohorts, whereas in the old FRG younger respondents were substantially more liberal on this issue than their elders. In 1991, only 39 per cent of the Ossis thought it was 'alright that there are many foreigners in Germany' (vs. 48 per cent of Wessis) – actually there are many more foreigners living in West Germany (see William Chandler, below) and there is a high correlation between being personally acquainted with foreigners and tolerant attitudes. Tolerance also is closely related to being ideologically more on the left rather than the right wing. The least tolerant, next to the radical right, are Christian Democrats. By 1992, the East German level of anti-foreign prejudice had roughly caught up with the lower one of West Germany. Ossis also disagree sharply as to whether the German economy needs foreign workers.[20] Two-thirds of East Germans believe it does not whereas about the same majority among West Germans thinks it does. Finally, having been drilled in the communist version of anti-fascism as their favourite displacement all their lives, they are notably more insistent that 'the shame about the crimes of fascism' should not be forgotten (18 per cent of all Germans oppose this attitude) while West Germans prefer more often to keep the 'shame of the crimes of [GDR] socialism' alive which, in the form of communism, had for so long been their favourite displacement.[21]

THE BROWN HERRING IN GERMAN IDENTITY

It did not take long for both categories of crimes of the German past to begin haunting the present. Crimes of the GDR élite were aired before the courts in the trials of trade union (FDGB) boss Harry Tisch, of border shootings, and of Erich Honecker and other GDR leaders (see the essay by Helga Welsh, below). The criminal character of the Third Reich was highlighted in the East German resurgence – the old FRG had exhibited waves of radical right extremism all along[22] – of neo-Nazi violence, a turn of events that had eerily been predicted by the departing communists. Three years after the actual unification, by 1992, the never-ending series of skinhead and neo-Nazi attacks on foreigners (see Chapter 23) once more fanned the fires of alarm in many countries, and especially among the earlier opponents of German unification who were anxious to say 'I told you so'. After Rostock, the *Los Angeles Times* (August 29, 1992) editorialised that 'the battle cry of the youthful Nazis – that Germany is for Germans alone – ominously recalls the darkest days of the country's past'. For survivors of World War Two and the holocaust, the symbolism must have been overwhelming,[23] even if the substance fell far short. The Israeli cabinet came close to approving demands for a ban on travel to Germany – some voices even called for a worldwide boycott and the severing of diplomatic relations – unless the Bonn government took stronger action against the neo-Nazi assaults. Prime Minister Yitzhak Rabin told newspaper editors 'you must crush the head of the snake when it's still small,' and a *Maariv* columnist, Yosef Lapid, wrote: 'we at least understood that this is not a fringe occurrence but something demonic that is happening in Germany'.[24] On the other hand, when the German government announced an agreement with Romania to repatriate tens of thousands of gypsies whose recent claim for asylum status in Germany had triggered many of the skinhead assaults on asylum hostels and aroused considerable local sympathy for the skinheads, some voices in the media abroad promptly excoriated the Germans for 'expelling a minority' that had been prominent among the victims of Nazi genocide. It was hardly a dispassionate report on Germany's problems with refugees and asylum-seekers. In the American press, for example, the 'brown herring' of linking the repatriation of gypsies with the holocaust was rarely salted down with salient comparisons, such as with the Bush administration policy of intercepting Haitian boat people and sending them back.

German reactions to the skinhead and neo-Nazi outrages of 1992 curiously match the foreign relations from one end of the spectrum to the other, especially along partisan lines. With the conspicuous exception of hard-boiled communist opinion (DKP/PDS),[25] the German Left not only condemned the anti-foreigner violence and their own government for 'not speaking out more forcefully' against it. It

strongly believed that, in the light of the German past and of the constitutional article 16 on asylum policy produced by this past, no efforts should be undertaken to curb the popularly feared, mighty influx
of refugees and asylum-seekers into Germany (see also Gerard Braunthal,
in Chapter 11). The few hundred anarchists, 'chaotics', and left wing
demonstrators who took over the grand anti-racist rally of 35 000 in
Berlin in November 1992 and threw eggs, tomatoes, and other objects at Federal President Richard von Weizsäcker – they had already
attacked Chancellor Kohl and headed him off under the Brandenburg
Gate – represented one extreme of this point of view. Sincerely dedicated to the ideal of a multicultural society in Germany, they called
the government leaders they attacked 'hypocrites' and worse, presumably for not supporting their own violent actions against neo-Nazis,
and effectively prevented them from speaking out against the racist
violence by shouting and disconnecting the public address system. The
rally itself, however, consisted of a broad spectrum of moderate left
and moderate right opinion. Like many rallies to follow, the moderates were anxious to show their strong opposition to violence against
foreigners but were not necessarily of one mind about whether to
permit the flood of refugees to increase without curbs.[26]

A short time after the débâcle in Berlin, there was a second mass
rally in Bonn which was of a rather different complexion, purely left
wing, and studiously avoided by all government representatives and
even by the prominent leaders of the Social Democratic opposition.
The theme of the rally was the defence against modification of article
16 of the constitution which has been described by at least one supporter, *Bundestag* deputy Burkhard Hirsch (FDP) as the German Statue
of Liberty: 'Give me your tired, your poor, the wretched refuse of
your teeming shores . . .' Most of the massive rallies against racist
violence that followed in big cities and smaller towns were more like
the Berlin demonstration than such straightforward defences of the
right of asylum for everyone.[27] In any case, the many thousands of
Germans who have demonstrated all over Germany against racism –
especially in small towns where asylum hostels are usually located –
of course constitute just as much an expression of German identity
today as do the groups of skinheads and neo-Nazis involved in the
attacks. The entire spectrum of opinion described here presents a range
of contemporary German concepts of what Germany is and what it
should be. Interestingly, many Germans on the left also echo Prime
Minister Rabin's notions that the anti-foreign violence could be the
beginning of a real Nazi revival and, therefore, needs to be stopped

when it is small. Some have even claimed that this is how the old Nazi movement did start, another echo of some international reactions, although this is demonstrably incorrect (see Chapter 23). Some small groups of militants on the left have been engaged in violent attacks on neo-Nazis all along, again not unlike the anti-Nazi militants of the ultra-rightist Kach party who have been reported arriving from Israel to go after the neo-Nazis.

The major parties of government (CDU/CSU and FDP) and of the opposition had been playing political football with the immigration issue for more than a year, each blaming the other side for inaction or indifference, when the escalation of anti-foreign violence finally forced their hand. Towards the end of 1992, the SPD leader Björn Engholm, who was under a lot of pressure to curb immigration from organised labour, committed his reluctant party comrades to a compromise with the liberal wing of the Christian Democrats and Free Democrats. The resulting agreement left the basic formula of the right of political asylum intact while setting up practical barriers to the claim for it. The formula of agreement was embroiled in contradictory statements from its very beginnings. The coalition of moderates behind the change insisted that its amendments – specifying that no one from a non-dictatorial neighbouring country, or in transit through such a country, should be permitted to ask for political asylum[28] – would hardly have any noticeable impact on the existing practices. The defenders of the right to asylum instead spoke of 'a total sell-out of the constitutional rights', pointing out, in particular, that the change made it impossible for real refugees to reach Germany by land as air and sea access had been blocked by earlier measures. The new formula effectively devolved the function of being the 'bouncer' of Germany upon neighbours like Poland which were expected to turn away asylum-seekers from the German gates.[29] Nevertheless, the coalition of moderate parties clearly communicated its own sense of German identity: against neo-Nazism and anti-foreign violence but also determined to curb the unlimited inflow of foreigners which had excited the broader public to exasperation and, in some cases, to a certain amount of sympathy for the radical right groups and their violent attacks on local hostels for asylum-seekers.

A look at public opinion polls towards the end of 1992 puts the dramatic events into perspective. The Mannheim *Politbarometer* asked a representative West German sample in November what they considered 'the most important problem in Germany at present'. The asylum-seekers received the highest number of mentions (52.5 per cent whilst among Republican supporters it was as high as 73 per cent), followed by 'foreigners' (22 per cent) and 'rightwing radicals' (11.2 per cent). The responses were however rather discriminating: 70 per cent believed that 'most asylum-seekers abuse their privilege', and yet 87 per cent approved of political asylum in Germany, and 65 per cent of the presence of 'foreigners' in the country. Furthermore, 77 per cent (92 per cent among the Republican supporters) also believed that 'we simply cannot absorb this flood of asylum-seekers' and 59 per cent wanted to change article 16 of the constitution.[30] The popular mandate for modifying the right of asylum was clear. On the other hand, there was clearly an anti-foreign minority present beyond the asylum issue: 30.3 per cent objected to the presence of foreigners and 11.6 per cent to the principle of political asylum,[31] and this even after the rash of violence.

An EMNID poll commissioned by *Der Spiegel* happened to catch the changing tide of public opinion caused by the killing of the Turkish women in Moelln. The poll had been scheduled to take place just prior to the outrage at Moelln and was quickly replicated right after the event. On the first occasion, respondents were asked if they agreed with the slogan 'out with the foreigners' and 32 per cent said 'yes', five per cent of them 'emphatically yes'. 67 per cent said 'no', 43 per cent of them 'emphatically no'. After Moelln, the ayes had shrunk to 19 per cent (four of them emphatic) while the noes now numbered 77 per cent, 69 per cent of which were 'emphatic noes'. In the same time span, the number of respondents who admitted that they could 'understand right radical tendencies' shrank from 33 per cent to 12 per cent, and those who indicated support for the Republicans dropped from 7 per cent to 5 per cent.[32] Evidently, the post-unification malaise had come to an end[33] and now the respondents even agreed to let in refugees from a civil war, at least for a while (90 per cent), while 62 per cent wanted a quota restricting the admission of ethnic Germans (*Aussiedler*) into the country.

Two thirds to three fourths were prepared to accept Engholm's constitutional formula for modifying the asylum law. Finally, the EMNID pollsters asked 'suppose there were two demonstrations in this town, one against xenophobia and one protesting against the flood of foreigners – what would you do?' 44 per cent responded they would not join either demonstration. But 40 per cent indicated their willingness to demonstrate against xenophobia, while a hard core of 11 per cent wanted to march against the foreign influx.[34] The percentages give us a rough idea of the prevailing balance, including the division among the non-demonstrating 44 per cent. It is a fair guess that most of them occupy the moderate-right to moderate-left middle ground and would support the Engholm compromise formula of curbing the influx while maintaining the principle of asylum for political refugees. Most of them also accept the presence of the millions of foreign residents that already live in Germany while sharing the apprehension of future waves of 'economic refugees' from Eastern Europe and the rest of the world.

This account of the partisan and ideological shadings of opinion on foreigners and especially asylum-seekers would not be complete without a differentiated look at those hostile to foreigners by degrees. It is not entirely a matter of partisanship: even among West German Green voters, 36 per cent wanted to restrict the number of political refugees admitted – among the *Bündnis 90* voters, it was 60 per cent! – and 22 per cent thought the presence of foreigners in Germany 'not o.k.' (33 per cent of *Bündnis 90*). These probably include the scions of bourgeois families that have maintained pre-World War Two bourgeois nationalist traditions common among the Greens. Among FDP and SPD voters, too, there are substantial minorities opposed to foreigners. On the other hand, it is of course true that those hostile to foreigners are concentrated among the right wing of the CDU and especially the Bavarian CSU. The large anti-foreign majorities among radical right parties such as the Republicans clearly mark the core of that sentiment, if not of the violent elements that are more likely to be found in small groups and without partisan ties.[35]

A LOOK AHEAD AT THIS BOOK

This book attempts to sketch, with the help of many contributors, just where the new Federal Republic of Germany stands after 45 years – only four since unification – and where it appears to be heading in 1995. With an enterprise such as this, it is unavoidable that some subjects are not covered, or inadequately considered. Prominent among these are public policies such as welfare and health care, even though policy concerns are often addressed indirectly in these pages. In any event, we shall try to mention the more obvious gaps as we go along with this preview of the chapters to come.

As will be obvious from this introduction so far, the central concern of this work is with the evolving united or disunited sense of identity, and we have already sketched some salient features of this uncertain identity: the striking differences between East and West German views, German pacifism and national pride, and the many shadings of opinion towards foreigners and the right of political asylum. The attitudes towards foreigners, among other things, not only tend to improve with the level of education and personal contact with them, but differ sharply between the generations: over two-thirds of West Germans under 25 are tolerant of the foreign presence whereas nearly the same proportion of those over 60, i.e. the World War Two generation, are not.[36]

A number of contributors to this book address particular themes of German identity: Andrei S. Markovits and Simon Reich describe the popular views in 13 European countries about Germany, the country's unification, and its future role in Europe and the world. The authors carefully discuss and qualify what may at first glance seem merely snapshots of external perception. As I have pointed out above, the range of foreign opinion on Germany is paralleled closely by German views about their own identity, from benign visions to extreme fears about future developments. This essay is followed by a disquisition about the nature of the altered German identity by one of the deans of German studies – among other fields of comparative politics in which he distinguished himself – Arnold J. Heidenheimer. His essay explores identities against a background of political landscapes with changing boundaries, such as uniting Germany and disintegrating Yugoslavia, or the fulcrum of European integration and the raging ethnic rivalries of Bosnia. Eras of modern German history and political leaders they spawned are interwoven with German policies and political structures against the dramatic opening of Eastern Europe to German influence since, and even before, German unification. The new German role in European and United Nations policy towards Yugoslavia, finally, is linked to the difficulties of the Maastricht Treaty with smaller EC countries (see also the essay of Emil Kirchner, Chapter 21).

Gerald R. Kleinfeld, for two decades the *spiritus rector* of the German Studies Association and its review in the United States, follows Heidenheimer with an exploration of the German-American 'partnership in leadership' that was proclaimed by President George Bush in 1989. Since West Germany had so many years behind it in a kind of junior partnership to the U.S.,[37] and had become economically penetrated and Americanised like few other countries in the world, the evolving German identity can be described very well in terms of the changing German-American relationship from dependency to autonomy. Some observers even see in the fashionable anti-Americanism of parts of the German Left an assertion of German nationalism. The end of the Cold War threat has permitted Germany a quantum jump in autonomy and more intense integration into European processes of unification

– Foreign Minister Hans-Dietrich Genscher even promised the complete 'Europeanisation of Germany' – and yet its chilly reception by suspicious European neighbours also brought the country back to reliance on American guidance. The United States, for its part, is persuaded by its own economic and global-political problems to appreciate German cooperation with regard to the contexts evolving in EC, NATO, and GATT. New shared interests, such as in the stability and democratic development of Eastern Europe have evolved to take the place of factors in decline, that used to give the United States leverage with regard to Europe on the verge of greater unification. Although the natural course of events has tended to drive the U.S. and Germany apart, therefore, German unification also has the potential of bringing the two countries back together again.

The section on all-German identity ends with an illuminating essay by Joyce Mushaben, who wrote on a similar subject in *The FRG at Forty*, and elsewhere, on the sense of identity of a majority of both East and West Germans, namely women. As Professor Mushaben, who has also written on German youth, points out, their 'political-economic identity . . . will be subject to greater redefinition through the process of unification than will hold true for . . . men', though not necessarily implying great advances, at least not for East German women. Not only did a lot of rights and privileges for women fall by the wayside with the demise of the GDR but they took the brunt of the economic effects of unification, the loss of jobs and of childcare facilities. The hidden anti-female prejudices of East German society remained, while the official, ideological commitment to gender equality disappeared along with the communist regime. For West German women, on the other hand, unification with East Germany opened the door to some significant changes and initiated spirited debates which encouraged their mobilisation against age-old taboos.

The next section of the book is still about identity, but rather about what is left of East German identity. *Was bleibt* (what remains) was the title of the provocative (and much-criticised) essay the famous East German writer, Christa Wolf, published on the occasion of the final collapse of the GDR regime. Wolf had been an early idealist supporter of GDR communism who became progressively more alienated as the system turned into one great disillusionment after the other. Quite a lot actually remains of the old GDR within the new, united Germany, and much of it is rather a problematic part of German identity today, or of the uneasiness often expressed by East Germans within the larger system. Intellectuals like Wolf, as Ian Wallace, the editor of *German Monitor* demonstrates below, had to walk a tightrope between the demands made by the regime, including the Stasi, and the kind of integrity without which a writer gets no respect from the public. Many of them showed early support for the popular revolution – more often, however, for a reform communist GDR rather than for German unification – only to feel the painful loss of their cosy nest when the GDR merged with the much larger, pluralistic nesting area, and an intellectual battleground of Western writers and artists. It is small wonder that many East German intellectuals are ill at ease and unhappy about what for them was supposed to be a realm of greater freedom. The Unification Treaty of 1990, to be sure, obliges the government to 'preserve the cultural substance' of the old GDR but this is much easier said than done.

A major part of the residue of some 40 years of communist dictatorship is the *Vergangenheitsbewältigung*, or 'coming to terms' with the injustice meted out by the State Security Service (Stasi) and communist state party (SED). Rather than to 'draw a veil over the past in order not to poison the future', to speak with Professor Wallace, East Germans need to bring the very real criminals of the past regime to justice so that they can once more hold up their heads in pride and help to improve the whole country. Whether such a purge can be accomplished by court proceedings alone seems doubtful. Judging from other, similar undertakings,[38] East Germans and their West German friends who are themselves not yet all that far from their own denazification or *épuration* efforts, need to develop first a consensus of *what* should be punished, or what kind of conduct deserved exoneration after the fact. Professor Helga A. Welsh, a well-known specialist on the GDR, also treats the problem in a comparative, Eastern European context. Gregg O. Kvistad adds to this perspective a thoughtful examination of the related problems of what to do with the hundreds of thousands of communist bureaucrats left over from the GDR regime. On the one hand, much of the personnel is obviously needed to administer, teach children, and police traffic – not to mention to restrain skinheads and hooligans. On the other hand, most of the GDR personnel obviously bears a heavy political legacy, having obtained their careers with political favouritism, or an absence of resistance, and most of them have neither the training nor the attitudes expected of their equivalents in the West. It would have been a cardinal mistake simply to accept them all into the well-protected fortress of bureaucratic rights and immunities of the West German *Beamten* status. Screening them one by one, demanding they fill out a questionnaire – shades of

denazification in the U.S. zone of occupation, 1946–51 – outright dismissal, or consigning them to several months in the *Warteschleife* (mora-
torium) while their records were vetted were all deeply resented by the
East Germans affected by the process and their families (half the population!).

Other very important aspects of how East Germans see themselves
are the consequences of 40 years of economic misdevelopment and
of being held in communist and bureaucratic dependency at the local
level. Marilyn Rueschemeyer, who also has long been prominent in
the study of the GDR, now observes the rebirth of democratic local
government with an experienced eye, concentrating particularly on the
area of Rostock on the Baltic where she had conducted research on
communist local government before. Popular participation along democratic lines has a particularly tough road in East Germany where government neglect and advanced urban decay have made communities even
more dependent on administrative planners and self-willed investors
than in the West. Karl Kahrs wrestles with the perplexities facing efforts to privatise enterprises in a post-communist society where the
economy had been deprivatised over the decades until 80.7 per cent
of all property was state-owned or semi-statal, 14.7 per cent cooperative, and a mere 4.7 per cent in private hands.[39] In particular, he describes the efforts of the Trust Agency for the People's Property
(*Treuhand*), the holding company for practically all East German enterprises until they could be either sold, privatised, or shut down in
the extremely painful transition to a market economy. Contrary to
early promises and calculations, the work of the *Treuhand* is far from
completed and, in one form or another, will continue to preoccupy
both East and West German critics. East Germans will feel defensive
and second-class in united Germany for as long as their economy is
in its current depressed condition.

POLITICAL STRUCTURES AND FORCES

From surveying the changing German sense of identity, the book moves
to the evolving rules and structures of the unified state and to some
of the political forces that inhabit it. The unification of the two
Germanies took place by means of a simple accession of East German *Länder* (states) – which had to be reconstituted first after 38
years – to the old Federal Republic under article 23 of the West German Basic Law, that is without drawing up a new constitution. Nevertheless, the unification under the two unification treaties of 1990, the

great differences in state and society, and the now disturbed balance of political forces have brought about many changes and initiated public debates that, in some cases, are still going on. New issues have arisen, moreover, particularly those highlighting the future role of united Germany in the world – for example its participation in NATO or UN peacekeeping or enforcement actions – and those involving migrants to Germany from the east or south, and they are also likely to continue. Such institutional and rule changes naturally show a dynamics all their own as the third section of this book describes. In the end, however, the political forces and what motivates them also have the capacity of changing the ground rules and patterns at work (Part IV).

Our first concern (in Part III) was with the changing constitutional rules and structures. Here the well-known scholar of German affairs, Gerard Braunthal addresses himself particularly to civil liberties issues,[40] especially those pertaining to the migrants of various categories, from the 'guest workers' to the asylum-seekers of today. Professor Braunthal also discusses some of the solutions to the dilemmas of asylum and migration, as they have been proposed by various groups. The larger framework for this, of course, is the constitutional debate that has been proceeding along so many lines since the unification and is presented here by Donald Kommers, a distinguished student of German courts and jurisprudence, who has long been the guiding light of German constitutional studies in the United States. Focusing on the work of the joint *Bundestag-Bundesrat* Committee on [Federal] Constitutional Revision and with a sidelong glance at the new *Länder* constitutions in the east, Kommers brings out issues and dilemmas that were far from the original framers of the Basic Law in 1948–49. Inevitably, the changes of unification also had a major impact on the federal system familiar from the old FRG – and so different from American federalism. Arthur Gunlicks whose name has become almost synonymous with the study of German federalism and local government, addresses the current problems and attempted solutions in the evolving system.[41] For one thing, the age-old pillars of states rights, such as the key position of Bavaria, have been weakened and other changes are still going on.

Another line of approach in this book is the effort to chart the evolution of leadership in West and East Germany. In this connection, the wax and wane of Chancellor Helmut Kohl's stewardship through the turbulent seas of German unification and post-unification politics has been amazing. Kohl had been in a prolonged political slump in stature prior to the upheaval of 1989–90 which gave him an unexpected opportunity to play a more prominent role within the system and in Europe than any chancellor since Konrad Adenauer (1949–63). No sooner had he and his coalition won reelection (December 2, 1990), however, than his star began to decline again. His leadership since has widely been characterised as 'aimlessly drifting' and unassertive when he was expected to 'set signals', such as against the mindless skinhead violence against foreigners. The evolution of East German élites from before to after unity and on to today is even more revealing, because, as the long-time GDR specialist Thomas A. Baylis shows in Chapter 13, this case of élite transformation is quite different from others in that the overthrow of the old communist élite did not replace them with 'a preexisting counterélite', and not even with the leaders of the citizens' protest movements of 1989–90, but with West German decision-makers and some coopted East Germans, for example from the old 'bloc parties'. Professor Baylis examines the question whether this is a 'colonial' situation, how it compared to leadership change in other postcommunist societies, and where that leaves the East German public. The political structure of the media in East and West, also changed most significantly with unification and, today, is an important fulcrum of just how unified or disunited Germany is. Professor Baylis goes into the evolving press scene in East Germany and the extent to which the Ossis still do have a press voice of their own, insistent on a distinctive East German perspective on their fate and on West German manipulations. But the German press, radio, and television, over the period involved, underwent major structural changes. The conservative unifiers in the old FRG made sure that the East German media would be solidly under the control of the market forces centered in West Germany, but we can gather the limits of this takeover from the example of the flashy new tabloid *Super* which – though owned by the Rupert Murdoch syndicate and the West German *Burda* conglomerate – made its mark by boosting East German sensitivities and notably stepping on West German (government, bank, and business) toes.

The political forces of united Germany have not quite gelled into a stable group and party system comparable to that of the old FRG. Instead, they are still swayed violently back and forth by the current economic problems, the difficulties of integration between the two Germanies, the flood of refugees at the door, and the uncertainties about Germany's future role in the world. The foundation of a new body politic, the enterprise to which Kohl and the governing parties CDU/CSU and FDP – not to mention German business – committed themselves with broad if conditional support from the Left, continues to be a major fulcrum of issues, criticism, and controversies that are plaguing, and sometimes splitting, the Right. Gordon Smith describes for us what is unchanging and what is under challenge in the moderate German right from his long years as a prominent interpreter of German politics and political parties.[42] The CDU/CSU and FDP are after all in the same quandary as other conservative parties of the West: with the collapse of communism they have lost the major antagonist and 'enemy image' around which they had structured their own programme and identity for four and a half decades. Will the German Right in the long run evolve into something like the *nationalgesinnte Rechte* (nationalistic right) of Weimar as a result of German unification, moving with determination to assert German interests and, in the face of immigrant streams, reserving Germany for the Germans? How will it attempt to retain its power of integration, *Volkspartei-*(catch-all party)-style, its supporters from all the social classes and groups, its conservative-national, and its 'social-republican' wings, not to mention the 'homeless right' which has not had significant national representation since 1945?

Already, a gaggle of radical right parties – fortunately unity continues to elude them which frustrates their access to representation and power – and a militant but unorganised neo-Nazi and skinhead fringe are trying to capitalise on the weakness of the government. In the South, in particular, the Republicans (REPs) have made considerable inroads on Christian Democratic voters, if not quite to the extent that the latter's conservative or religious equivalents in Austria, Northern Italy, and southern France have been devastated by competition from the radical right.[43] In the last chapter of this book, I return, among other things, to the vivid picture of the rise of unorganised neo-Nazi and skinhead attacks in East and West Germany and the consequences in image and policy.

The impact of the well-deserved collapse of communism on the Left has been no less dramatic even though, ever since the decline of the 'social democratic consensus' of the seventies and the *Wende* (turnabout) of 1982, the Left had been in a tailspin for some time already. For the West German SPD, the eighties were lean years with only brief relief from this downward trajectory. The year 1990 was supposed to be a time of making a triumphant return to power and respect: with an attractive young candidate, Oscar Lafontaine, and a well thought-out new programme of combining economic growth with a strong commitment to a better environment, the party promised to sweep the next federal elections of December 1990. But then came the fall of the GDR and German unification which the SPD candidate simply did not take seriously enough. The Greens ignored it altogether. While Kohl's coalition government rode to victory on what Kohl had insisted on likening to a train about to depart, the 'unity train', the SPD received its worst trouncing in three decades and the Greens, for various reasons, failed to clear the five per cent hurdle for representation in the *Bundestag*. Only after that election, as the government was fumbling badly and wracked by internal divisions, did the SPD recover in the polls.[44] A good showing into the polls, of course, is not the same as winning an election, although the combined total of SPD and Greens or of an alternative coalition of SPD and FDP both promised parliamentary majorities.

In spite of such positive harbingers,[45] the loyalty of lifelong SPD supporters has been eroding progressively, and certainly more so with the fall and discredit of communist regimes even though the Social Democrats have always been at pains to distinguish their brand of socialism from communism. The widespread belief in the inexorable progress and eventual victory of the labour movement in industrial countries was badly shaken and the grim revelations about repression and secret police did not help. Worse yet, the refugee and immigrant issues along with the recrudescence of nationalism and ethnic conflict in Eastern and Southeastern Europe had considerable appeal among working-class SPD supporters. The party feared substantial losses if it turned a deaf ear to the anxieties and prejudices of its constituents, for example on the asylum issue. Andrei S. Markovits and the late Donald Schoonmaker discuss the uneasiness of SPD and Greens, respectively, with their current roles and outlooks in Chapters 15 and 16. Professor Schoonmaker, in particular, plumbs the depth of the present and future of the Greens.[46]

The section on the play of political forces is rounded out by an essay by the former head of the Council of European Studies and of the Conference Group on German Politics, M. Donald Hancock on the trade unions and one by William M. Chandler on the immigration issue. The German trade union federation (DGB) still plays a much bigger role in Germany than its equivalents in most other Western countries. It has been credited with making the West German 'economic miracle' of the fifties and sixties possible by getting workers to use self-restraint in work stoppages and strikes. But today, its most prominent role seems to have been in extracting wage increases in the East German *Länder* which prevent East German enterprises from catching up to the West in productivity and thus frustrate the economic recovery of the East. At the same time, the unionisation of the East by the DGB in place of the disintegrating communist state union, the FDGB, was obviously a major advance for democratic reconstruction and constitutes an important countervailing force against the domination of West German capital over East German workers and consumers. It would have been illuminating to have essays also on other organised interests, such as the manufacturers and agriculture, but considerations of space and the patience of our readers precluded this option. To end Part IV, we added a contribution on immigration and immigration policy by William M. Chandler who has long been known for his comparative studies of German and Canadian federalism and bureaucracy, among other things. The topic of immigration into Germany has become a crucible of contemporary political alignments, policy options, and prejudices related to whether or not Germans see their country as 'an immigration country' and are comfortable with the notion of a multicultural society. An ample majority, according to the 'Germany 2000' poll of January 1991, seems to like the idea of a multicultural society, at least in theory, so long as it does not cost much or attract a flood of foreign 'economic refugees' whom 79 per cent of them would rather stop – 52 per cent even wanted to stop the ethnic German *Aussiedler* from coming. At least one third were haunted by visions of 'too many foreigners' by the year 2000. For this book, in any event, it seems crucial to present the complexities and fine distinctions of this phenomenon in systematic form and with all the necessary detail, as well as *sine ira et studio*.

GERMANY'S ROLE IN THE WORLD

The foreign relations of the new Germany move in three overlapping circles. One is the Atlantic connection to the United States which in the past was both the economic and, through NATO, the defence lifeline of the old FRG. As we have seen above, in the essay by Gerald Kleinfeld, this linkage is far from outdated, and may even have gained new strength because of the changed circumstances. The second circle is the European Community which, as seen from the German perspective, has taken on a predominant role in the economic life of Germany even though the great hopes for the 'deepening' of the EC are in something of a holding pattern since the crisis year of 1992 when both the patterns of financial cooperation and the expectation of smooth ratification and implementation of the Maastricht Treaty were rudely disturbed. One of the offshoots of an increasingly autonomous (from

U.S. power) EC consisted in the development of a common European foreign and defence policy and the perception of a European 'security identity' separate from the common NATO perspective. The third circle is, for the most part, quite new and a major consequence of the fall of communism and the changed status of united Germany: it is the evolving linkage of Germany, so far mostly economic but potentially also political, to Eastern Europe and the successor states of the Soviet Union. These three circles are, to some extent, in competition and even in conflict with each other. But while Germany may at times shift its attention and emphasis from one to the others, it would be a great mistake to neglect any of them completely and for whatever reasons. The geographic location and recent historical development of the country, before and after unification, clearly demands attention to all three for German economic and defence security.

The German security and economic strategy for Europe and its relationship with the United States are explored here by James Sperling, who has recently emerged as an authoritative interpreter of the complex connections and interplay between economic and security relations in the Atlantic and European theatre. As Professor Sperling explains, the nature of interdependence between Germany and the West, not to mention Eastern Europe, has changed and this governs the future role of the country in Europe and with respect to the one surviving superpower in the world. Werner Feld adds to this a detailed examination of the development of a 'European security identity' out of the lap of NATO relations since 1991, at the intersection of the first and second circle, so to speak.

The European circle receives systematic 'coverage' by Emil J. Kirchner who for so long has written most knowledgeably about the European Community, among other subjects. Professor Kirchner reminds us that some of the recent German and other discontents with European integration have to be measured against the continuing high levels of German commitment to the country's 'Europeanisation'. Citing George Kennan's earlier statement that a united Germany would be tolerable only as an integrated part of a united Europe, he argues that 'there does not seem to be an alternative to the EC' now. In a manner of speaking, of course, the antecedents were the 'Americanised' old FRG and the 'Russified' GDR and their union is problematical indeed for the Germans as well as their neighbours. A truly Europeanised Germany would make sense and a lot more so than the 'Swissified' Germany of some escapist German fantasies. Given the inertia of the integration process and the understandable reluctance of some of Germany's neighbours, however, a substantial continuance of American influence is an obvious choice for helping both the Germans and other Europeans with this difficult transition. Its benefits would also reach into the third circle, German relations with Eastern Europe where the demand for German economic aid and trade and the old fears of the central European colossus otherwise balance each other. American interest and participation would certainly calm East European fears and suspicions of a united Germany which in turn might advance the process of 'widening' the EC by including at least some of the East European nations that are eager to join.

The third circle, Germany's new (and renewed) relations with Eastern Europe and the Soviet successor states is a crucial element of the new situation without which any analysis is clearly out-of-date. One of our contributors, A. James McAdams, addresses these subjects in a searching way. We could not cover the evolution of German relations to what used to be called the northern tier of communist satellites, Poland, Czechoslovakia (now two states), and Hungary. By now, there are German 'good neighbour' treaties with the first two on the books. The bitter historical memories of both countries and the hostility of German refugee lobbies from the Oder-Neisse area and the Sudetenland required a great deal of soothing of raw feelings on both sides. Hungary by comparison could simply go back to its pro-German past before 1945. All three have already benefited from substantial German investment and are clamouring for more.[47] German–East European relations are now much closer and warmer than the American media would lead one to expect.

Even more underreported and astounding is the *entente cordiale* between Germany and the successor states of what used to be the second superpower in the world. In particular the degree of rapprochement between Germany and the Russian Federation[48] through the succession of major changes on both sides described by A. James McAdams is quite remarkable. It is a further sign of the increasing freedom of action that united Germany possesses in the post-Cold War world. It has long ceased to be the state that had no choice other than complete dependence on the West, and indeed it was assured of this freedom at the time it was given its sovereignty at the end of the Two-plus-Four negotiations of 1990. What use it can make of this freedom after unity has been granted by the now defunct Soviet Union, and indeed how to cope with the uncertain situation in the successor states is another question to which Professor McAdams supplies a number of clues.

'The united Germans are still looking for their role in a changed Europe', an editorial of the *Frankfurter Rundschau* (Oct. 2, 1992) mused. 'Braggadocio is as inappropriate as is a policy of going it alone or abstinence from power'. Such abstinence, or *Machtvergessenheit*, (being oblivious to power relations) was said to be the extreme of the pendulum to which the old FRG swung from the extreme of *Machtbesessenheit* (Machiavellism or obsession with power politics) of the first half of the twentieth century, according to Hans-Peter Schwarz. Now is the time, Schwarz argues, for Germany to act with a mature *Machtbewusstsein*, a sense of its power without either excesses and for the benefit of all concerned. 'As an economically strong nation, a trading nation, Germany also has worldwide interests', the *Frankfurter Rundschau* continued. 'How it will make the most of them *as an involuntary great power* next to the U.S. and Japan remains a question mark' (italics supplied, P. M..)

Notes

1. Contrary to some *post facto* reinterpretations of 'a West German takeover', all East German parties in March 1990 favoured unification, even the communists, and an ample majority of the parties that promised the most direct route to this goal, namely the Alliance for Germany, the FDP and the SPD, won a huge mandate to pursue it. The democratic reform movements, unfortunately, won only 3 per cent of the popular vote in that parliamentary election. Forschungsgruppe Wahlen, *Wahl in der DDR. Eine Dokumentation der Volkskammerwahl vom 18. März 1990*, Mannheim, 1990, p. 07.
2. For details, see Merkl, *German Unification in the European Context*, University Park, Penn.: Penn State University Press, 1993, pp. 355–6.
3. See also the discussion in Merkl, *German Unification*, chapter seven and Christian Soe and Dirk Verheyen, eds., *The Germans and Their Neighbors*, Boulder, Col.: Westview, 1993.
4. Trade and Industry Secretary Ridley, a close confidant of Mrs Thatcher revealed his, and perhaps her, anti-German bias in intemperate remarks reported in the London *Spectator* and, as a consequence, was made to resign. The Prime Minister had earlier convened the Chequers Seminar of German experts to brief her on German national character in anticipation of a visit by Chancellor Helmut Kohl.
5. See especially the polls reported in *The Pulse of Europe. A Survey of Political and Social Values and Attitudes*, Washington, D.C.: Times Mirror Center for the People and the Press, 1991.
6. See also Merkl, *German Unification*, pp. 327–352.
7. Still in late 1989, Chancellor Kohl shocked Poland and many foreign observers, as well as his domestic critics, with a refusal to recognise the Oder-Neisse border, a political manoeuvre to appease German refugee

voters from there who were being wooed by the radical rightist Republican party. Actually, the border had already been recognised twice in the seventies and this German acceptance of World War Two territorial losses was repeated in 1990 by the East and West German parliaments. There ensued further squabbles over the language and autonomous rights of the German minority until these too were settled in a Friendship and Good Neighbour Treaty. For details, see ibid., chapter seven, pp. 342–51.

8. World War Two began with the alleged 1938 liberation of German minorities in Czechoslovakia – Conservative Prime Ministers Neville Chamberlain and Edouard Daladier gave in to Hitler 1938 in Munich not because they were excessively given to appeasement but because they rather believed his argument that the Treaty of Versailles had unjustly given the ethnic German Sudetenland to Czechoslovakia – and in Poland (1939).

9. The public opinion polls quoted in this section are from Merkl, *German Unification*, pp. 119–20 where their sources are identified. The best study of East German opinion is still Gebhard Schweigler, *Nationalbewusstsein in der BRD und der DDR*, 2nd ed., Düsseldorf: Bertelsmann, 1973, especially pp. 80–105 and 121–53. By 1969, fifty per cent of West Germans indicated their willingness to recognize the GDR and to accept the permanent loss of German Eastern territories in exchange for détente in Europe. *Ibid.*, p. 133.

10. Large minorities of West Germans were opposed to tax increases for financing unification from the very beginning and the Kohl government therefore claimed that it would not cost anything. A rising tide of economic growth would take care of it. When at last, after the all-German parliamentary elections of December 1990, the bills began to arrive along with hefty tax increases, West German voters turned on Kohl with a vengeance, calling him a *Steuerlügner* (tax liar). East Germans turned on the Kohl government for having misrepresented the pain and suffering of their transition to a market economy. See Merkl, *German Unification*, pp. 231–3.

11. See esp. Patrick Süskind's essay in *Der Spiegel*, 43, no. 38, Sept. 17, 1990, pp. 116–17, or in Ulrich Wickert, ed., *Angst vor Deutschland*, New York and Hamburg: Hoffman & Campe, 1990.

12. This is a word concoction combining 'Wessi' with 'Besserwisser', a schoolmasterly know-it-all.

13. The national survey 'Deutschland 2000' was conducted in the first days of 1990 by Infratest and published by the *Süddeutsche Zeitung*, January 4, 1990, supplement.

14. For details, see Merkl, *German Unification*, pp. 13–22, and the polls and sources cited there.

15. Details and the sources are in Merkl, *German Unification*, chapter four and conclusion. There is also a poll of the Allensbach Institut für Demoskopie of 1976 which differentiated the same percentage of 71 per cent 'proud' of the Eurobarometer by age groups: those under thirty included only 57 per cent claiming to be proud. Majorities of 56–61 per cent even rejected the word 'fatherland' in polls of 1975 and 1981. See *The Germans: Public Opinion Polls, 1967–1980*, Westport, Conn.: Greenwood Press, pp. 106, 108.

16. See Institut für praxisorientierte Sozialforschung (IPOS), *Einstellungen zu aktuellen Fragen der Innenpolitik*, ed. by Manfred Berger, Wolfgang Gibowski, and Diether Roth, Mannheim. These annual surveys have been conducted since 1984 in May/June of the year cited. The sources quoted are: IPOS, *BRD, 1990*, p. 76 and IPOS, *DDR, 1990*, p. 54; IPOS *1991*, pp. 23, and 82–3; IPOS *1992*, pp. 30–1.

17. See also Wilhelm Bürklin, 'Changing Political and Social Attitudes in the Uniting Germany', in *Politics and Society in Germany, Austria, and Switzerland* 4, no. 1 (Autumn, 1991), pp. 20–33, esp. 29–31.

18. See also Gert-Joachim Glaessner in Merkl, *German Unification*, chapter three.

19. See the details and sources in Merkl, *German Unification*, conclusion, pp. 416–21.

20. See IPOS, *DDR 1990*, pp. 62, 88, IPOS, *BRD 1990*, p. 42, IPOS, *1991*, pp. 55, 57–8, IPOS *1992*, pp. 80–4. Only 31 per cent of West Germans but 70 per cent of East Germans reported having no personal contact with foreigners. Perhaps it would be beneficial to expose them more to such contacts, especially among young people at the youth gang age.

21. On East German official antifascism, see especially Konrad H. Jarausch, 'Das Versagen des ostdeutschen Antifaschismus', in *Initial* 1, no. 2 (1991), pp. 114–24. On the desire to see the oppressive past rectified, see *Deutschland 2000*, the national survey published by *Süddeutsche Zeitung*, January 4, 1991, supplement.

22. See esp. Ekkart Zimmermann and Thomas Saalfeld, 'The Three Waves of West German Rightwing Extremism', in Merkl and Leonard Weinberg, eds., *Encounters with the Contemporary Radical Right*, Boulder, CO: Westview, 1993, pp. 50–74 and Merkl, ed., *Political Violence and Terror: Motifs and Motivations*, Berkeley and Los Angeles: University of California Press, 1986, pp. 229–56. See also my examples and explanations in the concluding chapter of Merkl and Weinberg, op. cit., pp. 204–25.

23. Simultaneous attacks on a holocaust memorial near Berlin and Jewish cemeteries and reported shouts of 'Heil Hitler' – the message taking responsibility for the killing of three Turkish women at Moelln also ended with a 'Heil Hitler' – increased the propensity of foreign observers to associate the violent incidents with the atrocities of the Third *Reich*. But there was also a report that Rostock police had threatened legal action against French and American television that had allegedly paid German youngsters to give the straight-armed 'Hitler salute' on film. *Los Angeles Times*, August 13, 1992.

24. *New York Times*, November 30, 1992.

25. Adherents of the East German PDS (communists), for example, warmed up slowly to the right of political asylum for which, in 1990, they could only muster a level of support lower than that of the East German FDP, SPD, and *Bündnis 90*, or the West German Greens. See IPOS 1992, p. 86. Only in 1992 was their support level as high as their position on the left-right dimension would have suggested.

26. Critics have associated the prevailing fear of very large numbers, 'a flood of refugees', among other culprits to a media campaign of alarmism.

Even the moderate papers and magazines, critics suggest, have brought exaggerated estimates and prejudicial images of the 'impending flood'. See *Die Zeit*, no. 50. Dec. 4, 1992.

27. Currently, German authorities permit only about 7 per cent of the hundreds of thousands seeking asylum to stay (i.e. acceptance as *political* refugees) but the others are housed and fed for many months until their status can be decided. See the essay by William Chandler, below. Also, *The Economists*, Nov. 14, 1992, p. 58.

28. This aspect of the new formula can be compared more or less to the change in American immigration practice that no longer gives an automatic welcome to refugees from former communist countries that are no longer dictatorships.

29. See also Robert Leicht, 'Eine Kapitulation, kein Kompromiss', *Die Zeit*, 47, Dec. 11, 1992.

30. Forschungsgruppe Wahlen, *Politbarometer November 1992*, Mannheim, pp. 67, 120–4, 126 and 131. 60 per cent thought Engholm's compromise formula would succeed in the *Bundestag*. p. 65. Cf. IPOS 1992, p. 80 which from a May/June survey obtained a much higher level of hostility to foreigners, namely 47 per cent West Germans and 46 per cent East Germans who think the presence of foreigners is 'not o.k.'. We must assume that the violent incidents changed many minds in the direction of tolerance. If true this would demonstrate considerable flexibility on this issue on the part of the German public.

31. *Ibid.*, pp. 120 and 122. In an EMNID poll of the same month, 24 per cent wanted to scrap and another 43 per cent to modify the constitutional guarantee of legal recourse against being turned down for asylum (art. 19). *Der Spiegel*, 46, no. 50, Dec. 7, 1992, p. 65.

32. German electoral law requires a party to get more than five per cent to be represented in parliament. In some state elections, however, the party has already surmounted this hurdle. On the EMNID poll, see *ibid.*, pp. 58–65.

33. The impatience of the German public with the ineptitude of their government is also evident from the responses to *Politbarometer* questions about satisfaction with government. *Politbarometer November 1992*, p. 40. Only 36 per cent expressed satisfaction (vs. 45 per cent noes).

34. *Der Spiegel*, 46, no. 50, December 7, 1992, p. 65. The special regulation permitting ethnic *Aussiedler* from Russia, Kazakhstan, Romania, etc. to come has also drawn criticism as a 'racist exemption', as has the German nationality law by parentage (*ius sanguinis*). Re. the *Aussiedler*, however, the government has argued that ethnic Germans since 1945 suffered a great deal of discrimination and persecution under Eastern communist regimes for which the German government feels a sense of responsibility.

35. See IPOS 1992, pp. 80–81, 89. See also Merkl, 'A New German Identity?' in Gordon Smith et al., eds, *Development in German Politics*, London: Macmillan, 1992, pp. 327–348.

36. Re. levels of education, both East and West Germans range from an elementary level (*Hauptschule*) with 30–35 per cent tolerant of foreigners to 66–80 per cent of the level entitled to enter post-secondary institu-

tions (*Hochschulreife*) – East Germans supply the lower end of these ranges. The age difference in opinion seems to be limited to West Germany. The long isolation of East Germany may account for this difference. *Ibid.*, p. 82.

37. See also Wolfram Hanrieder, *Deutschland, Amerika, Europa*, Paderborn, Munich: Schoeningh, 1991, pp. 361–88, 440–57.
38. See esp. Klaus-Dietmar Henke, ed., *Politische Säuberung in Europa. Die Abrechnung mit Faschismus und Kollaboration nach dem Zweiten Weltkrieg*, Munich: Deutscher Taschenbuch Verlag, 1991.
39. See also Merkl, 'The Impossble Dream: Privatizing Collective Property in the East Germany, 1990–1991', in M. Donald Hancock and Helga A. Welsh, eds., *German Unification: Process and Outcomes*, Boulder, Col.: Westview, 1993.
40. See also his essay, 'Public Order and Civil Liberties', in Gordon Smith et al., eds., *Developments in West German Politics*, London: Macmillan, 1989, pp. 308–22 and his book, *Political Loyalty and Public Service in West Germany: the 1972 Decree Against Radicals and its Consequences*, Amherst, Mass.: University of Massachusetts Press, 1990.
41. See also his *Judicial Politics in West Germany: A Study of the Federal Constitutional Court*, Beverly Hills and London: Sage, 1976.
42. See also his 'The New Party System' and other contributions to his *Developments in German Politics*, ed. with W. E. Paterson, Peter H. Merkl, and Stephen Padgett, London: Macmillan, 1992, pp. 77–102, and 9–51.
43. See also Merkl and Leonard Weinberg, eds., op. cit., pp. 1–4, chap. 1, and pp. 55–8, 226–7.
44. For details of the unification period, see also Merkl, *German Unification*, chapter four, By August 1991, the SPD registered 44.4 per cent (33.5 per cent in the December elections) in the polls and the Greens 8.1 per cent (3.9 per cent) for a total of 52.5 per cent indicating a willingness to vote for them. The CDU/CSU had dropped from 43.8 per cent in December 1990 to 35.1 per cent and its coalition partner, the FDP, from 11 per cent to 8.4 per cent. *Politbarometer August 1991*, p. 1.
45. The impressive showing of the SPD in 1991 also did not last: as the level of popular dissatisfaction with the Kohl government rose in the second half of 1992, the opposition did not reap the benefit of it, It rather went to small parties, including the REPs (5.6 per cent) and Greens/ Bündnis 90 (10.1 per cent), and to those expressing no partisan preference (7.5 per cent). The SPD and CDU/CSU were neck and neck in the 32–36 per cent range. *Politbarometer November 1992*, pp. 1–3.
46. See also his earlier work on this subject, especially his *Between Protest and Power: The Green Party in Germany*, with E. Gene Frankland, Boulder, Col.: Westview, 1992.
47. See also Merkl, *German Unification*, pp. 327–352 where Austria and the spell of the old Hapsburg empire are also brought into the picture, and public opinion polls in these states regarding attitudes towards Germany are discussed in some detail.
48. For details, see *ibid.*, pp. 307–15 and 403–4.

Part I

Elements of the New German Identity

1 Germany's Image in the New Europe: The Controversy Continues

Andrei S. Markovits and Simon Reich

And now moving right along to global events. I'm sure you have heard that Germany has re-united. The only question, I guess, is when it will go on tour again. (Jay Leno, Tonight Show Host).

INTRODUCTION

Leave it to comedians to encapsulate the essence of political problems. While often simplistic, on occasion even crude, the vernacular used by popular culture often gets to the crux of sensitive matters which politicians are too hypocritical to articulate, intellectuals too cautious to disseminate, and scholars too slow to investigate. Humourists and comics, just like court jesters of old, are essential to any democratic polity precisely because they tackle taboos.

In a flightier mode, Jay Leno's comments are also known as the 'German Question'. It is this issue which has played a crucial role in modern European history. Contrary to certain views, it was never laid to rest in 1945, just altered yet again. The history of metamorphoses continues unabated after November 9, 1989. The question is not new. It has merely attained yet another twist, a hitherto unseen character, a novel manifestation. What will the Germany be like that will go on tour? Indeed, was the tour not already long in progress when the band's preferred nickname was 'Bundesrepublik' and its members were fewer in numbers? What kind of tour will it be, if indeed there has to be one? A popular one, cheered by fans all over Europe and welcomed by local promoters and fans packing the stadia? Or will it be a tour of reluctance and recalcitrance in which the enlarged band, with a changed repertoire, a different choreography, and altered light affects will make its former fans uneasy, fearful, perhaps even angry?

Nobody quite knows the answers to these questions, neither the prospective audiences nor the band, its managers and entourage. These questions have preoccupied the European publics since Germany's unification however. They have grown in salience with the immense changes transforming all of Europe and the appalling developments within Germany which have led to a resurgence of political forces once considered all but extinct in the old Bundesrepublik. But, as already stated, Deutschland is not the Bundesrepublik. There is a new band playing in new arenas in front of new audiences. The Germans know and feel this as much as their European neighbours. Opinions, views, hopes and fears abound. This study is a brief summary of our extensive research which we have conducted on this complex topic for a number of years.[1] As with all summaries, this, too, combines the benefits of brevity with the detriments of generalisation. Thus it is by necessity incomplete.

EUROPEANS AND THE GERMANS

Our research analysed how public opinion in ten countries of the European Community (EC) plus Poland, Hungary and Finland felt about Germany in general. We were particularly interested in assessing the reactions to German unification. In doing this research, it became obvious to us that no matter how rigorous the methodology, it would prove 'scientifically' inadequate to permit a definitive and 'objectively measurable' evaluation of how each country's population felt about Germany and the Germans at any given point in time, especially such a turbulent one as ours. These publics have become too diverse for any observer to be able to arrive at a valid characterisation of composite values such as 'The French view of the Germans is . . .'. The complexity of Frenchness renders any measures of the totality of French attitudes impossible. Which French? The Parisians or the provincials? Men or women? Young or old? Working class or bourgeois? Blue or white collar? Elite or mass? Southern or northern? Urban or rural? Even the most well-designed and comprehensive survey will be unable to convey with certainty collective views of such complexity and amorphous character which – complicating matters still – are subject to enormous fluctuation. Just because these feelings, views, opinions and attitudes cannot be presented without a reasonable doubt, however, does not mean that they do not exist or that they are not important. Indeed, we argue that they are, because they influence people's behaviour, and thus their politics. Hence, even though we are fully aware of the fact that every time we speak of a people's collective attitude vis-à-vis the Germans we are reducing complexity to the point of a simplifying distortion bordering on a cliché, we also know that such distortions exist in reality as perceptions which influence collective behaviour. Even though we realize that societies are becoming increasingly fragmented in terms of their opinions, habits and milieus, there are still aspects of every society which are characteristic of a collective which is most definitely more than just the sum of its individual parts. Thus, we agree with the statement made by Ludwig Fleck in the context of studying collective characteristics and observing other nations that 'we look with our own eyes but we see with the eyes of the collective'.[2] Stereotypes and preformed judgments based on history might be unfair in guiding contemporary behaviour and social action. Alas, it is a real and understandable, even if unfortunate, ordering mechanism in an increasingly disorderly world.

Above all, the explanatory power of our entire project is only meaningful in a strictly comparative context: geographic, cultural, synchronic (i.e. comparing the British view of Germans and Germany with that of the French, Spanish, Italian and Irish) on the one hand; and historical, longitudinal, diachronic (i.e. comparing the French view of the Germans exhibited in the 1950s with that encountered in the 1980s) on the other. Thus, our interpretation and analysis of each country's climate of opinion only makes sense against the backdrop of all other countries' as well as against its own history and those of the other countries.

The data for our evaluation stem from three sources: public opinion surveys; newspaper and magazine articles; and secondary materials written by country experts and published in three very valuable anthologies.[3] In terms of a systematic analysis of the data, we concentrated on five key periods which proved of major significance in the development of German unification and the restructuring of postwar European (and global) politics: Period 1 comprises the week between November 10 and 17, 1989, in other words the week following the opening of the Berlin wall, arguably the single most important event in the process of German unification. Period 2 concentrates on the week between Christmas and New Year's 1989–90 during which the Brandenburg Gate was opened and in which many newspapers carried extensive retrospectives on the events of 1989, featuring, of course, the opening of the Berlin wall and other matters pertaining to the German Question. Period 3 centres on the week of February 14–21, 1990 in which the actual unification of Germany was decided and the '2+4' agreement devised for its implementation by the international powers in Ottawa. The week of March 19–26, 1990 constitutes our period 4. This was the week which followed the first – and last – democratic election in what was then still the German Democratic Republic (GDR). Lastly, period 5 features the first two weeks of July 1990 which, among other events of world historic proportions, witnessed the monetary unification of the two Germanies under the aegis of the Deutsche Mark, thus all but eliminating even the faintest hopes of having the former East Germany develop along anything but the capitalist conditions exacted by West Germany's market economy (thus died the 'third way' if it ever existed other than in the minds of certain intellectuals); NATO's historic London conference which officially acknowledged the end of the Cold War; the annual meeting of the G-7 countries in Houston; and, perhaps most significantly, the Soviet Union's completely unexpected concession of having a united Germany remain in (or join) NATO.[4] In slightly less than nine months, the world had changed to a degree not witnessed since 1945. Just as in 1945, furthermore, Germany was both object and subject of this enormous change. Thus, we believe that with the systematic selection of these five time periods we have been able to gauge in a meaningful way the reaction among Germany's European neighbours to the events which transformed Germany and its politics in 1989 and 1990.

A number of questions and hypotheses guided our investigation. Were the reactions to German unification and the new Germany more positive or negative? If the former, how did they express themselves? If the latter, how was the fear or apprehension articulated? Was it mainly dominated by memory, i.e. a historical fear, or was it more contemporary? If the latter, was it more economic or political? Were there any worries about Germany's turning away from its commitments to the Single Market (i.e. Western Europe) due to the sudden opening of the East? Were there significant inter- as well as intra-country differences in the reactions to the 'German question'? As to the former, were the reactions different in small as compared to large countries? What about countries which suffered from German occupation in World War II as opposed to those that did not? In terms of intra-country differences, we were particularly interested in any visible left-right cleavages and variations between élite and mass opinions.

As is always the case, some of our initial hypotheses were borne out, others less so. Here then is an abbreviated summary of our findings.

(1) Germany engenders strong feelings on the part of all Europeans. It is futile to deny this (as has been the wish of some German diplomats and officials) or to fight it (as have some on the left) by claiming that the Germans are nothing special, that they are like everyone else and that the old Federal Republic as well as the new Germany are little more than oversized versions of Switzerland.[5] By virtue of the size of its population, that of its economy, its history, and its geographical location, Germany matters. That, indeed, is the very nature of a hegemon. The United States matters, too. Thus, people have opinions, feelings, attitudes, views concerning Germany – just as they do vis-à-vis the United States – which are qualitatively different from views of smaller, less powerful countries. We argue that there exists anti- and pro-Germanism, just like there exists anti- and pro-Americanism. There is little sense in denying this.[6] Germany – just like the United States – 'suffers' from the elephant problem: even if it does nothing, it is noticed by virtue of its importance and size (which in this case denotes much more than a geographic quantity).

(2) While history is not the sole lens by which Europeans view the Germans, it is safe to say that it is a very powerful one, arguably more powerful than is used in gauging other nations. Be it through such innocuous references as the regular labelling of German soccer players by the Italian public as '*panzeri*' and by calling the German national team '*Wehrmacht*'; or the endearing usage of the term '*Aatus*' when referring to Germans in Finland which is the plural for the Finnish '*Aatu*', the diminutive of the German 'Adolf'; Germany's Nazi past continues to cast a long shadow over its contemporary presence in Europe.[7] In the case of no other European country does its recent past play anywhere near a comparable role in terms of its assessment by its neighbours as it does in Germany's. We encountered no case in which Germany's past did not play a significant role in terms of that country's view of things German, even if only to deny that it did.

(3) The past is receding everywhere. In all our cases a decisive majority had positive associations with the Bundesrepublik. Nearly everywhere – the notable exceptions being Poland and Denmark with the Netherlands being a distant, though significant third – an equally impressive majority welcomed German unification. The degree of the warmth and enthusiasm for this support varied widely, but the data from opinion polls are quite decisive on this issue: Europeans welcomed Germany's unification.

(4) We also discerned two levels of the Europeans' reaction to German unification and things German in general. The first one could label the 'official' or 'legal' level. Propelled entirely by reason, it is the reaction which the respondents voice publicly, which they find acceptable and *salonfaehig* (suitable for polite company). After all, prejudices and fears are not to be stated concerning an issue which lies in the past and which – given its contemporary configuration – lends itself to few worries. It is this manifest level which public opinion polls have no difficulty in measuring quite accurately. It is the second, less official, or 'real' level which is a good deal more difficult to ascertain. Propelled by feelings and fears instead of reason, this level is voiced at the dinner tables, in pubs and in private. As such, it is barely gauged by opinion surveys. Yet, it exists, even beneath the manifest form of repeating the achievements of the Federal Republic. One cannot help but have the feeling that in certain cases the repeated assurances of the democratic nature of today's Germany, the reliability of its institutions, the stability of its economy, the pacifism of its youth, its deep commitment to Western values and its moorings in NATO – in other words of *not* being like any of the past 'bad' Germanies, be they of the Wilhelminian, Weimar, or Nazi persuasion – is like whistling in the dark. They sound too much like badly needed self-assurances in a situation of acute uncertainty.

(5) A country's role as a 'player' matters as does geographic distance from Germany. As a rule, the further away a country is from Germany, the less intense are the collective feelings of its population vis-à-vis Germany. Thus, the Dutch and the Danes have more intense – and negative – attitudes towards Germany than do the Greeks or the Irish. In terms of countries being 'players', the more this is (or has been) the case, as for example in the instances of Britain and France, the more their rivalry will propel their publics to hold negative views of Germany. In this case, too, distance is a significant variable. Thus, for example, American attitudes on the élite and mass level have been much more favourable to Germany than has been the case in either France or Britain reflecting in part a greater security – as well as indifference – by the American public concerning America's relationship with Germany as compared to the comparable British and French situations. Both France and Britain, suffer from what one could safely term 'imperial envy' concerning Germany's newly-won importance. Especially within the élites and the political class (see

point 7 below), anti-German sentiments have been quite pronounced in Paris as well as London. For the French, German unification meant a substantial loss in political importance. In the old world of the Bundesrepublik, the division of labour was clear: France was to dominate Western Europe politically with the Federal Republic assuming the role of economic leader. The creation of Deutschland meant an inevitable demotion of France in the area of political leadership in Europe. While for the British political class the change was less drastic, it still re-affirmed the growth of a new continental power for. which the British had developed little affection over the years. Moreover, a politically powerful and confident Germany would inevitably use its economic muscle to prod the British closer to the European project which – as is well known – continues to lack enthusiasm, perhaps even legitimacy, in the eyes of a considerable segment of the British political class as well as the public.

(6) Pre-Nazi relations are also important in shaping contemporary attitudes. In that sense, the historical legacy which continues to influence the present reaches well beyond the trauma of National Socialism. Thus, for example, even though Nazi occupation was very brutal in Greece, this seems to have left few traces in the current Greek climate of opinion vis-à-vis Germany. The much more hostile attitudes towards Germany in Denmark and Holland, for example, as compared to Greece are in good part connected to the difficulties of Dutch–German and Danish–German relations preceding the Nazi period. The animosity exhibited by the Danes vis-à-vis the Germans has as much to do with the trauma of 1940 as it does with the one of 1864. Indeed, the substantial differences in views of Germany exhibited in Holland and Belgium are related to events which preceded the Nazi occupation of either country. The decidedly pro-German sentiments of the Finns and the Hungarians are also anchored in pre-Nazi relations. Germany's positive image in Finland emanates from the important role which its universities and intellectuals played in Finland's struggle for independence. In Hungary, the long-held association of Germany as the embodiment of the West has sufficiently powerful pre- as well as post-Nazi components to have 'crowded out' any potentially negative images which might have lingered from Hungary's relationship to Germany and the Axis powers during the Second World War.

(7) In every country, one can discern a clear differentiation in the

reactions by age, education, and position in the social structure. Thus, for example, everywhere mass opinion has been much more favourably disposed toward the Germans than élite opinion. Indeed, were it not for the intellectuals and the members of the political classes, the climate of opinion in each of these countries would be more favourable towards the Germans than is presently the case.

(8) In every case, the political left has exhibited greater hostility towards Germany than the right. Tellingly, the fear and antipathy have nothing to do with Germany's Nazi past but concentrate instead on its current position as an economic and political hegemon in the new Europe. Even in a country such as Greece, where the political left has been consumed by an anti-Americanism which openly welcomed Germany as a possible replacement for American imperialism, an apprehension exists concerning Germany's excessive domination and potentially unbridled power. The left, to nobody's surprise, dislikes hegemons and excessive concentration of economic power, regardless of the particular agent involved.

(9) Just as with studies that focus on philo/anti-Semitism and pro/anti-Americanism, our research, too, says much less about the Germans than it does about those holding opinions about them. Indeed, images of Germany and the Germans have in most cases nothing to do with the reality of Germans and virtually everything to do with the particular country's view of itself and its relations with the world. Thus, for example, the decidedly positive view of German unification and Germany on the part of the Irish public derives much more from that public's historical experience with Britain than it does with anything concretely German.

CONCLUSION

Ultimately, our study addresses the question of collective memory in Europe. If there is one decisive factor which renders the project of a united Europe so difficult, it must be the virtual lack of a collective European memory. Surely Greeks and Danes, just like Germans and French, see themselves as Europeans and are obviously representatives of the Judaeo-Christian tradition. In a more immediate sense, however, in terms of offering an operative 'conscience collective' in a Durkheimian manner, there is little positive that ties Europeans together. In great contrast to the collective memory of the United States, there

Table 1.1 First reactions to German unification in selected countries

	Polls on German unification:			Positive impact of united Germany[c]	
	for[a] %	against[a] %	for[b] %	good influence on (country) %	
France	68	16	61		
Italy	66	18			
Netherlands	62	21			
Sweden	71	17			
U.S.	67	16	61		
Britain	41	49	45		
Poland			41	41 (32 negative)	
Hungary				78	
Czechoslovakia				53	
Russia				52	
Ukraine				60	
Lithuania				46	

Sources:
[a]*Business Week*, April 2, 1990, p. 47. [b]*Los Angeles Times/Economist* poll of January 1990. *The Economist*, Jan. 27, 1990, p. 48. Polls in October 1989 had ascertained a level of 71 per cent of the French, 70 per cent of the British, 83 per cent of Italians, but only 56 per cent of West Germans in the affirmative *before the fall* of the Wall. Cited by Richard Davy in *Europa Archiv*, no. 4 (Feb. 15, 1990), pp. 139–144. [c]*The Pulse of Europe: a Survey of Political and Social Values and Attitudes*, Washington D.C.: Times-Mirror Center for the People and the Press, 1991, pp. 199 and 207 and the tables on pp. 59–60, 74–76 and 128–129. The polls were taken in May 1991.

exists no common European memory which unites. Rather, it is a memory of division, of negation, of the 'other'. In this collective of negative memory, 'there appears to be a black thread which runs through the collective minds of the otherwise divided memory of the Europeans, and that is a largely negative image of the Germans'.[8]

Notes

1. Some of the publications emanating from this research have been: Andrei S. Markovits and Simon Reich, *Good Guys Finish First: German Hegemony in a New Europe* (Ithaca: Cornell University Press, forthcoming); 'Germany's Image in a New Climate of Opinion: Optimists and Pessimists Thirteen European Publics', Paper presented at the 1992 Annual Meeting of the American Political Science Association, The Palmer

House, Chicago, Illinois, September 3–6, 1992; 'Deutschlands neues Gesicht: Ueber deutsche Hegemonie in Europa' in *Leviathan*, (March 1992), pp. 1–49; 'The Latest Stage of the German Question: *Pax Germanica* in the New Europe' in *The Journal of Arms Control: Contemporary Security Policy*, Volume 12, Number 3, (December 1991), pp. 60–76; 'Modell Deutschland and the New Europe' in *Telos*, Number 89, (Fall 1991), pp. 45–63; 'The New Face of Germany: Gramsci, Hegemony and Europe' in the Center for European Studies, Harvard University Working Paper Series, September 1991; and 'Should Europe Fear the Germans?' in *German Politics and Society*, (Summer 1991), pp. 1–20.

2. Ludwig Fleck, as cited in Ingo Kolboom, 'Deutschlandbilder der Franzosen: Der Tod des Dauerdeutschen' in Guenter Trautmann, *Die haesslichen Deutschen?*, p. 213.

3. In addition to gathering local surveys from as many of the countries as we could, we also relied on a number of cross-European surveys which gauged the perception of Germans by Europeans. Most notable among these pan-European surveys were the ones conducted by *The Economist*, the Belgian newspaper *Le Soir*, the French paper *Libération* and the Allensbach Institute in the *Allensbacher Berichte* of 1990.

   As to the newspapers used in our analysis, here is a comprehensive list:

   Greece: *Anti, Avghi, Eleftheros Tipos, Kathimerini, Ta Nea, To Vima.*
   Portugal: *Correio da Manha, Expresso, Journal de O Dia, O Diario.*
   Spain: *ABC, Diario 16, El Pais, Ya.*
   Ireland: The *Irish Independent*, The *Irish Times.*
   Belgium: *Het Laatste Nieuws, La Libre Belgique, Le Soir.*
   Holland: *De Telegraaf, Het Parool, NRC/Handelsblad.*
   Denmark: *Politiken.*
   Italy: *Corriere della Serra, Il Messagero, La Repubblica, La Stampa, L'Expresso, L'Unita.*
   France: *Le Canard Enchainé, L'Express, L'Humanité, Le Figaro, Le Monde, Le Nouvel Observateur, Le Point, Libération.*
   Britain: *New Statesman*, The *Economist*, The *Financial Times*, The *Guardian*, The *Independent*, The *Spectator*, *The Times.*
   Hungary: *Magyar Hirlap, Nepszabadsag.*

   The three anthologies which proved immensely useful for our research are: Ulrike Liebert and Wolfgang Merkel (eds.) *Die Politik zur deutschen Einheit: Probleme – Strategien – Kontroversen* (Opladen: Leske und Budrich, 1991); Guenter Trautmann (ed.) *Die haesslichen Deutschen? Deutschland im Spiegel der westlichen und oestlichen Nachbarn* (Darmstadt: Wissenschaftliche Buchgesellschaft, 1991); and Harold James and Marla Stone (eds.) *When the Wall Came Down: Reactions to German Unification* (New York: Routledge, 1992).

4. This periodisation was first used by Andrei S. Markovits in his contribution to the Liebert/Merkel volume entitled 'Die deutsche Frage – Perzeptionen und Politik in der Europaeischen Gemeinschaft' in Liebert/Merkel, *Einheit*, pp. 321–341.

5. For a prototypical example of such an assessment which views Germany's politics and power merely as 'grossschweizerisch,' see Lothar

Kettenacker, 'Englische Spekulationen ueber die Deutschen' in Trautmann, *Die haesslichen Deutschen*? p. 207.

6. Thus, we find studies which try to deny the existence of anti-Americanism (or anti-Semitism for that matter) by showing its allegedly minoritarian quantitative presence in public opinion as assessed by survey data very limited, indeed severely flawed in their interpretation. A particularly egregious example of such flawed interpretation can be found in Steven K. Smith and Douglas A. Wertman, 'Redefining U.S. – West European Relations in the 1990s: West European Public Opinion in the Post-Cold War Era' in *PS*, Volume 25, Number 2, (June 1992), pp. 188–195. To demonstrate that only a minority – though as the authors' data clearly convey often not an insubstantial one – of European publics exhibits hostile attitudes towards the United States is perfectly reasonable, though hardly novel. To then conclude that anti-Americanism is all but negligible in its presence in European politics, culture and the world of decision makers – in other words that it does not matter – is erroneous.

7. For a nice analysis of how German sport teams and sport stars are invariably associated with warlike images, particularly hailing from World War II, see Manfred Schneider, 'Die Erotik des Fernsehsports. Beobachtungen zur heroischen Mystik des Alltags.' (unpublished manuscript delivered as a lecture on the panel 'Forum 2: Sport im internationalen Fernsehgeschaeft' at the Cologne Conference – Medienforum, Cologne, Germany, June 1, 1992.) Schneider also mentions how German soccer players in England are often referred to as 'tanks'. The Dutch regularly refer to German soccer players as 'Landsknechte'. That images of World War II, militarism and national socialism are regularly conjured up by sportscasters and the yellow press whenever the German national team plays its arch rivals, the Dutch, as well the French, the Danes and the English is yet further testimony to the fact that the Nazi interlude has not yet disappeared from European popular culture. On the positive connotation of 'Aatu' in Finnish, see Antti S. Vihinen, 'Das Deutschenbild aus finnischer Sicht – viel Positives, selten Negatives' in Trautmann, *Die haesslichen Deutschen?* p. 268.

8. Rusconi, as quoted in Luigi Vittorio Ferraris, 'Die haesslichen Deutschen' in Trautmann, *Die haesslichen Deutschen?* p. 245.

2 Germany, Maastricht and Yugoslavia: Altered Identities and Abiding Demarcations

Arnold J. Heidenheimer*

German politics remained easier to analyse when Germany was divided neatly between East and West than it has become now that so
many of the familiar political and conceptual boundaries and labels
have been transformed. Where Ostpolitik and West European integration once were distinct policy goals to be balanced out, since German
unification the overlapping of arenas has proceeded apace. East Germany became part of the European Community, but at the same time
all of Eastern Europe posed diverse additional problems for the EC on
the eve of its scheduled forward thrust toward economic and political
integration. For those who gathered to sign the crucial treaty at Maastricht
in December, 1991, ensuing developments transformed 1992 into a year
of great disappointments.

During the first year after the fall of the Wall, it appeared that the
consequences of German unification might on balance help more than
hurt the impetus toward Community integration. But then the German
reliance on high interest rates and other by-products of the unification
process began to generate contrary effects. Highly visible on the European
panorama was the inability of the leading EC members to agree on
how to handle a problem of violence on their doorsteps, in Yugoslavia.
How can one approach the problem of how changes in German policy
toward the dismemberment of Yugoslavia possibly affected attitudes
toward the conditions of European integration in the period following
the signing of the Maastricht Treaty in December, 1991?

I THREE LANDSCAPES

In this essay I will attempt to explore some neglected connections by
overlaying three sets of political landscapes and interaction systems.

44

In one large-scale background landscape the focus will be on the two state systems of Western and Central Europe which were being transformed the most during the quinquennium since 1989, one experiencing fusion, Germany, and the other experiencing fission, Yugoslavia.

The second landscape will be constituted by the party and governmental leadership constellation of the Federal Republic, with a focus on its two most important decision-makers, Chancellor Helmut Kohl and Foreign Minister Hans Dietrich Genscher, both of whom had joined as teenagers in 1946 the parties they later came to head, and a younger cohort of politicians who entered political careers some two decades later, in the 1960s. It will be drawn in greater detail.

The third landscape is both more skeletal and more two-dimensional, accommodating both the spatial demarcations and the dynamics which connect short-term convulsions to longer-term memories and identities. A pair of cities on the peripheries of historical German influence, both with symbolic resonance, exemplify polarities. The Bosnian capital of Sarajevo, site of infectious violence in 1914 as in 1992, symbolizes the inheritance of national and ethnic rivalries and conflicts. Maastricht will stand for the European attempt to eclipse these traditions through the European Community's plan to have the 1990s become a period of supra-national economic and political integration.

II CONCEPTUAL MARKERS AND LINKAGES

The rationale for pairing Germany with Yugoslavia is grounded in the attempt to relate the short-term events of 1989–92 to the *longue durée* processes of nation-building and nation-dismantling, which straddled the preceding two centuries.[1] As nation states consolidated and standardised the reach of national programmes in the 19th century, they caused intra-national regional differences to diminish, whereas identity-shaping policies like those of taxation, military service and education, became more heterogeneous than previously on the other sides of sets of national borders. Hence one can hold, with Charles Tilly, that for the century leading up to 1914, conditions 'homogenized within states, and heterogenized among states'.[2]

These tendencies came to be altered greatly a half century later, especially during the decades from the 1960s to the 1980s. During this period cross-country differences came to be diminished in distinct but nonetheless symmetrical ways as among both the West and

East European countries. Applying the same criteria to the situation which developed after the fall of the Wall leads one to conclude that the Federal Republic achieved a very distinctive status as a consequence of unification.

For since 1990 one can discern that political 'fusion' heterogenised conditions within the expanded Federal Republic to a degree far exceeding similar trends in any other European Community country. At the same time the degree of homogenisation among states, and the porousness of national boundaries, advanced greatly as regards Germany and both its sets of western and eastern neighbours.

Poland and Hungary at times played instrumental roles in setting up the conditions that led to German unification. It is Yugoslavia, however, which merits being paired with Germany in our context because, more than any other former communist country, the changes induced by 'fission' of the 1989–92 period also led to great increases of heterogeneity within its former state boundaries. It is this broad complementarity to developments in Germany that may have helped generate a fateful nexus between the two transformations.

Differences that developed from fusion among East and West German *Länder* did not approach the intensity of conflict that ensued from fission as among Croatia, Bosnia and Serbia. But fusion/fission developments in both arenas were to create problems, each in their own way, for the integration efforts of the European Community, which had counted on harnessing German along with other West European energies so as to achieve maximal supra-national economic and political homogeneity by the year 2000.

The demarcations on the western and eastern borders of the Germanies of 1990–91 were embedded in elements with both temporal and spatial dimensions. Thus the question of agreeing to a German-Polish and Croatian-Serbian border entailed not only markers like the Oder and Neisse rivers, but also key dates like '1914', '1939' and '1941'.[3] That the reemergent Croatia was stressing continuity to the Nazi client state of the 1940s was clear to both its friends and enemies. Entitlements to the territories initially allocated to World War I successor states, like Poland and Yugoslavia, had to be re-confirmed by politicians like Kohl and Genscher. They in turn belonged to a generation born around the late 1920s, or about midway between the outbreak of the first and the end of the second of the two great conflicts waged and lost by Germany. As politicians of those '*Jahrgang*' vintages, they were members of what came to be called the cohort of the '*Flakhelfer*', teenage males in war-time Germany who did military service with units like anti-aircraft batteries in the last phases of the war.

In line with Mannheim's concepts, Kohl and Genscher, as members of a generation with a common location in socio-political time and space, were disposed toward 'a certain characteristic mode of thought and experience and a characteristic type of historically relevant action'.[4] In terms of Federal Republican chronology they were members of the third generation of post-war politicians, coming after those like Adenauer and Schumacher, who were already adults during the first war, and those like Kiesinger and Schmidt, who served as either civilian or military officials during the 1939–45 conflict.

Of the two, Kohl may be distinguished as a more mainstream or system maintenance type of politician, while Genscher may be approached as a more explorative, innovative or even transcendent representative of this political cohort. As the younger of the two, Kohl (b. 1930) experienced in the 1940s even more what he himself labelled the *'Gnade der späten Geburt'*. Only a little more than a year elapsed between his induction as a flak-helper on his fifteenth birthday, one month before the end of the war, and his entry into the CDU as a Gymnasium student in Ludwigshafen. Repeatedly setting new marks as the youngest office holder he was able to quickly climb the ladder of the Federal Republic's dominant party in one of the heartlands of CDU power. Genscher (b. 1927), by contrast, experienced regular military service for several years, and pursued his education in the Soviet zone and the GDR. Coming from a family with German national orientation, he had more difficulty finding a party political 'home', which then initially became the Liberal Democratic Party in the Saxon university town of Halle. His subsequent record of ministerial longevity in Bonn may be viewed as especially unusual for someone who only moved to the Federal Republic in 1952, at the age of 25.

III   GENSCHER AND KOHL'S POLICY INHERITANCES

When Kohl and Genscher negotiated the terms of German unification, they were capping careers which constituted very different trains of ideological and policy inheritance in the Federal Republic. Both avowed to follow in the steps of great political figures: Adenauer in the case of Kohl, Stresemann for Genscher, but the linkages were different ones. Kohl entered CDU politics next-door to Adenauer's Rhineland base, and earned his elevation through yeoman service,

as *Landtag* deputy, Fraktion chairman, and then head of *Land* government in Mainz, and later as reinvigorator of the party's Federal organisation in the 1970s. Entering FDP politics in the 1950s, Genscher
benefited from sponsorship by Thomas Dehler, in a period when the
FDP's opposition to Adenauer's policies led it it to oppose the Treaty
of Rome, which founded the EC. Being in the vanguard of the group
that later prepared the FDP's 1960s coalition switch, led to Genscher's
appointment to the Interior Ministry in Willy Brandt's SPD-FDP government in 1969.

A considerable gulf separated Genscher from Kohl especially with
regard to their parties' *Ostpolitik* and *Deutschland* policies in the 1970s.
When he switched to the Foreign Office in 1974, Genscher inherited
not only Ostpolitik, but also new opportunities created by Germany's
admission to the UN in 1973, and then by the opening for further
East-West exchanges created by the Helsinki Declaration of 1975. Kohl,
as opposition leader in the Bundestag, had to cope with the bitter resistance to Ostpolitik which led the CDU to join the Albanian communists and the Italian neo-fascists as the only parties which refused to
endorse the Helsinki Accords, and coaxed the CDU to cut itself loose
from this ballast by the time that it regained Federal office.[5]

When the two party leaders joined in the 1982 coalition government, Genscher represented the junior partner but, as his biography
puts it, 'Kohl in a way became Chancellor under Hans-Dietrich
Genscher.'[6] Genscher was ahead of Kohl by 13 years of federal ministerial experience, and his talents for Bonn infighting had been honed
in having to assert himself against Helmut Schmidt's tendency to grab
the foreign policy helm.

Throughout the next decade Genscher was able to maintain strong
FDP influence in the Foreign Office, guarding its autonomy partly by
keeping committed Christian Democrats from occupying the politically
sensitive top positions. CDU influence on international affairs thus was
channelled primarily through the Defence Ministry, leading to the quip
that 'Genscher modernizes thinking, while we modernize weapons'.
Among frustrated Christian Democrats it bred the feeling that in foreign affairs the small FDP was wagging the large CDU dog, especially
as the Genscherites also kept the CDU chairman of the Bundestag Foreign
affairs committee at arm's length.

Kohl laid a basis for changing this pattern by ignoring the precedent of recruiting his Foreign and Security Advisor from the Foreign
Office, and instead filling this position with Horst Teltschik (b.1940)
who had served as his ghost writer in Mainz and Bonn for the preced-

ing decade.[7] Teltschik had experienced childhood expulsion from the Sudetenland, became a student of Soviet politics, and Stephen Szabo recounts that while a Christian Democratic student politician at the Free University, he had been 'close to Richard von Löwenthal', (an elevation to the noblesse de robe which would have amused the latter). He later came to like being described in the press as the 'German Henry Kissinger', as members of Kohl's staff tried to give the Chancellery more of a foreign policy voice, with the result that 'Teltschik had a very poor personal relationship with Genscher and with the foreign minister's top aides.'[8] With Kohl's conservative young Turks in touch with their Reaganite peers in Washington, there were plenty of sparks between the two offices, but generally the foul-ups like Bitburg were debited against the Chancellery.

Whereas previous chancellors had often enjoyed a so-called 'Chancellor bonus' over their parties' survey ratings, it was Genscher and not Kohl who became the most popular politician of the late 1980s. While Kohl never managed to become more popular than his party, Genscher did engender such a lead, particularly after he laid down the FDP chairmanship in 1986. Another contrast lies in their facility with the English language. Both men initially lacked a good command of English, because they had their schooling in the Soviet and French zones of occupied Germany, respectively. Genscher, through great effort, developed a good speaking ability, whereas Kohl continued to rely totally on interpreters.

The curious interaction that developed between the two leaders' reputation and popularity in the 1980s was influenced by the equilibrating pro-détente tilt which the Federal Republic's foreign policy carried over under Genscher into the CDU-FDP government. The Foreign Office basked in extraordinary domestic acclaim, based partly on an unusual ideological congruity between its East-West and European policies, and grassroots West German developments like the growth of the peace movement. The media both at home and abroad began to speak of 'Genscherism' as shorthand for détente maintenance. The second half of the 1980s was a period of great political opportunity and declining threat, as the EC's Single European Act and the consequences of Gorbachev's rise caused the 'heterogeneity between states' to diminish at a perceptible, though measured pace. Slow shifts in the tectonic plates underlying the political and military alliances helped Genscher's popularity to stay ahead of that of Kohl, as the CDU experienced new lows in both the 1987 Federal and 1989 European elections. Probably a good part of Genscher's edge is attributable to the support of adherents of the far-flung and pre-dominantly Protestant German peace movement. How these loyalties would be channelled after the falling away of the East-West military confrontation would hence structure a choice arena where Genscher's interests could intersect with those of members of the 1960s genera-tion who espoused some of the movement's positions within both the Social Democratic and Green parties.

IV YUGOSLAVIA AND POST-UNIFICATION DIPLOMACY

Then ensued the historic opportunity played out during the eleven months between the fall of the Wall on November 9, 1989, and the formalization of unification on October 3, 1990. The terms of the unification process helped dismantle the jurisdictional barriers delimit-ing the Chancellery's role, since inter-German, foreign and defence policies were inextricably mingled in the negotiations. Inevitably the staffs of Genscher and Kohl competed with each other so that at times they did not communicate or failed to consult each other.[9] Logs were closely scrutinised as to how many times Teltschik met with Gorbachev, or how many hours Genscher spent with Shevardnadse. American of-ficials, some of whom still harboured suspicions that Genscher might make unnecessary concessions to the Soviets, helped move the ball to Kohl when they could. For this and other reasons, as the negotiations progressed 'Kohl took a larger role, eventually relegating Genscher to a secondary position.'[10]

The question of Yugoslavia's dismemberment was put on the Ger-man policy agenda via the chancellery's back door. In late August 1990, Teltschik made time in his schedule for a contact which his CSU colleagues had been cultivating for the previous four years, by holding a secret two-hour talk with a personal emissary of the Croatian President, Franjo Tudjman. He conducted it 'without the knowledge of the Foreign Office', and was told that the Croats 'oriented themselves exclusively toward Germany', and were requesting the Federal Repub-lic's recognition of their sovereignty.[11] This encounter led to the emergent Yugoslav civil war becoming the 'one situation in which German for-eign policy exhibited a high profile', and subsequently 'provoked the most concern'.[12]

Until Croatia and Slovenia declared independence in June 1991, German policy had been aligned with that of that U.S. and the EC in favour of maintaining Yugoslav unity. In late spring of 1991, as the outbreak of open hostilities between Serbs and Croats began, a vast and almost unprecedented pro-Croat campaign swept German public and party opinion. The Bavarian CSU, with whom the prosperous post-1945 Croat community had strong links, led the way, along with other organizations reflecting Catholic support. The anti-Serb campaign won legitimation because it was orchestrated by one of the publishers of the *Frankfurter Allgemeine Zeitung*, Johann Georg Reissmuller, who published almost daily articles which influenced other news and TV journalists. Then it came to be supported by influential political groups within all three major parties and the media close to them. This support from almost all quarters, right across the Left-Right spectrum, developed to a degree apparently unparalleled in any other Western country, including the United States, where Croatian-Americans were also well-organised.

The terms on which they had achieved their own unification apparently encouraged something of a missionary consciousness, as in the argument of 'numerous German politicians' that 'having granted self-determination to the East Germans, they could hardly do less for others seeking to go their own way'.[13] Among the supporters were SPD political leaders who had become familiar to the public since their role in the '1968 movement' and the Young Socialists, like Karsten Voigt (b.1941) and Norbert Gansel (b.1940).

On June 18, 1991 all the Bundestag parties except the PDS passed a resolution supporting self-determination in Yugoslavia. A week later Slovenia and Croatia declared independence and two days after that Gansel and Voigt demanded that they be given diplomatic recognition. The pressure on Genscher was intensified at a July 1st meeting of the Bundestag Foreign Policy Committee at which both CDU and SPD demanded that Germany actively push the European Community to adopt a policy similar to Germany's.[14]

Counsels against a unilateral German recognition policy, because of its repercussions both to the East and West, were then undercut by the Moscow coup in August, 1991. The argument that Yugoslav disintegration should not be allowed to serve as a model for the Soviet Union, became moot as the Soviet republics split away.

If disappearances of the familiar East-West landmarks produced disorientation among experienced Cold War veterans of the Genscher-Kohl generation, the Yugoslav dilemmas posed particular problems for leading members of the 1960s generation who had by the late 1980s come to occupy key positions especially within the SPD parliamentary party. For them Yugoslavia was not just a Balkan country, but rather it represented a political system to which many developed deep attachments in the 1970s. Furthermore, the consequence of Yugoslav fission also rubbed political sore points that had developed during German fusion. For the rebuffs encountered by the SPD in the Neue Länder called into question their attitude toward movements aiming for self-determination, as they had been manifested both before and after the fall of the SED regime. Given the potential for shaping a new German policy toward the Eastern territories, they were willing to transcend critical attitudes like those toward Tudjman and the Croat nationalists, which had been rooted in the 1940s, a time when they, like Teltschik, were still children.

Although Tudjman had been received by Kohl on July 18, 1991, a formal policy follow-through toward recognition occurred only in the autumn, when Genscher overcame his qualms. According to one observer, one factor for his reversal was that the above-mentioned press campaign led some CDU supporters of the previous position to fall away. Another was seen as Genscher's conviction that the Germans especially, having just achieved their full sovereignty 'could not deny support to others in their striving for sovereignty'. But the decisive influence is attributed to the position of key Social Democrats – Karsten Voigt, Norbert Gansel, Guenther Verheugen (b.1944) and Gernot Erler (b.1944) – with whom Genscher had regularly discussed Yugoslavia in the summer and autumn of 1991. Voigt and Gansel finally succeeded in persuading the SPD Bundestag Fraktion to support rapid recognition against the advice of the East European specialist, Erler. This led to overwhelming support from the SPD and Greens, as well as government deputies, for a Bundestag resolution on November 14, 1991.[15]

German diplomats, aware of the likely consequences of recognition, made an attempt to get Genscher to hold out against it. When the Muslim President of Bosnia went to see Genscher in November, 1991 to plead against recognition, because it would invite Serbian and Croatian aggression against Bosnia, he was briefed by the German ambassador to Belgrade. Other groups in the Foreign Office, however, were broadening alliances with those who espoused the pro-recognition policies of Austria and the Vatican. In November Genscher had a key conversation with the Pope, just as the pressure to oppose the relevant organs of the UN and the European Community was building up in Bonn. The EC had in September set up a commission under Robert Badinter to establish criteria in terms of minority rights and majority consensus, for the recognition of breakaway Yugoslav republics.[16] Since Croatia was never certified as having met the minority rights tests, the Germans' pressure for recognition was in 'direct conflict with the commissions findings'.[17]

V THE GERMAN RECOGNITION POLICY AND MAASTRICHT

As European Ministers approached the conference at which they were due to approve the community's treaty at Maastricht, both history and geography caused Yugoslavia to be 'seen as a problem that Europe/the EC should solve on its own', now that its leading powers 'were cemented together institutionally'. Invoking the spirit of Maastricht, Mitterrand got Kohl to agree 'that any recognition of Croatia and Slovenia would only occur by EC members acting together', and German diplomats largely favoured this common front. On the eve of the conference, however, Genscher unleashed an unprecedented campaign to outmanoeuvre UN conciliation efforts being pursued through Cyrus Vance, and to counter the efforts of the other EC members to delay the German steamroller.

The German cabinet declared on December 11 that it would recognise Croatia and Slovenia, and in subsequent days German diplomacy unleashed all-out efforts to get the other EC members to overcome their reservations. Utilising 'an unusual amount of arm-twisting and muscle-flexing', and driven by previous commitments and 'domestic considerations', Germany made evident in an unsubtle manner that it intended to 'demonstrate that it was determined to take the lead on this issue'.[18] *The New York Times* of January 7, 1992, duly reported that 'an era drew to a close as a united Germany challenged the authority of the United Nations Secretary General and Washington, long Germany's big brother across the sea. By sweeping away British and French objections, reunited Germany did, for the first time, what rump Germany had never dared, forcefully elbowing through an unpopular move it perceived as crucial to its own interests'.

It is fascinating to note how the activities and roles of Genscher and Kohl complemented each other, especially over the weekend of December 13–15, 1991. While Genscher was overseeing the German diplomatic Blitzkrieg focused on the EC and the United Nations, Kohl was preparing to meet with Blockflöten of the East German and other party colleagues at the first all-German CDU party convention in Dresden. The topic was mutual accommodation of the East and West German Christian Democrats, even as his government was moving ahead of others to recognize Croatia and Slovenia.

Der Spiegel reports how Genscher mobilised spatial resources of the Foreign Service by placing dozens of phone calls to government heads and foreign ministers around the globe, in a successful effort to cash in IOUs and to secure backing for his tough reply to UN Secretary General Perez de Cuellar's request that Bonn delay its intended recognition. In preparing for what a Genscher advisor is quoted as calling the 'mother of all battles', Genscher pulled Roland Dumas over to his side by arguing that 'it could not be accepted that the Americans through the UN undermine the peace efforts of the Europeans'. With this alignment shift, the EC foreign ministers gave way to the German demand to recognise Croatia, though there was a compromise on the timing.

On Monday, December 16, the Germans persevered in a ten-hour marathon session of EC ministers in Brussels, which led to a formula on Yugoslavia which Gensher claimed exceeded the expectation of the Bonn Government. But *Der Spiegel* commented, 'Nicht jeder Sieg ist auch ein Gewinn' (not every victory is a gain), and also reported that President von Weizsaecker had wondered whether the pressure exerted by the Germans had not nurtured avoidable resentment against the reunited Germany.[19]

Meanwhile Kohl was utilising centre stage in Dresden to intrigue his audience through artful counterfactual history. Recalling that he had joined the CDU in Ludwigshafen in 1946 at the age of 16, he speculated on what he *might* have done if he had been living in Leipzig instead. He suggested he would probably have followed the opportunities for a young politician, by pursuing a career in the East German CDU, even though it meant following the prescribed roles laid down for politicians of a 'block-party'. Of course it was Genscher who had faced just such a dilemma when he joined the LDP in Halle as a 19-year old in 1946. His stand for détente, as foreign minister, had allowed him to make frequent trips back to Halle as a private visitor in the 1980s. The personal popularity which he had built up was no doubt a factor in the excellent showing of the FDP in the first all-German elections; the CDU had done well, but the FDP had done even better in the new Länder. But whereas the CDU was encountering severe problems in coping with its own internal heterogeneity, as shown by what happened to the CDU Minister Presidents who were hold-overs from the East German CDU, the FDP was less vulnerable.

In the weeks after Maastricht the key question of why the Germans had actually implemented recognition a month before the agreed January 15, 1992 date was one about which Western politicians heard differing versions. When they talked to Genscher they were told he was willing to be patient, but had a problem of managing Kohl's impatience. When they talked to Kohl, the attributions had the reverse flip. Probably both were utilizing tactics which they had honed during the 2+4 negotiations, but at the same time it was evident that they were also jockeying so as to maximize the credit which their role in officially implementing recognition would garner with the German public, where there were points to be scored on both the left and right spectrum.

VI SMALL COUNTRIES AND 'THE NEW ASSERTIVENESS'

The year 1992, long touted as due to mark a seminal turning point for European integration, in fact became a year of disappointment for advocates of that goal. Key milestones on the timetable – the buildup to a common currency, the cementing of European political cooperation (EPC), and the strengthening of Community institutions – suffered grievous impairment. Derailment was most obvious on the road toward European monetary policy, but anxieties raised by the Yugoslav conflict and influx of asylum-seekers from Bosnia reminded political élites of their failure to cope with ethnic problems that had proved the bane of previous generations. Politicians and diplomats, no longer basking in eulogies, sought to shift the blame.

Most unsettling were the votes of low or limited confidence cast by several key national electorates. The fact that the French, whose government had shared the pro-integration leadership, only barely endorsed the Maastricht treaty in the September 1992 referendum, came as a shock. This was unexpected, since the negative outcome in Denmark in June had set the mood of scepticism, which was echoed again later, as in the Swiss referendum defeat of the EEA treaty on December 6. Given their propinquity to Germany, this raised the question of whether some Danish and Swiss 'No' votes were triggered not only by suspicions toward EC bureaucracy, but also by reactions against the increased assertiveness of post-unification German economic and foreign policies, as in the Yugoslav case.

Contesting interpretations were presented in the 'non-German media'. Harald Müller criticised the overreaction to Germany's 'new assertiveness', and asked for due recognition of the 'full awareness of the shadows cast by its past' having 'become a remarkable quality of German foreign policy during the past twenty-five years'.[20]

Nonetheless, significant components of élite and mass opinion among Germany's small neighbours may well have reacted against some by-products of German priorities. Thus in the autumn of 1991, the Dutch opposed the German push for Croatian recognition, 'partly because they saw German pressure and action as incompatible with the Maastricht process.'[21] More Danes may also have been led to question whether binding Germany through enhanced integration would 'mitigate German dominance or only make the unified country more powerful. This latter assumption in part fuelled Danish rejection of the Maastricht treaty in June, 1992'.[22] In Denmark those who viewed the ongoing German unification process favourably in January, 1990, were outnumbered two to one by those holding negative views. Fifteen months later many factors influenced the negative vote on Maastricht, but there could be 'no doubt that the Danes' profound suspicions and dislike of Germany played a role in their decision.'[23] The Germans had agreed to a clause in the Maastricht treaty which would allow the Danes to prevent Germans from buying up their beach houses, but perhaps visions of an emergent German beachhead in Croatia may have inflated rather than diminished latent
apprehensions.

As the European unification project lost its élan and impetus after the Danish vote in June, the key architect of German foreign policy was no longer in office. Genscher's resignation in April, 1992 was not totally unexpected, since after 18 years in office the pace had come to show some effects on his health. But to many of his colleagues, it appeared that he chose the timing partly because 'he had misjudged a European issue right on his doorstep'.[24]

As politicians who had personal memories of wartime violence and Nazi brutality, Genscher and Kohl might have been expected to display in the Yugoslav case some of the sensitivities which they eventually demonstrated with regard to the Polish frontier. They were aware of the fears of the smaller neighbours of becoming German client states, but in the Yugoslav case they were competing for the support of younger supporters and voters, for whom the Serbian provocations aroused unprecedented moral indignation. After the divisions aroused by German abstention during the Gulf War, voters of the younger and middle-aged generations were concerned about the loss of direction in handling the consequences of both German fusion and Yugoslav fission. In this setting, Kohl may have seen an opportunity to seize the initiative from Genscher, as he had at times during the unification talks. Thus some observers interpret the events of late 1991 as a period in which

Genscher 'came under pressure from Chancellor Kohl, who was already predisposed to recognition'.[25]

The contrary interpretation was articulated by Rudolf Augstein, who asked: 'What is motivating the experienced German foreign minister to entice his Chancellor and all of us into this trap? Does the Greater German Federal Republic have no other mission than to rely on the Deutsche Mark so as to align other EC Countries into position for the Croats and against the Serbs. To provide the Croats verbal assistance against the Serbs, even though one disposes over no military means borders on "Grössenwahn" (megalomania)'.[26] By early 1993, with the relocation of violent conflict to Bosnia having brought about possibly the most extreme worst case scenario foreseeable in 1991, other Germans joined in criticising their government's recognition policy in harsh terms.[27]

REVIEW

In the 15 months following the European Community's acceptance of the German demand for early recognition of Slovenian and Croat sovereignty, awareness has grown that far from narrowing the conflict, its timing had greatly exacerbated it. The names of the two cities to which this tale is linked have become synonymous with blasphemy. Sarajevo has come to stand for the failure to stop the slaughter of civilian populations by political means. Maastricht has for a wider range of reasons caused politicians in Britain and other EC member countries to 'avoid mention of the dreaded M-word as if it might invoke a curse'.[28]

It is not the purpose of this analysis to try to anticipate what the ultimate most dispassionate judgment of these processes of disintegration will come to be. Rather, it is to try to discern what factors may have impelled German leaders to shift policies in both substance and style so radically at such a delicate juncture. Contributing to this outcome, I find, was the recasting of competition among German policy coalitions for whom the evaluation of alternatives was strongly shaped by generationally distinctive priorities in relation to sets of potential allies and adversaries. The thesis advanced here holds that the coinciding of some side-effects of German fusion and Yugoslav fission weakened the European Community's ability to cope with ethnic conflicts on its borders and to advance integration within its core.

Notes

* Among the numerous people who helped greatly in the course of this research, I would like to acknowledge particularly the assistance of Marina Achenbach, Chris Cordes, Herbert Korfmacher, Harry Pross and Stephen Szabo. The writing was concluded in April 1993.

1. Arnold Heidenheimer. 'Zeitliche und Raümliche Bezugsrahmen der Entwicklung der Bundesrepublik', Bernhard Blanke and Hellmut Wollmann (eds.) *Die alte Bundesrepublik*. Opladen: Westdeutscher Verlag. 1991. pp. 33–44.
2. Charles Tilly. *Coercion, Capital and European States*: 1990–2. Cambridge: Blackwell. 1992. p. 116.
3. Carlos Widmann. 'Ohne 1941, Kein 1991', *Der Spiegel*. 1991 Nr. 40, p. 217.
4. Karl Mannheim. 'The Problem of Generations', in *Essays on the Sociology of Knowledge* (ed., Paul Kecskemeti) London: Routledge and Kegan Paul. 1959. p. 291.
5. Clay Clemens. 'Power in Moderation: Helmut Kohl and Political Leadership in Germany, 1973–89', Paper presented at the German Studies Conference, October 1–4, 1992.
6. Helmut R. Schulze and Richard Kiesler. *Hans-Dieter Genscher: Ein deutscher Aussenminister*, Muenchen: Bertelsmann, 1990 p. 54.
7. Werner Filmer and Heribert Schwan, *Helmut Kohl*. Düsseldorf: Econ. 1990. p. 230.
8. Stephen F. Szabo. *The Diplomacy of German Unification*. New York: St. Martin's Press. 1992. p. 25.
9. Ibid. pp. 25, 74.
10. Ibid, p. 82.
11. Horst Teltschik. *329 Tage*. Berlin: Seidler, 1990 pp. 347–48.
12. Harald Müller, 'German Foreign Policy after Unification', in P. B. Stares, ed. *The New Germany and the New Europe*. Washington: Brookings 1991. p. 150.
13. John Newhouse, 'The Diplomatic Round: Dodging the Problem', *The New Yorker*, August 24, 1992. p. 63.
14. Gabriele Haasen, and Steven E. Sokol, 'Where is the Spirit of Maastricht? EC Foreign Policy and the Yugoslav Crisis' Ms., Washington, DC. School for Advanced International Studies, 1992. p. 80.
15. Andreas Zumach, 'Die UNO und der Krieg', in Erich Rothfelder, ed *Krieg auf dem Balkan Hamburg*: Rowohlt, 1992, p. 135–6.
16. Newhouse. op. cit. p. 65–66.
17. Ulrich Albrecht, 'Parteinahme für eine Seite; Die Deutsche Politik, Europa, die Institutionen und der Krieg' in Rothfelder, op. cit. p. 157.
18. Müller, op. cit. p. 152.
19. *Der Spiegel*, 1991, Issue 52, p. 18.
20. Müller op. cit., pp. 161–5.
21. Trevor C. Salmon, 'Testing Times for European Political Cooperation: The Gulf and Yugoslavia 1990–2', *International Affairs*, 1992, vol. 68, no. 2, p. 252.
22. Anne Marie Le Gloannec, 'The Implications of German Unification for

Western Europe', in P. B. Stares, ed. op. cit. p. 266.
23. Andrei Markovits, and Simon Reich. 'Germany's Image in a New Climate of Opinion,' 1992 APSA paper.
24. Newhouse, op. cit. p. 66.
25. Salmon, op. cit. p. 252.
26. Rudolf Augstein, 'Sondern auch Wut und Hass' *Der Spiegel*, Issue no. 2, 1992 p. 23.
27. Marina Achenbach, 'Interview mit Horst Grabert', Freitag. June 15, 1992; Korfmacher, Heribert (1993) Deutsche Jugoslavien–Politik: Vortrag vor dem Ostinstut der FU Berlin, February 6. Ms.
28. Bagehot, 'The M Word Again', *The Economist*, February 13, 1993, p. 62.

References

Agh, Attila (1989) 'Central Europe and the European Identity', *World Futures*, vol. 26, pp. 123–40.
Heidenheimer, Arnold (1991) 'Zeitliche und raumliche Bezugsrahmen der Entwicklung der Bundesrepublik', in Bernhard Blanke and Hellmut Wollmann (Hrsg.), *Die alte Bundesrepublik* (Opladen: Westdeutscher Verlag) pp. 33–44.
Kelstrup, Mortem (1992) 'Societal Insecurity in the New Europe: National and International Responses to New Challenges', APSA Conference Paper.
Le Gloannec, Anne Marie (1992) 'The Implications of German Unification for Western Europe', in P. B. Stares (ed.), *The New Germany and the New Europe* (Washington: Brookings Institution) pp. 251–78.
Markowitz, Andrei and Simon Reich (1992) 'Germany's Image in a New Climate of Opinion', APSA Paper.
Mueller, Harald (1991) 'German Foreign Policy after Unification', in Stares op. cit, pp. 126–76.
Mannheim, Karl (1959) 'The Problem of Generations', in Paul Kecskemeti (ed.), *Essays on the Sociology of Knowledge* (London: Routledge Kegan Paul).
Newhouse, John (1992) 'The Diplomatic Round: Dodging the Problem', *The New Yorker*, August 24, pp. 60–71.
Papcke, Sven (1992) 'Mitteleuropa, in Werner Weidenfeld and Karl Rudolf Korte (eds.) Handwoerterbuch zur deutschen Einheit, (Frankfurt: Campus) pp. 473–8.
Rothfelder, Erich (ed.) (1992) *Krieg auf dem Balkan* (Hamburg: Rowohlt).
Schulze, Helmut R. and Richard Kiesler (1990) *Hans-Dieter Genscher: Ein deutscher Aussenminister* (Muenchen: Bertelsmann).
Salmon, Trevor C. (1992) 'Testing Times for European Political Cooperation: The Gulf and Yugoslavia 1990–92', *International Affairs*, vol. 68, no. 2, pp. 233–53.
Szabo, Stephen F. (1992) *The Diplomacy of German Unification* (New York: St. Martin's Press).
Teltschik, Horst (1991) *329 Tage* (Seidler).
Tilly, Charles (1992) *Coercion, Capital and European States: 1990–1992* (Cambridge, UK Blackwell).

3 Partners in Leadership? The Future of German–American Relations

Gerald R. Kleinfeld

'The United States and the Federal Republic of Germany have always been firm friends and allies. But today we share an added role – partners in leadership. Of course, leadership has a constant companion – responsibility. And our responsibility is to look ahead and grasp the promise of the future.'[1] With these words, President George Bush complimented and flattered his German hosts at Mainz on May 31, 1989. The British were miffed, because the United Kingdom had always felt themselves the United States' closest ally in Europe. Although the German reaction was positive, most observers failed to note the American President's call for responsibility. For Bush, the Germans would be partners in leadership if they would also lead.

In many respects, the Federal Republic of Germany was already leading. Bonn was leading the way towards a united Western Europe, a European Community ever tighter together, and Germany was the primary continental member of NATO, furnishing more troops closer to the fault line with the Warsaw Pact than any other country. Within the EC, as 1992 approached and the commonality envisaged by the dropping of remaining internal barriers would become reality, the Germans favoured freer trade with the rest of the world, a position appreciated by the Americans. Within NATO, only the Federal Republic had all of its military within the Alliance. On relations with the Soviet bloc, German Chancellor Helmut Kohl was encouraging USSR President Mikhail Gorbachev in his process of reforms. The West Germans were also encouraging environmentalism in Europe and in the Third World, and were involved in a respectable programme of aid to underdeveloped countries.

But the world did not stand still. Gorbachev's reforms did not keep the Soviet empire together. Rather, they helped it to peaceably disintegrate. One by one, the East European countries threw off communism and attempted to establish democratic societies based upon market economies. Later that Autumn, when the German Democratic Republic celebrated its 40th birthday, the process of internal collapse had reached so far that the ageing leadership of the Socialist Unity Party could no longer keep their people in check. Massive demonstrations revealed even to the most jaded apologists for the régime that the people were vastly dissatisfied. On November 9, when the Berlin Wall was opened, Germans from the East poured across to greet their countrymen. Willy Brandt remarked, 'Now let come together what belongs together.' Within a single year, by October 3, 1990, the two German states had united and the Soviet Union itself was on the verge of total collapse. At the end of 1991, Gorbachev resigned as the USSR dissolved, and a Commonwealth of Independent States feebly represented what had become independent countries emerging from the USSR. A Russian flag fluttered above the Kremlin. The Baltics were independent, and so were Ukraine and Kazakhstan, while the world learned the names of many new states and sought to locate their capitals on a map. The Warsaw Pact was tossed into 'the garbage heap of history'.

Washington and Bonn sailed through these upheavals in amazing tandem. As it became clear to the Americans by the end of 1989 that there would be a united Germany again, the United States supported that development.[2] Presidents from Harry S. Truman to George Bush had endorsed self-determination for the Germans. Moreover, after a century of catastrophe, there was little sentiment in West Germany for a *Sonderweg*, an isolated and independent role in Europe. Thus, a free and independent Germany would remain part of the West, and also a part of the security structure that tied the United States to Europe. Bush and his Secretary of state, James A. Baker III, assisted the Germans in achieving their goal while most of Europe hesitated. Despite Bonn's policies over 40 years, neither in Western Europe nor in the newly freed East was there much enthusiasm for German unification. The United States, gently paving the way for Soviet acquiescence, encouraged the rest of Europe by reaffirming its presence on the continent and by leading in a reform of NATO to accomplish new goals once the Cold War had ended.[3]

Before the Germans had an opportunity to analyse the results of their first post-unity national elections in December, 1990, and to consider the role of Germany in that new world, Iraq invaded Kuwait, and the United States turned to the United Nations as a vehicle for international military intervention. The Security Council, in which

Britain and France, but not the European Community or Germany, were represented as Permanent Members, supported Washington, and a coalition dispatched an American-led expedition to expel the Iraqis. For days, the Germans vacillated. The Kohl–Genscher government did not believe that the Basic Law would permit Germany to send troops, but also did not immediately issue a strong statement of policy. The American public was taken aback by the delay. Bonn soon provided substantial logistic and financial support, but quietly, and more out of alliance solidarity rather than a very public conviction, despite opinion polls showing German support for the coalition effort. Kuwait was freed, but the Americans continued their process of military reductions that had begun when the Soviets collapsed. Whether the United States would have the capability to repeat such an engagement a few years hence, assuming they had the will, would be a new topic of discussion in Washington. The amount and nature of German assistance in the Gulf War proved again how important Germany was to the relationship, even as it demonstrated what could, and what could not, be expected.

But the world had changed. With the unification of Germany, the European continent was no longer the same as when Bush had made his speech in Mainz. Neither was the rest of the world. With the collapse of the Soviet Union, and the end of the Cold War, something old had been restored, and something new had come about. For a time, political leaders in Bonn and Washington continued to speak in the same patterns about German–American relations, while West Europeans continued to move towards the integration foreseen for 1992 as if nothing had happened. The treaty of Maastricht was both a move in that direction and an effort to act before the populations realized that significant changes were upon them. As both Germans and Americans began to ask, 'Why NATO?,' West Europeans also queried 'What form of European Community and which new members from the East?' as well as 'Who will govern this new Europe, whatever its borders?' George Bush referred to the changes as a 'new world order', seeming to overlook the contradiction that the old world alliances and relationships would remain the same within a new, altered world.

Whatever the nature of this new world, and whether or not it was a new world order, it was clear that German–American relations would involve new factors as well as old, and that both Germany and the United States would be seeking new identities in the changed environment. Several factors were involved, many of which were apparent long before the fall of communism in Europe, but only became more obvious and significant with the dramatic developments of 1989–91. First, with domestic concerns rising in importance and with the end of the Cold War, the United States was re-examining its role in world affairs. Then, with a changed Europe, united Germany needed to re-examine the traditional role of what had been 'West Germany' and seek its role in European and world affairs. The future of German–American relations will develop in the context of these changes and of the search by the two countries for their new identities.

The American situation was substantially changed. Some of these changes were not introduced by the collapse of the Soviet Union and the end of the Cold War, but became more obvious in the altered global environment, while others were a product of that new global environment. Even before the fall of the Soviet Union, the state of the United States economy was becoming a cause of concern both for domestic political leaders and in foreign relations. By the end of the Reagan presidency in 1988, the federal deficit had risen to over $400 billion, the national debt to more than four trillion dollars, and the balance of trade had also reached alarming negative numbers.

The American economy was no longer as dominant in the world as it had been in decades past. With a large domestic market and industries which had never needed to export to thrive, the United States was becoming increasingly flooded with imports. Although there was a public perception that this was exclusively due to lower cost production in Third World countries or in Japan, and to unfair trading practices, there was also a significant American component to the weaker economic showing. Many domestic industries had made poor decisions, losing competitive edge and failing to adopt new technology and new concepts. A combination of aggressive foreign competition and inappropriate domestic response caused a loss of ground in home markets without a compensating achievement of foreign sales. Entire industries had disappeared. Challenged both by Asians and Europeans, with a weakened manufacturing base and suffering massive trade deficits with Japan, the United States by the mid–1980s increasingly realized a need to rebuild its economic strength. The end of the Cold War meant that the defence industry would be radically cut back and that new investment in other areas would be necess-ary to provide employment opportunities for those affected. As the Soviet Union collapsed, a domestic debate began over the role of government in such a realignment and revitalization. The economy was still huge, and largely flexible. It had large resources and significant sectors were powerful competitors, but the 1990s drew a picture for most Americans that their country was not responding satisfactorily to the economic challenges and needed to do so. Although protectionist political candidates failed to win broad support, the recession that began in 1990 focused public attention on the long-term condition of the domestic economy. Part of the populist appeal of H. Ross Perot during the presidential campaign of 1992 turned on the flamboyant Texan's criticism both of business and political leadership on economic issues. The end of the Cold War meant a re-evaluation of priorities and capabilities.

Both social and economic challenges would have to be met. In addition to revitalising the economy, the United States faced the absorption of millions of new immigrants as well as issues relating to chronic unemployment, minority relations, the inadequacy of the school system to meet the challenges of education for a modern work force, a growing elderly population, the decline of the inner cities, and a variety of problems affecting infrastructure. In short, the problems were social, economic, and significant. The size of the defence establishment would continue to be reduced, and new goals set. A sense of proportion and a new global foreign policy would be required, one that reflected the post-Cold War period and the new domestic realities.

By 1992, the United States and Canada had joined in a North American Free Trade Association, to aid both in competition with the European Community and Asian trading partners. Mexico joined in 1993. Together, they form a zone of over four hundred and fifty million people. The growing sense of proportion in American economic strength was accompanied by an awareness that global security interests no longer reflected a conflict between two power blocks. While the military forces of the states which have emerged from the Soviet Union contain substantial nuclear destructive capability, the possibility of war in the near future with the United States has substantially evaporated, and there has appeared to be political and economic advantage in cooperation with Russia, Ukraine, and the other successor states. On the other hand, instability and conflict in Europe within what had been the Soviet sphere now has emerged as a fact.

The reduction in the size of the American defence capability has, therefore, two origins. On the one hand, there is increasing realisation of the need for domestic economic investment and, on the other, the end of the Cold War has initiated a re-evaluation of the nature and requirements of the security structure. A small military with concentration on other capabilities has entered into strategic planning. Both American major political parties emphasize this new development. Richard Gephardt of Missouri, Majority Leader in the House of Representatives, reiterated in August, 1992, his view that the basis of American strength in the world was economic power and that he believed it to be essential to rebuild that power. George Bush, fighting a battle for re-election, made the same point in several speeches. He proclaimed that his Administration would lead forces for change which would rejuvenate that power. His opponent, Governor Bill Clinton of Arkansas, had already asserted that Bush did not represent the path towards improved economic strength. He did.

While the political debate concentrated on domestic issues, there has been a corresponding reduction in American popular concern about international crises. Since the Cold War has ended, such crises are no longer seen as threatening the existence of the United States or as contributing to a larger threat. In a 1991 analysis, the Chicago Council on Foreign Relations reported that American opinion leaders were still virtually unanimously in favour of the United States retaining an active role in world affairs by the fall of 1990, but the general population was far less interested in the United States pursuing such a policy. Both leaders and the general public agreed that economic decline had contributed to a loss of American influence.[4]

Apart from the focus on domestic economics in the lingering problems inherited from the 1980s, there are objective concerns discussed within the American political élite about the legitimate long-term role of the United States in international affairs. An economy no longer dominant, with a currency still powerful but no longer universally so, and a military smaller than at the height of the Cold War, leave a superpower less super and more relativised. The United States is still a strong power, but less dominant. Allies are less concerned about the threat of imminent destruction, rendering the mutual defence service provided by the United States less crucial. This holds for Germany, as well, because the German situation has also changed. Otto Count Lambsdorff, Chairman of the Free Democratic Party, has observed that 'there is new reality in Germany ... Germany is acquiring a new status. It is starting to shift from being the *object* to being the *subject* of world history.'[5]

The German goal of integration into Europe has historical, political, and economic justification. The Basic Law laid the groundwork for German participation in west European integration, and Chancellors from Adenauer to Kohl have given high priority to this goal of Bonn's policy. The cooperation with France, symbolised by the Elysée Treaty and endorsed by a clear consensus of the German public, is part of this policy of western integration. Moreover, the European Community has been good for Germany. Integration has meant an unprecedented openness of borders, and a growing feeling of European-ness. For years, Western German trade within the European Community has been profitable, and absorbed a major share of exports. German investment within the Community, from Portugal to Britain to Italy, has sown the seeds of interdependency. The mergers and consolidations of European businesses and their expansion across frontiers make them better able to meet the challenges of American, Japanese, and other Asian competitors. The European Community, now, after 1992, the European Union, is not a region of states of equal economic stature, nor are its people happy with the continuing growth of decision-making power in Brussels, but its success is substantial, and the sense of cooperation a remarkable contrast to the crises of Eastern Europe. The German dilemma in the European Union is how to continue this growth and this integration when a larger Germany is a partner within, and when other states wish to join as well.

The more-or-less comfortable relationship between Germany and France has been possible within the existing balance of economic interests and of geopolitics. It has been easier because of the growing sense of European consciousness among younger generations, even if the stress between national goals and European identity has been less simple for the political élite to resolve. Both the larger size of Germany and the changes in Eastern Europe make this balance more difficult
to maintain. Three factors enter into consideration for the European Union: integration policy, expansion, and relations with Eastern Europe.

Each country within the European Union has its specific goals for integration, and united Germany will need to address its own needs, just as Portugal, Britain, or France. Germany's increased size will also have to be taken into consideration. The location of a new factory, whether in the new federal states, or in Portugal, or in the Czech Republic, is a part of the concern in economic terms for all of the partners. Common policy of shipbuilding, on agriculture, on trade, and the function of a centralised currency, all have a role in which a united Germany has somewhat different interests than before 1989. Then, there is the increasing pressure towards what is known as subsidiarity. Subsidiarity refers to the reversal of the concentration of decision-making authority and the delegation of powers to more local or regional levels. The Danish vote in the Spring of 1992, rejecting the Treaty of Maastricht by a narrow majority, represented a protest against centralization of authority. The Danish people reversed their decision in 1993, and agreed to accept Maastricht under slightly revised conditions. But the message was clear. Democratisation, or regional-ism, or whatever form may succeed in the institutionalisation of subsidiarity, must deal with the specific interests of the people in each state and dampen the urgency of their political élites to achieve cen-tralisation. The weight of Germany in these decisions could well reflect the increasing tensions of German domestic needs since unification and of pressures on Germany from the east. The same is true for ex-pansion.

Expansion of the European Union to include EFTA is less of a prob-lem than expansion into Eastern Europe, but even this is not easy. A preliminary stage, already negotiated, looks forward to just such an expansion. EFTA countries, such as Switzerland, Austria, and Norway are wealthy, and could aid Germany in burden-sharing with economically less strong members, such as Portugal or Greece. Nevertheless, their entry would dilute the membership and raise questions of the relative influence of France, Germany, Britain, and other larger states versus those of the smaller states and their smaller economies. Expansion to Eastern Europe, where the countries have not yet developed stable de-mocracies or market economies, would create even further complica-tions. These states would not contribute wealth, but would be recipients of assistance, much of which would fall to Germany. While expansion of the European Union to include other wealthier states would help share this burden, it is a burden for which there is little enthusiasm.

In the meantime, German investment in Eastern Europe is growing, far more rapidly than that of other European Union members. With their economies tied ever tighter to Germany, these states would rep-resent a new factor in any expanded European Union, recipients of assistance with unsteady democratic societies, but with strong trade and other relationships to Germany. Yet, German ability to assist is weakened by the continuing recession at home.

Today's Germany has two huge economic problems: meeting the challenges of integrating the former communist-run east and remaining competitive in a world economy where employee compensation and pro-duction costs on every continent are lower than in Germany. Because eastern Germans went on a buying spree after unification, they helped consumer production in the western German states, and delayed some-what the reckoning with a competitive world market that German in-dustry was sure to face. By 1994, in both east and west, Germans had begun to realize that their costs of production were high, and that hard decisions were ahead on how to remain globally competitive.

The integration of the new federal states has been both more costly and slower than had been expected. German deficits grow, dissatisfaction with the economic situation is rampant in East and West, and unemployment is higher than any would like. Business leaders make dire predictions that German products are too expensive, and that future factories will be built elsewhere. Attention to these domestic problems forces Germany to take decisions which cannot fail but impact the economies of neighbouring countries, who have their own problems. The fate of the monetary union is still not clear, but re-thinking has begun in European capitals. While a few years ago, just after unification, some world leaders were seeing Germany as so strong an economic juggernaut that all of Eastern Europe would be sucked into its net, the new German weakness has an impact of its own. It underscores the need to develop the framework of European integration.

Thus, German integration into Europe is still as certain as before, but the nature of that emerging European Union is not as clear. Before 1989, the European Community appeared comfortably within its existing frontiers, perhaps adding most or all of EFTA. Since then, the question of ultimate expansion eastward has been opened. The evolution of Central-Eastern Europe and of the former Soviet Union pose new questions for German policy in the 1990s.

From the Baltic to the Balkans, communism has been replaced by various attempts to create market economics. At the same time, nationalism and ethnic strife paint an image that harks back to the 1920s. While developing economies can offer fruitful opportunities for German investment, political instability and conflict as well as economic collapse pose a different security threat to Germany than in the 40 years of the Cold War. This has been dramatically demonstrated in the collapse of Yugoslavia, with two million refugees under way by the autumn of 1992. The separation of Slovakia out of the Czech and Slovak Republics creates one more state with serious economic problems and a substantial ethnic minority – in this case, Hungarians. Nor is the problem of Macedonia solved. During the Cold War, Germans looked east to a seemingly monolithic and harmonious region controlled by the Soviet Union, without democracy and with crumbling economies, but stable. Germany now borders upon a region of considerable instability, where conflict is not unlikely and where democratic evolution is not universally assured. There is less likelihood of such evolution within some of the successor states of the Soviet Union.

The problems of this region are more complex for Germany. Prospects for democratic evolution are not encouraging in Belorus or Ukraine, and Russia has neither made significant gains nor removed all troops from other states in the area. There are also still Russian troops in Eastern Germany. It is not impossible that further disintegration will result, and also economic dislocation that leads to further refugee movements. The role of the military could become significant should pressures increase.

With the two countries seeking to re-evaluate their identities and their international roles, economics will play a greater role in German-American relations. Count Lambsdorff commented in February, 1992 that 'The military threat from the East is a thing of the past. The new currency of power is primarily economic. And Germany is strong in economic terms.'[6] The most prominent public manifestation of German-American cooperation over the past four decades – alliance solidarity against possible aggression in Europe – has become less imperative.

Despite protectionist tendencies both in the European Union and in the United States and NAFTA, both countries remain committed to the principles of free trade. This has not prevented serious difficulties arising at the meetings of GATT and in discussions over import regulations. Domestic economic difficulties, differing cultural patterns in purchasing practices, and the requirements of trading partners have contributed to the hard negotiations that have characterised recent years. In the GATT negotiations, President Clinton looked to Chancellor Kohl to help move the European Union closer to the American position. The United States counted on German free trade principles to help persuade other Europeans, mainly the French. That Clinton was not more successful was due both to Germany's own domestic economic problems and to the German unwillingness to press their alliance with France.

Agricultural products have been among the more significant areas of dispute. The United States produces considerable surpluses, and counts on sales abroad not only to take up these products, but also to offset balance of trade deficits in manufacturing. The American farm industry produces efficiently at low cost, partly due to the larger size of American farms and to the success of agribusiness. Germans have smaller farms, but the place of the farmers in German society is traditionally significant, even if their numbers have dwindled. Eastern Germany is an additional complication, because increased efficiency will boost agricultural production there, thus adding to the German surplus, and any cutbacks there will impact on the problems of German integration. Like manufacturing, farm products are no longer exclusively a matter of bilateral negotiation. Instead, since Germany is a member of the European Union, they came within the agricultural policy of the Union. German domestic interests and economic policy have a role, an important one, in Union policy, but one that must be reconciled with the policies of other member states. As the Union moves ever closer towards the single market approach, and as NAFTA also acquires more commonality as a free trade zone, reaching agreement will depend upon even more complex factors.

One of these factors is trade in manufactured products. The United States has traditionally held a balance of trade surplus with the European Community. Similarly, exports to the United States are crucial to certain German industries and play a major role in others. It was an order from United Airlines which helped guarantee the profitability of Airbus Industrie, competitor of Boeing. Recently, Boeing and Deutsche Aerospace, a prime member of Airbus Industrie's production group, have discussed development of a new jumbo jet. Although German industry expects trade with the Third World and with Eastern Europe to be increasingly important, trade between the United States and Germany, because of its size and involvement in certain specific products, has to be significant for both countries.

The continuing advantages of transatlantic investment have created a further level of interdependency. Whereas American investment in West Germany accumulated rapidly after 1945, German investment in the United States has been growing in recent years. Despite a majority of trade with other countries, mutual investment has risen to a level reinforcing interdependency in a number of ways. The size, wealth, and stability of one another's markets encourage further investment. The level of technology and the cross-cultural involvement in business and trade have also stimulated investment. Further opportunities will open as global cooperation and competition in high-technology industries continues. Konrad Seitz has suggested that Germany faces a combined 'Japanese and American challenge.'[7] But, German corporations have already entered into strategic alliances both with American and Japanese firms and have invested so heavily in the United States that they have a stake in the success of the American economy.

As the generation of West Germans who built financial security in the years of the *Wirtschaftswunder* begins to pass their savings and investment to the next generation, which has also achieved financial security, further investment movement is likely. Thus, further German investment in the United States, not only by businesses, but also by individuals, appears assured. If Count Lambsdorff is right, then economic activity will mandate significant attention in German-American relations. The level of that activity requires that efforts be made in Washington and in Bonn/Berlin to ensure that relations are satisfactory.

A second area of mutual concern is Eastern Europe, where Germany has both opportunity and challenge. The opportunity lies in future cooperation, and in investment and economic ties. No other European country has invested so heavily in Eastern Europe. On the other hand, instability can lead to even heavier flows of refugees, and conflict can cause further conflict, and interrupt the flow of prosperity for Western Europe. Various means have been tried to assist the democratic and market economic development of Eastern Europe, but with varied success or lack of success. While there is not enough available capital in North America, Japan, or Western Europe to make a major impact on all of these countries' efforts to achieve economic advance, economists and political scientists agree that success cannot come from foreign investment alone. Domestic political and economic conditions must be created which stimulate local activity, and a long period of growth must be anticipated. Economic nationalism, and old-fashioned nationalism, have split for Czechoslovakia and Yugoslavia, and strife threatens both Moldova and Romania. Poland has not proven successful in its attempts to improve the economy, and even Hungary is experiencing difficulty. The Baltic states have both nationality and economic difficulties. Russian nationalists have not accepted their independence. The German interest lies in advancing economic development in Eastern Europe in an atmosphere of stability, particularly lest tens of millions of refugees begin heading westward. The United States has a similar interest.

Political stability and economic progress in Eastern Europe are as important to the United States as to Germany. Furthermore, the future of the states that were within the Soviet Union is still an unsettled question. Stability here is also both in the German and American interest. The vastness of Russia, of Kazakhstan, of Ukraine, and the explosions that could result within them dictate a concern for ordered economic and political development. Among the open questions are the various security and stability organizations and formulae that have grown over the decades since the Second World War.

Nato is the most successful, and many Eastern European countries, anxious for their own security, would like to join. The evolution of NATO began before the unification of Germany, and is continuing. The original function of NATO, to defend the West against Soviet and Warsaw Pact aggression, is gone. The concept of defence and security for its members is still there, but has lost some of its popular appeal now that the Soviet Union has disappeared. On the other hand, there is continuing, even escalating concern that instability in Europe is still a threat, and that security is still a valid need. How, and whether, this security umbrella can be extended to Eastern Europe is a new problem for Germany and the United States. The development of the North Atlantic Cooperation Council was a first, tentative, step. Expanding NATO would be a major decision, but not one that all members are yet ready to take. Instead, President Clinton offered as a substitute the 'Partnership for Peace' plan, wherein NATO and countries of the former Soviet bloc could cooperate in joint exercises. While full membership was preferable to these Eastern European countries, they accepted the Partnership for Peace as a temporary step, hoping that full membership would come. Both Germany and the United States have important decisions to make. Should they be admitted to NATO, even if Russia would object? Should Russia be able to veto NATO expansion? Would Germany and the United States be ready to defend Eastern European states against aggression? If not, what message would this send, and would European security and stability be weakened by the lack of such a guarantee? Could NATO survive such a guarantee? Could NATO survive without it? Is the question for NATO to expand or to disappear?

For Germany, NATO expansion is coupled with a decision process concerning the future role of Germany in international peacemaking and peacekeeping. Would an expansion of NATO mean that German troops might be stationed in Eastern Europe, where memories of the Second World War have not yet altogether grown cold? Again, with Germany united, is Germany now a 'normal power', ready to undertake peacemaking and peacekeeping obligations alongside other countries? These questions are part of a German decision process on the role of united Germany in the world. They are part of the search for identity that Germany and the United States are both undergoing.

These issues have more than regional importance. With conflicts developing in Eastern Europe, in the Persian Gulf, and elsewhere, the question of German participation in peacekeeping or peacemaking forces was bound to emerge. Since there is a divergence of opinion on the nature of the restrictions imposed by the Basic Law, a domestic debate has begun on German cooperation. Recently, a University of Trier political scientist has suggested that the United States undertake peacekeeping and peacemaking ventures, while Germany defines the moral framework of such activities through public discussion. Such an extreme position has met with ridicule across the Atlantic, where American political scientists have suggested that the United States, or other countries, are just as capable of seeking moral high ground as Germany.[8]

Most of the German discussion has centred around the use of German troops in peacekeeping functions, and not in peacemaking, but the thrust of the argument has reinforced the views of those who, like Count Lambsdorff, suggest that Germany has now become a *subject* of world affairs, rather than an *object*.

Germany has become a key factor in the new aspects of European-American relations. West Germany was always significant in American policy towards Western Europe. A larger Germany in a changed Europe with a coalescing European Community plays a major role. There is no prospect of Germany seeking a *Sonderweg*. Whatever the future structure of the European Union, Germany will be within it. Whatever activities Germany undertakes in Eastern Europe, they will be as a country firmly anchored in the west. Whatever security needs develop in the east, they will require – for the Germans – a joint response. But German activity will be significant, for reasons both of economics and geography. In addition, German success will be demonstrative, and instructional. German democracy is stable, and a model for much of Eastern Europe. This, in itself, is supportive of American interests.

The Clinton Administration in Washington took over at a crucial time. Government partnership with business to foster a resurgent manufacturing economy, particularly in key industries with relatively high paying jobs and promise for future technological advances, was a major element in the Clinton campaign. While officially rejecting protectionism, Clinton promised to support American trade interests abroad, and to concentrate on domestic economic progress in ways that would bring permanent reward. The new, young president and vice president represent a different generation than George Bush. They promise to help revitalize the economy while redefining the American international role to fit the new times and the new economic realities. Such a domestic focus does not mean international passivity. Instead, an active policy was begun in many world regions. With a campaign pledge to restructure the defence establishment to fit the needs of the changed world, Clinton's first steps continued and increased the budget cuts in defence proposed by the Bush Administration. But the Clinton Administration's activism met a Germany not ready to move out of its own domestic problems. 'That does not go down well,' observed Rolf Clement, writing in the *Rheinischer Merkur*, 'with a new Administration that is in the process of laying the groundwork for the next four years of American foreign policy.'[9]

The integration of the new federal states and problems relating to the admission of new refugees from the east captured the attention of the majority of Germans in 1992. As expenditures and the deficit rose, Bonn responded by cutting the German defence budget and anticipating even further cuts. In addition, not only was Germany unable to participate in the coalition for military action in Kuwait because of constitutional implications, but even the sending of troops to Somalia proved a source of considerable debate, lest the soldiers come into an area in which shooting might occur. As the Americans waited patiently for Bonn to assess its constitutional questions over the use of forces outside of the NATO area, difficulties arose over German troops manning AWACs equipment when these would be used to support United Nations endeavours in Bosnia. When the size of the German military establishment was being further reduced, additional questions began to be raised in Washington about Bonn's seriousness in expecting American troop levels in Europe to be maintained as scheduled. In short, by the early months of 1993, there was scarcely a partnership in leadership. Wherever the Americans turned in crisis areas – from Kuwait to Somalia to Bosnia, the Germans might provide food packages and some funding, but a contribution to international military engagement, even under the United Nations, was missing. This was offered by the British, the French, and a considerable contingent of other countries. Nevertheless, the German public ultimately accepted, with pride, the service of the Bundeswehr in Somalia. It was considered a successful venture, and was helpful to the domestic debate.

Official Washington was understanding of the German problems with such activities, but had to go ahead. For an absence of German troops in the Balkans, American heads nodded in understanding. Yet, there were still no American troops on the ground in Bosnia. If there were? Bonn and Washington must still sort out their security partnership. The old litanies of adherence to NATO no longer seem to fit the new realities. Despite Somalia, the question of what has been termed 'out of area' use of German troops has not yet been resolved.

With the Clinton Administration redefining American international behaviour, the absence of a clear German relationship will force decisions resting on other supports. While some change appears evident, the slow pace is bringing patient criticism. There is no doubt why Germans are reluctant, and understanding is there. *The Economist* expressed it thus:[10]

> It would take a Martian to ask why Germany feels inhibited. For two generations, talk there of military force, on left and right, took place against a backdrop, first of Hitlerism and defeat, then of fear

that a Germany stuck in the middle of Europe would be a nuclear battleground. Force was something to be threatened, not used. The need for armed humanitarianism in places like Yugoslavia or Somalia seems to Germans a particular contradiction in terms.

To some Americans, German policy has only partly come to terms with the changes of the past years. The drive to complete Maastricht seemed part of a policy to complete western European union before the pressures of the newly independent eastern part of the continent would force new decisions. Investing and lending money in Eastern Europe and Russia appeared as a means to help the transition to freedom and a market economy, but also to secure the removal of Russian troops from German soil. It was not accompanied by a clear policy of what the German role was to be in all of Europe, and what to do with the eastern European states. It was, therefore, cautious and hesitant. A more positive view holds that the completion of European union was a precondition for any eastward expansion, and economic aid and investment was a contribution to change. After this, Germany would support more open trade with the east, and work both to expand the European Union and to complete a security arrangement for Eastern Europe in cooperation with the United States. What is clear is that the German public opinion and the domestic economy were not willing to support more than Germany has already done, but must be prepared to support an evolution of this policy in the future. Germany and the United States have not yet evolved a clear policy towards Eastern Europe.

With both countries deeply concerned over their respective budget deficits and domestic issues, even the relative impact of German economic investment in Eastern Europe failed to make a substantial impression in the United States. Instead, German reluctance to accept ever larger imports from the newly non-communist states of Eastern Europe seems to indicate a growing determination to deal with domestic issues. With the United States facing similar pressures, the search for cooperative policy continues. Their parallel interests in many situations notwithstanding, the two countries were finding it difficult to bring their actual endeavours into harmony.

Even weakened by present economic difficulties, Germany is critically important in Europe, and in the world at large. As Daniel S. Hamilton has recently written:

> If Germany and the United States, together with their partners, are to drive the democracies forward, the character of the relationship must change to reflect new realities. Whether Americans have the

patience to assemble ... coalitions ... and whether Germans will develop the broader understanding of their responsibilities that must underpin such coalitions are open questions that will test leadership in both countries.[11]

When Hamilton writes of coalitions, he refers to the new position of the United States that has developed both in economic and security terms over the past decade. The search for a new American role, a new identity, involves an understanding of the limits of American power. Both Germany and the United States seek to harmonise their interests with their values. There are strong reasons for a continued transatlantic partnership based upon the new realities of the present world.

In economic terms, Germany within the European Union is a focus of American efforts to limit trade restrictions and to develop mutually acceptable concepts of free trade and the elimination of subsidies between the European Union and the United States. German support for these principles is essential if the Union is to follow them. In security affairs, the German membership in both transatlantic and exclusively European organizations will be important in working out interaction between Europe and the United States.

The United States is also tied to Germany by a community of values that has emerged in the 40 years of relationship with West Germany. While contacts with Eastern Germany, the five new federal states, have been limited since 1933, a kaleidoscopic array of different types of interactions have developed with the Western federal states. Many of these are now being expanded to the East. From sister cities partnerships to youth exchanges, university exchange and bilateral arrangements to internships, a cooperative network has developed, only a small part of which is publicly funded. The process of *Westbindung* in Germany involved more than a military alliance and a developing economic cohesion in Western Europe. It embraced a mind-set tied to Western Europe and even to a transatlantic connection. The very process of Europeanization of postwar generations and the development of a common culture strengthened this. Thus, the German-American common system of values is far different than such a value system in the early part of this century. It represents a pattern that is present both among élites and ordinary citizens, and continues to influence both the leadership and the society. It is reinforced, in turn, by a somewhat similar tradition that has developed in the United States.

The historical process of cooperation with allies in Western Europe, and the gradual development of a close relationship with West Germany has also left a significant impact on sectors of American society, even beyond the traditionally Europe-oriented eastern seaboard. For both the German connection with the United States and the American with Germany, this was reinforced by economic developments and by long-term stationing of American military in Europe. The various exchange opportunities among young people and university students affected a cross-section of the population. Transatlantic study has been a major factor in tying together not only élites but also large numbers of ordinary citizens. During the upheavals of 1989, various opinion surveys analysed American perceptions of Germany and German perceptions of the United States. The large majority in the United States in favour of unification, over ninety per cent, testified to the strong popularity of Germany among most Americans and to the trust felt in a united country. Polls conducted by the Chicago Council on Foreign Relations and by researchers of the University of Michigan confirm a generally high level of popularity of Germany among both élites and the general population. For tourism, Germany is also a significant destination. German tourists as well, particularly including Eastern Germans, have the United States as a major tourist destination.

To be sure, there are negative stereotypes and considerable criticism of social and cultural characteristics in both countries about each other. Surveys indicate that the majority of citizenry develop their views from television, and television contains a mix of features. News reports are not the only means of information. Almost no German television programmes reach American audiences, but a substantial percentage of German television consists of American imports. These impart only a partial view of American society and mores. As the American military presence in Germany is scaled down, and German as well as American interests are focused on post-Cold War realities, particularly on tough transatlantic economic negotiations, there are opportunities for the spread of negative stereotypes and for a lessening of cultural and social contacts. Bonn has responded to this danger by attempting on a small scale to institutionalise the contact among élites, in order to guarantee access to the next generation of American leadership. An American response, organised by Washington, would not be typical.

History is full of watersheds, and there is a general recognition that the changes in Europe beginning in the late 1980s have been fundamental. The priorities of German-American relations are responding both to the evolutionary and radical changes that have taken place. The future of German-American relations will reflect these new priorities. If, as Count Lambsdorff argues, 'the currency of power is primarily economic,' then the economic development of Europe and North America will play a major role in those relations. But, economic development requires stability, and Europe to Germany's East has not charted a firm course. Both Germany and the United States have an interest in democratic, successful evolution in that region, with advancing market economies. In addition, Germany will now be under increasing pressure to play a global role as a *subject*, rather than an *object* of events. The obligations, or responsibilities as Bush implied in his Mainz address, are not placed by the United States, but by the dimensions of German economic power and strategic location. One of the new challenges of this changed world is for Germany to develop a concept of more global responsibility. One of the new challenges for the United States is to reconcile the American sense of global responsibility both to new domestic and international realities, and to develop partnerships that are supportive and effective. The long-term relationship between the two countries will be positive and interactive, with both economic and cultural interaction growing. To what degree an actual 'partnership in leadership' between the United States and Germany can function in this changed world remains to be seen.

Germany will be increasingly important in an increasingly united Europe. Whatever the form of the developing European Union, the Union will be a significant force in Europe and in the world. As the United States develops new post-Cold War policies, cooperation with Europe will enter a new phase. For Germans, cooperation with the United States will be essential to help secure the global concerns of both peoples. The nature of the German-American partnership does not have to mirror that of the Anglo-American or any other. In a true partnership, each contributes what it can. As each country seeks to define itself in the new world, it might prove as inappropriate to expect American strategic intervention or economic support at each global crisis point as it may be to expect that Germany will be there as well. As both countries search for new roles in the world, cooperative relations can have many faces.

Notes

1. U.S. Department of State, Bureau of Public Affairs, *Current Policy No. 1179*, p. 1.
2. See Gerald R. Kleinfeld (1991) 'Die Verwirklichung des Unwahrscheinlichen: Amerikanische Aussenpolitik und deutsche Wiedervereinigung'

in Wolfgang-Uwe Friedrich (ed), *Die USA und die Deutsche Frage 1945– 1990* (Frankfurt/M.: Campus).

3. See Stephen F. Szabo, *The Diplomacy of German Unification*, New York: St. Martin's Press, 1992.

4. *American Public Opinion and U.S. Foreign Policy 1991*, Chicago: Chicago Council on Foreign Relations, 1991, pp. 6, 27.

5. 'The United States and Germany: New Challenges and Opportunities', Speech delivered at the Friedrich Naumann Foundation and the American Council on Germany in Washington, D. C., February 25, 1992.

6. 'The United States and Germany: New Challenges and Opportunities', February 25, 1992.

7. Konrad Seitz, *Die japanisch-amerikanische Herausforderung: Deutschlands Hochtechnologie-Industrien kämpfen ums Überleben*, 3. Auflage, Bonn: Bonn Aktuell, 1991.

8. See Hanns Maull, 'Zivilmacht Bundesrepublik Deutschland', in *Europa Archiv*, 10, 1993.

9. 'Jenseits des Atlantiks wächst die Ungeduld', Nr. 9, February 26, 1993.

10. *The Economist*, February 27 1993, p. 52.

11. Daniel S. Hamilton, *Beyond Bonn: America and the Berlin Republic*, Carnegie Endowment Study Group on Germany, Washington: Carnegie Endowment, 1994, p. 97.

4 Second-class Citizenship and its Discontents: Women in the New Germany
Joyce Marie Mushaben

> The essence of justice is a condition under which both my fulfillment and yours become possible.
>
> B. W. Harrison, 1985.

Accounting for roughly 52 per cent of Western citizens and 53 per cent of the Eastern residents, women comprise a majority of the New German population whose fundamental rights and roles have been redefined by the breathtaking merger of two formerly adversarial systems. The last 40 years have effected an unquestionable transformation of the socio-political roles and economic rights commonly ascribed to women in the former Federal Republic, as well as in the now defunct German Democratic Republic. Yet neither state had witnessed a transformation so complete by 1989 as to render the status of the *citizeness* equal to that of her male counterpart.

It is easy to argue, in retrospect, that the struggle for gender equality was often impeded on both sides of the Wall by a lack of positive, consensus internal to the movement and, consequently, by the stop-and-go character of various movement initiatives. Both the specific tactics employed and the particular aims pursued by women in each state reflected, more often than not, their differences and constraints immanent to the system. Developments of the 1990s may nonetheless infuse unified (though hardly united) feminists with new energy and a new sense of urgency: women have begun to recognise a mutual need to guard against a substantial 'roll-back' of hard-won opportunities in view of the pressing economic problems confronting post-unity Germany.

Setting a new agenda for the nineties is complicated by the fact that the struggles of women in both parts of Germany have derived from very different historical-legal foundations since 1949. Finding common ground is all the more imperative, in the light of this author's contention that the political-economic identity of German women, both Eastern and Western, will be subject to greater redefinition through the processes of unification than will hold true for Federal Republican men. As East-Berlin writer Daniela Dahn noted in the spring of 1990, 'the bill for our new freedom is arriving promptly, and the price is obviously higher than we expected. . . .'[1] For women in the newly democratized Eastern states [known colloquially as *Neufünfland*], the impact of unification can be summarized in paradoxical fashion: greater freedom equals fewer rights.

THE THEORETICAL FRAMEWORK

Citizenship is too often misconstrued as a discrete act, whereby a bestowal of membership automatically activates an extensive catalogue of rights and responsibilities. It is easier to grasp a vast array of paradoxical conditions besetting liberal-democratic societies if we recognise citizenship as an ongoing process. For all too many members of the polity, citizenship entails a continuing if unfulfilled 'quest for inclusion'.[2]

Eminent civic culture theorists (most of whom are men) accord a certain respect to the notion of 'balanced disparities' as contributing to the stability of democratic systems.[3] In reality those recognised disparities are quite imbalanced, owing to 'the "hidden masculinity" of Western political theory.'[4] As Carole Pateman argued in *The Civic Culture Revisited*, the institutional arrangements of liberal-democracy have themselves been

> treated as separate from, and irrelevant to, the formal equality of citizenship . . . yet the most striking finding . . . is that civic culture is systematically divided along lines of class and sex. The relationship between such a culture and the formal equality institutionalized in the political structure is never confronted or seen as a problem.[5]

The civic culture, with its emphasis on stability, reveals itself as an undeniably male culture:

> The civic culture rests not on the participation of the people, but on their nonparticipation. Its political focus is on the role of the upper SES (male) citizens, as participants and decision makers. The

balance of the civic culture is one that allows these élites 'to get
on with governing' in the absence of a politically active people ...
Rather systematically structured inequalities appear as individual psychological and personal attributes that happen to be distributed in a
particular way.[6]

In other words, particular segments of society are excluded from active participation in the system, due to a personal lack of self-compe-
tence which, in actuality, is structurally reinforced throughout the
socialisation process.

Judith Shklar pushes the citizen-qua-participant argument one step
further. Citizenship needs to be recognised not only as formal membership, i.e. in the sense of nationality; more importantly, it must be
construed as a significant mechanism for the allocation of SOCIAL
STANDING. Traditionally viewed as a 'certificate of full membership in society', access to the ballot box allows individuals to attain
a 'minimum of social dignity' at best.[7] As pertains to many disadvantaged strata of society, however, the 'struggle for citizenship ... [is]
overwhelmingly a demand for inclusion in the polity, an effort to
break down excluding barriers to recognition, rather than an aspira-
tion to civic participation as a deeply involving activity.'[8] The conditions which have historically rendered particular subgroups 'unfit' for
citizenship, such as gender, race or insufficient economic means, have
been socially contrived rather than naturally selected. The case of the
New Germany proves no exception to the rule.

THE LEGAL FRAMEWORK

Not a single woman is prominently featured in any of a myriad of
photo-documentations focusing on key unification processes and events.
The first step toward formal unification, namely the State Treaty establishing a Monetary, Economic and Social Union signed on May
18, 1990, contained but a single reference to the future regulation of
policies directly affecting women: it read, 'Consideration shall be given
to the interests of women and disabled persons' (Art. 19). Its phras-
ing is reminiscent of the 1850 Prussian Law on Associations, the purpose of which was to bar 'female persons, the mentally ill, school
children and apprentices' from membership of political organisations.

A second accord, formally designated the Unity Treaty of September 6, 1990, (to go into effect Oct. 3) offered a slightly greater meas-

ure of reassurance that policymakers would not seek to turn back the clock on the statutory rights of women already established in the GDR. As outlined in Article 31:

(1) It is the task of the all-German legislators to develop further legislation on the equality between men and women.
(2) ... in recognition of the different legal and institutional starting conditions in the employment of mothers and fathers, the legal situation is to be shaped from the point of view of *the ability to combine career and family* [my emphasis].
(3) In order to secure the further maintenance of day-care institutions for children in the territory named in Article 3, the Federal Government will participate in the costs of these institutions for a transitional period through June 30, 1991 [now moot].
(4) It is the task of all-German legislators to establish a regulation no later than December 31, 1992 which *guarantees the protection of unborn life and the constitutionally-conform mastery of conflict situations* [my emphasis] arising from the legally secured claims of women, especially in relation to counseling and social assistance, as is currently the case in both parts of Germany. To attain these goals, the Federal Government will immediately provide financial assistance towards· the creation of an encompassing network ... of counseling centers under the direction of various sponsors. The counseling centers are to be equipped with personnel and finances in a manner which ensures fulfillment of their mission to advise pregnant women and to provide them necessary forms of aid beyond the point of birth. ...

The language contained in these treaties explicitly if not exclusively emphasises women's roles within the family – in addition to affirming in no uncertain terms the conservative position that 'life begins at conception.' According to Berghahn and Fritzsche, the treaty amounts to a 'social clear-cutting' of all special protection rights for women once established under the GDR.[9] Its condescending recognition of the so-called *double* (in fact, *triple*) *burden* suggests that what it actually seeks to promote is the re-domestication of the East German citizeness. The Treaty guarantees no rights of self-determination for women as women; rather, it begins with the premise of separate spheres of responsibility for male and female citizens, institutionalising the precept of separate as inherently unequal.

It is important to note at the outset that GDR women were consistently less enthusiastic about the idea of unification than men, as demonstrated initially by the changing composition of the autumn 1989 demonstrations. Based on two anonymous polls encompassing 2000 'demo' participants, researchers at the now 'dissolved' Zentralinstitut für Jugendforschung (ZIJ) in Leipzig determined that one-third of those who regularly attended the candle-lit, silent marches were women, from October through December of 1989. Their banners called for reform, not revolution, with demands focusing on free elections, the right to travel and reconstruction of the GDR under the rubric of 'socialism with a human face'. An estimated one-half of all first-wave protesters were under the age of 35, drawing largely from the ranks of students, intellectuals, church or ecology activists, and salaried employees.

The period January through March of 1990 witnessed a shift in the tone and composition of the protests; demonstrators resorted to rowdier calls for a 'Germany united Fatherland', accompanied by much flag-waving and chanting (occasionally directed against pro-reform activists). During this phase the proportion of female marchers fell to under one-fourth; the restless masses were largely comprised of working class males, mixed with salaried employees.[10]

Further evidence rests with the findings of the first five 'scientifically correct' polls which were executed by the ZIJ shortly after the opening of the Wall (see Tables 4.1 and 4.2).[11] In late February/early March 1990, 88 per cent of the men compared to 80 per cent of the women polled *favoured* unity; by the end of April, the proportions had shifted to 92 per cent among males versus 80 per cent among females. Out of these figures, the group '*strongly in favour of*' encompassed 58 per cent of the males, as against 41 per cent of the females; among those classified as 'workers,' the supporters numbered 61 per cent for men, 43 per cent among women. Those *opposed* to unity stood at 20 per cent for females, in contrast to only 8 per cent males. When questioned further as to the time-frame they considered most appropriate for forging the two systems, 43 per cent among men and 38 per cent among women cited the end of 1990; the idea of delaying the process until *after 1992* garnered the support of 12 per cent of the former but tallied 21 per cent among the latter.[12]

Many Eastern women sided with the party of rapid unification as the lesser of two evils, that is, they accorded greater weight to the immediate dissolution of the old regime than to personally articulated fears regarding loss of their own jobs, rising criminality and a potential resurgence of right wing radicalism (always trust your instincts, women-readers!). Over the next ten years one can nevertheless expect the processes of unification to trigger an important paradigmatic shift

Table 4.1   Attitudes towards reunification

Question: How do you stand regarding the unification of the GDR and the FRG?

	Very much in favour		Sooner for than against			Sooner against than for	Very opposed
Total (Feb./March)							
M				=	88		
F				=	80		
Total (April)	49	+	36	=	85	12	3
M	58	+	34	=	92	7	1
F	41	+	39	=	80	16	4
Workers							
M	61		31			6	2
F	43		34			17	6
Salaried Employees							
M	55		38			6	1
F	43		38			16	3
Age groups							
15–24	41		36			18	5
25–44	47		38			12	3
45–64	54		35			9	2

Question: What is your opinion regarding the speed with which unification is proceeding?

	Too slow	Too fast	Just right	No opinion
Total	21	39	32	8
M	23	37	36	4
F	19	40	29	12
Workers				
M	29	31	36	4
F	19	33	35	13

Source: Förster and Roski, *Wende und Wahl*, 1990, p. 60, p. 63.

in the balance of power between the sexes in the unified FRG, both in terms of new voter preferences and with regard to an intensified debate over select 'women's issues'.

Table 4.2 Negative associations with unification

Question: How strongly threatened do you feel based on the following developments? (In per cents)

	Very strongly	*Rather strongly*	*Rather weakly*	*Not much*
... through pollution and poisoning of the natural environment				
Total	56	29	13	2
Male	56	27	15	2
Female	56	30	12	2
... through an increase in criminality				
Total	47	36	13	4
M	43	38	16	3
F	52	34	10	4
... through the increase in egotism in human relations				
Total	40	38	16	6
M	36	39	18	7
F	41	38	15	6
... through an increase in aggression and violence				
Total	38	42	15	5
M	31	45	18	6
F	44	39	13	4
... through an increase in the cost of living				
Total	29	40	25	6
M	23	41	28	8
F	33	40	23	4
... through the possibility of one's own unemployment				
Total	21	27	33	19
M	16	26	36	22
F	25	28	30	17

Question: How strongly threatened do you feel by the possibility that you might become unemployed?

Total	21	27	33	19
Workers				
M	15	28	37	20
F	32	28	29	11
Age group				
15–24 years	29	26	28	17

continued on page 87

Table 4.2   *continued*

Question: How strongly threatened do you feel based on the following developments? (In per cents)

	Very strongly	Rather strongly	Rather weakly	Not much
25–44 years	19	28	37	16
45–64 years	19	30	30	21
Party-voter				
CDU	12	21	43	24
SPD	21	32	25	22
PDS	31	34	22	13
Feelings about speed of unification				
just right	13	25	41	21
too slow	17	23	34	26
too fast	25	32	27	16

Question: How personally threatened do you feel by the spread of right-wing radicalism?

Total	33	35	23	9
M	29	33	26	12
F	37	37	19	7

Source: Förster and Roski, *Wende und Wahl*, p. 86, p. 88, p. 109.

INSTITUTIONAL VARIABLES AND THE POLICY CONTEXT

A general comparison of political representation in the parliamentary institutions of East and West prior to the free elections of March 1990 suggests that the Eastern state may have been the more 'German Democratic Republic' – at least on the surface. While the proportion of seats occupied by women in the GDR *Volkskammer* [People's Chamber] rose from 25 per cent in 1960 to 32 per cent in 1988, the share of female mandates in the Bundestag increased from only 9 per cent in 1960 to 15 per cent in 1989.[13] The first signs of roll-back emerged immediately after the March 18, 1990 elections. Although women had been virtually guaranteed one-third of the parliamentary seats under the old system, they accounted for only one-fifth of the delegates to the first democratically elected *Volkskammer* – and only one-sixth of the leading party's caucus (viz., the *Alliance for Germany*). Neither the Eastern-based Liberals, the Farmers' Party nor the right wing DSU counted any women among their mandated ranks. Naturally one can argue that the old chamber was little more than a rubber stamp for the designs of the Politburo.[14] Inhabiting a world so obviously dominated by spin-doctors and sound-bites, however, we have all come to recognise that in politics the symbolic is often as important as the real.

Nearly all of the frictions inherent to the 'cold fusion' of two diametrically opposed political cultures are bound to be reflected in the realm of women's politics. Conversely, both the short- and long-term prospects for a united front among women of the New Germany remain contingent upon the very structures of political power over which they exercise little effective control.

The first all-German Bundestag, constituted on December 20, 1990, boasts an all-time high of 20.5 per cent female membership. It is worth noting that the absorption of the Five New States into the federal system also precipitated an increase in the size of the parliament itself, from roughly 522 to 662 members. An increase in the number of legislative mandates held by women cannot be ascribed to this factor alone, however, especially in view of the losses incurred by the two parties which have most actively pushed for quotas since 1983, namely, the SPD (whose share fell by approximately 4 per cent) and the Greens (who dropped from 44 seats to none) in the new parliament.

The first post-unity government under Helmut Kohl boasts of the largest number of ministerial posts occupied by women in postwar German history. Yet in this case, female does not necessarily translate into feminist-politicians. The Chancellor initially resorted to the age-old strategy of divide-and-conquer, by chopping up the former Ministry of Youth, Family, Women and Health into three new components: the Ministry of Health (Gerda Hasselfeldt), the Ministry of Family and Elderly (Hannelore Roensch), and the Ministry of Women and Youth (Angela Merkel, X-GDR) – referred to rather irreverently by parliamentarians as *das Dreimädelhaus*. The fourth, the Ministry of Regional Planning, Construction and Urban Development, was placed under the direction of FDP coalition-partner, Irmgard Schwaetzer {trounced in a most unchivalrous manner during her bid to succeed Genscher as Foreign Minister in 1992}. Political segmentation is crossed with overlapping competencies – from the beginning the new ministers have been cognisant of the fact that they are 'a little responsible for everything but rarely holding the pen that signs off on anything.'[15] Day-care matters have been assigned to the Women's Ministry, since it is 'obviously' this half of the species which bears primary responsibility for such (even if 'Women' and 'Family' can no longer be linked in one administrative breath). Abortion is no longer defined as a 'women's question', being regulated instead by the Minister of Family and, ultimately, by the Ministry of Justice and the Federal Constitutional Court.

Prior to the events of 1989–90, over 90 per cent of all GDR women aged 15–60 were engaged in paid labour (compared to 48–54 per cent in the old *Länder*). Having accounted for 48 per cent of the total workforce under the former regime, women comprised 58.8 per cent of the newly unemployed by August 1991, many of whom had been forced out of the market with the disappearance of child-care facilities. {Roughly one-third of all children since the early eighties were born to single mothers – day-care costs in the West range from DM 250 to DM 1500 per month.} This proportion excluded those who had ceased 'looking' for work and hence were not registered as officially unemployed; by late 1991 women had been selected for only one-third of the federally funded *ABM-Stellen* (job-creation programmes). During interviews conducted in June/July 1992 I was repeatedly told that only 20 per cent of the Eastern women are now gainfully employed.

As the backlash against the welfare state in many countries suggests, the 'do-somethings' (taxpayers) are ultimately pitted against the 'do-nothings' (aid-recipients). Under the market system, a lack of paid employment, whether intentional or not, precipitates a loss of standing, both subjectively and objectively speaking. This condition is not unique to capitalism. Orthodox Marxism emphasises not only the exploitative nature of the capitalist production system; it also sees in human labour a higher form of self-actualization – hence the constitutional 'right to work' and the glorification of the 'workers' state under the former East European regimes.

The link between subjective perception and citizen competency is elaborated by Shklar:

> The unemployed may feel that they have been disgraced for no particular fault of their own, and that they have become less than citizens. You can think that the boss is a slave-driver but you may feel more like a real slave when you are unemployed. And there is nothing illusory about these experiences. You have been expelled from civil

society, reduced to second-class citizenship . . . this loss of one's social position is itself felt as a loss of competency, which is inevitably enhanced when the unemployed person must seek help from others . . . May they not, as is now often the case, be treated with that mixture of paternalism and contempt that has always been reserved for the dependent classes? They are not citizens of civil society, and they are not accepted as such.[16]

The new/old dependency created by the loss of personal income, and the gradual re-exclusion of women from the public sphere finds reinforcement in other policy arenas. Contraceptives are no longer free for the women of the East. The ramifications are immense, in view of a 1981 study by researchers at the Central Institute for Youth Research revealing that, on the average, one's first experience with intercourse occurred in the GDR at 16 years, 9 months of age.[17] The 'birth benefit' paid to all women after delivery irrespective of income has been cut from 1000 East-Marks to 150 West-Marks – despite the fact that salaries in the new *Länder* are currently equivalent to only 35–40 per cent of West German earnings (with women earning only 70 per cent of that). Prices in some locations exceed those in the West, and rents have risen some 200–500 per cent since the October 1991 termination of subsidies. The Ministry of Family and the Elderly estimates that there are now as many as 50 000 homeless women in the old states alone.[18] It is therefore not surprising that the Eastern *Länder* have registered a 50 per cent drop in the birthrate and a 400 per cent increase [for Berlin] in the number of sterilizations since 1991.

The dramatic decline in fertility rates, real and potential, is directly linked to fears regarding the possible elimination of the long-standing right to terminate unwanted pregnancies, under the rubric of paragraph 218. In 1990 Kohl appointed Claudia Nolte to head the parliamentary Task Force on Women and Youth which was to deliberate the issue. Currently the youngest Member of the Bundestag (born 1966), Nolte is a practising Catholic from Thuringia who told me in a June 1990 interview that she favoured a tightening of the FRG's already tough 218 requirements. Maria Michalk, another fervent Catholic from the Sorbin community in Dresden, was named to chair the CDU-caucus group deliberating this issue. Nolte and Michalk have been instrumentalized by Conservatives to demonstrate that a 'silent majority' in the East wants to terminate the 'tri-semester' approach country-wide.

A 1990 *Spiegel* survey published in January testified to a largely 'pro-choice' orientation among the German publics at large, however.

Abortion . . .	FRG		GDR	
1. should remain unpunishable	32%		35%	
		= 59%		= 68%
2. should be permitted during the first 3 months	27%		33%	
3. permissible only on medical or social grounds	28%		21%	
4. only when life of the mother endangered	13%		18%	

Women supporting (1) and (2)	FRG	GDR
Total	57%	69%
Ages 18–29	71%	79%
Conservative voters	54%	59%
Social-democratic voters	58%	75%

Source: Barbara Bertram, "Zurueck an den Herd?" *Spiegel Spezial, Das Profil der Deutschen*, Nr. 1, 1991, pp. 62–6.

Respondents chose among the following legal options:
Out of this sample, Eastern women evinced generally higher support levels for their own 'trimester' framework than their Western counterparts:

Of the three female Ministers charged with the regulation of more conventional 'women's issues', all actively opposed the principle of unfettered choice; Rönsch even sponsored the draft law securing compulsory medical documentation for purposes of eventual criminal prosecution of physicians performing abortions. Only former GDR-citizen Angela Merkel (interviewed by this author in June 1990) initially sought to leave the *ultimate* decision up to the woman, albeit subsequent to mandatory 'pro-life' counselling. In fact, she toed the party line in June 1992, voting to grant final authority to physicians but declaring that she would not join in a constitutional challenge to the coalition version. The day after the final parliamentary vote, a photo in the *Leipziger Volkszeitung* depicted Chancellor Kohl patting Minister Merkel's hand in a rather paternalistic fashion with the caption, 'Gut gemacht, Angela.'

West German regulations throughout 1992, rooted in the Criminal Code of 1871, specifically outlawed abortion on a trimester basis. Instead, a woman was obliged to seek certification from a doctor that she fell under one of four 'indicators' [medical, eugenic/fetal deformity, criminal/rape or incest, or extreme socio-economic hardship] in order to escape prosecution. In reality, only eight out of potentially 700 000 convictions were meted out in 1990.[19] A 1972 reform-law in the East permitted abortion upon demand for the first three months, and usually in consultation with a physician during subsequent stages. It was because of its highly controversial nature that the regulation of abortion was intentionally excluded from the first State Treaty and the Unity Treaty.

Instead of legal certainty, women were initially subjected to a lousy political compromise – the application of both laws through December 1992, based on the 'operative site' principle [*Tatortprinzip*], as opposed to the even more restrictive 'residency' principle [*Wohnortprinzip*] conservatives originally sought to impose. The untenable consequences of the current dual-system approach through 1992 became self-evident in the case of 'Kathrin K.', as well as in the follow-ups to the 1987 Memmingen decision.[20] In short, the Treaty deliberately violated the constitutional precept of 'equal protection before the law'.

In accordance with the deadline for a common regulation set by the Unity Treaty, the Bundestag commenced deliberations on six distinctive drafts of a new law in September 1991. On June 25th, the Bundestag approved the 'trimester solution' with mandatory counselling by a vote of 357 to 283; of the 32 renegade votes cast by conservatives, 19 hailed from the East. One of the most significant contributors to the final outcome was no doubt the composition of the legislature itself: 527 men and 135 women in 1992, compared to 468 men and 28 women in 1974 (the earlier reform law passed by a vote of 247 to 233). On August 4, 1992 the Federal Constitutional Court imposed a temporary injunction, prohibiting full-scale implementation.

Rejecting the legislators' framework by a vote of six to two (with one separate and one dissenting opinion) on May 28, 1993, the Constitutional Court proposed its own 'Interim Law' which took effect on June 16, 1993; the Bundestag has until December 1994 to generate a new statute based on its restrictions. Abortion has been declared *rechtswidrig aber straffrei* ('illegal but free from punishment'). Officially approved advisors must 'encourage' (*ermutigen*) all women to continue their pregnancies by outlining all available forms of public assistance. The cost of abortions falling outside the medical, criminal and embryopathic indications (ranging between DM 300 and DM 1400) will no longer be covered by the health insurance system (*Krankenkasse*). The ruling thus eliminates the 'social hardship' indicator, which formerly accounted for 80 per cent of all certified abortions.

A final example of the politics of exclusion (not to mention flagrant violation of Article 3 of the Basic Law) rests a little closer to home, namely, in the world of academia. Article 38 of the Unity Treaty provides the legal foundation for *Abwicklung*, a process of liquidation as renewal; its purpose is to purge Eastern universities and research institutions of the ideologically suspect and the substantively unqualified. Key targets were the Humanities and Social Science faculties where, unfortunately, the concentration of women has been the highest.

It cannot be said that the GDR's adherence to the principle of 'equal opportunity' was beyond reproach; in fact, most policies ensuring special benefits for members of the female labour force were not pro-woman, they were pro-natalist in essence. The proportion of female professors in the GDR was roughly equivalent to that in the old FRG, a mere 8–10 per cent. The pattern is a familiar one: women were generally the last to be hired, concentrated in particular disciplines (in 1989, women comprised 8.8 per cent of the social science professors, 1.7 per cent in math, natural sciences), the first to be fired, and now the last to be rehired.

Some 2800 of 7200 staff members have been forced to leave their jobs at the Humboldt University since 1990, many because of ties to the Stasi. Now facing an extreme financial crisis, the HU must undertake another round of deep cuts, eliminating 190 of 769 professorial positions and 326 of its 1578 *Mittelbau* staff. Women accounted for 21.9 per cent of the permanent research staff positions in the natural sciences, and 52.8 per cent of the *Mittelbau* in the social sciences; both may be reduced by a total of 80 per cent within five years.

The renewal process falls under the direction of two specially created post-secondary education commissions, the *Landeshochschulstrukturkommission* and the *Struktur- und Berufungskommission*, which set the parameters for an extensive hiring campaign in 1991. By the summer of 1992, 52 full professors had been appointed, only four of whom were women (two in education, two in law). One of the four is 58 years old – although the Unity Treaty urges those over 55 to take advantage of early retirement. All four women are 'carry-overs,' compared to 15 men who have been reappointed to their former departments. *No* women were hired at the rank of full professor in the fields of sociology and political science. The major chairs have all gone to West German males.

The hiring process itself appears to violate two laws designed to level out the playing field for applicants. According to the Berlin

Amendment to the Law of Higher Education of July 18, 1991, the State Structural Commission was to consist of three professors each, from East and West, recommended through complicated institutional channels. In actuality, the Commission consisted of 19 men and one woman whose task it was to recommend members for appointment to the Structure and Recruitment Commission. At the HU, recruitment committees for education, economics and philosophy had no female members; law and the social sciences committees had one Easterner each, history had two.

Nor did the hiring process meet the requirements set by Berlin's State Anti-discrimination Law (LADG) which took effect on January 13, 1991. Recruitment committees were to contain equal numbers of women and men, jobs had to be advertised publicly, and if insufficient numbers of women applied, the ad process was to be repeated: only 11.4 per cent of the social science applications came from women, suggesting that the process should have been reopened. Equal numbers of women and men were to be interviewed in those fields in which females were traditionally underrepresented. No women were placed first on the short-list for eight openings in sociology/political science. Presuming equal qualifications, women were to be preferentially hired until the proportion stood at 50 per cent. Neither the Berlin parliament nor the *Wissenschaftssenator* took objection to the improprieties of the recruitment process when the details became public. The only silver lining in the process of 'renewal' at the Humboldt University has been the election of its new president, a 48 year old sociologist named Marlis Dürkop who is a former *Bündnis '90*/Green member of Berlin parliament – a *Wessi* but a woman nonetheless.

IN SEARCH OF SOLIDARITY: ISSUES FOR NEW GERMAN WOMEN

Recalling the significance of symbolism in politics, the most significant constitutional-legal victory to date appears to be the right to retain (paraphrasing Virginia Woolf) 'a name of one's own'. The Federal Constitutional Court decreed in March 1991 that Paragraph 1355 of the Civil Code (BGB) violates the equality provisions of the Basic Law. That article obliges married partners (a) to assume the name of the man (or woman, but only if both agree); or (b) to trudge through marital life with an unmanageable double-name [triple in the case of remarriage]. A few of the more prominent examples resulting from the previous stipulations include: Herta Däubler-Gmelin, Margarete Mitscherlich-Nielsen, Sabina Leutheusser-Schnarrenberger, Renate Schweizer-Schulz-Darup, Hedwig Meyer-Wilmes-Mueller, and last but not least, Elisabeth Noelle-Neumann-Maier-Leibnitz.[21] The law still insists, however, that newborns only receive first-names which immediately identify their gender, for which state committees serve as the ultimate authority.

With regard to more substantive issues, there are certain grounds for optimism based on generational factors. In the first survey comparison of Eastern and Western youth attitudes conducted in June–July 1990, 83.4 per cent of all respondents (82.1 per cent FRG, 84 per cent GDR) cited 'equal rights for women' as an inalienable [*unverzichtbare*] component of their understanding of democracy. Young women concurred at the rate of 90 per cent, while male support differed according to levels of formal education, especially in the West. Some 60 per cent of the FRG group and 53 per cent of the GDR sample went so far as to reject the idea that 'housework is actually a woman's matter' {'Who does the laundry currently?' 85 per cent of the FRG women, and 79 per cent of the GDR women said they do}.[22]

Hence, the feminist theme for the next decade, as noted by this author in *The Federal Republic at 40*, remains unchanged: 'the women's question is now a men's question'. Without fundamental changes in the consciousness and behaviour of men, beginning with the equitable distribution of family and household responsibilities, there can be but limited progress in the campaign to secure for women the full rights of citizenship. Demographics will compel policy-makers to undertake an equalization of pensions and the provision of adequate child-care facilities – and hopefully anchor the liberalisation of abortion laws. Equally important for women will be the problems of acid rain and pollution, toxic and nuclear waste disposal, hazards of genetic research, and the deployment of German troops in out-of-area conflicts – arenas once deemed 'a man's world' which have drawn ever more women into politics since the early eighties.

For the time being, the status of women in the New Germany will fall under the ruling 'more freedom means fewer rights', or as Andrea Göhler phrased it, *Männer planen, Frauen baden aus* [men do the planning, women suffer the consequences]. Deprived on a number of fronts of their ability to earn, women are unlikely to enjoy political participatory rights commensurate with men. The women of *Neufünfland* are justified in perceiving that they do not yet enjoy the social standing promised them under the banner of unified German citizenship.

The effective deconstruction of GDR identity and the eventual internalisation of liberal-democratic ideals will require much more than mere emulation of the behaviours and attitudes of Federal Republican men. The Brandenburg Gate is now open, but on both sides there persists an extraordinary need for mutual social adjustment and a mutual recognition of social standing. The understanding of citizenship as an on-going process signifies that the 'German [Gender Equality] Question' is far from closed. The New Women of the Federal Republic still need to engage in significant prodding among the many Old Men who need to catch up with them. As the German adage prescribes, *Ohne Frauen ist kein Staat zu machen* (without women you can't have a decent state).

Notes

1. Daniela Dahn, presentation '*Ohne Frauen ist kein Staat zu machen*,' delivered at the American Institute for Contemporary German Studies in Washington, D.C. on April 16, 1990, pp. 1–2. Citation derives from a written draft graciously supplied to this author at the time.
2. For a compelling philosophical treatment, see Judith N. Shklar, *American Citizenship. The Quest for Inclusion*, Cambridge/London: Harvard University Press, 1991.
3. Gabriel A. Almond and Sydney Verba, *The Civic Culture Revisited*, Boston/Toronto: Little, Brown & Company, 1980, p. 19ff.
4. Tuija Parvikko, 'Conceptions of Gender Equality: Similarity and Difference', in Elizabeth Meehan and Selma Sevenhuijsen, eds., *Equality Politics and Gender*, London/Newbury Park: Sage, 1991, pp. 36–51.
5. Carole Pateman, 'The Civic Culture: A Philosophic Critique', in Almond and Verba, *Civic Culture Revisited*, pp. 59–60.
6. Pateman, p. 79, p. 98.
7. Shklar, p. 2.
8. Shklar, p. 3.
9. Sabine Berghahn and Andrea Fritzsche. *Frauenrecht in Ost und Westdeutschland. Bilanz, Ausblick*, Berlin: Basisdruck, 1991, p. 14.
10. Peter Förster and Günter Roski, *DDR zwischen Wende und Wahl. Meinungsforscher analysieren den Umbruch*, Berlin: LinksDruck Verlag, 1990, p. 161ff.
11. The study applied 'western standards,' that is, samples and questions not subject to ultimate Politburo approval. The Central Institute for Youth Research was established in 1966, and was formally subordinate to the Office for Youth Questions under the Council of Ministers. Its findings were generally classified as 'top secret,' accessible only to members of the Politburo and Ministers of State. Margot Honecker attempted several times to dissolve the Institute after 1981, its ever more negative findings

reflecting a significant loss of legitimacy for the régime in the eyes of younger citizens. Shortly after unification it was *abgewickelt* (closed down as having been too 'regime-friendly') and absorbed by the Deutsches Jugendinstitut housed in Munich.

12. Förster and Roski, p. 54, p. 60, p. 65.
13. Rainer Geissler, 'Soziale Ungleichheiten zwischen Frauen und Männern – Erfolge und Hindernisse auf dem Weg zur Gleichstellung in den beiden deutschen Staaten,' *Sozialwissenschaftliche Informationen*, Nr. 19, 1990, p. 185ff.
14. Not a single woman ever served as a voting member of the Party's ruling Politburo throughout the entire history of the GDR. Its two 'candidate' members, Margarete Mueller and Ingeburg Lange, were appointed in 1963 and 1973, respectively. Nor were there any women to be found in the Presidium of the Council of Ministers, the highest organ of government. Responsible for Education [*Volksbildung*] since 1963, Margot Honecker – known as the 'purple dragon' because of her blue hair-rinse – was the sole female minister at the time of the regime's collapse in October 1989. Only four others have ever enjoyed equivalent rank, compared to the eight female Cabinet members who had occupied posts in the *Bundesregierung* prior to the first all-German elections of 1990.
15. 'Ministerinnen: Ein bisschen zuständig,' *Der Spiegel*, Nr. 8, 1991, p. 70, p. 73.
16. Shklar, pp. 93–4, p. 98.
17. Uta Schlegel, Hrsg., *Junge Frauen Heute. Wie sie sind – was sie wollen*, Leipzig: Verlag für die Frau, 1986, p. 69.
18. Reported in *The Week in Germany*, September 25, 1992, p. 7.
19. 'Abtreibung: Pure Einbildung,' *Der Spiegel*, 45. Jg., Nr. 39, 23. September 1991, p. 38. This edition featured as its title story the German refusal to allow the marketing of RU 486, an abortifacient pill produced by a French subsidiary of the Hoechst Corporation – the result of which would be to enable women to terminate pregnancies immediately after conception without surgical procedures. Hoechst has argued that its historical culpability as a producer of chemicals (used for concentration camp exterminations) requires it to exercise a special responsibility for the preservation of life, now defined in terms of embryo/fetus.
20. In the former case, a married mother of 22 was arrested on suspicion of abortion while crossing the border between Holland and the FRG. Subjected to a forced vaginal exam in a state hospital, Katherine K. became a cause célèbre when it was revealed that she had fled to the West from Jena in 1988 – where the procedure is still considered legal. 'Abtreibung – Zwangsuntersuchung an der Grenze,' *Der Spiegel*, 45. Jg., Nr. 10, March 4, 1991.

The Memmingen case involved the Bavarian government's decision to expropriate a doctor's private records containing the names of 500 women who had terminated pregnancies over a period of two decades. Their names were published (many were practising Catholics), all were investigated, and 279 were criminally convicted based on a judge's refusal to accept their 'hardship' certification. Most of the latter faced sentences of DM 900–1500 in fines or 30 days in prison and were subsequently registered in police computers as having criminal records. See 'Magdalena wehrt sich, Memminger Hexenjagd geht weiter,' *Emma*, Nr. 7, July 1990, pp. 4–5. Further, 'BGH bestätigt Memminger Urteil gegen Frauenarzt weitestgehend,' *Der Tagesspiegel*, vol. 4, December 1991 no. 20.

21. 'Namensrecht: Im Zweifel durchs Los,' *Der Spiegel*, Nr. 16, April 15, 1991; and 'Recht: Los oder Elfmeter,' *Der Spiegel*, Nr. 14, April 1, 1991.

22. *Deutsche Schüler im Sommer 1990 – Skeptische Demokraten auf dem Weg in ein vereintes Deutschland. Deutsch-deutsche Schüler-befragung 1990*, Hrsg., Deutsches Jugendinstitut e.V., DJI Arbeits-papier 3–019, Munich, 1990, p. 33ff.

Part II

East German Identity, an Irreducible Residue?

5 East German Intellectuals in a Unified Germany
Ian Wallace

Divided Germany is at last unified, but nothing is quite so divisive as unification, it would seem. And nowhere is the new divisiveness more apparent than in attitudes towards the intellectuals of what used to be the GDR. Exactly who is and who is not to be seen as an intellectual within the context of a debate which broke out immediately after the Wall fell and which continues to rage today is the subject of competing theories and definitions. My intention here is to limit myself to the critical literary intelligentsia, although in my conclusion I call upon an academic and a leading member of the citizens' movement New Forum, Jens Reich, as my final witness.

INTELLECTUALS STAND CONDEMNED

'Call upon as a witness' – the language of the court-room is not out of place in this context. Beginning with the well-documented and much-discussed attacks on the moral integrity and, to a lesser extent, literary stature of the internationally famous novelist Christa Wolf, the GDR's literary intelligentsia has effectively been on public trial for well over two years now. Necessary and inevitable though this trial may be in the wake of the GDR's collapse, the spirit in which it has been conducted has been largely unforgiving, sometimes hysterical, and not without a strong whiff of vindictiveness. The bitterness has at least two principal sources. It is firstly, and paradoxically, a reflection of what in my view is the exaggeratedly exalted stature generally accorded to writers in the GDR. In line with a problematic German tradition which the GDR essentially continued, writers and readers alike tended to overestimate the power of the word. When this illusion was exposed to full public view by the complete bankruptcy of the GDR, critical writers felt the backlash. Secondly, powerful and censorious critics in the West with their own agenda to pursue unleashed a furious debate in the columns of newspapers and journals. Although it can be argued that the debate generated more heat than light, it did have the effect of reinforcing the impression that the writers had fallen short of what was expected of them. Disappointed expectations means failure.

What may be perceived to be the main elements of that failure from today's vantage-point? The most spectacular and damaging aspect is the revelation that leading critical writers collaborated with the State Security Police (commonly referred to as the Stasi). Sascha Anderson and Rainer Schedlinski, the leading lights in a supposedly autonomous, that is politically disengaged group of young writers living in the Prenzlauer Berg area of East Berlin, are the most prominent cases, but older writers such as Heinz Kahlau and even the notoriously non-conformist Helga Novak have also been forced out into the open. In January 1993, no less a figure than Christa Wolf had to confess to writing apparently relatively harmless reports for the Stasi at an early and vulnerable stage in her life. As yet unsubstantiated rumours abound about the likely number of well-known writers who allegedly assisted the Stasi on an unofficial basis as so-called 'IMs' or 'Inoffizielle Mitarbeiter' (roughly: unofficial assistants). Klaus Schlesinger is one who found it necessary to defend his reputation publicly (and credibly) against what he saw in effect as a whispering campaign. With the laudable exception of Hans Joachim Schädlich, none of those former colleagues who had impugned his integrity apparently felt it necessary subsequently to apologize.

A particular problem arises where, by virtue of his or her very prominence and status, a leading writer became – perhaps as a matter of conscience rather than by choice – the vehicle by which other, less prestigious literary figures conveyed their worries and wishes to the political authorities. By supping with the devil in effect, such writers exposed themselves to the charge of complicity, for the boundary between negotiation and collaboration is not always easily drawn, particularly when this is attempted in retrospect, from a defensive position, and on the basis of frequently unreliable and incomplete evidence. Heiner Müller, widely regarded as Germany's most accomplished contemporary dramatist, is one whose reputation has been challenged on this basis – but also vigorously defended by some of those he helped. More problematic is the case of Hermann Kant, formerly President of the GDR Writers Union. In his volume of memoirs, *Abspann* (1992), Kant devotes much space to denying any knowing involvement with the Stasi, despite his prominence in the Union, his oft expressed pride in being a Party functionary, and the long-standing accusation by his former professor, Alfred Kantorowicz, that Kant had been assigned to spy on him by the Stasi while a student at the Humboldt University in East Berlin.[1] As subsequent allegations in the weekly magazine *Der Spiegel* demonstrated, however, Kant's pre-emptive strike in self-defence did not make the issue go away.

The effect of this potent mixture of fact and rumour was to give substance to the otherwise contentious claim that critical writers were in a particular sense no more than servants of the state (*Staatsdichter*). Not even the confession by Wolf Biermann, the dissident poet and singer who had been exiled and deprived of his citizenship in 1976, that he too might, but for good fortune, have finished up working for the Stasi as a young man, or the appeal by another exiled poet, Günther Kunert, for understanding now the fall from grace of young and essentially weak colleagues like Anderson (this understanding did not extend to older writers, however) could reduce the impact of the shock that writers too are human and therefore corruptible. That this should come as a shock to anybody is surely just another reflection of the unnaturally exalted stature which, as noted above, GDR writers had hitherto enjoyed.

Ultimately the most damning accusation against the critical writers, because it is the one which has general application and against which it is most difficult to defend themselves, is that their criticism only served to stabilise an oppressive system since it always fell well short of demanding its overthrow. As Heiner Müller has admitted, it encouraged the illusion that 'critical solidarity' with the system held out the real promise of meaningful, fundamental reform. In fact – so the charge goes – it only made the GDR more habitable. In the words of the novelist Hans Joachim Schädlich, the help it offered to readers in facing the problems of their daily lives (*Lebenshilfe*) was the kind which well-meaning prison visitors offer to those condemned to spend their lives behind bars. The apparent courage of their criticism barely conceals the much greater cowardice of a privileged group. They were, in Biermann's words, the GDR's 'brave and cowardly intellectuals' ('*tapferfeige Intellektuelle*').[2]

The ambivalence inherent in this mixture of courage and cowardice is one of which the critical writers were themselves demonstrably conscious. It is implicit, for example, in the words which the narrator of Christa Wolf's story *Was bleibt* (What remains) addresses to herself every day:

Every day I said to myself that a privileged life like mine could only be justified by attempting from time to time to cross the frontiers of the sayable in the knowledge that frontier violations of any kind are punished.

[Jeden Tag sagte ich mir, ein bevorzugtes Leben wie das meine ließe sich nur durch den Versuch rechtfertigen, hin und wieder die Grenzen des Sagbaren zu überschreiten, der Tatsache eingedenk, daß Grenzverletzungen aller Art geahndet werden.][3]

The fierce controversy surrounding the appearance of Wolf's text in 1990 became the stage on which the battle about the alleged political failure of the intellectuals was fought out, with Wolf playing the part of the ritual scapegoat. The battle took place at two levels. Firstly, in what became a kind of second *Historikerdebatte* (historians' debate), the underlying aim of the most vociferous Western critics (notably the journalists Frank Schirrmacher of the *Frankfurter Allgemeine Zeitung* and Ulrich Greiner of *Die Zeit*) was to consign the past to the darkness of oblivion and to construct a new future free of such an embarrassing reality. With both GDR literature and West German literature safely out of the way, the path would be clear for a new, national consciousness and a cultural renewal founded on more conservative values. Secondly, it took the form of a particularly bitter assault on the integrity of critical writers by former colleagues who had chosen or been forced to leave the GDR, typically in the wake of the Biermann affair of 1976. This began even before the Wall fell, as Biermann's journalism proves, and as late as April 1992 Monika Maron was still excoriating with undiminished fervour the Johnny-come-latelys who turned into revolutionaries only after October 1989 – in other words, when it was safe to do so, and she clearly has Wolf in mind.[4]

There were those, among them large numbers of the GDR population including upright members of the citizens' movement, who felt it would be better to draw a veil over the past in order not to poison the future. This lay behind the poet and essayist Rainer Kirsch's wish that the archives of the Writers' Union should not be made accessible to the public. Helga Königsdorf, a writer whose journalism throughout 1990 reflects many of the hopes and disappointments of socialist intellectuals at the time, took a similar view of the staggering mountain of files left by the Stasi, although she did make an exception where cases of serious crime were concerned. This was not a view shared by the émigrés, who believed that it was imperative to know the full truth if only, as Jürgen Fuchs argued, to reveal the history of resistance in the GDR. The suspicion persisted, however, that these positive reasons really camouflaged the urge to take revenge by exposing misdeeds. To

some, the fact that Fuchs, Biermann, and others repeatedly say revenge is not their motive sounds disingenuous and in fact only serves
to draw attention to the (subconscious) possibility. As Martin Ahrends
has pointed out, 'Aufklärung' should not be confused with 'Aufarbeitung'.
Unlike the first term, the latter presupposes the willingness of both
sides to engage with one another in the shared wish not just to expose
but to come to terms with the past.

A further charge levelled at critical writers like Wolf, Müller,
Königsdorf, Volker Braun, and Stefan Heym is that, although it may
be accepted that their work had done so much to prepare the ground
for the upheavals of 1989 (the so-called *Wende*), they failed when the
revolution did come to comprehend the wishes and ambitions of their
compatriots and then belly-ached about what they saw as *Anschluss*,
colonisation, and the destruction of even the best aspects of the GDR's
inheritance by the West Germans. Self-pitying, moralising, self-
righteous, and unrealistic are just some of the adjectives used to describe this attitude. Königsdorf, for example, celebrated the *Wende* as
a 'work of art', but the freedom which followed it was 'the freedom
of the other side' ('die Freiheit der anderen').[5] Similarly, in one of the
strongest literary texts inspired by the *Wende*, Volker Braun draws
attention to his own part in helping to bring about change

Here I am still: my country is going west
(. . .)
I was the one who booted it into action
[*Da bin ich noch: mein Land geht in den Westen*
(. . .)
Ich selber habe ihm den Tritt versetzt][6]

but then bemoans the direction taken by that change and the devastating sense of loss it means for him. The search for a so-called third
way between capitalism and Stalinism, articulated most clearly and
controversially in the declaration *Für unser Land* (For our country)
issued by Braun, Heym, Wolf and others, proved a disastrous miscal-
culation. A further, and in all likelihood equally unsuccessful attempt
to snatch victory from the jaws of defeat can be seen in the move in
July 1992 to set up Committees for Justice in Eastern Germany. Of
the eight signatories of the lengthy statement ('Diskussionsplattform')
which accompanied the appeal issued by 69 intellectuals from East
and West, three were writers from the former GDR – Heym, Müller,
and the poet Stephan Hermlin. There are good reasons to sympathise

with the statement's protest against the frequently insensitive and humiliating treatment of citizens from the former GDR since unification and against the hasty rejection of GDR institutions and what are termed East German values and achievements, but the call for a third parliamentary forum to sit beside the two existing parliaments (the *Bundestag* and *Bundesrat*) and to consist of individuals, not parties, elected to represent the particular interests of citizens from the former GDR always looked like another dead-end.

A third reproach made of the critical writers was that, when the revolution did not follow the path they had marked out for it, they took refuge in wounded silence. Even more damaging is the charge that, like a rabbit reduced to fear-stricken immobility by the blinding headlights of the unification juggernaut, the writers refused in their literary work to deal with the revolution or to engage in *Vergangenheitsaufarbeitung*, that is, coming to terms with the GDR's past. But this silence can have more than one cause, for instance Müller's sense, shared with Hein and Wolf, that it would be simply absurd to try to provide an instant literary accompaniment to the revolutionary process.[7] Müller also points to the sinking of the Spanish armada, the decisive event of the Shakespearean age which, he declares, is not thematized in any of the plays written in that richest of all periods in the theatre. More generally, however, writers and other members of the critical intelligentsia were increasingly deflected from their work by the painful realisation that the actual and threatened disappearance of most of the cultural institutions which had in the past supported and promoted that work required the rapid development of survival strategies.

THE INTELLECTUALS FIGHT BACK

Following the demise of the Writers Union and, after much more of a struggle, the Academy of Arts (both in effect swallowed up by their counterparts in the West), the only GDR cultural institution of note to survive the unification process largely unscathed has been the PEN Centre, although even here the overwhelming likelihood is of an eventual union with the Western PEN Centre. Thus in its new statutes agreed on 1 February 1991 the organisation gave itself an explicitly temporary name: German PEN-Centre (East). The aim was clearly to preserve at least one important forum at which GDR writers could continue, for a time, to assert their identity and come to terms with their new circumstances without being steamrollered. Equally important was the opportunity to renew itself from within – for instance, by appointing a new President (Professor Dieter Schlenstedt) and, after some initial hiccups (Pastor Friedrich Schorlemmer, a leading figure in the citizens' movement, and the writer Joachim Walther were just two candidates who were not elected to membership and who therefore – very embarrassingly – were quickly offered membership by the Centre's counterpart in the West), by radically overhauling its membership.

That these were not purely defensive measures taken by an embattled élite set on defying the advance of political change is clear, for example, from its programme for 1992. This reveals a determination to engage with the issues which preoccupied and divided writers in East and West. One such was the conflict between writers who had chosen to stay in the GDR, notably after the Biermann affair, and those who for one reason or another had left. Entitled somewhat tendentiously 'Abhauen oder dableiben?' ('Run away or stay here?'), which tended to suggest that those who had left had not so much been forced out as decided to go of their own free will, this discussion was led by one representative of each side of the argument, Stefan Heym and the poet Bernd Jentzsch.[8] The latter also became the new director of the Johannes R. Becher Institute, an institution which was set up in the 1950s for the education and training of socialist writers, was initially earmarked for closure after the *Wende*, but finally re-emerged in a form which appears highly unlikely to protect those GDR values for which the PEN Centre has so far achieved a precarious and, almost certainly, short stay of execution.

The survival of a separate PEN Centre in the East is one indication that – although the critical writers rapidly lost their place at the forefront of events after that remarkable moment at the great mass rally on the Alexanderplatz on 4 November 1989 when they appeared to be the very voice of the 'gentle revolution' – it is an exaggeration to say that they generally withdrew into stunned silence. Certainly there were occasions when, under a hail of criticism, they saw discretion as the better part of valour, but they did also on occasion fight back vigorously, especially against the attacks of the émigrés. For example, Königsdorf questioned the motives not of those who had stayed but of those who had *left* the GDR:

> Why did they leave and not fight the good fight right here? So much for those who compare us unfavourably with Vaclav Havel. And we have the right to ask why this privilege was used, the privilege to

leave, when everybody else was not able to do so.
*[Warum ist man gegangen und hat nicht vor Ort den Kampf gefochten?
Denen ins Stammbuch, die uns Vaclav Havel vorhalten. Und man
wird fragen dürfen, warum dieses Privileg genutzt wurde, das Privileg
zu gehen, wo doch alle anderen nicht gehen durften.]*[9]

This was echoed in Friedrich Schorlemmer's evident admiration for
those who had stuck it out in the GDR as opposed to those who had
made it in time to the West ('rechtzeitig noch die Kurve nach Westen
gekratzt hatten') – that is, had taken the easy way out.

As for Wolfgang Thierse's idea of a tribunal (also argued for by
Schorlemmer) as a means of allowing East Germans to achieve their
own moral purification by coming to terms with the past of their own
volition rather than at the West's behest, Volker Braun of course agrees
that GDR criminals must be brought to justice. Indeed, he is second to
none in condemning crimes committed by the GDR's rules (*'Herr-
schaftskriminalität'*) and the way the socialist alternative in Germany
was sold down the river by the oppressive, semi-colonial society produced by Honecker's 'real existing socialism' (*'die Verwurstung der
sozialistischen Alternative in Deutschland durch die "realsozialistische"
(unterdrückerische, halbkoloniale) Lebensform'*).[10] He insists, however,
that equally necessary is an investigation of what he calls the 'ruler
mentality' (*'herrscherliche Mentalität'*) of successive Federal German
governments (he mentions aggressive armaments policies as well as
the controversial claim to be the only genuine representative of the
German people – the *Allein-vertretungsrecht*) and of something he describes as 'quite palpably criminal' (*'ganz greifbar kriminell'*), namely
the destruction or *Abwicklung* of the GDR's economic and cultural
potential by the current Federal government and its instrument, the
Treuhand.

The GDR's leading critical writers varied in their reaction to the
new situation of literature and writers after the *Wende*, but none seems
to have seen it as a serious threat to their continuing productivity. It is
true that Christa Wolf appeared at least momentarily vulnerable and
disoriented when asking her readers what it was they expected of her
under the new social and political conditions, but this appears to have
been the exception rather than the rule. Christoph Hein actually welcomed the change of circumstances as a release from the old obligation to meet the non-literary needs of his readers for information of
the kind which could now be found in the news media. This reaction
was shared by Müller, who welcomed literature's new autonomy and

freedom to pursue its real goal of subverting reality as it is presently constituted (*'die Wirklichkeit, so wie sie ist, unmöglich zu machen'*).[11] Volker Braun asserted that, for him, unification made no essential difference to literature's continuing duty to ask (new) awkward questions, puncture (new) ideological certainties, and to provide a safe haven for the utopian impulse:

> Who would prevent us from and who can relieve us of being the critic of the new half-measures and illusions too and of encouraging reason to think on a world scale.
> [*Wer will uns hindern, [wer] kann uns abnehmen, der Kritiker auch der neuen Halbheiten und Illusionen zu sein und die Vernunft zu ermutigen, in der Dimension der Welt zu denken.*][12]

It is clear on this evidence that the end of the GDR cannot mean the end of these authors' work. As might have been anticipated, first published reactions to the *Wende* took the form of single statements, speeches, and newspaper articles. These were followed by collections of the same (e.g. Königsdorf) as well as by diaries and memoirs (e.g. Müller, Werner Heiduczek, Thomas Rosenlöcher), not all of them without a strong dose of self-justification (notably Kant). A publication such as *Grenzfallgedichte. Eine deutche Anthologie* (The fall of a frontier. A German anthology of poetry), edited by Anna Chiarloni and Helga Pankoke in 1991, provides valuable proof that individual poems were being written on the *Wende* virtually as it happened. By 1992 the first complete volumes of what might be termed *Wende*-inspired literature were already appearing, notably Heym's *Auf Sand gebaut* (Built on sand: written between January 1991 and January 1992), Braun's *Die Zickzackbrücke. Ein Abrißkalender* (The zigzagbridge. A tear-off calendar: consisting, as the sub-title suggests, of a diary-like succession of poems and texts written between 1987 and 1991), Königsdorf's *Gleich neben Afrika* (Right next to Africa: 1992), and in the theatre Braun's *Böhmen am Meer* (Bohemia on sea) and *Iphigenie in Freiheit* (Iphigenia in freedom), as well as Jochen Berg's *Fremde in der Nacht* (Strangers in the night).

EX ORIENTE LUX

As we have noted, Braun argues that the literary intelligentsia has a duty to preserve the utopian impulse in German society. Jens Reich is another who sees this role for (Eastern) intellectuals in a united Germany, describing them in his book *Abschied von den Lebenslügen* (A farewell to life-lies) (1992) as the sourdough upon which Germany's future will vitally depend. As this claim suggests, the book's title is misleading since its main claim to our attention is not its revisitation of the old theme of the intellectuals' past failures but its assertion of the special role of intellectuals in the peaceful revolutions which, in Reich's view, are ahead of us and to which the 1989 revolution was simply a preliminary. An alternative title might have been *Das Licht aus dem Osten* (The light from the East), for what he holds out is nothing less than the promise that the world *can* be saved from the seemingly inevitable self-destruction towards which Western consumer ideology is catapulting it. In this scenario, the saviour will be the self-denying Eastern intellectual who, unlike his cynical counterpart in the West, has not signed a corrupting pact with the devil of consumerism. What we have here is a remarkable inversion of roles. Without in any way denying the sins of Eastern intellectuals in the past, Reich asserts that it is they who now have the better cards with which to face the future thanks both to the experiences of 1989 and to the (relative) lack of consumerism in the GDR before that:

> We can conceive of our situation as a start, as a tabula rasa. Having conformed and adapted, the intellectuals in the west are hanging on the wall bars with a heavy rucksack attached to their stomach. We have got rid of the rucksack.
> *[Wir können unsere Lage als Start auffassen, als Tabula rasa. Angepasst und eingefügt hängt die Intelligenz des Westens in der Sprossenwand, mit schwerem Rucksack vor dem Bauch. Wir sind den schweren Rucksack los.]*[13]

Thus October/November 1989 was essentially only a prelude to future changes (a *'Wetterleuchten in die Zukunft'*) whose full significance has still to be realised. The revolution did not represent a defeat for Eastern intellectuals, nor should they now withdraw from the scene and simply wait for a later generation to fight the good fight more effectively. On the contrary, Reich ascribes to them what sounds like a mission to shape Germany's active response to the challenges of the future:

> We make for home unbeaten, and it is not our grandchildren who shall make a better fight of it but we who must become the sourdough which spreads through the whole of Germany.
> *[Nicht geschlagen ziehen wir nach Haus, und nicht unsere Enkel*

sollen es besser ausfechten, sondern wir müssen der Sauerteig werden, der ganz Deutschland durchdringt.]

Whether we find Reich's analysis persuasive or not, it is important as a rallying cry to Eastern intellectuals, as a signal that they may and indeed should recover their self-confidence, and as an indication that they continue to have a distinct identity which separates them from intellectuals in the West:

They [the intellectuals] should not simply fall into line with the western model. Despite all the dents in their helmet they are not less well equipped for the future.
[Sie [die Intelligenz] soll nicht einfach aufs westliche Vorbild einschwenken Trotz aller Beulen am Helm ist sie für die Zukunft nicht schlechter gerüstet.][14]

Whether or not this particular argument is seen as simply Don Quixote's last tilt at the windmill, it is clear that leading writers and thinkers from the former GDR have no intention of simply leaving to others the redefinition of the role of intellectuals in the new Germany.

Notes

1. Hermann Kant, *Abspann. Erinnerung an meine Gegenwart*, Aufbau: Berlin and Weimar, 1991
2. Wolf Biermann, 'Tapferfeige Intellectuelle. Über Stefan Heyms Roman *Collin*,' in: *Wolf Biermann. Klartexte im Getümmel. 13 Jahre im Westen. Von der Ausbürgerung bis zur November-Revolution*, Keipenheuer & Witsch: Cologne, 1990, pp. 135–43
3. Christa Wolf, *Was bleibt*, Luchterhand: Frankfurt am Main, 1990, p. 22
4. Monika Maron, letter in *Die Zeit*, April 17, 1992
5. Helga Königsdorf, *1989 oder ein Moment Schönheit: eine Collage aus Briefen, Gedichten, Texten*, Aufbau: Berlin and Weimar, 1990, p. 5
6. Volker Braun, 'Das Eigentum', *Die Zickzackbrücke. Ein Abrisskalender*, Mitteldeutscher Verlag: Halle, 1992, p. 84
7. Heiner Müller, *Zur Lage der Nation*, Rotbuch: Berlin, 1990, p. 23. Cf. Christoph Hein, 'Kunst strickt nicht gern mit heißer Nadel', *Die fünfte Grundrechenart: Aufsätze und Reden*, Luchterhand: Frankfurt am Main, 1990, p. 193; Christa Wolf, *Im Dialog*, Luchterhand: Frankfurt am Main, p. 138, where Wolf states that 'it will take years before this process can be critically assessed by literature' ('(. . .) ehe dieser Prozeß von der Literatur aufgearbeitet werden kann, dauert es Jahre')
8. *Zur Lage der Nation*, p. 89
9. Helga Königsdorf, 'Deutschland, wo der Pfeffer wächst', *Die Zeit*, July 20, 1990.

10. Cf. Braun's letter to Wolfgang Thierse, published in *Die Zeit*, 46, November 8, 1991.

11. *Zur Lage der Nation*, p. 21

12. Volker Braun, 'Das unersetzliche wird unser Thema bleiben', *Neue deutsche Literatur*, vol. 6, 1990, nos. 6–9, p. 9

13. Jens Reich, *Abschied von den Lebenslügen. Die Intelligenz und die Macht*, Rowohlt: Berlin, 1992, p. 165. The other quotations in this paragraph can be found at the same place.

14. Ibid., p. 157

6 Shadows of the Past: Germany and the Legacy of SED Rule

Helga A. Welsh

BACKGROUND

Contemporary politics in Eastern Germany (as well as in most of Central and Eastern Europe) are characterised by a necessity to address the past in order to build the future. Unearthing and coming to grips with events since communist takeovers after the end of World War II is one of the primary concerns of the revolutions in Eastern Europe. The range of tasks this implies only begins with the revelation of injustices and the rehabilitation of victims of communism: there are streets to rename, statutes to topple, unmarked graves to locate, national identities to redefine.[1] Other critical components that require historical perspective in the transition from communist regimes to those based on principles of polyarchy and market economics include assessment of the lingering impact of the communist political background on current political culture;[2] restitution, which is central to the whole privatisation process; the appraisal of communist party assets, and the critical evaluation of the past and future role of the former nomenklatura and state security agents.

At the end of the Second World War, much of Europe was caught in a similar effort to deal with the legacy of a particular form of dictatorship and its national interpretations, Italian fascism and German National Socialism.[3] Now, again, after the fall of 1989, the search for justice and rehabilitation and the problems inherent in dealing with major decision-makers and their collaborators and accomplices seem to be particularly pronounced in Germany's case. To explain why this is so and to look at the process of *Vergangenheitsaufarbeitung* in the context of present-day Germany will be the focus of this chapter.

THE PROBLEMS

Are controversies surrounding the selection of measures to adequately proceed with political purges, are the accusations and suspicions inherent in the lustration process worth the time and effort? Is too much political energy being spent on settling the past instead of focusing on the important economic and social issues that will determine the future? Is pondering the past particularly painful because it further undermines the identity and self-assertion of Eastern Germans towards Western Germans? To what extent have revelations made public from state security files served as important political weapons to discredit political opponents and to undermine the credibility of new political institutions in the East? It is one thing to punish and another to rehabilitate. What about the pressing issues of collective guilt, of reconciliation, of understanding the 40 years of communist rule in Eastern Germany?[4]

Political crimes, the destruction of personal lives, the denial of freedom, the humiliations suffered under the rule of the SED call for justice and rehabilitation. The replacement of a system in which the rule of law was undermined to conform with political objectives – and in which private lives often could be protected only if public lives were built on conformity, subservience, and public lies – can be successful only if values such as trust and tolerance toward others, and the accountability of the rulers over the ruled are established. The exercise of these values should also guard against witch-hunting and revenge for its own sake.

During transitions from authoritarian rule to democratic rule difficult decisions have to be made concerning the extent of the political purge. The replacement of those in leadership positions in areas of public life such as public administration, education, and law is relatively uncontroversial, but what about those hundreds of thousands who joined the Socialist Unity Party (SED) and who practised a profession according to the rules laid down by those in power? Who does the selecting and what are the criteria for dismissal or retention? On the one hand, one can argue that fellow-travellers and accomplices helped in creating and maintaining a dictatorship. Therefore, there is a *need to assess their role*. However, democracy should not be based on the exclusion of large segments of the population but should invite healing and chances to right wrongs in fractured societies marked by high levels of stress and distress. Thus there is a *need to forgive*.

Ignorance breeds intolerance and promotes myth-building. The greater the knowledge of the workings of the communist system of government, the greater the chances that economic, political, and social crisis periods under conditions of democratic rule will be mastered. For many Eastern Germans life under communism had acquired a sense of normalcy and predictability; for others it symbolised repression and injustice; others again walked the tightrope between accommodation and subservience.[5] The extent to which the regime discredited itself in the eyes of its citizens is marked by individual memories. There are clear-cut cases of victims and perpetrators, but the never-ending revelations regarding the involvement of collaborateurs (*inoffizielle Mitarbeiter*) in the network of the state security (Stasi) have also highlighted the difficulties in distinguishing between victims and perpetrators. Information and documentation are necessary to correct and to set into context both the failures and the limited nature of the accomplishments of the communist regime in the former GDR. Hence there is a need to *know*.

Finally, there is a need *to punish* those who committed crimes under the rule of the SED. But can justice be done now when many of the most adverse events, such as the disappearance of opposition politicians and citizens in Soviet labour camps or special internment camps, or the brutal crushing of the 1953 uprising, occurred a long time ago? This time lag also raises the issue of the statute of limitations for prosecution,[6] and the prosecution itself is handicapped by the fact that many key witnesses are no longer alive and that most of the accused are elderly and often too ill to stand trial. The ascription of guilt is further obstructed by the involvement of Soviet decision-makers in the domestic affairs of the former GDR.

The last several years have seen legal proceedings against former East German border guards on manslaughter charges, against former GDR judges and public prosecutors, and against some of the former leaders of the SED regime, notably Erich Honecker, Erich Mielke, Willi Stoph, Heinz Kessler, and Hans Albrecht, as well as numerous inquiries and legal investigations into crimes associated with the previous communist-government regime. Advanced age and health-related problems notwithstanding, the trials against some of the most visible former political leaders of the GDR were more important for the fact that they took place than for their outcomes or even for the charges levied against these leaders, which were often insignificant in view of the magnitude of power abuses. Without ever being able to address all issues associated with these abuses of power, addressing the most egregious cases, these trials were important for the endorsement of legal principles, despite the unavoidable sensationalism surrounding the trials. But it is also true – and probably unavoidable – that they failed to give those who had suffered under communism the kind of inner satisfaction they had hoped for. Overwhelmed by the sheer number of cases that still await trial, criminal prosecutors caution that legal proceedings cannot bring justice to 40 years of injustice.

However, both political purge and legal proceedings alone are only part of the reappraisal of the East German past for which other kinds of political and scientific tribunals seem to be more appropriate, not the least because the latter act against tendencies to personalize guilt in the hands of a few. Indeed, the special characteristic of the German approach to dealing with the communist past lies in its emphasis on public information, documentation, and educational efforts. As a result, special research agendas have been defined and have received public funding. Public fora (the most important of which is the Commission of Inquiry, composed of parliamentary deputies and scientists) have been assigned to investigate the history and consequences of the regime in the former German Democratic Republic truthfully, objectively, and in a non-partisan manner.[7]

THE SPECIAL CASE OF GERMANY

It was asserted at the beginning of this chapter that the lustration process in the former East Germany is more thorough and pronounced than elsewhere in Central and Eastern Europe – with the possible exception of the former Czechoslovakia. The relative vigour with which lustration issues have been handled in Germany is the product of a number of interrelated factors, the most important of which will be discussed in the following.

Penetration

The extent to which the communist party and its security and police apparatus have discredited themselves in the eyes of the public varies considerably across Central and Eastern Europe. In those countries where the opening of the political system evolved over a longer period of time and where the communist party encouraged a slight opening of the political space, as in Hungary or Poland, the role of the state security was visible but less pronounced than in Czechoslovakia or East Germany, where political and economic reforms were severely restricted and often not much more than window dressing. Intelligence networks were particularly fine-meshed and effective in those cases where communist party rule was perceived as weak and where the influence of the West was considered as particularly destabilising. In the case of the former GDR, the geographical front-line position between East and West, the problem of national identity, and the apparent paranoia of its leaders helped in creating the 'monster' of the Stasi. From a population of 16.3 million, the State Security Service (Stasi) employed about 85 000 full-time staff members, and its network of informers entailed between 180 000 and 200 000 people. According to estimates, files on over six million people (four million relating to East German, two million relating to West German citizens) have been secured; at the Stasi headquarters in Berlin and elsewhere in the former GDR, the files laid end-to-end would reach nearly 178 kilometres.[8] In comparison, it has been estimated that in Poland – with a population of approximately 37.7 million people – the number of full-time officers in the secret services only amounted to 24 000; no reliable estimates as to how many collaborators worked for the security services have been obtained.[9] In Czechoslovakia, where the lustration process has been particularly thorough, the network of intelligence agents and informers of the security police amounted to between 110 000 and 140 000.

The extensive network of surveillance was just one of the mechanisms that was intended to pervasively penetrate all levels of society. If the extent of largely mobilised political participation is measured in terms of membership in political organisations, the GDR ranked high among its East European neighbours. Almost 20 per cent of the adult population were card-carrying members of the Communist Party and, on the average, every citizen over 14 years of age was a member in at least three mass organisations or political parties.

The extent of penetration in itself is not a sufficient measure to trace the worst abuses of power committed under communism. However, it is indicative of the rigour with which the regimes in question intruded into public and private lives and therefore created a heightened sense of awareness of the severe restrictions of civil and political rights among the public.

Implosion

In the literature on regime transitions much emphasis is being given to the (pre-)conditions under which democracy can prosper and on the best ways of institutionalising the new political order. One such issue in the democratisation process centres on this question of dealing with the past. Much in the literature assumes that the power of authoritarians needs to be diffused without completely disarming them. Central to this argument is the idea that the authoritarian regime is more likely to agree to a peaceful transfer of power and to the principles of democratic rule if a policy of clemency is part of the political transition process.

Although the transitions in Central and Eastern Europe were largely negotiated transitions,[10] in the case of East Germany the implosion of the communist regime was particularly expeditious and unexpected. In the winter months of 1989–90, the authority of the SED continued to wane during the round-table negotiations which started as a way to control and veto communist policy initiatives but soon had expanded into power-sharing. Finally, the political initiative moved from old to new political forces: even the representatives of the successor organisation of the SED, the reformed Party of Democratic Socialism (PDS), no longer had any right to legitimate rule. As a result, the future set-up of the former GDR and the issues of punishment and purge were decided without them.

On the other end of the political spectrum, in Poland, the opening of the political space clearly was contingent on a political pact between old and new political forces. Although many of the details regarding the outcome of the round-table negotiations have been kept secret, rumours persist that the Solidarity negotiators agreed to a settlement that safeguarded those who had acted on behalf of the former communist government.[11] Lacklustre prosecution of those involved in domestic repression and the indecisiveness with which the new democratic political forces have dealt with the issues of former communists and police collaborators may be the direct outcome of a policy of clemency that was part of the political deal negotiated in the spring of 1989.

Unification

Germany stands out as the country in Central and Eastern Europe where citizens now have personal access to their secret police files. In the Czech Republic individuals can obtain a certificate which clarifies whether or not they are listed as having collaborated with the secret police, but personal access to the files is closed. In Bulgaria, the state security files have been sealed for 30 years, in Romania for 40 years, and similarly lengthy time restrictions have been discussed for Poland. In those countries where files have not been public disclosed, the rationale has been the unreliability of the files and the dangers of widespread witch-hunts. A Polish commentator has suggested that Poland's unstable democracy might not survive a lustration process similar to the one in the former East Germany. In his opinion, the relative rigidity of the lustration process in East Germany has been possible only by virtue of the security blanket provided by Western Germany.[12] In this reasoning the dislocations resulting from a thorough vetting of former officials did not result in social unrest and work-related disruptions because of the financial help and the manpower provided by the West.

Since unification resulted in the absorption of the former GDR into the economic, political, and legal system of the Federal Republic, the uncertainties with regard to the process and the outcome that are inherent in the transition processes from authoritarian to democratic political rule were somewhat less crucial than in the neighbouring countries of Central and Eastern Europe. In some cases, this allowed for swifter and more thorough action. The financial and manpower reserves are greater as well: in no other country is there an equivalent to the Gauck Agency for which the Federal Diet has appropriated a yearly budget of more than 200 million DM and the number of employees is well over 3000.

This is not to claim that the side effects of unification were only positive in character. The role of West Germans in the lustration processes, the availability of Western manpower, the almost complete dominance of the Western media in the 'marketing' of the history of the former GDR, the widespread lack of knowledge about the East in the Western part of Germany are some of the factors further contributing to misunderstandings and to perceptions of élite 'colonisation' at the expense of many Eastern Germans. In this setting, the question whether the replacement of professional experts was necessitated by political reasons or on grounds of competency often became blurred.

Legacy of the Past

Presently, Germany is confronted yet again with having to come to terms with its history, this time while shadows of its National Socialist past still darken the picture. In the former GDR the discussion of the National Socialist past was largely left to its West German counterpart. Fascism, militarism, and imperialism were often referred to as those elements of the German past with which the socialist German state had nothing in common. The self-portrayal of the GDR as a state in which fascism had been exterminated served to legitimate a policy of demarcation from its West German neighbour and was supposed to aid in the effort to establish a separate national identity. However, as has been pointed out by Western observers, antifascism was built on a false representation of history and decreed upon the people. Potential efforts to grapple with feelings of collective as well as individual guilt were foreclosed.[13] Former members of the Nazi party were judged according to the membership in a particular group (social or occupational), and not so much on the basis of their actual behaviour during the Third Reich.

In the West, the deficiencies of efforts to adequately deal with the legacies of the Third Reich, in particular the problems inherent in the workings of the denazification commissions (*Spruchkammern*), the alleged repression of the past, and the continued use of Nazi personnel in many sectors of society have long been criticised.

Already a few years after the end of World War II, the basic tenet in all of Germany was – within certain limits – that it is politically less important where one comes from than where one is willing to go.[14] However, it was particularly true for the Soviet Zone of Occupation that the greater one's readiness for political activism on behalf of the new political order, the higher the probability one could be freed from the onus of one's past.

Is Germany to repeat some of the mistakes of the past or have lessons been learned that are instructive in the present circumstances? The dangers of the personification of guilt by a select few at the top of the leadership hierarchy, the tendency of many fellow-travellers to point to orders from higher-ups and not to personal responsibility, the impossibility of bringing justice to injustice are some of the shared characteristics between 1945 and 1989. Compared to 1945, however, there is a heightened level of awareness that the past can and should not be repressed, and years of critical discussion about the failures of denazification have also heightened the level of awareness of what can and what cannot be accomplished by a political purge. In line with the peaceful character of the transformation of the political and economic systems, the process of lustration generally has not been marred by witch-hunting or resort to extra-legal methods of revenge-seeking.

Certain positions and occupational groups (such as officers of the Stasi) were particularly affected by dismissals. In general, however, there was a shared understanding that the attribution of collective guilt should be avoided and that indictments and dismissals were supposed to be based on specific charges and not on membership in certain political institutions. However, once a general assessment of purges is available, it is probably this aspect of lustration that will present the most problems in its execution. For instance, the forced retirement of many civil servants, the closing of research institutes, the adaptation of the East German occupational system to that of West Germany affected those whose professional careers were particularly tied to membership in the SED but many others as well.

TO COMPARE IS NOT TO EQUATE

The policy of rapprochement between the East and the West more generally, and the efforts to normalise relations between East and West Germany since the 1970s further undermined tendencies to equate uncritically the national socialist dictatorship under Hitler with the communist dictatorship under Ulbricht and Honecker. Under the current circumstances in which the dictatorial character of the SED governments has come under extensive scrutiny, the lines have become somewhat blurred. It is still true that most scholars continue to highlight the distinctions when it comes to applying terms such as totalitarianism to different historical settings. What has changed is the heightened attention that is being given to the comparative study of dictatorships in twentieth century German history.

To name some of the most important similarities, both dictatorships have severely abused civil and political rights, have tried to impose absolute control over most areas of public and many areas of private life, have usurped the rule of law for political purposes, and have pushed the rule of the select few – who remained unaccountable to the public – to its limits. But there are important aspects in which they have been different.[15]

Adolf Hitler was in power from 1933 to 1945, of which more than five years were spent under the special and extraordinary circumstances of war. By contrast, communist rule in East Germany lasted for more than 40 years and, for most who did not chose to leave for the West, life acquired an aura of normalcy. Under communist government the majority of the current population was born and socialised; for them, the GDR was not just fate (*Schicksal*) but home (*Heimat*). It can also not be overlooked – authoritarian power structures notwithstanding – that the actual mechanism of coercion, control, and repression underwent changes in the 40 years of the existence of the GDR. The limits of permissible behaviour remained severely circumscribed and means of surveillance and control became more refined and widespread but overt political terror, defined as the arbitrary use of severe coercion against individuals and groups exercised by organs of political authority, decreased considerably from the heyday of Stalinism in the late 1940s and early 1950s. Although the negative sides of political and economic stagnation became very pronounced during the 1980s, there were times of change and of hope as well.

It seems a reasonable assumption that the equivalent of 'denazification' is 'decommunisation'. However, it is worth noting that the current inquiries into the communist past are hardly ever portrayed as 'decommunisation', i.e. the need to eradicate the ideology of Marxism-Leninism which was used to legitimise the rule of the East German political élite but rather as 'de-Stasification' or 'de-Stalinisation'.[16] This differentiation takes into account that the ideologies of communism and fascism are qualitatively very different; most important, however, few would disagree that the implementation of socialist ideals was an aberration in the name of domination. It is for this reason that phrases such as 'actual existing socialism' were invented to draw a distinction between ideal and reality and that the experience of communist rule is often portrayed as one of Stalinist or Bolshevik socialism. While the ideology of National Socialism was specific to the German setting, the actual execution of socialism in the GDR carried few traces of a home-made revolution or carried with it national specifics. The resort to Stalinist socialism draws attention not only to the dominance of Soviet interpretations of Marxism-Leninism but also to the deformation of the original ideals, and it also indicates how difficult it is to avoid the temptation to portray the imposition and implementation of socialism in the GDR as the work of the Soviet Union and its native puppets.[17]

The misguided execution of communism seems to have put to rest any serious concern about the resurgence of communism in Germany. The rule of the communist party collapsed like a house of cards and with it any legitimate claim to rule. The former ruling élite has been robbed of its power privileges and their resurfacing seems out of question. The Party of Democratic Socialism (PDS), the successor party of the SED, has been losing in membership but has been able to maintain and, more recently, to strengthen its political role on the territory of the former GDR. However, its future prospects as a regionally-based party remain uncertain.

The self-image or identity of the Western part of Germany has always been defined to a substantial degree in opposition to communism. This is also true of the West German leftist intelligentsia for whom the 'ideology of domination' in the GDR was the background to a critique of Marxism-Leninism. In the words of Helmut Dubiel, the collapse of actual existing socialism was not the reason for 'melancholy and mourning' but rather the abrupt ending of the dream of a 'Third Way'.[18] In contrast to 1945 where there was a perceived need to eradicate the ideology of National Socialism, therefore it would seem superfluous to eradicate the idea of communism as implemented in the GDR since it took care of its own demise, even if one detects a certain nostalgia for some specific elements of the past.

Last but not least, in 1933 Hitler came to power by popular vote. By contrast the superiority of the Communist Party in East Germany was established only through the use of severe political pressure and extensive manipulations of the electoral system. In 1945, the demise of National Socialism was ordered by foreign forces, whereas in 1989 the ideology of Marxism-Leninism was rejected by the East German people. The need to eradicate values and attitudes associated with previous dictatorial regimes is therefore clearly less pronounced now than was the case after 1945.

One of the most important distinctions between the period of Nazism and Communism in Germany has to be seen in the workings of the two different ideologies. In the name of communism, coercion, repression and the violation of human rights occurred to secure the existence of a separate German country whose very existence became a pawn in the rivalry between East and West. In the name of the other, National Socialism, the superiority of a certain race was proclaimed and the reign of Germans extended over much of Europe. As a consequence millions of people suffered, died, or lost their professional or material existence. The atrocities associated with the Hitler regime were unique in character, and, without minimizing the suffering of regime opponents and ordinary people in the former GDR, revealed the darkest side of human behaviour.[19] In 1945 the desire for revenge and rehabilitation was not limited to German opponents of the Hitler regime – it transcended geographical boundaries. Denazification proceeded under the watchful eyes of a world wide population; nowadays the issue of 'destasification' is one that is left to the Germans.

The fact that after the Second World War political priorities took precedence over moral analysis in both parts of Germany was often seen as the cornerstone of a failed *Vergangenheitsaufarbeitung*. But isn't it almost inevitable that in view of 'the unique criminal character of the German regime all attempts of expiation and rehabilitation indeed could function only as helpless scrapping on a mountain of historical guilt?'[20] In other words, from the very beginning, the task was monumental and – measured in purely moral assessments – it may have been inevitable that the process remained incomplete: the Holocaust cannot be rectified. However, in political terms, the overall assessment of German denazification and purification should centre not only on what it failed to do but also on what it has accomplished.

The relative ease with which most Germans have seemed to put to rest the whole process of denazification after the Second World War has often been remarked upon critically. Then and now it would be unrealistic to expect that the issue of the past will remain at the very centre of attention for a very long time. But neither will it be forgotten readily. The sheer number of cases that need to be heard and decided is immense and will be on the political agenda for years to come. In its first two years of operation, the Gauck Agency received 1.42 million requests to peruse files of the former State Security Services (Stasi); by October 1992 roughly 27 000 had been brought to a close. It is estimated that more than 100 000 people (some estimate close to 200 000) who had been imprisoned, tortured, forcefully resettled, or had suffered professional discrimination will file under the rehabilitation law to ensure compensation for the victims of the former Communist regime in the GDR. There are approximately 2.5 million registered claims for the return of companies, real estate, money and other property in Eastern Germany, but the settlement of these cases has been extremely slow.

At the same time, however, after the dust over the initial political scandals – with the cases of the Prime Minister of Brandenburg, Manfred Stolpe, and the first and only democratically elected prime minister of the GDR, Lothar de Mazière, among the most important ones – had settled, these headlines are no longer on the front page, and for good reason. After all, for the majority of Germans the issue is only of passing importance and, fortunately, the lustration process has been characterised by a remarkable, shared understanding among the major political parties. On balance there was no exploitation of the lustration issue for political gain and the dominance of West Germans in the political process in the Federal Republic – as unfortunate as it may be in terms of political representation – may have helped in avoiding some of the most destabilising consequences. The dissidents of the former GDR have done much to keep alive the necessity to investigate the past but had to learn relatively early on that the interests of their countrymen had shifted to matters of unemployment, and more generally to coming to terms with a changed political, economic, and social environment in the aftermath of German unification. This should not be surprising. However, in contrast to the need to limit the period and extent of the purge to a reasonable time, the working through one's past, i.e. the issue of *Vergangenheitsaufarbeitung*, cannot be limited to a certain time span.

CONCLUSION

Overall, the past years have been characterised by a policy of moderation, not of revenge-seeking. There is no doubt that the historical legacies of national-socialist and communist authoritarian rule have made Germany a special case. At times it appears, and rightly so, that mistakes of the past are rectified by a more enlightened approach that takes into consideration the possibilities but also the inherent limitations in assessing the past.

Vetting procedures and inquiries into the past should not become an end in themselves but they should combine the needs for punishment and rehabilitation with efforts to prevent the recurring of abuses of power in the name of certain ideologies. To learn about the past is therefore to understand the aberrations of the past so that the likelihood of repetition is reduced. The analysis of the past is not only of importance for Eastern Germans but for those in the West as well, if for different reasons. Just as the grace *of late birth* (Kohl) was never a sufficient excuse to escape the need to come to grips with the National Socialist past, the *blessing of Western birth* is also only of limited validity. To be sure, the personal entanglement of West German citizens with the communist regime was limited to very few but only because of the blessing of being Western and not because of heroism. This should not be forgotten nor should the common responsibility for the future of Germany: 'We have a shared burden of inheritance, and maybe it was the only thing which has united us over the decades and in particular which has shaped us although we did not realise it. And now we have a common future, and I want it to be democratic.'[21]

Notes

1. Jerzy Jedlicki, 'A Colloquium: The Revolution of 1989: The Unbearable Burden of History', *Problems of Communism*, vol. 39 (July–August 1990), pp. 39–45, 39.

2. Friedrich Schorlemmer, theologian and political activist in the former East German opposition movement, for example mentions the misuse of the term solidarity and the appeals to humanity under the communist regime as examples which have lasting consequences on the attitudes and behaviour of the people in the former GDR. Friedrich Schorlemmer, 'A Plea for the Establishment of a Political Tribunal', *Universitas*, vol. 1 (1992), pp. 13–19, 15.

3. For an interesting recent account see Tony Judt, 'The Past is Another Country: Myth and Memory in Postwar Europe', *Daedalus*, vol. 212, no. 4 (Fall 1992), 83–118.

4. For a lengthier discussion of problems inherent in coming to terms with the past see, for example, Stefan Wolle, 'Die vergiftete Gesellschaft. Das Stasi-Akten-Syndrom in der ehemaligen DDR,' *Transit*, 2 (Summer 1991), 180–2, in particular, 190–2; Claus Offe, 'Bestrafung, Disqualifizierung, Entschädigung? Strategien rechtlicher "Vergangenheitsbewältigung" in nachkommunistischen Gesellschaften,' *Berliner Journal für Soziologie*, vol. 2 no. 2 (1992), pp. 145–51.

5. The general willingness of the public to endorse the communist political system has been pointed out by a number of writers. See, for example, György Bence, 'Political Justice in Post-Communist Societies: The Case of Hungary,' *Praxis International*, vol. 10, nos. 1/2 (April and July 1990), pp. 80–9, 80: 'Communism pressed the citizen into active complicity with the system, unless he was prepared to drop out of normal civil existence. Therefore, it is wrong to condemn him simply because he tried to survive.'

6. Cf. Rudolf Wassermann, 'Die strafrechtliche Aufarbeitung der DDR-Vergangenheit,' *Recht und Politik*, vol. 28 (1992), 121–34.

7. Efforts by former GDR dissidents to create another public forum for discussion failed in part because of the unfortunate choice of the word 'tribunal.'

8. Joachim Gauck, *Die Stasi-Akten. Das unheimliche Erbe der DDR*. Ed. by Margarethe Steinhausen und Hubertus Knabe (Reinbek bei Hamburg; Rowohlt, 1991), 11–12; Stefan Wolle, 'In the Labyrinth of the Documents: The Archival Legacy of the SED-State,' *German History*, vol. 10, no. 3 (October 1992), 352–65.

9. Anna Sabbat-Swidlicka, 'Problems of Poland's State Security Office,' *RFE/RL Research Report*, 28 February 1992, pp. 15–20, 17; 'Interview with Zdzislaw Rurarz,' *Uncaptive Minds*, vol. 4, no. 4 (Winter 91–92), pp. 29–34, 33.

10. For a detailed discussion of the concept of negotiated transition see Helga A. Welsh, 'Political Transition Processes in Central and Eastern Europe,' *Comparative Politics*, vol. 26, no. 4 (July 1994), 379–94.

11. Rurarz, pp. 32–3; 'Verzicht auf eine Hexenjagd als Preis für die Macht,' *Süddeutsche Zeitung*, pp. 28–9 December 9, 1991.

12. Janusz Tycner, 'Wohin man packt, man greift in Dreck,' *Die Zeit*, March 20, 1992, 21.

13. For a critical evaluation of the East German posture toward the National Socialist past see, e.g., Ralph Giordano, *Die zweite Schuld oder Von der Last Deutscher zu sein* (Hamburg and Zürich: Rasch and Röhring, 1987), pp. 215–228.

14. Hermann Lübbe, 'Der Nationalsozialismus im deutschen Nachkriegsbewußtsein,' *Historische Zeitschrift*, 236 (1983), 570–99, 594. (In the article the statement refers to West German attitudes.)

15. The following discussion owes much to the analysis presented by Jürgen Habermas, 'Bemerkungen zu einer verworrenen Diskussion. Was bedeutet 'Aufarbeitung der Vergangenheit heute?' *Die Zeit*, April 10, 1992, pp. 17–19.

16. See also Dieter E. Zimmer, 'Die Zeit. Das Geld. Die Schuld.,' *Die Zeit*, October 4, 1991, pp. 17–18

17. Tony Judt, 'The Past is Another Country,' p. 110.

18. Helmut Dubiel, 'Linke Trauerarbeit,' *Merkur*, vol. 44, no. 6 (June 1990), pp. 482–91; reprinted in English in *Praxis International*, vol. 10, nos. 3/4 (October 1990/January 1991), pp. 241–9.

19. For a summary of the *Historikerstreit* in West Germany during the 1980s see Konrad H. Jarausch, 'Removing the Nazi Stain? The Quarrel of the German Historians,' *German Studies Review*, vol. 11, no. 2 (May 1988), pp. 285–301.

20. Klaus-Dietmar Henke, 'Die Trennung vom Nationalsozialismus. Selbstzerstörung, politische Säuberung, "Entnazifizierung," Strafverfolgung,' in Klaus-Dietmar Henke und Hans Woller, eds., *Politische Säuberung in Europa. Die Abrechnung mit Faschismus und Kollaboration nach dem Zweiten Weltkrieg* (Munich: Deutscher Taschenbuch Verlag, 1991), pp. 21–83, 22.

21. Brigitte Rauschenbach, 'Erbschaft aus Vergessenheit – Zukunft aus Erinnerungsarbeit,' *Deutschland* Archiv, vol. 25, no. 9 (September 1992), 934–42, 941.

7 What to do with Communist Bureaucrats from Bureaucratic Communism: The German Case

Gregg O. Kvistad*

Many studies of communist regimes have relied heavily on Max Weber's theory of the routinisation of chiliastic rule. These studies suggest that breaks with the inequalities and cleavages of traditional societies have been led by revolutionary militants who win mass support for radical programmes of wealth redistribution. Upon coming to power, these militants ('chiefs,' in Weber's terminology) create the institutional means to deliver their revolutionary programmes with party/ bureaucratic élites ('administrative staff') that not only implement policy, but also serve as a reservoir of support and protection for the ruler.[1] These studies further suggest that a tension between the chiliastic revolutionary vision and its institutionalisation will typically develop and that bureaucratic routinisers will ultimately hold sway. 'Neo-traditional stagnation' is the result, with huge institutional apparatuses maintaining status and privilege at the expense of both political freedom and economic viability.[2]

LEGITIMATION AND REVOLUTION

As Guiseppe DiPalma points out, however, this focus on the bureaucratic routinisation of communist rule can help to account for regime stagnation, but it helps little for explaining regime breakdown. The breakdown is realised, according to DiPalma, as it was in Central Europe in 1989 and 1990, when a civil society of citizens emerges in a 'metademocratic movement of collective identity'.[3] Such a revolutionary movement attempts to relocate the authentication of legitimacy from a state that defines away political opposition as contrary to 'objective' reality, to a citizenry demanding participation and control.[4] If this metademocratic movement is successful, it constitutes a new regime that must deal with an unavoidable question: what should be done with the 'administrative staff' of the old?

POST-COMMUNIST BUREAUCRACY

Central European states now attempting to consolidate post-revolutionary regimes are heavily burdened in answering this question. Most of them are home to an abstract if not absent civic culture that allowed revolutionary mobilisation, but not the construction of 'normalised' sovereign democratic rule. Few of these revolutionary 'metademocratic movements of collective identity' will be able to stabilise quickly and successfully.[5] Most are also burdened by a widespread lack of expertise beyond the 'administrative staff' – however politicised that was – of the old order. These states lack even the blueprints for these transformations that must remain consistent with democracy, economic productivity, and existentially-vital imperatives of international organisations. While these factors very much complicate the answers that post-communist regimes will give to the question of what to do with old communist bureaucrats, the answers they give are nonetheless existentially vital.

The East German uprising and regime change in 1989–90 was unique among the transformations experienced by Central European states in this period. One more or less sovereign German regime collapsed and acceded to another. Because of the instrument used in this transformation – Article 23 of the West German constitution, mandating the accession of new *Länder* without a constitutional revision – East Germany disappeared and became part of the Federal Republic in a process that neither founded nor refounded a new regime.[6] The Federal Republic of Germany grew in territory, population, and in at least short-run social-economic problems, but the East German uprising, contrary to the determination of many of its activists, created institutionally nothing new in the wake of its destruction.

Instead, the East German public appears indirectly to have acquiesced to allowing West German civil service law to answer the question of what to do with old East German communist bureaucrats. This implicit choice would seem to bode well for realising the 'meta-democratic' political legitimation needs of the ex-East German citizenry. Civil service law in the Federal Republic is informed by the 'traditional principles of the professional civil service' which place central importance on the political 'reliability' of civil servants. The Federal Republic as a successor regime would thus appear likely to be able to avoid some of the perils faced by other Central European states on this question. The East Germans acceded to a stable institutional arrangement amidst a liberal democratic civil culture and a well-entrenched body of civil service law according central importance to the political beliefs and actions of state officials.

Not only cross-nationally, relative to other Central European states in the early 1990s, but also cross-temporally, relative to its own problematic past, Germany would seem to be advantageously positioned to answer this question in a manner contributing to political legitimation and stability. New German regimes facing this question in 1918 and 1949 did not have the institutional, political-cultural, or manpower advantages now enjoyed by the unified Federal Republic. As a result, many argue that wrong answers were given to this question in 1918–19 and 1949, with problematic if not disastrous consequences. Commentators view the failure of the Weimar Republic in 1918–19 to purge nationalist anti-republican Wilhelmine officials from the civil service as contributing directly to the collapse of the regime and indirectly to the rise of the Nazi dictatorship.[7] Others also see the half-hearted and incomplete effort at administrative de-nazification after World War II, which was followed by a 're-instatement' in 1951, as contributing to the questioning of regime 'legitimacy' by the student protest movement in the 1960s and 1970s.[8]

German Civil Service Reform

Civil service reform has periodically been a topic of broad and intense political debate in the Federal Republic of Germany since the state's founding over 40 years ago. In the early 1970s, the new Social Democratic government confronted what it saw as a decentralised, cumbersome, and functionally-inadequate institutional impediment to domestic reform. The new government convened a Study Commission for the Reform of Civil Service Law in 1970 charged with producing a report within two years that addressed 'the place and role of the civil service in today's society'.[9] If the conveners of this Commission did not initially appreciate Ernst Forsthoff's observation that, in Germany, 'every civil service reform not limited to minor things is a *Staatsreform*,'[10] they did after the Commission produced five thousand pages of briefs, opinions, and academic commentary calling only for the 'most consistent possible implementation of existing [civil service] law.' Some 'looking over' of the law was appropriate, but it was 'not necessary' to amend or get rid of the nineteenth-century 'traditional principles of the professional civil service' ensconced in Art. 33 of the Federal German constitution. Reformers found more to their liking political scientist Kurt Sontheimer's minority report, published as a separate volume, calling for overcoming the state/society dichotomisation with an efficient, rational, service-providing, user-friendly institution to replace Germany's traditional professional civil service.[11] Though civil service reform went nowhere in the Federal Republic in the 1970s, debate about it did not cease.

Civil service reformers in the early 1970s could have learned something from the experience of the Allied Powers right after World War II. In its occupation zone, the Soviets were able to dictate the dissolution of the professional civil service and its replacement with 'workers in the state administration' stripped of traditional privilege and status.[12] Less willing to use force, respectful of some measure of self-determination, and calculating its own foreign policy advantage, the Western Allies were deeply mistrustful of the German bureaucratic state but ultimately unable to initiate fundamental reform. The Americans and the British demanded the end of civil servants' passive voting rights, the construction of a party-neutral 'Civil Service Commission,' and the replacement of a career-ladder by merit-based promotion. Virtually all of Western Germany's nascent political parties, trade unions, and interest groups circled their wagons and rejected these demands as the superficial meddling of naive Anglo-Saxon reformers. By early 1952, the Allies gave up and the Federal Republic adopted the 'traditional principles of the professional civil service'.

To defenders of the German civil service, Western Allies in the late 1940s and reformers in the early 1970s appeared to be not just overly zealous or motivated by a party-political agenda. They saw such efforts as attacking the very foundation of the German state, and in so doing, the one German political institution that had survived since the nineteenth century basically intact, serving governments in many different regimes, dedicated to promoting the general interest over party politics, and internationally praised as a model of institutional organisation and efficiency. For them the civil service, though tarnished, was one of the few distinctly 'German' institutions that the nation could salvage from its problematic political history. They viewed it not as problematically malleable – able equally to serve a constitutional monarch, a genocidal dictator, and a parliamentary democracy – but rather as a distinctly German institution vital for the country's most democratic, stable, and economically successful regime. Indeed, some commentators saw the absence of that institution in the former GDR as one of that regime's most serious defects.

This 'institution' has its roots in the Stein-Hardenberg Reform Era in early nineteenth-century Prussia. Its 'traditional principles,' appearing in Art. 33 of the Federal Republic's constitution and reaching back to the constitutional monarchy, posit a dichotomisation of state and society and a corresponding location of civil servants in the state and of ordinary citizens in society. The state is a realm of hortatory politics in which civil servants, legally bound in conscience and action to serve the common good at all times, pursue an above-party universalism. Society, in contrast, contains self-interested, mainly economic citizens with particularistic motives who at best engage in a 'lower' and less 'reliable' kind of political activity.[13] These nineteenth-century ideas directly inform the pension, insurance, and tenure privileges of contemporary German civil servants, as well as their special loyalty relationship and career-ladder system of promotion.

Challenges to the Institution

Since the mid-1970s the institution of the civil service has come under increasing attack in the Federal Republic from a variety of quarters. Two main dimensions exist to this challenge. First, the German public, like that of every other Western industrialised state, began to support 'post-materialist' and quality-of-life issues that directly challenged the denigration of ordinary citizens in Germany's civil service ideology. 'Anti-political' citizens' movements challenged, 'from below', the legitimacy of traditional state institutions in advanced industrial countries.[14] In the Federal Republic, this challenge was particularly fuelled by the so-called anti-radicals decree (*Radikalenerlass*), issued in 1972, with the stated intent of keeping left- and right-wing extremists out of the civil service, but with the result of mobilising millions of West Germans to address the question, among others, of the proper relationship between civil servants and citizens.[15] The Greens appeared at the end of the decade and focused this question somewhat more explicitly.

By the 1980s, some of the popular political challenge to the civil service abated, with *Länder* governments significantly reforming or claiming to drop altogether the provisions of the politically-restrictive *Radikalenerlass*. Civil service reform thus lost some of its theological character, and the institution's economic viability became a concern. The German civil service was brought into focus not only as a political agent for the protection of German society, but also as an institution with its own material interests. These material interests – which civil service ideology posits as 'needs' to ensure dutiful service – increasingly came under the popular attack in the Federal Republic in the 1980s as unwarranted privileges of an underproductive part of the working population.[16] While this was not a groundswell of critique or popular animus, German private sector employees and taxpayers increasingly began to question the validity of the benefits, career-ladder promotion, and security for the roughly sixteen per cent of the working population employed by the West German state.

In short, what March and Olsen call the 'logic of appropriateness' that once marked a 'shared history, shared interpretation and common understanding embodied in rules for appropriate behavior' and provided an institutional identity for the German civil service, had broken down in the Federal Republic by the end of the 1980s. The German civil service no longer enjoyed the relatively hegemonic identity that it had for over a century, even among conservatives. At issue in this breakdown was not the particular functioning or personnel of a particular office in the late 1980s. This was not, in other words, a '*Bürokratiekritik*', of which many have appeared since the institution's appearance.[17] Instead, the challenge was to the institution as such, to the ideal reality of the German civil service, not to particular practices or incompetent personnel that required adjustment or replacement. As a challenge to the traditional élite political identity of the institution, it bears directly on Germany's answer in the early 1990s to the question of what to do with the state employees of the ex-GDR.

GERMAN POLICY AND TWO LEVELS OF LEGITIMATION

To return to our earlier discussion, then, what Germany is facing in deciding what to do with the old communist bureaucrats of East Germany is mediated by the Federal Republic's own simmering political and economic debate over the future of the institution of the professional civil service. Two different sources of legitimacy are at stake: the more immediate political and material needs of ex-East Germans, on the one hand, and the less immediate political and economic needs of West Germans who support some measure of civil service reform, on the other. While these are not necessarily in conflict, they are also not necessarily compatible, nor of equal weight in setting the policy agenda. The political legitimacy needs of ex-East Germans may best be met by retaining the old political reliability criteria of the 'traditional principles' and adopting a conservative civil service policy to keep all traces of the 'political class' of the ex-GDR out of the institution. West German legitimacy needs, in contrast, may best be met by a fundamental reform or 'reinterpretation' of those 'traditional principles' and the institution's Europeanisation, rationalisation, and general depoliticisation. Instead of summary dismissal on political grounds, this would suggest a civil service constituted of East and West Germans with competence and aptitude (which may include less stringent political criteria) – fit for a leaner and more efficient state service-providing institution.

Germany's advantages for answering the question of what to do with the communist bureaucrats from bureaucratic communism are therefore complicated by two very different and potentially incompatible sources of legitimation at stake in any answer that is provided. In other post-communist Central European regimes, civil service policy may need to walk the line between the material and political legitimation needs of a recently liberated population. But that policy need not, as it must in Germany, also be consistent with the pressing needs of a post-industrial, liberal-democratic society demanding efficiency and rationality in its march toward European integration. As we shall now see, West German needs have largely superceded East German needs on this question. To the extent that Germany's current party élites understand the political dimensions of this question for ex-East Germans at all, their answer is more focused on integrating the 'political class' of the old regime into the Federal Republic than on the political needs of ordinary citizens. More relevant for these élites than either of these political dimensions, however, are the material dimensions of a forward-looking functionalism driven by impending EC integration, private sector competition, and state fiscal crisis. A backward-looking concern to allow the ex-GDR's citizenry a 'genuine political response' to their past – which is *not* provided simply by opening the Stasi files – has not been supported by Germany's current party élites.

THE CDU/CSU PARTY-POLITICAL DEBATE

Within the governing CDU/CSU, debate about the civil service since 1989 has been mediated by two major developments, each of which bears on the party's answer to the question of what to do with the communist state employees of the ex-GDR. The move toward European political and social integration, on the one hand, and serious fiscal demands on the state, on the other, create a context for the CDU/CSU in which a functionalist rather than political logic holds sway. EC integration requires community-wide standards for state employment that would allow foreign nationals into Germany's historically most venerable 'German' political institution. Cost competition from the private sector and the heavy burden of German unification have not only impeded the expansion of this very expensive institution, but have even suggested to the CDU/CSU the possibility of privatisation. These forward-looking concerns combine with the end of the Cold War – which is not, however, explicitly acknowledged in this CDU/CSU debate – to promote functionalist rather than political criteria for determining what to do with ex-GDR officials.

European Integration

European integration has been generally supported by the CDU/CSU and Kohl government as defining Germany's future since the Single European Act of 1986. The Federal Republic usually cooperated with France in the late 1980s to maintain the drive toward European integration, and unification appears not yet appreciably to have diminished the German commitment to Europe. While the goals of the original European Coal and Steel Community of 1951 – to reconcile France and Germany, to anchor the Federal Republic in the Western alliance, and to promote peace in Europe – have been the goals of the CDU/CSU, EC integration nonetheless has important consequences for German institutions in addition to giving up (most likely, anyway) the German Mark.[18] Article 48 of the European Economic Treaty of 1957 mandates the right of the freedom of movement of member-state workers within the community. Nonbinding provisions of the original treaty also included the imperative of member-states to engage in a close collaboration of labour law and working conditions. The right of free movement was reiterated in the non-binding European Social Charter adopted in Strasbourg in December, 1989. The Social Charter stated, consistent with Art. 48, that any member-state citizen may exercise any trade or occupation within the Community on the same terms as those applied to nationals of the host country.[19] Civil service employment was not excluded from this right of European free movement. If the CDU/CSU were thus to support continued EC integration, some amendment to Germany's 'traditional principles of the professional civil service' would be needed.

On the one hand, CDU officials addressed a convention of the Federation of German Civil Servants (the *Deutsche Beamtenbund* – DBB) in early 1991 to laud European integration generally and to suggest that EC civil service regulations were minimally problematic for extant German civil service law. State Secretary Franz Kroppenstedt, from the Interior Ministry, argued that even with Art. 48, the EC must 'retain room for member states responsibly to determine the structures of their national administrations in keeping with their own traditions'. The CDU/CSU declared 'not to allow the process of European integration become a means for getting rid of the professional civil service.' This was partly a question of maintaining a respectable and respected political/institutional identity. Interior Minister Schaeuble noted in late 1989, 'The professional civil service is a part of our stateness.' Three years later, he observed that the 'German public administration and the civil service have enjoyed a good reputation in Europe and throughout the world.'[20] Some suggested that its structure should be the model for the EC civil service.

On the other hand, the CDU/CSU acknowledged a 'growing interstate mobility of employees in the civil service'. Such mobility would require an amendment to 'ease' the employment of non-German Europeans as '*Beamten*', the highest category of the civil service, now prohibited by civil service law, but 'European development provides no reason to alter the constitutionally-anchored structure of our civil service.' Since more than 20 000 foreigners were already employed in the German civil service, though not at the highest *Beamte* level, civil service law would need only to be 'loosened' to permit that. The party argued that this would affect neither the tripartite structure of the German civil service, nor the positive demand for loyalty to the German constitution. Political loyalty would not be a problem for foreign civil servants in Germany because 'all EC states are committed to the common values of a free and democratic constitutional-law state.'[21]

These are notable statements from a party that has historically supported the proud and particular history of the German civil service and – with the backing of the DBB – has always resisted (especially in the 1970s during the *Radikalenerlass* debate) any comparison with institutions of other European states. Indeed, CDU/CSU ideology in the 1970s contributed to making the civil service what Peter Katzenstein has called a 'hard trunk' impervious to the 'pocket-knives' of political reformers.[22] It was a distinctly German institution to be protected not only from reformist pocket-knives, but also foreign critics and 'communist' mail carriers and locomotive engineers who might be working for the GDR. Now the CDU/CSU sees this institution also as European, and it calls for a functionalist 'loosening' of the body's identity – including, apparently, its political restrictiveness – to serve European integration. While the party ritualistically still insists that a 'loosening' will not fundamentally alter the institution's traditional identity, the German civil service has never tolerated a minimalist or 'lukewarm' loyalty to the German political order among its personnel. To get more than that from other Europeans may be asking something that they neither can nor are required to provide. An EC-inspired functionalism within the CDU/CSU has thus appeared precisely when retaining the institution's traditional political restrictiveness – which the party supported throughout the *Radikalenerlass* debate of the 1970s – could positively serve the political needs of Eastern German citizens coming to terms with their institutional past. This functionalism is buttressed within the CDU/CSU by concern about growing state fiscal constraints.

Fiscal Constraints
By the late 1980s, the CDU/CSU began to argue that the civil service needed to introduce flexibility to ensure competitiveness, especially given rapid technological and demographic changes. These voices of reform, though not very loud, have been heard more frequently since 1989. In a speech to the DBB, the CDU's Kroppenstedt stated that 'the civil service may not be uncoupled from General developments in the economic and financial world.' Kroppenstedt advocated a more 'flexible' system to reward initiative and merit with a 'market-equivalent salary'.[23] Contrary to the traditional ideology of the German civil service, the CDU/CSU thus suggested that the civil service relationship was not entirely different from private sector employment. While the party began adopting this functionalist perspective before the fall of the Berlin Wall – in January, 1989, Federal Postal Minister Christian Schwarz-Schilling argued that 'individual performance incentives' for postal employees were needed – after unification it became more pressing.

In early 1991, CDU parliamentarian Paul Laufs told the DBB that, 'Tremendous challenges lie before us to equalize the standards of living in Germany. Promises for concrete measures in the areas of benefits and salaries would be frivolous.' Three days later, a colleague concluded, 'We must further reduce the size of the civil service in the next few years. Potential for reduction exists especially in the postal service, the railway, and the armed forces.'[24] Concrete numbers were attached in a press report in October 1991, stating that the federal government planned to reduce the size of the senior-level civil service (*Beamten*) of 1.8 million by more than one-half. While immediately denied by the Interior Ministry and the CDU/CSU parliamentary spokesperson for domestic affairs, the denial stressed the formidable *legal* impediments to such a reduction, not its undesirability. A debate over privatisation in 1991 further demonstrated that the professional civil service was neither the CDU's 'sacred cow' nor 'golden calf.'

In 1991, CDU Postal Minister Schwarz-Schilling proposed a privatisation of the postal service. While requiring a constitutional amendment via two-thirds vote in the parliament, the Minister confidently invited the opposition to 'jump over the trench and lay the foundation for an efficient postal service'. Not just Social Democrats, however, many of whom supported the proposal, but also many Christian Democrats, the DBB, and the German Postal Workers' Union who rejected it out of hand, would have to do some jumping. One CDU parliamentarian stated that personnel problems existed within the service, but neither the Chancellor nor the parliamentary fraction supported putting privatisation on the agenda. He went on to say that his party 'clearly and unmistakably supported the professional civil service'. and that anyone 'who would question the fundamental principle of civil service law, must clearly show what he intends to gain by that'. He nonetheless agreed that better 'promotion of efficiency' was desirable within the postal service[25] By early autumn, over sixty per cent of the German people reportedly favoured the proposal and Schwarz-Schilling could claim that he had Chancellor Kohl's general support. At the end of October, the Interior Ministry acknowledged that discussions about privatising the postal service and the railway had indeed ensued.

In early November, Interior Minister Schaeuble nonetheless repeated on television the CDU/CSU's old catechism that, 'a general attack on the professional civil service is not itself justified and would not find any support within the federal government or the coalition'.[26] But the party certainly was supporting civil service reform if not 'attack'. That reform entailed the incorporation of a functionalist perspective to accommodate EC integration and cost competition from the private sector. While a more political understanding of the institution continued to appear in almost ritualistic defences of the 'traditional principles of the professional civil service', the party increasingly viewed the political dimensions of those principles as less paramount. This is abundantly clear in the party's answer to the question of what to do with the old officials of the GDR.

What to do with ex-GDR State Officials: CDU/CSU

The CDU/CSU's answer to this question at the federal level has been to support the professional German civil service in name, yet to loosen the traditionally very restrictive political demands on individual state employees, for ex-GDR officials. This reveals the functionalist lenses for viewing a post-Cold War landscape – ground according to EC specifications for a customer in a competitive market – through which the CDU/CSU has come to view this institution. Functionalism was evident in a battle erupting in 1990, when Western officials were asked to 'go East' to provide their services. Like most Western civil servants, the CDU/CSU dismissed the idea that Western officials, because of their special loyalty relationship, were obliged to go East to assist a vulnerable East German society in overcoming its hardship. Instead, the party adopted a more functionalist position and asked why West German civil servants should sacrifice their quality of life when others were not forced to. Schaeuble stated that whatever the East's need for Western officials, legally no German civil servant could be forcibly transferred. Instead, what was offered – and defended by the CDU/CSU leadership – was a quite generous package of wage, benefit, and promotion incentives as an inducement. Chancellor Kohl noted that if private sector employees received monetary and career incentives for working in the East, then 'why shouldn't civil servants receive the same?'[27]

Four months after the fall of the Berlin Wall and just prior to East Germany's first and last free election, CDU Interior Minister Schaeuble announced his opposition to a 'new denazification' for East German officials and stated that only those who had committed 'severe crimes' should be denied public employment in a unified Germany. Schaeuble called for an 'internal reconciliation and new beginning' that would categorically exclude no former GDR official, even those who worked for the Stasi, from public employment in a unified Federal Republic. While it was unclear what exactly about denazification offended Schaeuble, here he unambiguously stated that the participation of ex-GDR officials in the old regime would be no handicap for state employment in the Federal Republic. In other words, the 'administrative staff' of the old regime would not be a viable target for post-revolutionary action in united Germany. Though it is hard to imagine that the prospect of attracting the 1.7 million votes of GDR state employees was not a factor in CDU/CSU thinking here, the party was also articulating an increasingly functionalist and depoliticised understanding of one of Germany's most venerated institutions. It was, the Interior Minister stated, the 'bloated size' of the GDR state service that would prevent its 'global takeover' by the Federal Republic, not its political role in the old regime.

The 'traditional principles of the professional civil service' thus became a lot less traditional for the CDU/CSU. Self-admitted 'severe crimes' would be grounds for exclusion, but not previous membership in any party, organisation, or state security institution. CDU parliamentarian Gerster declared that applicants would need to 'explain their earlier activities and state that in the past they had not committed any crimes against humanity [*Verbrechen gegen die Menschlichkeit*] while in the employ of the Stasi.'[28] A Federal Interior Ministry circular in September, 1990, repeated the traditional demand that all German civil servants guarantee a readiness to uphold the free democratic basic order at all times, and noted that for ex-SED members 'doubts' were warranted, as were 'grave doubts' for ex-Stasi employees. But if applicants could make 'believable' their rejection of the 'communist system' in an interview, these 'doubts' would be lifted. The federal government required no 'routine questioning' of ex-GDR applicants about possible past Stasi activity.

Nonetheless, an Interior Ministry official stated in January, 1991, that 'competence is not the only issue'. In keeping with the 'traditional principles of the professional civil service', which the CDU/CSU continued to defend, the politics of future state employees in the Federal Republic also mattered. But how much did they matter? After the end of the Cold War and collapse of East Germany the party's main personnel concerns were not just the political reliability of state civil servants, but also the drive toward European integration and competitive pressures from the private sector. The political pasts of ex-GDR officials mattered, but relatively little compared to the party's concern about the politics of state employees during the *Radikalenerlass* controversy of the 1970s. The Interior Ministry suggested that

> Every person who wishes to enter or remain in the civil service needs self-critically to ask himself whether his earlier behavior accords with the trust that is necessary for his position. That certainly depends upon the particular function for which he is applying in the civil service.

To ask an ex-GDR official to judge for himself his level of 'trust' reveals a curious shift in the CDU/CSU's concerns about the political legitimation needs of the ex-GDR citizenry. Here, indeed, the 'vast majority' of ex-GDR officials should have no problems, as the Interior Ministry official stated. But what about the 'trust' accorded these officials by the 'vast majority' of the ex-GDR citizenry?

At the same time, the CDU/CSU was not impervious to other dimensions of the legitimation needs of former East German citizens experiencing the Federal Republic as a successor regime. The party has viewed those needs primarily in material terms. Contrary to much expert advice, the CDU/CSU supported a speeded-up German monetary union on economically-indefensible terms as required 'social' policy in the summer of 1990. Since then the party has repeatedly referred to the indispensability of a well-functioning civil service to meet the dire needs of the Eastern German citizenry. In late 1990, Paul Laufs argued, 'the quicker the construction of a civil service in the new *Länder*, the quicker the equalisation of living standards with Western Germany.'[29] State Secretary Kroppenstedt similarly argued:

> The people want quick progress and they frequently lack the necessary patience for that . . . The consummation of German unification demands more than accepting a constitution and the creation of a realm of legality. Necessary is also the creation of a uniform standard of living in unified Germany. It is to the credit of the members of the civil service that they are meeting the difficult challenges of the unification process.

The CDU/CSU thus attributed to the ex-GDR citizenry material legitimation needs that were largely consistent with a functionalist view of a state institution approaching EC integration and constrained by competition from the private sector. The possible political needs of a citizenry coming to terms with an institutional arrangement that attempted to legitimise itself 'from above' for forty years was not central in the party's deliberations.

SPD PARTY-POLITICAL DEBATE

As the opposition party at the federal level, the SPD has not been as intensively concerned with the question of what to do with ex-officials of East Germany as the CDU/CSU. This has partly to do with the SPD's inability to find much to oppose in the federal government's position. Though the parties take very different routes, the SPD and the CDU/CSU basically agree that ex-GDR officials must be considered on their individual merits and that functionalist criteria are more relevant, except in extreme cases, than politics for determining who are fit for the German civil service. For the CDU/CSU, this position is a response to the end of the Cold War and the imperatives of EC integration and private sector competition, and it is mediated by a lingering support for the traditional, more political, identity of the institution. For the SPD, in contrast, functionalism is informed by EC integration and the need for 'modernising' the institution, but most importantly by a long-standing critique of the professional civil service and the nineteenth-century 'traditional principles' that inform it as alleged anti-democratic relics of an authoritarian statist past.

European Integration

The SPD has supported a 'United States of Europe' as a peace-keeping institution since the 1920s. In its Basic Programme of 1989, the party called for the 'further development of a unified economic, monetary, and social space'. Like the CDU/CSU, the SPD's support for EC integration is also somewhat tempered by concern about the fate of German institutions that the party holds dear. One of those institutions for the CDU/CSU, as we saw, is the professional civil service, however much the party professes a 'European' perspective on this question. If the professional civil service is not a sacred cow for the CDU/CSU, it is at least revered. For the SPD, in contrast, 'exemplary social achievements of individual countries' – such as co-determination in industrial relations – 'should be made useful for the entire Community.'[30] These 'achievements' for the SPD do not include the professional civil service. Indeed, the SPD views the EC integration as a cattle prod to send the CDU/CSU's revered cow to slaughter, or at least to the diet farm.

In early 1989, SPD parliamentarian Egon Lutz argued that the CDU/CSU was either disingenuous or ignorant in claiming that Art. 48 of the EC Treaty did *not* pose grave challenges to the current organisation and personnel of the German professional civil service. Lutz held that Art. 48, guaranteeing freedom of movement within the Community for all member-state citizens, 'contradicted' German civil service law stating that only Germans may become *Beamten*, and that they must be given preference in all state hiring. He further noted the European Court's ruling that only 'specifically sovereign activities' within national state bureaucracies may continue to be governed by national law. According to Lutz, only the 'core of the administration', such as

police and justice, may continue to enjoy German civil service jurisdiction; all other elements, like education, the postal service, and the
railway, must, according to the EEC treaty and Court of Justice, be
open to all Europeans.

Contrary to Lutz's claim, we saw that the CDU/CSU does acknowledge the differences between standing German civil service law and
the EEC treaty. We also saw, however, that the CDU/CSU minimises
those differences by suggesting that consistency may be reached simply by 'loosening' the requirement to hire German nationals. Lutz
and the SPD, in contrast, view EC integration as an opportunity for
fundamental institutional reform. They focus instead on the EC's
definition of the 'sovereign core' of the institution for which particular national law takes precedence. In the name of good European citizenship and not socialist transformation, the SPD advocates fundamental
civil service reform that reduces the professional body to the 'sovereign core' of state activity. As SPD parliamentarian Hans Martin
Bury stated in July, 1991: 'Of course the professional civil service
must remain for the areas of sovereign activity. But then only there.'[31]
While the CDU/CSU wanted to 'widen' the *Beamte* pool to all qualified
Europeans as a means of saving the institution, the SPD wished to
'deepen' the *Beamte* status to apply only to the 'sovereign core' German state activity. SPD support for 'deepening' this status, however,
is part of a functionalist agenda the party has been advocating since
the 1970s. Stymied in the politicised context of the 1970s, the SPD
now can portray civil service reform as 'European' and at least partly
endorsed by the CDU/CSU.

Fiscal Constraints
Like EC integration, state budget deficits caused by German unification
are also an impetus for the SPD to support functionalist civil service
reform. But the party views these fiscal constraints, like EC integration, as *further* justification for reform that it has supported 'for some
time', not as sufficient policy motivations themselves. The SPD has
neither welcomed nor minimised the impact of those current deficits
– apparently to its electoral detriment in December, 1990 – but it also
does not regard civil service reform as primarily budget-driven. The
party has long viewed the traditional structure and ideology of the
professional German civil service as anachronistic for the needs of a
modern industrialised society. Unlike the CDU/CSU, the SPD has not
had to wrestle much with the lingering presence of the nineteenth century idea of the civil service as a protective and hortatory political

institution for the rest of German society.

Party chair Björn Engholm argued that it is only 'sensible' for the civil service to 'catch up' with the 'fast changes in economic and societal organisations that today are functioning highly effectively'. First must be determined 'what tasks really need to be handled in a ministry and what tasks do not'. Unsupportive of what he calls 'simple privatisation', Engholm suggests that most important is the rational organisation of the institution: 'The main task is to make the public administration as small as possible and as effective as the most modern organisations in other areas of society.' That requires 'decentralisation' and differentiating within civil service offices between 'sovereign' and service-providing activity.[32] The ultimate goal, according to Engholm, is a 'modern and more effectively organised state'.

The privatisation proposal for the postal service by Schwarz-Schilling was positively received by many in the SPD. Parliamentarian Arne Boernsen announced support for privatising the institution and introducing 'performance-based criteria' for promotion that would improve 'competitiveness'. His colleague Hans Martin Bury similarly greeted Schwarz-Schilling's initiative by saying it would 'improve the competitiveness of the enterprise . . . [given] the ever more complex areas of activity of the postal system'. Engholm, however, refused to project simple 'privatisation' as the solution:

> the issue here is the modernisation of civil service law, not privatisation. The railway and postal service are existential for the infrastructure and the provision of necessary services. This also concerns the basic right of informed self-determination. That all appears in the constitution as core tasks of the state. We agree with that.

What was needed was an 'organisational form for the state that can in the future provide services better for a modern and more democratic society', and that required exploring many different options.[33]

Political Critique
Since the Brandt government promised 'more democracy' in 1969, the SPD has supported a reorganisation and reorientation of the German civil service to reduce the 'distance' between the institution and the people and encourage democratic participation. This political critique is most responsible for the SPD's functionalist answer to the question of what to do with the ex-officials of the GDR. The party programme of 1989 stated,

We need an administration that is close to the people [*bürgernahe*] and efficient. Free from the traditions of the authoritarian state, its workings must be transparent and controllable. It should promote and not stifle citizen self-help initiatives, citizen responsibility, and citizen participation.[34]

Institutionally, the SPD has long called for a unitary civil service law for all public employees, including the right to strike, now expressly forbidden to *Beamte*. Instead of viewing the civil service as one of the few distinctly German political institutions that is exemplary and deserves preservation in its traditional form, the SPD has advocated fundamental reform and rationalisation. As part of that reform, the SPD has supported a relative depoliticisation of civil service personnel policy, especially since the divisive battle over the *Radikalenerlass* in the 1970s.

While conflict over the *Radikalenerlass* had substantially subsided when the question of what to do with the state employees of the ex-GDR appeared, the effects of this episode on the SPD were still being felt as the party addressed the question. In 1989 party leader Hans-Jochen Vogel referred to the 'psychological climate in the Republic' that the decree had damaged:

The intention was entirely proper, namely to defend the democracy from illoyal civil servants. The implementation was in contrast often very bad. It led less to the defence of the constitutional order than to its impairment, because it produced a type of consciousness testing. The loss of credibility among the youth has one of its roots here. The Social Democrats got rid of this decree, piece by piece, in every *Land* that it governed. But the memory of this mistaken decision is still painful today.[35]

Many party leaders, Chancellors Willy Brandt and Helmut Schmidt evidently among them, literally could not believe how problematic making political demands on civil servants could become in West German society in the 1970s. The practice was, after all, consistent with the institution's 'traditional principles'. But those 'principles' were increasingly inconsistent with needs and identities in West Germany's modern liberal democratic society. As SPD parliamentarian Hans Martin Bury noted,

most civil servants have come to consider their service relationship to be a normal work relationship. Getting rid of the professional civil service thus only executes a development in our society that has long been completed. Holding fast to old structures does not really help anyone.

The SPD did 'hold fast to an old structure' as it initially – and apparently unreflectively – supported the *Radikalenerlass* in 1972. Untangling itself from the traditional institution of the professional civil service was a long and divisive process for the party in the 1970s that it clearly did not wish to repeat. As 'once-burned children' who had made explicit political demands on state employees and paid for it, the SPD was adamantly opposed to see this practice re-instituted, even for the ex-officials of the GDR.

What to do with ex-GDR State Officials: SPD

From the foregoing discussion, we see that the context for the SPD's answer to this question is less complicated – but perhaps no less problematic – than the context for the CDU/CSU. While the CDU/CSU was pulled in one direction by an institutional ideology that saw the political reliability of state officials as paramount, and in another direction by EC integration and recent fiscal constraints suggesting reform, partial privatisation, and a general depoliticisation of the institution, the contextual cues for the SPD, in contrast, more or less all pointed in one direction: EC integration suggested reducing the civil service to core 'sovereign' activities; fiscal constraints further justified the institution's 'modernisation;' and a powerful political critique of the 'authoritarian state' tradition of the German civil service, sharpened by the party's battle over the *Radikalenerlass*, suggested a pragmatic functionalism for determining the political fit of ex-GDR officials. This context pushed the party to adopt relatively depoliticised criteria for determining the fit of ex-GDR officials for the German civil service. The question of what to do with the old officials of the GDR, in short, got subsumed by the SPD in the general question of what a modern civil service should be in a post-industrial society.

Discussing the needs of the new *Länder*, one SPD official stated in August, 1991: 'our most crucial goal is really not to produce *Beamten*, but rather to construct an efficient administration.' Efficiency and functionalism over politics was the clear message of Gerhard Schroeder, SPD Minister President of Niedersachsen, in July, 1990: 'Membership, such as in the SED, can certainly not be a reason to prohibit a person for all time from practising the profession of teaching.' With regard to 'higher functions' – 'sovereign' activities – a single-case test must be applied in accord with civil service law and 'practical reason'. But even the single-case test must be administered with considerable restraint because, Schroeder suggested, to ask individual former-SED members to explain their motives for joining the party – as was promoted by some CDU/CSU leaders – is 'totally absurd'. The result would be 'extensive investigations of conscience that would both hurt the state and encourage people to lie'. No former member of the SED would admit to anything more than 'fellow-traveler' status.[36]

The party's misbegotten experience with the *Radikalenerlass* was clearly evident in its response to this question. Throughout the 1970s and 1980s during the *Radikalenerlass* debate, the SPD supported the single-case test to determine political fit for the civil service, and it came eventually to reject the 'routine check' with the Office for the Protection of the Constitution for each applicant. These relatively more liberal positions were resisted by the CDU/CSU, but finally, by the end of 1991, the 'routine check' was also lifted in CDU/CSU-governed *Länder* of Baden-Wuerttemberg and Bavaria, with the stated justification that East German applicants would have no file at the Western Office for the Protection of the Constitution for the hiring authorities to check. By the time the question of what to do with the state personnel of the ex-GDR appeared, the SPD had been promoting a functionalist reform of the West German institution for about 20 years. To drop the functionalism and readopt a systematic political vetting of all applicants for state employment – however arguably justified by the political legitimation needs of the ex-GDR citizenry – would have meant abandoning civil service reform, forgetting the problematic experience of the *Radikalenerlass*, and applying criteria inconsistent with a modern service-providing state administration.

The broader implications of the SPD's response to this question are similar to those of the CDU/CSU's response. Its Western German focus neglects a direct consideration of the political needs of former East German citizens. While the material needs of those citizens may be addressed by an efficient provision of services, their political needs in coming to terms with their past may be compromised by the appearance of ex-GDR officials in continued positions of authority. Recent German historical experience suggests that even if inspired by a moral desire to forgive, such a policy can come back to haunt policymakers for years after it first appears. *Not* systematically ridding a new regime of the 'political class' of the old may be morally defensible, but also extremely difficult for a once-repressed population 'or its children' to accept.[37]

CONCLUSION

The Federal Republic of Germany, as a successor regime to the GDR, has chosen a generally depoliticised functionalist response to the question of what to do with the state employees of the old regime. Given the muted but continued resonance in the Federal Republic of a nineteenth century institutional ideology that focuses on the political reliability of individual state actors, and the decades-long party-political fight over precisely this issue spawned by the *Radikalenerlass*, the level of multi-partisan agreement among Germany's political élites on this issue at the federal level is high, somewhat surprising, and potentially distressing to ex-East German citizens. To meet as they did, the CDU/CSU was driven by the imperatives of EC integration and state budget deficits with the backdrop of the end of the Cold War, while the SPD combined an appreciation of these with a long-standing critique of the idea and the institution of Germany's professional civil service. In short, these factors, having much more to do with the needs of a mature post-industrial liberal democracy than a post-revolutionary society repressed for four decades by the 'administrative staff' of a Leninist regime, largely determined the answer to the question of what to do with the state employees of the old order.

Germany's response to this question, however, is not the only one we have seen in Central Europe. The former Czechoslovakia's 'lustration' law (Latin for 'sacrificial purification'), passed by parliament and reluctantly signed by President Vaclav Havel, was intended to keep all persons with virtually any official ties to the former regime from public employment for five years. This represents a radical political targeting of the 'administrative staff of the old regime' by a mobilised citizenry striving to authenticate a new legitimation 'from below'. It generated a divisive national political and moral debate, with many of the old regime's most prominent victims, like Havel himself, opposing the law and its assumption of collective guilt. Nonetheless, the 'lustration' law, however crude and categorical, may go further in meeting the deeply complicated legitimation needs of the former Czechoslovakia's post-revolutionary citizenry than the functionalist position adopted at the federal level by Germany's political élites.

In the former Czechoslovakia, Jeri Laber wrote of a population 'with a guilty conscience . . . taking revenge for their own humiliation'.[38] In Germany, we see a mass private obsession with the 125 miles of Stasi files, in which people learn of their betrayal by friends, physicians, therapists, and even husbands. Is the private poring-over of Stasi files partly a response to the lack of a more distinctly *political* effort by the Federal Republic to come to terms with its reality as a successor regime to the GDR? Has private catharsis so far substituted for an absent political catharsis?

Notes

* Initially prepared for the Eighth International Conference of Europeanists, Chicago, Illinois, March 27–29, 1992. The author wishes to thank Spencer Wellhofer and David Ost for comments, and Peter Munkelt, archivist of the SPD in Bonn, for access to materials.

1. Andrew C. Janos, 'Social Science, Communism, and the Dynamics of Political Change', *World Politics*, vol. 44, October, 1991, pp. 82–4.
2. Giuseppe DiPalma, 'Legitimation From the Top to Civil Society: Politico-Cultural Change in Eastern Europe', *World Politics*, vol. 44, October, 1991, p. 54.
3. DiPalma, pp. 63–78.
4. See DiPalma, p. 55, note 20; and Mike Dennis, *German Democratic Republic: Politics, Economics and Society* (London: Pinter Publishers, 1988), p. 113.
5. Grzegorz Ekiert, 'Democratization Processes in East Central Europe: A Theoretical Reconsideration', *British Journal of Political Science*, vol. 21, Part 3, July 1991, pp. 286–9; 312–13.
6. Klaus von Beyme, *Das politische System der Bundersrepublik Deutschland nach der Vereinigung* (Muenchen: R. Piper & Co. Verlag, 1991), pp. 48–57. Also Uwe Thaysen, *Der Runde Tisch oder: Wo blieb das Volk?* (Opladen: Westdeutscher Verlag, 1990); and Robert Leicht, 'Viel Rauch and wenig Feuer', *Die Zeit* Nr. 14, 3. April 1992.
7. See Theodor Eschenburg, *Die improvisierte Demokratie: Gesammelte Aufsaetze zur Weimarer Republik* (Muenchen: R. Piper & Co., Verlag, 1963); and Karl Dietrich Bracher, *Die Aufloesung der Weimarer Republik* (Koenigstein/Ts., Duesseldorf: Athenaeum Verlag/Droste Verlag, 1978).
8. Lutz Niethammer, *Die Mitlaeufer Fabrik: Die Entnazifizierung am Beispiel Bayerns*, 2nd. ed. (Berlin, 1982).
9. See Peter J. Katzenstein, *Policy and Politics in West Germany: The Growth of a Semisovereign State* (Philadelphia: Temple University Press, 1987), pp. 260–6, and Studienkommission fuer die Reform des oeffentlichen Dienstrechts, ed., *Bericht des Kommissions*, Bd. 12 (Baden-Baden: Nomos Verlagsgesellschaft, 1973).
10. Quoted in Frank Rottmann, *Der Beamte als Staatsbuerger: Zugleich eine Untersuchung zum Normtypus von Art. 33 Abs. 5 GG* (Berlin: Duncker & Humblot, 1981), p. 13.
11. See Studienkommission, *Bericht*, pp. 163–66; and Kurt Sontheimer and Wilhelm Bleek, *Abschied vom Berufsbeamtentum? Perspektive einer Reform des oeffentlichen Dienstes in der Bundesrepublik Deutschland* (Hamburg: Hoffmann and Campe, 1973).

150   *What to do with Communist Bureaucrats*

12. Henry Krisch, *The German Democratic Republic: The Search for Identity* (Boulder: Westview Press, 1985), pp. 35–6; Bernd Wunder, *Geschichte der Buerokratie in Deutschland* (Frankfurt: Suhrkamp, 1986), pp. 153–64.
13. Kenneth H. F. Dyson, *The State Tradition in Western Europe: The Study of an Idea and an Institution* (New York: Oxford University Press, 1980).
14. Wunder, *Geschichte*, p. 156; and Suzanne Berger, 'Politics and Anti-Politics in Western Europe in the Seventies', *Daedalus*, vol. 108, no. 1, Winter, 1979, pp. 27–50.
15. Gregg O. Kvistad, 'Radicals and the State: The Political Demands on West German Civil Servants', *Comparative Political Studies*, vol. 21, no. 1, April, 1988, pp. 95–125, and Kvistad, 'Between State and Society: Green Political Ideology in the Mid–1980s', *West European Politics*, vol. 10, no. 2, April, 1987, pp. 211–28.
16. See Gerard Braunthal, *Political Loyalty and Public Service in West Germany* (Amherst: University of Massachusetts Press, 1990), but also Peter Meier-Bergfeld *'Staats(ver)diener?' Der Oeffentliche Dienst* (Zuerich: Edition Interfrom, 1983), for a colourful yet informative treatment.
17. James G. March and Johan P. Olsen, *Rediscovering Institutions* (New York: The Free Press, 1989), pp. 160–1; Peter Graf Kielmansegg, 'The Basic Law – Response to the Past or Design for the Future?' *Forty Years of the Grundgesetz*, Occasional Paper No. 1 (Washington: German Historical Institute, 1989).
18. Emil J. Kirchner, 'The Federal Republic of Germany in the European Community', in Peter H. Merkl, ed., *The Federal Republic of Germany at Forty* (New York: New York University Press, 1989), p. 428, and Stanley Hoffmann, 'The European Community and 1992', *Foreign Affairs*, Fall 1989, vol. 68, no. 4.
19. T. Hitiris, *European Community Economics*, 2nd. ed. (New York: St. Martin's Press, 1991), pp. 251–71.
20. *Der Bundesminister des Innern teilt mit:* 'Ansprache von Staatssekretaer Franz Kroppenstedt', 8. Januar 1991, pp. 4–5, and *CDU/CSU Fraktion im Deutschen Bundestag*, 8.1.1991, No. 547, pp. 2 and 5.
21. *CDU/CSU Fraktion im Deutschen Bundestag*, 26.7.1991, p. 2, and 13.8.1991, ID3302/52.
22. Katzenstein, *Policy and Politics*, p. 271.
23. *Der Bundesminister des Innern teilt mit:* 'Rede von Bundesinnenminister Dr. Friedrich Zimmermann', 10. Januar 1989, pp. 20–1, and ibid., 8. January 1991, pp. 15–16.
24. '"Zu viele Beschaeftigte beim Staat"' *Stuttgarter Nachrichten*, 11. Januar 1991.
25. *CDU/CSU Fraktion im Deutschen Bundestag*, 26.7.1991, pp. 1–2.
26. BPA – Nachrichtenabt. 7.11.1991, No. 1107–10, p. 2.
27. BPA – Nachrichtenabt. 9.4.1991, No. 04094; 'Ueber allem Schwebt die Treue zum Dienstherrn', *Handelsblatt*, 27. Maerz 1991. Also 'Kohl verteidigt Beamtenzulage', *Stuttgarter Zeitung*, 12. April 1991.
28. *CDU/CSU Fraktion im Deutschen Bundestag*, 24.8.1990, No. 2603, and 'Schonzeit fuer Staatsdiener', *Handelsblatt*, 18. September 1990.
29. *CDU/CSU Fraktion im Deutschen Bundestag*, 26.11.1990, No. 484.
30. *Grundsatzprogramm der Sozialdemokratischen Partei Deutschlands*, ed.

Vorstand der SPD (Bonn: 1989), p. 36.

31. See *ppp*, 40. Jhrg., Nr. 7, 10. Januar 1989, p. 6, and *Sozialdemokratischer Pressedienst*, Nr. 144, 31. Juli 1991, p. 3.

32. '"Ersatzlose Abschaffung des Berufsbeamtentums nicht in Frage"', *Bonner Behoerden Spiegel*, Oktober 1991, and '"Oeffentlichen Dienst so klein und effektiv wie moeglich machen"', *Sueddeutsche Zeitung*, 6. Juli 1991.

33. 'SPD macht bei Post Kehrtwende', *Frankfurter Rundschau*, 10. August 1991.

34. *Grundsatzprogramm*, p. 49.

35. *Presseservice der SPD*, No. 656/89, 18. Oktober 1989; Willy Brandt and Helmut Schmidt, *Deutschland 1976: Zwei Sozialdemokraten im Gespraech* (Reinbek bei Hamburg: Rowohlt, 1976), pp. 47–9.

36. 'Berufsbeamte falsch am Platz', *Berliner Zeitung*, 24. August 1991. Also, '"Bonbon fuer die Wendehaelse"', *Der Spiegel*, No. 30, 23. Juli 1990.

37. See '"Hetzjagd auf unbescholtene Genossen"', *Sueddeutsche Zeitung*, 10. November 1990; 'Die Anfrage soll kuenftig nicht mehr die Regel sein', *Stuttgarter Zeitung*, 15. Dezember 1990; DDP 200, 3. Dezember 1991. Also Vaclav Havel, 'Paradise Lost', *The New York Review of Books*, vol. XXXIX, no. 7, April 9, 1991, pp. 6–8.

38. See Jeri Laber, 'Witch Hunt in Prague', *The New York Review of Books*, vol. XXXIX, no. 8, April 23, 1992, pp. 5–8, and Havel, 'Paradise Lost', p. 8.

8 Participation and Democracy: Residential Communities in the Former GDR

Marilyn Rueschemeyer*

I INTRODUCTION

With the dismantling of the wall between the two Germanies and the end of the regime of the former German Democratic Republic, a radical transformation of East German society was not only possible but necessary. Two issues mattered and continue to matter most in this transformation: economic restructuring and the grounding of democratic politics. This chapter will deal with the beginnings of democratic life in the new towns of East Germany, residential areas generally surrounding major cities.

Focusing on these local communities gives me the chance to build on earlier work, done before 1989, in which I studied the social and political life in the new towns in the GDR. In addition, this focus on the local level offers perhaps the best opportunity for observing the interface between people's daily life and their experience with the new political situation. Although grassroots organisation and participation in local political life are not in themselves synonymous with democracy, they do give an indication of how people respond to the introduction of democracy in the five new German states. And as they establish linkages to the more remote forms of democratic politics and influence the acceptance of the new political system, they may be important in shaping future developments.

With unification, West German legal and political institutions were introduced in the East. This instantly established the forms of democracy, it extended the reach of West German parties, unions and other organisations, and it opened opportunities for a new kind of participation in the political process. Yet unification also brought unexpected and potentially devastating problems and left many wondering what democracy and the new economy really entailed for them.

Did popular participation in political parties and in politically relevant voluntary associations, once freed from the fetters of the old regime, shoot up or did it develop sparsely, burdened with old attitudes and current problems? Did people embrace the new politics with fervent hope or did they meet it with hesitant scepticism? Did the new social and economic problems stimulate or blunt social and political participation? What were people's hopes for the new beginning? What were their conceptions of democracy? And how did their experience with the new political life relate to their hopes and anticipations? These are the questions I explore in the following pages.

My work has concentrated on the city of Rostock, with some comparative observations on Berlin. Rostock lies at the Baltic Sea, about two hours north of Berlin. It is part of the new German state of Mecklenburg–Vorpommern. In Rostock, nearly two-thirds of the residents live in new residential areas of 20 to 30 000 people each. The huge apartment house complexes around East Berlin are much larger; Marzahn, for example, has approximately 160 000 inhabitants. And the problems that developed there even before unification were also different from the situation in Rostock. Nevertheless, in spite of such variation in size, design, environment as well as problems, the residential communities of the former GDR had and still have a similar overall character.[1]

Today, these urban residential communities still contain remnants of their earlier organisational life, and the residents, of course, reflect on these and act in ways that are shaped in part by their past experiences. On the other hand, we find in the new towns all the new institutional structures and attempts at social and political restructuring that take place throughout East Germany, and these, too, are being observed and evaluated. People's past and present experiences as well as their reflections and reactions find crystallised expression in their willingness to participate in the organisational life of their communities.

After a brief retrospective based on my earlier research in the residential communities around Rostock, this chapter will describe a number of changes in the new towns that have taken place since unification. It will attempt to explore the extent and modes of social and political participation as well as people's initial evaluations of what for them constitutes the democratic alternative to their past social existence.

II RESIDENTIAL LIFE IN THE FORMER GDR

The huge blocks of flats found everywhere in the former German Democratic Republic were clearly a response to the need for building inexpensive housing as quickly as possible. The shortage of housing and the poor condition of existing buildings were for years major problems in the German Democratic Republic. Yet in discussions of what these communities should be, the architects and planners were asked to develop more than mere bedroom communities. They were to introduce a number of institutions that would make these areas into cities of a new type. Some people talked about a new 'socialist' way of life; but that concept remained vague. More concretely, the residential areas had to be built so that both men and women could participate in the labour force. That meant that each area needed child-care facilities, schools, and shops as well as other services. In actuality, however, the 'additions' or 'extras' were rather limited; there were only a few shops and meeting places for social or cultural activity even if the most necessary institutions were provided.

The residential areas also were to have a special social and political character. They were to be organisationally rich, including not only a social framework in which the residents would take responsibility for the buildings and public spaces but also the mass organisations such as People's Solidarity, a welfare organisation, the Free German Youth, or the Democratic Women's Federation – as well as a number of smaller committees. These organisations were to integrate and involve the people in their communities much as similar organisations were supposed to do in the workplace. And the different units were to be coordinated by the National Front, an umbrella organisation that included the mass organisations and parties under the control of the Communist Party.

Associational activities in the residential communities nearly always took place in a context that was regulated. In fact, before the mid-1980s, virtually no participation in public life was allowed outside that context. At the same time, if people were willing to participate at all, at least some of their interests had to be served. The protection of individual interests – avoiding sanctions and even advancing one's career – could often be accomplished by mere paper activity, and much of the officially registered public participation was just that. But there also existed some significant actual participation in the GDR, and that participation required that the organisations serve some real interests of their members. Furthermore, the system had to offer the participants some control from below, however limited, if they were to get involved at all. Where this happened, however, if it happened at all, was at the place of work, at the lowest level of the trade union organisation – in the 'work collective'.[2] That led to some interesting developments in the mid- to late-1980s before unification, and it affects what is happening now.

Clearly, the formal institutional network in the residential communities, and the formal arrangement of organisations that offered the opportunity for participation, does not describe how they were evaluated by the residents and how residents responded to them. For understanding the strength and influence of these organisations and committees, it is critical to examine how they related to spontaneous neighbourhood interaction, and to the most strongly felt needs of the population, and to determine where people turned for help, for the fulfilment of their cultural, social, and recreational interests and needs, and for assistance with housing and neighbourhood problems.

In previous research, several committees and organisations were examined in relation to the needs of specific groups in the residential area.[3] To take one example only, families in the new towns as well as in the inner city were organized into *Hausgemeinschaften*, house organisations. These were to help maintain order, cleanliness, and stability in the living area but also to give support to the political programmes introduced. The chairs of the house organisations met regularly with the community coordinating committee; Rostock had on average 13–15 such committees. It was through these community coordinating committees that the National Front, the umbrella organisation of parties and all social organisations, was to play an important role in the residential area. One might see these *Hausgemeinschaften* in analogy to union work collectives and expect that, where they were successful, they were similarly capable of absorbing, integrating, serving and shaping the informal and spontaneous tendencies of association in a block of flats and the neighbourhood. Linking informal local interaction and people's concerns for company, help, etc. to the wider organisational structure would have constituted a major achievement for the regime. By and large, however, this strategy was singularly unsuccessful.

The residents faced frequent problems with the delivery of services of all kinds and with repairs in the buildings. That these problems remained unresolved related directly to a general unwillingness of the residents to become active. In fact, many did not believe that *any* formal institution responsible for the residential area was capable or willing to respond to these needs. Even if they initially had come with some enthusiasm – and most people were delighted to get a flat in the new residential areas of Rostock – they became less active in the Hausgemeinschaft, unwilling to respond to public campaigns for cleaning up the area, and so on. In the end, the house organisations confined themselves to the tasks of order and cleanliness, and with some difficulty most achieved those goals. The men and women active in house committees whom I interviewed agreed that most importantly one should not spout the words of the Party: 'No politics.'[4]

GDR citizens had the right to complain formally, and such petitions could be sent to the branch of the city administration that existed in the residential area, the representative of the National Front, or the Party. Functionaries of the city and of the various political parties of the National Front spent a lot of time answering complaints, many of which revolved around housing, and some of these were resolved. Yet when this did happen, the resolution in most cases was an individual matter and did not involve any need for organisational activity. Furthermore, there was no collective recognition of anything positive that the National Front had done. Overall, it is a fair judgment that the residential house committees and the various linking organisations did not have particular clout. Some may have exerted pressures and occasionally succeeded in bringing about some improvements in the new towns; but generally they were not seen as responding to people's needs. For this reason, especially, these organisations had difficulty attracting people, not to mention exerting any influence on them.

It is possible to do a similar analysis of the needs of adolescents and the role of the Free German Youth in the community, or the needs of working women and the role of the Democratic Women's Federation. Perhaps People's Solidarity, a welfare association that particularly served the older residents of the community, achieved greater success than the other organisations; even with new West German welfare associations competing in the community now, it manages to retain a number of its former members and continue its activities.

Overall, however, people stayed away from organised activities in the residential community as much as possible. In contrast to the organisational obligations clustered around the workplace, which were hard to avoid whether one was willing to get involved or not, life in the residential areas was dominated by the idea of privacy, a concept that accorded of course with prevailing and rather uncontested ideals of family life.

The Party eventually tended to withdraw from the residential areas after considerable internal discussion about these matters. Some argued that its subsidiary for young people, the Free German Youth (FDJ), should intensify its work in the Neubaugebiete; but many believed that the FDJ's representatives would not be accepted by the residents. There also was widespread discussion at the lower levels of the Party about the need for flexibility and open debate with the population responding to the interest in and support for Gorbachev-style *Glasnost*. But neither did this lead to a different official policy nor is it clear that if the attempt had been made, it could have – after all these years – convinced people to become involved in official organisations in their communities. In effect, the Party gave up its attempt to organise the residential communities in any politically significant way. The desire for privacy was too strong; and the residents would only become involved when they could have some impact on their environment, and their ability to achieve this was extremely limited.

The organised groups that tried to bring about change were mostly tied to the Protestant church, which also served as an umbrella organisation for a number of other groups with specific interests, especially concerning environmental issues and questions of peace. There were also some discussions at the lower levels of mass organisations, in professional associations that were under the general trade union umbrella, and even in the lower levels of the Party about introducing more democratic procedures, responding to the frustrations of the members, etc. Certain elections were affected in professional associations, which at least helped to prepare a certain grounding for what was to happen later in the GDR. But the kinds of issues that can be addressed in professional associations are not as encompassing as those brought out in a more general community setting, or in the Free German Youth or the Union, more broadly based mass organisations. And the higher ranking officials of the party and mass organisations were not willing or able to introduce significant change.

Conceding the residential areas as spaces virtually free of social and political obligations may have served to stabilise the state socialist regime, because the insistent demand for privacy was thus tacitly acknowledged. Yet this withdrawal also underscored the failure of the Party–State to respond effectively to major needs of the population. Furthermore, the regime lost in this way the opportunity of engaging people in a sphere of life – of family and friendship and of leisure activities – that was growing in importance with increasing levels of education and prosperity. Finally, and perhaps most important in the long run, the combination of this withdrawal with the repression of autonomous associations neutralised the community as an arena in which wide-ranging discussion and shared action could develop. This was important for the way the regime collapsed; it probably also shaped the aftermath of the regime, leaving communities with little from which to develop meaningful and voluntary participation.

III   THE IMPACT OF UNIFICATION

In 1990 and 1991, the West German constitution, legal procedures, and political and social institutions were introduced into Eastern Germany. The processes involved in unification and national elections evoked a mixture of reactions in the new residential areas but generally many people were initially joyful and hopeful about their future lives in a united Germany. They believed that it would now be possible – given the introduction of democratic institutions – to finally exert some control over their own lives.

It is no exaggeration to say that nearly every social problem plays itself out in the residential area. But the core issues are declining industrial production and a dramatic rise of unemployment, a problem unknown before. In Eastern Germany, the unemployment rate is now 40 per cent if one counts those who have no work at all, those who were forced to retire early, those who work short (and often very short) hours, and those who are in retraining programmes. Unemployment is particularly high among women. Before 1989, women had represented 49 per cent of the workforce and contributed 40 per cent of the family income; now they comprise 63 per cent of the unemployed!

The result of these levels of unemployment is not only economic hardship, disruption of life routines, and loss of self-esteem (though the latter is mitigated by the very mass character of the problem); the main effect is a great uncertainty and fear about the future experienced by many.

There are many other disruptions and problems. Prices are high, and inflation exceeds West German levels. Rents, which had been nominal user fees, have risen substantially and are expected to rise further. Some child care facilities have been eliminated, the others now charge modest fees, and there is great concern about the maintenance of these day care centres in the future.[5] A number of doctors abandoned the polyclinics because of pressure and initial support for privatisation. Schools and universities are still in a state of flux – in their personnel as well as in their curriculum. There is a continuing emigrating of young and skilled workers and professionals to West Germany.

Not much has changed in the facilities of the new towns. In the new towns of Rostock, the *Treuhandanstalt*, the agency responsible for privatisation and restructuring, has sold a number of buildings which will be used for new purposes. Though there are a few restaurants and services, generally very few new shops have opened in the residential communities. In the meantime, some cultural institutions and youth clubs were closed, cutting down on the opportunities for entertainment and leisure activities in the residential areas. This is the more serious as more unemployment leaves people with free time. There are new open markets, but here again unemployment is visible – many people are hanging around without work. Only a third of the students leaving secondary school in Rostock are able to get apprenticeships.[6]

A rise in crime and in particular a heightened incidence of violence must be seen in the context of these social and economic problems. One of the most dramatic attacks on foreigners in the East took place in Rostock. In Lichtenhagen, a residential community between Rostock and the sea resort of Warnemuende, an overcrowded house reserved for asylum seekers was attacked by right extremists. While the police – ill-equipped and not prepared for crowd control – were extremely ineffective, the attacks escalated and were supported by some of the residents.

IV EFFECTS ON PARTICIPATION

How did these developments affect social and political participation? There is every reason to get involved in the residential area, in civic initiatives, in voluntary associations, and in the new political parties. And there are many reasons why this is not happening.

First of all, there is the expectation, arising in part out of a sense of futility, that someone else 'or some other group' is responsible for what is happening and will take care of what has to be done. This is, of course, the classic free rider problem, but it is intensified by the number of private problems without visible solutions that many East Germans are experiencing[7]: the opportunity costs of participation, as economists put it, have risen drastically. Secondly, there is a lack of familiarity with the new institutions and organisations that have emerged. Thirdly, the experiences with former political organisations and institutions make people hesitant to become involved. And this leads, fourthly, to a particular sensitivity to similarities with the past, similarities not so much in the language used, though that may produce an allergic reaction, but in the actual experience of the new politics.

In the Rostock new towns, there are citizen centres where a number of groups in the residential areas meet. Although many people are not aware of the different new organisations and associations emerging in the new towns, they do turn up at the Renter's Association for advice, for legal advice of all sorts, to the welfare organisations if there are special needs, though where subscriptions are required, people often turn up without joining.

There has been a marked change since the immediate aftermath of the collapse of the regime. The number of spontaneous groups which developed during the transition period has been reduced significantly since unification, and the new leadership that emerged at the end of the regime lost a good deal of its support.

Seemingly spontaneous voluntary organisations often rely on a few people who are paid for with public funds. The people working there depend on grants budgeted for one year. Sometimes these grants can be extended for a second year, but if they fall through, and they are very insecure, the frail organisational attempts to involve people may fail altogether. Will these initiatives then be picked up by spontaneous, volunteer activity? There are reasons for doubt.

One critical question is whether these groups will have an impact on the decisions made about their communities. Small grassroots organisations will have difficulty making a difference and the citizen's centres, for instance, are paid for by public supplements under any condition. In addition, we must consider here that expectations about democracy were running extraordinarily high. Many people in the former GDR developed an idealistic notion of democracy; democracy means being able to affect your work conditions, your living conditions, your community. Idealistic conceptions of 'real influence from below' now clash with the realities of a system that is majoritarian and representative and in which administrative decision making has considerable weight.

That the elected political parties have so much power in the community and yet are not very responsive to the most urgent problems 'as people see them' is experienced as an indication that politics as it is carried out does not work for the people. Even if most people are glad and feel generally better now than in the old regime, many claim that they had nothing to say then and they have nothing to say now. There is a similar disappointment with the new unions. They sustained some loss of membership, which very quickly had shot up after unification due to fears about the new problem of unemployment.

Some interesting survey results from the Institute for Social Analysis Study in Berlin-Bonn give us an indication of attitudes among the population. To the question, 'The Wall has been gone for 2 years. How do you see this today?' a little over a third thought it was good, and another third thought that the advantages outweighed the disadvantages, but a full third thought the advantages and disadvantages equalled each other or the disadvantages outweighed the advantages. Thirty-six per cent said they would not vote the way they did in 1990. Fifty-one per cent disagreed with the statement that socialism from the beginning was an error, the same per cent agreed fully that the idea of socialism was good but poorly developed, and an additional 33 per cent mostly agreed with that statement. Only 22 per cent thought socialism would return in better form, while 41 per cent agreed fully or mostly that as an idea it is important as a counterpoint to the market economy.[8] These results indicate that problems experienced now affect perceptions of the past. And they will continue to influence perceptions of possible future developments and the willingness to become involved in shaping a new Germany.

Though the major parties are not completely unresponsive to the difficulties in the East, they have not thus far succeeded in developing locally strong units in the five new German states and have in fact lost members. The Party of Democratic Socialism (PDS), the renewed former communist party[9] attempts to work in the community more extensively than the others, though in the different residential areas one or the other political party may be particularly sensitive to the problems at hand.[10] The discussion of an Eastern movement, Committees for Justice, by prominent people of all political persuasions[11] was a very interesting development. Even with its difficulties, it indicated, among other things, the frustration with the major political parties, especially with their inadequate response to the difficulties in the East.[12] A further consequence, from the point of view of the political party itself, is its failure to socialise a new and important constituency which could come to believe, support, and work for its party programme.[13]

In addition to initiatives, associations and parties, there are new forms of local self-administration. In the winter of 1992, each residential area of Rostock had a local council comprised of about 15 people chosen according to the percentage the parties received in the elections. Many residents remain uninformed about these councils and their activities. Public meetings are announced in the paper, and between a dozen and 20 people have attended these meetings thus far – the largest number turned out to discuss traffic problems. Will these councils have an impact on what happens in the residential areas?

Local democracy has to compete with administrative decision making. The local government, the city of Rostock, though working within the framework of policies set by the federal government and the state, attempts to play a mediating role, pursuing its own vision of what is good for Rostock in the face of rapid political and economic change. The political heads, planners, and architects involved in the development of the residential areas of Rostock share a collective orientation and commitment of this sort, even with their rejection of the old regime. At the same time, many developments which formerly were the responsibility of government now are steered by market forces. My impression is that the core group of planners and administrators is trying to control the impact of some of these forces. For example, there are plans to develop more housing or commercial areas in the new towns. Rostock needs investors, but the chief architect calls for a planned framework for development, a model, which is presented to the potential investor. That does not mean that the architectural firm that created the model gets the contract or that the construction company will be local, not at all, but that, for example, natural spaces will be preserved, or that the size of the houses built should fit the community, or that segregation by social class will be minimised.

How do these administrative efforts look from the local council's point of view? Two brief examples will be instructive. After one interview with a council head, I attended a meeting at city hall with the Senator responsible for the sections of the city and six other people. The Senator spoke, the architect charged with developing new plans for housing spoke, the woman who was head of the council softly mentioned that they wanted to preserve the natural spaces. The response was 'It's being taken care of.' She said no more and the meeting continued. Most likely, the matter was indeed being taken care of but the concern of the council and even its existence were barely acknowledged. It appears that the council is there to moderate intense reactions from the population, to inform people and to involve them somewhat in decision-making, but they are not part of the development and shaping of policy.[14]

Another discussion concerned a development project in the same residential area which included transforming one of the apartment house complexes into a hotel. That would have resulted in older residents and large families having to move elsewhere. The head of the council said they immediately formed a *Mieterbeirat*, a renters' council (which by law they found out they were entitled to do) and invited WIRO, the public housing authority, and the investor. The investor decided against building the hotel. The chief architect, however, explained that the investor decided there would be too many structural problems in transforming the building into a hotel; he never even mentioned the renters' council.

In Marzahn, the large residential community in Berlin, there is an institution called *Plattform Marzahn* which meets every four weeks; organised by a private firm and for the time being financed by the Senate, the Berlin administration, it is supposed to further dialogue between inhabitants, planners and investors. It brings together representatives of the state administration, housing enterprises, and party caucuses of the district parliament. The question is whether we must not see this organisation primarily as a symbolic happening that is a substitute for action which is not yet possible, creating merely a sense of democratic participation.[15] But this limited structure and the still undeveloped Rostock councils may have consequences that in the long run are problematical for democratic development. If it, too, exists mainly to inform and get the cooperation of the residents and to moderate the most severe problems, the residents are not learning how to negotiate, how to arrive at compromises, or how to develop projects together. As Anne Saeterdal put it: 'Participation is the first step to active political engagement. Participation in local planning may, if properly arranged, involve people who are not used to political and/ or public activities. They may, through participating on a familiar ground, get encouraged to further their political activity.'[16] However, without the feeling that there is a real chance to influence what is happening, people will not see sense in this society either in wasting time or by becoming involved in meaningless activity.

In the instances mentioned, which could be multiplied, there is evidence of some effort in the community and some structural possibility to control developments in the residential areas. And, at the same time, we find politicians and professionals in the city committed to strong notions of the 'public good.' There is a conflict between democratic participation and administrative ambitions to 'get things done'. The professionals and local politicians have their hands full with political[17] and economic pressures from the outside. They did set up some democratic structures, and they do think these are important, but they do not worry much about real participation and building a democratic basis. Neither do the major political parties.

Finally, the many obstacles to active participation are compounded by old and new tendencies not to become involved in any activity that goes beyond their private sphere. Two poignant examples in Rostock come to mind. People complain that adolescents who are caught in wrongdoing, in car theft for examples, easily walk the streets again. The police claim they need witnesses but people are afraid to be witnesses; they fear that the response from the wrongdoer will be anger, that their car will be stolen, that they, the witnesses, will 'get it' in the end. Similarly, people have expressed approval of the mediation commissions set up in neighbourhoods to deal with minor neighbourhood issues; these commissions, which existed also in the former GDR, are not able to find members. Residents do not want to take on the work; they do not want to become involved.

V CONCLUDING REMARKS

Unification brought new opportunities for democratic participation. It also brought problems of social and economic transformation of a magnitude few anticipated. Yet popular participation in public affairs is quite limited for various reasons. The main explanation may be found in the pressing private problems many people now encounter. Other factors relate to people's past memories and their conceptions and perceptions of democracy:

(1) For many, the freedom *not* to be socially and politically active is the important new option.
(2) Perceived similarities in the unresponsiveness of parties, organisations, and institutions lead to similar reactions of withdrawal.
(3) Often democracy is seen as the promise of full self-determination. Such conceptions of democracy – the opposite of the experience of the old regime – may be idealistic and unrealistic, but the reality of democracy is judged by these standards.
(4) There are many and huge problems of public policy; that they remain unresolved is likely to affect sympathies for and commitment to democracy, though for the time being even people hit hard by, say, unemployment still look at their situation in a broad context of promise and hope.
(5) Where people do engage in democratic participation they often

encounter fairly cohesive administrations with their own commitments to action for the public good and a tendency to neglect democratic participation as too cumbersome. If unchecked, this may in the long run sap the strength of emerging democratic developments.

(6) All of this must be seen in the broader context of the interaction between West Germany and East Germany. There is a widespread sense that the West is controlling all developments in the East and that East Germans have little say in determining their own fate.

This complex picture leaves no doubt about one conclusion: The rejection of an undemocratic past, which is indeed widespread and nearly universal, is not in itself a strong basis for a vital democratic political life.

Notes

* I am very grateful to the International Research and Exchanges Board for supporting this earlier work as well as the current project; to Peter Voigt, Andreas Schubert, and Christoph Weinhold for their ongoing help with my work in Rostock; to Wolfgang Schumann and Martina Buhtz, who are involved in research and community work in Marzahn; and to Anders Aslund for his kind invitation to spend the Fall semester of 1992 at the Stockholm Institute of Soviet and East European Economics, where this paper as well as other projects were completed. I had useful discussions with Dietrich Rueschemeyer and I would also like to thank the Swedish Collegium for Advanced Study in the Social Sciences in Uppsala, where Dietrich Rueschemeyer was a fellow at the same time, for the warm hospitality and support extended to both of us.

1. For a detailed description, see my 'New Towns in the German Democratic Republic' in M. Rueschemeyer and C. Lemke, eds., *The Quality of Life in the German Democratic Republic: Changes and Developments in a State Socialist Society*, New York: M. E. Sharpe 1989, pp. 117–43. In the former GDR, the new towns were called *Neubaugebiete*; after unification, they are usually referred to as *Grossiedlungen*. In East Berlin, half of a whole, about a quarter of the population is so housed; the residents live in *Grossiedlungen*; on Eastern Germany see Bernd Hunger, 'Wohnen am Stadtrand,' *Gruenstift-Forum: Gross-Siedlungen, Gross-Städte*, July 1991, pp. 8–9.

2. See Marilyn Rueschemeyer and Bradley Scharf, 'Labor Unions in the German Democratic Republic,' in A. Pravda and B. Ruble, eds., *Trade Unions in Communist States*. London and Boston: Allen & Unwin 1986.

3. For a more extensive analysis, see my article, 'Participation and Control in a State Socialist Society: The German Democratic Republic,'

Working Paper Nr. 17 of the Center for European Studies, Harvard University, 1989, revised in *East Central Europe*, vol. 18, No. 1, 1991, pp. 23–53.

4. This general judgement about the role of the Hausgemeinschaften should not be taken to mean that there were no successful house committees. Where these worked, people were able to undertake a number of repair projects together as well as celebrations. Some of these continued after unification, typically though confined to the care of the building and achieving some unity in the face of new problems, rent increases, etc.

5. There are substantial differences in opinion about the desirability and the quality of institutional care for children under three. See my article on women in Eastern Germany in M. Rueschemeyer, ed., *Women in the Politics of Post-Communist Eastern Europe*, London, and Armonk, New York: M. E. Sharpe, 1994.

6. Interestingly, Mecklenburg-Vorpommern has the highest degree of alcohol consumption in any German state. *Ostsee Zeitung*, June 10, 1992.

7. In some of the residential communities, whole sections are unemployed, for example all the workers employed in ship-building.

8. 'Ein Jahr danach, Sozialstrukturelle Umbrueche und sozio-kulturelle Veränderungen ein Jahr nach Inkrafttreten des Einigungsvertrages,' Institut fuer Sozialdatenanalyse, Berlin/Bonn, December 1991, pp. 5 and 13.

9. The PDS is unlikely to again be represented in the federal parliament because it needs 5 per cent nationally in the next election. It has had some success locally; in the Berlin elections in May 1992, for example, it continued to do well in the Eastern districts; in Marzahn, Hohenschoenhausen, and Hellersdorf, three of the largest new towns, it received the support of approximately a third of the voters. There, the CDU received approximately 14 per cent of the vote. The *Republikaner,* a party of the extreme right, received in these three communities about 6 per cent of the vote. The *Republikaner,* a party of the extreme right received in these three communities, about 6 per cent of the vote. Federally, the Socialist Democratic Party (SPD) is likely to gain in the next election. (In the Berlin elections in these three communities, it received about 28 per cent of the vote.) The Free Democrats, with 3–4 per cent in these residential areas, have attempted to work more frequently with the SPD in addition to the CDU and Alliance 90 in the East, modifying some of its views in response to its Eastern constituency.

10. In Marzahn, for example, the large housing development in Berlin, the Social Democratic Party had only 180 members; every sixth member is an elected official. In Eastern Germany as a whole, in 1992, the Social Democrats had 30 000 members compared to 900 000 in the West. The CDU, which took over the Christian satellite party of the communist past, the Eastern CDU, had 660 000 members in the West and approximately 85 000 in the East; the FDP, which also profited from taking over a former satellite party, had approximately the same number of members in the East and West, 70–80 000. The old bloc parties do not, however, prove to be stable in membership; thus, the FDP has lost members in the East; previously, the party had 138 000 members in the new German states.

11. They include Gregor Gysi, former chair of the PDS and Peter-Michael Diestel, former chair of the CDU party caucus in the state parliament of Brandenburg.

12. A poll done by the EMNID survey institute indicated that 87 per cent of the Easterners interviewed saw themselves still as second class citizens while 57 per cent of the Westerners saw their living conditions as nearly the same. *Berliner Zeitung*, April 30, 1992.

13. See Bernhard Wessels, 'Gruppenbindung und rationale Faktoren als Determinanten der Wahlentscheidung in Ost-und Westdeutschland,' Manuskript fuer die Tagung des Arbeitskreises Wahl-und Einstellungsforschung der DVPW, Bamberg 1992.

14. For an interesting discussion of these issues in the West, see Nico Nelissen, 'Methods of Public Participation in Western Europe. Experiments with Public Participation in Urban Renewal in West European Municipalities,' in Tjeerd Deelstra and Oleg Yanitsky, eds., *Cities of Europe: the Public's Role in Shaping the Urban Environment*. Mezhdunarodnye otnoshenia Publishers, Moscow 1991, pp. 53–68.

15. *Bruno Flierl*, who has written extensively on architecture in the former GDR, commented similarly on the Stadtforum. He asks if the Stadtforum for Berlin can accomplish anything given the large role of politics in the capital. He criticises the relevant political head for backing down from putting limits on the size of buildings in the competition to build the Potsdamer and Leipziger squares. See his 'Hochhäuser für Berlin – wozu und wo?' in Hans G. Helms, ed., *Die Stadt als Gabentisch*, Leipzig: Reclam-Verlag 1992, pp. 445–64 esp. p. 462. He is not the only critic of these developments. Krätke and Schmoll write that the Berlin Senate waived urban planning requirements, ignored requests for involving the public in this important decision of awarding the site (Potsdamer Platz area) to Daimler-Benz at a very favorable price.' See M. Krätke and F. Schmoll, 'The Local State and Social Restructuring,' *Journal of Urban and Regional Research*, Vol. 15, No. 4, 1991, pp. 542–52.

16. Anne Saeterdal, 'Participation as a Learning Process. The Norwegian Context.' *Cities of Europe, op.cit.*, pp. 329–42, esp. p. 341.

17. Including advisers appearing regularly from the West. Rostock, for example, is advised by Bremen. The councils that were set up in the residential communities follow the Bremen model, though the West German councils have far greater funds at their disposal.

9 Treuhand: The Privatisation of a Planned Economy
Karl H. Kahrs

The Cold War was fought essentially over two fundamentally different ways of organising society, both with claims to universal validity. When the judgement of history was in, the losers hurried to embrace the winning formula: democracy and – the market system.

The prospects for rapid transformation were particularly rosy for East Germany. Where other Eastern European countries were breaking apart after the fall of communism, the GDR was united with the more affluent and larger Federal Republic of *Wirtschaftswunder* and DM fame. The German Democratic Republic had been economically the most successful of the COMECON countries, it had a well trained labour force, a relatively high standard of living, and a long industrial tradition reaching back to pre-communist days. And now the helping hand of the mighty FRG . . . It looked like an invitation to move into a glamorous home, with some loving relatives co-signing the mortgage and making the first interest payments.

It turned out that even under these exceptionally advantageous circumstances the conversion of a system of command planning and public ownership into a market system with private ownership of the means of production is a very difficult and painful process. Much of the anger and criticism over this was directed against the agency commissioned by the government to privatise the state-owned companies if possible and to close down the rest.

TREUHANDANSTALT: A VEHICLE FOR TRANSFORMATION

On March 1, 1990, the last communist government of the GDR, headed by Prime Minister Hans Modrow (SED), established the *Treuhandanstalt* (Trustee Agency) in order to convert state-owned enterprises into western-type joint stock corporations or limited liability companies capable of operating in a market system.[1] While the privatisation of small and medium-sized firms was part of the plan, public ownership was to remain an important element of the restructured East German economy. The emphasis was on enabling western capital to enter into joint ventures with East German companies.

The government of Prime Minister Lothar de Maizière (CDU), formed after the elections of March 18, 1990, committed itself immediately to rapid unification with the Federal Republic of Germany. One of the more practical steps toward this goal was the enactment of the *Treuhandgesetz*, a law clarifying the assignment of the already existing Trustee Agency and focusing it on privatisation. The first paragraph of the law states clearly:

> The state-owned property is to be privatised. In cases to be determined by law, state-owned property may also be transferred into the ownership of local communes, cities, counties, and states (*Länder*), as well as public agencies.[2]

The Unification Treaty of July 31, 1990, put the *Treuhandanstalt* under the authority of the Finance Ministry in Bonn and affirmed one more time the statutory mandate of the agency in Article 25 by charging it with 'restructuring and privatising the formerly state-owned enterprises and to prepare them for the demands of a competitive market economy'.[3] In cases where the transfer to new owners should prove impossible on account of a lack of economic viability, a liquidation of the firm would be called for.

The task ahead was formidable indeed. The publicly owned enterprises to be privatised included some 8500 state-owned industrial enterprises, substantial property holdings, and about 25 000 small shops, restaurants, hotels, cinemas, etc. The *Treuhand* had to take immediate control without the benefit of financial balance sheets or profit-and-loss statements; in fact, it was not even aware of the existence of all the establishments it was to take charge of. As temporary custodian of the East German economy the *Treuhandanstalt* had become overnight the world's largest holding company. The independence bestowed upon the privatisation agency was as unprecedented as it was necessary to allow the *Treuhand* to make the difficult and often unpopular decisions that lay ahead.

An Unprecedented Transformation

The course from a planned economy to a market economy was uncharted; there was no blueprint to follow. The pace of unification, on the other hand, was relentless. By July 1, 1990, the monetary, economic and social union between the Federal Republic of Germany and the German Democratic Republic took effect, only two weeks after the *Treuhandanstalt* had received its statute. The agency's leadership had to improvise. Mistakes were made; corruption occurred. Adjusting its course by trial and error, the agency exposed itself to criticism from all sides. Businessmen complained about red tape and delays, trade unionists were alarmed by lost jobs, the media emphasised the hardships imposed, bankers saw good money being thrown after bad – and the people were befuddled and resentful, seeing the efforts of 40 years of socialism go to waste. Exposing the rotten legacy of 'actually existing socialism' backfired on the messenger.

Treuhand president Detlev Karsten Rohwedder, who had previously made a name for himself as a top aide in the economics ministry in Bonn and then as CEO and rescuer of the ailing Dortmund steel combine Hoesch, became the real organizer of the *Treuhandanstalt* in its pioneering period. As president he chaired a management board of nine, headquartered in Hermann Goering's old Air Ministry in East Berlin. This management team is operating under the watchful eyes of a 23-member supervisory board, consisting of the prime ministers (governors) of the new federal states, representatives of the employers, trade unions, and banks. Even a foreigner from Belgium is included. The affairs of the larger combines are handled directly by the Berlin office, which employs about 3000 people. Only about a third of these employees are easterners. There are also fifteen regional branch offices, responsible for the privatisation of firms with less than 1500 employees. At the outset, East Germans headed these regional branches, but in October of 1990 all 5 of them were replaced, some because they had incriminated themselves politically, others for lacking professional competence.

The predominance of Westerners in the leading positions is resented in Eastern Germany understandably, but the reasons given for this apparent imbalance are convincing. There is a lack of Eastern experts, versed in (Western) corporate law, business accounting, and international banking and management practices. The *Treuhand* estimated at one time a shortage of 13 000 managers for the companies under its control. A certain arrogance of the know-it-all Westerners ('*Besserwessis*') certainly contributes to the resentment, but the problem has its origin in differences in training and experience of managerial personnel. Management in the old GDR was production-oriented, i.e. the production goals were set by the planning authorities, and management had to meet those targets timely and efficiently. This is quite different from

market-oriented management, where marketability of the products is
the alpha and omega of management concern. A good part of the
friction between Ossis and Wessis has its origin right there. While the
former feel frustrated by the existence of idle capacities and hands,
the latter sweat over product design, cost analysis, marketability, service arrangements, advertising, and, last but not least, the bottom line
of the balance sheet.

The unification negotiators added another complication by impos-
ing the entire body of West German law on the new *Länder* – commercial and corporate law, tax and zoning laws, environmental and
consumer protection, administrative law, labour and welfare regulations, etc. Naturally, the new *Länder* lacked the administrative experts
capable of handling this complex legal system. This led to delays and
frustration, and to the need for help from Western bureaucrats.

Taking the Heat

The late *Treuhand* president Detlev Karsten Rohwedder set the agency's
priorities in a memorandum which was to become his legacy:

• fast privatisation
• resolute restructuring
• prudent closure.[4]

Critics claimed that the agency's policy is one of selling off as many
companies as possible as quickly as possible and that this was de-
stroying the socio-economic fabric of the five new federal states.
Rohwedder was very much aware that the *Treuhand* was becoming
the 'whipping boy of the nation'. In a shocking way President Rohwedder
became a victim of all this. On April 1, 1991, he was shot dead in his
Duesseldorf home by a sniper of the Red Army Faction (RAF), a terrorist group tracing its history to the infamous Baader-Meinhof gang
of the sixties and seventies. In their twisted minds they apparently
believed that they were committing a popular deed by killing the man
who sold the 'people's property' to capitalist owners.

The search for a successor ended with the appointment of Birgit
Breuel, who comes from a well established Hamburg banking family,
is a member of the CDU, and had previously served as cabinet minister for economic affairs in the western state of Lower Saxony. She is
sometimes compared with another pugnacious lady, Margaret Thatcher,
because of her stern demeanour and strong belief in a free market
economy.

Policies and Performance

As of the end of 1991, almost 5000 enterprises had been sold and the new owners had pledged to invest some $62.5 billion in the years ahead. Early in 1992 the *Treuhand* was selling off an average of 20 companies a day. About 800 companies had been closed down. The privatisation of small commercial establishments, such as retail shops, bookstores, cinemas, restaurants, small hotels, pharmacies, and travel agencies, was actually completed. Some 22 300 units had found new owners, more than 70 per cent of them being Easterners. However, other firms were shut down, and only 120 000 of 280 000 jobs were saved. President Birgit Breuel felt confident that her Trustee Agency would finish its original objective by the end of 1994. Only contract controlling would be required beyond that.[5] That may be easier said than done, however. The choice properties (*'Filetstuecke'*) were gone by now, and the remaining enterprises had to be reorganised or split up, debts had to be forgiven, or new management had to be brought in. Other firms needed loans or loan guarantees.

Nevertheless, at the beginning of 1994 the *Treuhand* still held 950 companies with 233 000 employees. Most of these firms were to be privatised shortly or shut down. For 266 enterprises with about 100 000 employees no plans existed. The agency's deficit was expected to reach DM 275 billion by the end of 1994, its final year of operation.[6]

At the outset it was assumed that the well-established export connections of East German firms with the COMECON trading area would be an important asset. However, as East Germany was becoming a hard-currency area of July 1, 1990, the former Soviet bloc countries were turning one by one toward market reforms and opening up toward the world market. The attempt to sustain the old trade relations in order to keep East Germany's capacities busy and the workers employed was largely futile because most of the old customers were either no longer able to pay or, to the extent that they did have hard currency, they could now shop on the world market. Most Eastern German companies lost out against Western and Asian competitors. Even if they were able to match quality, they could not cover their costs without government subsidies. The insulated COMECON market, in which the GDR had played a star role, was simply disappearing.

Further complicating the work of the *Treuhand* was the need to settle the ownership question before selling any property. Some claims go back to the Nazi period (1933–45), others result from expropriations under GDR authority (1949–89). In a joint declaration of the two German governments from June 15, 1990,[7] all expropriations undertaken by the Soviet occupation power in the years from 1945 to 1949 were accepted as irreversible. An appeal challenging the constitutionality of this agreement was rejected by the Federal Constitutional Court on April 23, 1991. This was a significant relief for the *Treuhand* because some 45 per cent of the properties in its trust involved expropriations from 1945 to 1949.

Nevertheless, it will probably take up to ten years to settle the 1.2 million applications, representing some 2 million claims pending. So far only 67 000 cases have been resolved. Saxony's minister president, Kurt Biedenkopf (CDU), called the principle of 'restitution before compensation' a 'major mistake'. Disputes over property rights have deterred investors, delayed plant construction and industrial development. The property law has been twice amended, but now it is so complicated that inexperienced local authorities are afraid of making decisions for fear of lawsuits.[8]

A particularly depressing example of the compound problems of industrial restructuring presents itself in the area of Halle/Merseburg and Bitterfeld/Wolfen. Based on the locally mined potash and brown coal, this region had developed into a centre of chemical industry and also one of the most polluted areas of Europe. Water and air quality have been improved since unification, but mainly as a consequence of drastically reduced production. In 1989 the chemical industry employed 155 000 people here; in 1990 production was down by 60 per cent and the labour force was reduced to 90 000. It is estimated that employment will ultimately stabilise at 20 000.[9]

In the meantime, the Trustee Agency has sold off the oil refineries of Leuna to an international consortium by packaging them together with a chain of Minol gas stations. The Buna A. G., after being switched from brown coal to oil-based production, has been taken over by the state of Saxony-Anhalt. In May of 1992, the *Treuhand* decided to help the teetering Chemie A. G. of Bitterfeld-Wolfen by granting an interest-free loan of DM 80 million toward the implementation of its restructuring concept, despite a recorded DM 100 million loss in 1991. Attempts to privatise the photographic and chemical plants had failed. The new plan is to separate the viable ORWO film business from the rest of the complex, which would continue as property management company only. It will try to sell off the remaining real estate and individual plants in an effort to create a more diversified industrial park. The effort is clearly motivated by the need to provide some social stability in this region that had once been the pride of the GDR and its lionized chemical workers.[10]

The record card of the agency after two years in operation is rather impressive. By the end of June 1992, 8175 firms and parts of companies[11] had been sold and 8048 pieces of real estate had been privatised. Some 1500 divestments were by management buy-out. All these sales together resulted in investment pledges of DM 144 billion (about $97 billion). The agency claimed to have thus secured 1.22 million jobs.[12] On the down side, it also needs to be reported that of the about four million people employed by the state-owned enterprises taken over by the *Treuhand* many have lost their jobs. While a good number have found work in private industry, others took early retirement or joined retraining programmes. About three thousand firms are still awaiting privatisation or shutdown. Presently only about a million people are still working in companies under the agency's control. It comes as no surprise that there have been workers' demonstrations at the doorsteps of the *Treuhand*.

A Clearance Sale with Complications

Those who had hoped that privatisation would pay for itself were certainly wrong. The balance sheet deficit of the 8,500 state-owned companies entrusted to the *Treuhand* was calculated with hindsight to have amounted to DM 209 billion (about $139 billion) on July 1, 1990. According to the same independent report the companies represented a value of not more than DM 81 billion.[13] Obviously, the *Treuhand* is in no shape to generate a profit. By the end of June, 1992, the agency had brought in DM 30.7 billion (about $21 billion) in revenues. But its total debts were estimated to reach DM 135 billion (about $90 billion) by the end of 1992. This includes DM 55 billion in new liabilities and DM 85 billion in pre-unification debts assumed by the agency and compensation of former owners of sold properties. It does not include the costs for cleaning up environmental damages. By the end of 1994 the overall debt of the Trustee Agency is expected to exceed DM 200 billion, excluding still undetermined environmental costs.

Selling off enterprises should, of course, bring in money, but the *Treuhand* had to consider other factors than the highest bid. It looked at trade-ins, such as investment pledges and job guarantees. This meant, for example, that the German chemical giant BASF paid nothing for a plant in Schwarzheide near Dresden, but obligated itself contractually to invest DM 500 million. Needless to say, such promises are secured by contractual penalties, to be imposed in case of unfulfilled pledges. The *Treuhand* can also improve the attractiveness of a company for prospective buyers by unburdening the firm of debt obligations accrued before unification or of environmental cleanup costs. After all, it makes no sense to privatise and see the new owner go into bankruptcy, as has happened.

All of this makes the privatisation transactions not exactly transparent. Foreigners in particular have complained about unfairness, but *Treuhand* has made extra efforts to refute such charges. Actually, foreign companies have bought shares in 523 Eastern German companies. In general, the Europeans have shown the greatest interest in buying agency-held companies; but the *Treuhandanstalt* has also opened offices in New York and Tokyo in the hope of generating interest. American corporations, such as Ford, General Motors, Philip Morris, Reynolds, Coca-Cola, Procter & Gamble, and Otis Elevator, have already made major commitments in the former GDR. U.S. management consultants, like Goldman, Sachs & Co, are under contract to assist prospective buyers with their special expertise.

CRIME AND CORRUPTION

In this somewhat opaque environment there is also, of course, the opportunity for outright corruption. A fair price for privatisation is hard to establish. There are no market values to go by, and the capitalisation of potential future earnings is equally difficult. The temptation of extending special favours to friends or partners and accepting bribes or kickbacks in return is enormous. After all, millions are being made here!

The German buzzword referring to the old-boy network of former communist officials is '*Seilschaft*', literally a roped party of mountain climbers. Such cliques in some cases managed to plunder the 'people's property' through embezzlement or fraudulent shifting of assets to firms controlled by their partners in crime. They also often tried to secure their loot by taking in western equity participation to extend West German legal protection of private property to their dubious acquisitions. Needless to say, con artists from Western Germany also ventured out on their own, by filing fraudulent claims, cheating unsuspecting Ossis out of real estate or business property, or selling their questionable know-how.

The chief public prosecutor assigned to deal with such business crimes believes, however, that the greatest damage was done by another scheme, which is much more difficult to uncover. In these cases managers of Eastern German firms or even employees of the *Treuhand* deliberately mismanaged state-owned companies to drive down the purchasing price for the benefit of Western co-conspirators, who sometimes paid nothing or even got substantial bonuses, just to take these apparently worthless objects off the *Treuhand*'s hands. After privatisation such firms often recovered rather miraculously.

Many Easterners are furious that some of the former communist functionaries who helped to run the GDR into the ground, continue to thrive as businessmen, protected by their clique's network. The *Treuhandstalt* has instituted an ombudsman to whom citizens can report dubious transactions. However, the agency has difficulties following up on thousands of reported cases. Many documents have been destroyed. It will take many years for the judicial authorities to deal with the backlog.[14] This makes it the more puzzling that the *Treuhand*'s in-house prosecutorial office, which had uncovered embezzlements involving some DM 3 billion and initiated some 300 criminal investigations leading to the dismissal of 70 agency employees, was abolished in the autumn of 1992. This leaves the prosecution of future cases to the already overburdened state attorney's office in Berlin.[15]

The Trustee Agency has also been accused of perpetuating the monopolistic structure of Eastern German industry by favouring privatisation in large units. While medium-sized industrial companies are the backbone of the West German economy, the development of this sector has been lagging behind in the new federal states. To achieve a similar structure as in the West, some 20 000 small and medium-sized firms would have to be created, but only a fourth of that have actually been set up. The situation in the trade sector is also characterised by an over-representation of large companies. Experts are warning against the domination of regional markets by single companies. In the eyes of the common Ossi all of this looks suspiciously like 'monopoly capitalism', the bogeyman of the communists.[16]

UNDER FIRE FROM LEFT AND RIGHT, EAST AND WEST

There is one kind of criticism that is historically irrelevant by now and deserves little more than polite sympathy. It comes from people having difficulties in letting go of their socialist dreams; and among them are by no means only diehard communists but also some of the most courageous and admirable revolutionaries of 1989. They would have liked to try socialism just one more time and to do it right this time around. To their misfortune, there was no constituency for another socialist experiment. When the people had the choice between 'the socialist alternative on German soil'[17] and the FRG's 'social market economy', they opted overwhelmingly for the latter. One may regret that, but that is that.

Citizen activists have complained that because of the absorption of the GDR by the overpowering Federal Republic, the East Germans never had a chance to bring into the unification bargain their very own social experiences and desires. There is no denying however that, for example, the results of the Round Table discussions were simply swept aside by a wave of enthusiasm for 'Deutschland, einig Vaterland!' The government in Bonn certainly did its part to fire up this patriotic groundswell, but the demonstrators in the streets of Leipzig also threatened to go West: 'If the DM is not coming to us, we'll get to it by bus!'[18]

Unfortunately, some of the disgruntled critics of unification have become apologists of the old system. It comes as no surprise, then, that they see nothing but failure in the work of the *Treuhand*. The East Germans demonstrated and voted for unification with the more successful and larger Federal Republic. The West Germans, on the other hand, were in no mood to renegotiate their social contract. To put it cruelly: once the DM steam roller got moving, Bonn called the shots and that meant privatisation and transformation in line with the Western model. The *Treuhand* is, in a sense, carrying out the verdict of history; it is completing the restoration of Germany's bourgeois society.

One should also not overlook the environment of the European Community. The enlarged Federal Republic of Germany became part of the Single European Market on January 1, 1993. The rest of Europe would have been scared to death by a united Germany heading down another '*Sonderweg*'. In all likelihood they would have found a way to block it. The privatisation of the Baltic shipyards demonstrates the influence of the European Community. After long negotiations with prospective buyers, regional politicians, and trade unionists, the Trustee Agency awarded the Rostock shipyards to the Norwegian Kvaerner group and the Wismar yards to Vulkan of Bremen. The agreement required, however, the approval of the EC because of the government subsidies involved. The European Community concurred, contingent on a reduction of the shipbuilding capacity by 40 per cent. This implied slashing the workforce to 10 000 in an industry that had once employed 51 650.[19]

A quite different position in the debate is articulated by the advocates of laissez faire. To them the job of the *Treuhand* is to preside over one big bankruptcy sale, pure and simple. They believe in speedy privatisation at any cost, the mythical healing forces of the market, and 'creative destruction' (Joseph A. Schumpeter) for those enterprises that can not find a buyer, because they are not viable. Coddling ailing enterprises is a waste of resources to them. This, however, is much too narrow a view and hardly a responsible public policy option, because it ignores or belittles all wider social ramifications. What about unemployment caused by such reckless policy, emigration of the jobless, political unrest? The advocacy of unfettered free enterprise as the only economically rational solution is little more than the lobbying position of self-centred business interests.

Keeping corporations in business creates social benefits not fully reflected in profit-and-loss accounting. The avoidance of unemployment is the obvious one, but retaining a functioning workforce and keeping experienced research and development teams together are additional advantages over starting from scratch. If there is a market for its products at all, salvaging the enterprise incurs fewer social costs than letting it collapse.

While the Trustee Agency was commissioned to privatise the planned GDR economy and to release its components into a competitive environment, the desired result was certainly not cut-throat capitalism. 'Social market economy' has been the trademark of the West German economy since the days of Ludwig Erhard. During the 1950s various subsidy programmes existed to support basic industries, housing, shipbuilding, etc. There is ample precedent for public support of ailing industries. In the same spirit, the *Treuhand* has set out to buffer the social impact of the unavoidably painful transition. But the *Treuhand* is not set up to function as a super-ministry – a central planning commission, if you wish – responsible for industrial and structural policies, regional planning, employment and social policies. Such policies would have to come from the national and state governments.

The *Treuhandanstalt* has been called a 'slaughterhouse' (Fritz Steinkuehler, I. G. Metall), 'complacent and a failure' (Heiner Geissler, CDU), and it has been accused of 'calculating firms out of business' (Manfred Stolpe, SPD).[20] The main thrust of the criticism appears to be that the agency thinks exclusively in terms of the alternative between privatisation and liquidation. If an object cannot be sold, the trustees do little more than downsizing the company (sometimes at the expense of R. & D.) and providing liquidity until a buyer comes along. Critics demand a more constructive reorganisation effort through providing support for product development, for modernisation and marketing. However, the original assignment of the *Treuhand* did not include such entrepreneurial responsibilities.

Keeping companies in public hands is, as such, hardly objectionable if a credible viability plan exists. Carl Zeiss Jena was saved by a DM 2.8 billion subsidy from *Treuhand*, designated to streamlining the company. Management of the firm will be in the hands of the western German company with the same name, while Jenoptik GmbH, owned entirely by the state of Thuringia, will hold 49 per cent of the capital. Carl Zeiss Jena will keep only 2800 of the 25 000 employees, but Jenoptik will employ another 6800. This solution, combining public and private resources, is crucial for the entire region of Thuringia.[21]

Even though there is little enthusiasm for public solutions in the present Bonn government, the political pressure has forced them to ease up on seeing only the alternative of privatisation or close-down. The Trustee Agency has recently created ten management holdings to assist more vigorously with reorganisation and to hold off on massive closings. Such expanded support will, of course, require even greater expenditures by the *Treuhand*. The agency's limit for raising loans had been DM 25 billion annually. The Federal Government has now asked the Bundestag to increase the limit, allowing the *Treuhand* to go an additional DM 114 billion into debt till 1994.[22]

Some enterprises will undoubtedly remain in public hands for quite some time or for good. Even if a buyer can not be found, it can not be ignored that the economic survival of entire regions often depends on the fate of a single employer. In those cases local and provincial governments will have to take control with or without federal support. The danger is, of course, that such state-holding companies might become permanent sick bays for ailing industries, requiring a never ending flow of subsidies.

But then, publicly owned corporations are not entirely unknown in Western Germany either. Not only the railways, the postal and tele-communications services are public in the Federal Republic, but a great number of savings banks, insurance companies, and utilities are. Despite all postwar efforts to divest itself of industrial holdings, the government is still a shareholder in Lufthansa, Volkswagen, Saarbergwerke, etc. However, Bonn is again considering to sell off these vestiges of the past. Thus there is little enthusiasm for taking on an entrepreneurial role in Eastern Germany. But political pressure resulting from mass unemployment and looming deindustrialisation of the new *Länder* may force the hands of the reluctant.

CONCLUSIONS

The belief that a clearance sale of public enterprises, combined with the introduction of the almighty DM and a little help from the mystical forces of the free market, would lead to an instant *Wirtschaftswunder* in the former GDR has turned out to be an illusion. With hindsight it is easy to detect mistakes that were made. Critics see a nightmare of errors, misjudgements, and omissions. One can hardly accuse Bonn of not spending enough in the new federal states; the problem is, though, that much of the money was squandered. Why didn't they think this through before acting? The truth is that a perfectly planned transition from a planned economy to a market economy is probably as much of an illusion as a perfectly planned economy.

The *Treuhandanstalt* has done a respectable job in privatising thousands of formerly state-owned enterprises. It has been criticised mainly for doing what it was supposed to do: privatise, reorganise, and close down. Criticism is not going to subside because the toughest calls are still ahead. Almost the entire mechanical engineering sector, parts of the chemical industry, and steel making are still under trusteeship without viable buyers in sight. All of these industries suffer from their loss of markets in the East, their inability to export to the West due to their high production costs, the strong DM – and the recession. But they also used to be the core sectors of industrial employment.

A clear separation of governmental policy functions from the custodial asset management assigned to the *Treuhand* seems to be just as desirable as the separation of the latter from the entrepreneurial function, which should remain with the individual firm. If the government does not want a particular closing for political reasons, it should intervene and not hide behind a bureaucratic agency made up of experts on reorganising ailing companies or liquidating them. The creation of the *Treuhand* was once praised as a 'master-stroke', because it set up a perfect scapegoat while removing the decision makers from direct political accountability. However, in the case of clearly political rather than technocratic decisions the *Bundestag* and the *Länder* parliaments should exercise their due responsibility.

In 1991 DM 170 billion of public monies were transferred from the old to the new German states, and in 1992 it was DM 218 billion. In December 1993 the official unemployment rate in the Western part of Germany was 8.1 per cent; in the Eastern part it was 15.4 per cent. The real unemployment in the five new *Länder*, including the redundancies hidden behind early retirement and retraining, is likely to exceed twenty per cent. The GDP of Eastern Germany came to DM 183 billion, which was about 6.6 per cent of the overall GDP of Germany. According to calculations, the non-commercial sector (government, private households, non-profit organisations) generated 23.7 per cent of the eastern GDP in 1991, as against only 14 per cent in the West.[23] These figures prove that much of the increased living standard in Eastern Germany is earned in the West, and that will remain so for some time to come. It will take major investments on the part of private industry to rectify this imbalance. Without it, the migration from East to West will continue and so will the resentment of the taxpayer in the West.

In the end the '*Aufschwung Ost*' (recovery-East) may not come from the successful sale of the old GDR industries, but from new investments, starting from scratch, avoiding the messy heritage of established firms. The Japanese and many MNCs clearly prefer this route. With the help of Bonn's efforts to put in a new infrastructure (roads, telephone networks) brand new projects must ultimately create the jobs lost in the old industries. But many companies that have profited most from unification by supplying the new markets with goods produced in the West have not been ploughing their profits back into Eastern Germany. The *Bundesbank* estimated that West German firms invested in 1991 about DM 100 billion abroad but only DM 25 billion in the new *Länder*. Responding to an economic downturn, some major companies, like Mercedes-Benz, Heidelberger Druckmaschinen A. G., and Holtzmann & Cie. A. G., have actually backed away from earlier commitments to invest in the East.[24]

The trade unions have made mistakes too. With productivity in the East being only a third of what it is in the West, the demand for equal wages will remove the competitive edge of Eastern enterprises. On the other hand, workers in the West fear that their jobs may wander Eastward, following the comparative advantages offered by the new *Länder*. Taxpayers, business, unions, and governments will have to pull together behind a major national effort. But even with such an effort it will take a little longer to close the gap between East and

West than Chancellor Kohl had promised – and it will take an upturn in the global economy.

Notes

1. Beschluss des Ministerrates der DDR zur Gruendung der Anstalt zur treuhaenderischen Verwaltung des Volkseigentums (Treuhandanstalt) vom 1.3.1990 and Verordnung zur Umwandlung von volkseigenen Kombinaten, Betrieben und Einrichtungen in Kapitalgesellschaften vom 1.3.1990, *Gesetzblatt der DDR*, Teil 1, Nr. 14/1990.
2. Gesetz zur Privatisierung und Reorganisation des volkseigenen Vermoegens (Treuhandgesetz) vom 17.6.1990, *Gesetzblatt der DDR*, Teil 1, Nr. 33/1990.
3. Presse und Informationsamt der Bundesregierung, "Einigungsvertrag," *Bulletin*, Nr. 104, Sept. 9, 1990, p. 883.
4. Detlev K. Rohwedder, 'Brief an alle Mitarbeiterinnen und Mitarbeiter der Treuhand-Anstalt', *Die Zeit*, April 15, 1991.
5. Birgit Breuel, 'Der Aufschwung im Osten beginnt im Sommer', *Hamburger Abendblatt*, Dec. 27, 1991; and *Die Wirtschaft*, Nr. 35/1991, p. 2.
6. German Information Center, New York, *The Week in Germany*, February 11, 1994, p. 5.
7. Cf. Anlage III of the Unification Treaty ('Gemeinsame Erklaerung... vom 15. Juni 1990) as well as Art. 41(1), which establishes the legal status of the declaration.
8. Cf. Michael Piazolo, 'Ungeklaerte Eigentumsfragen als Hauptinvestitionshindernis in den neuen Bundeslaendern', *Deutschland-Archiv*, Vol. 25 (May 1992), no. 5, pp. 484–91.
9. Cf. Peter Joachim Lapp, 'die neuen Bundeslaender: Sachsen-Anhalt', *Deutschland-Archiv*, vol. 24 (Dec. 1991), no. 12, pp. 1266ff.
10. Manfred Schulze, 'Sunshine reaches out to a blighted town', *Rheinischer Merkur*, June 2, 1992; translated and reprinted in *The German Tribune*, June 19, 1992.
11. The *Treuhand* claimed in 1990 to have taken on only 8000 state-owned firms. This figure was later corrected to about 11 800 units because of the breakup of companies.
12. German Information Center, New York, *The Week in Germany*, July 31, 1992, p. 4.
13. Ibid., Oct. 23, 1992, p. 4.
14. Ferdinand Kroh, 'Cliques and Old-Boy Networks: Power Retention Strategies of the former East German Power Elite', *Aussenpolitik*, (English Edition), vol. 43, no. 2 (2nd Quarter 1992), p. 150.
15. 'Nur noch selektiv', *Der Spiegel*, Oct. 19, 1992, No. 43, p. 169.
16. Thomas Bastar, 'The debt piles up as the Treuhand begins winding down its operation', *Deutsches Allgemeines Sonntagsblatt*, August 21, 1992, reprinted in *The German Tribune*, Sept. 4, 1992, p. 6.
17. Appeal 'Fuer unser Land', Nov. 28, 1989.
18. This is my liberal translation of an authentic poster inscription, reading in German: 'Kommt die DM nicht nach hier, gehen wir zu ihr!'

19. German Information Center, New York, *The Week in Germany*, June 26 1992, p. 4.
20. *Kieler Nachrichten*, Jan. 25, 1992.
21. See reprinted articles in *The German Tribune*, June 30, 1991, p. 8.
22. *Der Spiegel*, Apr. 20, 1992, no. 17, pp. 160f.
23. German Information Center, New York, *The Week in Germany*, June 5, 1992, p. 4; and December 11 1992, p. 4; and January 7, 1994, p. 4.
24. *Der Spiegel*, November 9, 1992, no. 46, pp. 192 ff.

Part III

New Political Rules and Structures

10 The Basic Law and Reunification
Donald P. Kommers

In *The Federal Republic of Germany at Forty*, I summed up the Basic Law's significance with these words: '. . . the Basic Law has been firmly woven into the fabric of West German society and politics; it has become the fertile source of an ever-deepening and widening constitutional tradition. Today . . . the Basic Law enjoys the status of a genuine constitution framed to last in perpetuity.'[1] Now, however, four years later, after Germany's sudden and unexpected reunification, another stocktaking of the Basic Law and its future seems timely, for reunification has sparked new demands for constitutional reappraisal and reform, a task recently undertaken by a newly created parliamentary commission on constitutional revision. In structuring this brief commentary, I (1) describe the setting of the current campaign for constitutional revision, (2) comment on proposed changes in the Basic Law, and (3) assess the likelihood and propriety of constitutional change in reunited Germany.

I BACKGROUND

The Basic Law, as we know, was not conceived in perpetuity. It emerged in 1949 as a provisional document pending Germany's reunification. As originally drafted, the Basic Law would expire on the day when the German people as a whole freely adopt a new constitution. By 1989, however, time – and West Germany's successful experiment in democracy – impressed the Basic Law with the seal of ostensible permanence. In the space of 40 years, Germany had managed to create what Justice Felix Frankfurter once called 'the most difficult of all social arrangements', namely a constitutional democracy that fuses popular government with liberal controls on majority rule. The Federal Republic's architects designed a parliamentary democracy modelled on the institutions and practices endorsed by the Weimar Constitution of 1919, but yoked it to constitutional and structural innovations calculated to secure political stability while guaranteeing individual liberty.[2] Already in 1956, with West Germany on the threshold of an extended era of peace and prosperity, the Federal Constitutional Court confidently announced that the polity created by the Basic Law conformed to the political and social convictions of the German people.

Reunification, however, changed the character and profile of the German people. With the expansion of the Federal Republic's territory to the banks of the Oder-Neisse, which added the German Democratic Republic's 16 million people to its population, Germany became more Protestant, more eastern-oriented, more socially and politically diverse and, owing to decades of communist indoctrination and propaganda in the GDR, more secular and non-religious in its outlook on life. For many people, Germany had taken on a new identity, raising questions about the 'fit' between West Germany's Basic Law and the new Germany. German unity, be it remembered, occurred at a moment of extraordinary political mobilisation, a moment that Germans might have seized to reconstitute themselves as a nation through the adoption of a new constitution. But for well-documented reasons, East Germans chose to become part of the Federal Republic within the framework of the Basic Law.

On the other hand, it is worth recalling that the dissident groups in the vanguard of the GDR's bloodless revolution were concerned mainly with the constitutional identity of East Germany. For these groups, dominated by educators, artists, and clergymen and headed by 'The New Forum', a rare transformative moment had arrived. Basking in the glow of a victory that led to the breaching of the Berlin Wall on 9 November 1989, they seized the moment to draft a new constitution that would chart a third way between capitalism and state socialism.[3] They had no plans to unify Germany, at least in the short run. Rather, they wanted to put an end to the police state, to democratise their political system, and to retain the values of sociality and solidarity that would provide socialism with a human face. These plans and hopes were dashed, however, in the March 18, 1990 East German election, the first free election on East German territory in nearly 60 years, when GDR voters themselves dictated the stride of history. They chose immediate reunification and largely on West German terms. A few months later the GDR became part of the Federal Republic under the accession clause of Article 23, thereby extending the reach of the Basic Law to all of Germany.

Constitutive moments in history do not last long. If they are not seized when the popular mood is ripe for transformative change, they may be lost forever. Its original initiative having been rejected by the voting masses, the New Forum lost its chance to transform East Germany into a model socialist state.[4] Its loss, however, provided Germans with yet another constitutive moment, for the Basic Law itself, as already noted, offered *reunited* Germany a chance to make a fresh start under a new constitution. One possible scenario, sanctioned by Article 146 of the Basic Law, envisioned the dissolution of both German governments, the drafting of a new constitution by an elected all-German constituent assembly, its ratification in a popular referendum, and then the election and formation of an all-German government in accord with it. Cogent arguments supported such a reconstitution of the German people: one claimed that a new constitution would more accurately reflect the identity and values of the new Germany; another insisted that its popular ratification would bestow on it the legitimacy never enjoyed by the Basic Law.

These arguments, however, succumbed to the impatience of German leaders determined to remake East Germany in the image of the West. The State Treaty on Monetary, Economic, and Social Union, ratified within a month of the 18 March election – a constitutive moment in its own right – set the pace of events. Any de-escalation of the pace to allow time for the crafting of a new constitution may have blocked the path toward instant unity. The international context was also critical. A thaw in U.S.–Soviet relations, Gorbachev's policies of *glasnost* and *perestroika*, and the liberal revolutions taking place in the satellite countries of Eastern Europe set the stage for German unity and the Two-Plus-Four Peace Treaty that closed the door on the Second World War. Opportunistic West German leadership, backed by the ballots of GDR voters, seized this particular moment in history to achieve unity *now* under the Basic Law. Lest the previous sentence be construed as faint praise, it could also be argued – as many Germans did argue, in contrast to those who would have preferred a new constitution – that the Basic Law itself reflected the best hopes and aspirations of the German people as a whole.

Nevertheless, forging unity within the framework of the Basic Law required some constitutional surgery. Indeed, as we shall see, besides amending the Basic Law in crucial respects to reflect the reality of a changed Germany, the Unity Treaty urged the GDR and FRG governments to consider certain changes in the Basic Law within two to five years. Of course, the Basic Law was never a settled script. No living constitution is, for any such document is always in the process of recreation, by interpretation if not by amendment. 'Every society,' as Alasdair MacIntyre has written, 'enacts its own history as a more or less coherent dramatic narrative, a story in which each of us has to find his or her own place as a character, in order to know how to participate in it and how to continue it further.' When East Germans were given the opportunity to vote freely, they rejected their existing government. But did they reject their history or, as Lothar Maizière put it, the 'personal biography' of the East German people?

The Basic Law and its authoritative interpretation over a period of 45 years, in times both of stress and calm, has spun a dramatic and impressive epic in constitutional democracy. The question is whether East Germans are ready to become full participants in this grand narrative or whether something more is required *constitutionally* to integrate East Germans into the Federal Republic's common life. Current efforts to graft features of East Germany's 'personal biography' on to the Basic Law, and more generally to update it, are calculated, at least in part, to bring a feeling of oneness to the German people, thus averting another identity crisis.

II REAPPRAISAL

The Unity Treaty: Catalyst for Constitutional Reform

Out of consideration for East Germany's vital interests, the Unity Treaty amended the Basic Law in several particulars. We can pass over provisions that repealed Article 23 and expunged all other references to the goal of unity or the recovery of other lost German territory. These changes, together with parallel provisions in the Two-Plus-Four Treaty, froze the all-German border at the Oder-Neisse line, legally foreclosing any further German claims to territory lost as a consequence of the Second World War. We can also pass over modifications in the Basic Law's federal structures and relationships necessitated by the 'accession' (*Beitritt*) of five new eastern *Länder*.[5] More important for present purposes are provisions of the Treaty (1) creating a new Article 143, (2) amending Article 146, and (3) recommending future amendments to the Constitution.

The Unity Treaty's insertion of Article 143 into the Basic Law showed that the Berlin Wall was not the only barrier separating East and West Germans. In short, the new article allowed the Eastern *Länder* to deviate from the terms of the Basic Law for a limited period in those areas where compliance with it would be impossible under existing social and economic conditions or inflict considerable hardship on former GDR residents. Sensitive policy areas temporarily released from the Constitution's grip were abortion, property-settlements, and federal-state relations dealing with the apportionment of tax receipts, equalisation payments, and revenue sharing. The deviations permitted here were very few but necessary to keep the unity train on its fast track.

Accordingly, as with abortion,[6] different policies would be followed in the old and new *Länder* until the adoption by a specified date, of a national uniform policy. Whether the Basic Law could be suspended in this way, even for a good purpose, was itself a matter of constitutional debate, but for present purposes the resolution of this complicated issue is less important than our discussion of the perceived need for some rethinking of the Basic Law in the face of east-west differences. A rethinking of the Constitution might have gone forward even in the absence of German unity, for constitutional reform has long been on the agenda of both liberal and conservative groups in the Federal Republic, with proposals ranging from a few institutional adjustments to the total revision of the Basic Law.

The Unity Treaty's amendment of Article 146 added to the pressure for constitutional revision. Germans fully satisfied with the Basic Law and convinced of its applicability to all of Germany argued originally in favour of repealing Article 146. Instead, at the insistence of Social Democrats and their East German supporters, it was retained in amended form. Recall that under Article 146, the Basic Law provided for its own termination on the day when a reunited Germany freely adopts a new constitution. Article 146 now reads: 'This Basic Law, *which is valid for the entire German people following the achievement of the unity and freedom of Germany*, shall cease to be in force on the day on which a constitution adopted by a free decision of the German people comes into force' (amended part in italics). The retention of the Article's main clause appears to continue the Basic Law's contingent status.

It is also possible to suggest that Article 146 as amended is a meaningless appendage on the Basic Law in the light of the GDR's accession under Article 23, the provision that automatically extends the reach of the Basic Law to former German territories voluntarily 'acceding' to the Federal Republic. Article 146 appears to have been retained at the insistence of West Germans, particularly Social Democrats, resolved to secure the popular approval of the Basic Law itself. (The Basic Law was originally ratified by the parliaments of the various states.)

Actually, Article 146 as amended needs to be read in the light of the Unity Treaty's Article 5, pursuant to which an all-German parliament would consider additional amendments to deal with the reality of a reunified nation. Among the possible changes mentioned were the introduction of state objectives into the Constitution and the invocation of Article 146 for the purpose of holding a popular referendum on the Basic Law. The reference to a referendum confirms the prevailing view that the intent behind Article 146 was not the drafting of a new constitution, but rather to keep open the possibility of a referendum on the existing constitution which, if approved, would render Article 146 superfluous, effectively repealing it.

Joint Commission on Constitutional Reform

In the Spring of 1991, the ruling coalition of Christian and Free Democrats, rejecting a Social Democratic proposal to form a 120 member extra-parliamentary council to propose revisions of the Basic Law, established a joint legislative commission on constitutional revision chaired by Rupert Scholz (CDU), a distinguished constitutional scholar and respected figure in the Bundestag. Composed of 64 members, 32 from the Bundestag and 32 from the Bundesrat,[7] the commission's mandate, following the recommendation of the Unity Treaty, is to consider incorporating state objectives and other changes into the Basic Law as a consequence of German reunification. The commission convened on January 16, 1992; its recommendations would be ready by March 31, 1993.

The original skirmish over whether to create a parliamentary commission or a council of revision independent of parliament was really an intra-German debate over how much constitutional change was necessary. Those who favoured fundamental alterations in the Basic Law preferred a council of revision with wide public representation, whereas those in favour of a parliamentary commission were inclined to minimise the need for major constitutional surgery. Also colouring the disagreement were attitudes toward the East. Those who felt that the experience and condition of the old GDR offered important lessons for organising the common life of all Germans spoke up for an independent council. Those favouring a parliamentary commission were unconvinced of the reality of a *qualitatively* new Germany in the wake of reunification; in their view, all that was necessary were constitutional adjustments designed to meet the needs of an expanded territory and the movement for a more perfect European union.

It would indeed appear that a commission dominated by legislators with a vested interest in existing political and constitutional arrangements was unlikely to endorse fundamental changes in the Basic Law.[8] The commission, however, has solicited and considered proposals for constitutional change from a wide circle of governmental and nongovernmental sources. These include state and federal governments, political parties, and a large number of constitutional scholars ranging from Ulrich Preuss (Bremen University) and Erhard Denninger (Frankfurt University) on the left to Klaus Stern (Cologne University) and Josef Isensee (Bonn University) on the right. The following list includes the most important of the suggested changes in the Basic law. The listing warrants some general remarks.

Proposed Amendments

Subject of Amendment	*Article Amended*
A. Privatisation of Aviation Control	article 87d
B. Privatisation of Federal Postal and Railway systems	new provision
C. Basic Law and European Community	
– expanded right of consent for Bundesrat	article 24
– voting by EC citizens in local elections	article 28
– relation between German & EC central banks	article 88
D. Division of Powers between Federation and *Länder*	
– enumeration of reserved powers of *Länder*	article 30
– expansion of Bundesrat's right of consent	article 72 (1)
– exclusive federal authority extended to refugees and compensation for victims of war, imprisonment, and persecution	article 73 (5)
– exclusive federal authority extended to federal highways and long-haul traffic	article 73 (12)
– curtailment of framework legislation over education, press, and film industry	article 75
– expansion of framework legislation over protection of German cultural treasures, real estate transactions, land law, and agricultural leases	article 83
– curtailment of certain joint tasks between	

federation and *Länder*	article 91a
– expansion of Constitutional Court's power to hear federal-state conflicts	article 93 (2)

E. State Objectives and Basic Rights

– protection of minorities	new provision
– protection of natural environment	new provision
– fostering peaceful relations among nations	new provision
– guaranteed right to employment	new provision
– guarantee of adequate housing	new provision
– education and culture as public tasks	new provision
– guarantee of social market economy	new provision
– guarantee of social security and medical care	new provision
– right to informational self-determination	new provision
– labour's right to codetermination	new provision
– expanding definition of citizenship	article 116
– limiting right to asylum	article 16 (2)

F. Parliamentary Law and Citizen Participation

– expansion of rights of investigating committees and opposition parties	article 44
– right of Bundestag to dissolve itself	new provision
– extend parliamentary term from four to five years	article 38
– determination of legislative salaries by extra-parliamentary body	new provision
– public financing of political parties	new provision
– limit federal president to one 7 year term	article 54 (2)
– adoption of initiative and referendum at federal level	new provision
– application of article 146	article 146

G. Right of Resident Aliens to Vote in Local Elections

	new provision

H. Military Affairs

– employment of military forces out of area	article 87a
– renunciation of ABC weapons	new provision
– prohibition of weapons exportation	new provision
– equalization in length of time spent in military and civilian service	article 12a (2)
– extending military draft to women	article 12a (1)

I. Combining the *Länder* of Berlin and
    Brandenburg   preamble

J. Changes in Federal–State Fiscal Relations   articles 104a–115

First, some restructuring of federal–state relations appears inevitable. The proposed amendments reflect a need to restructure federal–state relations. Many of the suggested changes have been advanced by the Bundesrat itself or by the Conference of *Land* Parliamentary Presidents. These bodies hope to strengthen the *Länder* vis-à-vis the national government and to ensure that the Maastricht Treaty and other efforts to enlarge the authority of the European Community do not erode the limited sovereignty of the *Länder* governments. In fact, they want to breathe more life into the principle of subsidiarity, a rule of governance already embedded in the Basic Law. The rule postulates that the lowest unit of government capable of effective action on a given matter should be responsible for that matter.

Accordingly, the *Länder* – and to some extent municipal governments – have proposed retrieving certain powers earlier surrendered to higher levels of government and specifically to identify those powers reserved to the *Länder's* exclusive authority. And so, for example, the above list includes proposals (1) to repeal provisions empowering the national government to pass framework legislation dealing with 'the general principles governing higher education' (Article 75 [1a]), (2) to terminate the national government's concurrent authority over the regulation of hospitals (Article 74 [19a]), and (3) to cut back on the national government's participation in certain 'joint tasks' under Article 91a.[9] Equally important are the Bundesrat's proposals to enlarge the scope of its consent power, the most consequential of which would require the Bundesrat's consent to any transfer of sovereign power under Article 24 to international institutions, particularly if such power affects the *Länder's* legitimate interests. (This proposal derives from the growing power of the European Community.) A related proposal to require its consent for laws falling into the domain of the Federation's concurrent legislative power would virtually transpose the Bundesrat into a legislative body coequal with the Bundestag.

Secondly, state objectives are prominent on the list of constitutional repairs desired by many East Germans and their progressive allies in the western *Länder*. These goals would oblige the state to protect the environment and to provide all persons within its jurisdiction with a place of work, adequate housing, comprehensive medical care, higher levels of social security and welfare, and the benefits of culture and education. These proposals have been the subject of intense debate in the commission, much of it centring on whether, if codified in the Basic Law, they would be transformed into judicially enforceable rights. The prevailing view is that such state objectives are merely declaratory. Even so, except for the goal of environmental protection, opposition to putting them into the Constitution is strong. Some argue that constitutionalising these goals would create expectations unlikely to be fulfilled; others that many of these goals are already implicit in the Basic Law's command that the state respect 'human dignity' (Article 1) and in the principle of the 'social welfare state' (*Sozialstaatsprinzip*) (Article 20).

A strong egalitarian impulse, emanating largely from the Eastern *Länder*, but also strongly supported by certain parties and groups in the West, sustains the drive for the constitutional recognition of the socioeconomic goals just mentioned. The impulse flows from gross inequalities existing between the Eastern and Western *Länder* and in society generally.[10] The incorporation of socioeconomic objectives in the Basic Law, many argue, would put the state on notice that specified human needs must be placed at the top of the government's agenda, even though resources may be insufficient to accomplish these goals. In short, constitutionally mandated goals, although nonjusticiable, would place lawmakers on notice that they would violate at least the spirit of the Basic Law if they do not strive conscientiously to implement them.

It may be observed in this connection that the protection of the environment as a state objective has been pushed with particular zeal by nearly all parties to the debate on constitutional revision. There are of course differences over what 'environment' means. Some would include a textual reference to the protection of 'plants and animals'. The strongest proponents of defining environmental protection as a state objective propose adding the words 'and creation' to the preambular declaration acknowledging the German people's 'responsibility before God and men'. They would make the protection of the environment a 'special duty of the state' and even charge individuals with this burden by 'obliging everyone to contribute to [this goal] by his [or her] own behavior'.[11]

In the matter of state guarantees, there are additional proposals to defend the rights of linguistic and cultural minorities (including communities marked by unorthodox life-styles), to equalize the power of labour and management, and to protect persons against the disclosure of personal information stored in data banks or recorded by any number of official and unofficial 'custodians' in an increasingly automated society. The Federal Constitutional Court has already seen fit to vindicate these rights in judicial decisions. In 1983, for example, in striking down parts of a census statute, the Court created a new right of 'informational self-determination',[12] just as it sustained the constitutional validity of a national codetermination statute in 1979 over the objection that the law violated the constitutional right to property.[13] The feeling is strong, however, that these rights, like some other guarantees, have taken on such great importance at the threshold of the 21st century that they ought to be frozen into the Basic Law itself.

Third, proposals to further democratise the political system and to expand rights of political participation have been greeted with more controversy than the project on behalf of state objectives. Certain groups in West Germany, notably the Greens and many Social Democrats, have been fighting for years to introduce methods of direct democracy, such as the initiative and referendum, at the federal level, a movement resisted by conservative constitutional scholars fearful of any modification in the *representational* character of the German political order. Proposals to have the Bundestag dissolve itself and to extend the vote to resident aliens and EC citizens living and working in Germany would help to break up what many perceive as a frozen political order dominated by entrenched élites and an ossified party system. (The proposal to allow resident aliens to vote in local elections would reverse recent decisions of the Federal Constitutional Court nullifying the extension of the franchise to non-Germans.) For others, however, these proposals pose the danger of fragmenting the electorate, thus undermining the political stability and balance that constitutional arrangements adopted in 1949, such as the constructive vote of no confidence, were designed to secure.

Fourthly, the pressure to amend Article 16 (2) to curtail the right of asylum and to amend Article 87a (1) to allow the deployment of the military forces outside the area covered by the North Atlantic Treaty Organisation and for purposes other than the defence of Germany has been gathering force in recent months. The tension surrounding the issue of asylum is so acute nationwide that the initiative for change has been seized by groups outside the constitutional reform commission. Indeed, at this writing, months before the recommendations of the commission are due, the Bundestag began debating legislation that would amend Article 16 substantially to limit the categories of persons eligible to claim a right to asylum.[14]

In the matter of military forces there is a deep divide between broad and narrow constructionists. Broadly read, the Basic Law can easily be interpreted to permit the use of German forces in collective peace-keeping operations anywhere in the world. Narrowly read, the same provisions can be interpreted to ban such deployments except in defence of Germany itself or in the event of an attack on a NATO ally. Most German politicians, Christian and Social Democrats alike, have tended to accept the narrow interpretation over the dissent of numerous constitutional scholars.[15] The issue has been brought to a head with Germany's reunification and the enlarged role the nation is now expected to play in world affairs. Largely in response to pressures from the United States and the United Nations, German political leaders, against the backdrop of considerable domestic opposition, are seeking to amend the Basic Law expressly to permit the deployment of the armed services outside the theatre of NATO operations.

III   ASSESSMENT

Several German constitutional lawyers have suggested that most of the problems of reunited Germany can be dealt with within the framework of the existing constitution; doubtless, this is true. Except perhaps for proposals to incorporate the mechanisms of direct democracy, the Basic Law is not expected to be amended in its essential core. Indeed, the Basic Law itself prohibits any amendment that would change the nature of the *federal* system or alter the basic legal and political values set forth in Article 20 and the personal value of human dignity laid down in Article 1.[16] In any event, the Federal Constitutional Court would have the final word on the constitutionality of any amendment arguably in conflict with the Basic Law's core values. In this respect, incidentally, it is worth pointing out that despite the fierce criticism that has often greeted decisions of the Constitutional Court, no proposed amendment would curtail its jurisdiction or tamper with its institutional autonomy. In fact, the one proposal that does touch the Court would enlarge its authority to hear disputes between the *Länder* and the Federation. There is of course some tension between the apparent determination of Germans of all political persuasions to maintain intact the juridical democracy created by the Basic Law and the effort on the part of some groups radically to democratise the political system. Any substantial tilt in the direction of plebiscitary democracy would potentially disturb the existing balance between liberalism and democracy and threaten to change the character of German constitutionalism. For this reason, less drastic changes focusing on parliamentary reform, party financing, and the extension of the franchise to resident aliens, are likely to be more successful than any mechanism of direct democracy.

What does seem probable is the adoption of certain directive principles of state policy, especially one committing the nation to the protection of the natural environment. A revised constitution may also commit the state to certain socioeconomic goals that even economic liberals should be able to accept on the assurance that what is being promoted is a state goal rather than a subjective right. After all, the objection cannot be to the idea of a state goal, for such goals have long been part of the Basic Law, the most obvious of which has been the goal of German unity. Another, appearing in Article 6 (1), obliges the state to confer its 'special protection' on marriage and the family. Constitutionalising such goals matters. In the case of German unity, for example, the Federal Constitutional Court never ceased to admonish German political leaders of their responsibility under the Basic Law affirmatively to strive for reunification with all the tools at their disposal.

Perhaps the most critical decision facing the constitutional revision commission is whether to propose the submission of the Basic Law itself to a popular referendum. It seems clear now that despite the literal wording of Article 146, which would authorise reunited Germany freely to adopt a new constitution, the Basic Law will continue in perpetuity as the nation's fundamental law. Its fundamentality has been reinforced and solidified by 40 years of authoritative interpretation, overlaying the Basic Law with a solid veneer of permanence and esteem. Article 146 would be effectively repealed, however, removing any lingering doubts about the Basic Law's permanence or legitimacy, if it were to be submitted to and overwhelmingly approved in a popular referendum.

A constitution's legitimacy, however, need not depend on its popular approval. One could argue that the Basic Law has stood the test of time, having nurtured a stable and durable political order marked by respect for liberal values and limited government. One could also argue – and it will be argued – that longevity confers legitimacy; in the last 40 years a large majority of Germans – between 70 and 90 per cent of the voting population – has given its tacit consent to the Basic Law in 11 federal elections. As for the Eastern *Länder*, they too consented to be governed by the Basic Law, first in the election of March 18, 1990 and then again when East Germany's parliament voluntarily acceded to the Federal Republic. Finally, as just suggested, the Federal Constitutional Court has won the applause of a grateful nation for helping to turn the Basic Law into a tried and tested instrument of constitutional governance.

The again cogent arguments would support any recommendation to proceed with a referendum on the Basic Law. After all, the Basic Law was conceived, written, and ratified within the womb of legislative politics. *Länder* parliaments even chose the members of the original constitutional convention, and those same parliaments ratified the Basic Law. And, as mentioned, the current constitutional reform commission is made up of members of the Bundesrat and Bundestag. Perhaps the time has come, at this strategic moment in Germany's postwar constitutional history, to place the fate of the Basic Law in the hands of a larger public so that it can be said that the people as a whole have reconstituted themselves as a nation committed to constitutional democracy.

On the other hand, any decision to submit the Basic Law to a popular vote would raise difficult problems. For one thing, the Basic Law lays down no procedure for the conduct of such a referendum. For another, in the event of a referendum, what would Germans be asked to approve? The Basic Law as a whole, each of its major sections, or its main principles? And what kind of majority would be required? Simple, absolute, or qualified? In all of the *Länder* or in a majority of them? As a way of getting around these difficulties without losing the value of a popular vote, Germans might be advised to hold a referendum on the repeal of Article 146. A simple 'yes' vote to repeal – perhaps in two-thirds of the *Länder* and by a simple majority – would probably be sufficient, finally, to breathe perpetual life into the Federal Republic's Basic Law.

IV POSTSCRIPT

This postscript updates the story of constitutional revision in Germany. The Joint Commission on Constitutional Revision finished its work on July 1, 1993, three months later than originally expected and long after this chapter had been submitted for publication. These concluding remarks centre on the principal amendments approved and recommended by the Joint Commission and on two other developments of major constitutional significance.

One major development was the revision of Article 16 on the right to asylum. Because of the urgency of the problem caused by the influx of asylum seekers – well over a million since 1980 and 435 000 in 1992 alone – the Bundestag itself initiated the move to adopt a new Article 16a after months of negotiation between Social and Christian Democrats. Adopted in June of 1993, the new article retained the original declaration that politically persecuted persons 'shall enjoy the right of asylum'. Subsequent paragraphs of Article 16a, however, deny asylum to persons arriving on German soil from any member state of the European Community or any third state in which it is statutorily determined that political persecution does not occur. In addition, aliens from states designated by statute as countries in which political persecution is absent may not claim the right to asylum under Article 16a. The assumption of non-persecution is rebuttable; aliens from safe countries may not be deported if they can present facts showing that they would be persecuted upon being forced to return to their country of origin. As Gerald L. Neuman remarks, this new constitutional standard 'does not imply that Germany has power to narrow the definition of the human right to asylum, only that Germany can limit the conditions under which that right may be invoked in Germany'.[17]

The Joint Commission, on the other hand, initiated the proposal resulting in a new Article 23, replacing the repealed article under which German unity took place. Known as the 'Europe Article', Article 23, along with proposed amendments to Articles 24, 88, and 28, were ratified as a 'single package' by the necessary two thirds vote in the Bundestag and Bundesrat and entered into force on December 21, 1992. Each of these amendments to the Basic Law deepened Germany's commitment to European integration.

Article 23 commits the Federal Republic to the Maastricht Treaty and permits the transfer of its sovereign rights to the European Union, but only if the transfer accords with the basic principles laid down in Articles 1 and 20 of the Basic Law.[18] A new clause in Article 88 authorises a European central bank to take over the functions and authority of the Germany's Federal Bank (Bundesbank). Article 28 was amended to allow citizens of member states of the European Community resident in Germany to vote in local elections, a proposal that effectively reverses a recent decision of the Federal Constitution Court invalidating foreign resident voting in such elections. Finally, a new paragraph in Article 24 permits the *Länder*, with the approval of the Federal Government, to transfer their reserved powers to regional institutions.

To compensate for the transfer of powers to the European Union, Article 23 seeks to increase parliament's control over Germany's relationship to Europe. As noted, sovereign rights may be assigned to the European Union, but only in the form of a law requiring the Bundesrat's approval. Other provisions of Article 23 require the national government to enter into detailed consultation with the Bundestag and Bundesrat on matters relating to European affairs. On matters involving the vital interests of the *Länder*, the national government must reach its decisions in cooperation with the Bundesrat. To insure that such consultation and cooperation take place, proposed amendments yet to be ratified authorise the creation of committees on European affairs in both Bundestag and Bundesrat.

The principle of subsidiarity reaffirmed in Article 23 finds renewed resonance in proposals (1) to strengthen local government and to curtail the Federations's discretionary authority under Article 72 (2) to pass laws within its concurrent legislative authority. Under one proposal, the Bundestag could exercise this authority – and thus preempt *Land* legislation on the same subject – only when necessary to establish uniform living conditions in the Federation as a whole or to secure legal unity in the national interest. A proposed amendment to Article 93 would authorise the Federal Constitutional Court to enforce this limitation.

The Joint Commission's remaining recommendations include proposed amendments to establish environmental protection as a state goal, to protect the identity of ethnic, cultural, and linguistic minorities, and to reinforce the equality of the sexes. The last of these recommendations would oblige the state to promote 'the actual equality of men and women' and 'to remove existing disadvantages [to the effective enjoyment of equality in German society].' Each of these proposed amendments secured the approval of the Joint Commission. The Commission rejected proposed constitutional amendments to introduce institutions of plebiscitary democracy at the national level. Also rejected was a proposal to elect the Federal President by popular vote.

Finally, two important constitutional issues, emerging respectively out of the Unity and Maastricht Treaties, have been resolved by recent decisions of the Federal Constitutional Court. Recall that under the Unity Treaty the all-German parliament was to enact a new abortion law applicable to Western and Eastern Germany by the end of 1992. A new law legalising abortion within the first trimester of pregnancy subsequent to obligatory counselling was passed in June, 1992. In an opinion handed down on May 28, 1993, the Constitutional Court nullified this law, declaring that abortion must remain a criminal offence at all stages of pregnancy. The Court went on to declare that women who nevertheless procure an abortion within the first trimester, after pro-life counselling and guarantees of state assistance, will not be prosecuted. Such abortions, however, may not validly be financed under the national health system. This ruling is now supreme law in all of Germany.[19]

On October 12, 1993, the Constitutional Court sustained the constitutionality of the Maastricht Treaty. The Court ruled, however, that any transfer of sovereign power to the European Community within the terms of the new Article 23 would have to conform to the principle of democracy laid down in Article 20 of the Basic Law. This simply means that representatives of the people freely elected under Article 38 of the Basic Law must approve by majority vote any transfer of sovereign power to a supranational institution. 'Democratic legitimation,' declared the Court, 'derives from the link between the actions of European governmental entities and the parliaments of the member states.' The Court also made clear that it would retain final authority to determine whether any governmental decision under the Maastricht Treaty would violate the sovereign rights of the people as represented in the Bundestag or the rights of the *Länder* as represented in the Bundesrat.[20]

Notes

1. Donald P. Kommers, 'The Basic Law of the Federal Republic of Germany: an Assessment After Forty Years' in Peter H. Merkl (ed.), *The Federal Republic of Germany at Forty* (New York: New York University Press, 1989), p. 133.
2. For a discussion of these innovations and a comparison of the Basic Law with earlier German constitutions see Kommers, Ibid., pp. 134–41.
3. 'Entwurf: Verfassung der Deutschen Demokratischen Republik', Arbeitsgruppe 'Neue Verfassung der DDR' des Zentralen Runden Tisches (Berlin-Niederschönhausen, April 4, 1990).
4. In assessing the impact of the March 18, 1990 election, Klaus von Beyme remarked: 'From this moment on it was clear that the GDR was doomed, that no separate GDR institution was wanted and needed and the basic ideas of the draft [constitution] had little chance of entering the amendment procedure for the German Basic Law.' 'The Effects of Reunification on German Democracy', *Government and Opposition*, vol. 27, pp. 158–76 (1992).
5. For a detailed description of these changes and related constitutional issues

see Peter E. Quint, 'The Constitutional Law of German Unification', *Maryland Law Review*, vol. 50, pp. 516–41 (1991).

6. On the matter of abortion, the Unity Treaty permitted the eastern *Länder* to follow a policy incompatible with West German constitutional law. GDR policy had legalised abortion on demand during the first trimester of pregnancy, whereas prevailing West Germany policy, following a decision of the Federal Constitutional Court, obligated the state to protect the fetus at all stages of pregnancy unless an abortion was warranted for certified reasons specified by law. Certain West German groups allied themselves with East German leaders in securing this arrangement. Under the terms of the Unity Treaty, a new all German policy on abortion was to be in place by the end of 1992.

7. *Gemeinsame Verfassungskommission* (Stenographischer Bericht), 1. Sitzung. Bonn, Donnerstag, den January 16, 1992, p. 1. Among the Bundestag's members on the Joint Commission, 15 are Christian Democrats, 11 Social Democrats, 4 Free Democrats, and 1 each from the Party of Democratic Socialism and the Greens. The Bundesrat's members include 2 delegates from each *Land*, giving the eastern *Länder* 10 of its 32 members.

8. On this point see Dieter Grimm, 'Verfassungsreform in falscher Hand? Zum Stand der Diskussion um das Grundgesetz', *Merkur: Deutsche Zeitschrift für Europäisches Denken* (1992), pp. 1059–61.

9. Article 75 authorises the federal government to pass 'framework' laws (*Rahmengesetzen*) which lay down general guidelines for the regulation of specified topical areas normally within *Land* jurisdiction, but permits the *Länder* to flesh out the details and administer the policy. Article 91a allows the federal government to assist the *Länder* in carrying out so-called 'joint tasks' (*Mitwirkungsbereiche des Bundes bei Läandesaufgaben*) mainly in the area of the federal government's concurrent legislative authority.

10. On the other hand, certain western interests would like to constitutionalise the social *market* economy, stressing the value of economic freedom, competition, entrepreneurship, and the right to property. As a directive principle of state policy, any such guarantee would surely conflict with the egalitarian presuppositions of other socioeconomic guarantees.

11. The 'special duty' language of this proposal would not be unusual. Under Article 6 (1) of the Basic Law, 'Marriage and [the] family shall enjoy the special protection of the state', just as Article 6 (4) announces that 'every mother shall be entitled to the protection and care of the community'.

12. 65 BVerfGE 1. A partial translation of this decision may be found in Donald P. Kommers, *The Constitutional Jurisprudence of the Federal Republic of Germany* (Durham, N.C.: The Duke University Press, 1989), pp. 332–6.

13. 50 BVerfGE 290. For a translation see Kommers, op. cit., pp. 278–82.

14. The proposed amendment was adopted and entered into force on July 1, 1993. For details, see the postscript to this chapter.

15. See, for example, Torsten Stein, 'Die verfassungsrechtliche Zulässigkeit einer Beteiligung der Bundesrepublik Deutschland an Friedenstruppen der Vereinten Nationen', in Jochen Abr. Frowein and Torsten Stein, *Rechtliche*

Aspekte einer Beteiligung der Bundesrepublik Deutschland an Frieden-struppen der Vereinten Nationen (Heidelberg: Springer-Verlag, 1990), pp. 17–30.

16. Art. 79 (3) of the Basic Law.

17. 'Buffer Zones against Refugees: Dublin, Schengen, and the German Asylum Amendment', *Virginia Journal of International Law*, 33 (1993), 519.

18. Article 23 commits the Federal Republic to a European Union that governs democratically, abides by the rule of law, is federal in character, subscribes to the principle of subsidiarity, and protects rights and liberties comparable to those already guaranteed by the Basic Law.

19. See Judgment of May 28, 1993, *Entscheidungen des Bundesverfassungs-gerichts*, 88 (1993), 203–358.

20. The full text of the Maastricht decision is reported in *Europäische Grundrechte Zeitschrift* (EgGRZ), 20 (1993), 429–46.

11 Civil Liberties: The Issue of Migrants

Gerard Braunthal*

In 1948, the United Nations adopted the Universal Declaration of Human Rights. It was a manifesto proclaiming the importance of human dignity and freedom, and the need of the state to respect the life and uniqueness of every individual. The declaration became a benchmark in the history of the struggle of individuals to achieve more rights and liberties against an ever more powerful state.

If it had not been for the barbarism committed by Nazi Germany against millions of its own citizens and those in other countries the Declaration might never have been issued. The United Nations realised that national law alone could not effectively protect individuals against the state. Thus a new dimension was added to international law. The Declaration articulates and safeguards fundamental values that are not unique to specific states but cut across state lines. Even though it is not binding on United Nations members, it sets minimum standards of conduct that states should maintain in relation with the people living in their territory.

In 1950, the Council of Europe approved the European Convention on Human Rights, influenced by the UN declaration. The Council set up a commission and a court to implement the convention. The Federal Republic of Germany (FRG) signed the UN declaration and the European convention. In 1988, on the fortieth anniversary of the UN declaration, Chancellor Helmut Kohl reaffirmed his government's commitment to the basic values listed in the documents. These are also enunciated in the 1949 Basic Law (constitution) of the FRG and, since 1990, of the united Germany.

The first 19 articles of the Basic Law spell out the basic rights, some applying only to Germans and others to all persons residing in the FRG, regardless of citizenship. The basic rights include protection of human dignity; right to develop one's personality; equality before the law; freedom of faith and conscience; freedoms of expression, assembly, and movement; the right to choose one's trade, occupation, or profession; inviolability of the home; guarantee of property; socialisation of the economy (subject to parliamentary action); deprivation of citizenship, extradition, and right of asylum; and right of petition. Article 19 states: 'In no case may the essential content of a basic right be encroached upon.'

This chapter focuses on one current major civil rights issue: the degree of liberties enjoyed by foreigners (including asylum seekers), ethnic Germans in Germany, and East German migrants to Western Germany. It tests what has happened in practice to the government's commitment to defend human rights as enunciated in the supranational and national basic charters. Has the government abided by Kohl's statement in 1988: 'No one should make light of, let alone support, threats to human life or racial, religious and political discrimination, even if only by their silence'?[1]

FOREIGN MIGRANTS

One of the toughest and most explosive problems facing German politicians (as well as politicians in other West European countries) in the early 1990s has been what policies to adopt to cope with the mounting number of foreigners seeking admittance into their countries. Many of these foreigners had come to Germany in the 1960s and early 1970s when companies were eagerly recruiting foreign workers ('guest workers') to fill vacant semi-skilled and unskilled positions. In 1973, when the oil crisis led to a ban on the influx of foreigners from non-European Community (EC) countries, the foreign population in Germany stood at close to 4 million, of whom 2.6 million were workers; by the end of 1992 it had risen to 6.5 million, representing an over 7.5 per cent share of the united German population. About 25 per cent of foreign workers and families had lived in the FRG for at least fifteen years.[2]

In 1991, half of the foreign workers were employed in industry and about 20 per cent in the service sector. Every twelfth worker and employee was a foreigner, working often in jobs that Germans preferred not to take. Given the absence of a multicultural society and equality of opportunities, few foreigners have been able to rise into managerial or professional positions. A minority have opened small firms, especially grocery shops, creating new jobs. The foreign labour force has generated a sizeable proportion of the country's gross national product, in effect contributing to German economic strength. But most Germans are not aware of the benefits that accrue from having a foreign labour force in their midst and the necessity to maintain one, or even expanding it, as an underpinning of the country's economy.

Instead, many citizens grumble about foreign workers and their families who receive the same social benefits, such as subsidised housing, unemployment and health insurance, as they do. Moreover, they have erected a social barrier against foreigners, many from Turkey, the former Yugoslav republics, Italy, Greece, Portugal, and Spain. As a result, foreigners, despite the attempts of some private organisations to integrate them, face social isolation, engendered by a media that highlights crimes committed by some of them. Foreigners are also the target of prejudice, discrimination, rejection, and, on a smaller scale, violence. They consider such treatment as a violation of their human rights, especially because most of them are legally in the country, having received a residence permit.

ASYLUM SEEKERS

In addition to the foreign workers, many persons since the late 1970s and again the late 1980s seek political asylum in Germany. The Basic Law contains Article 16, a provision on asylum ('Persons persecuted on political grounds shall enjoy the right of asylum'), which is the most liberal of industrialised nations. It was included as a gesture of atonement for the Nazi past and the inability of many emigrants from Nazi Germany to gain asylum in other countries.

In 1991, more than 250 000 asylum seekers, of whom the bulk came from Eastern and Southern Europe (former Yugoslavia, 75 000; Romania, 40 000; Turkey, 24 000; Bulgaria, 12 000), sought permission to stay in Germany. In 1992, the number rose to 438 000. While the courts decide their fate, they are housed in camps, and receive medical services and an allowance to cover living expenses. Upon application, many are allowed to work (87 000 in 1991–92). If they can prove they fled their country for bona fide political reasons, a concept often narrowly interpreted by judges, then they can stay. But fewer and fewer (4–8 per cent) fall into this category. Most come for economic reasons, and, once denied permission to stay, remain illegally. Their presence is tolerated by the government, which hesitates to be accused again of mass deportations, such as in the case of 60 000 Romanians, primarily Gypsies, who were sent back in 1992 to Romania.

Since 1978, the government has sharpened asylum procedures seven times in order to curb the number of asylum seekers. In July 1992, a new law went into effect, after heated partisan discussion in Parliament, to speed up the application process of asylum seekers coming into Germany and to spare local communities from having to accommodate a stream of economic refugees for years until their cases were decided. The *Länder* will have to provide the assembly camps. Cases of applicants who stand no chance of being granted asylum will be decided within a maximum period of six weeks. If the decision goes against them, they would have to leave the country or be deported immediately. But the implementation of the law is slow, given the shortage of judges. In addition, most of those rejected for asylum remain illegally rather than face deportation.[3]

According to the CDU/CSU-led government, Germany's ability to absorb further asylum seekers and refugees from war zones or hardship areas is limited. It pointed out that because of the country's liberal asylum policy, two-thirds of all persons seeking asylum in one of the West European countries come to Germany. State and local governments are faced with serious problems in providing for their accommodation and care. Because of the high numbers of asylum seekers coming at a time when economic problems were multiplying in Eastern Germany, the authorities have been faced with increasing protests from German citizens about the financial and social costs involved, the acute shortage of adequate housing, and the right-radical violence against foreigners in their midst.

Accord on a New Asylum Policy

In late 1992 the government shifted its attention to the 1951 Geneva convention on refugees as justification to restrict Article 16. The convention stipulates that people who have a justified fear of persecution because of their race, religion, nationality, membership in a social group, or political conviction *may* be entitled to asylum (rather than '*shall be*' in Article 16). In October 1992, the governing parties passed a resolution in the Bundestag to make Article 16 conform with the convention and sought the support of the SPD, whose approval was necessary for the minimum two-thirds majority needed in Parliament to amend an article in the constitution. For more than a year, the SPD had been deeply split on weakening Article 16. In mid-November, however, at a special SPD convention, delegates, aware that public opinion had shifted from a full support of Article 16, agreed to its restriction. In December, the parties reached a final accord that, after a dramatic Bundestag debate in May 1993, was enacted into law on July 1, 1993.

The law, amending Article 16, stipulates that people who are politically persecuted have the right to asylum. But the right to asylum will not be granted to anyone coming from an EC member state or another country that provides asylum under the provisions of the Geneva convention or the European Convention on Human Rights. These clauses mean that unless asylum-seekers fly into Germany non-stop from their home countries, or flee from a country adjoining Germany, and are carrying documents that prove political persecution, they will not be admitted into Germany to claim asylum. This provision would apply, for example, to refugees fleeing Turkey, who would pass through several countries, including Austria, on their way to Germany or those fleeing an Asian or Latin American country in which the aircraft stops over in Paris on its way to Germany. In such cases, the asylum seeker will be sent back to the third country, say Austria or France, to seek asylum there.

The law also stipulates that asylum seekers from 'safe' countries, free of political persecution, as determined by the Ministry of the Interior, will not be admitted into Germany unless they can prove that in their cases persecution had taken place. This provision has affected especially asylum seekers from Romania and Bulgaria.

Another provision in the law deals with refugees from crisis areas such as the former Yugoslavia, who will no longer fall under asylum provisions but in the category of civil war refugees. They will be allowed to stay in Germany until peace returns to their homeland. In 1994 the German government planned to send home many Croatians on the ground that fighting had ended in their republic. The decision produced a storm of protest among the refugees who had lost their homes and possessions and faced a bleak future in Croatia.

The German government has provided financial assistance to the Polish and Czech governments, which provide momentary asylum to the many who had transited their countries for Germany, but were blocked at the German frontier. As a result of the new law the flood of asylum seekers streaming into Germany has fallen drastically. In 1993 a total of 323 000 applied for asylum, in contrast to 438 000 in 1992. Yet the number of illegal immigrants has risen sharply since Article 16 was amended.

SUPRANATIONAL SOLUTIONS

The CDU/CSU in Bonn has also attempted to solve the asylum problem at the supranational level. Germany and other EC countries signed the Schengen (Luxembourg) agreement of June 15, 1990, which, as in the German law of July 1993, stipulates that the state handling a refugee's application for first asylum entry (say, France) remains responsible for that person and agrees to take back any refugee who goes on to another state (say, Germany) that is a party to the agreement.[4]

CDU/CSU ministers want to include all non-signatory East European countries in the Schengen agreement or conclude bilateral accords with them, thereby hoping to throttle the influx of asylum seekers, who mostly come from that area. One German newspaper, critical of Schengen and its restrictive asylum policy, said that European agreements call for the disappearance of frontiers, but that refugees are to be treated as if the frontiers still existed. It wrote: 'It all sounds like the regulations of the German penal institutions which lay down when and which prisoners are to be transferred to which other prison.'[5]

The EC has not come up with an asylum policy, primarily because the member states fear an interregional sharing of the burden from the influx of immigrants. EC immigration policy goals are limited to uniting families, meeting labour requirements, and fighting illegal immigration and illicit work. Whether EC countries will harmonise asylum laws in coming years remains doubtful. But if right wing movements make political capital out of the asylum crisis, then the EC states might come more quickly to an agreement, which will be to further curb the immigration of foreigners into Europe.

Ethnic Germans and East Germans

In addition to the problem of asylum seekers, the German government must deal with the mass immigration of ethnic Germans coming primarily from the former Soviet Union, Romania, and Poland. During communist rule, these minorities, some of which had emigrated from Germany in the 18th century, some earlier, were at times persecuted; as a consequence West Germany encouraged their resettlement. In the late 1980s, when the communist regimes fell, they began to immigrate in large numbers. In 1990 close to 400 000 arrived, but since then the number has declined somewhat. Even when no longer facing persecution in the countries in which they grew up, most of those remaining still have expressed a desire to emigrate to Germany.

They wish to 'live as Germans among Germans' and to better themselves financially. But with the wave of asylum seekers coming into Germany, the government began to negotiate with East European states and the former Soviet republics to improve the conditions of ethnic Germans there and permit German cultural activities and German language courses as a spur to fewer emigrating to the FRG. To this end, it has also made a procedural change: potential emigrants must satisfy in their home countries all entry formalities, including compiling documentary evidence that their ancestors had emigrated from Germany to the East, before they receive authorisation to enter Germany. In the 1993 amendments to immigration policy, one provision states that the number of incoming ethnic Germans will not be allowed to grow in coming years.

Upon arrival, they are entitled, under the Basic Law's 'right of return' provision, to German citizenship. But not speaking the language and holding different values, such as strong religious ties, they constitute a new minority among native-born Germans. They face many of the same problems as other foreigners: few jobs commensurate with their experience, competition for adequate housing, hostility against their presence because they receive government benefits, and the difficulty of integration into a nearly alien society. Consequently, according to one study, family relations often deteriorate, as parents find integration into society more difficult than their children.

The government has also had to cope with the flood of East Germans (350 000 alone in 1989) who have fled to Western Germany seeking a better life since the Wall crumbled in 1989. It has assisted them in their search for housing and jobs. To facilitate the task, the government set up quotas to distribute them more evenly among the *Länder* and communities. The minister of the interior announced that the quotas were not meant to abolish freedom of movement, but rather to reduce the concentration of those resettling in a few municipalities. Such concentration made tight housing and labour markets even tighter.

In March 1990, the Bonn government announced that it was ending the special resettlement benefits they had received upon arrival. The decision meant that East Germans moving to Western Germany had to fend for themselves to find housing and jobs. Bremen became the first city to shut its doors to them. The mayor announced that if any more came, they would go homeless or be shipped back. Justifying this harsh action, he said that 7000 Bremen residents were waiting for housing and 14.5 per cent were unemployed. Five gymnasiums had been converted to emergency barracks; when the city tried to take over a sixth, the local sports club occupied the building to keep out the East Germans.

Bremen's action epitomised the dilemma other West German authorities faced. The city's blocking of East German refugees limited the freedom of movement guaranteed to citizens, thus restricting their civil rights. But such a ban had to be equated with the Bremen residents' inability to find housing and jobs, perhaps not inalienable rights but rights nevertheless. There was no easy solution to the dilemma, which government authorities also had to address in their dealings with asylum seekers and ethnic Germans. President Richard von Weizsäcker stated, in another context: 'The rule of law is a manifestation of the practical knowledge that we humans have no automatic access to absolute justice.'[6]

Government officials' attitude in treating East German refugees hardened mainly because of a shift in public opinion in West Germany. When East Germans were fleeting to the FRG through Hungary and Czechoslovakia in 1989, 63 per cent of West Germans polled said every one should be accepted. By February 1990, only 22 per cent polled held the same view.[7]

VIOLENCE AGAINST FOREIGNERS

Right-wing extremist groups and skinheads have capitalised on a growing sentiment in the population against the costs of having foreigners in their midst. Members of right wing groups lash out at foreigners because right-wingers reject a pluralist society that values democracy and human rights. Right-wingers are xenophobic, racist, anti-Semitic, and intolerant of minorities. Some of them have smeared anti-Semitic graffiti on buildings and desecrated Jewish cemeteries. In the new *Länder* especially, many have turned against foreign workers from Asian and African countries, viewing them as interlopers who attacked German women, imported AIDS, received preferential treatment from the state, and were better off than the average German citizen. Such views did not correspond to the facts, but provided an easy rationalisation for the violence they committed.

In 1991 and 1992, the number of attacks by right-wingers, skinheads, and hooligans against foreign workers and Romanian Gypsies in Eastern (and Western) Germany reached a peak, not matched since the violence of the early Nazi years. In 1992 alone, more than 2000 serious attacks and 10 000 other right-wing incidents occurred, in which 17 people were killed and hundreds injured (see also Chapter 23, below). Until late 1992, the government response was timid compared to its tough responses against leftwing terrorism in the 1970s. The rightists' vicious attacks against defenceless foreigners, of whom, paradoxically, there were proportionately few in the new *Länder*, were sparked, among other reasons, by the political suppression of young people in the GDR. The end of the regime gave them freedom to vent their anger and frustration. Unemployed and shiftless, coming from broken homes, dropping out of school, lacking a trade, many joined gangs to end their social isolation.

Thus, in the early 1990s, they firebombed a number of hostels for foreigners in Hoyerswerda (northern Saxony), Rostock, and other cities, often with insufficient police present to quell the riots. Some residents encouraged the attackers, chanting slogans like 'Germany for the Germans' and 'Foreigners out'. But most German citizens deplored the rightist actions, capped by the death in a firebombed house of three Turkish nationals in Mölln, a small town in Western Germany, in November 1992, and five Turkish nationals in Solingen in May 1993. One encouraging sign was that the deaths sparked in many cities numerous mass protest demonstrations, in which hundreds of thousands participated, against the assailants.

Although polls indicate that only a minority of Germans are racist or ethnically hostile toward foreigners, a 1990 study in eastern Germany indicated that more than 70 per cent of the foreigners polled said that Germans (presumably the minority) had insulted or reviled them; 20 per cent reported physical abuse. Many said that they were afraid to leave their apartments in the evenings.[8]

Chancellor Kohl said after the Rostock attack in 1992, rather belatedly, that violence against foreigners 'will be confronted with the utmost legal firmness and strictness. The most important thing is that we jointly, all democratic parties, make it clear to the world that xenophobia is totally unacceptable, that xenophobia is a disgrace for our çountry.'[9]

SOLUTIONS TO INTRACTABLE PROBLEMS

German politicians, human rights specialists, church leaders, and academics have advanced a number of proposals to solve the problems arising from the migration of persecuted or poor people across national boundaries to Germany. Right wing politicians have insisted that 'the boat is full'; hence immigration must be drastically curbed. Conservative politicians may concur with this sentiment, but have been more circumspect in their public pronouncements.

Alliance '90/Greens deputies, with some support from SPD and FDP deputies, have suggested that legal immigration into Germany be introduced, yet controlled by setting national quotas for immigrants from various countries, comparable to United States practice. But the CDU/CSU has opposed this, claiming, not too convincingly in the light of millions of foreigners in Germany, that Germany traditionally has not been a country of immigration.

Human rights specialists and others have advocated broadening the concept of citizenship, which is currently determined by blood or kinship and not by place of birth. Thus, ethnic Germans in Russia who have never seen Germany are entitled to German citizenship while Turks who have lived or were born in Germany, paid taxes, and speak the language fluently, are considered foreigners. Any foreigner between the age of 17 and 23, however, is entitled to apply for citizenship after eight years' residence, including six years' attendance at a German school. In addition, any foreigner who has resided in Germany for 15 years (and spouse and children for less time) can apply for citizenship before January 1996, but may not have dual citizenship. The procedures, however, are complex, time-consuming, and costly.

To integrate some foreigners more into German society, SPD-controlled Hamburg and Schleswig-Holstein wanted to grant voting rights in municipal elections to foreigners from EC countries. But upon petition by the CDU/CSU, the Constitutional Court ruled against the SPD because such a practice violates the constitution's provision that only German citizens can vote in elections. This restrictive ruling was partly offset by the court encouraging the national government to enact new legislation granting all foreigners the right to vote in local elections. The government has not responded positively, but it will abide by the provision in the Maastricht EC treaty to allow EC citizens living in other EC countries the right to vote in local elections. Thus, Portuguese or Greek immigrants, for example, will be able to vote in Hamburg but not in a German national election.

Critics of limited immigration also have said that national solutions to migration problems will not work unless international efforts are undertaken to remove the causes producing large-scale movement of poor people to the wealthier nations. They say that for the German government and other West European governments to try to buttress a Fortress Europe policy, in effect erecting a new 'wall', will fail as long as the gap widens between the First World (United States, Canada, and Western Europe), on the one hand, and the Second World (former communist bloc states) and Third World (most Asian, African, and Latin American states), on the other hand.

They cite the projected increase of the world's population in this decade from 4.5 to 6.5 or 7 billion, most of it in the world's poorest states. Many of these people will suffer in their home countries from hunger, human rights violations, oppression, or will be innocent victims in civil wars. Some of them will seek to migrate to Germany and other Western states, which have only a limited capacity to absorb them. One alternative is for these states to share more of their wealth with poorer states in order to slow down the exodus of people. Another is to adopt an international social charter that would provide minimum protection for workers and families in their home countries on a global scale. Still another is for the wealthy states to adopt a foreign economic policy that would assist, rather than harm, Third World states.[10]

In 1992, Alternative '90/Greens deputies in the Bundestag introduced bills that sought a humane solution to the multiple problems caused by immigration. The bills reflect the deputies' opposition to unlimited immigration because the feelings of German citizens and the inability of the German social system and infrastructure to cope with such an influx had to be taken into consideration. As noted, they favoured instead immigration based on a quota system, with full integration provided to all foreigners. They also wanted to grant foreigners after five years of residence more civil rights than they currently possess and German citizenship for children of foreign parents born on German soil.[11]

These bills are not a panacea to the problems but would provide some solutions and expand the scope of civil rights and liberties granted foreigners. CDU/CSU politicians and the conservative media were opposed once again to such 'radical' alternatives, but the politicians seem ready to make some concessions on the integration issue to placate the SPD for its major concessions on the asylum issue.

CONCLUSION

This survey of the civil rights of foreigners in Germany covers only a small segment of the wide range of human rights issues confronting the country's inhabitants. Because of space constraints, there could be no discussion of equally important issues, such as the human rights situation in Eastern Germany, state surveillance of residents, data protection for individuals, increasing powers of the intelligence services and the police, the concentration process in the media, violence in public demonstrations, equal rights for women, and the treatment of homosexuals and other minorities. Nor could there be a discussion of the planned establishment of an EC-wide police central register and more intensive contacts between European Police and intelligence services. These could serve to enhance, but also endanger, the liberties of residents in EC states.

Chancellor Kohl's 1988 speech, cited in the introduction of this chapter, reflects the government's commitment to defend human rights. Has practice matched the theoretical commitment? On the question of foreigners, the chancellor's record has not matched it. His government has responded belatedly and not firmly to the increasing number of violations of human rights encountered by foreigners. They are confronted by racism and neo-Nazi groups' violence, not to speak of people's hostility to their integration into German society. Policy and attitudinal changes will be needed to remedy some of the problems; others will remain intractable.

No country has a perfect human rights record. Democracies, such as the FRG, have less repression than authoritarian states, such as the former GDR. But less repression still means some repression. Government agencies restricted civil rights in West Germany in the 1970s when the fear of left-wing terrorism and domestic communism was at its height. Restrictions included the enactment of laws that infringed on the civil liberties of all residents, censorship of radical literature and plays, and keeping political extremists out of the civil service. The fall of communism has lessened the likelihood that such restrictions will occur again to the same degree, although in Eastern Germany the wholesale loss of jobs limits some basic rights (human dignity, the right to choose one's profession).

On the civil liberties agenda there are some issues that were relevant during the decades of West Germany's existence, are currently relevant, and will continue to remain relevant. Among them are the expansion of surveillance agencies, protection of data, the integration of foreigners into a mainstream society that is not multicultural, curbs on demonstrators, and less competition within the media (meaning fewer dissenting voices will be heard).[12] Other issues, such as ethical dilemmas resulting from breakthroughs in medical research and technology, will assume greater importance in the coming decade. If Germany cannot escape the social and economic tensions besetting many industrialised countries, then the civil liberties situation will worsen as the state seeks to maintain its prerogative of maintaining law and order in the face of mounting popular protests. Restrictions on individual liberties will then occur regardless of which major party heads a government.

Notes

* The author thanks Hannelore Koehler and Wolf-Dieter Narr for their constructive comments on this chapter.

1. Statement to the Bundestag, Dec. 9, 1988, reprinted in 'A Manifesto of Dignity and Freedom,' *Statements & Speeches* (German Information Center [GIC], New York), vol. XI, no. 24 December 10, 1988, p. 2.
2. GIC, *The Week in Germany*, July 17, 1992; February 19, 1993.
3. *The Economist*, May 23, 1992.
4. *Süddeutsche Zeitung*, Feb. 3, 1992. See also *Der Spiegel*, April 6, 1992. The Schengen agreement is paralleled by a corresponding European Community convention on the responsibility for asylum applicants signed at Dublin.
5. *Saarbrückener Zeitung*, April 18, 1992.
6. Address on receiving the Heine Prize 1991, Duesseldorf, December 13, 1991, reprinted in GIC, *Statements & Speeches*, vol. XV, no. 2.
7. *Der Spiegel* poll, cited by *New York Times*, March 1, 1990.
8. Study by a Cologne research institute, cited in GIC, *The Week in Germany*, March 1, 1991.
9. *New York Times*, August 26, 1992.
10. See Wolf-Dieter Narr, *Flüchtlinge, Asylsuchende, die Bundesrepublik Deutschland und wir*. Issued by Komitee für Grundrechte und Demokratie (Einhausen: hbo-druck, 1991).
11. Bündnis '90/Die Grünen, *Für eine offene Bundesrepublik* (Cologne: Farbo, 1992).
12. See Gerard Braunthal, 'Public Order and Civil Liberties,' *Developments in West German Politics*, eds. Gordon Smith, William E. Paterson, and Peter H. Merkl (Houndmills, England: Macmillan, 1989), pp. 308–22.

12 The 'Old' and the 'New' Federalism in Germany

Arthur B. Gunlicks

When the Wall came down on November 9, 1989 the two Germanies had dramatically different political systems. The most obvious of the differences could be found in the political party, administrative, and judicial systems and their ideological underpinnings as well as the contrasts these reflected in virtually all areas of public policy. Another major difference lay in the territorial–administrative organisation of the two states, that is, in the federal organisation of the West German Federal Republic and the unitary structures of the East German Democratic Republic (GDR). This difference was not in principle the direct result of the democratic-capitalist system in the West and the communist-dominated party dictatorship in the East. Most democratic systems are also unitary states, and, at least in theory if not in practice, the Soviet Union and Yugoslavia were federal states under communist party leadership.

With the fall of the Wall, the long-desired but unrealistic goal of German unification seemed within reach. At first, there was widespread agreement that unification would have to come slowly, not only because of anticipated objections by Germany's neighbours – and especially by the Soviet Union – but also because of the difficulty of uniting two states and societies that had gone off in very different directions after 1945. On November 28, 1989 Chancellor Helmut Kohl proposed a ten-point plan with unification as the final goal.[1] For our purposes, three steps were especially important:

(1) Chancellor Kohl proposed that the GDR and the Federal Republic should enter into a *Vertragsgemeinschaft* ('contractual community'). This is a vague concept in international law, but Kohl said it meant concluding treaties affecting economic relations, science and technology, culture, and, especially, the environment.

(2) Kohl proposed that confederative structures be developed. This would require democratic legitimacy in the GDR, to be achieved through free elections, after which numerous common institutions could be formed.

219

(3) Finally, unification would be achieved in a series of small steps, leading to a federation, a *Bundesrepublik*.

Soon after Kohl's statement, it became clear that unification was probably the only realistic alternative to the various options under consideration (including retaining the GDR as a separate state that would be neither capitalist nor socialist in the sense of past communist practice), and that it would have to come about much sooner than at first thought. About 2000 people were leaving the GDR every day for West Germany, a situation which neither German state could tolerate for long. East German elections were moved up from May to March, and the prospect that unification might occur in early 1991 or even in 1990 began to sound less and less unrealistic.

What kind of state would a unified Germany be? It was clear, of course, that it would be a democratic capitalist welfare state, like the other states of Western Europe. But it was also clear that unlike France, Italy or Great Britain, it would have to be a *federal* state, a requirement of the Basic Law (Article 79) not subject to amendment. More important, perhaps, was the fact that there was a consensus in West and East Germany that a unified Germany should be a federal state whatever the Basic Law said.

STATES AND LÄNDER BEFORE UNIFICATION

Why was there so much support for federalism? One answer would be that throughout their long history, with the exception of the 12 years of Hitler's Third Reich, Germans had only known some form of association of states. The Holy Roman Empire, which at least on paper lasted until 1806, was a semi-confederation of hundreds of mostly German states, including numerous city-states, and the German Confederation of 1815 was another loose collection of 39 sovereign German states. The first real 'German state' (if one ignores the federation of 1867) was a federation put together in 1871 by uniting 25 formerly sovereign states.

The collapse of Bismarck's Kaiserreich in 1918 led to the formation of the Weimar Republic, which was organised as a federation of first 18, then 17, states, now called *Länder*. When Hitler assumed power in January 1933, he not only established a one-party dictatorship but also eliminated the federal system.

At the conclusion of World War II in 1945, most of Pomerania,

Silesia, and the southern half of East Prussia were given to Poland, while the northern half of East Prussia was annexed by the Soviet Union. What had been the middle quarter of Germany was placed under Soviet occupation, while the Western half of the country was divided for occupation purposes among the United States, Great Britain and France. This western half became the Federal Republic of Germany in 1949, when the Basic Law, or constitution, was approved by the Western Allies and adopted by the parliaments of the previously created West German *Länder*. With the exceptions of Bavaria and the city-states of Bremen and Hamburg, these were not *Länder* with a long history of independence or autonomy but rather creations of the Allies. Lower Saxony, for example, was formed in 1946 by the British occupation authorities from the Prussian province of Hanover and the three small former *Länder* of Braunschweig, Oldenburg, and tiny Schaumburg–Lippe. North Rhine–Westphalia, Schleswig–Holstein, Hesse, the Rhineland-Palatinate, the Saarland, and Baden–Württemberg (formed in 1952) were also more or less artificial creations. West Berlin, of course, was a special case, and was legally though less in practice under Allied occupation until 1990.

Many people in the West were surprised to learn or had forgotten in 1989–90 that the East Germans had also established five *Länder* between December 1946 and February 1947 and provided them with democratic constitutions. These went so far as to guarantee private property and free enterprise, but they also provided a number of social welfare rights. In two cases they also limited private farm holdings to 100 hectares, in conformity with the Soviet–sponsored *land* reforms of 1946.

The five *Länder* were (1) Mecklenburg, created from the old *Länder* of Mecklenburg–Schwerin, Mecklenburg–Strelitz, and Vorpommern, the western part of the Prussian province of Pomerania; (2) Brandenburg, formed from the Prussian province of Brandenburg that lay west of the Oder River; (3) Saxony-Anhalt, a combination of the former *Land* of Anhalt and the Prussian province of Saxony; (4) Thuringia, the pre-1933 *Land* that had been formed in 1920 from several old Thuringian principalities; and (5) Saxony, the old *Land* of Saxony with a long history as an independent kingdom.

In 1945 the Allies in Potsdam called for decentralised political structures and local self-government in post-war Germany. The creation of the five *Länder* in the Soviet Zone of occupation was a result of that agreement. The 1949 constitution of the newly established GDR also provided for a federal system with five *Länder*; however, by the early

1950s it was clear that the Socialist Unity Party (SED) and the Soviets preferred a highly centralised unitary state, and in July 1952 the five *Länder* were reconstituted in *Kreise* (counties) and 15 *Bezirke* (districts), including East Berlin. In the process of drawing boundaries for these 15 districts, the old *Land* boundaries were often ignored.

Soon after the Wall fell, people in the GDR began to agitate for the re-establishment of the East German *Länder* created after the War.[2] Even though three of five of these had had little or no tradition and the East German experience with them had been short-lived, there was evidence that most East Germans identified with them more than they did with the GDR (now – 1993 – there is talk of a certain GDR 'nostalgia' which hardly existed in 1990). On June 21, 1990 a bill (*Ländereinführungsgesetz*) that amended the GDR constitution and provided for five *Länder* went through its first reading in the East German parliament, the *Volkskammer*. The bill provided not only for the five original *Länder*; it also saw united Berlin as a *Land*. It called for the formation of the *Länder* based on the boundaries of the *Bezirke*; however, the questions of which border territories (counties) should go to which *Land* were to be settled in nonbinding referenda (*Bürgerbefragungen*) by July 31, 1990.

The *Ländereinführungsgesetz* bill was passed into law on 22 July 1990. The five *Länder* with the border adjustments noted above came into being on 3 October, the day on which German unification took place. East Berlin, however, was joined with West Berlin as a result of the law of 22 July. In contrast to the five 'territorial states' that held their first elections on October 14, 1990, elections in Berlin were not held until 2 December, when the new *Bundestag* (federal parliament) was elected. The law contained provisions permitting additional boundary adjustments, and even before unification more than 140 cities and towns indicated they wished to change their territorial status, some even hoping to belong to West German *Länder* along the former border. After 1990 other adjustments continued to be made by state treaties between the individual *Länder*. The 15 *Bezirke* were abolished on May 31, 1990.

THE EXPERIENCE OF FEDERALISM IN THE WEST

A second important reason for the consensus concerning a united *federal* Germany lay in the generally positive experience with West German federalism. Of course, not all West Germans were entirely happy with federalism in a country about the size of the state of Oregon or Great Britain. They argued that federalism was too costly, inefficient, and unnecessary in a relatively small but densely populated country with little ethnic, cultural or religious conflict. Some complained that the federal system had been 'imposed' on them by the Western Allies, ignoring the long tradition of federalism in Germany and the general agreement among the founding fathers of the West German state that some form of federalism was desirable. Some also complained that federalism was a 'conservative' device to prevent uniform (and, of course, 'progressive') standards in various policy areas, especially education. Finally, there were and are those who argue that as desirable as federalism might be in the abstract, modern technology, the welfare state, the demands for 'uniform living conditions', and now increasingly the European Community, to name only some of the most obvious pressures, are requiring ever more centralisation of policy-making.[3]

In spite of the doubters, evidence from opinion polls and other sources suggest that most Germans support strongly the federal system and, in contrast to federalism in the Kaiserreich and Weimar, identify it with a highly successful if imperfect postwar democratic Germany. With the weakening of the particularism that did exist before the War due to: the millions of refugees who streamed into West Germany after being expelled from the Eastern territories or fleeing the GDR; the formation of new and artificially created *Länder*; the decline of religiosity; and the rise of a national welfare system, a national (and international) market, national television networks, and national standards for all kinds of activities, it might seem surprising that federalism would enjoy such support. This support probably derives from a generally positive experience with federalism in practice rather than any kind of theoretical position.

Thus a traditionally strong system of local government was preserved in the eight 'territorial' *Länder* (i.e. excluding the city-states Bremen, Hamburg and West Berlin). Under federalism, German local governments and *Länder* were able to experiment with policies that were sometimes adopted elsewhere but at other times were opposed in other regions. The traditional focus on administration even of most national laws by the *Länder* and local governments preserved important responsibilities for regional and local politicians and officials and probably reduced the bureaucratic 'overload' alleged by many to exist in the highly developed – and mostly unitary – states of Western Europe.

The existence of *Land* parliaments in addition to local councils has provided voters with additional opportunities to influence policies and personalities through regional elections and multiplied many times the number of politicians who were successful in participating in politics above the local level but did not or could not serve in the *Bundestag*. *Land* cabinets as well as parliaments have provided politicians with practical political and administrative/managerial experience above the local level and with a base of operations not found in unitary states. The unique institution of the *Bundesrat* makes it possible for regional leaders to participate even in national affairs, since the *Bundesrat* considers all national legislation with the right of either a suspensive or an absolute veto. Indeed, today the *Bundesrat* has an absolute veto over more than 50 per cent of all national legislation, i.e. those bills that affect the *Länder* in ways that permit the application of the absolute veto.

Regional leadership opportunities have contributed to the quantity and quality of political leaders available for national office. The existence of regional as well as local bases of political operations has also made it possible to create and maintain a non-centralised party system with regional leaders not infrequently willing to challenge the national leader or leaders. Federalism probably made it possible for some parties to come into existence (the Greens), for others to remain in existence (FDP), and for the major parties to lick their wounds and regenerate themselves (the CDU from 1969 to 1982 and the SPD since 1983). Thus federalism has served to promote and sustain party competition in ways that are not available to the British or French parties, for example.

DEVELOPMENTS OF GERMAN FEDERALISM, 1949–89

In both the United States and Germany, the concept of 'dual federalism' is frequently applied. In the American context, it means a division of powers between the national and state governments. The federal government as well as the state governments legislate, execute and adjudicate their own laws. Each level is responsible for financing its own public policies. There is little overlap; however, in case of conflict in an area of concurrent powers, federal law is supreme. This concept of dual federalism, while never applied in a pure form, prevailed until federal policies, identified mostly with the New Deal and, later, the Great Society, brought the federal government into areas previously considered to be the responsibility of the states or, in the view of some conservative critics, to be outside the area of any government's responsibility. Many of these policies called for some form of cooperation, for example, through shared financing between the federal and state/local governments, which led to what came to be called 'cooperative federalism'. Lyndon Johnson's Great Society programme brought about a dramatic increase in cooperative policies in which the national, state, and local governments shared in numerous ways the administrative and fiscal responsibility for most public services and activities. Since then the network of complex interrelationships among governments in the United States has been frequently referred to as 'intergovernmental relations' and has led to demands, such as those reflected in the 'sorting out' or 'swap' proposals of Ronald Reagan's 'new federalism', that efforts be undertaken to return to something more like the old dual federalism.

Germans also sometimes refer to the traditional German system of federalism as 'dual federalism', but here the concept can mean something quite different from the American term. What Germans usually mean is that federalism in the German tradition is characterised by policy-making in most areas at the national level and policy implementation at the *Land* level. The *Länder* are not, however, mere administrative subdivisions of the national government. They enjoy a large degree of autonomy in their administration of national policies. In addition, municipalities – in contrast to the *ultra vires* tradition in the Anglo-Saxon countries that restricts local government to the activities permitted them in their charters – have enjoyed considerable discretionary powers since the early nineteenth century, that is, the right to engage in any activity that does not violate national or *Land* law.

While German federalism has been characterised since the *Kaiserreich* by the delegation of national laws to the regional and then local governments for administration, the Bonn Basic Law did provide for some dualism in the American sense. For example, cultural affairs (including all aspects of education), police and administration of justice, local government law, and the administration of their own and national laws on their own responsibility were made *Land* functions. The original idea was also to have separate tax systems for the national and *Land* governments.

Thus the Federal Republic began in 1949 with a relatively strict division of powers.[4] However, as the years went by, centralising pressures were felt and a general transfer of legislative powers from the *Länder* to the federal level took place. By 1955–6 previously separate income and corporation taxes were made joint taxes, shared between the federal and *Land* governments. Increasing reliance was placed on federal government grants to make up for inadequate own source revenues of the *Länder*. These developments and others led many to conclude that without some kind of reform, federalism in Germany would be seriously undermined.

The Finance Reform of 1969 was designed to bring about some needed changes. Value added tax (VAT) was added to the income and corporation taxes as joint taxes shared in different proportions between the federal and *Land* governments, thus reducing *Land* dependency on federal grants. The *Länder* also expanded their self-coordination and 'horizontal' cooperation among functional ministries and through common institutions. 'Vertical' cooperation between the federal and *Land* governments also increased in a number of policy areas.

But the joint tasks (*Gemeinschaftsaufgaben*) that the 1969 Reform provided for in key amendments to the Basic Law in fact served to undermine further the autonomy of the *Länder*. Joint planning, decision-making, financing, and, to some extent, administration, became oriented toward certain tasks for which the *Länder* originally had been responsible. Accountability for policies became increasingly difficult to assign. Intergovernmental actions, a German version of 'cooperative federalism', had come to replace the 'dual federalism' of 1949.[5]

From 1949 to 1989 there were 35 amendments to the Basic Law. More than 20 of these had some effect on German federalism, above all in the expansion of powers for the federal government. In no case were the *Länder* given expanded powers. To the extent that they were compensated, it was in the form of increased *Land* cabinet participation in decision-making in the *Bundesrat*, not in more power for the *Land* parliaments. By the end of 1989 one expert on German federalism went so far as to conclude that 'the losses suffered by the *Länder* have led to a serious erosion of the substance of federalism, although the institutional structures of a federal system still exist. A unitary and centralised state form has been established behind the federal facade.'[6]

This same expert noted that a number of changes that seemed to indicate a reversal of the centralising trends were made by the new government of Chancellor Helmut Kohl after it took office in 1982. The *Länder* received a larger proportion of VAT, 'mixed financing' in some areas was eliminated or reduced, and the federal government removed itself or exercised self-restraint in other areas. These policy shifts, in addition to the comfortable CDU/CSU-FDP majorities in both the *Bundestag* and *Bundesrat*, which reduced some of the previous gridlock between the SPD-FDP-controlled *Bundestag* and the CDU/CSU-dominated *Bundesrat* that made life more difficult for SPD-Chancellor Schmidt (1974–82), seemed to set a new trend more favourable to federalism. The general result was a degree of disentanglement and decentralisation that represented a significant break with the past.

However, by the mid–1980s the fiscal situation of the federal government and the general political environment began to change in ways that were less favourable for federalism. The federal government took the initiative in a number of policy areas without seriously consulting the *Länder*. Divisions over finances between and even within the parties grew, and relations between the CDU-FDP central government and SPD *Land* governments became more tense. The CDU and FDP began to lose votes and even control over a number of *Land* governments, thus threatening the government's majority in the *Bundesrat*, which by the late 1980s did fall under the control of the opposition SPD. By the end of the decade it was clear that Kohl was not able to sustain his friendly position toward the *Länder*. The federal government returned to the previous focus on federal solutions to major problems, and it cut grants to the *Länder*. A 1988 federal law authorising supplementary aid to nine of the eleven West German *Länder* (*Strukturhilfegesetz*) has not been an adequate substitute for the cuts.[7]

This is not to say that the *Länder* have been left out of the decision-making process. Since the *Länder* administer most national laws, since the most important taxes are shared, and since the joint tasks involve the *Länder* by definition, the role of the *Bundesrat* has actually increased over the past decades. This provides opposition parties in control of *Land* governments, and even dissenting *Land* prime ministers associated with the governing coalition in Bonn, with additional opportunities to influence national decisions. But the *Bundesrat*'s role in lawmaking involves *Land* governments (cabinets), not parliaments, which are frequently left with the responsibility of merely ratifying actions of the *Bundesrat*.

In the meantime the *Länder* continue to complain of inadequate financing from their own source revenues, and they have objected to the cuts in federal grants. Tension between the 'poor' North, where many of the old smokestack industries are located, and the 'rich' South, where the high tech industries, Mercedes-Benz and BMW are found, have exacerbated the conflicts among the *Länder* with respect to fiscal equalisation policy.

The Unification Treaty of August 31, 1990 went into effect, then, in the context of a strong but troubled federal system in which national policy making, *Land* and local administration, shared taxes, joint tasks and joint planning had resulted in a complex system of shared powers and responsibilities (*Politikverflechtung*) subject to much criticism by numerous constitutional experts.

FEDERALISM IN THE UNITED GERMANY

As we have seen above, there seemed to be a popular consensus that federalism had been successful in the West German Federal Republic in spite of certain problems – not unlike many developments and trends in the United States – that needed to be addressed if federalism were not to become a mere front for increasing central government control. All previous challenges now seem minor, however, when compared to the situation confronting German federalism after unification in October 1990.

The most obvious of these challenges include the financing of the federal system, and especially fiscal transfers to the new eastern *Länder*; the impact of the five new *Länder* on the complexity of decision-making in the *Bundesrat* and other federal institutions, such as the conference of *Land* prime ministers; the issue of territorial reorganisation that would reduce the number of *Länder* with the goal of creating financially stronger regional units; the increasing integration of Europe and, in particular, the implications of the Maastricht Treaty on European Union for German federalism; and the numerous constitutional changes these challenges require or make desirable.

Fiscal Equalisation[8]

Unlike the United States, where each level of government determines which taxes to raise and at what rates, the most important German taxes are shared by the different levels while regulated by federal law; however, federal tax laws must be approved by the *Bundesrat*, which represents the *Land* governments. The shared taxes in Germany are those placed on income, corporations, and sales of services and products (VAT), which together are called joint taxes (*Gemeinschaftssteuern*). These account for more than two-thirds of all tax revenues in the Federal Republic. Since 1980 the municipalities have received 15 per cent of the income taxes derived from the payments of local citizens.

The remaining 85 per cent of the income tax and all of the revenues from the corporation tax are divided equally between the *Land* and the federal governments. The VAT, which is less sensitive to economic conditions than the income and corporation taxes, was added to the shared taxes by the Finance Reform of 1969. It was 14 per cent before January 1993, when it was raised to 15 per cent. The *Länder* received 35 per cent of the VAT until January 1993, when it was raised to 37 per cent (to be raised to 44 per cent in 1995).

Separate taxes, shared or common taxes, and federal grants to the *Länder* are all a part of what is called in Germany 'vertical fiscal (or tax) equalisation'. In order to provide a more equitable distribution of tax revenues than vertical equalisation alone can produce, a 'horizontal fiscal equalisation' among the *Länder* and municipalities has been added as an important feature of the *Land* and local tax systems. While the virtually uniform tax system does not produce the differences among the *Länder* that are found among the American states, the systems of vertical and horizontal tax equalisation are designed to assist the *Länder* still further in providing conditions approaching 'uniform living conditions'.

Though it was clear even before the Wall fell in November 1989 that the system of fiscal equalisation was in need of reform,[9] a political solution did not seem to be in sight. With unification approaching suddenly and unexpectedly, the situation changed dramatically.[10] Unless a temporary separate regulation for the five new *Länder* could be found, the former West German fiscal equalisation system would be overwhelmed. Equalisation funds would rise from DM 3.5 billion to DM 20 billion. All of the West German *Länder* with the exception of Bremen and perhaps the Saarland would become paying *Länder*, and they would all have to give up their supplementary federal grants. Because this scenario was unacceptable to the old *Länder*, provisions were made in the Treaty of Unification that was signed on August 31, 1990 for a special set of arrangements for the new *Länder*. In May the old *Länder* and the federal government had agreed to share the projected East German deficit on the basis of the ratio of one-third old *Länder*, one-third federal government, and one-third East German *Länder*. The West German share was set at DM 115 billion through 1994, to be paid through a specially created 'German Unity Fund'. DM 20 billion were to be raised by the federal government from savings gained from costs once attributed to the division of Germany (e.g. aid to West Berlin, aid to border regions). The rest was to be divided between the federal and *Land* governments and raised by borrowing. This would leave the old *Länder* with a DM 47.5 billion bill to pay.

The German Unity Fund was established by the old *Länder* in compensation for excluding the new *Länder* until January 1, 1995 from the normal vertical and horizontal fiscal equalisation schemes provided by the Basic Law. Experience soon showed these arrangements to be completely unsatisfactory, and a number of corrections were made in February 1991. The new *Länder* received their *full* share of VAT funds as of January 1991, although some division between East and West was retained. The federal government also gave up the 15 per cent of the German Unity Funds that it had intended to use for 'central' purposes. These changes increased aid to the new *Länder* by an additional DM 10 billion, and an additional DM 31 billion by 1994. Another special fund was also created that was to send DM 12 billion to the East in 1991 and 1992 for investments and work programmes. In spite of earlier assurances by Helmut Kohl that taxes would not have to be raised to finance unification, certain taxes were raised in 1991 when it became clear that the costs of unification were higher than anticipated. These tax increases were to provide an additional DM 46 billion to the East.

In addition to these measures, serious partisan controversy emerged toward the end of 1991 concerning an increase in the VAT from 14 to 15 per cent and an increase in the *Land* share in the VAT revenues from 35 to 37 per cent. The proposal passed in the *Bundestag*, but the SPD threatened to use its new majority in the *Bundesrat* to defeat the measure. The only *Land* in the East governed by the SPD, Brandenburg, deserted the national party, however, and voted with the Bonn government coalition parties in February 1992 to uphold the change.[11] The new *Länder* were to receive DM 23.4 billion in 1993 and 1994 from this change,[12] and they were to benefit as well from a DM 31 billion increase in the German Unity Fund between 1992 and 1994.[13]

Taken together, various transfers to the East are amounting to very large sums indeed, and it is clear that large transfers will continue in the coming years. In 1991 they amounted to DM 153 billion (almost $100 billion). The federal government, the German Unity Fund and the Trusteeship Agency (*Treuhandanstalt*) responsible for privatising the approximately 8500 businesses in East Germany (later separated into about 12 500 units) contributed DM 128 billion, the Federal Labour Office DM 19 billion, and various West German *Länder* and municipalities DM 6 billion. About 62 per cent of these funds were spent for various social measures (unemployment compensation, subsidised wages, etc.), and 38 per cent for investments.[14] Projections show that transfers to the East of about DM 180 billion will be required for the remainder of the 1990s.

In the meantime widespread dissatisfaction and pessimism in the East have resulted from high unemployment and underemployment, the relentless closing down or shrinking of whole industrial branches, and a feeling that the East Germans are misunderstood by their sometimes arrogant and contemptuous 'big brother' in the West. The expected rush by West Germans and other Westerners to invest in the East has not materialised as hoped: a largely neglected and decaying infrastructure (highways and roads, railways, telephone systems, etc.), outmoded industrial equipment, the collapse of markets in Eastern Europe, catastrophic environment pollution, inadequate and decaying housing, continued uncertainties regarding property ownership, and other serious deficiencies, in some cases not recognised or anticipated sufficiently in the West before unification, have too often discouraged would-be investors. In a *Bundesbank* report published in March 1992, it was noted that with 20 per cent of the population, the East was producing only 3.5 per cent of the German GDP.[15] In spite of the massive investments now taking place and planned for the near future, some observers are now suggesting that with luck the East Germans may be producing goods and services at 55 per cent of the per capita rate in the West by the end of the century.[16] Others have suggested that the East is about forty years behind the West in economic development.[17]

Given the economic conditions in the East, the heavy burdens on the federation and the realisation by the old *Länder* that admitting the new *Länder* to the West German system of fiscal equalisation would have devastating consequences for them made it clear that the federal government and *Länder* would have to devise a new financing system before 1995, when the new *Länder* were scheduled to join the equalisation system as regular members.

As a result of these pressures, the finance ministers of the 16 *Länder* formed in September 1991 a working group, 'Finance Reform 1995'. This group met regularly until the spring of 1993, during which time some of the larger, economically stronger, *Länder* promoted reform proposals generally opposed by the smaller, economically weaker, *Länder*.

The new *Länder* were, of course, interested in being included as soon as possible in the fiscal equalisation measures. But no model of reform could garner a majority.

The disagreements between the federation and the *Länder* were also a barrier to reaching consensus on a reform model. This encouraged the *Länder* to work together in order to counter the federal government's efforts to push through reforms that the *Länder* could see as disadvantageous to them. After many months of wrangling between the federal government and the *Länder* and among these as well, a 'solidarity pact' was finally reached in the spring of 1993.

Basically, the solidarity pact was a victory for the *Länder*. They succeeded in getting the federal government to agree that it was largely responsible for carrying the burden of subsidising the new *Länder* in the East. The result was that the proportions of the VAT shared by the federation and the *Länder* will be changed after 1995 from 63:37 to 56:44. The old *Länder* will contribute to the new *Länder* via the currently operating horizontal finance equalisation scheme as well as through certain changes in federal grants, and the federation will provide the new *Länder* supplementary grants for the next 10 years in the amount of 57 billion DM per year.[18] These changes have taken place, however, without constitutional amendment. Thus the fundamental reform that some observers thought essential was not part of the process described below.

More Complex Decision-Making

Federations are inherently complex systems. By definition they must resolve disagreements between central and regional authorities over the division of political and administrative powers. Disputes over taxes and revenues are endemic. High courts – in Germany the Federal Constitutional Court in Karlsruhe – are key institutions in conflict resolution in federal systems, but they have a limited role in making policy and accommodating interests on a routine basis. The institution designed to do this more than any other in Germany is the *Bundesrat*, an organ given the constitutional function of representing the interests of *Land* governments, i.e. cabinets (and not the *Land* parliaments) in the policy-making process. According to the Federal Constitutional Court, it is not really a second house of parliament, even though it is often viewed as such. It is not a popularly elected body but rather one in which specially designated *Land* cabinet ministers cast from three to six block votes. The *Bundesrat* votes on all laws passed by the *Bundestag*, exercising an absolute veto over questions affecting the *Länder* (more than half of all bills) and a suspensive veto over other matters. In fact most disagreements between the *Bundestag* and

Bundesrat are dealt with in mediating (conference) committee meetings called for the specific purpose of reaching a compromise between the two legislative bodies. Before unification there were ten *Länder* with 41 votes in the *Bundesrat*, not counting West Berlin's 4 consultative votes. Each of the largest West German *Länder* – North-Rhine Westphalia, Bavaria, Baden-Württemberg, and Lower Saxony – received 5 votes; Hesse, Schleswig-Holstein, and the Rhineland-Palatinate received 4; and the Saarland, Hamburg, and Bremen received 3.

When the five East German *Länder* joined the Federal Republic, 3 votes were given to Mecklenburg-West Pomerania and 4 each to the other 4 *Länder*. In order to reduce the disproportionate weight that the smaller West German *Länder* and the new *Länder* would have, and especially to prevent them from forming a two-thirds majority for the purpose of amending the Basic Law, the Unification Treaty of August 31, 1990 raised the number of votes for the largest *Länder* to 6 each. This has increased the total number of votes in the *Bundesrat* to 68. With about 23 per cent of the total population of Germany, the five new *Länder* are still overrepresented with 28 per cent of the votes. On the other hand, there is no East German *Land* that is large enough to receive 6 votes (which requires a population of 7 million) and serve as a partial counterweight to the large *Länder* in the West.

The expanded size of the *Bundesrat* will undoubtedly complicate the decision-making process and make the federal system even less transparent than it was with eleven *Länder*. The larger number of *Länder* will also make somewhat more unwieldy the various conferences of the *Land* prime ministers and functional ministers as well as the numerous bodies that meet within the framework of the joint tasks.[19]

Territorial Reorganisation

The creation of five new *Länder* in the East has revived an old and divisive debate in Germany regarding a *Neugliederung* or re-ordering and re-organisation of the *Länder*. In general the restructuring of *Land* boundaries in Germany has occurred only under severe pressure from the outside and/or as the result of war.

In the late 1960s there was much discussion of territorial reform in Germany, including boundary reforms for the villages, towns, cities, counties, and, of course, the *Länder*. Major territorial reforms were enacted at the local level in the eight territorial *Länder*,[20] and a commission was formed to look at the *Land* boundaries. This commission, called the Ernst-Kommission, recommended major boundary changes.[21] It proposed that the Federal Republic have either five or six *Länder*. Nothing ever came of these proposals, due in part to the Finance Reform of 1969 and the rise of 'cooperative federalism'.

Since early 1990 discussions concerning a re-ordering of boundaries and a reduction in the number of *Länder* have continued unabated. There is relatively little controversy over the proposal to combine Berlin and Brandenburg into one *Land*, but proposals to incorporate the smaller and weaker *Länder* in the West, especially Bremen and the Saarland (Hamburg has indicated a willingness to consider consolidation with one or more of its neighbours), into larger neighbouring *Länder* and to reduce the number of *Länder* in the East have led to heated debate. As an alternative there has also been some discussion of cooperative arrangements between *Länder* to promote common goals.[22]

There are powerful arguments both for and against a redrawing of *Land* boundaries and a reduction in the number of *Länder* from 16 to 8 or 10.[23] It seems clear at the time of writing, however, that with the possible exception of Berlin and Brandenburg, there will be no consolidations or redrawing of boundaries. The *Länder* that are the most obvious targets in the West, namely Bremen and the Saarland, are the most vehemently opposed to consolidation; and it would not be easy to convince the *Länder* in the East that they should merge after having just been re-established.

Nevertheless, the joint constitutional commission (see below) has recommended changes in Article 29, which deals with territorial reorganisation. The key change would allow the *Länder* to negotiate state treaties for the purpose of altering boundaries. Whether affecting a small boundary region or an entire *Land*, the treaty would be subject to popular approval by referendum. The required majority would have to constitute no less than 25 per cent of the eligible voting population. In essence, the recommendations make boundary changes somewhat easier to achieve; however, the required referendum is still a high barrier.

The Länder and the European Community[24]

As the only federal system in the EC, the German *Länder* have been caught in the dilemma of supporting European integration while at the same time finding it necessary to resist developments that threaten to or actually do undermine *Land* autonomy in certain functional areas. An important constitutional provision in this regard is Article 24 of the Basic Law, paragraph 1 of which states that 'The Federation may by legislation transfer sovereign powers to intergovernmental institutions'. This means that the federal government can transfer not only its own but also *Land* powers to the EC without the approval of the *Länder*, in spite of Article 79 which guarantees federalism in Germany. In addition, Article 235 of the EC Treaty grants 'implied powers' to the EC, including education, broadcasting, and media, i.e. *Land* powers. Because of the growing influence of the EC in European policy-making in general, the *Länder* fear increasing marginalisation.[25]

The *Länder* have been concerned about the effect of the European Community on their autonomy from the beginning, and initial efforts by the *Bundesrat* to protect *Land* interests proved ineffective.[26] Between the late 1970s and the late 1980s, however, the *Länder*, via the *Bundesrat*, won several important concessions from the federal government and gained some influence over federal policy-making with respect to the EC.[27] To help them anticipate issues that needed to be raised in the *Bundesrat* and to keep informed generally about EC matters, the *Länder* opened their own information offices in Brussels.[28]

In July 1990, before unification in October, the prime ministers of the German *Länder* met and produced a document on 'cornerstones' (*Eckpunkte*) of German federalism. Among other things, the document calls for a revision of Article 24 to give the *Länder* a greater voice in transferring powers to intergovernmental organisations (primarily the EC). Later, Article 5 of the Unification Treaty of August 1990 called for constitutional revisions in order to adapt the German Basic Law to the changes unification had brought about.

At the same time pressures for more European integration, the result in part of German unification, were serving as a powerful incentive to adapt the Basic Law to a more integrated Europe. These pressures culminated in the Maastricht Treaty on European Union which was negotiated in December 1991. This treaty required two specific revisions of the Basic Law: Article 28, which deals with local government, had to be revised to allow citizens of the EC with residences in Germany to vote in local elections; and Article 88 had to be changed to allow the transfer of the functions of the Bundesbank to an EC central bank. But other changes were called for as well.

When the joint constitutional commission (see below) met for the first time in January 1992, it was clear that one of the most important revisions of the Basic Law would have to concern the relationship of the *Länder* to the EC. As a result of the deliberations of the commission, the old Article 23, which had been used as the means of uniting the two Germanies in 1990, was replaced entirely by a new Article 23 which deals with the European Union (as it is now called under the Maastricht Treaty). The new Article 23 notes the participation of Germany in the development of a democratic European Union with the purpose of achieving a united Europe. It mentions specifically the principles of federalism and subsidiarity and the guarantees of basic rights. It states that the federation, with the approval of the *Bundesrat*, can transfer sovereign rights to the EU. The federal government is required to take into consideration the views of the *Bundestag* in its decision-making process regarding the affairs of the EU; however, it is not bound to follow these views. In cases where the functions involved belong to the federation, the views of the *Bundesrat* must also be taken into account; however, where *Land* powers are affected, the federal government must for all practical purposes follow the wishes of the *Bundesrat*. Article 23 even goes so far as to allow the representative of a *Land* government to exercise the rights of the Federal Republic in the Council of Ministers when the issues at stake involve *Land* powers. In order to carry out these provisions, Article 45 was revised to create a 'Europe Committee' in the *Bundestag*. Article 52 allows the *Bundestag* to form a 'Europe Chamber'. In both cases these committees are responsible for dealing with the federal government under the provisions outlined above in Article 23. Unlike other recommendations by the joint constitutional commission for changes in the Basic Law, the recommendations described above regarding the European Union were approved by the *Bundestag* and *Bundesrat* in December 1992.

Constitutional Reform and Federalism

There were two impulses after 1989 that required serious consideration of constitutional reform. The first of these was Article 5 of the Treaty of Unification which 'recommends' that the *Bundestag* and *Bundesrat* take up the issue of constitutional revision, looking especially at provisions affecting the relationship between the *Länder* and the federation and at the possibility of consolidating Berlin and Brandenburg. It also suggests that consideration be given to the issue of adding to the Basic Law certain goals of the state (*Staatszielbestimmungen*) and to the application of Article 146.

Some constitutional changes occurred already under Article 4 of the Treaty of Unification. Thus Article 23, under which the five new *Länder* joined the Federal Republic, was repealed. The preamble of the Basic Law was changed to add the five new *Länder* to the list of *Länder* in Germany and to state that the Basic Law now applies to all Germans. The four largest *Länder,* all located in the West, were given six rather than five votes in the *Bundesrat.* And, in addition to other changes, Article 146 of the Basic Law was revised to read: 'This Basic Law, which applies to the whole German people following the realisation of unity and freedom, will lose its validity on the day on which a new constitution goes into effect which has been freely accepted by the German people.'[29]

In March 1991 the *Bundesrat* formed a 'Commission Constitutional Reform' for the purpose of recommending changes in the Basic Law that would strengthen the *Länder,* and it submitted a report in May 1992. In the meantime, during the debate in the *Bundestag* in May 1991 concerning the recommendations of Article 5 of the Unification Treaty, it became clear that the governing and opposition parties had different views on how implementation was to proceed. The CDU/ CSU–FDP coalition advocated the creation of a constitutional committee with 32 members, 16 each from the *Bundestag* and *Bundesrat.* The SPD urged the formation of a much larger constitutional council with 120 members, including not only politicians but also representatives from the scientific, cultural, economic, labour, and other walks of life. These proposals symbolised significant differences over the nature of the changes to be made, i.e. minor adjustments or a thoroughgoing review. Not surprisingly, the Greens and Bündnis 90 called for a 'total revision', whereas SPD spokespersons indicated their commitment to the major points of the Basic Law but also their support for numerous changes. The CDU/CSU and FDP objected to a general review and to participation by persons outside of parliament. The governing parties also rejected the proposal of the SPD to hold a referendum on the revised Basic Law.[30]

Finally, a 'Joint Constitutional Commission', consisting of 32 members each from the *Bundestag* and *Bundesrat*, was formed in January 1992. It considered the *Bundesrat* recommendations as well as the proposals made by other bodies, but it did not consider itself bound by any of them.

From January 1992 to the fall of 1993, the joint constitutional commission met 26 times and held nine hearings. It considered eighty proposals for changing the Basic Law and looked at one-half of the Basic Law's articles in the process.[31] We have already reviewed briefly the changes made by the commission concerning territorial reorganisation and European Union. Also of considerable significance for our purposes were the numerous recommendations made in general areas of federalism.

For many years there has been concern in Germany regarding the increasing centralisation of functions and weakening of the *Länder* brought about not only by the fiscal relations described above in an earlier section, joint tasks, federal grants, and European integration. Also of great significance have been federal preemptions of concurrent powers and detailed federal regulations via the framework laws. In order to strengthen the *Länder,* at least with respect to concurrent powers and framework laws, the commission has recommended a number of changes.

For Article 72, which deals with concurrent powers, the recommendation was made to insert more precise language to limit federal preemptions to specific laws rather than to allow the federation to absorb a broad function based merely on a partial preemption. Another recommendation gives the federation preemption rights in order to secure legal uniformity or '*equivalent* living conditions' around the country rather than '*uniform* living conditions' as before. Since it is obviously difficult to interpret this provision, a proposed revision of Article 93 gives the *Bundesrat,* a *Land* government (cabinet), or a *Land* parliament the right to go to the Federal Constitutional Court for clarification in specific cases.[32]

Article 75 provides for federal framework laws. The commission's recommendations make more precise language which gives the federation the right to pass framework legislation regarding higher education by limiting the legislation to several areas rather than talking about 'general principles of higher education'. The recommendations also discourage detailed federal regulations. The recommendations for Article 76 would grant the *Bundesrat* nine rather than six weeks to react to federal government proposals 'for important reasons'; the federal government may still impose a three-week time limit in certain urgent cases. The recommendations would also harmonise the provisions regarding legislative initiatives of the *Bundesrat,* i.e. these may be sent to the *Bundestag* for its deliberation within nine weeks rather than the normal six weeks (instead of the previous three months) if the federal government so requests 'for important reasons'. The *Bundesrat* may also request action within three weeks for urgent matters. Both the *Bundestag* and the *Bundesrat* are to complete their deliberations within a reasonable period of time.

Other important recommendations relevant to German federalism concern Articles 24 and 28. The proposal for Article 24 would grant the *Länder* the right to transfer, with approval by the federal government, certain sovereign powers to transnational border authorities for the purpose of dealing with common problems. A recommended addition to Article 28 calls for including the principles of autonomous financial responsibility in the guarantee of local self-government. It is not entirely clear what this really means, since it is not supposed to be interpreted as committing the federation to a guarantee of financial support for local governments.

All of these and other recommendations made by the joint constitutional commission will be considered by the *Bundestag* and *Bundesrat* during the winter of 1994. Since they all received the required two-thirds majority in the commission, which included party representatives in proportion to their strength in parliament, they are all expected to pass. On the other hand, there may be some efforts on the part of critical elements within the various parties to change certain parts of the 'package' proposal. If such efforts should be successful in one or more cases, certain key recommendations and even the whole package may be at risk.

CONCLUSION

When the two German states united on October 3, 1990, they faced the challenge of bringing together two societies that had lived under radically different political, social, and economic systems and political cultures for at least forty years. It was apparent from the beginning that the new Germany would look rather like the old West Germany, whereas very little of what had been the East German political and economic systems would survive. It was also taken for granted that, like the former West Germany, the new Germany would be a federal system. This was not only because of a long tradition in Germany of federal, confederal, or semi-confederal states or associations, and Article 79 of the Basic Law which requires the federal organisation of Germany, but also because of the generally positive experience and high regard for federalism that had developed in West Germany over the years.

West German federalism had been generally successful, but – not surprisingly – it was also an imperfect system. Strong centralising pressures had been felt from the beginning, and political practice as well as constitutional amendments, whether intended or not, had forced the *Länder* to share or even give up numerous powers to the central government. This applied to the system of taxation and fiscal equalisation in particular. The end result was somewhat analogous to 'intergovernmental relations' in the United States, which the Germans called 'cooperative federalism' and then *'Politikverflechtung'*. As in the case of American states, certain efforts were undertaken to strengthen the *Länder* vis-a-vis the federal government, but these were neither dramatic nor lasting.

With unification, German federalism faces a set of additional and in part new challenges. Among the most obvious of these are

- tax and fiscal equalisation systems badly in need of reform in order to provide the *Länder* with the resources necessary to carry out their functions adequately;
- a more complicated decisionmaking process due to a larger number of *Land* representatives in the *Bundesrat* and in various committees established to make or coordinate decisions involving, vertically, federal and *Land* governments or, horizontally, *Land* prime ministers and functional cabinet ministers;
- dramatic differences among the *Länder* in size, population, and tax revenues and the demands by many experts to redraw *Land* boundaries in order to create fewer and more viable regional units that are more likely to maintain their autonomy and are less dependent on federal grants;
- a serious challenge of the European Community to the authority and autonomy of the *Länder*;
- various proposals to amend the federal Basic Law, some of which have been from the beginning or have become controversial and divisive.

To some extent 'solutions' to some of the older problems and newer challenges of German federalism may be found in the proposals for constitutional revisions that were considered and recommended in 1992 and 1993 by the joint constitutional commission established in January 1992. These do seem to address seriously some of the problems of growing centralisation in German federalism and threats to *Land* autonomy through the transfer of sovereign powers to the EU (formerly EC) and through the actions of the EU bureaucracy. It is clear, however, that no constitutional amendments can answer all of the questions or deal with all of the issues affecting the health and future of German federalism. Federalism in Germany will remain an important subject for scholarly attention and dispute for a very long time to come.

Notes

1. *Das Parlament*, December 8, 1989, pp. 4–6.
2. For a more detailed discussion of plans and developments concerning the re-establishment of the Eastern *Länder*, see Arthur B. Gunlicks, 'Federalism and German Unification', *Politics and Society in Germany, Austria and Switzerland*, vol. 4, (Spring 1992), no. 2, pp. 52–66.
3. See also Arthur B. Gunlicks, 'Some Thoughts on Federalism and the Federal Republic', *German Politics and Society*, no. 15 (October 1988), pp. 1–7.
4. For a discussion in English of the development of German federalism from 1949 to 1989, see Hartmut Klatt, 'Forty Years of German Federalism: Past Trends and New Developments', in Arthur B. Gunlicks (ed.), 'Federalism and Intergovernmental Relations in West Germany: A Fortieth Year Appraisal', special issue of *Publius: The Journal of Federalism*, vol. 19, (Fall 1989) no. 4, pp. 185–202. Another version of this chapter can be found in *German Federalism Today*, ed. Charlie Jeffery and Peter Savigear (New York: St. Martin's Press, 1991), pp. 120–137.
5. Klatt, 'Forty Years', p. 189.
6. Ibid., p. 191.
7. Ibid., pp. 199–200.
8. Much of the following discussion is taken from my chapter, 'The Future of Federalism in a Unified Germany', in *The Domestic Politics of German Unification*, ed. by Christopher Anderson, Karl Kaltenthaler and Wolfgang Luthardt (Boulder: Lynne Rienner Publishers, 1993), pp. 159–64.
9. Ulrich Exler, 'Financing German Federalism: Problems of Financial Equalisation in the Unification Process', in *Federalism, Unification and European Integration*, ed. by Charlie Jeffrey and Roland Sturm (London: Frank Cass, 1993), pp. 22–37.
10. The following discussion is based on Wolfgang Renzsch, *Finanzverfassung und Finanzausgleich* (Bonn: Verlag J. H. W. Dietz Nachf., 1991), pp. 274–81.
11. See *The German Tribune*, February 28, 1992, p. 3.
12. Ibid.
13. BNA's *Eastern Europe Reporter*, vol. 2, no. 5 (March 2, 1992), p. 172.
14. Bundestag *Report* 6/91 (October 12, 1991), p. 12.
15. 'Die Zahlungen an Ostdeutschland verringern', *Frankfurter Allgemeine Zeitung*, March 19, 1992, p. 15.
16. Peter Christ, 'Der Osten schreibt rot', *Die Zeit*, North American edition (March 6, 1992), pp. 7–8.
17. Lothar Julitz, 'Die Investitionslücke schliessen', *Frankfurter Allgemeine Zeitung*, March 13, 1992, p. 15.
18. For a brief review of the 'solidarity pact', see Wolfgang Renzsch, 'Die Finanzverfassungsreform blieb aus', in *Das Parlament*, vol. 2 (January 14, 1994), p. 14.
19. See also Hartmut Klatt, 'Der kooperative Bundesstaat: Entwicklungslinien und neue Herausforderungen', in *Föderalismus in der Bewährungsprobe: Die Bundesrepublik Deutschland in den 90er Jahren*, ed. Arthur B. Gunlicks

and Rüdiger Voigt (Bochum: Universitätsverlag Dr. N. Brockmeyer, 1991), pp. 256–7.

20. Arthur B. Gunlicks, *Local Government in the German Federal System* (Durham: Duke University Press, 1986), ch. 4; and *Local Government Reform and Reorganization: An International Perspective* (Port Washington: Kennikat Press, 1981), ch. 10.

21. Bundesministerium des Innern, *Bericht der Sachverständigenkommission für die Neugliederung des Bundesgebietes* (Ernst-Kommission) (Bonn, 1973).

22. For an excellent analysis of the problems of territorial reorganisation and a discussion of regional cooperation as an alternative, see Arthur Benz, 'Redrawing the Map? The Question of Territorial Reform in the Federal Republic', in *Federalism, Unification and European Integration*, pp. 38–57.

23. Ibid. See also Gunlicks, *The Domestic Politics of German Unification*, pp. 155–9; Uwe Leonardy, 'Into the 1990s: Federalism and German Unification', in *German Federalism Today*, pp. 143–7. For a strong pro argument in German, see Ulrich Penski, 'Die Vereinigung beider deutscher Staaten als Problem und Herausforderung für das föderalistische System in Deutschland', in Föderalismus in der Bewährungsprobe, pp. 265–71.

24. For a more detailed discussion, see my chapter in *The Domestic Politics of German Unification*, pp. 167–71.

25. Michael Burgess and Franz Gress, 'German Unity and European Union: Federalism Repulsed or Revitalised?', in *Regional Politics and Policy*, forthcoming; for a list of policy areas in which the *Länder* see EC interference, see Rudolf Hrbek, 'German Federalism and the Challenge of European Integration', in *German Federalism Today*, pp. 86–7.

26. Klaus Otto Nass, 'The Foreign and European Policy of the German *Länder*', *Publius: The Journal of Federalism*, vol. 19, no. 4 (Fall 1989), pp. 175–6.

27. Ibid., p. 178; Hrbek, 'German Federalism', pp. 94–6.

28. Hrbek, 'German Federalism', pp. 96–7.

29. The text of the Treaty of Unity of 31 August 1990 can be found in *Europa Archiv* (25 October 1990), pp. D 515–D 536.

30. *Bundestag Report* 4/91 (May 29, 1991), pp. 2–4.

31. For a useful set of articles summarising the background, work, and accomplishments of the constitutional commission, see the entire issue of *Das Parlament*, vol. 44, no. 2 (14. January 1994). The official government publication which deals with the constitutional commission in considerable detail is *Bericht der Gemeinsamen Verfassungskommission*, Deutscher Bundestag, 12. Wahlperiode, Drucksache 12/6000, dated November 5, 1993.

32. A discussion of this and the following recommendations can be found in the *Bericht der Gemeinsamen Verfassungskommission*, Drucksache 12/6000.

13 Leadership Change in Eastern Germany: From Colonisation to Integration?

Thomas A. Baylis

One mark of a revolution is the comprehensiveness with which old élites are replaced by new ones in the most influential political, economic, and cultural positions of the society in question. At least in this respect, there is no question but that the upheaval in the former German Democratic Republic that began in the autumn of 1989 was a genuine revolution. In other cases of revolutionary élite transformation, however, the old leaders were replaced by new ones drawn from a pre-existing 'counterélite,' with those who led or at least participated in making the revolution generally taking over the most important posts. Here the East German case deviates from the revolutionary norm; the most important positions influencing the fate of East Germans today are occupied by outsiders – West Germans – whose role in the revolution was at best that of interested spectators. East Germans, with some exceptions, find themselves in subordinate roles – although a few of these might be classified as secondary élite positions. The new élite thus resembles an authentic revolutionary leadership far less than it does a classic colonial one.

Kolonisierung, like *Anschluss*, is a term with unhappy connotations for Germans, and those who use it are likely to face some of the bitter recriminations that have tainted so much of the German debate over the process and consequences to date of unification.[1] Since the fact of West German élite dominance in the 'five new *Länder*' or 'accession area' (both terms that unconsciously reflect the *Anschluss* mentality) is difficult to gainsay, defenders of what one might term real existing unification are inclined to argue that no feasible alternative to it ever existed.[2] The communist-era élite, they urge, was too thoroughly discredited, and the numbers, education, experience, and popular credibility of any potential East German 'counterélite' too

243

small to offer a realistic alternative to a West German élite takeover. The at best chequered performance of indigenous postcommunist élites elsewhere in East Central Europe could easily be cited in support of such a conclusion. Such commentators also suggest, with some accuracy, that the Western takeover simply responded to the desires of East Germans, expressed most emphatically in their overwhelming vote for the CDU and its allies in the March 1990 elections. Thus what took place might justly be described as 'self-colonisation'.[3]

I am suspicious of the frequently voiced assertion that no path to German unity other than the one actually taken in 1990 was practicable in the atmosphere of crisis that reigned at the time. My purpose in this chapter is, however, not to speculate about foregone alternatives but rather to describe the extent and nature of élite colonisation in the post-GDR and to explore some of its consequences. The question of élite composition and character in present-day Eastern Germany, as elsewhere, is not just a matter of sociological description; it is a question of 'voice' and identity. To what extent can the new élite speak for, or on behalf of, a now deeply disgruntled population? What can the present configuration of élites tell us about the struggle in both parts of the Federal Republic to find a satisfactory post-Cold War identity? What – a closely related problem – is the potential under these circumstances for building élite *consensus*, sometimes identified as the hallmark of stable democracies?

THE PATTERN OF ELITE COLONISATION

Poland, Hungary, Czechoslovakia, other East European countries and the newly independent members of the Commonwealth of Independent States had no alternative but to look within for their new élites. Initially, leadership change in the GDR followed a pattern much like those of its neighbours. Beginning with the deposing of Erich Honecker and Günter Mittag, the 'old' communist leadership was in a matter of weeks replaced by a younger set of party leaders committed in varying degrees to political and economic reform. These in turn entered into 'Round Table' negotiations with figures from the former opposition, who ultimately agreed to a form of power-sharing arrangement and even produced the draft of a new GDR constitution. The democratic elections promised by the reformers then brought the formation of an anti-communist government made up of East Germans, only one of whom, Rainer Eppelmann, had been a prominent figure in the opposition prior to the fall of the Berlin Wall; most of the rest had been little-known figures with no apparent links either to the SED or to the opposition.[4]

Well before the elections, however, West Germans had begun to play a prominent role in East German life. The weakness of the newly formed East German parties and the poor credibility of the former 'satellite' parties, combined with the competition of the major West German parties for favour among both their existing and prospective electorates, led to a campaign dominated by the westerners. West German politicians offered rapid unification as the only answer to mounting economic uncertainties and the continuing exodus of East Germans to the West; they also argued that the 'window of opportunity' for union offered by Gorbachev's policies might not remain open for long. With honourable exceptions, they failed to discuss the costs of unification.[5] Understandably, East German voters paid much more attention to them than to their own fledgling party leaders. Meanwhile, West German businessmen in search of investment and sales opportunities hurried to the East; the first West German professors took up posts at East German universities (e.g. Kurt Biedenkopf, who went to Leipzig as a visiting faculty member in April 1990). East Germans, facing the pervasive uncertainties of the transition period, had every reason to seek allies in important West German institutions as quickly as possible.

The terms of economic and political unity that the new East German government quickly agreed to made the need for Western personnel still more pressing. The agreement to introduce a market economy almost instantly as the necessary prerequisite for currency union; to adopt West German law, educational structures, bureaucratic practices, and social security provisions; and otherwise to replace the GDR's institutions with West German ones, created a massive need for West German personnel. East German negotiators – conservative, inexperienced, and operating from a weak bargaining position – were rarely moved to insist upon the retention of significant elements of the GDR's system; Western negotiators were even less inclined to grant such concessions. Under severe (albeit self-imposed) time pressures, the argument that adopting 'proven' Western institutions wholesale would be far easier than working out painful compromises with the 'failed' institutions of the GDR seemed too compelling to resist. The implications of these institutional decisions for the configuration of the postcommunist élites were largely irresistible.[6]

Thus thousands of West Germans – albeit far fewer than were said

to be needed – moved East to occupy key positions in East German
governments, bureaucracies, and universities, as well as in business
sold to or launched by West German firms or still under the control
of the *Treuhand*. Some came out of retirement to do so, others were
'seconded' by their public or private employers, generally for limited
periods of time. Some came from genuine idealism, others under pressure
from their employers or because the new posts seemed to offer career
opportunities and financial rewards not available to them at home.
Many were unable or unwilling to settle their families in the East,
choosing instead to commute back to the West at weekends.[7] Their
skills at operating within the framework of West German law and
administrative practice and their experience at capitalist management
were probably indispensable under the circumstances. But their understanding of the context in which they now must act was often deficient.
One suspects that, in common with most of their countrymen, they
knew little about the GDR prior to the upheaval of 1989, and the
depth of their commitment and their sensitivity to the plight of their
East German subordinates and colleagues varied widely.

That former high SED officials would be barred from public positions of importance – even in the SED successor party, the PDS, itself – was clear from the outset.[8] But lower-ranking party officials,
most of those with connections of any sort to the state security police, the Stasi, and those trained in politically suspect fields such as
the social sciences, law, or philosophy have also been largely excluded. The very extent of Stasi operations and the degree to which
ideological criteria penetrated the educational system and influenced
career advancement in the old GDR assured that many of the most
gifted, well-trained, and experienced East Germans were effectively
barred from taking important positions in the new German order. Much
more so than in Poland or Hungary, entrance to higher education and
most careers had been dependent on party membership and/or other
evidence of social activism in support of the old regime. More than
one out of every six adult GDR citizens had belonged to the party,
with the proportion roughly twice that among university and *Fachschule*
graduates.[9] The rigour with which the SED suppressed internal efforts
at reform, intra-party factionalism or dissent also made it difficult for
former SED members to demonstrate that they had worked for fundamental change from 'within' – although some in fact had. The 'reform communists' of the SED's successor party, the PDS, while for
the moment represented in the *Bundestag*, were forced into the role
of an ostracised opposition, since other parties viewed them as a pol-

itical embarrassment and refused to risk the opprobrium of dealing with them.

The pervasive control, internal discipline, and ideological rigidity of the old SED was mirrored in the weakness of the GDR's political opposition. While Poland's Solidarity movement and Czechoslovakia's Charter 77 provided something of a pool for members of the new élite in those countries, nothing of comparable dimensions ever emerged in the GDR. The small circles of dissenters protected by the Evangelical Church played a catalytic role in the events of autumn 1989, and the writers and other cultural figures who gave voice to measured criticism of the regime helped lay some of the groundwork for the upheaval. But the numbers of both were relatively small; also, most such groups, we now know, were extensively penetrated by the Stasi. The dissenters – pastors, natural scientists, artists – had had little opportunity to acquire political or administrative skills. Their previous advocacy of a 'humane socialism' or 'third way', while sometimes dictated by tactical considerations, worked to their political disadvantage in the postcommunist era. Thus while representatives of *Neues Forum* and other opposition groups took a prominent role during the immediate transition from communist rule, only a few have enjoyed much influence since unification.

Something of an intermediary position between former SED members and opposition figures is occupied by those who belonged to the former 'satellite' or 'bloc' parties, especially the CDU and LDPD (Liberal Democrats), which have now merged with the West German CDU and FDP. In the old GDR, membership of such parties, whose policies and pronouncements rarely deviated from those of the ruling party, provided a means by which some citizens could meet the state's demand for social engagement without joining the SED itself. As beneficiaries of the 1990 GDR, *Land*, and national elections, a number of lower-ranking officials and members of the old CDU and LDP obtained important posts in the unified parties, the new governments, or even in Bonn. Some have since lost their jobs because of revelations of Stasi ties or other questionable past activities, while others have come under attack owing to their reputations as veteran 'Blockflöten'.

However much responsibility ordinary East Germans share for the dominance of West Germans in the new élites, many of the former now bitterly resent the fact that their future is being shaped by forces over which they believe they have little or no control. Many have come to view the West and its political class, as *Der Spiegel* has remarked, not as guarantors of freedom and well-being, but as 'new conquerors and exploiters'.[10] They see no one speaking for them in Bonn, and few in their own *Land* capitals. The numerous East Germans still in middle-ranking positions in the economy, the state bureaucracy, the educational system, or elsewhere, usually find themselves the subordinates of West Germans, and harbour predictable resentments toward them. The West Germans, for their part, often complain of the lack of initiative or poor work habits of their underlings. Clichés about arrogant 'Besserwessis' and whining and ungrateful Ossis flourish in such an atmosphere, offering little hope that the East–West cultural and psychological divide can be overcome in the near future.

THE POLITICAL ELITE

The meagre representation of East Germans in the Federal government and in the leadership of the major parties can be viewed both as a product of the shortage of able personnel and of the desire of West Germans to leave the accustomed patterns of the country's politics as little disturbed as possible by the accession of the former GDR. Just three in the Kohl government named after the 1990 elections ministers came from the former GDR, none of them in critical ministries: the controversial Minister for Transport, Günther Krause, formerly the GDR's chief negotiator over the unification treaty; the Minister for Youth and Family Affairs (and CDU Deputy Chairperson) Angela Merkel; and the Minister for Education, Rainer Ortleb (FDP). By early 1994, only Merkel remained. The GDR's former Prime Minister, Lothar de Maizière, was forced to give up his cabinet position and party posts in the wake of charges (which he continues to dispute) of links to the Stasi. It is also worth noting that the former Ministry for Inner-German Relations has been dissolved; no new ministry for East Germany's reconstruction has replaced it, in spite of suggestions to that effect. Four Parliamentary State Secretaries (in effect, junior ministers) are from the ex-GDR.[11]

The Eastern States send some 140 members to the *Bundestag* and are represented in the *Bundesrat*, although the number of votes in the latter given to the larger West German states was increased in order to dilute the impact of the small new *Länder*. No East German is a deputy *Bundestag* president, and few are found in leading positions of the three major parties: just two of the 13 members of the SPD's *Vorstand* are East Germans, for example. Only a handful of East German deputies can be said to enjoy any prominence as spokespersons for their part of the country; the SPD's Wolfgang Thierse – 'the most aggressive, the loudest and the most conscious politician from Eastern Germany who now holds a leading political position in the united Germany' – is the best-known of these. In June 1992 the 63 east German CDU deputies and, separately, some 20 East German deputies from all three major parties provoked some discomfort among their Western colleagues by forming groups to promote their joint interests.[12]

In the new *Länder*, two of the five Minister-Presidents are from the West, and the Governing Mayor of Berlin is from the Western part of the city. Kurt Biedenkopf, once the West German CDU General Secretary, heads the government of Saxony, the largest of the East German states and the one with the most favourable economic prospects; he has been an outspoken advocate, and perhaps the most effective one, of East German interests since unification.[13] Two other West German politicians replaced long-time East-CDU members as the Minister-Presidents of Saxony–Anhalt (in mid–1991) and Thuringia (January 1992): Werner Münch, a former deputy to the European parliament and, after unification, the Saxon–Anhalt Finance Minister, and Bernhard Vogel, earlier the Minister-President of Rhineland–Palatinate. Münch and three 'West' ministers were forced to resign in December 1993, however, in the wake of a scandal over their inflated salaries; Münch's successor is an East German. In Mecklenburg–West Pomerania political squabbling over the fate of the state's shipyards led in March 1992 to the fall of Alfred Gomolka and his replacement by another East German, Berndt Seite.[14] The East's only other 'native' and only SPD Minister-President, the former Evangelical Church leader Manfred Stolpe, has remained in office in spite of a hailstorm of political attacks on him by the CDU, *Der Spiegel*, and some former opposition figures. These attacks, based on his contacts with the Stasi during his years as spokesman for the Church, have undoubtedly compromised his effectiveness as an advocate of East German interests, although he remains overwhelmingly popular in his home state.

As of mid-1992 fourteen of the 49 ministers of the East German state governments were from the West, as were 13 of the 16 members of the Berlin executive, the Senate. Presumably because of the special expertise required, the positions of *Land* Finance Minister, Economics Minister, and Justice Minister were especially likely to be filled by Western imports. All but a few of the state secretaries named to head the administration of the new ministries come from the West – most of them either from Western *Land* governments or from Bonn.[15]

Bureaucracy

Leihbeamten – 'loaned' officials from the West ' – also occupy many of the most important positions in east German *Land* bureaucracies. In Brandenburg, for example, 391 of the 1428 persons employed in government ministries in June 1991 were westerners; in the 'higher service' the proportion reached 51.6% – in the Justice Ministry 43 out of 60. Most come from Brandenburg's West German 'partner state', North Rhine–Westphalia. In Saxony, similarly, about one-quarter of the officials of the state chancellory and ministries are from the West, particularly Bavaria and Baden–Württemburg; at the level of division (*Abteilung*) director 32 of 57, at the level of section (*Referat*) director, 122 of 216. Nevertheless, a number of such positions have gone unfilled because of the difficulty of recruiting enough Westerners and the unwillingness of the government to employ those who are not 'politically pure' (*sauber*). The shortage of judicial officials is said to be particularly desperate, owing to the introduction of the new legal system and the mountain of pending litigation over such matters as property rights, employment questions, and the correction of alleged injustices from the communist past. According to an early 1991 estimate, the five new states were short of some 4500 judges, state attorneys, and judicial administrators.[16]

   Political standards for employing East Germans in bureaucratic and judicial posts appear to be particularly rigid in Saxony, where a pastor once severely persecuted by the Stasi is now Interior Minister. Former party officials, those with any past connections with the Stasi, and even graduates in certain politically corrupted disciplines – law, the social sciences – are barred from employment. As a result, only a handful of the thousands that apply for state jobs are hired. In other *Länder* and Berlin, such criteria appear to be applied less consistently, and court challenges occasionally overturn dismissals on political grounds. Bur the pressures from sections of the public and from politicians to deny public employment to those who might have benefited from the old order – and particularly those revealed to have received the somewhat ambiguous classification of 'IM' (unofficial collaborator) in Stasi files – often seem to override the need for expertise and any consideration of individual circumstances (see Gregg Kvistad, above). Ironically, East Germans applying for jobs in public service in the West do not generally face such rigorous screening.[17]

   With administrators from the West occupying most of the higher positions and those from the East predominating in subordinate positions the potential for friction in the relationship between the two is evident. A study carried out beginning in the autumn of 1990 comparing middle-level officials in the East Berlin *Magistrat* (n – 46) and the West Berlin *Senat* (n – 54) reveals differences that may well be typical for the former GDR as a whole. Reflecting the different 'administrative cultures' from which they came, East Berlin bureaucrats approached more closely the 'classical' model of élites of reseacher Robert Putnam and West Berlin ones his 'political' model. Nearly four-fifths of the East Berlin group criticised the degree to which 'the identity and originality of East German society' had been crushed in the process of unification; one-third saw citizens of the former GDR as a group whose legitimate interests were being neglected. Westerners criticised Easterners for a supposed lack of initiative, an 'underdeveloped capacity to apply critical and constructive thought to policy proposals', and a dependence on detailed guidance from above. East Berlin officials criticised Western ones for 'narrow-mindedness', the maintenance of an 'undesirably cool and formal working climate', and a superficial or non-existent understanding of specific East German needs and problems. Only 20% of the Eastern respondents 'classified themselves without qualification as being fully accepted by their Western colleagues'.[18]

Economic Elites

Even before the GDR's last communist government was swept from power by the elections of March 1990, the state's economic enterprises were put under the control of a giant trusteeship agency, the *Treuhandanstalt*, 'the largest holding company in the world' (see Karl Kahrs, above). By March 1992, the central *Treuhand* (considerably transformed and now responsible to the German Finance Ministry) had sold 7092 companies and closed some 800, with 4863 still awaiting privatisation. Fifteen regional subsidiaries had sold 22 300 small-scale enterprises, such as retail shops, restaurants, and cinemas. While more than 70% of the small business had gone to East Germans, most of the large enterprises were sold to West German firms, and just 366 (about 5%) to foreign interests.

Thus the emerging *de facto* economic élite of Eastern Germany is to be found among the owners and managers of West German banks and business firms, or in the hierachy of the *Treuhand* itself, headed by Westerners, although 70% of its 4000 employees are said to be from the new states. At the intermediate and lower levels, to be sure, many East German managers remain in place. But by the end of July

1991, the *Treuhand* had fired just 1400 heads of firms, 400 because of Stasi connections or membership in the SED Central Committe, and the rest because of incompetence; 1000 Western managers replaced them. Although some 20 000 new managers were said to be needed, the *Treuhand*'s original intent of hiring an experienced manager from the West for each of its companies proved unrealisable.[19]

It is widely believed in East Germany that managers and other members of the former *Nomenklatura*, taking advantage of old *Seilschaften* (connections), retain significant posts in the economy and in some cases have flourished. There are instances in which figures of some standing in the old regime, such as Wolfgang Rauchfuss, former Minister for Material Economy, and the former Foreign Trade Minister Gerhard Beil, have been hired by Western capitalist firms. The shortage of able Western managers willing to suffer the risks and inconveniences of moving to the East helps explain this phenomenon,[20] as does the experience of the old managers. 'The Treuhand feels that these managers must be kept on, because only they understand the workings of their companies and have close contact with suppliers and customers,' writes one source. 'Ordinary East Germans who have been laid off see this as an injustice, especially when these same managers get offered an MBO [Management Buyout] on the cheap'.

Officials of Western firms often have misgivings about the ability of East German managers to adapt to a market environment. One recent study suggests that such managers (not surprisingly) suffer especially from their lack of understanding of marketing, West German economic law, and European Community requirements; to a lesser extent they face psychological and motivational 'deficiencies' presumed to be inherited from their earlier experience. But, the author reviewing the study contends, 'there is no alternative to the existing élite' in this sphere; the only question is that of who is to be employed in which position.[21]

Leadership in the now all-German trade unions largely follows the pattern we have observed in other German institutions. Following the opening of the Wall, the GDR's official trade union organisation, the FDGB, shed its old top leadership and embarked on a path of reform; largely autonomous branch unions, paralleling those in West Germany, were created. The Western unions belonging to the DGB then moved in, often cooperating with East German reformers, but refusing to consider a formal merger with their East German counterparts. Instead, members from the latter were accepted on an individual basis, and in many unions reform-oriented former FDGB officials were permitted to occupy intermediate and lower-level leadership positions (in part because of a shortage of Western personnel to fill these posts). Total membership of all the unions expanded, by some four million in 1990 and another half million in 1991; the proportion of union members in the East is in fact higher than that in the West. But the unions remain essentially West German in their leadership and orientations – and as a result have experienced tensions with their East German clientele similar to those we have observed elsewhere, with Western officials often seen as arrogant 'conquerors' possessing only a superficial knowledge of special east German conditions. The fact that a large proportion of the DGB members in the East are now unemployed, for example, presents the Western leadership with issues it did not have to face in the west.[22].

Higher Education and the Media

Higher education and the mass media were both highly politicised during the years of communist rule, and have received correspondingly close attention from the West German authorities since unification. The much higher level of staffing in East German universities and research institutes compared with that in West Germany provided an additional justification for the professional and political screening process carried out by joint commissions of scholars and more arbitrary measures decreed by political authorities. The results have been predictably controversial, leading to legal challenges and student protests at several universities. Whole institutions – e.g. the Academy of Economics (Berlin) and the Academy for State and Law (Potsdam) – as well as politically suspect faculties and departments have been *abgewickelt* ('wound up'); new institutions, notably in Brandenburg, have been opened. Berlin's Humboldt University and the Karl-Marx-University of Leipzig have been particular centres of controversy. The rector of the former, a theologian elected to his post after the 1989 revolution, was summarily fired by the Berlin science senator because of (unclarified) Stasi contacts. Several members of the group of young Humboldt social scientists that cautiously explored reform proposals prior to the old regime's fall have lost their jobs; others have thus far been retained, but are under fire.

'Almost everywhere' in the social sciences and humanities, writes one former Humboldt philosopher, 'one or two [pre-*Wende* faculty] remain in temporary and marginal positions, otherwise positions are filled by Wessis.' As in the case of the new state administrations and business, Western recruits are often placed in supervisory positions over the remaining East Germans. But severe financial constraints and the inadequacy of research facilities and equipment have made it difficult for most Eastern universities to attract established scholars from the West.

The former GDR Academy of Sciences, employing some 25 000 persons, and modelled after the Soviet Academy, included much of the research capacity of the east German states. It has been closed down, but many of its less politicised institutes, following review by the West German Science Council (*Wissenschaftsrat*), were designated for restructuring and/or incorporation into universities or other research institutions. One economist who had fled to the West in 1986 has described the screening process as a 'pitiless steamroller'.[23] Moreover, the financial constraints on implementing the Council's more positive recommendations are severe.

The former GDR's mass media have also undergone a far-reaching transformation, although not always along anticipated lines. East German readers have shown surprisingly little enthusiasm for West German newspapers, an interesting indicator of their ambivalence over unification and their desire to cling to something with a distinctive East German identity and history. The beneficiaries of this preference have been primarily East German regional newspapers, such as the *Berliner Zeitung* or the *Leipziger Volkszeitung*, once controlled by the SED but now owned by Western firms. If the owners and many of the editors of these publications are now Western, the majority of the journalists are holdovers from the communist era, and the coverage has a distinctive East German flavour. The critical perspective on unification they offer also helps explain the spectacular initial popularity of the new East German publication, the Murdoch–Burda tabloid *Super!*, which built its readership on 'a brash mixture of sex, East German boosterism, and bashing of Western Germans'.[24]

In the years of communist rule, the GDR's population neglected the often tendentious offerings of the state television networks in favour of western programming. The political upheaval of 1989, however, brought about a startling transformation. 'Young media Turks' took over the networks, renamed them, and drastically altered their approach to programming. Thus, the decision to replace the East's DFF (Deutsche Funk– und Fernsehen) with new regional networks on the West German model was resented by many on the grounds that their elimination would mean the loss of still another bit of East German identity. The new services initially retained a few popular GDR programmes, and public pressures have persuaded them to restore additional ones. The most important of the new networks is the Mitteldeutscher Rundfunk (MDR), covering Saxony, Thuringia, and Saxony–Anhalt; Brandenburg has established its own network (ORB), and East Berlin is now covered by West Berlin's SFB, while Mecklenburg–West Pomerania has joined North German Radio, the service of the Western states of Hamburg, Schleswig–Holstein, and Lower Saxony. MDR is headed by a Bavarian, Udo Reiter, and all but one of the service's directors, appointed after a bitter partisan struggle, are West German. On the other hand six of the eight deputy directors are East German, and Reiter has voiced his intention of keeping East Germans 'behind the microphones'.[25]

The Cultural Intelligentsia

An élite group rather different from those discussed to this point is made up of East German writers and other cultural figures. Especially during the last 20 years of Communist rule, many of the best-known of them – such as Christa Wolf, Heiner Müller, Stefan Heym, Christoph Hein, Volker Braun, and Stephan Hermlin – took on an extraordinary role as public critics of the failures of the GDR's 'real socialism' in the name of a more genuine, humane, indeed utopian socialist order. In a society in which journalism and social science were kept on tight ideological reins, the writers were often able to outmanoeuvre an inconsistent censorship, Stasi surveillance, and sporadic acts of repression, to acquire a visibility and social importance in the GDR and in the West normally denied authors in democratic societies.

After the collapse of communist rule, their prestige withered under a ferocious assault from conservative West German critics and several former GDR writers who had earlier been forced into exile in the West. The writers had, it was charged, legitimised and lent their prestige to the regime while enjoying special privileges under it; even in their criticisms they had only tried to 'improve the conditions of incarceration' without challenging incarceration itself (see Ian Wallace, above).[26] The sharp decline in interest in literature and culture that the former GDR shares with the other East European states, and the writers' loss of the unique position they occupied under the dictatorship as a 'substitute public,' has also eroded their standing.

They have not by any means been cowed into silence.[27] Their ability to speak for their former countrymen, however, and to influence political decisions on their behalf, is at the moment greatly attenuated.

Since several of the most celebrated of them, such as Wolf, Heym, and Müller, openly advocated a humane socialism, their audience in a country in which the failure of the GDR's political and economic system is routinely (and, I think, improperly) characterised as the failure of 'socialism' in general, is likely to remain sceptical for some time to come. Still, in concert with sympathetic West German intellectuals, like Günter Grass and Walter Jens, they remain among the few advocates for the ex-GDR capable of obtaining a broad hearing.

CONSEQUENCES

I suggested earlier that the question of élites is closely tied to the matters of voice and identity. East Germans, it is clear, have little voice in a process that is drastically altering the conditions under which they. live. For them, the critical decision-makers sit in government offices in Bonn, in Western corporate board rooms, in the headquarters of the *Treuhand* in Berlin, in Western publishing houses, and so on. Even in their own *Länder*, the most important positions are more often than not held by West Germans. They have a few eloquent advocates – often West Germans themselves, such as President von Weizsäcker or Minister-President Biedenkopf – but their voices are more often than not ignored by the Western élite.

The lack of an effective voice both reflects and reinforces the crisis of East German identity. The continuing attachment of many East Germans to their regional newspapers, the surprising survival of *Jugendweihe* (an SED-nurtured counterpart of confirmation), and the strong showing of the PDS in local elections in East Berlin and Brandenburg suggest a surprising nostalgia for the past, a resistance to unrelenting westernisation, and above all an effort to cling to something familiar in a sea of uncertainty. But the proliferation of Western automobiles, sex shops, and much of the other paraphernalia of West German life suggests that others are quite prepared to put the GDR past behind them. Aside from the declining majorities of East German opinion polls calling for a reckoning with the SED and Stasi, there is no evident agreement on GDR *Vergangenheitsbewältigung*, on how such an exercise should be carried out, or whether it is necessary or would be meaningful (see Helga Welsh, above). East German Bundestag deputies, state government officials, and cultural figures also do not agree on these matters, although they find some common ground in the advocacy of the East's more concrete material interests, and in a diffuse resentment of Western tutelage.

The identity question is by no means confined to the East. The character of the West's élite colonisation, in particular its unwillingnesss to tolerate the survival of any institutions or values associated with the old GDR or the presence of East Germans in anything but subordinate positions, betrays a Western unwillingness to come to terms with the idea of a new Germany understood to be anything other than the old Federal Republic with expanded borders. Continuing resistance to moving the country's capital to Berlin is one symbol of this reluctance. The undeniable success of the West German political and economic system and the equally undeniable crimes and failures of GDR communism have made it easy to ignore the flaws of the former or the pockets of virtue in the latter. East Germans who call the public's attention to either, particularly if they were once SED members or otherwise situated on the left, are subject to vilification. The exclusion of East Germans from the élite to that extent may be evidence of a bad Western conscience, but more plausibly it simply reflects the universal human discomfort at contemplating fundamental change.

It has been suggested that, in particular, the frenzy over Stasi revelations has been consciously used by conservative forces in the West to frustrate any serious consideration of the redefinition of German identity, and also as a club for discrediting the left in the West as well as the East.[28] Certainly one result has been to undermine the credibility of some of the more articulate advocates for the East, such as de Maizière, Stolpe, Gysi, Wolf, and Müller. On lower levels, the exclusion of those with alleged Stasi connections (usually without any consideration of individual circumstances) or other significant ties to the old regime has denied Eastern Germany the services of thousands of able individuals, however emphatically they may have renounced their past convictions and attachments. Here, however, East German opposition figures and ordinary citizens have joined in the clamour for exclusion. They reject as too facile the defence that the perpetrators (*Täter*) were simultaneously among the victims (*Opfer*) of GDR communism, and insist that real individuals and not just 'the system' must be held responsible and punished for the oppression of the old regime.

The proposal launched in June 1992 by the East German CDU leader Peter Diestel and the PDS leader Gysi for some sort of movement to promote Eastern interests that would cut across party lines, even including the PDS, unleashed something like panic among West German politicians, who saw it as a call for an Eastern 'party' that would inevitably deepen the division of the country. Critics voiced the fear that such a party might produce a Western backlash that could be used as an excuse for curtailing assistance to the east. The SPD's Wolfgang Thierse argued that the formation of a separate East German party would have 'devastating consequences', but also pointed to the 'furious resignation' in the former GDR that helped provoke it. 'The dominance of the German West,' he wrote, 'was and is unavoidably necessary in the economic sphere. Nevertheless, I ask whether it might be possible to create a kind of balance in other areas, giving the economically, socially, and politically weaker East Germans the chance to participate as genuinely equal partners in the shaping of this common Germany?'[29]

Realising Thierse's vision would require the emergence of a stronger and more self-confident East German élite than presently exists. It is true that most of the West Germans now in leading economic and administrative positions in Eastern Germany expect to return home, and that a new generation of East German leaders may emerge from the universities, western training courses, or as protégés of the Westerners. But the development of such a *Nachwuchs* is at its early stages.

There is evidence that the tensions between transplanted West Germans – 'Wossis' – and their East German subordinates are diminishing over time, as the understanding of each for the other's perspective grows. The greatest obstacle toward building a new élite 'consensus' may instead be the divergence between Western élites in the old Federal Republic and a coalition of West German and East German leaders in the new states. Their differences will be fuelled by the ongoing *Verteilungskampf* – the battle over the distribution of resources, symbolic as well as material – that seems certain to colour relations between the two parts of Germany for years to come.[30]

Notes

1. See the sharp attack on American specialists on the GDR for cultivating the 'cliché' of West German colonial conquest in Reiner Pommerlein, ' "Ihr müsst doch stolz und glücklich sein" ', *Die Zeit*, May 1, 1992, p. 15. Pommerlein goes so far as to suggest, rather implausibly, that leftist American scholars may have 'hindered the opposition in the GDR and contributed to the stabilisation of the SED regime'.
2. In this vein, see Klaus von Beyme, 'The Legitimation of German Unifi-

cation between National and Democratic Principles', *German Politics and Society*, Spring 1991, esp. pp. 5–10.

3. I owe this term to Michael Brie, speaking at the 18th New Hampshire Symposium, June 1992.

4. See the short biographies in *Informationen* (Bundesminiterium für innnerdeutsche Angelegenheiten), April 27, 1990, 12–18.

5. For an illuminating discussion of the changing strategies of unification, see Gerhard Lehmbruch, 'Die deutsche Vereinigung: Strukturen und Strategien', *Politische Vierteljahresschrift*, vol. 32 (December 1991), 585–604.

6. Even when East German negotiators sought to resist Western pressures, most notably on the question of property rights, they were unsuccessful in winning more than token concessions. 'In Bonn the general line in the negotiations over the treaty of unity was determined early – that the institutional mantle of the GDR should be entirely liquidated. So far as possible, there should be no institutional continuity.' Lehmbruch, p. 596.

7. Werner Scheib, 'Go East Young Man – Then Come Back and Get promoted', *Magdeburgische Zeitung Volksstimme*, August 19, 1991, translated in *German Tribune*, September 1, 1991, p. 6. Most West German bankers working in the East 'fly in on Monday mornings, returning to their homes and families in West Germany on Friday evenings. Flights at these times are booked months in advance, while flights during the week are half-empty.' Peter Lee, 'Common Goals, Divided Loyalties', *Euromoney*, February 1992, pp. 41–2.

8. See Stefan Scheytt and Oliver Schröm, 'Lebenslängliche Bundesbürger', *Die Zeit*, June 26, 1992, pp. 7–9, who discuss the fates of former members of the Politburo, State Council, and Council of MInisters; all but a few are in retirement.

9. Calculated from figures in Gert-Joachim Glaessner, *Die andere deutsche Republik* (Opladen: Westdeutscher Verlag, 1989), pp. 127, 129, 326.

10. *Der Spiegel*, June 15, 1992, p. 19.

11. Thomas Kröter, 'MPs from Eastern Germany Begin to Find Their Bearings in Bonn's Corridors', *Kölner Stadt-Anzeiger*, March 5, 1991, translated in *German Tribune*, March 17, 1991, p. 4.

12. Joachim Neander, 'Both Bouquets and Brickbats for an Abrasive Ossi Social Democrat', *Die Welt*, July 16, 1991, translated in *German Tribune*, July 28, 1991, 4–5; 'Ostdeutsche Abgeordnete formieren sich', *Süddeutsche Zeitung*, June 17–18, (1992), p. 2; and 'Angst vor einem Phantom', *Der Spiegel*, June 15, 1992, 19.

13. Kurt Biedenkopf was born in Chemnitz, but grew up in West Germany; similarly, the Berlin Governing Mayor Diepgen was born in Pankow in East Berlin but grew up in the Western part of the city. See Ralf Hübner, 'Vote of Confidence for Man Who Carries Saxony's Hopes', *Neue Zeit*, December 9, 1991, translated in *German Tribune*, December 22, 1991, 4, and the interview with Biedenkopf, 'Statt Ausbau im Westen lieber Aufbau im Osten', *Die Zeit*, June 19, 1992, p. 5.

14 See Christoph Dieckmann, 'Der Spuk im Schloss', *Die Zeit*, April 3, 1992, p. 6.

15. Irma Hanke, 'Die "dritte Republik:" Wandel durch Integration?', paper delivered at 18th New Hampshire Symposium, June 18–25, 1992. Also

'Staatssekretäre in den neuen Bundesländern Sachsen, Mecklenburg–Vorpommern und Brandenburg', *Informationen* (Bundesminister für innerdeutsche Beziehungen), January 11, 1991, pp. 13–16.

16. See *Der Tagesspiegel*, August 9, 1991, p. 7, and Horst Zimmermann, 'Friction Between Eastern, Western Officials', *Hamburger Abendblatt*, July 16, 1991, translated in *German Tribune*, July 28, 1991, 3. Some East Germans have suggested that 'NRW,' the abbreviaton for the West German state, really stands for 'Nun Regieren Wir' – we rule now. Barbara Tewes, press spokesperson for the Interior Ministry of Saxony, supplied the information for that state at the 18th New Hampshire Symposium, June 1992. Also Gisela Helwig, ' "Wer langsam hilft, zahlt doppelt"', *Deutschland Archiv*, 24 (March 1991), pp. 227–9.

17. See 'Pastro Survived a Hospital's "Treatment"' *Nürnberger Nachrichten*, January 10, 1992, translated in *German Tribune*, January 24, 1992, 14; 'Putzfrau für Mielke', *Der Spiegel*, May 18, 1992, 68–72. As a number of critics have acidly noted, those who served the Nazi regime but were needed in public positions in the period after World War II faced no such rigid screening either. See Alfred Diamant, 'Who's Alfraid of the Big Bad Wolf or Deutschland: Ein Wintermärchen', paper delivered at Eighth International Conference of Europeanists, Chicago, March 27–9, 1992.

18. Eckhard Schröter, 'When Cultures Collide: The Case of Administrators from East and West Berlin', paper delivered at the Eighteeth New Hampshire Symposium, June 18–25, 1992. Putnam's basic distinction is to be found in Robert D. Putnam, 'The Political Attitudes of Senior Civil Servants in Western Europe', *British Journal of Political Science* 3 (July 1973), 257–90.

19. See Bernd Stadelmann, 'Privatisation to be Over by Next Year', *Stuttgarter Nachrichten*, May 11, 1992, translated in *German Tribune*, May 22, 1992, 7; *Deutschland Archiv*, vol. 24 (August 1991), p. 896; Also Hans Luft, 'Die Treuhandanstalt', *Deutschland Archiv*, 24 (December 1991), 1276 and Ralf Neubauer, 'Quantensprung im Osten', *Die Zeit*, May 29, 1992, p. 11.

20. See the rather undifferentiated attacks on holdovers from the old regime in Gabor Steingart, 'Genossen raus', *Der Spiegel*, May 20, 1991, 130, and an interview with Mecklenburg–West Pomerania Economics Minister Conrad-Michael Lehment, *Der Spiegel*, July 1, 1991, pp. 93–5. Some question the qualifications of certain of the Western recruits, including some former elected officials, see ' "Wer kennt einen, der passt?",' *Der Spiegel*, January 14, 1991, pp. 90–3.

21. Reinhard Myritz, 'Elites ohne Alternative', *Deutschland Archiv*, 25 (May 1992), pp. 475–83.

22. The above is based primarily on Michael Fichter, 'From Transmission Belt to Social Partnership? The Case of Organized Labor in Eastern Germany', *German Politics and Society*, Summer 1991, 21–39; Fichter, 'The East–West Dichotomy and the Process of Integration: The Organizational Expansion of Labor Unions Throughout Eastern Germany', paper delivered at Eighth New Hamshire Symposium, June 18–25, 1992. See also Ralf Neubauer, 'Warnsignale von der Basis', *Die Zeit*, July 3, 1992, p. 9.

23. Conservatives, however, continue to complain that the old SED 'team' is still largely in place in the universities. See 'Die alte Mannschaft ist noch im Boot', *Süddeutsche Zeitung*, July 9, 1992, p. 5. On Western attacks on two of the key figures of the Humboldt reform group, Michael Brie and Dieter Klein, see Norbert Kostede, 'Doktor Brie wird abgewickelt', *Die Zeit*, July 12, 1991, p. 4; Also Roland Kirbach, 'Ein Fall von Professoren-Kungelei?', *Die Zeit*, August 21, 1992, 6 and Rainer Land, 'Abwicklung und Neugründung: Gespräche an der Friedrich-Schiller-Universität Jena', *Berliner Debatte*, No. 4, 1992, 28. Furthermore, Neuordnung der deutschen Forschungslandschaft', *Deutschland Archiv* 24 (September 1991), 910–12 and Hans Harald Bräutigam, 'Notwendige Grausamkeiten', *Die Zeit*, July 5, 1991, p. 22.

24. John Tagliabue, 'East-West Differences Still Foil German Papers', *New York Times*, March 9, 1992, C7, cited in Richard L. Merritt, 'Normalizing the East German Media', paper presented at the Eighteenth New Hampshire Symposium, June 18–25, 1992, p. 19. See also Francine S. Kiefer, 'No Reunification for German Papers', *Christian Science Monitor*, October 24, 1991, P. 12; Hans-Joachim Höhne, 'Eastern Newspapers: Red-Cloister Graduates Skulk Between Screaming Headlines', *Rheinischer Merkur*, May 15, 1992, translated in *German Tribune*, May 29, 1992, p. 6. Höhne describes a study done for the German Interior Ministry comparing the content of these East German papers to that of West German ones.

25. See the informative account in Merritt, 20–8; also Irene Charlotte Streul, 'Zum Stand des Rundfunkwesens in den neuen Bundesländern', *Deutschland Archiv* 24 (October 1991), pp. 1073–83; Otto Köhler, 'Der Osten wird stumm', *Die Zeit*, July 5, 1991, pp. 17–18. Köhler presents a dismaying account of the brutal treatment of DFF and its staff prior to its dissolution. Also 'Warten auf das Frühlingserwachen', *Die Zeit*, April 24, 1992, p. 6.

26. Hans Joachim Schädlich, as cited in Wolfgang Emmerich, '*Affirmation – Utopie – Melancholie*: Versuch einer Bilanz von vierzig Jahren DDR-Literatur', *German Studies Review*, vol. 14 (May 1991), 327. Emmerich's essay offers an unusually insightful interpretation of the German *Literatenstreit*.

27. Christiane Zehl Romero, 'New Voices – No Voices', paper delivered at Eighteenth New Hampshire Symposium, June 18–25, 1992.

28. See Peter Marcuse, 'Das Feindbild Stasi sichert dem Westen den Status quo', *Frankfurter Rundschau*, May 14, 1992, p. 18.

29. The formation of the 'Committee for Fairness' was officially announced on July 11. In addition to Diestel and Gysi, signers of the group's appeal included the writers Heym and Müller, the former Humboldt University Rector Fink, Gottfried Forck, a retired Evangelical Church bishop, Heinrich Albertz, former mayor of West Berlin, Michael Sontheimer, the editor of the leftist Berlin daily the *Tageszeitung*, and the rock singer Tamara Danz. Stephen Kinzer, 'New Movement Seeks to Defend East Germans', *New York Times*, July 12, 1992, p. 8, Heribert Prantl, 'Die Volksfront im Osten', *Süddeutsche Zeitung*, June 17–18, 1992, p. 4, and Thierse: 'Ostpartei wäre verheerend', *Süddeutsche Zeitung*, June 17–18,

1992, p. 6; Wolfgang Thierse, 'Zwei Welten – oder eine?', *Der Spiegel*, June 1992, p. 22.

30. See ' "Du passt nicht mehr in unser Weltbild" ', *Der Spiegel*, July 13, 1992, pp. 32–5. Gerhard Lehmbruch, p. 602, suggests that cross-cutting alliences between East and West German interests, as in the abortion question, may serve to reduce the intensity of the struggle; I am sceptical.

Part IV

The Play of Political Forces

14 The Moderate Right in the German Party System

Gordon Smith

What can broadly be described as the 'moderate right' in the German party system is occupied by just two party formations, the CDU-CSU and the FDP. Yet the problem is that neither party can be labelled as definitely belonging to the right of centre, and both the Christian Democrats and Free Democrats have firmly resisted being pushed in that direction. Their resistance has had a significant consequence in creating a wide gap between the established parties, the CDU–CSU and FDP, on the one hand, and non-established, right wing parties such as the German People's Union (DVU) and the Republicans on the other. These last two are generally regaded as 'extremist', although neither has been found to be unconstitutional. They are certainly unacceptable to other parties and are not regarded as coalitionable. What are the reasons for this pronounced party 'gap' on the moderate right, and what are the possible implications for German politics?

THE WEAKNESS OF GERMAN CONSERVATISM

One important area of explanation of the structuring of the party system concerns the fate of German conservatism. Conservative traditions have had very little influence on the development of the Federal Republic. Its weakness goes a long way in accounting for the diffuse and uncertain expression of the moderate right in present-day Germany. Why did conservative politics enter such a steep decline after 1945, and what, too, are the chances of a revival?

In the past, during the time of Imperial Germany and later in the Weimar Republic, conservative parties were well represented, and they took a considerable role in the party system, winning a maximum of around 20 per cent in both periods. In the Federal Republic only one, the Deutsche Partei, looked to have potential to become a federal-wide conservative force. But despite some early successes it disappeared by the end of the 1950s.

Several reasons can be advanced for this apparently terminal decline; some have to do with the nature of German conservatism, others with the positive appeal of Christian Democracy. Not surprisingly, the failure of conservative politics after 1945 was in large measure due to its association with the overthrow of German democracy, and the word 'conservatism' became linked with 'reaction' as well as having an authoritarian connotation. Conservative politics was strongly national in spirit, but this central value had little to offer in the situation of West Germany in the years after 1945: it was not seen as relevant to their needs by the mass of the electorate; there was a nostalgia for many aspects of Germany's past, but conservatism was not a viable option.

The international environment was also unfavourable: West Germany was an artificial creation and relied less on national sentiments to establish itself than on supranational ones. The heavily dependent position of the new Federal Republic, together with the apparent invincibility of the Soviet Union, simply made it unrealistic to hope to win strong support for platforms based on, say, German reunification or the return of the lost Eastern territories. Behind these specific handicaps, however, there was evidence of a more deep-rooted malaise affecting the German right. Kurt Sontheimer drew a sharp contrast between the Weimar Republic and the Federal Republic. In the lattter, the idea of the 'intellectual' – academics, writers, and journalists – from the outset became the preserve of the left; there was no equivalent on the right.

> The absence of a right-wing intelligentsia with a truly critical potential is one of the most remarkable and historically important differences between the political landscapes of the Bonn and Weimar republics. In Weimar, the critical intelligentsia stood either on the far left or the far right, hardly ever in the centre . . . the right-wingers of the national, conservative-revolutionary tradition of the Weimar Republic have scarcely figured in Bonn but have assumed a new position of relatively moderate and liberal conservatism.[1]

Yet even this brand of conservatism was unable to sustain itself as a separate and identifiable political force. It had become a bankrupt political ideology, since it could make no positive contribution to the social and economic situation of post-war Germany, a period, at first, of great deprivation and basic social change. In these circumstances, conservatism – to survive at all – had to be subsumed in a wider political movement, Christian Democracy, that was better suited to tackle the pressing problems of the time.

POLITICAL INTEGRATION; THE ROLE OF CHRISTIAN DEMOCRACY

The CDU was founded as a party of mass, democratic integration in which traditional conservatism could not play a major part. The new party was located towards the centre, but at the same time sought to attract conservatives and others who were further to the right. The prominence of right-wingers within the CDU was a source of suspicion to political opponents, such as the SPD leader, Kurt Schumacher; he argued that there was less to fear from right-wing parties than from the right wing of the CDU. This threat, however, did not materialise. That rightwing forces within the CDU failed to assume a leading role is shown by the lack of intense or prolonged polarisation of the party system.

Such was the integrative power of Christian Democracy in the 1950s that the CDU and CSU were able to absorb the supporters of right-wing regional parties – the Deutsche Partei and the Bayern Partei – as well as the Refugees' Party (BHE). Christian Democracy was strongly attractive to a wide range of voters because it heralded a new start for West Germany, not a hangover from the Weimar Republic. It received wide support, too, because it promoted the idea of social solidarity, modifying the disruption to society of the war and its aftermath. But all that would have been insufficient had not economic recovery and growth been sustained over a period of several years.

As a broadly based Volkspartei from the outset, the CDU-CSU was helped in not having a firm ideology, and no one faction could claim for itself to represent the 'true' nature of Christian Democracy. Yet the consequence has been that the party has always had to accommodate a number of disparate groupings. Just how variegated the CDU-CSU has remained is shown by Peter Glotz in examining the position in the 1980s. Glotz describes the party winning office in 1982 as a 'precarious coalition' consisting of social-republicans, Christian-socials, national-conservatives and market liberals. These distinctive standpoints also give rise to several power blocks (Machtgruppen), five in all, but six if the special position of the CSU is taken into account.[2]

The party leadership has always had to preserve some kind of balance between these competing tendencies, in particular between the left-leaning social-republicans at one extreme and the national-conservatives at the other. Apparently, however, the CDU has experienced less difficulty in shifting towards the centre than in tilting to the right. The risks for the party in making a right wing appeal were shown in the 1980 federal election when the CSU leader, Franz Josef Strauss, was adopted by the CDU-CSU as its chancellor candidate. Strauss sought deliberately to polarise politics and put the Christian Democrats on a conservative course, and the reputation that the CSU had for its brand of clerical-conservatism and that of Strauss as a fiery demagogue ensured that the party lost heavily at the election.

This experience may show that the CDU is unlikely ever to make a decisive shift to the right. But despite the appeal the party has for the electoral middle-ground, it is difficult to locate it at the centre. Thus, in von Beyme's view, electoral success does not resolve the question of where the party is positioned: 'The main obstacle to the Christian Democrats' image of themselves as a Centre Party is their own success.'[3] In other words, a centre location is not just a matter of a party's self-definition or its electoral support, but dependent on the presence of other parties being on its left and right. With the initial disappearance and then the long-term absence of right-wing parties, the CDU – if even only by default – was bound to encompass the conservative right. With the growth of right-wing support at *Land* and local level from the late 1980s onwards, the problems for the CDU in defining its position in the party system are likely to grow, especially if a party such as the Republicans wins federal representation.

THE AMBIGUOUS ROLE OF THE FREE DEMOCRATS

The Free Democrats exemplify the problems of locating the moderate right in German politics, even though the composition of the party is far less complex than the CDU. The character of the FDP has features common to European liberalism in general, and they stem from the difficulty of accommodating Liberal parties on the usual left–right axis. As a result, allowance has to be made for two distinctive party expressions of liberalism, the left-inclined 'liberal-radical' parties and those with a 'radical-conservative' orientation belonging to the moderate right. The liberal-radical strand emphasises the importance of individual freedom, civil rights and constitutional reform, whilst the liberal-conservative strand stresses the value of economic liberty, private property and the market system.[4]

The particular problem posed by the FDP is that both these strands are combined within a single party, in contrast to the party systems in Imperial Germany and the Weimar Republic, both with two Liberal parties each representing the different facets of liberalism. This bifurcation made location far easier, and there was no doubt, for instance, in the Weimar Republic that the German People's Party (DVP) stood on the right and that the German Democratic Party (DDP) was on the left. But where does the FDP stand?

This question was fairly easy to answer in the early years of the Federal Republic, since the FDP combined a liberal-conservative economic philosophy with a strong 'national' emphasis seen, for example, in the party's insistence that German unification should keep a prominent place on the agenda, despite the weakness of West Germany's position at the time. These features put the FDP firmly with the right in the party spectrum and made the CDU its natural coalition partner. Changes in the party leadership in the 1960s led to a complete switch in the FDP's Ostpolitik in favour of reconciliation with the countries of Eastern Europe, and this change in direction of the party's 'national' stance provided the basis for the long-lasting coalition with the SPD. Yet the FDP's move back to the CDU in 1982 – a coalition that has proved to be just as durable – indicates that German liberalism is apparently still subject to these historic pressures, even though they only periodically affect the FDP at the level of government.

It would be wrong, however, to interpret the behaviour of the FDP purely in ideological terms. Equal attention has to be given to the question of the party's strategy, how it can best preserve itself in the context of a party system dominated by the two Volksparteien. FDP party strategy is based on maintaining a high profile for the party, and that is best ensured by the party being in the governing coalition rather than opposition. The purposeful manner in which the FDP has followed this course is shown by the fact that since 1949 it has served in government far longer than either the CDU or the SPD, and because the support of the FDP has been critical in forming a governing majority, it has been able to stake an almost permanent claim to important government positions. Its control of the foreign and economic ministries ensures that the party's presence will be consistently in the public's eye. Yet at the same time the FDP has shown itself to be a past master in practising 'opposition from within' and in using its de facto power of veto over a chancellor's policies.

The 'ambivalence' of the FDP thus operates on two levels: on one it relates to the party's mixed ideological character and is determined by which expression, liberal-radical or liberal-conservative, holds sway over the medium term; on the second level it concerns the party's 'survival strategy', in other words how it can best ensure its place in federal government. The two levels are often compatible, but not necessarily so, and it may be difficult to determine which one is operative at a particular juncture. For example, when the FDP deserted the SPD-led coalition in 1982 and joined with the CDU-CSU in ousting Chancellor Schmidt, both considerations were important. On the one hand, the leadership of the party was concerned to restore the FDP's reputation in defence of the market system by reducing the expanding federal budget, an aim that it seemed could be realised only in partnership with the CDU. But, on the other hand, the fear of being 'dragged down' by the SPD was a potent factor, since the SPD was showing itself to be increasingly divided, and Chancellor Schmidt had become isolated from his own party. Moreover, a danger signal – always taken as an indication by the party – was its poor showing in a number of preceding Land elections. The switch from the SPD to the CDU caused severe dissension within the ranks of the FDP, since the change of course appeared to many as simply opportunist; the substantial loss of support in the following 1983 election makes it apparent that the FDP has to be wary of changing direction too readily.

How is the FDP likely to behave in the future? Given its outlook and its experience over so many years, the strategic imperative is likely to prevail over other factors. The FDP has no wish to be tied to the CDU if – chiefly as a consequence of the problems of German unification – the fortunes of Chancellor Kohl and the CDU-CSU rapidly decline. For its own good, the FDP would have to look to a new alignment on the left, even toying with the idea of a federal 'traffic-light' coalition to include the Greens should a majority with the SPD alone be insufficient. This scenario is plausible, and it would have the effect of reducing the weight of the 'moderate right' in the party system to a significant extent.

PROBLEMS OF THE CDU AS A VOLKSPARTEI

The ability of the CDU to continue to act as a party of wide political integration has increasingly come under question. The doubts affect the SPD as well as the CDU, and can be conflated to the level of a general disillusion with the established political parties. Such a general trend is supported by several indications: falling electoral turnout, a drop in party membership, and a decline in the share of the federal vote going to the two Volksparteien. The problems thus not only affect the CDU, in almost all respects the SPD has fared worse, but the consequences of a weakening of the moderate right could be more significant for future political development. However, it is important not to place undue emphasis on the negative factors, since to an extent persuasive counter-arguments can be made.

The decline in electoral participation has certainly become appreciable in recent years. In contrast to the very high figures in the early 1970s of over 90 per cent, by the time of the 1990 all-German election it fell to 77.8 per cent, and this trend was also reflected in subsequent *Land* elections. But how significant is this decline? Seen from a comparative European perspective, the Federal Republic is just becoming more 'normal'. The 1990 federal election was also exceptional in that, for East Germans this was the third free election in the course of the year; it was hardly surprising the voters lost their first enthusiasm. Both the CDU and SPD have lost members, but in the case of the CDU this fall (taking Western Germany by itself) only brings it back to the level of the mid-1970s; at around two-thirds of a million in 1991–92, the party's voter/member ratio compares favourably with other European mass parties.

Perhaps the most persuasive evidence of the weakness of the Volksparteien is the steady fall in their aggregate share of the vote (from 91.2 per cent in 1976 to 77.3 per cent in 1990). Admittedly, the SPD has been more affected, but the CDU-CSU in 1990 scored its lowest share of the vote since 1949. It may, of course, be somewhat misleading to concentrate solely on the proportion of the vote a party attracts. In the German case the electorate has increased substantially over the years, and the CDU-CSU in particular has been successful in attracting a substantial part of the new electorate, so that the party has been more than able to compensate for losses in percentage terms.[5] This qualification is especially important in considering the performance of the Christian Democrats in the 1990 election: German unification meant that, compared with 1987, the electorate increased from 45 to 60 million, and – despite the slight fall in its share – the CDU-CSU was spectacularly successful in securing an initial integration of the new electorate.

The major doubt concerns the strength of this integration of the East German electorate. At that time support for the CDU and for Helmut Kohl was still coloured by the successful achievement of unification, and a decline would anyway have to be expected. But the extent of a fall in support for the CDU depends critically on two factors – the performance of the economy and the leadership provided by Chancellor Kohl. The problems encountered in making the rapid switch from a state-run economy to a market system have had two kinds of negative effect on the CDU: one in Eastern Germany resulting from the high levels of unemployment and the consequent social dislocation, the other in Western Germany as a result of the increased burdens: higher taxation and measures to deal with the escalating public debt, as well as the possibility that the outcome would be a severe economic recession.

Allied to the problems of securing the economic integration of the two parts of Germany are those of consolidating political integration. In retrospect, both kinds of difficulty were seriously underestimated, since the immediate effects of economic, monetary and social union seemed beneficial, and the CDU won resoundingly in the new Länder, first in the Land elections and then the Bundestag elections. These successes were largely ascribed to the key part played by Helmut Kohl in bringing about unification. By the same token, however, the strong identification of Kohl with unification led to increasingly negative judgements once the harmful economic and social results began to become apparent.

Any discussion of the moderate right in Germany is bound to be dominated by assessments made of the CDU; in turn, the medium-term outlook for the CDU is mainly dependent on Chancellor Kohl and the kind of leadership he is able to provide. But what kind of leadership is that? His performance during the process of unification was outstanding, both resolute and decisive, but it is not representative of his long period of office. Neither between 1982 and 1989, nor subsequent to 1990 could Kohl be counted as a strong government leader, although that is also due to the nature of the CDU and the political system. Thus, Kohl's earlier efforts to implement a 'Wende-politik' – cutting down the state's social and economic commitments – were frustrated by conflicting interests in the CDU and by the political structures, as Steen Mangen concludes: 'It is the nature of the German polity that renders single-minded New Right social reform impossible.'[6] However, Kohl proved adept all along at exercising general control over the CDU, and despite his moderate to low standing with the electorate, he led the party to victory in 1983 and 1987, largely because of the extreme weakness of the SPD, Yet by 1989 dissatisfaction within the CDU made his position precarious, and if the chance of German unification had not appeared, Kohl may well not have survived. Unification not only saved Kohl and held the CDU's electorate together, it enabled him to control the disparate forces in the CDU. The reprieve could be short-lived: the problems facing post-unification Germany brought disillusion in east and west Germany, gave rise to tensions in the coalition, and caused dissension within the CDU.

None of these developments gives any certainty as to the future direction of the CDU, whether it will move more to the right, or its electoral prospects. But it is unlikely that the CDU will be able to maintain its 1990 level of support, especially not in east Germany. Moreover, disunity in the CDU will increase if the economic situation sharply deteriorates. That would also mean that the CDU-CSU would have to contend with strong competition from parties of the radical right. Would the Christian Democrats be inclined to move a little in that direction as well? Such a shift could be represented as closing the 'gap' on the moderate right, and it raises a further question: How great is the distance from the moderate right to the radical right?

THE MODERATE RIGHT AND THE RADICAL RIGHT

Can the gap between the moderate and the radical right be bridged, and if so on what terms? Two broad lines of development can be envisaged. First, it could involve the CDU-CSU shifting towards the right; an alternative would be for important segments of the party to break away in frustration with the moderate course pursued by the leadership. Secondly, the gap would be narrowed if one or other of the parties of the radical right toned down its platform and became more 'responsible'. A combination of the two lines of development would result from a significant body of CDU-CSU party members moving across to one of the existing radical parties.

It is reasonable to take the position that any speculation on the possibility of 'rehabilitating' the radical right in Germany should be carefully phrased, since it inevitably imparts a gloss of pseudo-respectability to political extremism. Certainly, the discussion of political tolerance in Germany is clouded by historical experience as well as by the ideological foundations of the Federal Republic. The description of the political system as a 'streitbare Demokratie', that is, as a militant democracy or a 'democracy on guard', is a good indication of how seriously West Germany took its responsibility to avoid the erosion of the democratic system as happened in the Weimar Republic. That ideological standpoint was reinforced by the provision of Article 21 relating to parties undermining the constitutional order and a similar provision allowing the banning of organised extremist groups under Article 9. The fact that these constitutional rules were seldom applied is beside the point; they were sufficient, for example, to justify in part setting up the Office for the Protection of the Constitution, the Verfassungsschutz, and – less directly – issuing the Radikalenerlass (the so-called 'Berufsverbot') aimed at preventing the employment of proven radicals in the public service. The fact that the attention of the Verfassungsschutz and the application of the Radikalenerlass were preponderantly applied to organisations and individuals of the left has naturally led to demands that, in the context of contemporary politics, equal attention should now be directed at the radical right.

West German politics in earlier years had a peculiar, if easily explicable character: the left–right axis of party politics was sharply truncated, reflecting the two 'traumas' of German experience, National Socialism on the right and, on the left, the communist dictatorship in Eastern Germany.[7] This truncation – the inadmissibility of left and right extremes – produced a constricted party system, a political centrality, that was only partially lifted in the 1980s with the rise of the Greens. Their arrival, somewhere on the left of the party spectrum, could imply that a party on the right, such as the Republicans, should also be acceptable. If so, it would signal the end of 'centrality', and it would also show that the Federal Republic had finally 'normalised' its politics and joined the European mainstream.

Yet it is also clear, taking the example of the Republicans, that it is insufficient for a right wing party to disavow any connection, for instance, with Nazi ideology without at the same time convincingly setting out proposals that have no connection with that ideology. It is ironic that parties like the DVU and the Republicans took much of their initial sustenance from the growth of anti-foreigner sentiments, and yet in order to achieve a measure of acceptance from the wider public they would have to make a range of positive appeals, though not necessarily conformist. On a charitable view, the radical right as represented by the Republicans can be described as a single-issue 'protest' party, concentrating mainly on the issues raised by the high influx of foreigners into the Federal Republic. A less charitable interpretation is that behind the formal statements and publications a whole syndrome of right-wing extremism can be detected. It is not strictly necessary to decide between these evaluations at present, since such parties are still fluid in their make-up, and it is clear that, whatever their underlying nature may be, the kind of support they muster is principally of a 'protest' character. Voters, defecting from the larger parties, SPD as well as CDU-CSU, use the radical right in protest against the perceived immobilism of the political establishment in dealing with particular issues. Such support is notoriously ephemeral, and for the leaders of the radical-right parties concerned, strategic choices have to be made as to how to retain and build upon their initial support, whether to risk a more explicit switch to the right or not. If not, then it is possible to foresee a movement towards a more moderate position, that is, an attempt to fill the 'gap' on the German right by carving out a conservative–national niche.

This option may be attractive, but not so easy to put into practice. First, once a radical party becomes orthodox it loses its interest for voters who see it as a vehicle for incisive protest. Second, it may be difficult to co-exist in closer competition with the Christian Democrats. However, the CDU for its part could encounter problems if it gave a one-sided attention to the conservative–national elements of the party's appeal. Third, it is as yet by no means clear what potential the radical right has in Eastern Germany; it may be that radical protest, with a relatively unstructured and potentially volatile electorate, promises more than a conservative–national orientation could offer to disgruntled East Germans.

Yet, whatever a party of the radical right seeks to do in the way of promoting a more responsible image, what actually results is heavily dependent on the attitude taken by the established parties, especially the Christian Democrats, and both the CDU and the CSU are ambivalent in their attitudes, at least as far as the rank-and-file is concerned. Perceptions and motives are understandably mixed. On the one side, a small minority sees an affinity on the basis of common conservative-national aspirations, and – equally relevant – sees a possible line-up with the Republicans as a way of avoiding a dependency on the FDP for coalition-building. But, on the other side, a large majority opposes what they see as a dangerous shift to the right by the CDU-CSU. There is, too, a well-founded fear that it would make the party electorally vulnerable, losing votes both to the left and the right.

The CDU's majority viewpoint was confirmed at the 1992 party conference with the adoption of an 'incompatibility' resolution, and is committed to a strategy of 'exclusion'. In addition, the move taken to have the Republicans put under the observation of the Verfassungsschutz, on the grounds that the party is hostile to the constitution, effectively precludes any party of the radical right being accepted as having a legitimate role in the democratic process. The 'gap' on the German right looks set to persist.

From this discussion some conclusions can be drawn about the future of the party system. Even allowing a generous meaning to the idea of the 'moderate right', it is unlikely that it will find an independent expression in the party system. A move by the CDU in this direction would risk splitting the party or losing substantial electoral support – probably both. From the other direction, any attempt, however genuine, by the Republicans, say, to improve the party's image and become an orthodox conservative–national force is likely to fail: it could not easily remove the label of 'extremist', and if it did succeed, the chances are that it would lose its major attraction as a protest party.

The Christian Democrats face difficulties whether they make a move to the left or to the right. That was always the case, but now there is an important difference: the era of the all-dominating Volkspartei is coming to an end, and smaller parties have better chances with the electorate. This development need not lead to a destabilising fragmentation, but it could mean that the CDU is far less able to straddle the centre-right of the party system as effectively as in the past.

Notes

1. K. Sontheimer, 'Intellectuals and Politics in West Germany', *West European Politics*, vol. February 1, 1978, no. 1 pp. 30–41.
2. P. Glotz, *Die deutsche Rechte. Eine Streitschrift*, Stuttgart: Deutsche Verlagsanstalt, 1989, pp. 77–8.
3. K. von Beyme, *Political Parties in Western Democracies*, Aldershot: Gower, 1985, p. 97.
4. G. Smith, 'Between Left and Right: The Ambivalence of European Liberalism', in E. Kirchner (ed.), *Liberal Parties in Eastern Europe*, Cambridge, Cambridge University Press, 1988, pp. 16–28.
5. P. Mair, 'The Myth of Electoral Change: The Survival of Traditional Parties in Western Europe', Stein Rokkan Lecture, Limerick, ECPR, April 1992.
6. S. Mangen, 'Social Policy, the Radical Right and the German Welfare State', in H. Glennerster and J. Midgley (eds.), *The Radical Right and the Welfare State*, Harvester Wheatsheaf, 1991, p. 122. See also D. Webber, 'Kohl's Wendepolitik after a Decade', *German Politics*, vol.   , August 1992, no. 2, pp. 149–80.
7. G. Smith, 'The German Volkspartei and the Career of the Catch-All Concept', H. Döring and G. Smith (eds.), *Party Government and Political Culture in Western Germany*, London and Basingstoke: Macmillan, 1982, pp. 59–76.

15 The German Left: Dilemmas and Uncertainties of Power*

Andrei S. Markovits*

This essay asks questions and offers some answers as to why the West German left has – with virtually no exceptions – reacted with despondency, often bordering on hostility, to the monumental events transforming East Central Europe and the Soviet Union in 1989–90.[1] To be sure, the West German left was as surprised by the structural magnitude and alacrity of these epoch-making developments as the rest of the world. Nobody foresaw the appearance, let alone the far-reaching consequences of this *annus mirabilis*, perhaps not even the subjects of this historic change themselves. Moreover, it is no secret that the transformations in Eastern Europe and the total disappearance of the Soviet bloc have caused substantial crises of identity for virtually all left-wing movements and parties in the West. Most of them have responded with some ambivalence, perhaps even trepidation concerning their own future. But none seemed as reticent, sceptical, critical, even outright hostile regarding these events as the West German left. One German observer astutely referred to this mood as an 'anti-position'.[2]

While there have been a number of excellent accounts of this anti-position and fine descriptions of its various manifestations, none of these contributions has attempted to give a comprehensive analytic answer as to *why* this has been the case.[3] This is precisely what this analysis attempts to do. Concretely, it will discuss a number of items which will demonstrate the uniqueness of the West German left among its counterparts in the rest of the advanced capitalist world. As will be clear, all these items are inextricably linked to Germany's recent past, thus rendering the West German left's particularly negative reactions to the events of 1989–90 an integral part of modern German history. As such, the 'Germanness' of these reactions cannot be denied.

THE WEST GERMAN LEFT'S PROBLEMS WITH NATIONALISM

If one had to point to perhaps the most consistent and arguably fatal Achilles heel of the European left's strategic thinking over the last 100 years, it surely would have to be the left's woefully inadequate understanding of nationalism as a major force and a powerful agent of collective identity. Hailing from the cosmopolitanism and international existence of the early socialists, as well as from Marx's correct assessment that modernisation entailed an increasingly internationalised and global exploitation of labour by capital, leftist intellectuals by and large concluded that progressive politics had to be *ipso facto* international. Above all, international seemed always to mean a- or even anti-national. Whereas the left generally assumed identities derived from the 'universalistic' realm of production to be progressive, it viewed identities stemming from the 'particularistic' areas of geography and culture with suspicion. Most of the time the left viewed the latter identities as *a priori* reactionary. Only in the context of Third World liberation movements did the left ever accept nationalism as a legitimate *and* progressive expression of collective solidarity. Specifically, the left accorded nationalism its *Salonfähigkeit* mainly in the context of its struggles with the United States or its allies, that is, when forces confronting American and/or capitalist hegemony used nationalism in support of their cause. Whenever conflicts arose which involved the Soviet Union as a repressor, the left either remained silent, sided with the Soviets, or – in its more liberal version – rallied to the cause of the oppressed, always emphasising that the support accorded the anti-Soviet combatants was given for their lack of civil rights and autonomy, not their inability to express their national identity. This remained constant from the East Berlin uprisings of 1953, through the Hungarian revolt of 1956, the destruction of the Prague spring of 1968, the various Polish incursions in the course of the 1970s and Afghanistan in 1979.

In addition to these 'generic' problems which virtually all left-wing parties of the First World have exhibited for nearly one century, the German left has had to confront additional complexities in its dealing with nationalism which reflect key peculiarities of modern German history. Unlike the British, the French and even the Italian left, nationalism with all its complexities already played a crucial role in the debates of the nascent socialist movement in Germany. With the processes of state and nation building incomplete, socialist politics in

Germany became inevitably intertwined with issues pertaining to them. Should one attain social and political progress via a unified national German state, even under the aegis of a semi-feudal Prussia, as the Lassalleans argued, or was it better for the left first to support broad progressive, bourgeois-led coalitions whose task it would be to topple the reactionary aristocracy prior to constructing a united Germany based on the parliamentary principles of liberal democracy?[4] Even though Bismarck's international and domestic triumphs rendered the debate void by rapidly eliminating the second option, the role of nation and nationalism, as well as socialism's relations to them, had entered the left's world on a permanent basis. The particular acuteness of this topic in the case of the German left stemmed from the fact that it had to confront two simultaneous problems in the complex formation of class and national identities. In contrast, socialist movements in western Europe were by and large 'only' faced with one of these problems.

Nationalism most certainly did not endear itself to the German left because even before the official institutionalisation of the newly established nationalist German Reich, the state used the rhetoric of national interest to outlaw socialists. With nationalism becoming increasingly more rabid towards the turn of the century in circles generally hostile to the German left, nationalism's ambivalence and its pejorative meaning grew for socialists. It also became a major topic of programmatic and strategic debates. How were class and nation to be reconciled by socialists? Could nationalism be progressive under certain circumstances? If yes, which ones, where, and when? While, for obvious reasons, never as keenly debated by German socialists as by their Austrian comrades, Rosa Luxemburg's polemics on nationalism inside German social democracy simply have no west European counterparts.

Nationalism continued to matter to the German left throughout the troubled Weimar years. While increasing its hostility to German nationalism, which by then had become the virtual prerogative of the reactionary right, there were definite attempts by the left to use nationalism for its own purposes, as in the case of the communists' strategy of 'national Bolshevism'.[5] While this and similar experiments were simply no match for the right, it is clear that nationalism played an existentially crucial – albeit largely negative – role in the German left's identity during the Weimar Republic. The German left's traditional aversion to nationalism received unprecedented support with Hitler's rise to power.

Hitler and Auschwitz not only changed German history but all the conventional parameters of nationalism. It is through the lasting legacy of this change that one has to analyse the West German left's uniquely troubled relationship to its own (that is, federal republican) and German nationalism, as well as to nationalism in general. It is quite true that, following the war and well into the 1950s, it was the German left – particularly the Social Democratic Party (SPD) – which pursued a strategy of a single German state. In marked contrast to Adenauer's policy, which aimed at Germany's integration into the West – even at the cost of unity – as the only possibility to overcome Germany's errant ways of the past and guarantee a prosperous and democratic future for Germany and Europe, the German left believed that only a socialist Germany was a plausible guarantee against a recurrence of fascism on German soil. This socialist Germany was to be demilitarised, pacifist and not belonging to any political alliance. Since the left's electoral bastions lay in what became the German Democratic Republic in October 1949, unification for the Social Democrats also had a pragmatic-instrumental dimension which should not be underestimated. Thus, although explicitly pro-unification and single-statist, the West German left pursued these policies more in the name of socialism and a fundamental restructuring of class power in Germany, than in the name of conventional nationalism. Paradoxically, those sentiments remained strong, though often subdued, in the officially two-statist Christian democratic right.

The 'Westernisation' of the Federal Republic's left was complete by the late 1950s, and the existing two-state solution became one of the fundamental ideological pillars of the West German left. Being a German nationalist in any way, shape or form simply became unacceptable for any leftist. With the belated discovery of the Holocaust in the course of the 1960s, any kind of German nationalism was discredited in leftist circles. Indeed, it was during this time – and not immediately after the war – that much of the West German left developed the notion that Germany's permanent division was one of the just costs exacted from the German people for Auschwitz. In no other West European left did nationalism evoke such embarrassment and conflicting emotions as in the Federal Republic. Thus, it was *de rigueur* for West German leftists to support Algeria in its soccer match against the Federal Republic at the World Cup in 1982. Similarly, one of the major cleavages between West German and French socialists was their different sensibility toward nationalism, particularly their own, but also – as we will see – those of Eastern Europe and the Soviet Union. It would have been unthinkable for the West German left to welcome the deployment of a German nuclear force as a sign of the Federal Republic's national independence even from the much-hated United States, similar to the French left's often enthusiastic approval of the *force de frappe*.

One of the major tenets of virtually all West German leftists was the complete acceptance of the German Democratic Republic as a legitimate German state. That this was the case is best illustrated by the left's complete misreading of what exactly happened on 9 November 1989. Well into the winter of 1990 – in some cases such as major segments of the Green Party, until the East German elections of 18 March 1990 – the bulk of the West German left simply refused to acknowledge the fact that an undeniable majority of East Germans wanted – for whatever reasons – to have their country join West Germany, thereby ending a 40-year episode which defined the post-war European order. All kinds of explanation for this attitude were given by the West German left, ranging from the evil machinations of Helmut Kohl to the slightly more élitist version that the East Germans obviously do not know what is good for them if they sell their souls for Western consumer goods. Whence this assessment of the German Democratic Republic by the West German left? Let us now turn to this discussion.

THE GDR'S REAL EXISTING SOCIALISM: UNLOVED BUT BEYOND REPROACH

For the West German left, the GDR's legitimacy hailed from many sources. Foremost among them was the universally held view within the West German left that for all the GDR's shortcomings it – rather than the Federal Republic – represented a true break with Germany's fascist past.[6] By establishing the first socialist experiment on German soil under adverse domestic and international conditions, the GDR – in notable contrast to the FRG – came to terms with Germany's past simply by being socialist, which, after all, was antithetical to capitalism, perhaps the single most compelling social arrangement favouring the rise of fascism. The establishment of socialism extended the GDR a 'legitimacy bonus' in the eyes of the West German left which the latter bestowed on few other countries outside the Third World. The GDR's dictatorial ways and bureaucratic repression, although meeting with the West German left's disapproval, were simply no match for the system's true achievement, namely the abolition of private property. With this major step the GDR had obviously initiated a structural change which made it in the eyes of most West German leftists qualitatively superior to any capitalist society. Even compared to social democratic success stories such as Sweden, for example, the West German left perceived the GDR as qualitatively more progressive. Of course it was flawed, but in its essence it was socialist, which was certainly not the case with Sweden. Not only was the GDR socialist, but it was so on German soil: it embodied the legacy of Marx, Engels, Liebknecht (more son than father), Luxemburg, Thälmann, Brecht in a country where Hitler had ruled not long before. The GDR, though deformed, did represent – in principle and structure at least – the good Germany.

The GDR's perception by the West German left is inextricably linked to the latter's political fate inside the Federal Republic as well as to the developments of West German politics at large. As in so many other things in the Federal Republic, the major watershed in the perceptions of and relations with the GDR occurred in the late 1960s.[7] Until then, virtually all public discourse in the Federal Republic was engulfed by an anticommunism bordering on an article of faith if not outright hysteria. In no other European country did anti-communism play such a fundamentally system-affirming role as in the Federal Republic. Indeed, much of the West German left – led by the pro-unity, one-statist Social Democratic Party – shared this antipathy for everything communist throughout the 1950s and much of the 1960s.

Enter '68. West German public life experienced a fundamental transformation 'from above' as well as 'from below' in both of which the GDR, communism, eastern Europe, and the Soviet Union were to play a decisive role. As to the changes 'from above', the most important and lasting centred on the Willy Brandt-initiated Ostpolitik, which in many ways has to be viewed as *one* of the decisive contributors to communism's collapse 20 years later. Secure in its explicitly reformist position in an increasingly prosperous Federal Republic, West German social democracy began a strategic initiative which completely contradicted its main tenets of the 1950s: Replacing their earlier anti-communism with an acceptance of it, the Social Democrats began pursuing relations with the GDR, thereby giving further evidence to their apparently final departure from a one-state solution and their legitimisation of two sovereign German states. The essence of the SPD's policy was what its intellectual architect, Egon Bahr, called *'Wandel durch Annäherung'* (change through *rapprochement*).

Ostpolitik's dialectic could best be summarised by the following quotation from Willy Brandt: 'In order to shake up the status quo politically, we had to accept the status quo territorially.'[8] Following initial opposition to Ostpolitik from West Germany's conservatives, this policy became a bipartisan pillar of the Federal Republic's relations with the GDR and all of Eastern Europe, thus making Ostpolitik the most lasting and successful component of the social democrats' reform initiatives of the late 1960s and early 1970s.

As to the reforms 'from below', it was the West German student movement and the New Left which challenged virtually every convention and institution in the Federal Republic, including anti-communism and the postwar order. Critical of communism's reality in the GDR and eastern Europe, the New Left was equally vocal in its opposition to anti-communism's repression as part of the Cold War atmosphere which built the Federal Republic. Explicitly dismissive of the old left's (that is, social democracy's and communism's) bureaucratic, centralised and heteronomous qualities, the New Left and its legacy nevertheless transformed the characterisation 'anti-communist' into an epithet – a genuine '*Schimpfwort*' – in most West German intellectual circles by the mid-1970s. That the Social Democrats were not enamoured with the rapidity and direction of the New Left's reforms and that they still feared being labelled 'red lovers' in a society barely shedding its Cold War past was best exemplified by their feeling compelled to pass the so-called 'Radicals Decree' which was to screen all applicants to the civil service for communists and other 'enemies of the constitution'.[9] There can be little doubt that the SPD-initiated Radicals Decree was in good part a domestic pacifier for Ostpolitik.

The New Left's creative and euphoric movement phase of the late 1960s disintegrated in a number of directions by the early 1970s. Some new leftists began their 'long march through the institutions', most notably the world of social democracy with its party-affiliated research institutes, and ancillary labour organisations. Others formed the core of a number of leftist organisations which – in opposition to the SPD and the establishment – adhered to a variety of orthodox Leninist positions. A minority even joined organisations close to the West German Communist Party (DKP) which had been re-admitted to the West German political scene in 1968 following a 12-year constitutional ban of communism at the height of the Cold War. While these worlds were very different from each other and were often consumed by bitter ideological rivalries, they also developed certain commonalities which clearly identified them as 'the left'. One of the shared values in this milieu was never to criticise the GDR and other communist regimes in eastern Europe, even if one disapproved of certain concrete measures and policies. In this world of the post-68 West German left, 'real existing socialism' was without any doubt preferable to any capitalist arrangement, hence worthy of at least tacit – if not explicit – approval. This led to the shameful situation in which the West German left became perhaps the most solid Western supporter of the status quo in Eastern Europe and the Soviet Union throughout the 1970s and 1980s publicly and consciously forsaking the plight of opposition movements.

Examples abound. Unlike in France, and to a lesser degree in Italy, where Alexander Solzhenitsyn's *The Gulag Archipelago* caused considerable consternation and soul-searching among left-wing intellectuals, the West German left's response was a scolding of its French comrades for drawing the wrong conclusions about socialism and the Soviet Union from Solzhenitsyn's book. Above all, the West German left decried Solzhenitsyn's nationalism and criticised the French for overlooking such an obvious shortcoming in their effusive praise of the author which seemed part of the French intellectuals' zealous quest for the discovery of liberalism and the shedding of their Marxist past. Teaching about the Soviet invasion of Afghanistan was repressed in one of the trade union movement's most important youth education programmes. The trade unions' youth organisation refused to condemn the Soviet invasion even though this condemnation was to have occurred in a balanced way by having the Central American involvement of the United States criticised in equally harsh terms. A leading member of the printing, media and writers' union (currently IG Medien, formerly IG Druck und Papier) condemned union members who – as German authors – protested against the dissolution of the Polish writers' union. He called them a 'fifth column' which helped to destabilise Poland by 'offering resistance against the regime'.[10] Others in this union called KOR, the organisation of Polish intellectuals explicitly formed to help workers and closely associated with Solidarity, 'a questionable organisation which transforms Solidarity into a political resistance movement'.[11] Many railed against the 'Catholic-reactionary' nature of Solidarity, and one member even dared to compare Polish activists with Hitler's storm troopers, the SA.[12] It has been common knowledge that in certain West German unions members who tried to organise symposia in favour of dissident movements in Eastern Europe met with massive resistance on the part of the union leadership and fellow unionists. That this tacit approval of the communist status quo reached the highest echelons of the social democratic hierarchy was best exemplified by that bizarre – though telling – coincidence of December 1981 when Helmut Schmidt spent a sequestered weekend tête-à-tête with Erich Honecker in the latter's country house in the GDR while General Jaruszelski's troops imposed martial law in Poland. Worst of all, Schmidt did not find the events sufficiently disturbing to leave his meeting with Honecker.[13] The East European dissidents' disappointment concerning this betrayal on the part of the West German left runs deep. This sentiment was best conveyed by the Czech intellectual Pavel Kohut in his speech to guests gathered in Berlin for the celebration of Willy Brandt's 76th birthday: 'You will have to analyse it yourselves why you dropped us in the 1970s, why you – instead of allying yourselves with the beaten – preferred the beaters, or at best stayed neutral.'[14] There are no comparable feelings in eastern Europe *vis-à-vis* any other Western left.

WEST GERMANY'S SPECIAL RELATIONSHIP WITH THE UNITED STATES

As a consequence of the Third Reich's destruction and Germany's broken national identity ever since, the United States assumed a very special role in the formation and weaning of the political reality known as West Germany, something the United States has not replicated anywhere else in western Europe and perhaps not even in Japan due to that country's continued cohesion as one sovereign entity. The special texture of German–American – as opposed to British–American, French–American, or Dutch–American – relations clearly lies in the broken nature of Germany's national identity and historical legacy. For just as in West Germany, so, too, has the United States continued to exert a hegemonic authority in military and political relations vis-à-vis virtually all west European countries since the end of World War II. Again, in a clear parallel with the German situation, the United States emerged all over western Europe as the first and foremost economic and cultural power since 1945. And yet, American missiles and Coca-Cola embodied a very different symbolic – thus political texture in West Germany as compared with any other west European country. Both have been appreciated or rejected by different people at different times in France, Britain, or Italy; in no instance, however, did American missiles or Coca-Cola play a key part in the post-World War II identity formation of the French, British, or Italians. One could take or leave either (as in the case of the French, who despite themselves decidedly opted for Coca-Cola and spurned American missiles) or both without any of the choices implying something beyond the manifest nature of the choices themselves. In other words, in contrast to the West German case, there never existed an intermediate level of understanding and experience, beyond the manifestly political and cultural, in America's relations with the countries of western Europe. Without a doubt, the creation of the Cold War and Germany's position as a front-line state in an antagonistically divided Europe made American penetration of the Federal Republic's political, military, economic, and cultural life a lot more pronounced than anywhere else in the West. But more than geography, it was the broken continuity of German history and the ensuing uncertainty of German national identity which lent the United States willy-nilly a role in West Germany's post-1945 existence that in this form existed nowhere else in Europe. The United States has been qualitatively different toward the Federal Republic than toward any other political and military ally, just as Americanism as a socio-cultural phenomenon has meant different things to post-World War II Germans than to other Europeans.

As already mentioned, nowhere in Europe was the belief in the evils of communism as essential to the formation of postwar political identity as was the case in the Federal Republic. Indeed, this commonly shared distrust and hatred of the Soviet Union and communism created an important bond between the United States and the Federal Republic, and formed a major pillar of what was to become the much-vaunted 'specialness' of German–American relations. It bears mention, of course, that this 'special' relationship was from its very inception profoundly unequal in America's favour, which is not to say that the West Germans did not derive major benefits from it on all levels. But therein lay many of the problems which have since emerged. Had the United States only been repressive and exploitative vis-à-vis the Federal Republic, there would not have developed any conflict and ambivalence by the Germans towards the United States and Americans. A relatively straightforward aversion would have arisen with little need for explanation and analysis. The United States, however, resembles a rich uncle with annoying foibles, much generosity, and definite demands, one who is admired *and* needed by an initially poor, young, and talented nephew. The nephew may even appreciate the uncle and emulate him. But would he love him? Would he accept him without any resistance and resentment always knowing – and being reminded of – the uncle's initial generosity with material and spiritual support? Would there not be constant jockeying for more control on the part of the uncle and greater autonomy on the part of the increasingly independent nephew? It is in this ambivalence, unique to German–American relations in the context of postwar European history, that anti-Americanism attained a special quality in West Germany.[15]

Nowhere has this attained a more pronounced and acute reality than in the Federal Republic's leftist milieu.[16] For the West German left, America is a priori politically dangerous and morally reprehensible by virtue of its power as the leading capitalist actor in a capitalist-dominated world. The West German left sees the United States as dominating, domineering, and intimidating due to its might and its willingness to use it without much restraint. By being the world's leading capitalist power, the United States – for the West German left – cannot but be imperialist, thus predatory, bellicose, and brutal. In addition to a structural critique of the political and economic arrangements in the United States and the profound scepticism vis-à-vis America's very existence, the West German left also paid considerable attention to particular American policies which it saw as prima facie evidence for America's unsavoury role in the world. Beginning with the Vietnam War and continuing with American assistance to Israel and the United States' involvement in Central America, the West German left had ample opportunities to have its general views about America empirically corroborated.

Yet the left's anti-Americanism attained a different quality in the course of the early 1980s. Starting with the neutron bomb debate in the late 1970s and accentuated by the deployment of intermediate-range nuclear missiles in 1983, the West German left began to see the United States as an evil and dangerous occupying power whose reckless policies were to lead to Germany's physical annihilation.[17] The victims of American aggression metamorphosised from Salvadorian peasants to German housewives. Whereas in its pre-1980s anti-Americanism the West German left viewed the Federal Republic as a quasi junior accomplice to the United States in the two countries' joint quest to exploit the Third World, Germany (N.B. *not* just the Federal Republic) had in the left's eyes joined the Third World as one of America's most threatened victims at the height of the Euromissile debate. Thus opined a grafitto on a Frankfurt wall: 'The FRG = El Salvador'. Never was this dichotomised view of America The perpetrator and Germany the victim more emphatically articulated than during the Gulf War, when the German left's anti-Americanism reached proportions of mass hysteria.

In this context the West German left added yet another favourable dimension to its already relatively benevolent picture of the former Soviet Union and its east European allies. While still scorned for its bureaucratic centralism and excessive heteronomy, the Soviet Union was perceived by the left in the Federal Republic not only as a socialist country but as a peaceful, defensive and reactive global power which naturally had to arm itself in its legitimate defence against the American aggressor.[18] Only very unusual West German intellectuals, such as Peter Schneider, who have been explicitly using the events of 1989–90 to come to terms with their own past as leftists, have now publicly confessed their bewilderment and shame when the Kremlin, following Gorbachev's accession to power, openly admitted to having deployed its own intermediate-range missiles as part of a premeditated offensive strategy against the West.[19] This revelation should come as no surprise since the Soviet Union consistently escaped rigorous criticism by the West German left well before the Euromissile crisis.

THE GERMAN LEFT'S EXCESSIVE STATISM

In its Communist as well as social democratic version, the German left has traditionally exhibited a greater degree of 'state fixation' than any of its west European counterparts.[20] Developing without the substantial anarchist and anarcho-syndicalist traditions of the Latin lefts and not sharing the British labour movement's autonomy in civil society, the history of the German left has been inextricably linked with a strong state on virtually all levels: the state as creator of a nation; repressor; provider of welfare and protection; regulator and mediator among groups and classes; initiator of political reforms; guardian of an acceptable industrial relations system.

In the realms of the political economy – in notable contrast to issues pertaining to civil liberties – the West German left has by and large continued to view the state as good. One can detect a clear liking for a '*verstaatlichte Gesellschaft*' (a state-dominated society) which by and large enjoys a preference vis-à-vis any other social arrangement in West Germany's leftist milieu.[21] This 'state fixation' has led union politics in the Federal Republic – certainly a key carrier of progressive causes in the country – to be among the most 'juridified' anywhere in the advanced capitalist world.[22]

One of the corollaries of this 'state fixation' has led to a deep-seated suspicion of the market. Crudely put, much of the West German left adheres to the notion of 'state good, market bad' regardless of the issues involved. If the state remains associated with solidaristic measures and a structural propensity to foster collectivism, the market is seen as the state's exact opposite, undermining all solidarities and encouraging privatisation. Above all, the market is associated with the furthering of individual choice and liberty, certainly among the most disdained concepts inside the West German left. Thus, it should have come as no surprise to the late Petra Kelly of the Green Party that few of her party colleagues and comrades in the West German left supported the Chinese students who dared challenge the Chinese communist regime with that ultimate bourgeois symbol, a replica of the statue of liberty.[23] Kelly compared the West German left unfavourably to the Italian, which did in fact demonstrate on behalf of the Chinese students' quest for liberal reforms in China. Much more characteristic of the West German left's antipathies towards any movement clamouring for individual liberties is the opinion of a leading intellectual, and veteran of the West German student movement of the late 1960s, cited by Kelly in her article.

We don't have a clear picture . . . what did the demonstrators mean by democracy? Did they have a clear program? One also has reservations about becoming engaged on behalf of the movement, since photographs from China showed violent students and demonstrators indiscriminately attacking tanks, vehicles and soldiers with rocks and rods.

Another leading leftist simply resorted to racism and the worst kind of 'First-Worldism': 'What were the first three men called who were executed? One cannot even remember their names'.[24]

CONCLUSION

None of this is to say that the West German left will be spared soul-searching discussions in the coming years about socialism and its own past as it transforms itself from the West German left into the German left. These will be trying times for many individuals and a collective which deserves enormous credit for having made the Federal Republic by far the most humane, enlightened and democratic polity that ever existed on German soil. At this early juncture one can detect the roots for the following contradictory but also complementary lines of argument.

Total denial: socialism is superior to capitalism. The Soviet Union and its East European allies were socialist, regardless of their short-comings. They were thus superior to the West in every possible way. Everybody will soon realise that the former Soviet Union and Eastern Europe will be governed by various forms of neo-fascist and ultra-nationalist regimes beholden to crude consumerism and a market capitalism creating hitherto unprecedented social inequality, economic hardship, and ethnic strife. Only socialism, whose defeat is temporary, could prevent these countries from returning to barbarism. This openly Stalinist whitewash which continues to sing the unmitigated praises of real existing socialism represents the voice of a small minority within the West German left.[25]

Partial denial: much more prevalent are various interpretations which admit to some problems but continue to extol the socialist 'project' and the moral – if not economic and political superiority of social-ism. The number of themes comprising partial denial is best charac-terised by the following quotation: 'What did not exist does not necessarily have to be wrong; and: The opposite of something wrong need not by necessity be right.'[26]

The first part of the statement denies that socialism ever existed anywhere in the world, most certainly in the Soviet Union and East-ern Europe. Whatever system ruled those countries – Stalinism, bu-reaucratic repression, state-led accumulation, modernisation from above, a deformed workers' state – it most certainly was *not* socialism. Hence, as the former Green leader Jutta Ditfurth argued at a panel discussion at the Humboldt University in East Berlin, there simply is no need to re-examine socialism's validity as a model, because it was not social-ism that was defeated in eastern Europe and the Soviet Union, since these systems were never socialist.[27] This exoneration of socialism is extremely widespread in virtually all facets of the West German left. It is often accompanied by a quasi-religious extolling of socialism, not so much as a political and economic reality, but as a moral mission. As a leading West German leftist intellectual told the author over the telephone, 'One is simply a more righteous person if one is a socialist'. It is interesting that people with such views continue seeking to make socialism into an orderly 'science' superior to capitalism's chaos even though none of science's most elementary qualities (such as falsification, for example) and all of religion's (unquestioned ad-herence to dogma) pertain to their political approach and general *Weltanschauung*.[28]

The second part of the above-mentioned quotation warns against any extolling of capitalism simply by virtue of socialism's ostensible failure. This *faute de mieux* embracing of capitalism as the lesser of two evils – understandably so prevalent among East European and Russian intellectuals – need not worry the author of those lines in the German case. Most German leftists have remained completely immune to capitalism's lure throughout thse momentous events and will hardly concede anything positive to it in economics or politics. Much more prevalent, however, will be the debate concerning the next line of argument.

The frenzied search for the elusive 'third way'. Everybody seems on a treasure-hunt for the elusive 'third way', combining the humane collectivism and solidaristic protection of the socialist model with the efficient accumulation and allocation, plus the individual liberties, of a market-dominated capitalism. A number of points constantly appear in this ubiquitous debate: first, there is a woeful absence of empirical examples. With Yugoslavia's disintegration into barbarism, nobody extols the Yugoslav model as the much-vaunted panacea along the third way. Second, there is still the assumption that real existing socialism – of the GDR variety in particular – created a certain solidarity among people, and a serenity and humaneness in interpersonal relations which ought to be (re)introduced into the brutal, commodified and ratrace-dominated West with its individualistic and pushy *'Ellenbogengesellschaft'* (elbow society). Third, everybody wants to go 'beyond social democracy'. Systems such as Sweden's or Austria's, for example, are always mentioned in a 'yes, but' mode. Of course the Federal Republic – let alone any other Western country – never serves as a model for anything. Lastly, there still continues the search for the all-encompassing solution, the total transformation of politics and economics, the definitive answer, the new – and completely moral – human being.

The latter point is particularly surprising as well as disappointing coming from a left which has arguably included perhaps the most effective and powerful new social movements anywhere in the world. It may go to show that despite these movements' insistence on being neither left nor right but ahead – in other words in being quintessential representatives of 'post-modern' politics – they are actually much closer to the traditional left than they might like to admit. The greenish subculture of the Federal Republic maintained a surprisingly strong reddish hue over the years. Despite the many post-modern claims to the contrary, Socialism with a capital 'S' still possesses a powerful spell over the German left.

Instead of moping, it behoves the German left to rejoice about the following immense improvements in European and global politics to which paradoxically – perhaps even unbeknown to itself – it contributed through its activism of the 1970s and 1980s: the end of the Cold War meaning the beginning of an era of true peace and integration in Europe, not just an extended cease-fire; the end of Germany's division; the long overdue liberation for the left of having to bear the millstone of Stalinism and Soviet-style despotism around its neck whenever the word 'socialism' is mentioned in any context; and the extension of liberal democracy from Portugal to the Ural mountains for the first time *ever* in European history.

Thus, the German left should forget about salvaging *anything* 'socialist' from Eastern Europe and the German Democratic Republic. Those who argue that these societies were not socialist should be consistent: they really weren't. Contrary to widespread belief among the West German left, almost everything in the GDR turned out disastrously, including the much-vaunted day-care centres. The solidarity in the GDR was based on shared misery and scarcity, exactly the opposite of the socialist view which envisions the creation of a solidarity based on personal choice and abundance. Above all, the left in the Federal Republic should give itself credit for having created in 1968 something that has proved to be so woefully absent in the world of real existing socialism. Instead of living socialism (small 's') through the emancipatory struggles which transformed the Federal Republic and other Western societies 'from below', the GDR and its East European cohort were decreed Socialism (capital 'S') 'from above', which led to a wholesale state-run 'emancipation' that treated citizens like wards, thereby amounting to no emancipation at all. Just look at how '*salonfähig*' racism, anti-Semitism, sexism, authoritarianism and all other bad 'isms' remained through 40 years of real existing socialism after the left had made them all but unacceptable – though far from non-existent – in the West, including the Federal Republic. The left in Germany has to come to the bitter realisation that the GDR and real existing socialism have bequeathed nothing positive for the left at all. Sad – and incredible – as this may sound, the experiences of the Soviet Union and Eastern Europe can only serve as negative examples and warnings for Western leftists in their continued legitimate and necessary struggle to improve the human condition. If anything, the long overdue Leninist débacle will soon enhance the validity of socialism as an emancipatory project. Whether socialism will ever become the hegemonic system of an advanced industrial economy with a democratic polity nobody can tell. It is perhaps better that way.

Notes

* This chapter is reprinted, with minor editing, from *German Politics*, vol. 1, no. 1 (April 1992) pp. 13–30 (London: Frank Cass).

1. In this essay the West German left comprises all Old Left groups to the left of the Social Democratic Party (SPD) such as the Deutsche Kommunistische Partei (DKP) and the broad legacy of the '68ers and the New Left. Thus, it includes all the factions of the Green Party ranging from the 'Fundamentalists' on the party's rejectionist or maximalist wing through its mediators in the middle, the so-called 'Aufbruch' group, to the party's accommodationists known as 'Realists'. The West German left also encompasses all facets of the so-called 'new social movements' (feminists, peace activists, antinuclear demonstrators) who defined the agenda of progressive politics in the Federal Republic throughout the late 1970s and much of the 1980s. Lastly, I will also count a good part of the West German trade union movement and the Social Democratic Party as belonging to the left. Definitely as a consequence of 1968 and its subsequent legacies, a number of trade unions such as IG Metall and IG Medien – those I have elsewhere termed 'activists' – have been very much part of all aspects of leftist politics in the Federal Republic. The same pertains to the left wing of the SPD.

2. Sven Papke, 'Links und kleinmütig?' in *Gewerkschaftliche Monatshefte*, vol. 41, July 1990, no. 7, pp. 463–74; Papke uses the wonderful German term 'Missmut', best translated as ill-humouredness, despondency, sullenness, discontent, as a section heading for the part of his paper where he describes the concrete reactions by the West German left to the events of 1989–90.

3. In addition to Papke's fine piece, they are Walther Mœller-Jentsch, 'Entzauberung eines historischen Projekts: Der Sozialismus ist im Osten gescheitert und im Western über der Zeit überholt' in *Frankfurter Rundschau*, August 1, 1989; Norbert Roemer, 'Politik sozialer Partnerschaft – Stellungnahme zur gewerkschaftlichen Sozialismus Debatte' in *Gewerkschaftliche Monatshefte*, vol. 41, April 1990, no. 4, pp. 217–25; Wolfgang Kowalsky, 'Zur Kritik linker Deutschlandpolitik' in *Gewerkschaftliche Monatshefte*, vol. 41, April 1990 no. 4; pp. 226–32; and above all Peter Schneider, 'Man kann ein Erdbeben auch verpassen' in *Die Zeit*, April 27, 1990 and reprinted in *German Politics & Society*, No. 20, Summer 1990, pp. 1–21.

4. Werner Conze and Dieter Groh, *Die Arbeiterbewegung in der nationalen Bewegung: Die deutsche Sozialdemokratie vor, während und nach der Reichsgründung* (Stuttgart: Klett, 1966).

5. Louis Dupeux, *National Bolchevisme: Stratégie communiste et dynamique conservatrice* (Paris: H. Champion, 1979).

6. To emphasise the structural characteristics and capital-dependent nature of the Nazi regime, as well as to show the ubiquity of many of its features, the West German left has consistently preferred to refer to this epoch in German history by the generic 'fascist' instead of the specific 'National Socialist' or 'Nazi'. See Andrei S. Markovits, 'Germans and

Jews: An Uneasy Relationship Continues' in *Jewish Frontier*, April 1984, pp. 14–20.

7. It might be a consequence of personal bias, but I for one am convinced that it would be virtually impossible to exaggerate the importance of 1968 as a watershed for virtually every development in the Federal Republic's private and public life.

8. Willy Brandt, *Begegnungen und Einsichten: Die Jahre 1960–75* (Hamburg: Hoffmann und Campe), p. 642.

9. For a recently published fine study on the Radicals Decree, see Gerard Braunthal, *Political Loyalty and Public Service in West Germany: the 1972 Decree Against Radicals and its Consequences* (Amherst: The University of Massachusetts Press, 1990).

10. As quoted in Schneider, 'Man kann ein Erdbeben auch verpassen', *German Politics and Society*, p. 6.

11. Ibid.

12. Ibid.

13. Friends who attended a demonstration on that Sunday in Frankfurt protesting against the imposition of martial law in Poland were very surprised by the low turnout in a town known for its political activism and social engagement on the part of its sizeable and readily mobilised leftist subculture.

14. As quoted in Schneider, 'Man kann ein Erdbeben auch verpassen', p. 8.

15. Much of the above analysis relied on my previous research on German–American relations as well as Americanism and anti-Americanism in the Federal Republic. See, Andrei S. Markovits, 'Anti-Americanism and the Struggle for a West German Identity' in Peter H. Merkl (ed.), *The Federal Republic of Germany at Forty* (New York: New York University Press, 1989), pp. 35–54; and idem, 'On Anti-Americanism in West Germany' in *New German Critique*, No. 34, Winter 1985; pp. 3–27.

16. For a particularly egregious example of this attitude and conviction, see the journal *Prokla*'s editorial 'Aufgeklärte Blindheit; Plädoyer für einen linken Antiamerikanismus' in *Prokla*, vol. 19, March 1989, no. 74; pp. 2–10.

17. The usage of language associated with the Holocaust was unmistakable. Thus, judging by the West German left's rhetoric, Americans were ready to do unto Germans what Germans had done unto the Jews in the Holocaust.

18. Jeffrey Herf, *War by Other Means* (New York: The Free Press, 1991).

19. See Schneider, 'Man kann auch ein Erdbeben verpassen', p. 4.

20. On the useful concept of the German left's – particularly social democracy's and the labour movement's – 'state fixation', see Bodo Zeuner, 'Solidarität mit der SPD oder Solidarität der Klasse? Zur SPD-Bindung der DGB-Gewerkschaften' in *Prokla*, vol. 6, 1977, no. 1, pp. 1–32.

21. On the issue of 'verstaatliche Gesellschaft', see Christiane Reymann, 'Für manche Linke bricht ein Haus aus Selbsttäuschung zusammen' in *Frankfurter Rundschau*, October 21, 1989.

22. On the notion how 'juridification' has on the one hand helped West German labour attain many important reforms and positions of power while at the same time stymieing its radical potentials, see Andrei S.

Markovits, *The Politics of the West German Trade Unions: Strategies of Class and Interest Representation in Growth and Crisis* (Cambridge: Cambridge University Press, 1986).

23. Petra Kelly, 'Wiegen die Menschenrechtsverletzungen Pekings weniger schwer?' in *Frankfurter Rundschau*, August 3, 1989.

24. Ibid.

25. For a representative statement see Hermann L. Gremliza, 'No deposit, no return' in *Konkret*, December 1989, p. 8. Parts of the Hamburg left have developed in this direction.

26. Karlheinz Hiesinger, 'Wider die Politik persönlicher Denunziation' in *Gewerkschaftliche Monatshefte*, vol. 41, July 1990, no. 7, p. 459.

27. In mentioning the well-known Ditfurth incident, Peter Schneider comments on it in the following brilliant way: 'Wonderful. Our images intact, we can carry on as usual. Exhibiting the same determination, a young SA-fascist could have said in 1945: the collapse of the Third Reich does not affect me in the least, since true fascism has not even begun to be implemented anywhere in reality.' Schneider, 'Man kann ein Erdbeben auch verpassen', p. 10.

28. Steffen Lehndorff, a supposedly converted, that is 'critical', West German communist still is trying to make Marxism into a better science. See Steffen Lehndorff, 'Für manche Linke bricht ein Haus aus Selbsttäuschung zusammen', in *Frankfurter Rundschau*, October 21, 1989.

16 Unifying the Greens
Don Schoonmaker

THE ALL-GERMAN GREEN ALLIANCE: MARRIAGE OF
CONVENIENCE?

The proper way to understand the coming together and future prospects of an All-German Green Party is to look at how the epochal
events of 1989–90 affected the more experienced Greens of the West
and the recently formed Alliance 90/Greens, the collection of opposition citizen movements, who are the Eastern counterpart to the Western Greens. The rapid unification of Germany confounded and confused
both of these 'Green' party movements by presenting them with the
issue of national unity. Strong proponents of democracy and equality,
they both had difficulty in accepting the popular will for a united
Germany. The Greens of the West tried to avoid the issue by down-
playing it and emphasising ecological concerns. Their leaders issued
conflicting statements which ranged from supporting two separate German
states, to a possible confederation, but they only succeeded in confus-
ing, and, eventually, alienating potential voters. (Kitschelt, 1991).

Alliance 90/Greens of the East suffered a very similar fate. The major
groups – New Forum, Democracy Now, Initiative for Peace and Human Rights, Independent Women's Union, Greens – which were so
influential in mobilising the crowds in Leipzig, East Berlin, Dresden,
and Halle which helped bring down the one-party communist (SED)
state, also were wed to the idea of a separate East German state. Their
cry was 'wir sind das Volk' (we are the people) not 'Wir sind ein
Volk' (we are one people), and they wanted an East Germany which
was democratic, socialist, and constitutional which would negotiate a
modus vivendi with the powerful West Germany. Only in late January
and early February of 1990 when their work on the Central Round
Table (Thaysen) was complete and the major parties had manoeuvred
to have the national election moved from May to March did the key
leaders of the 'peaceful revolution' realise that their idea of a separate
East German state was shared by a very small minority of the *Volk*.
(Philipsen) The results of the March election – the first and last free
national election in East Germany – shocked the citizen movement
groups. A very solid majority of their fellow citizens clearly opted for

a rapid path to a unified Germany with the clear understanding that West Germany would be setting the tempo and the conditions. The civic opposition groups lamented that the press of time was such that no real debate had taken place with the accelerated pace of events, but it can also be said that they were simply out of touch with the popular will of East Germany on the unification issue. (Hamilton, Hartung, Philipsen).

Thus, the Green parties, East and West, found themselves preparing for the first all-German national election of December 1990 without either enthusiasm or a well-formulated position on the most salient issue of the campaign: national unification. The Western Greens straggled alone, dispirited and disorganised, in the autumn campaign, and were ousted from the Bundestag when they gained only 4.8 per cent of the vote. They had received 8.3 per cent in 1987. Favoured by a very friendly electoral provision and a Federal Constitutional Court decision which allowed small parties to run separately in either East or West Germany, the Alliance 90/Greens managed to garner 6 per cent of the vote, which gave them eight seats in a German parliament of almost 600 members. The day after the election, December 3, 1990, Joschka Fischer and Antje Vollmer, two prominent Green leaders, held a news conference in Bonn. Representing the reform wing of the party, they declared the electoral defeat to be deserved and listed the changes the party had to implement if the Green tradition of constructive opposition was to be maintained in the new Germany. Most of the journalists at the news conference were sceptical about the Greens renewing themselves. Their analyses on the second day following the election read more like obituary notices for a Western Green party which had had considerable impact on the issues and political culture of the Federal Republic in the 1980s. Their assessments about the long-term future of the small eight member Alliance 90/Green were also not hopeful.

Three years later, in 1993, the Western Greens and the Eastern Alliance 90/Greens formed into one party to be called formally Alliance 90/Greens, and informally the Greens, an all-German national party which will run a common slate of candidates in the national election of 1994. What were the forces that brought this new party together? What are the differences and similarities of these two 'Green' parties which have united – on the slow not the fast plan – and how will they find a niche for themselves in a Germany party system that is very much in flux? What are the possibilities for this Green party obtaining national power, and what role would they play in the political system of the new Germany?

To answer these questions, it is necessary, first of all, to keep in mind the very different origins and patterns of development of the West German Greens and Alliance 90/Greens before they cast their lot together in 1993. The sweeping historical events of 1989–90 prompted both Eastern and Western Greens to do some serious rethinking about their role in the evolving German political party system. The events of 1991–3 indicate how each of these parties reacted to the challenges of recovering from the electoral rebuffs, and how the 'slow' unification of the parties came about. We must first look at these events from both Eastern and Western perspectives before an analysis about the future of this new party can be undertaken.

Variations on the Green Theme in the East and West

The contrasts in the historical experiences of the leaders of the new Green party are striking. The West German Greens represented a generational core of middle class radicals who eventually became reformers. They grew up in a stable, economically prosperous constitutional democracy which they felt needed more democratisation, more concern for environmental issues, and less willingness to accept – in their view – the well-mouthed pieties of the established parties about the need to expand military power, nuclear weapons and nuclear plants. The Green party developed from a grass-roots local base before slowly moving on to gain power in the state legislatures, the national and European parliaments. Except for Petra Kelly and a small number of Green leaders, the Western party paid scant attention to the struggles of the opposition dissidents, a factor which rankled with the counterparts of the East. Finally, earlier criticisms notwithstanding, after 15 years the Greens on the Western side had become quite experienced with the rhythm of campaigns, the tactics of parliamentary manoeuving, the framing of issues, and dealing with the media.

Alliance 90/Greens of the East, in contrast, had been in existence only since 1989. It did not represent a particular generation, but there was the same high level of educated professional middle class in the leadership cadre as you have on the Western side. What you have on the Eastern side are more pastors and natural scientists and few trained in the social sciences. Social science in East Germany would simply have been Marxism. The dissident opposition, especially the older generation, lived through Nazism, a Soviet occupation, and a one-party dictatorship which tried to be the model socialist nation-state among the satellite states of the Soviet empire. Instead by building a

Wall, dunning its citizens with endless propaganda, and creating a spy-state in which over one-third of the people – perhaps a modern day record – had been observed, they only managed a fragile, artificial legitimacy which cracked asunder when someone leaned on it. While the activists of the East understood the ideals of a civil society, a constitutional democracy, and a tradition of vigorous dissent, they did not have much experience with these habits and institutions. As one member of the Berlin Parliament noted in an interview: the whole legal system of the West, the intricacy of the parliamentary process, the constant harassment by the media were, at times, too much to take in.[1] The East German oppositionists also had some negative impressions of the West German Greens which were shaped by the Western television they watched. This media image certainly played up the confrontational style and factional disputing of the Greens.

For all these differences in origins, context, and experience, both parties had a rightful claim, in clear distinction to the other parties, to the issues of decentralised power, widened democracy, ecological concerns, gender equality, demilitarisation, and expanded civil and human rights. Both Green parties were also on the left side of the spectrum in looking at capitalism with a sceptical eye without having any interest in a command socialist economy. For both, the excesses of capitalism needed constant critical attention and regulation. The Western Greens in recent years shed their quasi-Marxist and dogmatic socialists and are quite close to their Eastern wing on reforming a social market economy so that it checks the powerful economic interests and provides a measure of equity in opportunity for all of its citizens.

Despite these commonalities, the union of the two movements might never have occurred but for the December 1990 election. In 1990, it was difficult to say whether the election defeat in December was the final blow that SPD politician Walter Momper of Berlin wanted it to be or whether it was the shock therapy that would galvanise the Green party. However, there were a series of challenges in state elections in the next two years that tested the adaptability of the Greens, and these results showed the party on the rebound.

The state elections of 1991 and 1992 show largely positive results for the long-term Green project, but we must add a note of caution. (Frankland and Schoonmaker; Mannheim Studies; Poguntke, 1992) The radical leftist wing had decreased in importance in the Greens of the West, and the move from radical to reform politics had been accomplished by better organisation, improved campaign techniques, a recovering of some of the younger voters, and a diversification of

the occupational backgrounds of Green voters. But the percentage of
the floating vote is still quite high, and the party still gets voters more
interested in sending a message of dissatisfaction to the traditional parties
(CDU and SPD) than in settling in with a permanent link with the
Greens.

The 1990 elections illustrated that there were some very pragmatic,
electoral reasons why the Greens of Western Germany would consider uniting with the eastern movement. Their common interests on
basic issues of human rights, opportunities for women, demilitarisation, and democratisation also encouraged a natural kinship. However, the practical problems of negotiating a merger first needed to
be overcome through painstaking negotiation before the benefits of
the union could be realised.

Stages of a Courtship to Make a Green Union: Party Conferences of Berlin, Hanover, and Leipzig

It was clear from the beginning that the suitor in this courtship of the
East German party was the Western Greens. One of their strong cards
has been their highly successful, pragmatically electoral campaign
conducted in the western states. They proposed to Alliance 90 that
they meet in the summer of 1992 at which time, if their membership
was willing, a negotiating commission would be set up with equal
member representation from east and west. This negotiating commission
would then present a Contract of Association to two separate party
conferences in Hanover in early 1993. That is, the Greens of the west
and Alliance 90 would hold separate discussions of the proposed
rules for merger, vote separately – it would need a two-thirds majority from each conference – and then come together in one common
meeting, hopefully to celebrate the union. Lastly, the calendar called
for a unified party conference in May of 1993 in Leipzig, symbolically in East Germany where the dissidents had challenged the old
SED state. Between late January and May of 1993 a general vote of
the entire membership of each party – 38,000 in the West, 3,000 in
the East – would vote on the new union, and in Leipzig two major
speakers for the national party, one Eastern, one Western, would be
chosen. There was a well-conceived 'method to this madness' of bringing
the parties together through these stages. Both parties wanted to show
the grass roots decision-making style that manifested their ideals of
participatory democracy. They also wanted to contrast their way of a
slower pace with adequate time for debate with the manner in which

the West German parties had taken over and dominated the Eastern German parties in 1990. In short, they aimed to reproach the traditional parties for their hierarchical power structures and highlight the Green tradition of grassroots democracy by showing, by example, how their actions match their ideals. And, of course, they hoped that this contrast in internal party politics would help attract the younger, often idealistic, educated voters who had provided electoral strength in the past.

The Berlin Conference of Alliance 90, May, 1992

The Western Greens were pleased with the outcome of the Federal Delegate Conference of Alliance 90 in Berlin in early May. The final report of the three-day discussion by the eastern citizen movements stated their principles, noted that they had a natural inclination to ally with the Western Greens, and set down further details as to how a new party might emerge. Debates during the conference also gave evidence of problems for the future union.[2]

In a very carefully drawn protocol of the conference, the Alliance 90 leaders reaffirmed their commitment to democracy, human rights, and ecology. They spoke of the need to correct the excesses of capitalism while praising market mechanisms instead of central controls, and they talked of a new party which would combine parliamentary and extraparliamentary actions. Most of this information was close to echoing Western Green positions. However, in a pointed reference to earlier Green internal party decision-making, Alliance 90 roundly criticised factional in-fighting, personal conflicts which showed little overall tolerance, and the promotion of a *Streitkultur* (a culture of polemical argumentation) which could hamstring a party. With that said, the final report noted:

> The alliance should be concluded with the Greens, an historic force which emerged from the ecological, social, and democratic citizen movements of West Germany. In spite of all differences in experience in totally different political systems, they are our authentic partner. Our common political initiatives will develop a significant momentum for an alliance for democracy, ecology, and human rights. (Berlin Protokoll, May 1992).

The conclusion of the report talked about the details of the procedures for unifying the parties. A negotiating team would meet over the summer of 1992 to prepare the Contract of Association which would be voted on in late January 1993 by the delegates to the party congress. Alliance 90 leaders recommended the name, Alliance 90/ Greens, and they pushed for all decision-making bodies in this new party merger to be organised with equal numbers from East and West. Given their much smaller size and experience, that suggestion was bound to rub against the Western Greens. Finally, the conference brought problems to the light of day with which the parties had to contend. For example, some easterners feared that the new party would not be as tolerant of centre and right political views and they resented being 'swallowed' by the larger Western party. A second problem was the split in New Forum between the purists who wanted the group to remain a movement, not a party, and the pragmatists who welcomed the chance to ally with the Western Greens in order to have a national voice. Despite these problems, the key decision to set the merger action in motion was approved by overwhelming majorities in both party conferences. The first stage of the courtship had succeeded; now the details of the union had to be hammered out in the negotiating commission and debated in Hanover.

Party Conference of Alliance 90 and Greens in Hanover, January, 1993

The Hanover conference signified both a new beginning for the Greens of Western Germany and a formidable challenge for them to develop a competitive opposition party with the help of Alliance 90 of the East. The veteran journalists who had followed the Greens through years of turbulent organizational and personal disruptions were surprised by the orderly style of the conference and the large majorities of East and West approving the Contract of Association which merged the parties. They all agreed the union was not a *Liebesheirat* (marriage of love), but they were uncertain just how to label this new political combination. And so, it was either a *Vernunftehe* (marriage of reason), a *Zweckehe* (a marriage of convenience) or even a *Zwangsehe* (shotgun marriage). Obviously the complex motives did not fit within a neat label. The staid *Frankfurter Allgemeine Zeitung* wrote that the party conference's desire for unity had never been so high. Joschka Fischer, Green leader and environmental minister in the state coalition of Hesse spoke of a 'merger of the West German protest movement that grew out of 1968 with the democratic resistance to the East German dictatorship'.

The negotiating committee had done a thorough job. It had not solved all the difficult problems, but those issues caused minor disruption. A large part of the explanation for the relatively smooth fusion of the two political forces that had eyed each other with great suspicion earlier was the concessions offered by the Western party to the smaller party. It was agreed that the name of the party would be Alliance 90/Greens with the suggestion that it informally be called the Greens. The Easterners were sensitive on issues of identity and symbolic names. The negotiating commission recommended that civic movements be allowed to form groups within the party, and this was accepted even though the Greens assumed these would be like the work/study groups (Arbeitsgemeinschaften) which had been used in the past to channel extraparliamentary group suggestions to the parliamentary party. The Easterners' fear of being dominated was allayed by granting a veto right on the State Council – an important organisation of the party – but not in the Federal Executive Committee. Every member would have the right to bring a motion to the floor (Antragsrecht) in the annual Federal Delegate Conference. The party would be led by two speakers, one from each side, and the Eastern Alliance 90 would be guaranteed four or five seats on the powerful Federal Executive Committee. Considering that the Eastern party had only 7.5 per cent of the total membership of the new party from a section of Germany with roughly 20 per cent of the population, obtaining almost 45 per cent of the seats in this body was a major accommodation. All of the major provisions from the negotiating commission, save one, were approved by the separate party conferences with majorities of over 80 per cent.

By any criteria, the Hanover conference was a resounding success. The two parties met on the final afternoon and declared boisterously that 'We are the Opposition'. The next order of business was approval of the Contract of Association by the general membership of both parties, and a united party conference in Leipzig in May of 1993 to celebrate the union and elect two national party speakers. One of the sections on the principles of the new party reads:

> With the party unification of Alliance 90 and the Greens, the experience and the rightful claims of a political citizen movement and an alternative party are directed toward a common project. This merger of equal partners is not the end of present developments but the beginning of a qualitatively new type of cooperation as a common organisation in united Germany. This union is based on quite diverse background experiences, common values, and overarching goals. (TAZ, Jan. 18, 1993).

The Leipzig conference was also a success. The membership had approved the union and the Greens were on the way as a national party. The new party survived all the critical conferences which tested the patience and will power of the two parties. An overall summary of the tensions and commonalities of this all-German Green party suggests that it has a reasonable chance to obtain parliamentary representation in 1994. What are those tensions and commonalities?

Consensus and Cleavage in the All-German Green Party

The Berlin conference cleared the air about Alliance 90's intentions, the Hanover conference created a united party, and the Leipzig conference gave the party members a chance to celebrate and to inform their fellow German citizens that the Greens were back and that Germany needed an intelligent, active, reform-oriented – not radical – constructive opposition. The new beginning for the Greens had taken much cajoling, patience, and willingness to make concessions to Alliance 90. But the year of negotiating and forging reasonable compromises was a good sign for the future.

On the most basic issues, especially when not pitched in great detail, the two parts of the united party had much in common. A major point of consensus in the new Green party is their critique of the present political system. Both see the traditional parties as tied to special economic interests through which interlocking corporatism distributes valued goods – health, education, clean air – unequally. It creates parties whose short-term perspective undermines long-range planning and the interest of the commonweal. Not only are these dominant parties locked into powerful economic interests – management or labour unions – but they are undemocratic, centralised, bureaucratic structures which feed voraciously from an overly generous public finance system, and who are still beset with financial scandals. The Greens contend that their autonomy and detachment from the aggressive clients of the major parties makes them an indispensable critic and beneficial opposition party. To break this concentration of economic and political power, both Eastern and Western parts of the newly united party call for decentralisation, regionalisation, and further democratisation. Lastly, both groups of the new party have great suspicion about the powers of the State. The German historical legacy, especially the double dose of dictatorship in Eastern Germany, has created political activists in the new Green party especially concerned with human rights and civil rights. That gets at the core of what pulled these parties together: human rights, democratisation of polity and society, a concern for the environment, and, in reaction to concern for individual development, a dismantling of a patriarchal value system which prevents gender equality.

There are differences but no great gap in the new party on issues of foreign policy. Both Greens and Alliance 90 favour the European Community but not one dominated by multinational corporations. The Greens want to strengthen the European parliament and reduce the power of the more powerful and less approachable European Community Executive Council. Of all the parties in the new Germany, the new Greens will be most critical of the Federal Republic's interest in a military projection of power. Although there are differences in details, the centre of gravity within the new Green party is for a multi-cultural society in which foreigners can obtain citizenship and refugees can find asylum. Protection of minority rights is part of how human civil rights apply. It also speaks to the Green sensitivity to racism, extreme nationalism and discrimination against the 'other'. All of these viewpoints have been part of the Greens' programmes since the early 1980s.

It would be highly unusual for there not to be points of friction between two groups of highly talented, ambitious, and energetic politicians and activists given the extraordinarily diverse historical experiences of the last half-century. The Germans have a common language and *somewhat* of a common political history, but to have been a citizen of the satellite German Democratic Republic tyrannical regime and to have been a citizen of the stable, prosperous constitutional democracy of the Federal Republic means that your beliefs, attitudes, and values about politics will be quite different. After months of work on the Contract of Association which was presented at Hanover, Ludger Volmer, one of the main speakers of the Greens, said that 'one of the most important experiences of both negotiating delegations was to recognise that even a common language is not readily understood but must be acquired by effort in difficult discussions, and that this was a lesson that all members of the party, east and west, had to catch up on' (*Punkt Null*, 6). There are four areas of possible tension; they involve historical memories, the decision-making and organisation style, the emphasis on different values, and differences on policies. The dissidents of Alliance 90 still harbour resentment at the way in which the Greens of the West neglected or disregarded the human rights movement in the East. Petra Kelly's courageous demonstration in Alexanderplatz, East Berlin in 1983 notwithstanding, the Greens, in the eyes of their new partners, accepted the East German status quo too easily. All of us are captured by past memories and images and many Alliance 90 activists have the Greens frozen in time with media coverage of the mid- to late 1980s when they were regularly 'washing their own dirty linen' in public, engaging in shoot-from-the-lip verbal radicalism, and speaking to the electorate with too many discordant voices. Guenter Nooke of Brandenburg in 1993 still has the Greens on the far end of the left-alternative spectrum supporting a centralised state, an unrealistic assessment of the present party. Lastly, the feeling of inferiority that 'Ossies' feel toward 'Wessies' because of the tragic failure of their social and political experiment of forty years is aggravated when Westerners attempt to 'run the show'. Since some Alliance 90 people have a past image of the Green leaders as brash and arrogant, that could impede honest communication.

It is too early to really tell, but there appear to be different styles of argumentation which characterise Easterners and Westerners in this new party. The Greens are used to – some think they thrive on – a confrontational style which emerged out of the adversarial culture of the student movement of the late 1960s. The dissidents of the East are no shrinking violets, but years of both courage *and* caution marked their ways of dealing with a one-party dictatorship. The attitude toward conflict resolution is simply more moderate on the Eastern side.

The Easterners are a minority in a new party of experienced Green politicians, some of whom have been active in competitive politics and party organisation for over 15 years. The negotiating sessions for the Contract of Association spent considerable time shaping a decision-making structure which honoured both majority decisions and minority rights. Those provisions have been discussed – a veto right in the state council, a guaranteed number of Alliance 90 seats in the Federal Executive Committee, recognition of separate 'citizen movements' within the party – but the real test will come when controversial decisions confront the party. If the necessary mutual trust develops through common experiences and a sense of tolerance, the structural provisions of the Contract of Association will work. There are other organisational problems of lesser weight which merit noting. There is still a touch of traditional partriarchalism on the Eastern side which manifests itself in reaction to gender quotas. The Greens have been the most progressive party in that area, and the national election shows a strong female vote from the East (60 per cent to 40 per cent) whereas the gender figures for the West were 52 per cent to 48 per cent. Again, the issue of media politics and party discipline has always been a most thorny problem for the Greens, and, given the experience of the Alliance 90/Green Bundestag delegation, 1990–93, a similar one for them. Elected officials and party leaders in both groups have been notable in their disdain for *Fraktionszwang* (party discipline). That leads to too many conflicting press releases which blur the image of the party with its supporters. The individualistic, libertarian style may appeal to some who abhor the 'party line' approach, but programmatic party coherence has its merits.

A last issue of media politics involves the use of prominent leaders (Promis) in major campaigns. The Greens, from their beginnings, reacted against the 'cult of personality' approach to politics and stressed issues, but they carried this anti-personalisation inclination to a fetish where they used no media consultants and featured their popular figures – Petra Kelly, Antje Vollmer, Joschka Fischer – only sparingly. Now Joschka Fischer has convinced the pragmatic 'realo' wing of the party that campaign planning, including the effective use of the media, is necessary. (Panebianco) This may rub the Easterners the wrong way. Their own inexperience and their horror at the March, 1990 and December, 1990 elections which the major Western parties dominated created inhibitions they will have to work through.

In the area of policy differences, the Easterners have special issues – the role of the Stasi, the concern about constitutional changes, the need for a thorough assessment of the workings of the GDR – to which the Western Greens may not accord high priority. But the larger issue of difference may come on transforming the East. The Greens have been a postmaterialist party where quality of life meant a participatory society, a clean environment, and a demilitarised international setting. The task of economically improving the Eastern party of Germany is a very materialist issue of which Alliance 90 members have been highly aware and sensitive. However, it may be that this tension encourages the new Green party to formulate more specific economic proposals.

In summary, on many issues the Eastern Alliance 90 is to the right of the Western Greens. Some Greens see several Easterners as suffering from 'free market euphoria' after the experience of state socialism. There is more concern for existential values, religiosity, and family values than on the Western side. It could well be that the Western Greens are more secular than sections of Alliance 90. However, put in perspective, the areas of common agreement still make these two groups natural partners. The question will be whether – as is often said – the 'Wall' in the heads of these active citizens and leaders can also come tumbling down. In the 1980s, the Western Greens spoke often of an organisational model which would be characterised by extensive decentralisation of power, tolerance, and civility. Except for the first value – which lowered their effectiveness – they did not practise what they preached. Now with the party renewed by reforms and a new Eastern partner, they can try to shape an internally democratic, externally effective opposition party in united Germany. To do that, it is necessary to assess this newly united party's chances in the electoral arena, and whether the changing party system offers them a niche.

A Changing Electorate in a Party System in Flux

The value of Ronald Ingelhart's work on the politics of post-industrial polities is that he alerts students of German politics to the transnational trends that have affected electorates and party systems in a variety of advanced industrial democracies. (Inglehart, 1977 and 1991) Leaning on Daniel Bell's work on the coming of the post-industrial society, Inglehart analyses how changes in social structure and educational opportunities have affected political attitudes and actions. In short, the postwar long run of economic development produced middle class societies in which an increasingly larger segment of the population became educated. The decrease of the working class because of technology, and the rise of an expanded, educated, new middle class are signs of a change from an industrial society based on manufacturing to a postindustrial society providing services, especially in the organisation and application of knowledge. Some of the younger members of these societies, especially those born after the war, have been raised in relative security and affluence. Their opportunity for post-secondary education has engendered, for some, a concern for a different set of political issues than those of the previous generation. These are the postmaterialists who have been interested in quality-of-life issues: the environment, peace, opportunities for participation, and gender equality. This New Left is critical of large bureaucratic organisations which, in its view, inhibit opportunities for self-development. A New Left developed in almost all postindustrial polities, spawning a cohort of younger, educated voters who challenged the traditional parties, the powerful state, and the philosophy that economic growth – with relatively few restraints – was the key to the good society. The Greens of West Germany took the slogan, 'limits to growth', and made that a major part of their appeal.

The political agenda for most of the years of the Federal Republic was dominated by issues of economic reconstruction and development. As Dahrendorf said many years ago, it was a society 'bathed in an economic light'. Except for the foreign policy issues of the eastern treaties and promises of further democratisation (risk more democracy) in the 1972 election, this emphasis on continual enlargement and division of the economic pie was not broken until the 1980s with the Green challenge to the policies of the traditional parties about the consequences of rapid economic growth on the environment. The Greens also challenged some of the basic assumptions of the foreign policy consensus and called for more decentralisation of power in all spheres of the society and political system. With a reunited Germany a new set of issues, some quite controversial, are becoming more salient, and these issues further complicate party strategies and voter choices. The costs of unification, the new role of Germany in world affairs – the UN, NATO, the European Community – especially its military role, and the complex problems related to asylum, refugees, immigration, citizenship, and the multicultural society, are all issues which do not lend themselves to easy solutions. How does this new political setting affect the possibility of an all-German Green Alliance?

CONCLUSION: THE WAXING OF OPPOSITION?

The Western Greens successfully improved their organisational machine, and with their 'second founding' with their Eastern partner, they enter another experiment in adaptation. As a party built up from the grassroots with good support on the local and state levels, the Greens have accumulated experience and core supporters over a 15-year period. Their Eastern wing, part of the same radical democratic tradition, is smaller in number but equally convinced that Germany needs a well-informed constructive opposition of the left. Raschke sees the Greens as a professional framework party of small membership, educated activists and voters, who act as the gadfly toward the traditional parties. They are also the tugboat that helps push the big tankers of over-bureaucratised parties, heavily freighted with special interests, in the right direction when they ignore important issues. It could well be that Germany will be moving to a party system in 1994 of two Volkspartien, two framework parties of a very different sort (FDP and Greens) and probably a rightwing populist and nationalist Republican party which exploits the issues of economic discontent, refugees and foreigners, the citizenship debate, and supranational organisations. This party will be reaching again for the rhetoric of German nationalism.

When Otto Kirchheimer wrote his essay in the late 1960s on 'The Waning of Opposition' he used the West German case to make a general comparative argument. The West German *Volksparteien* were the catch-all parties who attempted to integrate a multiclass clientele through blurring of the issues, softening of any ideological principles, and using market principles to find out what the consumer-voter wanted. His analysis was convincing because these habits of Peoples Parties are especially pronounced in flush economic times when the economic pie is expanding. But the present context involves a newly united Germany with a host of problems, domestic and foreign in an economically unfavourable climate. That puts an edge to ideological viewpoints, makes it harder to integrate groups that see themselves as winners and losers, and makes for a peevishness toward those exercising power. In this situation, the task of a new all-German Green party is to offer to voters a reflective and thoughtful critique of what the governing parties propose. That is their challenge in the 1990s.

Notes

1. The interviews with parliamentarians, party workers, and party officials in Bonn were conducted in the summers of 1991 and 1992. The interviews with the party workers on the grassroots level were conducted in Leipzig, Dresden, Berlin, Rostock, and Schwerin. The interviews with the state legislators of Brandenburg, Saxony, Saxony–Anhalt, and Thuringen were carried out in the summer of 1992. Interviews with key leaders of the Federal Executive Committee and with the Bundestag members of Alliance 90/Greens were conducted in 1991 and 1992. All of the interviews were an hour or more in length and all are with people connected with the Greens, west, and Alliance 90/Greens. The particular interview cited here is of note. The Berlin delegation is the only one which has put together an Ossie-Wessie Fraktion. The merits and limitations of that model may have implications for the new party.

2. As of yet, there have been no scholarly analyses of these conferences. The quotations and information in the text is derived partially from the following German newspapers from January 16–22, 1993.: *Rheinische Merkur, Die Zeit, Neues Deutschland, Berliner Zeitung, Frankfurter Rundschau, Frankfurter Allgemeine Zeitung, Stuttgarter Zeitung, Stuttgarter nachrichten, die Tageszeitung, Neue Zeit, Allgemeine Zeitung, Hamburger Abendblatt, Koelner Stadt-Anzeiger, Augburger Allgemeine, Berliner Morgenpost, Sueddeutsche Zeitung, Handelsblatt*, and *der Spiegel.*

References

Frankland, E. Gene and Donald Schoonmaker (1992) *The Greens of Germany: From Protest to Power* (Boulder: Westview).

Hartung, Klaus (1990) *Neunzehnhundertneunund achtzig* (Frankfurt: Luchterhand).

Inglehart, Ronald (1990) *Culture Shift in Advanced Industrial Society* (Princeton: Princeton University Press).

Kitschelt, Herbert (1991) 'The 1990 Federal Election and National Unification', *West European Politics*, 14 (October) pp. 121–48.

Mannheim Forschungsgruppe Wahlen, e.V. (1993) *Politbarometer*, 2/93.

Panebianco, Angelo (1988) Political Parties: Organisation and Power (Cambridge: Cambridge University Press).

Philipsen, Dirk (1993) *We Were the People: Voices from East Germany's Revolutionary Autumn of 1989* (Durham: Duke University Press).

Poguntke, Thomas (1992) 'Goodbye to Movement Politics? Organisational Adaptation of the German Green Party', American Political Science Association Paper, Chicago (September).

'Protokoll Beschluss of Alliance 90' (1992) Document of the Intent to Unite with the Greens of Western Germany' Berlin (May).

Punkt Null: Magazin der Gruenen (1993) 'Georg- die Null in der Mitte: Der Assoziationvertrag zwischen Gruenen und Buendnis ist unterzeichnet', Frankfurt, 5–6.

Thaysen, Uwe (1990) 'Der Runde Tisch. Oder: Wer war das Volk?, Teil I und II' in Zeitschrift fuer Parlamentsfragen, vol. 21, no. 1 (pp. 71–100) und no. 2 (pp. 257–308).

17 Reinventing Trade Unionism in Unified Germany

M. Donald Hancock

German unification in 1990 entailed not only the extension of Western-style capitalism and the Federal Republic's constitutional-institutional system to the former German Democratic Republic but also the establishment of social organisations on West German patterns. Key among them are regional branches of the 17 national trade unions that make up the national Confederation of German Trade Unions (*Deutscher Gewerkschaftsbund*, or DGB). With the parallel reconstitution of democratic trade unions and employer associations throughout the five new *Bundesländer*, unified Germany embraced Western Germany's system of industrial relations. The interim outcome, however, has proved anything but a continuation of established practices of collective bargaining and industrial peace.

Harsh economic realities in the aftermath of unification coupled with Western Europe's continuing (if somewhat hesitant) movement toward greater regional integration confront organised labour in Germany in the 1990s with a dual strategic challenge of historic proportions. For the remainder of the decade and beyond, the DGB and its member unions face nothing less than the reinvention of German trade unionism in the face of uncertain change on both the national and regional levels of political economy. The success – or failure – of union leaders and rank-and-file members to meet this challenge will determine whether organised labour in Germany can remain a viable social partner in the decades ahead.

The need to adapt to an unprecedented combination of contemporary national and regional economic, social, and political change is by no means limited to Germany. The demise of communism in Central and Eastern Europe, the end of the Cold War, and continuing processes of economic globalisation pose both risks and opportunities throughout the emergent 'new world order'. If the Federal Republic is distinctive, it is because the demonstrated achievements of the postwar 'German

312

model' of sustained economic prosperity and political stability are now on trial.

THE GERMAN MODEL: PRINCIPLES AND PERFORMANCE

Scholars and politicians alike employ system abstractions like the 'German model', the 'Scandinavian model', and the 'English sickness' to encapsulate the socio-economic and political essence attributed to particular nations or regions[1] – often with implicit ideological or over polemical intent. *Das Modell Deutschland* is no exception. Appropriated for partisan electoral purposes by the Social Democrats in the 1976 parliamentary campaign, the concept of a special German model of advanced industrial society has subsequently elicited both praise and scepticism in scholarly discourse and the domestic political debate.[2]

Analytically, as I have suggested elsewhere,[3] the concept of a German model encompasses an exceptional combination of political and performance characteristics which in fact distinguish the Federal Republic from its ill-fated Weimar predecessor and most of its European neighbours. Politically, the postwar emergence of a national two-and-a-half party system and a consensual democratic civic culture stands in sharp contrast to Germany's historical legacy of party fragmentation as well as more complex multiparty systems in other contemporary European nations. Socially, the Federal Republic ranks as one of the world's most advanced welfare states on the basis of its comprehensive array of social services and adaptive educational reforms. Economically, West Germany achieved from the 1950s into the 1970s and during most of the 1980s an objectively impressive pattern of economic growth, material prosperity, and long-term labour peace. While none of these achievements is unique to Germany, their confluence in the political and economic development and performance of the Federal Republic from 1949 onward establishes an empirical benchmark for comparative analysis – not the least with respect to Germany's own future.

The success of the German model is a result of multiple international and domestic factors. These included Allied intervention during the occupation interregnum (1945–49) to promote political and economic decentralisation and recruit a reliable democratic counter élite to succeed discredited Nazi officials; the receipt of $4.4 billion in Marshall Aid grants and loans from the U. S. government to assist in the reconstruction of war-shattered industry and infrastructure; and formative constitutional decisions by postwar political leaders to establish a parliamentary form of government based on competitive elections, executive accountability, federalism, and the rule of law.[4] Economic recovery and rapid growth during the 1950s and early 1960s were facilitated by the implementation of an innovative 'social market' approach to economic management which combined reliance on the private ownership of most industry, land, and services with policy measures to facilitate monetary stability, encourage competition, ensure the survival of important socioeconomic groups such as farmers, and provide social benefits to individuals and groups in need.[5]

An essential component of postwar system transformation in Western Germany was the simultaneous creation of an effective system of industrial relations. This involved, as a first step, the reestablishment of autonomous trade unions and employer associations as the principal interest group representing labour and capital, respectively. During Germany's first two political regimes – the Imperial Reich and the Weimar Republic – organised labour had been ideologically fragmented among competing socialist, liberal, and Catholic organisations. Employers, in contrast, claimed a unitary tradition in the form of national federations dating from the Imperial era. The National Socialists' rise to power brought an end to political independence on the part of both labour and capital when party-state officials ordered the dissolution of unions in May 1933 and created in their place an authoritarian 'National Labour Front'.[6]

Trade union activity began to revive spontaneously with the end of the war and, under watchful Allied supervision, led in 1945–48 to the creation of democratic trade unions throughout the western zones of occupation. Most were established as industrial unions (rather than as craft unions on the British model), initially on a regional or zonal basis and later as national organisations encompassing the Federal Republic and West Berlin. Simultaneously, the employer associations were purged of Nazi sympathisers and reorganised themselves in two national federations with largely overlapping membership of individual firms: the Federal Association of German Employers (*Bundesvereinigung der Deutschen Arbeitgeberverbände*, or BDA) and the Federation of Industry (*Bundesverband der Deutschen Industrie*, or BDI). Unions as well as employer associations were both established on a federal basis consisting in each case of a national headquarters and staff and – for purposes of collective bargaining over wages and other terms of employment – regional structures corresponding approximately to the boundaries of the various federal states (*Bundesländer*).

Resolving to avoid a repetition of the Imperial and Weimar legacy of ideological conflict among disparate labour movements, union leaders convened in Munich in October 1949 to establish the German Confederation of Labour (DGB) in October 1949 as an umbrella association representing some 4.9 million workers organised in 16 national West German trade unions.[7] In terms of membership size, the principal members included the Metal Workers' Union (*IG Metall*); Public Services, Transport, and Communications (*Gewerkschaft Öffentlice Dienste, Transport und Verkehr*, or ÖTV); Chemicals, Paper, and Ceramics (*IG CHemie-Papier-Keramik*); Mining and Industry (*Gewerkschaft Bergbau und Energie*); and Construction, Stone, and Earth (*Industriegewerkschaft Bau-Steine-Erden*). Delegates at the DGB's founding congress affirmed their support of the newly-established Federal Republic while simultaneously endorsing a catalogue of 'fundamental demands' that called for selective nationalisation, central economic planning, and the 'codetermination of organised workers in all personnel, economic, and social questions of economic leadership and organisation' as essential economic adjuncts to formal political democracy.[8]

Communist party officials and trade unionists in the fledgling German Democratic Republic scorned the Western initiative by creating a rival 'Free German Federation of Labour' (*Freier Deutscher Gewerkschaftsbund*, or FDGB) based on the Marxist-Leninist practice of political control from the top down. In fundamental contrast to the Western pattern of representative interest group politics, the FDGB functioned primarily as an ideological and organisational extension of the governing Socialist Unity Party (SED); its key purpose was to mobilise workers in a concerted effort to 'build socialism'. Throughout the subsequent development of the GDR as a separate German state, the two national trade union organisations remained mutually antagonistic and organisationally distinct entities.

Alongside postwar organisation renewal, a second step in the development of an effective system of industrial relations was a succession of labour market reforms which accorded organised labour a voice in company and plant management. Among them was the introduction of a novel system of codetermination (*Mitbestimmung*) based on equal representation of workers and shareholders on the supervisory boards of Western Germany's iron, coal, and steel industries. This new experiment in industrial democracy began in 1947 in the British zone of occupation when employers sought to prevent the expropriation of heavy industry by offering workers a participatory role in managerial decisions.[9] Despite subsequent resistance by newly-confident employer groups, the Federal Republic's first parliament (Bundestag) endorsed legislation in 1951 to extend parity codetermination to all West German iron and steel companies employing more than one thousand workers. The 1951 law stipulated that the supervisory boards of such industries are to be composed of an equal number of worker and shareholder representatives. To oversee the day-to-day operations of companies, the supervisory boards appoint a smaller management board whose members designate a labour director with sweeping. responsibilities for company personnel management, the organisation of work, and a broad range of social matters. The labour director cannot be appointed if a candidate is opposed by the worker representatives on the supervisory board.[10]

Additional legislation extending worker rights followed. In 1952 the Bundestag enacted a Works Constitution Act (*Betriebsverfassungs-gesetz*), which sanctioned the restoration of works councils at the plant level[11] and provided for one-third worker representation on the supervisory boards of West Germany's remaining industries. Union officials were bitterly disappointed that the Works Constitution Act did not allow for parity representation of workers and shareholders in *all* larger companies, but they applauded its provisions governing rights of consultation in social, personnel, and economic decisions by the elected members of the works councils. A new Works Constitution Act, implemented in 1972, further strengthened the consultative rights of the works councils.[12] Finally, in 1976 the Bundestag passed a second codetermination law which requires an equal number of worker and shareholder representatives on the supervisory boards of all large enterprises that are not covered by the 1951 bill governing the iron, coal, and steel industries.[13] The 1976 reform falls short of full labour-capital parity, however, in that the worker representatives do not possess a veto power equivalent to that in the 1951 statute over the appointment of the labour director.

While opposition by employers and political conservatives thwarted efforts by organised labour to achieve complete industrial democracy, the codetermination reforms and reinstatement of works councils encouraged union leaders to work within the capitalist order on behalf of traditional bread-and-butter issues such as higher wages and improved working conditions. In the process, individual unions and their counterpart employer associations instigated a distinctive pattern of regional collective bargaining that yielded a largely sustained pattern of industrial peace during the initial forty years of the Federal Repub-

Table 17.1   Industrial conflict: per capita working days lost based on total civilian employment, 1965–69

Year	West Germany	France	Italy	Sweden	United Kingdom	United States
1965	.00	.05	.37	.00	.12	.33
1966	.00	.13	.78	.09	.09	.35
1967	.02	.21	.45	.00	.11	.58
1968	.00	n/a	.49	.00	.19	.65
1969	.01	.11	2.03	.03	.28	.55
1970	.00	.09	1.12	.04	.45	.94
1971	.17	.21	.79	.22	.56	.67
1972	.18	1.00	.00	1.06	.00	.37
1973	.02	.19	1.28	.02	.29	.36
1974	.04	.16	1.04	.01	.60	.61
1975	.00	.19	1.45	.00	.24	.41
1976	.02	.24	1.34	.01	.13	.48
1977	.00	.17	.83	.02	.41	.44
1978	.17	.10	.51	.01	.38	.43
1979	.02	.17	1.36	.01	1.19	.40
1980	.00	.07	.80	1.06	.47	.00
1981	.00	.07	.51	.05	.18	.00
1982	.00	.10	.90	.00	.22	.09
1983	.00	.06	.68	.01	.16	.17
1984	.06	1.13	.21	2.93	.01	.08
1985	.00	.03	1.28	.12	.26	.07
1986	.00	.03	1.88	.16	.05	.11
1987	.00	.02	1.54	.00	.14	.04
1988	.00	.05	n/a	.18	n/a	.04
1989	.00	.04	n/a	.09	n/a	.14

Source: Calculated from International Labour Office, *Year Book of Labour Statistics* 1970, 1980, 1988, 1989–90 (Geneva: ILO). Reprinted from M. Donald Hancock, David P. Conradt, B. Guy Peters, William Safran, and Raphael Zariski, *Politics in Western Europe* (Chatham, N.J.: Chatham Publishers, 1992), p. 549. Used by permission.

lic's existence. As indicated in Table 17.1, West Germany experienced significantly fewer industrial conflicts through 1989 than other comparable democracies with the qualified exception of Sweden. Strikes periodically occurred – notably during the early and late 1970s when unions pressed for catch-up wage increases in response to an inflationary jump in consumer prices and in 1984 when metalworkers and printers walked off their jobs for seven weeks to demand a shorter working week – but they proved the exception rather than the rule.

Institutionalised cooperation between labour and capital through vari-

Table 17.2   Average annual growth of real GNP/GDP, 1968–87
(in percentages)

	West Germany	France	Italy	United Kingdom	United States
1968–72	5.1	5.9	4.5	2.6	2.8
1973–77	2.4	3.1	3.0	1.9	2.6
1978–82	1.6	2.4	4.1	.0	1.4
1983–87	2.3	1.6	2.6	3.5	3.8

Source: Calculated from OECD, *Economic Outlook*, vol. 43, (June 1988),
p. 170.

Table 17.3   Average annual inflation and unemployment rates, 1968–87
(in percentages)

	Consumer prices average changes from previous year					Unemployment rate				
	West Germany	France	Italy	United Kingdom	United States	West Germany	France	Italy	United Kingdom	United States
1968–72	5.4	5.6	6.6	4.0	4.6	.8	2.6	2.6	5.3	4.7
1973–77	5.6	10.4	16.3	16.3	7.2	3.0	3.9	3.6	5.9	6.7
1978–82	4.8	13.6	12.0	16.8	9.8	4.3	6.7	7.8	7.5	7.3
1983–87	1.6	5.7	4.7	9.0	3.3	8.1	9.9	11.3	9.9	7.5

Source: Calculated from OECD, *Economic Outlook*, 43 (June 1988): 180, 187.

ous modes of codetermination and the relative paucity of industrial
conflicts contributed in turn to the positive economic indicators associated with the German model. Following rapid expansion during
the 'economic miracle' of the 1950s and early 1960s, when the annual
growth rate averaged 6 per cent, the average annual rate of Western
Germany's gross national/gross domestic product declined to more
modest but still internationally respectable levels during the 1970s and
1980s. (See Table 17.2) During the same period, Germany's per capita
gross domestic product (calculated in constant values) more than doubled
– increasing from $6038 in 1960 to $12 602 in 1988. This amount
exceeded that of France ($12 190), the United Kingdom ($11 982),
and Italy ($11 741). Among Germany's principal trading partners only
the United States (with per capita GDP of $18 339 in 1988) and Swe-
den ($12 991) achieved higher levels of material prosperity.[14]

Low inflation and virtually full employment accompanied the Federal Republic's largely sustained economic expansion through the early

1970s. The first international oil price shock of 1973–4 caused the average annual inflation rate to increase marginally by mid-decade, while the unemployment rate rose at an ever higher pace. Thanks to a combination of cautious monetary policies and wage restraint on the part of the unions, the average annual inflation rate subsequently dropped dramatically in 1983–7. Unemployment, however, continued a precipitous ascent from the late 1970s onward – albeit at lower levels than in France, Italy, and the United Kingdom. (See Table 17.3.)

Organised Labour as Ambivalent Insider

Throughout even the halcyon years of political stability, sustained material growth, and virtually full employment that characterised the maturation of the German model, organised labour has functioned as an 'ambivalent insider' within western Germany's socioeconomic and political establishment.[15] The DGB and its member unions are clearly inside players on the labour market. They also play an important role in the national administrative system and policymaking process. Formally, trade union officials participate alongside employer representatives in a number of tripartite administrative agencies such as the Federal Employment Office in Nürnberg. In addition, Germany's trade unionists perform familiar advisory and lobbying activities vis-à-vis the chancellor's office, federal and state ministries, and the Bundestag, comparable to 'pressure group politics' in other industrial democracies. From 1967 to 1977 the federal government institutionalised such inputs by convening, on a regular basis, executive-level consultations on national economic policy with the DGB, its principal members, and employer associations. These sessions, known as 'concerted action' (*Konzertierte Aktion*), were designed to enlist the support of both social partners in the government's continuing quest for economic stability and growth.[16] Union officials utilised concerted action as a forum for presenting their views on fiscal and employment policies, but ultimately they refused further participation in 1977 when employer associations filed a suit with the Federal Constitutional Court challenging the constitutionality of the 1976 law on codetermination.[17]

Politically, organised labour has exercised maximum influence on three occasions during the course of postwar German politics: (1) toward the end of the occupation regime, when union leaders capitalised on the temporary weakness of private capital to engineer the first experiment in codetermination; (2) the founding years of the Federal Republic, when the unions threatened a political strike to induce the

Adenauer cabinet to agree to parity codetermination in the iron and steel industries throughout Western Germany; and (3) during the early to mid–1970s, when a Social Democratic-led government sponsored the extension of worker rights under the Works Constitution Act of 1972 and the codetermination law of 1976.

Despite their multiple insider roles and periodic victories on behalf of industrial democracy, union officials retain an ambivalent orientation toward system performance and development in the Federal Republic. Germany's labour movement has neither achieved progress toward its long-term programmatic goal of economic democracy nor does it exercise assured influence on policy priorities and executive decisions. These omissions reflect economic and political realities that restrict organised labour's relative power in contemporary German society. Within the economic system, private capital enjoys preponderant strength based on its greater financial resources and constitutionally-guaranteed rights of ownership.[18] The organisational representatives of private capital – notably the BDA and the BDI – conscientiously wield capital's considerable economic resources both during collective bargaining processes with organised labour itself and with respect to authoritative political outcomes. Its ideological alignment with the right-of-centre Christian Democratic and Free Democratic parties accords private capital a consistent voice in macro-economic management, particularly in light of long-term executive governance by the CDU/CSU and FDP. On the eve of the 1994 parliamentary election, the Christian Democrats had dominated cabinet office (usually in coalition with the FDP) for 32 years (1949–69, 1982–94). In contrast, the Social Democrats – who are the DGB's nominal political allies in policy and legislative matters – have held office for only 13 years (1969–82), and then only in coalition with the more conservative FDP.

Helmut Kohl's election as federal chancellor in October 1982 relegated organised labor once again to its accustomed role as subordinate partner to private capital and political conservatism. For the remainder of the decade, the CDU/CSU–FDP cabinet pursued policies conducive to moderate economic expansion accompanied by low inflation. From 1983 through 1989, western Germany's growth rate averaged 2.6 per cent annually while the annual inflation rate was only 1.9 per cent. Strike activity proved negligible, with persisting high unemployment – which gradually moderated from 7.7 per cent in 1983 to 5.6 per cent in 1989 – encouraging the DGB and its member unions to refrain from confrontational tactics against employers.

The unexpected onset of mass agitation in 1989 throughout the GDR in support of political and economic liberalisation caught union leaders – as it did virtually all West Germans – by surprise. The nation's subsequent rush to unity, coinciding with simultaneous moves within the larger European Community toward closer economic and political integration, confronted Germany's unions with compelling challenges of organisational renewal and policy relevance at the very time when organised labour was at one of its periodic nadirs in political influence. In the short run, unification has brought a significant expansion of union membership. At the same time, economic and political trends in the aftermath of unification raise fundamental questions about the continued viability of the German model – including the future role of organised labour as one of its central pillars.

Unification and the Reconstitution of Organised Labour and Employer Associations in the East

With Erich Honecker's forced resignation as East German head-of-government and First Secretary of the SED in October 1989, a counter élite of trade unionists began its ascent to organisational power within the FDGB – thereby setting into motion a process of institutional and political renewal that resulted in the extension of West German unions to the territory of the former GDR. In parallel moves, the West German BDA and BDI established new regional organisations to represent the interests of reprivatised industry. The culmination of these dual initiatives has been the establishment of an all-German system of industrial relations on the West German model.

The formation of Western-style unions and employer associations in Eastern Germany proceeded through successive phases of creation, merger, and internal consolidation.[19] Following the March 10, 1990 election to the Volkskammer, which resulted in a decisive victory by the CDU–dominated 'Alliance for Germany', non-communist labour activists effectively dissolved the existing unions in the GDR and reconstituted new regional organisations modelled on those in the Federal Republic. The largest among them were *IG Metall*; Public Services, Transport, and Communications (*ÖTV*); Chemicals-Paper-Ceramics; Construction-Stone-Earth, and Mining and Industry. In May, union leaders created a temporary 'Speakers' Council' (*Sprecherrat*) to replace the discredited FDGB. The FDGB was formally disbanded at a special trades union congress in September.

East German managers pursued parallel initiatives to create

counterpart employer associations. In contrast to the unions, whose previous Marxist-Leninist leaders and organisational structures had enjoyed the official blessings of the former SED regime, employer representatives began their work in a veritable vacuum. Employer associations had simply ceased to exist on East German territory during the GDR's transition to socialism, and the Party and state had exercised a political monopoly over all decisions concerning the economy. As a hesitant first step toward filling the resulting institutional void, representatives of eastern Germany's principal industrial conglomerates (*Kombinate*) established an Industrial Forum (*Industrieforum*) in March 1990 to facilitate the exchange of economic and political views. Viewing this effort as too timid, officials at BDA headquarters in Western Germany swiftly proffered their services to help in the creation of Western-style employer associations 'from the top down'. They proceeded to establish 22 local and regional associations in the GDR representing each of the principal industrial sectors – including engineering, construction, chemistry, textiles, commerce, and energy.[20] By early July five state-level employer associations were in place, corresponding to the boundaries of the new *Bundesländer* which had been reconstituted in April as a prelude to Germany's pending unification.[21]

Organizational reform and rebirth were followed by a second phase of merger. The institutional integration of employer associations and organised labour began in the autumn of 1990 with personal unions among leaders of equivalent groups in the two parts of Germany (as was the case with the engineering associations in Hesse in Western Germany and Thüringen in East Germany) and culminated in a formal institutional fusion of both unions and employer associations by early 1991. Once the merger of unions was complete, the DGB opened regional and local offices of its own throughout the former GDR.[22]

The formation of all-German unions meant, in nominal terms, a significant increase in trade union membership. According to preliminary estimates by union officials, the total number of workers belonging to the DGB's member unions jumped from 7.9 million in 1989 to nearly 11.9 million a year later. This represented an increase of 49 per cent. *IG Metall* remains by far the largest union, with a combined membership of 3.7 million, followed by *ÖTV* with an estimated 2 million and – in descending order among the other larger unions – Chemicals-Paper-Ceramics, Construction-Stone-Earth, and Mining and Energy. The infusion of East German workers brought an increase in membership ranging from 29 per cent in the Chemicals-Paper-Ceramics union to fully 71 per cent in the case of Construc-

Table 17.4   Membership expansion as a result of union mergers, 1989–90
(1990 totals are estimates)

Organization	1989	1990	Percentage Gain
DGB	7 937 923	11 850 000	49
Principal Unions			
IG Metall	2 726 705	3 700 000	36
OTV	1 252 599	2 000 000	60
Chemicals-Paper-Ceramics	675 949	870 000	86
Construction-Stone-Earth	462 751	790 000	71
Mining and Energy	322 820	600 000	86

Source: Michael Kittner, ed., Gewerkschaftsjahrbuch 1992. Daten-Fakten-Analysen (Düsseldorf: Bund Verlag, 1992) pp. 82–111. The estimated 1990 totals are based on DGB calculations and preliminary estimates by the various unions. Percentages are calculated from the numerical change from 1989 to 1990.

tion-Stone-Earth. IG Metall experienced a 36 per cent gain. (See Table 17.4).

Coinciding with renewal and incipient merger was the extension of West German labour law to the new Bundesländer through the attainment of economic, monetary, and social union on 1 July. The 1951 and 1976 laws on codetermination became applicable throughout all Germany, as did statutory provisions governing the composition and functions of works councils. Separate collective bargaining procedures remained tentatively in place, with ministerial officials in the last government of the GDR negotiating interim wage settlements with union representatives during the summer and early fall of 1990. Following constitutional-political union on October 2, however, Germany's unions and associations assumed direct responsibility for collective bargaining procedures on the established West German basis.

A third· phase of reconstitution involving organisational consolidation and legitimation ensued in late 1990. In contrast to the relative case of reform, creation, and institutional merger, consolidation has involved formidable political and economic problems. Politically, unions had to cope initially with the absence of administrative structures in the new Bundesländer to enforce the extension of West German labour law and ensure its uniform application. Acting under enormous time pressure and often without adequate personnel, public officials only gradually established a requisite network of labour and social offices throughout the former GDR. Internally, union leaders face an ongoing task of organisational integration. Unions have sought to legitimise their all-German status by expanding their executive committees to include a visible contingent of East Germans. While these efforts have made union leadership more representative of organised labour within Germany as a whole, organisational consolidation remains incomplete on the level of rank-and-file membership. East German workers lack the day-to-day experience with democratic norms and procedures of their colleagues in the West. Many evince a high degree of political cynicism because of their persisting ideological antipathy toward the former FDGB.

Despite the enormous difficulties associated with political and organisational reconstruction in the new federal states, the unions appear to have made solid progress in their preliminary efforts at internal consolidation. Pessimistic predictions that they would lose membership have not proved correct, and union officials claim institutional and material success for their contributions to the ongoing process of social integration of the two parts of Germany.[23] Regional and national economic problems, however, remain far more intractible. Germany's Social Democrats correctly forecast during the 1990 national election campaign that unification would cost considerably more than the sanguine claims of both the Christian Democrats and the Free Democrats, but even they underestimated the difficulties of economic reconstruction and continued growth. The loss of traditional Eastern German export markets in Central Europe, redundancies and plant closings as a result of privatisation of industry in the former GDR, and the onset of Germany's worst economic crisis since the end of World War II have placed severe strains on the fledgling all-German system of industrial relations. The result has been a discernible erosion of labour peace.

ECONOMIC DOLDRUMS AND INDUSTRIAL CONFLICT

As an immediate consequence of unification, the German economy in the 'old' federal states experienced during 1991 its strongest growth rate (4.5 per cent) in fourteen years. Western German firms reported an 8.2 per cent increase in plant investments and a 12.1 per cent increase in new equipment as they swiftly expanded production, distribution facilities, and retail outlets to meet pent-up demands for consumer goods in the new *Bundesländer*.[24] Public officials and private enterprise also instigated a profitable construction boom as they launched a long-term strategy to modernise Eastern Germany's antiquated infrastructure and telecommunications facilities and build much-needed office space throughout the region.

At the same time, the Eastern German economy itself began to falter. Even prior to unification, ownership of the GDR's 12 515 state-owned firms (*volkseigene Betriebe*), collective farms, and public forests had been transferred to a public holding corporation, the Trust Agency for the People's Property (the *Treuhandanstalt* or '*Treuhand*' in less formal speech). The *Treuhand* was charged with the privatisation of state-owned enterprises through their return to previous owners or their sale to German or foreign investors. In the event a suitable buyer could not be found or a particular firm was deemed unprofitable, the Trust Agency was empowered to maintain it in operation through state subsidies or, alternatively, to close it down.[25] While by 1993 *Treuhand* officials had succeeded in selling the vast majority of enterprises entrusted to its care – most of them to Western German investors – they were compelled to liquidate many marginal firms.[26] Simultaneously, numerous companies – including both those privatised and those still in the hands of the *Treuhand* – have been forced to curtail their workforce drastically in order to remain reasonably competitive. As a result, the Eastern German labour force shrank fully a quarter during the first year after unification – declining from 9.2 million workers in 1990 to just over 6.7 million in December 1991. In 1992 an additional 700 000 workers lost their jobs as the labour force contracted still further to approximately 6 million workers.[27] During the same period, the number of registered unemployed jumped to 1.1 million (13.5 per cent). An additional 1.7 persons were engaged in part-time work (*Kurzarbeit*) or participated in job-training programmes.

Exacerbating mounting problems of structural unemployment in the new *Bundesländer* was a decline in exports from the region. The federal government reported that total exports from the former GDR fell 7.4 per cent in 1990 compared to the previous year's total.[28] By 1991, exports to Eastern Europe (including the former Soviet Union) plummeted fully 60 per cent. A primary reason for the decline was that following economic and monetary union in July 1990 Eastern German products became priced in hard currency Deutsche Mark (DM) – and therefore too costly for many traditional buyers in Central and Eastern Europe.

The federal government launched a massive aid package costing 120 billion DM to finance economic reconstruction and the steep increase in the expense of unemployment benefits and other forms of social assistance in the new federal states. To generate the requisite revenue for these efforts, the governing CDU/CSU–FDP coalition initiated legislation to raise personal and consumer taxes, effective July 1991.[29] The tax rise had an immediate dampening effect on economic performance in the old federal states. Economic growth slowed from an average rate of 4.6 per cent during the first two quarters of the year to 2.5 per cent during the third quarter as real incomes fell and wage-earners adjusted their consumption patterns accordingly. Coupled with the Bundesbank's dogged determination to maintain high interest rates as a policy hedge against excessive inflation, the cumulative effect of these measures was the onset of nationwide economic malaise by 1992 with concomitant negative consequences on unified Germany's labour market.

Deepening concern over the prospective loss of jobs and wage disparities averaging 60 per cent between workers in Eastern and Western Germany prompted the onset of labour unrest among East German workers in early 1991. In January, some 130 000 postal employees went on strike to demand higher wages. Later that same month, 9000 workers protested the closure of an automobile plant in Eisenach. In late February, tens of thousands of metal workers staged warning strikes in Erfurt, Halle, and Leipzig to demand job security. Simultaneously, thousands of dock workers took to the street to protest against plans announced by the *Treuhand* (which were later rescinded) to shut down the ship-building industry in Rostock. Members of works councils in Eastern Germany sent an open letter to the Bundestag criticising policies of the *Treuhand,* while officials at DGB headquarters in Düsseldorf warned of 'massive social unrest' if the unemployment surge in the new federal states continued.

Labour market conflict temporarily abated in Eastern Germany when the employer associations yielded to union demands for substantial wage rises and an agreement in principle to equalise salary differentials between the two parts of the country by the end of 1994. Workers in Western Germany, however, soon pressed their own claims for higher wages. In late 1991, *IG Metall* and *ÖTV* presented employers with demands for a 9.5 per cent and 11 per cent increase in wages, respectively, to compensate their members for their loss of purchasing power due to a combination of higher inflation (which rose to an annual rate of 3.6 per cent in 1991 from 2.6 per cent the previous year) and the effects of the July 1991 tax increase. When employers countered with offers less than half the amount the unions requested, labour officials declared their willingness to initiate strike activity if necessary.

Warning strikes began in the banking sector in March 1992 and were soon extended to include commercial, clerical, and technical employees. Although this preliminary skirmish ended in early April when the unions and employers agreed to a compromise settlement, tension mounted between *ÖTV* and government negotiators during collective bargaining sessions affecting public sector workers. Union leaders moderated their earlier demands in response to claims by federal officials that 'excessive' wage increases would contribute to domestic inflationary pressures and thereby undermine economic growth, but they adamantly refused the government's offer of 4.8 per cent. When government negotiators rejected a proposed compromise of 5.4 per cent suggested by an arbitration commission, nearly 90 per cent of *ÖTV* members voted to go on strike. Some 250 000 employees walked out during the last week in April, bringing to a temporary halt most refuse collection and disrupting rail and some air traffic, postal deliveries, and administrative health care services in the western part of the country. The public sector strike – which proved Western Germany's largest in 27 years – was briefly joined by sympathetic car workers who protested an even lower wage increase offered by employers in the engineering sector.

The conflict ended in early May when government negotiators reluctantly accepted the arbitration commission's proposal of a 5.4 per cent wage rise. Chancellor Kohl was not pleased with the result, declaring that the settlement posed 'incalculable risks' for the increasingly sluggish German economy and should not be viewed as a precedent for resolving the simultaneous conflict between metalworkers and employers.[30] That nonetheless proved the case a week later when *IG Metall* and the engineering associations accepted an identical compromise formula for a 20 month period. Restive building workers were similarly mollified, thereby averting a potential strike in the building industry as well.

The end of industrial conflict in Western Germany in May 1992 did little to assuage deepening economic gloom throughout the unified nation. Due to a combination of destabilising factors – including a burgeoning national debt due to transfer payments to the new federal states,[31] high interest rates charged by the Bundesbank, a slowdown in the rate of export growth, and sluggish activity throughout the industrialised world – the German economy faltered perceptibly through the remainder of the year into 1993. The annual growth rate in Western Germany declined from 3.1 per cent in 1991 to 1 per cent in 1992, and inflation inched upward from 3.6 per cent to 3.75 per cent. The jobless rate – already a painfully high 13.4 per cent in the new

Bundesländer – also began to climb in the old federal states. The number of unemployed West Germans rose from nearly 1.9 million (6.1 per cent) in November 1992 to more than 2 million by the end of the year (6.6 per cent). By early 1993, government officials formally declared that Germany was in a recession.

Despite the all-German economic doldrums, industrial conflict erupted again in early 1993 in the East. A strike threat began to loom in March when employers repudiated a 1991 contractual agreement to increase wages by 26 per cent for eastern Germany's 300 000 electrical, steel, and metal workers in a forthcoming round of collective bargaining. Instead, they offered only 9 per cent. This move meant, in effect, that the employers were unwilling to honour their previous agreement with the unions to equalise wages between the two parts of Germany by 1994. As reasons for their recalcitrance, employers cited increased competition from steel imports from Central Europe and higher unit production costs in the Eastern German steel industry than comparable rates in the West. Eventual wage parity, they declared, 'must be linked to productivity and economic growth'.[32] Union officials promptly characterised the employers' move – which was the first cancellation of a labour contract in postwar German history – as 'a direct attack on organised labour and the collective bargaining system . . .'[33]

When employers rejected a compromise proposal worked out by Saxon Minister-President Kurt Biedenkopf and a negotiator representing *IG Metall* to honour the promised 26 per cent wage increase while postponing for one year the wage equalisation timetable, thousands of East German metal and steel workers staged warning strikes in early April. The strike activity had discernible East-West overtones characterised by 'eastern antipathy for the predominantly western employers' and efforts by *IG Metall* to rally 'the rank-and-file behind resentment at being treated like second-class citizens'.[34]

Both sides to the conflict declared their willingness to resume negotiations as *IG Metall* scheduled a union vote among metalworkers in Saxony and Mecklenburg–Vorpommern and steel workers in all five of the new federal states on whether to stage a general strike. Union president Franz Steinkühler asserted that *IG Metall* was 'open to compromise', adding that the metalworkers' union would be willing to sign '"labour contracts with individual firms" as a temporary solution "until the employer association is once again a reliable collective bargaining partner."'[35]

Negotiations proved at first inconclusive, prompting a majority decision among rank-and-file workers in late April to instigate a formal strike. The strike – which was the first legal labour conflict in Eastern Germany in 60 years – began on May 3 in Saxony and rapidly spread to Thüringen, Sachsen–Anhalt, and Brandenburg–Berlin. Some 40 000 workers participated who were employed at 80 steel and engineering plants, most of them owned by West German firms or the *Treuhand*.[36] Workers at the Mercedes-Benz factory in Western Germany staged a brief sympathy strike in support of their demands.

After 12 days of strike activity, *IG Metall* and the engineering association announced a compromise agreement in Saxony on May 14. The accord, which was subsequently extended to the other four Eastern German states, provided for wage increases ranging from 17.5 to 18 per cent in 1993. This amount would equal 80 per cent of wage levels among metal and steel workers in Western Germany. The union and the employer association further agreed to seek wage parity by 1996 (two years behind the original timetable). Outside observers noted 'the compromise was a victory for western Germany's unions, showing that they can organise effective action in eastern Germany and push through their agenda even though the economy is in dismal shape'.[37] Significantly, however, the agreement contains an 'opt-out' clause whereby individual firms are authorised to negotiate lower wage increases with workers if 'economic hardships' at their plant justify a deviation from the general contract. Even though *IG Metall* and the engineering association must approve such exceptions, the opt-out clause constitutes an important departure from the established postwar German practice of industry-wide collective agreements.

Recurrent labour unrest since 1990 in both parts of Germany thus reveals an erosion of long-term labour peace as one of the central tenets of the postwar German model. Domestically, recent conflicts on the labour market are a direct consequence of the extraordinary economic costs and structural dislocations of unification. In the broader West European context, the incipient transformation of the German model has been accompanied since the early 1990s by the adoption of a regional Community Charter for Fundamental Social Rights, the attainment of a single European market, and movement toward prospective economic, monetary, and political union. Thus, alongside the pressing domestic imperative to respond to the sober economic and social realities of integration, Germany's trade unions confront a simultaneous challenge of adapting to an accelerating pace of internationalisation within the boundaries of the European Community.

TOWARD EUROPEAN ECONOMIC UNION

As a founding member of both the European Coal and Steel Community (ECSC) in 1951 and the European Economic Community (EEC) in 1957, the Federal Republic has been firmly committed to the West European integration movement since its inception. Successive federal chancellors – from Konrad Adenauer through Willy Brandt to Helmut Schmidt and Helmut Kohl – have played a key supportive role in both 'deepening' the Community's institutional powers and policy domain and 'widening' its territorial scope from the original core of six members to include the principal European industrial democracies. Even during the hectic pace of German unification in 1989–90, political and administrative officials repeatedly affirmed the Federal Republic's resolute support for the parallel round of regional diplomatic negotiations that culminated in the Treaty on European Union signed in December 1991 in Maastricht, Holland.[38] The Maastricht accord, once ratified and fully implemented, will extend trans- and supranational legal-political authority over a wide range of economic and social issues that traditionally have remained the prerogative of autonomous nation-states.

Alongside the 'high politics' of decisionmaking involving monetary, fiscal, security, and foreign policies on the executive-legislative levels of the European Commission, the Council of Ministers, and the European Parliament, organised interest groups and their clientele continue to dominate day-to-day activities affecting production, investments, distribution, and the provision of services within the EC's member states. Like the institutional development and accretion of power by the Community itself, however, such activities will increasingly be structured by international transactions. This prospect reflects the fundamental aspirations of postwar integrationists – as expressed in the Preamble to the 1957 Treaty of Rome – to 'to lay the foundations of an ever closer union among the peoples of Europe [and] ... to eliminate the barriers which divide Europe. ...'[39] The success of the ECSC and the EEC in dismantling such barriers and establishing a regional customs union during the formative first decade of the integration movement has indeed established the basis for 'closer union' among EC members through the subsequent adoption of common policies in such key areas as agriculture, fisheries, regional development, and currency exchange.[40]

Beginning in the early 1970s, Community officials began to address conditions of work and employee rights as a supplement to the

EC's initial emphasis on the elimination of legal barriers to regional trade and the free movement of workers. Their concerns reflected the radicalisation of domestic European politics during the 1960s, which had included renewed efforts among German trade unionists to extend workers' rights in the Federal Republic and demands by socialist trade unionists and party leaders to achieve *autogestion* in France. In an effort to institute a European-wide system of industrial democracy by requiring private capital to be more accountable for corporate decisions affecting employment (including contemplated plant closures and job redundancies), members of the Commission staff drafted a European Company Statute and a Directive on Company Law for submission to the Council of Ministers. Their objective was to establish the legal foundations for a social dimension within the European Community – through the enactment of appropriate Council directives – to complement parallel processes of economic and political integration. A central feature of both documents was the requirement that European firms would have to provide some form of worker participation in management decisions, preferably on the model of codetermination in the Federal Republic.[41]

Although the Council failed to enact either proposal in the face of opposition by Britain and employers in the member states, the Commission's initiative helped sustain internal EC and public interest in workers' rights in subsequent decades. Joining the debate were representatives of trans-national European organisations representing national trade union and employer associations, notably the European Trade Union Confederation (ETUC) and the Union of Industrial and Employers' Confederations of Europe (UNICE), respectively. Both organisations perform lobbying functions analogous to those of their member federations at home through their institutional and informal access to members of the European Commission, the Council of Ministers, the European Parliament, and the EC's advisory Economic and Social Committee.[42] Predictably, representatives of the ETUC endorsed efforts to extend the practice of industrial democracy, while most UNICE officials were opposed.

Despite the enactment of EC directives in 1975 and 1977 requiring European companies to notify employees about prospective redundancies and changes in firm ownership,[43] little substantive progress toward expanding the EC's social dimension occurred until the mid–1980s. Jacques Delors' appointment as President of the Commission in 1985 coincided with quickened interest on the part of public officials in a number of EC member states in relaunching the European integration movement. Delors, a French socialist and policy activist by political and ideological temperament, served as a crucial policy catalyst in implementing a rapid succession of important Council directives and treaty revisions which significantly expanded the authority and relevance of the EC as a regional actor. They included a Commission 'White Paper' of 1985, which recommended to the Council of Ministers nearly 300 concrete measures to achieve a more liberalised internal market by the end of 1992, the Single European Act of 1986, which affirmed the goals of European economic and monetary union and expanded qualified majority voting procedures in the Council of Ministers; the European Social Charter, which explicitly recognises a litany of social rights of workers; and the Treaty on European Union.

The White Paper and the Single European Act are significant to organised labour in Germany and other European countries primarily for macroeconomic reasons. Both facilitate the movement of capital, goods, and services across national boundaries and expand the decision making capacity of the Council to formulate common EC policies with respect to the implementation of the single market. Together with the provisions of the Treaty on European Union governing the convergence of regional monetary and fiscal policies and the contemplated introduction of a common EC currency under the aegis of a new European Central Bank by the late 1990s, the purpose of these objectives is to stimulate stable economic growth and attendant prosperity.

Of more direct relevance to organised labour in Germany and other European countries are new Community provisions relating to employee rights. Acknowledging that economic growth does not automatically ensure minimum social standards among citizens, the Council of Ministers confirmed in the Single European Act the need for a social dimension to accompany the attainment of a single market and longer-term economic and monetary union. In part, the Council's renewed commitment to the social rights of workers has entailed an expansion of existing Community support for regional development, the exchange of information and experience regarding vocational and higher education, and improved hygiene, safety, and health protection' at work.[44] In addition, the Council adopted – over British objections – a Community Charter for Fundamental Social Rights (the 'Social Charter') at a summit meeting of EC heads-of-government in Madrid 1989. It also incorporated an action programme on social policy as part of the Treaty on European Union.[45] Moreover, subject to future Council approval, the European Commission has drafted complementary directives to establish transnational European companies and works councils.

The Social Charter reaffirms a number of basic social rights which are already protected by Community and/or national laws in the member states – among them the right 'to engage in any occupation or profession in the Community in accordance with the principles of equal treatment as regards to access to employment . . .'; 'an adequate level of social security benefits'; freedom of association and collective bargaining (including the right to strike); and protection of younger, elderly, and disabled workers.[46] More controversial – especially in the view of British conservatives and private enterprise – is a formal commitment by the Council to achieve minimum standards of industrial democracy throughout the Community. To this end the Charter requires that member states ensure 'information, consultation, and participation in [company] decisions' involving 'collective redundancy procedures' and the introduction of technical changes, company restructuring, and mergers 'having an impact on the employment of workers'.[47]

Acting to ensure the implementation of the Social Charter, the EC heads-of-government incorporated (again without British endorsement) an 'Agreement on Social Policy' as part of the December 1991 Treaty on European Union.[48] Council members confirmed a Community interest in supporting and complementing activities in the member states with regard to 'improvement in particular of the working environment to protect workers' health and safety; working conditions; *the information and consultation of workers*; equality between men and women with regard to labour market opportunities and treatment of work; [and] the integration of persons excluded from the labour market. . . .' The Agreement specifically empowers the Council to adopt appropriate directives mandating 'minimum requirements for gradual implementation' of these objectives. In addition, the Council may enact by a unanimous vote of its members Commission proposals regarding 'social security and social protection of workers'; the 'protection of workers where their employment contract is terminated'; the 'representation and collective defence of the interests of workers and employers, *including co-determination* . . .'; and 'financial contributions for promotion of employment and job-creation. . . .'[49]

An innovative feature of the Agreement on Social Policy involves the participatory role of European capital and labour in the formulation of Community social policy. Article 2 of the Agreement stipulates that member states may entrust management and labour, 'at their joint request,' with the implementation of both the general and specific social objectives of the Treaty on European Union.[50] In addition, Article 4 affirms: 'Should management and labour so desire, the dialogue between them at Community level may lead to contractual relations, including agreements.'[51]

Even prior to the Maastricht summit, the European Commission had drafted proposals in 1989 and 1990 to formalise transnational 'social dialogue' in the form of a European Company Statute and a European Works Councils Statute, respectively. The former consists of a dual recommendation for the Council of Ministers to adopt (1) a regulation that would stipulate legal procedures for establishing a multinational European company and the creation of either an administrative board or a management board as its governing body; and (2) a directive regarding the definition of employee participation 'in the supervision and strategic development of the company'. According to the Commission, employee participation could take various forms: 'firstly, a model in which the employees form part of the supervisory board or of the administrative board, as the case may be; secondly, a model in which the employees are represented by a separate body; and finally, other models to be agreed between the management or administrative boards of the founder companies and the employees or their representatives in those companies. . . .'[52] The choice among these models would be left to the individual member states of the Community.[53]

Finally, the proposed European Works Council Statute would require multinational European companies employing a thousand or more workers (at least 100 of them in two or more EC member states) to establish works councils at the initiative of either the company itself or its employees. The composition and competence of the works councils would be subject to negotiation between the social partners, but minimally the councils would be accorded rights of information and consultation concerning management decisions. Works council members would enjoy the same rights and privileges as those provided under national law.

In combination (and if fully implemented), the European Social Charter, the Council's Agreement on Social Policy, and the Commission's proposed statutes on European companies and transnational works councils will vastly expand the potential scope of organisational activity on the part of the DGB and its member unions. As recounted above, Germany's trade unions have long experience with codetermination on both the company and the plant level within the Federal

Republic. The incipient Europeanisation of industrial relations – including new forms of transnational collective agreements and the extension of industrial democracy to multinational firms – remains, however, largely uncharted territory.

THE DOMESTIC AND EUROPEAN CHALLENGE

Prior to and even in the immediate aftermath of German unification, the DGB was actively involved in the construction of the 'new Europe'. Germany's unions as well as employer associations are well represented at the EC's headquarters in Brussels, and their representatives in the ETUC and UNICE have consistently been (in the words of a well-placed informant) 'on the inside track' of the integration movement.[54] Delors' presidency, with its resolute commitment to extending the EC's social dimension and promoting a transnational 'social dialogue' between Western Europe's labour market partners, energised the ETUC and its member confederations. The DGB launched an intensive information campaign on the implications of the Maastricht accord in the form of special conferences and publications for the benefit of union officials and rank-and-file members. Germany's employer federations were similarly engaged in support of prospective European economic union, although most UNICE members initially resisted the new social activism on the part of Community policymakers. Employer representatives subsequently endorsed the concept of social dialogue, however, 'when it became obvious that legislation was inevitable'.[55] According to a ranking official at UNICE, the instigation of a social dialogue on the European level 'has resulted in a much better understanding, on both sides, of the social aspects of a single market. It has proved a good learning process, and has been a successful tool in converting public opinion (including union views) about the internal market'.[56]

Consonant with the emphasis on the consultative rights of workers in both the Social Charter and the Agreement on Social Policy, approximately 20 European multinational corporations have already instigated European works councils on a voluntary basis. Most of them are French-owned firms, but at least four have corporate headquarters in Germany: Allianz, Gillette, Volkswagen, and Mercedes-Benz. While the experiment with European works councils is still too new for any definitive analysis, a preliminary assessment by a team of British scholars indicates that both partners to such agreements are generally satisfied with the results: 'managers stressed their value in promoting an international corporate identity and facilitating restructuring. Employee representatives emphasised among other things the importance of developing international contacts and co-ordination, and the value of obtaining information on corporate strategy direct from group headquarters which could then be fed into collective bargaining at the appropriate level'.[57] At the same time, some employee representatives voiced muted criticism about 'the infrequency of meetings and associated problems in following up issues'.[58]

While early experiments with voluntary European works councils encouraged Commission members and other EC actors to intitiate formal deliberations on the proposed European Company Statute and the European Works Council Statute during the Community's euphoric march toward the Maastricht summit in December 1991, the initial rejection of the Treaty on European Union by a narrow majority of Danish voters in a national referendum in June 1992 and a regional currency crisis later in the year perceptibly slowed the integration movement. Germany's economic doldrums in the intermediate aftermath of unification – coupled with a deepening economic malaise throughout most of Europe during 1992 and 1993 – contributed to the sudden onset of another cyclical round of 'Eurosclerosis'. Ratification of the Treaty on European Union suddenly seemed in doubt, and the Commission – conceding inopportune timing – has at least temporarily withdrawn both the Works Council and the European Company statutes from the Council's agenda.

Organised labour in Germany thus confronts disquieting economic and political uncertainty on multiple fronts. Within the European context, unexpected opposition to the Maastricht accord among disaffected citizens in Denmark and France as well as among parliamentarians and legal experts in a number of other member states has diminished hopes that regional economic, monetary, and political union can actually be achieved by the end of the 1990s. Consequently, trade union officials in Germany and elsewhere appear to have lost interest – at least for the time-being – in the Maastricht vision of economic, monetary, and political union.

Domestically, the DGB and its member unions have successfully joined with Germany's employer associations in creating an all-German system of industrial relations. Moreover, they have contributed significantly to ongoing processes of organisational and social integration within the newly-unified nation. Yet fundamental structural dislocations, wage disparities, and perceived inequities in the distribution of the economic and social costs of unification have provoked recent industrial conflicts which are symptomatic of organised labour's continuing unease as the subordinate partner on the labour market. *IG Metall*'s recent acceptance of an opt-out clause to permit individual firms in the new federal states to pay lower wages than the agreed-upon contractual norm is understandable in light of an overriding concern among rank-and-file workers in job preservation, but such exceptions violate the basic postwar principle of industry-wide collective agreements. This deviation poses a potentially risky precedent for both labour market partners. For their part, unions could suffer decreased organisational relevance if the trend continues. As a German scholar has observed: 'If collective agreements were to lose their binding power with the consent of the employees, the reasons to join or stay in a union might vanish'.[59] Employer associations face a comparable risk; if they lose their 'capacity to negotiate industry-wide agreements, [they], too, will lose membership'.[60]

To minimise such a prospect while simultaneously benefiting from new opportunities inherent in regional economic integration (with or without a formal treaty on European economic and political union), Germany's trade unions must rethink the future. While immediate domestic and regional problems necessarily preoccupy union officials in their day-to-day affairs, the long-term viability of organised labour will require a firm commitment – conceivably by a new generation of leaders – to organisational, strategic, and programmatic innovation. Each has both a domestic and regional component.

Organisational innovation will require, as a domestic imperative, the merger of at least some of Germany's smaller unions into larger, more effective collective bargaining agents. The existence of 17 national unions under the DGB umbrella – ranging in size from the Leather Union's 62,000 members to *IG Metall*'s 3.7 million – undermines the institutional efficacy of German trade unionism as a whole. The existence of fewer but correspondingly larger union federations would enhance the aggregate financial and organisational resources of organised labour in relation to private capital. An important consequence would be a more equal balance of power on the labour market, which in turn would prove a powerful incentive for individual workers to become or remain members. Because of inherent dangers of bureaucratisation and self-serving behaviour on the part of officials in all large organisations, structural rationalisation must simultaneously be tempered by adequate institutional and legal provisions to ensure leadership accountability to rank-and-file trade unionists. A possible means to institutionalise greater élite accountability and sensitivity to membership needs would be to introduce a version of codetermination within the unions themselves.

Regionally, the demonstrated utility of early experiments with European works councils is likely to encourage the creation of similar councils in a growing number of multinational enterprises in the years ahead – even in the absence of formal Council directives and national legislation requiring their formation. As this occurs, the affected unions in Germany, France, and other European countries will be encouraged to share information and experience about the functions (and deficiencies) of the European councils on an institutionalised basis. This could lead to the eventual emergence of transnational unions (and equivalent employer associations) as instruments of collective bargaining in at least some industrial sectors on the European level. Regional organisational innovation of such magnitude would be fraught with difficulties, not the least because workers (like most citizens) retain strong national identities that inhibit internationalism. But it is consistent with the logic of regional economic union within the single European market.

Strategically, Germany's trade unions face difficult choices with respect to both employment and wages. Union officials were compelled to deviate from traditional collective bargaining outcomes in 1993 in Eastern Germany largely because of persisting differences in levels of productivity between the two parts of the country and the prospect of increased unemployment if they had refused to compromise with the employers. Exacerbating the particular problems of economic reconstruction in the new federal states are general processes of structural change – accompanied by increased unemployment – throughout Europe and the rest of the industrialised world. Germany's trade unionists are therefore likely to make virtue of necessity and make similar concessions in other sectors of the economy. Differentiated wages will not necessarily lead to an exodus of union members, however, if trade union officials can convince rank-and-file members that a revitalised trade union movement will remain a reliable and effective bulwark of job security in a more flexible collective bargaining system.

For this strategy to succeed, Germany's trade unions must undertake meaningful programmatic innovation. This will require a 'modernization' of the DGB's programme to reflect the exigencies of an emerging new economic and social order characterised by economic internationalisation even as unified Germany struggles with its own domestic agenda of integration. Programmatic innovation will also necessitate concerted efforts by union officials to inculcate a stronger sense of solidarity among rank-and-file trade unionists with respect to shared individual burdens and organisational opportunities in unified Germany as well as the regional market. Abstract demands by organised labour for economic democracy can be meaningfully recast to include European variants of industrial democracy and an expanded insider role by the DGB and its member unions in the joint task of rebuilding Germany and constructing the 'new Europe'.

The 'reinvention' of trade unionism in unified Germany thus involves multifaceted initiatives which are synonymous with the redefinition of the industrial relations component of the postwar German model. Successful adaptation is by no means assured. Worsening economic conditions and inertia on the part of union leaders could forestall essential reforms and irreparably weaken the labour movement. Conversely, resolute innovation – even under conditions of recurrent economic instability – can help ensure organised labour's continued relevance in the twenty-first century.

Notes

1. Another example is frequent reference in scholarly literature to American (or French or Russian) 'exceptionalism'.
2. See the collection of laudatory and critical essays in Andrei S. Markovits, ed., *The Political Economy of West Germany: Modell Deutschland* (New York: Praeger, 1982).
3. M. Donald Hancock, *West Germany: The Politics of Democratic Corporatism* (Chatham, N.J.: Chatham House Publishers, 1989).
4. Allied and German measures to dismantle the Nazi regime and reinstitute, on firmer foundations than the Weimar precedent, constitutional and political principles of representative government correspond to what Dankwart A. Rustow depicts as the 'preparatory' and 'decision' stages in regime transitions from authoritarianism to democracy. A third phase in successful transitions is 'democratic habituation'. See Rustow, 'Transitions to Democracy: Towards a Dynamic Model,' *Comparative Politics*, vol. 2, (April 1970), pp. 337–63.
5. Germany's social market policies contrast in form and substance with less interventionist 'pure market' and 'regulated market' approaches to macro economic management and more interventionist 'coordinated market', 'étatist' and 'dirigiste' approaches. For a definition of these terms and an assessment of their consequences for different industrial and other economic policies, see M. Donald Hancock, John Logue, and Bernt Schiller, eds., *Managing Modern Capitalism. Industrial Renewal and Workplace Democracy in the United States and Western Europe* (New

York and Westport, Conn.: Greenwood Press, 1991).

6. Michael Schneider, *A Brief History of the German Trade Unions*, trans. Barrie Selman (Bonn: Verlag J. H. W. Dietz Nachf., 1991), pp. 204–13.

7. The number of member unions was increased to seventeen in the mid–1980s with the creation of a national media union (*IG Medien*).

8. *Die Grundsatzforderungen des DGB 1949*, reprinted in Dieter Schuster, *Die deutsche Gewerkshaftsbewegung*, 5th rev. ed. (Düsseldorf: DGB-Bundesvorstand, 1976), pp. 84–6.

9. Ibid., 247.

10. A good descriptive overview of codetermination on the company level can be found in Volker R. Berghahn and Detlev Karsten, *Industrial Relations in West Germany* (Oxford/New York/Hamburg: Berg Publishers, 1987), pp. 116–28.

11. Elective works councils had originally been established in Germany during the early years of the Weimar era as a preliminary experiment in industrial democracy, but they were suppressed under the Nazi regime. The Weimar era and postwar German precedents inspired similar legislation in a number of West European countries after World War II.

12. In a perceptive analysis of labour influence and the works councils, Jutta Helm observes that the Works Constitution Act 'has succeeded in forcing employers to be more cooperative and to consult and negotiate with employee representatives on a host of issues. In turn, many works councilors have learned to take advantage of the opportunities and resources the law provides. This is no negligible achievement.' Helm, 'Workplace Democracy in Germany', in Hancock, Logue, and Schiller, *Managing Modern Capitalism*, 184. Berghahn and Karsten provide a detailed legal description of the powers and functions of the councils in *Industrial Relations in West Germany*, pp. 106–116.

13. The 1976 law applies to enterprises employing two thousand or more employees; it excludes the news media, political parties, trade unions, religious groups, and educational and scientific organisations.

14. Robert Summers and Alan Heston, 'The Penn World Table: an Expanded Set of International Comparisons, 1950–1988', *Quarterly Journal of Economics* (May 1991): pp. 327–68.

15. This is the analytical theme of my chapter on 'The Ambivalent Insider: the DGB Between Theory and Practice,' in Peter H. Merkl, ed., *The Federal Republic at Forty* (New York, N.Y.: New York University Press, 1989), pp. 178–2.

16. 'Concerted action' was mandated by a 1967 Law to Promote Economic Stability and Growth. This German variant of democratic corporatism was apparently inspired by the prior creation by British Conservatives of a tripartite National Economic and Development Council (NEDC) in 1962. The declared purpose of both the NEDC and concerted action was to facilitate economic stability through voluntary agreements to exercise wage, price, and fiscal restraint on the part of labour, capital, and the government, respectively.

17. The court affirmed the statute in a 1979 decision, but concerted action was never resumed. While the employers' initiative proved the immediate impetus for the decision by DGB leaders to boycott future sessions,

union officials had already decided by then that concerted action favored employer and government interests more than their own. Hence, in the view of DGB officials, concerted action had become counter productive. Less formalised consultations took the place of concerted action in the form of 'bungalow discussions' convened by the federal chancellor at his residence in Bonn. On the rise and fall of concerted action, see Hancock, *West Germany: The Politics of Democratic Corporatism*, pp. 135–8, and Helm, 'Workplace Democracy in Germany,' pp. 175–6.

18. Article 14 of the Basic Law affirms that 'Property and the right of inheritance are guaranteed. . . .'

19. Michael Kittner, ed., *Gewerkschaftsjahrbuch 1992. Daten-Fakten-Analysen* (Cologne: Bund Verlag, 1992), pp. 72, 77–80.

20. Bundesvereinigung der Deutschen Arbeitgeberverbände, *Übersicht über die Verbandsgründungen in der DDR* (Cologne: BDA, July 1990).

21. This account of events is based on interviews by the author with knowledgeable BDA officials in Cologne in June 1991.

22. The DGB waited until December 1990 to authorise the creation of state-level offices in each of the five new *Bundesländer* (Berlin–Brandenburg, Mecklenburg–Vorpommern, Sachsen, Sachsen–Anhalt, and Thüringen). It authorised an additional thirty-three local offices in May 1991. Confederation officials in Düsseldorf had deliberately postponed establishing a DGB presence in the GDR 'to leave [the DGB] open to organisational alternatives during the course of [economic and political] reconstruction. . . .' Kittner, *Gewerkschaftsjahrbuch 1992*, p. 78.

23. While only 2.8 per cent of East German workers whom the DGB had surveyed in 1991 categorically rejected trade unions, 11.4 per cent of them spontaneously thought of 'deceit' or 'fraud' (*Betrug*) when they heard the word 'unions'. Over 90 per cent of those surveyed previously belonged to one of the FDGB unions. See Institut für empirische Psychologie, *Präsentationsunterlagen DDR – Trendmonitor* (Düsseldorf: DGB, June 4, 1991).

24. Kittner reports that during the initial phase of consolidation (1990–1), 'respectable material and employment successes were achieved. There was no alternative to establishing the unions [in the new federal states] on the basis of historically-proven and at the same time future-oriented structures.' Kittner, *Gewerkschaftsjahrbuch 1992*, p. 72.

25. Established by the last government of the GDR, the Trust Agency became politically accountable to the ministries of Finance and Economics in Bonn following unification. Peter H. Merkl provides a comprehensive assessment of the activities of the Treuhand in his chapter, 'An Impossible Dream? Privatizing Collective Property in Eastern Germany,' in M. Donald Hancock and Helga A. Welsh, eds., *German Unification: Process and Outcomes* (Boulder, Col.: Westview Press, 1994), pp. 199–221.

26. The *Treuhand* announced that some 10 669 firms had been sold by the end of November 1992. Another 1773 enterprises remained in *Treuhand* hands, while the remainder had been liquidated. Well-known casualties include the Wartburg and Trabant automobile plants and the former Eastern German national airline Interflug. Western German firms purchased more

than 90 per cent of the total; foreign companies bought 629. Reported in *The Week in Germany*, December 4, 1992, p. 2, and *The Week in Germany*, June 18, 1993, p. 5.

27. Among those unemployed were some half a million former public officials in Eastern Germany whom the federal government dismissed for political reasons in 1990.

28. *The Week in Germany*, February 15, 1991, p. 5.

29. Personal income taxes rose by 7.5 per cent; additional taxes were imposed on oil and tobacco.

30. Quoted in *The Week in Germany*, May 15, 1992, p. 4.

31. Public expenditures increased 9.2 per cent in 1992 to an unprecedented high of nearly 1.2 trillion DM while revenues totalled 1.1 trillion. By the end of 1992, Germany's national debt totalled 46 per cent of the gross national product (GNP), which constituted a 6 per cent increase over 1990.

32. *The Economist*, May 15, 1993, p. 78.

33. *The New York Times*, May 15, 1993.

34. *The Wall Street Journal*, May 4, 1993.

35. Quoted in *The Week in Germany*, April 23, 1993, p. 4.

36. *The Economist*, ibid.

37. *The New York Times*, ibid.

38. See Andreas Falke, 'An Unwelcome Enlargement? The European Community and German Unification,' in Hancock and Welsh, eds., *German Unification: Process and Outcomes*.

39. Office for Official Publications of the European Communities, *Treaties Establishing the European Communities* (Brussels and Luxembourg, 1987), p. 217.

40. Succint overviews of the development of the European Community, its institutions, and policies include Derek W. Urwin, *The Community of Europe: a History of European Integration since 1945* (New York: Longman, 1991), and William Nicoll and Trevor C. Salmon, *Understanding the European Communities* (New York: Philip Allan, 1990).

41. Beverly Springer, *The Social Dimension of 1992. Europe Faces a New EC* (New York: Praeger Publishers, 1992), p. 86.

42. For a brief description of lobbying activities in Brussels, see Nicoll and Salmon, pp. 81–3.

43. Springer, pp. 87–8.

44. European Documentation, *1992 – The Social Dimension* (Luxembourg: Office for Official Publications of the European Communities, 1990), pp. 78–9.

45. British government officials endorsed most of the charter's provisions but objected to an extension of Community regulations in the area of social policy. For a comprehensive statement of British views, see House of Lords, Select Committee on the European Communities, *A Community Social Charter. With Evidence* (London: HMSO, 1989).

46. European Documentation, *The Social Charter* (Luxembourg: Office for Official Publications of the European Communities, 1989).

47. Ibid.

48. Council of the European Communities, Commission of the European

Communities, *Treaty on European Union* (Luxembourg: Office for Official Publications of the European Communities, 1992), pp. 197–201.

49. Ibid., pp. 197–8. Italics added for emphasis.
50. Ibid., p. 198.
51. Ibid., p. 199.
52. 'European company Statute.' *Company Law*, 3 (January 1983), pp. 33–4. A Council regulation is directly binding on the member states, whereas a directive – which is also binding – must be implemented through national law.
53. Beverly Springer observes: 'Member states have the option of selecting one of the alternative forms of worker participation contained in the directive or incorporating all of them into national law and leaving the choice to be made by the employers and representatives of the employees in the companies concerned'. Springer, *The Social Dimension of 1992*, p. 95.
54. Author's interview with a ETUC officer in Brussels in March 1992.
55. Ibid.
56. Author's interview at UNICE headquarters in Brussels in March 1992.
57. Mark Hall, Paul Marginson, and Keith Sisson, 'The European Works Council: Setting the Research Agenda,' *Warwick Papers in Industrial Relations* (Warwick, England: Industrial Relations Research Unit, School of Industrial and Business Studies, University of Warwick, November 1992), p. 5.
58. Ibid.
59. Dieter Sadowski, 'The Effect of European Integration on National Industrial Relations Systems: The Ambiguous Case of Germany'. Paper presented at the Third Biennial Conference of the European Community Studies Association on 27–9 May 1993 in Washington, D.C., p. 21.
60. Ibid., 22. Sadowski notes that the Opel automobile factory in Eisenach and some of the *Treuhand*-owned firms have not yet joined the engineering association (*Gesamtmetall*).

18 Immigration Politics and Citizenship in Germany
William M. Chandler

Germany, like most European nations, has been traditionally a land of net emigration. Hence compared to North America, governmental concerns for both demographic inflow and the integration of ethnic/linguistic minorities have remained low priorities. Indeed, even today the idea that Germany is not a land of immigration has still to be officially denied, even though there is no doubt that migration patterns have been reversed. In the half century since the end of World War Two, peace, economic modernisation and sustained prosperity have made Germany, along with much of Western Europe, a compelling magnet for foreign populations attracted by high wages and generous social benefits. By the end of the 1980s, especially in the wake of disorder and economic chaos in many parts of Central and Eastern Europe, the flow of immigrants and refugees has accelerated beyond anyone's expectations.

Although we witness a generalised increase in immigration pressure across Western Europe, some unique circumstances apply to Germany. The horrors of National Socialism convinced the writers of the 1949 Basic Law of the need to protect refugees from political persecution. Article 16(2), which states that, 'Every politically persecuted individual has the right to asylum', enshrined this basic human right and assured Germany's openness to potential asylum seekers. It later created an effective means of entry for both economic and political refugees. The Basic Law also guaranteed the right of return for ethnic Germans under Article 116(1). Originally this article applied to Germans who after 1945 found themselves outside the now reduced German borders, but the provision was later expanded to include a broad definition of ethnic Germans. In the post-unity era, this has meant an open door for hundreds of thousands of Eastern Europeans from many lands who can claim German ancestry.[1]

Beyond these constitutional provisions, Germany retains a definition of citizenship based on blood (*jus sanguinis*) rather than soil (*jus soli*). The legal conditions whereby foreigners may obtain German citizenship remain restrictive, even with the 1991 revisions that make naturalisation possible after 15 years of permanent residence. The prohibition of dual citizenship blocks many from taking this option.[2]

Discussions of post-war demographics must also recognise that trends in the Federal Republic do not apply to the former German Democratic Republic (GDR). Indeed, patterns in West and East have been fundamentally divergent. While demographic movements have contributed significantly to population growth and changes in social structure in the Federal Republic, in the GDR the predominant phenomenon was one of steady decline after an initial influx of post-war expellees. In this regard the GDR became unique among modern states.

PATTERNS OF IMMIGRATION

During the first three decades of the Federal Republic the combination of a post-war babyboom and a massive in-migration resulted in a population increase from about 46 million in 1946 to 62 million in 1972.[3] From the early 1970s until 1989, both these trends abated and the total population levelled out. Scanning the entire post-war era, we can identify three formative episodes of mass influx, each with its own dynamic – the expellee, the *Gastarbeiter*, and the unification phases. The first wave (1945–50) was driven by the imperatives of post-war resettlement in an atmosphere of total devastation. The second (1960–73) corresponds to the achievement of Germany's economic miracle with its expansive labour market. The still unfolding third wave (1989–) has been shaped by unification and post-unification instability. Each phase provides a distinctive background for understanding immigration politics.

Within and across these three waves, at least five major categories of migrants should be noted:

(1) **Post-1945 German expellees and refugees.**
(2) **Cross-border migrants** between the two German states, of which there are two quantitatively significant groups: those between 1950 and 1961, prior to the *Mauerbau*, and those East German (*Übersiedler*) post–1989.
(3) **Ethnic German immigrants** (*Aussiedler*) – descendants of prior generations of German settlers in Russia, Romania, and elsewhere in Eastern Europe. These migrants have been able to enter the Federal Republic under a German ethnic quota, sometimes criti-

cised as a 'racist exception', with claims to German citizenship based on ancestry. Some of these descendant Germans have had no cultural or linguistic links to modern Germany and therefore often have constituted real immigrants in terms of social integration.

(4) **Foreign workers**, non-Germans without direct claim to citizenship.

(5) **Asylum-seekers**, political/economic refugees.

To these five categories one might add a residual group of illegal immigrants plus other unspecified entrants of diverse origin.

The Expellee Phase

The first wave of primarily German migrants began with the end of World War Two. All told over 9 million expellees and refugees would move westwards into the four zones of occupation from parts of the Reich lost in war and occupied by the Red Army. The three largest regions of origin were Silesia (3.2 mil), the Sudetenland (2.9 mil) and East Prussia (1.9 mil). During the same time, some 3 million ethnic Germans also migrated into the future Federal Republic from outside the borders of prewar Germany.[4] There were temporarily large numbers of displaced persons as well, many of whom would be either forcibly returned to the Soviet Union or were in transit to further emigration.

Although hardly a natural economic immigration, this special form of imposed migration by 1950 represented over 16 per cent of an expanding West German population. The conditions of devastation prevailing across all four occupation zones created serious problems of integration. However, the economic recovery of West Germany provided an essential opportunity for integration, and the new entrants constituted a relatively skilled and upwardly mobile labour force that was able, ultimately, to contribute to and take advantage of the economic take-off.

Politically, this first migration period is unique because it coincides with the founding of the two German states and the re-establishment of party politics. As the party system was taking form in the western zones, millions of expellees provided a potential mass base for a regionalist party of nationalist revindication. As a dispossessed minority, often without property, housing or jobs, the large expellee population was feared to be a possible source for a revival of rightist extremism. The early success of the BHE (*Bund der Heimatvertriebenen und Entrechteten*) demonstrated its electoral potential among Eastern resettlers.[5] In the longer term, both major parties attempted to attract portions of the refugee/expellee population, but Chancellor Adenauer and his governing CDU/CSU were the more successful in doing so. His first government in 1949 responded to expellee concerns with the establishment of a ministry for refugee affairs and, in 1952, with the Equalization of Burdens Act, which provided partial compensation for lost property and other assets. Facilitated by the implementation of the 5 per cent rule nationally as of 1953, Adenauer's catch-all strategy succeeded in coopting both activists and electorate from the BHE. This incorporation into the governing coalition also served to blunt the possibility of a purely irredentist party taking hold.

The initial surge of migration stabilised by 1950, but an ongoing repatriation process through subsequent decades meant a steady but limited inflow of cross-border and ethnic Germans. Into the next decade the most politically significant migration took a different form. From the founding of the GDR until 1961, a net migration from East to West of some 2.5 million Germans took place, averaging about 200 000 per year.[6] The exit of primarily young, skilled workers and professionals presented the SED government with a major problem. Ulbricht's decision to build the Wall was driven by the need to stem the loss of the GDR's economically active population. After 1961 all East German borders were effectively sealed, and the exodus dwindled to a trickle.

The Gastarbeiter Phase

In this phase German policy initiatives were defined by economic growth. This second wave was more gradual and less perceptible, but no less significant, in its impact than the preceding expellee phase. As a consequence of full employment prosperity, Germany's labour market strategy came to increasingly depend on the importation of workers. The *Gastarbeiter* of the 1960s were seen as a temporary solution to immediate labour shortages. Beginning in 1955, a series of bilateral treaties between the Federal Republic and various states in southern Europe set conditions for the recruitment of workers on limited term contracts. In the early years, Italy provided the greatest number of *Gastarbeiter*. By the mid–60s, Turkey and Yugoslavia became the primary sources of new workers.[7] For the first time large numbers of non-Germans began to arrive, often with quite different religious and cultural backgrounds.

In this transformation no thought was given to social integration because newcomers were defined as fixed-term, temporary workers who would later return to their homelands. The inaccuracy of this assumption only became fully evident as millions of foreigners took up effective permanent residence. The 1973 ban on further recruitment of foreign workers did not diminish their numbers. Instead the foreign population stabilised as family members arrived and a second generation was born. By the 1990s this would account in total for over 5.8 million non-citizen permanent residents or 8.2 per cent of the population.

During this second phase, because foreigners did not become voters, parties had no incentive to attract their support or defend their needs. Benign neglect characterised the attention given to problems of social integration. Although there was no direct impact on the party system, the status of foreigners did become a latent basis for subsequent conflict. Today it is clear that immigration has had societal effects extending far beyond employment considerations. Foreigners may have come for jobs, but they soon became permanent features on the fringe of German society. In the words of Swiss author Max Frisch, 'We asked for manpower, and we got human beings'.[8]

The Unification Phase

The third critical phase is directly linked to the collapse of communism and the consequent peaceful revolutions throughout Central and Eastern Europe. These events opened borders and provoked new demographic instability. Popular rejection of decades of political repression combined with deteriorating economic conditions increased both the likelihood of exodus from the former socialist states and of sustained pressure for entry into the wealthy regions of western Europe. The impact of this transformation has been greater and more sudden in Germany than elsewhere due to geography and a liberal asylum policy. Of course, the absorption of East Germany into the Federal Republic meant the instant admission of over 16 million who had grown up within a socialist economic and political system. Although Germans in the new *Länder* are hardly immigrants, their integration into the social fabric of the Federal Republic has presented social challenges not unlike some faced by foreign entrants.

In this phase, migration has involved a mix of three principal groups: a renewed exodus of east Germans (*Übersiedler*) moving westwards, ethnic Germans (*Aussiedler*) from Eastern Europe, and non-German asylum-seekers. This third category (*Asylanten*) has become the most politically sensitive as victims of socio-economic chaos and collapse to the East have swelled in response to economic uncertainty and political crises in their lands of origin.

As noted earlier, the intra-German *Übersiedler* phenomenon is not confined to this period. However, after 1961 the outflow of East Germans remained minute – until the effects of the Gorbachev revolution, including the implict disavowal of the Brezhnev Doctrine, prompted an unforeseen and uncontrollable pressure for exodus. The first major leak was opened up with the Hungarian decision to ease border restrictions. In this dramatic process, the automatic right to West German passports for all Germans turned out to have a catalytic effect. Mass pressure to open borders transformed a small leak into a flood, leading to the ouster of Honecker, the opening of the Wall on November 9, 1989, and the eventual demise of the GDR.

After unification, intra-German migration became relatively invisible but has continued at a rate of about 20 000 per month over the transition period and into the 1990s. An estimated one million have migrated in the first three years of unity. In addition, at least 30 000 East German commuters work in the West. Certainly, internal population shifts from the ex-GDR westward represent a continuing feature of demographic volatility for German politics.

The influx of ethnic Germans from across Eastern Europe, who are entitled to citizenship under Article 116, also accelerated in the wake of the collapse of communism. Moreover, long term prospects remain for new waves of ethnic Germans, depending on the extent and duration of economic chaos in Russia and other former Soviet-block states. There is a vast reservoir of potential refugees estimated at as many as 15 million, who may place new pressure on Germany's capacity to absorb.[9]

IMMIGRATION AND POLITICAL CONFLICT

As was true in the early phase, demographic volatility has had significant politicising effects. The destabilising shocks of the end of communism have generated insecurities and unexpected negative political reactions. These have combined with social and economic uncertainties to create urgent policy dilemmas.

As the GDR disintegrated, popular demands for rapid unification, voiced most clearly in the March 1990 *Volkskammer* election, determined an inevitable fusion. The West German Basic Law, along with administrative/legal systems, filled a vacuum and assured an immediate institutional stability. Rapid unification also meant the sudden elimination of GDR structures of control and security, which until then had encapsulated eastern society under austere yet predictable conditions. The associated economic collapse led to plant closings and job losses. It also exposed much previously hidden unemployment in an occupational structure bloated by the dogma that unemployment could not exist in a socialist state. Under such circumstances, it is not surprising that unification on the fast track generated stress for East Germans and anxiety for West Germans, conditions which have unavoidably accentuated endogenous social tensions.

Coincidentally, a set of exogenous developments also had direct impacts on German politics and society. Certainly unanticipated was the virtual collapse of East Germany's established markets for its industrial production in the former Soviet Union and other east block states. This undoubtedly intensified the explosion in unemployment in the Eastern *Länder*. Another factor was the mounting influx of immigrants, of two main types – ethnic Germans from Eastern Europe and, increasingly, asylum-seekers. Pressure from demographic instability of this character was intensified by economic and political crises to the south and east, particularly the disintegration of Yugoslavia into civil war.

These shocks have meant that attitudes toward immigration and foreigners in the post-unity era have been characterised by high public sensitivity and have provided fertile terrain for intolerance and extremism.

Popular Opinion

How do Germans perceive issues of immigration? One popular interpretation is that foreigners are tolerated but not accepted. Correspondingly, there is still limited acceptance of a multi-cultural society, both in public opinion and among political elites. The prevailing value system does not yet accept entry of foreigners as full members of society, that is, as citizens.

While there is a kernel of truth to such generalisations, in fact, the situation is rather more complex. Public attitudes towards foreigners have been characterised by contradictions and ambivalence. Recent survey evidence indicates that most respondents regard the presence of large numbers of foreigners as appropriate and normal. Furthermore, with respect to asylum, a stable majority supports in principle this basic right. However, most Germans also believe that the existing laws on asylum have been misused and should be revised. This, of course, helps to explain the pressure on political parties to find some compromise solution to the asylum question (see introductory chapter, and Braunthal, above).

Evaluation of public views on immigration is made difficult by the fact that easterners and westerners differ significantly in their political priorities. In the former West Germany, asylum and foreigner-related issues have consistently ranked as the most important (data for 1992), while residents in the new *Länder* rank unemployment as issue number one. Attitudes on immigration issues remained stable through the first half of 1992 and then experienced a dramatic upsurge in salience response to mounting violence against foreigners between August and November of that year.

Finally, it is worth noting that there exists a high level of scepticism among Germans about the competence of political parties and governing elites to deal effectively with such problems. Dissatisfaction with government performance increased significantly in the second half of 1992.[10]

Violence against Foreigners

Societal crises may stimulate latent xenophobia. Limited outbreaks of intolerance and violence against foreigners occurred with the first postwar recession in 1966–7, a period which also saw the temporary surge of the neo-Nazi NPD in several Landtag elections. Again in the mid–70s sporadic violence, especially directed against Turkish immigrants, developed in the context of economic slowdown and mounting unemployment.[11] In the post-unity period, a new atmosphere of crisis and insecurity has fuelled a new round of intolerance that has gone beyond opinions and spilled over into frequent episodes of xenophobic violence (over 2000 incidents recorded by the end of 1992).

Immigrants, both old and new, have become targets of rising social frustrations. The increasing frequency and intensity of racist violence have became evident across Germany, but disproportionately in the new *Länder*, where economic collapse has produced a crisis based on failed expectations and frustrations. In this atmosphere scapegoating of foreigners has been easy and has led to violent outbreaks, both provoked and spontaneous, involving organised extremists and unemployed, alienated youth (see concluding chapter below).

Although instruments for containing extremism exist in criminal law, the use of police power in the first instance proved ineffective, even half-hearted, as became evident in Rostock in August 1992. The next two months were marked by repeated violent attacks, culminating in the murder of three Turkish women in Mölln in November. This tragedy shocked public opinion and prompted a new government response to mounting xenophobia. As governments have recognised the pattern of concerted attacks by organised extremists, initiatives to outlaw extremist groups and to prosecute violators have increased.

PARTY SYSTEM ADAPTATION

The decline in support for both major parties is a trend evident at least since the 1987 Bundestag elections. Patterns of increasing electoral volatility and decreasing turnout attest to the incapacity of the established parties to mobilise their traditional bases of support. These trends correspond to a diffuse public disillusionment with parties and political elites.

The rise of extremist parties of the right provides an essential test of the extent of erosion within the existing party system. Even before the *Wende* of 1989–90, the far right *Republikaner* had captured a surprisingly strong protest vote in several elections, notably in 1989 in Berlin (7.5 per cent) and in the European Elections (7.1 per cent). The collapse of communism and the euphoria of unification appeared to deflate any significant support for extremist parties. However, within a year, their resurgence was observed in regional elections. In September 1991 in Bremen, the openly xenophobic DVU captured 6.2 per cent of the vote. In April 1992, these gains were repeated in Schleswig–Holstein, while the *Republikaner* shocked the nation with 10.9 per cent in Baden–Württemberg. By the start of 1993, supporters of the far right hovered around the critical five per cent threshold in response to the question of, 'How would you vote if an election were held next Sunday?' By early 1993 indications were that racist violence had, at least temporarily, diminished the acceptability of the far right for many would-be supporters.[12]

POLICY EVOLUTION

Long-standing components of German public policy concerning immigrants have included labour market goals, family reunion and protection of refugees from political persecution through asylum.

Post-war demographic patterns have brought new diversity, but governments in Bonn and the *Länder* are only now starting to realise the urgency of responding to these new circumstances. Immigration issues have become most pressing for Germany just as it has entered a new era dominated by the enormous costs and challenges of unification. Although unemployment in the Western *Länder* has remained moderate, in the new *Länder* it is pervasive, reaching levels of 30 or 40 per cent in some areas, and without job growth, refugees are often misperceived as threats in job competition. Since 1991, asylum-seekers may legally seek employment, but there is no evidence that this has deprived Germans of work. Of the 1.3 million immigrants who have found work since 1989, most are in jobs that Germans do not want. As of 1992 there were still 150 000 skilled trade apprenticeships open.[13]

Given the negative climate, there have been special problems of settling asylum-seekers in the new *Länder*, which were at first expected to provide temporary residence for about one-fifth of all incoming asylum-seekers. However, the lack of infrastructure and administrative capacity, combined with a lack of public understanding, created conditions for explosive animosity against foreigners.

Clearly immigration does not occur in a policy vacuum. The internal challenges of economic reconstruction in the former GDR interact directly with the need for social integration. Internal social welfare needs, housing shortages, and resettlement programmes illustrate the complex network of policy concerns that are inevitable with any significant immigration trend. The questions of asylum and citizenship pinpoint special dilemmas of German immigration politics.

Asylum Policy

As borders opened post–1989, there was a steady increase in asylum-seekers. From about 120 000 in 1989, this figure increased to over 250 000 in 1991, reaching 430 000 by 1992, and threatening to double in 1993. Political tension intensified as the influx increased.

The slow and inadequate administration of asylum applications produced a massive backlog of cases. Efforts to speed up the processing had little or no effect, with some cases taking several years to settle. The low rate of acceptance of asylum-seekers (about 5 per cent) only served to reinforce the popular impression of massive abuse of Article 16 and of the incapacity of politicians to resolve the problem. Meanwhile, increasing violence against foreigners intensified the controversy over asylum and forced political parties to adapt their thinking. Particularly after the gains of the far-right in Baden–Württemberg, a conservative bastion, the Christian Democrats became increasingly concerned about further electoral erosion. The Social Democrats, although originally opposed to restricting the right to asylum, found themselves out of touch with public opinion which supports change in asylum provisions. In internal party discussions, SPD Chairman Engholm warned that failure to address the asylum issue could lead to a right-wing backlash and even more violence.

Both major parties have been in decline in recent elections, a fact which has made inter-party compromise on revision of Article 16 all the more urgent. After months of bargaining the governing coalition and the opposition SPD were able to reach a provisional accord. (See Chapter 11 by Braunthal, above.) Also related to the asylum question were the initiatives seen in bilateral agreements on the return of foreign nationals, for example with Romania and Bulgaria. These agreements are based on return with substantial financial compensation.

Citizenship Policy

Citizenship might be seen as a natural and direct consequence of immigration, yet in Germany immigrants have remained excluded from German society, due in part to citizenship laws. Underlying the restrictive concept of citizenship is a myth of social and cultural homogeneity, which provides a justification for the lack of an integration policy. Much of the terminology commonly used to describe the status of foreigners in Germany (for example, *Ausländer* rather than *Einwanderer*) belies both popular belief and policy practice that newcomers are not perceived as future citizens to be socially integrated.[14] This perspective has the effect of transforming foreign immigrants into permanent outsiders.

At the governmental level, popular ambivalence about foreigners translates into an incomplete policy pattern. Germany has become a multicultural reality with neither a melting pot nor a social mosaic. In this sense Germany, like many of its neighbours, has yet to create a 'full-service' immigration policy. Taken together, these conditions have meant openness without a sense of social or political integration. This gap between formal definition and actuality means that there continues to be a glaring discontinuity between openness and acceptance. The inevitable admission of newcomers must be balanced by a more expansive policy of integration, which will depend, in part, on a relaxation of the conditions for citizenship.

Generally, instead of a comprehensive, adaptable immigration policy, Germany retains an aliens policy with limited goals.[15] The integrationist dimension has been neglected, and there exists no standing policy of social assimilation or multiculturalism. Except for the first (expellee) wave, which was really an internal migration, there has been little sense of permanence. The persisting pattern has been one of demographic transformation without any strategy for social integration or multicultural citizenship.

PROBLEMS AND PROSPECTS

The impact of demographic change on politics is generally assumed but seldom investigated. Post-war German experience provides a dramatic instance in which the necessity for evaluating transformations in population as a base point for political conflict and change appears primordial. Here multiple patterns of extensive, sometimes rapid, mobility, often reflecting unanticipated political and economic crises, have left their distinct imprints on modern German democracy.

Politics may also reshape populations. For example, unification has altered temporarily the demographic profile of Germany – resulting in a decrease in population density, greater regional disparity, a stronger agrarian component, and a younger age structure. However, long-term demographic trends suggest a continuing ageing of Germany. Prognoses indicate that the economically active 20 to 60 age group, which in 1990 equalled 58 per cent of the population, will by the year 2030 correspond to only 48 per cent of the total. Over the same time span, youth (20 years and under) will drop from 22 to 17 per cent, while the retirement age group (60 and over) will expand from 20 to 35 per cent of the German population.[16]

Two other overarching demographic realities will impinge on German politics for the future. One is a projected population decline for Germany, which will shrink the active population and create a long term need for new immigration. The second is a vast pool of potential refugees, dependent on external conditions in Russia and other eastern areas. The mass and timing of such future migrations remain great unknowns. Also uncertain are eventual forms of Euro-migration. Moreover, internal economic migration will also persist as long as income and employment disparities do.

German governments, from national to local levels, are likely to be confronted with new and recurring policy dilemmas rooted in demographic transformations. These will not be resolvable in the short-run or through band-aid solutions. To the east and south of Germany and its EC neighbours, persisting economic stagnation or decay and occasional political upheavals, like the civil war that has destroyed Yugoslavia, are likely to make immigration a pressing issue well into the next century.

Notes

1. Barbara Marshall, 'German Migration Policies', in Gordon Smith et al., eds., *Developments in German Politics* (London: Macmillan, pp. 247–8.
2. Klaus Grosch, 'Foreigners and Aliens', in Susan Stern, ed., *Meet United Germany* (Frankfurt; Frankfurter Allgemeine Zeitung, 1992), p. 139.
3. Rainer Geissler, *Die Sozialstruktur Deutschlands* (Opladen: Westdeutscher Verlag, 1992) p. 285.
4. Dennis L. Bark and David R. Gress, *From Shadow to Substance 1945–1963* (Oxford: Blackwell, 1989), p. 305. Estimates of the total number of expellees/refugees vary. According to the Statistisches Bundesamt, for example, in 1945 4.5 million Germans lived in Silesia, three in the Sudetenland, 2.4 million each in East Prussia and East Pomerania/Brandenburg, 1.5 in the Soviet Union and 1.3 in Poland beyond the Oder-Neisse line, with another 2.5 million elsewhere in Eastern Europe (P. Merkl).
5. Gordon Smith, *Democracy in Western Germany* (New York: Holmes and Meier, 1986), pp. 111–12; Wolfgang Rudzio, *Das politische System der Bundesrepublik Deutschland*, 2nd ed. (Opladen: Leske, 1987), pp. 114–8.
6. Geissler, pp. 297–8.
7. Dietrich Thränhardt, 'West Germany – an Undeclared Immigration Country', discussion paper, Institut für Politikwissenschaft der Westfälischen Wilhelms-Universität, Münster, 1989. pp. 21–5.
8. Quoted in Grosch, p. 138.
9. Marshall, p. 248.
10. Dieter Roth, 'The Painful Process of Unifying Germany, Political Attitudes and Preferences since the Last Election', Georgetown University, Washington, September 30, 1992; Forschungsgruppe Wahlen, *Politbarometer*, pp. 1–12, 1992.
11. Thränhardt, pp. 21–5.
12. *Politbarometer*, 12/1992.
13. Figures from the Institut der Deutschen Wirtschaft, reported in *German Brief*, June 5, 1992.
14. Thränhardt, p. 12.
15. Grosch, p. 139.
16. *Die Zeit*, June 12, 1992, nr. 24.

Part V

Germany's Role in the World

19 The German Architecture for Europe: Military, Political and Economic Dimensions

James Sperling

The fluidity of the current European state system stands in stark contrast to the constancy and predictability of the postwar order. The absence of order and the nostalgia for the comfort afforded by certainty and calculability have generated many 'architectures' for the post-Yalta European state system. The security architectures range from the Bush administration's ill-defined 'new world order' to the French conception of an independent and confederal Europe freed from the unnatural postwar alliances imposed upon the European states by the United States and Russia. The Germans have also articulated a security architecture for post-Yalta Europe. It emphasises the need for a pan-European collective security arrangement that serves as the foundation of a pan-European economic space. The two dimensions of the German security strategy, the economic and military-political, raise several questions: How do the Germans define their security interests in post-Yalta Europe? What is the institutional configuration of the German architecture in the military and economic spheres? What is the interrelationship between the economic and military-political dimensions of the German security strategy? What are Germany's strategic objectives in post-Yalta Europe? Is the German architecture likely to define or simply help shape the contours of the post-Yalta security order?

THE REDEFINITION OF GERMAN SECURITY INTERESTS

The turbulence of alliance relations and the uncertainties of the East–West conflict between 1949 and 1989 now appear, in retrospect, to have been a long period of continuity, certainty, and stability. The

content and direction of German security policy was narrowly circumscribed by the Federal Republic's membership in NATO and dependence upon the United States, and defined by the need to contain
Soviet power in Europe. The traditional preoccupation with guaranteeing Germany's territorial integrity has been pushed into the background by the changes that have taken place in the European state
system, particularly the unseemly and hasty Soviet retreat from empire and consequent internal disintegration, the process of western European political and economic integration, and the prospect of a
premature (and hence unwelcomed) American retreat from *its* empire.
The question has arisen, from whom and for what reason should the
Germans prepare to defend themselves militarily?

At the same time, the Germans have refined and broadened their
concept of security to conform with the pressures generated by, and
to exploit the opportunities offered by, the evolution of the European state system. Today, German security is threatened not by an
invasion of the Soviet army, but by the inability of Germany to control its borders in the event of mass migrations from eastern and
southern Europe driven by political chaos or economic deprivation;
and by threats to German economic security, broadly defined and encompassing issues ranging from environmental degradation to price
stability.

This broadened and evolving redefinition of German security interests also reflects a redefinition of the German state;[1] Germans have
welcomed and embraced the notion that Germany must play the role
of a 'civilian power' in Europe, since the role of a great or middle
power, defined militarily, has been proscribed by history, conscience,
treaty, and self-interest.[2] The Germans remain unwilling to contribute
to the military requirements of global stability; it is acceded that these
tasks are best left to the United States, France, and the United Kingdom.[3] Nonetheless, the German role in the future European order is
expansively defined economically, technologically, environmentally,
and politically. Germany desires full participation in the political and
economic reconstruction of Eastern Europe, in the creation of European political and economic union, in the restoration of the European
environment, and in the construction of a functioning pan-European
security structure resting upon the twin pillars of democracy and the
market economy. Germany remains satisfied to contribute to the economic requirements of security and to accelerate the demilitarisation
of interstate relations, particularly in Europe – a development that
plays to Germany's economic capacity and not coincidentally enhances

German influence in the reconstruction and recasting of the European order.

THE ECONOMIC STRATEGY

The political unification of Europe was intended initially as a method of burying European animosities built up after seven decades of intermittent war; and as a method of eradicating its source, Franco–German competition for European hegemony. For the Germans it also served the larger political purpose of reintegrating Germany into the society of western states after the second world war; and it eventually became the idiom in which German economic interests were expressed and identified. A combination of historical escape, tactical necessity, and strategic realism has left a legacy of a genuine German dedication to European political and economic integration, albeit increasingly on German terms.

Today leading German politicians describe the European Community as the 'sheet anchor' of Europe. The Germans argue that since the EC is the only 'area of stability' (*Stabilitätsraum*) in Europe, it demonstrates that stability on the European continent need not reflect or depend upon military power. The EC plays a quadruple role in the German strategy for Europe: first, it provides a mechanism for ensuring German predominance in Europe on economic affairs; second, the progress towards political union and economic and monetary union provides a magnet for the reforming states of central and eastern Europe that will contribute to the erasure of the '*Wohlstandsgrenze*' (prosperity border) between capitalist and protocapitalist Europe; third, the inevitable trend towards the creation of a common security and foreign policy will enable 'Europe' to function as a second pillar within NATO and assume responsibilities commensurate with Europe's economic and military power; and fourth, the political unification of Europe will create the framework for common immigration, asylum, and terrorism laws that will protect the German domestic order.[4] Moreover, the European Community (along with NATO and the CSCE) assures Germany's neighbours and partners that Germany is cognisant of and will respect the 'security needs and the feelings of all Europeans, understandably and above all our neighbours'; and German enthusiasm for the EC demonstrates, at least from the German perspective, that Germany has renounced, once and for all, the 'national unilateralism and the *Sonderweg*' that have shaped modern European history.[5]

The most important element of Germany's postwar foreign economic policy agenda in Europe – the economic and political integration of the member states of the EC – is nearing completion: the Single European Act (SEA) created a single internal market in the European Community and accelerated the institutionalisation of policy coordination in areas ranging from the environment to foreign policy; the treaty on economic and monetary union (EMU) targeted 1999 as the deadline for the creation of a European central bank and common currency; and the treaty on political union has established the rules for achieving 'an ever closer union among the peoples of Europe'[6] (see also Emil Kirchner, Chapter 21). But it is the transformed political map of Europe, particularly the unification of Germany, the disintegration of the former Soviet Union, and the trend towards democratisation and market liberalisation in north central Europe, that has redefined and reinvigorated Europe.

The Germans desire the integration of the north central European nations into a pan-European framework. Chancellor Helmut Kohl, following the French lead, suggested in mid-1990 that the preferred framework would be a European confederation anchored by a federal European Community. But in the German version, a federal European Community could not exclude Austria, Sweden, Norway or Finland; and the Visegrad nations – Poland, the Czech Republic, Slovakia, Hungary – should not necessarily be precluded from future membership. Thus the EC could envelop the majority of the EFTA states as well as select members of the former CMEA. The Germans, uneasy with a strategy precluding the European republics of the former Soviet Union or the states of southern Europe, have also looked to the CSCE as the framework for a single European economic space beyond that created by the EC–EFTA treaty. The German preference for a single European economic space, complemented by federal and confederal political and economic institutions, is located in Germany's commercial self-interest and in Germany's desire to allay the unspoken suspicions and fears of a united and untethered Germany.

The anticipated integration of the north central European nations – Poland, Hungary, the Czech Republic, and Slovakia – into a pan-European economic, monetary, and trade order reflects the economic calculation that cooperation is an important pillar of the pan-European security architecture. By the time of the Bonn CSCE economic conference in March 1990, the Germans made an automatic connection between the collapse of the communist regimes in Eastern Europe and the future integration of the (broadly defined) European economy. The Germans envisioned the EC as the 'motor of western support for the reform of the nations of central and eastern Europe'; as the core of a confederate Europe within the broader security and economic architecture of the CSCE.[7] Accordingly, the German government embraced that proposal of Jacques Delors, EC Commission President, to forge special association agreements between the EC and the nations of north central Europe as well as Poland's near-term association with and future membership in the EC; and in early 1991, then Bundesbank President Pöhl indicated the need to keep open the door for the future participation of the Visegrad nations (in addition to Austria, Sweden, and Norway) in the exchange rate mechanism of the EMS.

The tentative and differentiated role assigned the CMEA nations in German economic calculations differs significantly from the role assigned the EFTA nations. From the German perspective, the common denominators of the EC and EFTA nations – democracy and free market economies – initially made those nations natural partners in creating a single European economic area. The German desire for a tighter relationship between the nations of EFTA and the EC is in part a calculation of commercial interest: it forms the second largest trading partner of Germany after the EC. Closer commercial relations between the EC and EFTA would lead, inexorably, to pressures for stable exchange rates and consequently to EFTA participation in the exchange rate mechanism of the EMS, if not monetary union by the end of the decade. In either case, EFTA nations will be compelled to adopt economic policies conforming to German economic preferences and indirectly give the Germans leverage over those nations' macroeconomic policies. Moreover, it broadens the economic base of a single European currency and consequently enhances European (and German) leverage with the United States and Japan on related political and economic issues.

The move towards a single internal market is nearly complete. At the December 1991 Maastricht Summit the EC representatives agreed to establish EMU no later than 1999. The agreement to abandon national control of currencies is located in the need to complement the integration taking place in the real sector of the economy, in the need to provide a mechanism for counterbalancing the economic policies of the United States, and in the need to reinforce the progress towards political union. The German Chancellor and the Bundesbank have assured the German public that during the transition to full monetary union neither the statutory obligation of the Bundesbank to tar-

get price stability nor its political independence would be jeopardised. Both the German government and the Bundesbank jealously guard
the Bundesbank's domestic monetary autonomy and its informal role
as the manager of Europe's money. The German government and
Bundesbank established six general conditions for German participation in European monetary union: the completion of the internal market; price stability as the sole objective of any European central bank;
a federal structure for the European central bank; the political independence of that institution from national and Community institutions;
binding restrictions on the monetary financing of national or community budgets; and parallel progress in the convergence of economic
policies and performance. The treaty on EMU conformed to German
preferences, although the Bundesbank remains reluctant to commit itself to a 1999 deadline and has emphasised the necessity of parallel
progress on political union and EMU. The Bundesbank appears unwilling to forego its independence and ability to informally manage
Europe's money in the present arrangement in exchange for written
assurance that inflation will be the key target of a central European
bank that it will not necessarily dominate or control.

The Germans have insisted and gained agreement at Maastricht that
economic convergence among the member states of the EC – measured
by price stability, interest rates, gross indebtedness of the public sector as a percentage of GDP, financial balance of the public sector as
a percentage of GDP, and exchange rate stability – should precede
monetary union. Although the exchange rate mechanism of the EMS
established a framework for economic convergence and the convergence of national economic policies, the final stage of monetary union
– the incontrovertible fixing of national currencies and the introduction of a European currency – depends upon the actual convergence
of national economic performances and policies; and convergence has
come to mean conformity to the German preference for fiscal rectitude and price stability.

Despite EC efforts to accommodate the Germans on the principles
of monetary union, the definition of economic convergence, and the
institutional characteristics of the European System Central Banks
(ESCB),[8] the Germans remain fearful that their stable DM may be
sacrificed on the altar of European monetary union. This fear is reflected
in the Finance Minister Theo Waigel's suggestion that the Ecu be
rechristened the 'Europa-Mark' or 'Frank'; and the German demand
(subsequently met in 1993) that as a condition of participation in EMU,
the European Monetary Institute, the precursor of the European Cen-

tral Bank (ECB), and the ECB itself be located in Frankfurt. The Germans are aware that once the ESCB is established and the final stage of monetary union is completed, they will have to share the management of Europe's money with the Community's other (and less inflation averse) central bankers.

The German conception of European political union is both federal and confederal: the nations of the EC, EFTA, and north central Europe will form a United States of Europe that is confederated with the remainder of Europe, including the European republics of the former Soviet Union. The German conception of economic and monetary union is simply a single European economic space governed by German economic precepts; and secondarily, the aggregation of European economic power to create a pole of global economic power capable of competing successfully with the United States and Japan. The development of Europe politically and economically is contingent upon a number of variables, ranging from the German willingness (along with that of the French and the British in particular) to relinquish economic and monetary sovereignty to Community institutions to the continued demilitarisation of interstate relations in Europe.

The CSCE offers an additional mechanism for continuing Germany's economic agenda in Europe and more specifically for overcoming the 'prosperity barrier' (*Wohlstandsgrenze*) between the nations of Western and Eastern Europe with the establishment of a free market regime throughout Europe. The Germans argue that economic envy (*Wirtschaftsneid*) on the part of the immiserated nations of Europe, rather than the exercise or exploitation of Germany's economic power (*Wirtschaftsmacht*), is the important and very real threat to the stability of Europe, and consequently to the German polity and economy. Although the EC plays the dominant role in securing the economic dimension of German security, the CSCE provides an important mechanism for constructing a stable and prosperous European economic space.

The Germans proposed and hosted the 1990 CSCE Bonn conference on economic cooperation in Europe.[9] The Bonn CSCE document obligated the non-market economies of Europe to institute price reform, to implement policies that would lead to currency convertibility, and to adopt the principles of the market economy. The Germans believed that the Bonn document provides a stable framework for the creation of a single, integrated European economic space spanning the Atlantic to the Urals; that in effect it establishes a European economic regime favouring the principles of the social market economy. The emphasis on the economic aspect of the relations amongst the nations of Europe reflects the German redefinition of security. It also has had the practical consequence of altering the calculus of power in the European area: it shifts attention away from the military potential of a state to its productive capability and rate of technological innovation, a development that would further strengthen German diplomacy at the expense of France and Britain. Moreover, the German government assumes that security cooperation is contingent upon economic cooperation, an assumption that goes a long way to explain German enthusiasm for European economic and monetary union, the fourth enlargement of the European Community, and the Bonn CSCE document.

THE MILITARY POLITICAL STRATEGY

The redefinition of German security and the changed European state system have reshaped the role and promise of the existing institutions of European security. Germany, the key continental European partner of the United States in NATO, now faces a choice in the procurement of its security: whereas NATO had the character of an automatic alliance over the course of the postwar period, the collapse of the Warsaw Pact and the absence of a countervailing order in the eastern portion of the European continent has had the unsettling effect of providing Germany with choice.[10] While it remains true that NATO remains the essential institutional guarantor of security and stability in Europe and for Germany, it faces a longer term challenge from the Conference on Security and Cooperation in Europe (CSCE), the European Community (EC), and the Western European Union (WEU).

NATO

NATO, and the extended American nuclear deterrent, guaranteed German security in the postwar period, supported the German effort to achieve western European political and economic integration, and was considered essential to the eventual unification of the two Germanys. Prior to unification, the German adherence to NATO derived from the structure of power in the international system and the geostrategic position of Germany in Europe. The German–American security tie within NATO has been and remains essential for German security and

European stability.[11] But the sources of cohesion in the alliance have undergone a subtle, but significant change: NATO member-states, to be sure, share common security interests, but the Germans argue that the glue that holds the alliance together are the values common to them.[12] For the Germans, the American role in Europe has evolved into the explicit role of nightwatchman.

NATO has changed in three important respects since 1989. First, NATO membership has been effectively expanded to include the former member-states of the Warsaw Pact with the creation of the North Atlantic Cooperation Council (NACC) and the 'Partnership for Peace' programme.[13] Second, NATO has acknowledged that political, economic, and even environmental concerns are displacing the military mission of the alliance. And third, NATO has redefined its military mission and has jettisoned 'flexible response' as alliance military doctrine. The military purpose of the alliance has been irrevocably altered by the changed context of the European state system. In response to those changes, the alliance enumerated four principles of security policy: to provide the 'indispensable' foundation for a stable European security order and for the prevention of hegemony by any single nation; to serve as the primary forum for resolving disputes between alliance members on any issue of vital national interest; to deter and defend any possible threat of aggression against a member-state of NATO; and to preserve the Euro-strategic balance.[14] These so-called Copenhagen principles now define the 'fundamental tasks of the alliance'.[15] These military principles are reinforced by an updated and reformulated Harmel Doctrine, the prior touchstone of alliance policy. The dyad of détente and defence has been replaced with the triad of dialogue, cooperation, and collective defence capability within the alliance;[16] and the triad of dialogue, partnership, and cooperation between the member-states of the NACC.[17]

NATO remains attractive to the Germans because it provides them with a number of positive externalities: first, the stability afforded by the alliance contributes to the stability of the reforming nations of eastern and central Europe;[18] second, NATO, the NACC and the 'Partnership for Peace' programme provide institutional mechanisms that integrate all the nations of Europe into a pan-European security system, reinforcing (and possibly usurping) the role of the CSCE; third, the changes in NATO strategy promise a more secure Germany with a greatly diminished exposure to nuclear war; fourth, NATO serves as a hedge against neoisolationism in the United States; and finally, as former Defence Minister Stoltenberg noted, NATO is 'the single functioning security structure in Europe' and serves as a yardstick against 'fair-weather security structures' that are pretenders to NATO's role.[19] Within the German government there is general agreement that NATO, as the sole functioning security structure in Europe, is necessary for the foreseeable future. It is also clear that the Germans believe that without NATO, the CSCE and probably European political union would be nonstarters.

CSCE

The CSCE promises the institutionalisation of a pan-European peace order based upon the principle of collective security. The Germans argue that the security concerns of Germany's neighbours can only be resolved in a 'common European house'. Despite the German government's ambivalent attitude towards the CSCE, it frames Germany's security (and economic) aspirations in eastern and central Europe. At this stage of the evolution of the European state system, the Kohl–Kinkel government views the CSCE process as supplementary to NATO in the following sense: NATO provides insurance against any military threat to German territorial integrity, while the CSCE makes a positive contribution to European security by integrating the former Warsaw Pact member-states, including the former Soviet Union, into the western economic and political orbit. Yet, the Germans remain dependent upon the United States: the success of the CSCE requires a continuing American imprimatur to lend it legitimacy and effectiveness.

The CSCE plays an important function for the Germans that NATO cannot play and the EC is unlikely to play, now or in the future: CSCE provides an institutional mechanism for integrating the former republics of the Soviet Union into a pan-European security and economic space without necessarily compromising or threatening the geopolitical and military logic of NATO or undermining the progress towards European political union within the framework of the EC. The meaning and importance of the CSCE for the Germans may be located as well in former Foreign Minister Genscher's assertion in early 1991 that 'the German–Soviet relationship possesses a central importance for the stability of Europe'.[20] The fragmentation of the former Soviet Union and the uncertain future of the Commonwealth of Independent States makes it uncertain whether Germany will have a lone partner or a number of partners in the place of the Soviet Union. But if the Commonwealth of Independent States revives (or is replaced by a looser confederation of states conducting a common foreign policy) then only the CSCE provides a ready-made mechanism for ordering that relationship within a multilateral framework. The CSCE also unburdens Russo–German cooperation by diminishing the spectre of a second Rapallo, because the relationship between a Russian-dominated Commonwealth of Independent States and Germany will be conducted within and sanctioned by an established multilateral framework.[21]

The European Community and Western European Union

The benefits of a European security identity flow from the economic, social, and environmental problems facing Europe that NATO is ill-equipped to resolve. Thus, the Germans are dependent upon NATO – as reinsurance against the unravelling of the reform process in Eastern Europe and the former Soviet Union and as the nexus for the coordination of policy on a broad array of issues ranging from security to the environment to debt relief. But this has not precluded a European option for Germany, an option seen as complementary to rather than competitive with continued German membership in NATO or partnership with the United States.

The Germans view the process of European political union and the absorption of the WEU by the EC as a major contribution to the stabilisation of Europe and the creation of an effective second pillar in the Atlantic Alliance. The relationship between the European Community and WEU did not gain momentum until 1990, but a convenient starting point is the publication of the WEU 'Platform on European Security Interests' in October 1987. This platform drew in varying degrees on the Atlanticist, Gaullist, and Europeanist catechisms. American and European security was indivisible and the Alliance required a credible European pillar. But at the same time, the protection of European interests in the Atlantic area required the creation of a European security identity independent of the United States (see Werner Feld, Chapter 20 below). Moreover, the Europeans agreed that 'the construction of an integrated Europe will remain incomplete as long as it does not include security and defence;'[22] and the revitalisation of the WEU was linked to the process of European political union.

Two ambiguities arose from the envisaged role of the WEU. First, would it become the second pillar of the Atlantic Alliance or the security and defence policy arm of the European Community? And second, would it promise intensified security cooperation or conflict between the United States and Europe not only on security issues that were 'out of area', but on security issues within the purview of NATO as well? In 1990, French President Mitterrand and Chancellor Kohl agreed that both NATO *and* the WEU were essential to continued stability and cooperation in Europe; and that both institutions occupied the same 'security area' and needed to intensify their cooperation. President Mitterrand and Chancellor Kohl later proposed that the EC intergovernmental conference on political union consider how the WEU could be strengthened and how it could become merged with the European Community.[23] Their purpose was two-fold: the WEU could serve as a transitional institution prior to the creation of a federal Europe and would thus enable the Europeans to jump-start their security cooperation by grafting an existing institution on to the EC; and it would enable France and Germany to cooperate on security policy without forcing France to choose between security cooperation and an ever ephemeral (and pointless) security independence and without forcing the Germans to make an (increasingly irrelevant) choice between the United States and France, between NATO and Europe. The importance vested in the WEU reflects the German calculation that European political union has made the concept (and practice) of national military autonomy outmoded.

The institutional relationship between the WEU, NATO, and the EC became a highly charged affair in October 1991 when the Anglo–Italian declaration on the WEU, which outlined the future goals and institutional relationships of the WEU to NATO and the EC, produced a counterproposal by France and Germany. The Anglo–Italian and Franco–German declarations exhibited a fundamental schism: whereas the British and Italians preferred a WEU that continued to operate within an intergovernmental framework, protected the privileged position of the United States within the Alliance, preserved the intergovernmental character of defence cooperation, and facilitated cooperation 'out of area', the French and Germans clearly preferred a WEU that cooperated with NATO within Europe and 'out of area', but sought closer institutional ties between the EC and the WEU, viewing the latter as the core of the future defence identity of a European Union. The Franco–German proposal, if realised, could limit American influence in Europe on security matters by providing a politically coherent European pillar for the alliance; while the Anglo–Italian proposals, by retaining American dominance and an intergovernmental framework, provide the Americans with a ready mechanism for pressing the Europeans into 'out of area' duties.

At the December 1991 Maastricht summit, the Europeans largely agreed to the Franco–German position in substance, but employed language allowing the British to claim that the WEU will remain subordinated to NATO. The EC draft treaty on political union commits the member states to 'the eventual framing of a common defence policy, which might in time lead to a common defence . . .' and identified the WEU as an 'integral part of the development of the European Union'.[24] Although language in the treaty provided that the evolution of the relationship between the WEU and the EC be compatible with NATO, it is arguable that the Franco–German design for a separate security identity won the day.[25]

The exact institutional relationship between the WEU and the EC to NATO remains uncertain at this time; but that relationship will be determined as much by the foreign policy calculations of France and Germany as by the internal dynamics of European union.

THE GERMAN SECURITY ARCHITECTURE

The German architecture for Europe has three primary elements: the self-containment of German military power in order that Germany may use its economic power to influence its European neighbours to effect German policy objectives; the creation of an independent Europe capable of negotiating on an equal basis with the United States on economic issues; and the continued demilitarisation of Europe that depends upon the sustained growth of democracy and the free market in the former member-states of the Warsaw Pact.

The economic dimension of German security depends first and foremost upon the consolidation of the EC's role as the economic and political magnet for north central and nordic Europe, as the 'sheet anchor' for all of Europe, as the core of a future European (con)federation, and as the vehicle for ensuring the adoption and codification of German economic mores, particularly the triple imperative of monetary independence from political interference, price stability, and fiscal rectitude. The CSCE provides the framework laws lending legitimacy to the market economy in the reforming nations of central and eastern Europe. The military-political dimension of German security is supplied, in the short- to medium-term, by NATO. NATO is the premier vehicle for addressing the symptoms of the security dilemma facing the Europeans and Germans and for reinsuring Germany against a failure of the CSCE, the institution viewed as best suited to the task of resolving the conflicting demands of Germany's security interests. The

Germans consider the WEU the most promising European security institution, because it will allow a uniting Europe to forge a single foreign and defence policy without requiring the Europeans to jettison NATO prematurely.[26] The fortunes of the WEU, however, are dependent upon the process of European political unification.

The institutional solution to Germany's security dilemma – retaining the American extended deterrent, building a prosperous, politically stable and independent Europe, and creating an inclusive pan-European security system – can not be found in a simple choice between NATO, CSCE, the EC, or WEU. The Germans in fact reject the notion that a choice must be made. The Germans argue against the proposition that NATO, the EC-WEU, and the CSCE have conflicting purposes or conflicting logics; hence the slogan '*Sowohl-als auch*' (this as well as that) and the emphatic rejection of '*Entweder-Oder*' (either this or that).[27] For the Germans all four security institutions are compatible and mutually reinforcing. Each serves specific and interrelated tasks for the Germans. NATO reinsures against the unravelling of the post-Yalta order as the Germans (and other Europeans) construct a (con)federal Europe and a European security identity. The CSCE is inclusive (both the United States and the republics of the former Soviet Union are members), provides a framework for the continued demilitarisation of European foreign affairs with accelerated arms control and disarmament, and furnishes Europe with embryonic regimes that lend support to the embrace of the market economy and democracy in Eastern Europe and the republics of the former Soviet Union. And the EC and the WEU provide the Germans with a mechanism for ensuring a German voice in the evolution of the European order; for providing the Germans with the consummation of the constitutionally dictated objective of European unification; for engendering a European economic space that conforms to German economic imperatives; for creating a European security identity capable of contesting American pretensions in Europe; and for constructing a political entity capable of withstanding pressures from a renascent Russia. Despite the seeming compatibility of these institutions, the logic of the German security strategy leads inexorably to the conclusion that the CSCE and the EC will inevitably become the preferred institutions of European security. Thus, the Germans desire to have it three ways – NATO and the American security guarantee, the European Community and a single European security identity, and the CSCE and a pan-European security order. The Germans refuse to make an unambiguous choice between these institutions, partly because there is no compelling reason to make such a choice at this juncture and partly because these institutions are in fact complementary rather than competitive, at least for now (see Werner Feld, below).

CONCLUSION

The German security strategy for Europe has two dimensions, the economic and the military-political. The economic strategy has four objectives: to shape the direction, content, and objectives of the emerging and evolving institutions of European economic security; to impose German economic preferences upon its neighbours; to protect Germany's comparative advantage with its western European neighbours in the commercial sector of the economy via economic and monetary union; and to exploit the complementarity of the German and central and eastern European economies via preferential trade agreements. The military-political strategy has five objectives: to create a pan-European security structure that integrates Germany into Europe as an equal if not a leading state; to accelerate the demilitarisation of the European area in order to create an environment favouring German economic interests, a development that would increase German leverage with the other European states and minimise Germany's historically dictated disadvantage in the military realm; to retain the American presence in Europe as reinsurance against the failure of a demilitarised pan-European security structure; to ensure the integration of the republics of the former Soviet Union, especially Russia, Ukraine, and Belarus in that pan-European order; and to convince Germany's neighbours that it has renounced the objectives and instruments of *Realpolitik*.

The German security strategy offers Europe a bargain that Europe can hardly refuse: the most influential state in Europe, by virtue of geography, demography, economic capacity, and potential military power, has offered to entrap itself in integrative and constraining political and military structures in exchange for the right to lead Europe on economic affairs and more critically to set the framework conditions of the post-Yalta European economy. Thus, this bargain yields tangible economic returns to the Germans, while the Europeans are left with the intangible military-political gain of resolving the German Problem – the full and irreversible integration of Germany into a pan-European security structure that banishes once and for all the prospect of a German diplomacy conducted in the prewar idioms of war and territorial annexation.

The Germans seek the creation of a European order congenial to the instruments, concerns, and calculations of power and interest of a 'civilian power'. It remains questionable whether the final contours of the post-Yalta European order will conform to the cooperative security system and German-dominated pan-European economy anticipated by the Germans. A German-inspired Europe would require, at a minimum, the continued and permanent demilitarisation of European affairs, an economic, social, and environmental definition of security by the major players of the European system, and the acknowledgment and internalisation by national élites of the linkage between economic stability and political security. Put simply, the contours of the European state system will depend upon the stability of the Germans, Americans, and other Europeans to overcome the ingrained habits of the postwar order; and upon the acceptance of the German definition of security and economic probity as well as the success of the German strategy for demilitarising the political space occupied by Europe. These conditions require the transformation of the European state system from a system driven by the competitive logic of power and *Staatsraison* to a system ordered by the cooperative logic of economics and transnationality. It remains an open question whether the future development of the European state system will accommodate the Germans.

Notes

1. For a discussion of the redefinition of state and nation in Germany, see Ole Waever, 'Three Competing Europes: German, French, and Russian', *International Affairs*, vol. 66, (July 1990) no. 3, pp. 477–94.
2. See Theo Sommer, 'Die Deutschen an die Front?', *Die Zeit*, no. 13, March 29, 1991, p. 3; Hanns W. Maull, 'Germany and Japan: The New Civilian Powers', *Foreign Affairs*, vol. 65, (Winter 1990/91) no. 9, pp. 92–3; and Stephen Szabo, *The Changing Politics of German Security* (New York: St. Martin's Press, 1990).
3. On the potential role of the Bundeswehr in UN peacekeeping missions, see Peter Bardehle, '"Blue Helmets' from Germany? Opportunities and Limits of UN Peacekeeping', *Aussenpolitik*, vol. 4, (1989) no. 1, p. 381ff; Christoph Bertram, 'Wo nicht hin mit der Bundeswehr?', *Die Zeit*, June 7, 1991, no. 23, p. 1; and Foreign Minister Klaus Kinkel, 'Speech at the forty-seventh session of the General Assembly of the United Nations', *Statements and Speeches*, vol. XV, (September 23, 1992), no. 13.
4. For an overview of the problem of migration, see François Heisbourg, 'Population Movements in post-Cold War Europe', *Survival*, vol. XXXIII,

(January/February 1991), no. 1, pp. 31–44.

5. Defence Minister Gerhard Stoltenberg and Foreign Minister Hans-Dietrich Genscher, 'Sicherheitspolitische Fragen eines künftigen geeinten Deutschland', February 19, 1990, *Bulletin*, Nr. 28 (February 21, 1990), p. 218.

6. *The Economist*, December 14th–20th 1991.

7. Foreign Minister Genscher, 'Verantwortung des geeinten Deutschland für ein einiges Europa', October 14, 1990, *Bulletin*, Nr. 122 (October 16, 1990), pp. 1273–4.

8. For a summary of the ESCB, see Bank of England, 'The Maastricht agreement on economic and monetary union', *Quarterly Bulletin*, vol. 32, (February 1992) no. 1; Commission of the European Communities, *The Maastricht Conclusions on EMU: Six Points*, Brussels, February 1992.

9. For an analysis of the Bonn conference, see Hans-Christian Reichel, 'Die Bonner Wirtschaftskonferenz und die Zukunft der KSZE', *Europa Archiv*, vol. 45, no. 15 (August 10, 1990), pp. 461–70.

10. For an extended discussion of NATO as a 'fated community' (*Schicksalsgemeinschaft*), see Emil J. Kirchner and James Sperling, 'The Future Germany and the Future of NATO', *German Politics*, vol. 1, (April 1992), no. 1, pp. 50–77.

11. On this issue there is little disagreement. See Michael Broer and Ole Diehl, 'Die Sicherheit der neuen Demokratien in Europa und die NATO', *Europa Archiv*, vol. 46, (June 15, 1991) no. 12, pp. 372–6; Joseph Joffe, 'The Security Implications of a United Germany: Paper I', *America's Role in a Changing World, Part II*. Adelphi Paper no. 257 (Winter 1990/91), pp. 84–91; Robert D. Blackwill, 'The Security Implications of a United Germany: Paper II', *America's Role in a Changing World, Part II*, Adelphi Paper no. 257 (Winter 1990/91), pp. 92–5; Gerhard Wettig, 'German Unification and European Security,' *Aussenpolitik*, vol. 42, (1991), no. 1, pp. 13–19; Rupert Scholz, 'Deutsche Frage und europäische Sicherheit. Sicherheitspolitik in einem sich einigenden Deutschland und Europa', *Europa Archiv*, vol. 45 (April 10, 1990) no. 7, pp. 239–46; Michael Howard, 'The Remaking of Europe', *Survival*, vol. XXII (March/April 1990) no. 2, pp. 99–106; and Stanley Hoffmann, 'The Case for Leadership', *Foreign Policy*, no. 81 (Winter 1990/91), pp. 20–38. Contrary views are found in Earl C. Ravenal, 'The Case for Adjustment', *Foreign Policy* (Winter 1990–1) no. 81, pp. 3–19; and Christopher Layne, 'Superpower Disengagement', *Foreign Policy* (Winter 1989/90) no. 77, pp. 17–40. A sceptical view of NATO's future, relevant although written before the collapse of the postwar order, is found in David P. Calleo, 'NATO's Middle Course', *Foreign Policy* (Winter 1987–8) no. 69, pp. 135–47.

12. See Emil J. Kirchner and James Sperling, 'From Success to Uncertainty', in Emil J. Kirchner and James Sperling, *The Federal Republic of Germany and NATO. 40 Years After* (London: Macmillan, 1992), pp. 252–66.

13. The NACC is envisioned to perform specific and unique functions: it will serve as a forum for consultation with the 'liaison states' on issues such as civilian control of the military and the conversion of defence industries to civilian purposes; it may serve as a forum for negotiating further conventional arms control and confidence and security building

measures; and it has been suggested that the NACC play a peace-keeping role in Nagorno-Karabakh and other contested areas in the former Soviet Union and eastern Europe.

14. These principles have been complemented by a new force structure and strategy that emphasises smaller forces, enhanced flexibility and mobility, and a substantially reduced reliance upon nuclear weapons; and is accompanied by an abandonment of the linear defence posture in central Europe and a major reduction of the NATO stockpile of substrategic weapons in Europe. North Atlantic Council, 'Rome Declaration on Peace and Cooperation', November 7–8, 1991, *NATO Review*, vol. 39, no. 6 (December 1991), pp. 27, 29–32; Marc Rogers, 'NATO shapes up for new role', *Jane's Defence Weekly*, vol. 16, no. 20 (November 1991), p. 926.

15. See North Atlantic Council, 'The Alliance's New Strategic Concept', November 7–8, 1991, *NATO Review*, vol. 39, (December 1991) no. 6, p. 25–7.

16. 'Rome Declaration . . .', p. 19.

17. North Atlantic Cooperation Council, 'Statement on Dialogue, Partnership and Cooperation', December 20, 1991, *NATO Review*, vol. 40, (February 1992) no. 1, pp. 29–30.

18. Chancellor Kohl, 'Erstes Treffen des Rates der Aussenminister der Teilnehmerstaaten der KSZE', June 19, 1991, *Bulletin*, Nr. 72 (June 22, 1991), p. 579. This position reflected the outcome of the Copenhagen NATO Summit on June 6, 1991 where the allies made an effort to reassure the nations of the former Warsaw Pact with language that stopped short of offering a unilateral security guarantee. *New York Times*, June 7, 1991, A1.

19. Defence Minister Stoltenberg, 'Zukunftsaufgaben der Bundeswehr im vereinten Deutschland', March 13, 1991, *Bulletin*, Nr. 29 (March 15, 1991), p. 215; 'Das Selbstverständnis des Soldaten in der Bundeswehr von morgen', June 17, 1991, *Bulletin*, Nr. 70 (June 19, 1991), p. 566.

20. Foreign Minister Genscher, 'Eine Vision für das ganze Europa', February 3, 1991, *Bulletin*, Nr. 14 (February 6, 1991), p. 93.

21. Less relaxed appraisals of the new German–Russian relationship can be found in W. R. Smyser, 'USSR–Germany: A Link Restored', *Foreign Policy*, no. 84 (Fall 1991), pp. 125–41; and Marian Leighton and Robert Rudney, 'Non-Offensive Defense: Toward a Soviet–German Security Partnership?', *Orbis*, vol. 35, (Summer 1991), no. 3, pp. 337–94.

22. Western European Union, *Platform on European Security Interests*, The Hague, October 27, 1987, photocopy.

23. The logic of the Franco–German position is presented in Jacques Delors, 'European Integration and Security', *Survival*, vol. XXXIII, (March/April 1991), no. 2, pp. 99–110.

24. *The Economist*, December 14th 1991, No. 7737, p. 52. For post-Maastricht statement on the WEU and the EC, see Chancellor Kohl, 'Erklärung der Bundesregierung', December 13, 1991, *Bulletin*, Nr. 142 (December 17, 1991), p. 1156.

25. Nonetheless, German public support for an independent European army remains lukewarm at best. A public opinion survey conducted by the Sozialwissenschaftliches Institut der Bundeswehr found that 66 per cent of

the respondents believed that any European army should remain within the NATO framework and only 22 per cent believed that it should operate outside it. Poll cited in Hans-Joachim Veen, 'Die Westbindung der Deutschen in einer Phase der Neuorientierung', *Europa Archiv*, vol. 46, (January 25, 1991) no. 2, p. 35.

26. It is also the case, that the WEU allows the Europeans to side-step the immediate problems associated with Irish (and Austrian and Swedish) neutrality and the longer-term problems associated with the EC membership of former member-states of the Warsaw Pact, particularly Poland, Hungary, and the Czech and Slovak Republics.

27. See Chancellor Kohl, 'Die Rolle Deutschlands in Europa', March 13, 1991, *Bulletin*, Nr. 33 (March 22, 1991), p. 245; and 'Aufgaben deutscher Politik in den neunziger Jahren', May 20, 1991, *Bulletin*, Nr. 56 (May 22, 1991), p. 441. This formula was endorsed by Jiri Dienstbier, then foreign minister of the Czech and Slovak Federal Republic, in 'Central Europe's Security', *Foreign Policy*, no. 83 (Summer 1991), pp. 125–7.

20 Germany and the European Security Identity

Werner J. Feld

The concept of a European Security Identity has evolved over a number of years and the name has undergone slight changes. It was during a meeting of the Heads of State and Governments of NATO on November 7–8, 1991, that the emergence and development of a 'European security identity and defence role' was acknowledged by the participants. Recognising that it was for the European NATO members to decide what arrangements were needed for the definition of a common European foreign and security policy, the hope was expressed that there would be the necessary transparency and complementarity between the European security and defence identity (ESDI) as it emerged in the European Community and the WEU on the one hand and the NATO Alliance on the other.[1] Europeans living in the Community were anxious to see political union move forward as quickly as possible after the Maastricht agreement and may have looked at the emerging ESDI as an important tool to attain their goal. But the identity potential needs to be analysed carefully as to which existing structures in the EC, WEU, or perhaps CSCE would be useful for this purpose or whether new structures need to be established to make this identity a reality. It is not entirely clear, either, what kind of relationship to NATO may evolve, although the Alliance will remain a forum for consultation within Western and most likely Eastern Europe (the North Atlantic Consultation Council). Moreover, only NATO possesses at present the necessary strategic, tactical, and logistical means to assure the security of Europe as a whole.

The interests of Germany in this situation are not entirely clear. We may gain some insights from the evolution of ESDI over the last decade in which the Federal Republic played various roles. Considering that Germany has a very new foreign minister, Klaus Kinkel, and a relatively new defence minister, Volker Ruhe, Bonn's policies may be far from clear-cut. In any case, we will first explore in this essay the emergence of ESDI, then examine the impact of Franco–German military cooperation on this concept, explore the possible effect of the Maastricht agreement, evaluate the prospects of ESDI, and finally analyse possible German interests and options.

THE EMERGENCE OF ESDI

Concern with the general subject of European security and defence identity can be traced back to former U.S. Secretary of State Henry Kissinger's ill-fated initiative for the 'year of Europe' in 1973. In this initiative Kissinger declared that the United States had global interests while the European allies had only regional interests. These were not necessarily in conflict, but neither were they automatically identical. The Europeans, often displeased with their dependency in security matters on decision-making in Washington, disliked the regional role attributed to Europe by Kissinger. Nor did they like another aspect of Kissinger's initiative, namely to make a deliberate, indirect linkage of economic issues with defence and security. They feared that through this linkage Washington would want concessions in the trade and monetary fields in exchange for the maintenance of its security role, and of U.S. armed forces in Europe.[2]

Another attempt to strengthen European security considerations could be found in the Genscher–Colombo proposals leading to the Solemn Declaration on European Union in Stuttgart in June, 1983. The aim was to further develop European Political Cooperation, the method used by the EC member states to coordinate their foreign policies, by including in this coordination the political and economic aspects of security.[3] However, the Solemn Declaration was not accepted by the remainder of the EC member governments and therefore no progress was made in making security concerns part of the Community's agenda.

In the face of differing opinions among the EC member governments about how political integration and concerns for European security might be combined, and increasing concern about the part the EC should play within NATO, the foreign and defence ministers of the seven WEU members met in Paris on June 12, 1984, and decided to reactivate that organisation. WEU of course had never stopped to exist; it originated in 1948 as the Brussels Treaty but after playing a very important role in bringing West Germany into NATO in 1954, it showed little activity during the 1960s and 70s. After the WEU reactivation, West Germany's Foreign Minister Hans-Dietrich Genscher declared that this initiative was taken against the background of the negative attitude of many Europeans on America's role in NATO, but this did not mean that the reactivation of WEU was a step against the Atlantic Alliance.[4] Rather, WEU was to operate within the Alliance, perhaps developing into a significant part of its European pillar.

In October 1987, after many months of deliberations among the member states of the WEU, its Foreign and Defence Ministers Council adopted a 'Platform on European Security Interests'. It included a commitment to build a European Union in accordance with the Single European Act and emphasised that the construction of an integrated Europe would be incomplete as long as it did not include security and defence. 'We intend therefore to develop a more cohesive European defence identity.'[5]

Another source for the emergence of ESDI was Franco–German military cooperation and especially the Franco–German Committee for Security and Defence established in 1982 which was upgraded in 1988 to a Franco–German Council composed of the French President and the German Chancellor, the two foreign and defence ministers as well as the chiefs of staff of both military services. In the same year a joint Franco–German brigade was created that became fully operational by the end of 1990.[6]

The functions of the Council are, *inter alia*:

- the elaboration of common concepts regarding defence and security,
- the assurance of increasing concertation between the two states in all questions respecting the security of Europe including the control of armaments and disarmaments,
- decisions with respect to mixed military units to be formed with mutual consent,
- improvement in the inter-operability of weapons and equipment among both military forces,
- the development and deepening of the cooperation on armaments considering the necessity to assure the common defence through an adequate industrial and technological potential in Europe which needs to be maintained and strengthened.[7]

At present, the joint brigade encompasses 4200 men. It was initially commanded by a French brigadier general with a German colonel as its deputy commander, but these roles were reversed after two years and will be alternated in the future. The headquarters of the unit is located near Stuttgart in south western Germany and the troops are stationed in this area as well. While the brigade itself cannot be considered part of the European security and defence identity because it is too small and represents only two of the 12 EC countries, in October 1991 the French and German governments called for the creation of a corps-strength Western European Army as a step toward giving the region an independent defence capability. The two governments said that they would expand the joint brigade to perhaps 35 000 troops and indicated that units from other countries in the European Community could eventually join the force bringing it up to a strength of perhaps 50 000.[8] Belgium, Spain, and Italy showed an interest in joining the so-called 'Eurocorps', but so far definite decisions by these countries have not been made. Obviously, if such a development could be realised, ESDI would be enhanced materially. But Great Britain immediately challenged the French–German initiative as a potential threat to NATO (of which France is not a full member) because it would duplicate what the Alliance was already doing. Nor did Washington like the Eurocorps to be outside NATO. The U.S. had difficulty accepting the German claim that a 'European Army' was a long-term proposal and that if such an army were to be fielded under the WEU label, would complement NATO. Nevertheless, as a French spokesman noted: 'The identity of a European security system is being created. It is a fact. it exists.'[9] And such an army could be seen as an enhanced 'European pillar' of NATO.

During a meeting between President Mitterrand and Chancellor Kohl at the end of May 1992 more details about the Eurocorps were announced. The new force would be based in Strasbourg and would be ready in 1995. It would absorb the already existing French–German joint brigade and the units of the Corps would be called upon to intervene under the 'political cover' of the WEU, but according to German defence minister Volker Ruehe, there would be no WEU supreme allied commander because some of the German Corps units had already been allocated previously to NATO.[10]

Finally, as during 1990 the EC member states were moving toward the establishment of intergovernmental conferences (IGCs) regarding Economic and Monetary Union (EMU) as well as Political Union (PU), increasing consideration was given to security and defence cooperation which indirectly also touched on ESDI. During the European Council meeting in April of 1990 in Dublin, bringing together the heads of state and government of the 12 member states, it was declared that the future dynamic development of the Community had become an imperative not only because it corresponded to the direct interests of the 12 but also because it had become a crucial element in the progress that was being made in establishing a reliable framework for peace and security in Europe. This may require the transformation of the Community 'from an entity mainly based on economic integration and political cooperation into a union of a political nature, including a common foreign and security policy . . .'[11]

The inclusion of the security dimension in the EC framework may also prove beneficial for the EC efforts to move political union forward. The concept of creating military muscle for the use of the Community may appeal to a number of Europeans who would like to see Europe 'speak with one voice' and who chafe under the perception of being too dependent on America for their security and defence needs.

Considerable support for giving the Community institutions authority and competences in the security and defence policy fields has also been expressed on many occasions in the European Parliament beginning in 1989. Moreover, public opinion polls have indicated that many Europeans would favour security and defence policy decisions to be made by EC institutions rather than NATO although there are considerable differences in the views expressed in individual member states.[12] It is also necessary to point out that even after the Maastricht agreement the European Parliament has only limited political power and the attainment of its objective is often doubtful, especially when major structural changes of the EC are involved. But combined with even mildly supportive public opinion these circumstances are likely to bolster ESDI in future years.

THE MAASTRICHT AGREEMENT

During the deliberation of the IGC on political union, the attainment of a common foreign and security policy for the EC was a much discussed and controversial subject both in terms of substance as well as in policy-making procedure. While WEU was recognised as a legitimate organisation to be involved in security and, eventually defence policy, its operational role in these fields so far was extremely limited. However, this seems to be changing, as the defence ministers and chiefs of staff of the WEU member states will be meeting regularly and a planning unit (not a 'command') is being set up in Brussels in October 1992 with a military staff of 40 under the direction of an Italian general.[13] On the other hand, the EC up to now had no institutional competences in the security area at all, although this could be changed in the future.

Initially there was hope that the IGC operating the first six months of 1991 under the leadership of the Luxembourg presidency[14] would come up with an agreement on what the political union would look like. But no agreement could be reached by the end of June 1991 and consequently it was at the end of the Netherlands' presidency on December 9 and 10 that consensus was reached on what was then called 'European union', with the treaty having been signed on February 7, 1992. The treaty has to be ratified by the national parliaments of the EC member states which was to be accomplished by the end of 1992 and would lead to the amendments of the current EC, ECSC, and Euratom treaties. Although a Danish referendum in June 1992 rejected the Maastricht agreement initially, a second referendum in May 1993 endorsed the agreement.

The Maastricht agreement contained substantial steps toward a Common Foreign and Security Policy which foresee the possibility of joint actions binding on EC member states. This will notably cover disarmament and control of armaments in Europe, non-proliferation and economic aspects of security and, in the longer term, the formulation of a Common Foreign Defence Policy which may in time lead to a Common European Defence. WEU, which is scheduled to become an integral part of the new European Union, is expected to progressively work toward a true European identity on security and defence and increase European responsibilities in this domain. At the same time, WEU will become a defence component of the European Union and a means to reinforce the European pillar of the Atlantic Alliance.[15] This means that with no specific obligations assumed it will take several years to implement the eventual framing of European security and defence policies. The European Union agreement is anticipated to be reviewed in 1996 and it is not unthinkable that WEU, whose constituent treaty runs out in 1998, then will be swallowed up by an expansion and deepening of the EC institutional framework.[16]

PROSPECTS FOR ESDI

While the European Security and Defence Identity is recognised as a reality by the NATO leadership as we have seen in the beginning of this chapter, the continuing assumption, in particular by Washington and London, is that the Alliance remains the centrepiece of European defence policy. In July, 1991 the Secretary-General of NATO, Manfred Wörner, a former West German defence minister, engaged in an interesting discussion with members of the European parliament who were anxious to promote the ESDI. Mr. Wörner expressed the view that ESDI was neither a 'rival or substitute' for NATO. But he stressed that 'even a stronger, more united Europe cannot balance the immense geopolitical assets of the (then still existing) Soviet Union or uphold its interests beyond its shores except in close cooperation with the United States'. He added that 'realism was in order to acknowledge that neither the WEU nor the future political union will have for some time an operational defense capability able to be deployed without U.S. assistance in domains like air transport, strategic lift, logistics,intelligence, and communications'.[17]

Three factors may speed up the development of a more independent European security and defence policy.

(1) Despite the strong American interests to remain involved in European economic and political affairs through NATO, the costs involved in maintaining even 150 000 American troops may be too high for the U.S. budget, especially in a continuing recession, and the troop level will be gradually lowered further and eventually eliminated.

(2) Europeans are upset about American efforts to link issues of trade and military security. Threats have been made by American policy makers, i.e. former Vice President Quayle, that a breakdown of the Uruguay Round of trade negotiations between the EC and Washington could place in jeopardy the American military commitment in Europe.[18]

(3) There is continuing unease among many EC citizens, especially the more affluent and better educated, about European dependency on U.S. decision-making in world affairs and consequently they would like to have their own security and defence system. This of course will be a costly undertaking and will take time.

The problems of the Yugoslav conflict which is both a foreign policy crisis for the EC as well as a test of possible, low-level military involvement, have demonstrated that the EC must develop considerably more structures in the security field, beyond the modest achievements of the WEU, before the Community can stand militarily on its own feet. On the other hand, the creation of the North Atlantic Consultation Council (NACC) at the end of 1991, bringing members of the Commonwealth of Independent States to consult with NATO, has strengthened the latter in Europe as a whole and may have weakened ESDI. Finally, ESDI may be affected by perceptions of 'Euro-Gaullism'[19] which refers to Euro-Gaullist overtones in European defence cooperation. Obviously, the Franco–German initiative in the fall of 1991 and early 1992 calling for a 'European' army corps based initially on French–German military units – that could be expanded by units from other EC countries and that would operate outside NATO – may rekindle fears of Gaullist strategic concepts that had been expressed in the 1950s and 60s. There may also be fears in Washington and some EC countries that the build-up of European defence cooperation may not have the purpose to strengthen NATO's European pillar, but may seek to shift the centre of security and defence policy making more and more to the EC and WEU structures. Hence, ESDI must be handled very carefully if it is to grow and not to run into increasing opposition which could come mainly from America.[20]

GERMAN INTERESTS AND DEVELOPMENTS

French–German military cooperation goes back to 1963 and despite ups and downs in the overall relationships between the two countries and language problems among the troops in the joint brigade, interests in the further pursuit of the common military efforts has not faltered. The creation of the 'Eurocorps' of between 35 000 to 50 000 military personnel outside NATO puts the German government on the spot. It has always been a loyal supporter of the Alliance, but undoubtedly a compromise will have to be found between German continued cooperation with the United States and with non-Nato France which is considered essential for moving forward the creation of European union. In this connection a number of past aspects and developments need to be reviewed:

(1) The spirit of European unity was strongly kindled during the establishment of the Schuman Plan in 1950. The prospect of European unity now revives many of the ties between the two countries which originated during the creation of the European Coal and Steel Community and later the EEC (EC) and Euratom.

(2) The close cooperation between German Chancellor Helmut Schmidt and French President Valéry Giscard d'Estaing during the second half of the 1970s made possible the NATO agreement on the so-

called 'double-track' decision regarding the deployment in Europe of U.S. ground-launched Cruise Missile and Pershing-II systems and a parallel and complementary arms control effort to obviate the need for such deployments.

(3) There have been many complaints by the German people about NATO manoeuvres in the 1980s which caused considerable damage especially in rural areas and about low-flying American fighter planes during training exercises. While NATO's new strategic concepts emphasise rapid reaction forces and multi-national army corps, the German government must negotiate with its NATO partners on the basis of its fully restored sovereignty to determine under what international law conditions foreign troops will be allowed to operate on German soil. Both issues may have negative domestic overtones for the German government and may subtly influence its attitudes toward NATO in the 1990s.[21]

(4) Finally, a comment by former German defence minister Gerhard Stoltenberg may shed some light on the thinking of the Bonn government. In early 1992 he wrote, 'The formation of a European security identity and of a responsible role in the defence is based on the logic of the political integration process. . . . This development must not be pursued in competition with NATO, and should be seen as a division-of-labour and complementary addition to NATO which will strengthen the European pillar of the Alliance . . . and enhance the common European capability for action in the security and defence field'.[22]

Considering the above factors and the developments traced in this essay, a number of conclusions can be drawn:

(1) Germany has a strong commitment to building up ESDI based upon continued close Franco–German military cooperation including the Eurocorps with additional military forces from selected EC member states and outside of the NATO system.

(2) This does not mean giving up the NATO relationship altogether. Efforts will be made to remain a loyal NATO ally including pre-allocation of Germany military units to the Alliance and to look at the total defence strategy as a division of labour between NATO and European security forces as evolved from the Eurocorps and WEU.

(3) In the long run – perhaps eight to 12 years – ESDI will win out although the cost for the Europeans will be substantial and NACC will be a useful instrument for guiding East European countries

toward democracy and the market system, as well as increasing their self-confidence in these difficult times.

(4) The Yugoslav crisis is likely to affect the progress of ESDI; the more forceful WEU is during this crisis, the better the prospects for the European Security Identity.

Notes

1. See *NATO Review* (No. 6, December 1991), Documentation, pp. 19–20.
2. See Panayiotis Ifestos, *Nuclear Strategy and European Security Dilemmas* (Aldershot, England: Gower Publishing Company, 1988), pp. 31–33.
3. See excerpts of the Solemn Declaration in Press and Information Office of the Federal Government, *European Political Cooperation (EPC)*, Bonn: 1988, pp. 70–8, par. 1.4.2.4, Article 30.
4. See Ifestos, op.cit., pp. 366–7.
5. For the full statement see *ibid*. Appendix pp. 468–73, especially p. 469.
6. For details see Werner J. Feld, 'International Implications of the Joint Franco-German Brigade', *Military Review* 70, No. 2 (February 1990), pp. 2–11.
7. Press and Information Services of the Federal Government, *25 Jahre Elysee-Vertrag*, Bonn: 1988, pp. 45–8.
8. *New York Times*, October 17, 1991, pp. A1–7.
9. *Ibid.*, p. A7.
10. *Europe*, June 22, 1992, p. 5.
11. *European Community News*, No. 26/90, June 27, 1990, p. 8.
12. For a detailed discussion of this topic, see Werner J. Feld, 'Toward a European Security and Defense Policy', *Military Review* 71, no. 6, (July 1991), pp. 14–25.
13. *Europe*, June 20, 1992, p. 6.
14. The presidency changes every six months and is based on alphabetical rotation.
15. See Ambassador Andreas van Agt, Head of EC Delegation in Washington, D.C., whose article 'The Message of Maastricht: One European Partner', was published January 24, 1992.
16. See 'Making Sense of Maastricht,' *Europe* (Agence Europe), February 7, 1992, p. 1.
17. *Europe* (Agence Europe), July 3, 1991, p. 4.
18. *New York Times*, February 18, 1992, p. A19.
19. On Euro-Gaullism see John Roper, 'European Defence Cooperation', in Catherine McArdle Kelleher and Gale A. Mattox, eds., *Evolving European Defense Policies* (Lexington, Mass: D.C. Heath Co., 1987), pp. 39–58, especially pp. 49–51.
20. For an expression of American concern, see David M. Germroth and Rebecca J. Hudson, 'German–American Relations and the Post Cold War

World' in *Aussenpolitik* 43, (1/92), pp. 33–42. See also the report regarding the Pentagon's wish for the U.S. to remain the sole superpower in the *Gazette Telegraph* (March 8, 1992), p. 1 and *New York Times* (March 10, 1992), p. 10.

21. See also David T. Plesch and David Shorr, 'NATO Down and (Soon) Out', *New York Times*, July 24 1992, p. A15.

22. 'Sicherheit im Umbruch der Weltpolitik', *Europäische Sicherheit* (3/92), pp. 135–7 on 136.

21 A 'Federal Republic of Europe'?

Emil J. Kirchner

Whereas containment had been an important by-product of the FRG's history over the first 40 years, German dissolution into an EC framework became a main preoccupation in the aftermath of German unification. Developments surrounding the preparation and ratification procedure of the 1991 Maastricht accord indicated, however, that the latter would be a difficult process. Not only did some countries take a tough stand in the Maastricht negotiations by insisting on 'opt-out clauses', but public opinion on the agreement was generally divided within all countries. Some of these opinions, like the one expressed in the Danish referendum on the ratification of the Maastricht agreement, were coloured by government unpopularity and fear of potential German dominance.[1]

In Germany, the cost of German unification, the looming loss of the Deutsche Mark, and disappointment with the lack of progress on Political Union, as distinct from Economic Union, influenced opinions, and fuelled an already existing ambivalence toward EC integration. Hence four main questions were raised by mid 1992. Firstly, even if the German government would be willing to press on with European unification, would an ambivalent public, the *Bundesbank*, *Länder* authorities, and political opposition parties allow it to deliver within the next decade? Secondly, if Germany was ready to transfer essential elements of sovereignty to a supranational entity, would other EC countries be prepared to do the same? Thirdly, if one or more EC states refused to take far-reaching steps towards integration, whilst others moved ahead, would that make an EC of various speeds inevitable and thus impede the overall European unification process? Fourth, what role would Germany play in a more unified Europe and how could a potential German hegemony be avoided, diverted, or controlled? In some ways, the latter suggests similarities with the way hegemonial Prussia dissolved itself into the wider German state system over 120 years ago.

CONTROLLING OR ACCOMMODATING GERMANY?

Under the notion of 'double containment' NATO's main mission had been, as phrased by Lord Ismay, 'keeping the Soviets out, the Germans down, and the Americans in'. This objective had been complemented through such international organisations as GATT, IMF, OECD, and especially the EC. By and large this had allowed countries like France and the U.K. to maintain leading roles in political and military terms whilst enabling Germany to become an economic giant. It also contributed to growing economic interdependence and increasing levels of cooperation among West European countries. Although the EC gained in competences, decision-making was characterised more by a 'pooling of sovereignties' among nation states than by a 'supranational mechanism'. Despite the Court of Justice playing an influential role, only limited powers had been transferred from the national to the EC level until 1986.

This changed with the introduction of the single market programme of 1986, events in Eastern Europe in 1989, and especially German unification in 1990. The latter also raised important questions about the power distribution within and outside the EC. How would France, the U.K., and other EC partners respond to a larger, economically stronger and politically aspiring Germany? Whilst some EC governments saw the answer in a more federalised and centralised EC which would dilute German strength or prevent unilateral German actions, others were not willing to achieve such results at the expense of forgoing important spheres of national sovereignty. Instead they sought to continue with the principle of a balance of power in which a coalition of European countries would either check potential German preponderance/aggressiveness on their own, or solicit the help of the Americans. A federalised and centralised Europe was therefore seen as restricting national sovereignty, whilst possibly enabling German dominance from within the EC, and challenging or undermining American support and commitment to Europe. Such a view would be primarily attributed to the U.K., while the conviction of a more federal/central EC prevailed most strongly in France and to a lesser extent in Belgium, Italy, Spain, Greece, Luxembourg and Denmark. A desire to have the best of both worlds was held by the Dutch, Irish and Portuguese.

Independent of reactions and strategies by European governments on how best to relate to the unified Germany, two additional questions were of equal importance. Firstly, how would the Germans themselves want to proceed? Would they be willing, for instance, to forgo national sovereignty to a wider European unification, aspiring to peace and prosperity? In short, when push comes to shove would the Germans, accustomed to relatively high standards of living, be willing to invoke Article 24 of the Basic Law which stipulates that for the maintenance of peace, the Federation shall consent to such limitations upon its right of sovereignty as will bring about and secure a peaceful and lasting order in Europe and among the nations of the world. How would they take to a substitution of the ECU for the Deutsche Mark; would they tolerate deviations within the EC from their own principles of 'fiscal rectitude'; how would they respond to large requests of financial transfers to so-called disadvantaged countries/areas of either the present or an enlarged Community; and how would that part of the population formerly know as 'East Germans' be disposed towards a transfer of sovereignty?

Secondly, there was the question of the U.S. Would the U.S. prefer collaboration with a strengthened Germany rather than with the EC? Would the U.S. see a politically unified Europe more as a competitor than as an ally?

Reactions to the Maastricht agreement and to the Danish referendum of June 1992[2] offer important insights not only into the way Germany's EC partners line up with regard to further EC integration, but also into German and U.S. attitudes towards European unification. At stake in the negotiations leading up to Maastricht were crucial issues of control over monetary, social, immigration, foreign and security policy, as well as additional powers for the European Parliament (EP). Whilst the U.K. showed the least appetite for any of these measures, most of the other countries wished to 'pick and choose' from the available menu. That was not to the liking of the Germans who tied progress on EMU to progress on political union (involving immigration, foreign and security policy as well as EP powers) and hence threatened not to ratify the proposed European Monetary Union (EMU) agreement if there was no reciprocal progress on political union. The Germans also played a leading role in the convergence criteria that countries would have to meet in order to participate in the establishment of a European Central Bank and a single European currency. This amounted to tight controls over inflation rates and levels of public finance, and to a narrowing of interests and currency exchange rate differentials.

However, this German toughness concealed domestic ambivalence on EMU. In the first instance, this was reflected in the disagreement between Chancellor Kohl and Karl-Otto Poehl, president of the German Bundesbank, over how and when EMU should be introduced. The latter resigned prematurely from office in 1991. A further German domestic reaction followed after the Maastricht treaty was signed, and took the form of a belated, but concerted, public reaction to the proposed loss of the Deutsche mark. This, together with the no-vote in the Danish referendum, provoked the Kohl administration into a counteroffensive, warning that Europe could resort to the 'dark days of nationalism', pointing to the benefits of membership for peace and prosperity and urging compliance with the Maastricht agreement.[3]

In the following a brief examination will be made of the reaction of major actors within Germany to the Maastricht accord. These involve general public opinion, the Bundesbank, business groups, political parties, and *Länder* authorities.

German Domestic Factors and European Integration

A public opinion survey carried out by the Konrad Adenauer Foundation between June/July 1991 and January 1992 (see table 21.1) revealed that seldom has there been such an opinion change within six months.[4] Support in favour of integration sank from 46 per cent to 36 per cent over this period. But rather than indicating support for independent national policies (which actually decreased from 17 per cent to 16 per cent), those in favour of keeping EC integration at its present level rose from 36 per cent to 46 per cent. Consolidation rather than expansion appeared to be foremost in the mind of people. Preoccupation with internal problems over the assimilation of the five new *Länder* and heavy financial commitments to the reform process in the CIS states probably worried some people that Germany was taking on too much.[5]

However, a sudden but growing realisation after the Maastricht agreement concerning the loss of the Deutsche Mark also weighed in. On the specific question of substituting the ECU for the DM, 52 per cent of all Germans opposed it and only 25 per cent were in favour. There is no doubt that Germans view the Deutsche Mark as a powerful national symbol which embodies post–1945 success and stability; it might also be the prize East Germany voted for in 1990. From an 'East German' perspective, having just been through one currency upheaval, they may not be keen to face another. Resentment may also be due to the artificially devised term ECU, which is unfamiliar to most Germans and which has still to win their trust.

A majority of German respondents (usually in the 70 per cent range) saw negative repercussions with regard to pension payments, improve-

Table 21.1 Future role of Germany in Europe

	Political union should be advanced and national independence should be forgone						Political union should not be advanced, rather the EC should remain as it is						An independent national policy outside the EC should be pursued					
	June/July 1991			January 1992			June/July 1991			January 1992			June/July 1991			January 1992		
	Together	West	East	Together	West	East	Together	West	East	Together	West	East	Together	West	East	Together	West	East
	%	%	%	%	%	%	%	%	%	%	%	%	%	%	%	%	%	%
Together	46	43	53	36	36	35	36	38	33	46	47	40	17	18	12	16	17	16
18–24 years	49	48	55	40	34	59	33	33	31	38	41	22	17	18	13	20	21	17
25–29 years	48	44	57	42	47	32	37	41	29	42	38	51	14	15	14	12	11	14
30–44 years	48	46	57	39	37	46	35	36	29	42	43	40	16	17	11	17	19	12
45–59 years	46	45	47	34	35	32	36	37	40	50	51	45	16	17	11	15	15	20
60 years & over	40	37	54	29	27	39	39	41	32	53	55	42	19	20	12	18	17	19
CDU/CSU Supporters	45	43	56	39	39	39	40	43	29	46	48	39	13	13	13	14	13	21
SPD Supporters	48	46	55	39	38	48	33	33	36	43	44	40	17	19	10	17	18	10
FDP Supporters	58	57	52	31	32	30	27	26	29	42	45	37	15	17	19	27	23	33
Greens Supporters	52	55	76	56	65	43	27	25	17	36	23	48	20	21	9	9	12	8
Republ. Supporters	24	23	19	9	11	–	22	22	3	77	78	–	53	55	64	14	11	–

Source: Forschungsinstitut der Konrad Adenauer Stiftung Archive No 9101, 9102, 9201.

ments in social benefits, job protection and price stability. Even on the question of economic stability, 59 per cent foresaw unfavourable consequences. However, expectations regarding the completion of the internal market should be treated with caution. Whilst the share of those who had positive expectations dropped from 52 per cent to 35 per cent, the majority of respondents were 'undecided'. The latter might also contain respondents who resented the meagre progress made towards political integration at Maastricht.

Moving on from the general public to the business community, yet another survey[6], carried out in the Spring of 1992, showed that German business was the least enthusiastic in Europe about European union; 19 per cent judged the Maastricht treaty as poor or very poor, and less than 40 per cent found it good or very good. Taking these figures at face value would probably be a mistake, since different countries want different things from the EC. Whereas some countries put more emphasis on a single currency as a Community aim, German business seems to be keener on monetary and political stability. Hence they expressed fears that it was not enough to stress convergence as a condition of entry. German business appeared to be worried that currency union would create a club of inflationary sinners. Once a state joins the club then governments which are inclined to inefficiency no longer feel under any compulsion to exercise monetary/fiscal discipline. The implication was that the proposed EMU 'sanctions' would have no bite. This also seemed to reinforce images of 'richer' countries that would have to pay for the inefficiency of other countries and that Germans would sacrifice the Deutsche Mark and pay subsidies on top of that.

Public and business doubts, anxiety and hesitation were reinforced by the continued ambivalent position of the Bundesbank which criticised the 'haste and pressure of deadlines on the way to currency union', and considered the arrangements for political union inadequate. Hans Tietmeyer, the successor of Karl-Otto Poehl at the Bundesbank, insisted that Germany will be prepared to accept EMU only in the shape of community of stability (also involving budgetary discipline), and that 'when in doubt, the goal of monetary stability must have priority over exchange rate targets'. He also hinted that this could lead to clashes with finance ministers, who are to share responsibility with the European Central Bank for the latter.[7]

Henceforth, Bundesbank ambivalence gave political opposition parties and *Länder* governments/parliaments additional ammunition in their respective claims for further controls by the Bundestag and for the preservation of *Land* interests. To obtain ratification, the Kohl government needed first to obtain an amendment to the German constitu-tion that would allow the Bundesbank's powers to be transferred to the proposed European Central Bank. This required a two-thirds majority from both the Bundestag and the Bundesrat, which forced Kohl to deal with the federal states and the opposition Social Democratic party.

Although the U.K. alone explicitly reserved the right in the Maastricht treaty not to proceed to a single currency, Germany did retain a form of 'opt-out'. The *Länder* and the opposition SPD insisted that the German Parliament should have the right to decide (along with the government) in 1996 whether the economic conditions for EMU have been fulfilled by all member states intending to go to the final stage. The attached conditions had the potential to delay. In addition to these economic conditions, there was also an insistence that at this stage political union would have to be strengthened by, among other things, increasing the powers of the EP. In part, the stand taken by the *Länder* involved the question of who was to meet increasing EC payments: the *Länder* or the central government; the *Länder* had already successfully placed most of the burden of German unification on central government.

A more positive approach was taken by the major German banks in response to criticism by 60 German economists who had denounced the Maastricht resolutions as 'overhasty', short-sighted, and as damaging rather than benefiting the European cause. In one of their very rare joint initiatives, the big three German banks – *Deutsche, Dresdner* and *Commerzbank* – accused the professors of still living in the 1970s, of failing to see a single currency as a 'natural extension' of the EMS and of underestimating the danger that the Community will break up if it does not forge ahead now.

Given the fact that the Maastricht accord occurred one year after the German unification, it is interesting to see how the two groups responded. The population in the five new *Länder* tended to be more Euro-friendly, or positively inclined toward further integration, than those in the 'old' West Germany. There were also differences between the two groups on the question of whether German union has made European union more difficult. Whereas 41 per cent of the West German respondents felt that it made the latter more difficult, only 30 per cent of the East Germans agreed. Similarly, whereas 48 per cent of the West Germans thought union had made European union more important, 56 per cent of the East Germans supported this view. What Germans wanted most from the EC were: preservation of peace (86 per cent); fight against drug trafficking (84 per cent); aid for economic recovery in Eastern Europe (82 per cent); dealing with environmental problems (80 per cent); maintaining the alliance with the U.S.A. (78 per cent); and controlling immigration into the EC (69 per cent).

A number of observations about Germany's attitude towards Europe can be made. Firstly, the debate on the Maastricht agreement reached heights witnessed only once before on such a scale, namely in the 1950s when entry into the EC was an issue. Secondly, the nature of the European debate was more difficult to ascertain in Germany than in countries like the U.K. where nationalism is the preponderant component in the discussion on Europe. This is not to say that similar points were not being raised. As in other countries, German domestic reactions were critical of bureaucratic waste – also – prolonging the notion of Germany as a 'Zahlmeister' which made its entry in the 1970s – centralisation (the principle of subsidiarity is not only a favourite ploy of the Länder in dealing with federal authorities. It was also effectively reinforced in the concessions won by the Länder in the German ratification of the Single European Act in 1986), and loss of cultural identity. There were also fears that in future, Germans would no longer be masters of the Deutsche Mark, e.g. they could be outvoted in the council of Ministers and in the European Parliament.

In contrast to debates elsewhere, the federal structure is an important factor in German attitudes to and relations with the EC. This, together with what could loosely be called German ambivalence on European matters, is in part nationalism by other means and in part a phenomenon separate from the nationalism witnessed in other EC member states. The importance of 'Land' interests rather than national/federal interests again came to the fore in the ratification process of the Maastricht accord. A new clause was introduced into the German constitution which states that in those areas where the Länder traditionally enjoy 'exclusive powers', such as in education and culture, a state politician will represent Germany in the Council of Ministers. In other areas where Länder interests are 'affected', Länder opinion must be taken into account via the Bundesrat. However, in areas of foreign and security policy, the federal government's right to the last word has been preserved. Thus, there is not an overriding worry that national parliamentary sovereignty is being eroded, as is the case in the U.K., but rather that the preservation of Länder rights is maintained.

Furthermore, besides the criticism levelled against the erosion of state or federal interests, Germans expressed greater disapproval over the lack of progress towards Political Union than many other EC countries. Germany made the original post-national leap four decades ago – unlike the U.K. and France – therefore has almost no painful loss of nationalism to endure. There is a general consensus that Germany's future is only within a united Europe.

Germany has traditionally been in the forefront of promoting European integration and after German unification these efforts were reinforced. Not only did the constitutional references to European unification begin to surface more strongly within Germany, there were also domestic concerns that the worries of its neighbours over German unification should be allayed. The Spring 1990 Franco–German initiative on Political Union was a direct response to the latter. The Germans hoped that this would dispel any suspicion that a united Germany could turn its back on the West and return to a 'seesawing policy' between East and West as in the 19th century. In other words, German leadership wanted to demonstrate that it intended to build a greater Europe, not a greater Germany. There might also be a desire on the part of Helmut Kohl, as Pond suggests, to unite Germany into Europe before ceding his post to people less haunted by German history.[8]

Has Germany always behaved in a communitarian way? Resistance to CAP reforms, resistance to EC deregulation of road haulage, and in the telecommunication and insurance sectors, and insistence on continued state subsidies for certain industries have been examples to the contrary. The disregard by the Bundesbank for economic conditions in other countries represents an even greater indictment. Some EC partners go as far as to call the unilateral Bundesbank decisions 'interest rate dictatorship'. Undoubtedly, the persistence of high German interest rates, resulting either from the capital needs of unification or the Bundesbank's attempt to control inflation has put severe strains on the EMS, and in particular on countries such as France and the U.K. This lack of consideration for the interests of others has even provoked critical voices within Germany. According to Dieter Schröder of the *Süddeutsche Zeitung*

> From the very beginning there has been an element of hypocrisy in German enthusiasm for Europe. This singles us out from the British and French, who have never made a secret of the fact that they pursue national objectives with their 'Europe' policies.[9]

However, what can be viewed as German ambivalence or contradiction might reflect German consistency. Germany has insisted for some time that the price for transferring its own monetary authority would have to be the establishment of European rules on price stability and fiscal rectitude. There is of course a question whether unilateral, as well as diverging, German monetary policy (higher interest rates when most other countries desire lower ones) is conducive to the establishment of EMU. Only time will tell whether German monetary actions will help or hinder other countries to meet the stipulated convergence criteria to qualify for the introduction of a single currency.

FEDERAL VERSUS CONFEDERAL

In the meantime, there is the question of whether EMU needs Political Union to succeed. If so, this would require a substantial strengthening of the EC institutions. First and foremost, from a German perspective, it would necessitate a greater role for the EP and a reduction of the perceived 'democratic deficit' in EC decision-making. Increasing the practice of majority voting in the Council of Ministers would be another key element in this respect.

However, Political Union is not desired by some countries who see the future EC as a confederation in which the nation states continue to be the main actors. They propose greater coordination of foreign and security policy issues and an enlargement of the EC comprising both EFTA and Eastern European countries. In their opinion 'widening' should therefore come before a 'deepening' of EC integration, primarily in the institutional field.

Whereas France seems to take the view that any enlargement is disruptive to integration and preferably to be avoided, Germany sees virtues from enlargement both in terms of market potential and security and stability perspectives. However, like France, it wants to combine enlargement with deepening and do so gradually, starting with EFTA countries. Germany, being a quasi-neighbouring state, is concerned with the ethnic conflicts in Eastern Europe and with the danger of instability being exported to Western Europe.

The war in Yugoslavia has created the biggest flood of refugees in Europe since 1945. By mid–1992, some 1.8 million had been 'displaced' inside the ex-Yugoslav republics and as many as 500 000 had fled to countries in Europe. Indications then were that Germany was carrying a disproportionate burden of the humanitarian aid to victims of the war as well as accepting a much higher number of refugees than other EC countries. Generally, Germany takes more than 60 per cent of refugees coming to the EC: roughly 400 000 in 1992.

Besides the pressing problem of refugees, the EC was also confronted with the challenge of how to help Eastern European countries economically. It could be argued that economic aid and advice,[10] though welcome, are not substitutes for market access. In December 1991, Czechoslovakia, Hungary and Poland signed association agreements with the EC which opened western markets only slightly. Clearly, to make the common agricultural policy (CAP) more porous and subject to international competition does not seem to be easy, as shown in the protracted negotiations of the Uruguay Round. Equally, the EC might be accused of being short-sighted in its general economic policy by not appreciating that the accelerated development of Eastern economies would, in turn, help to stimulate Western European economies. As Hans-Dietrich Genscher points out: 'Western Europe cannot thrive in the long term if Eastern Europe continues to suffer'.[11]

Enlargement, as well as Political Union generally, also involves consideration of a common foreign and security policy (CFSP). It is lamentable but a fact that inspite of considerable economic clout the EC has no effective political influence in the international arena; the inept attempts at solving the Yugoslav crisis has been the most glaring example. The EC has not been able to move much beyond the informal framework, set up under European Political Cooperation (EPC), for mutual information and consultation, and for coordinating and aligning the member states' viewpoints. Since EPC is based on unanimity, each country can either delay actions or force a compromise. As Peter Ludlow suggests, foreign policy is founded on interest rather than innate solidarity'.[12]

These differing interests surfaced strongly in the debate leading up to the Maastricht accord, resulting in the decision to establish an intergovernmental arrangement for a common foreign and security policy (CFSP). Three fundamental issues arose. Firstly, should arrangements for CFSP come under acquis communautaire, i.e. have a binding nature and if necessary be subject to Court rulings, or become an extension of intergovernmental negotiations? Secondly, to what extent should the EC develop its own security, i.e. should it be complementary to, or independent of, NATO? Thirdly, should majority voting be used in EC foreign policy matters and if so, when and in what areas?

Agreements seemed to come about most easily on the first issue with Britain and France among the large EC countries in favour of an intergovernmental arrangement. Consent was also obtained on majority voting in well defined areas of EC foreign policy. Most controversy ensued over the second issue. Whereas France, and to some extent Germany, wanted to see the Community develop its own defence and foreign policy identity as a replacement for NATO (in the shape of

Western European Union), the U.K. was eager to prevent a split from the Americans and proposed instead that Western European Union form a sort of bridge between NATO and EC. Rather than settling the issue, the Maastricht accord has given rise to further ambiguities by stating the WEU should become 'the defence arm of the Union' whilst insisting that it also becomes the 'European arm' of NATO.

In the meantime, France and Germany have suggested a strengthening of their joint brigade (which was established in 1987); proposing a force of 30 000 soldiers. Belgium and Spain joined this 'Eurocorps' in 1993. Jacques Delors, the Commission president, has also hinted at a possible pooling of European nuclear forces. A WEU or EC solution may help Germany to get around its constitutional constraints. Article 87 of the constitution limits using German troops to purposes described in the constitution – Article 24 permits Germany to fight alongside allies in collective security pacts. As Helmut Kohl remarked in the Summer of 1992, 'Fewer and fewer people in our country understand the fact that important decisions are being blocked, particularly with regard to the inevitable need to amend the constitution'.[13]

Undoubtedly, the issue of security will surface again in 1996 when a general review of WEU is envisaged. Failure to deal with ethnic conflicts, like the one in Yugoslavia, and general pressures for more EC involvement in international problems will raise the temperature of discussion. But it will also expose more fully the problems surrounding the future of NATO, relations with the U.S.A. and the acceptance of Germany as a key player within the EC. Another factor earmarked for an intergovernmental conference in 1996, is a review of EC immigration policy, the third pillar of the Maastricht agreement. Though subject to intergovernmental negotiations, Maastricht accepted that not only asylum but also immigration policy is a matter of interest for the member states. However, it postponed a decision on which citizens of non-member states need only a visa to enter into the territory of the Community and which foreigners are not obliged to hold a visa.[14]

Maastricht proposes the establishment of European citizenship which would provide citizens of the EC with a greater sense of involvement in EC affairs. Put differently, the message is that the Community belongs to its citizens. This point takes on additional significance after the Danish referendum, which created the impression that governments were out of touch with popular sentiment. The Maastricht agreement enables nationals of EC countries to vote in local elections anywhere in the EC. Besides efforts to democratise and popularise EC decision-making, there is also the aim of promoting a European identity and a sense of commonality among the different nationalities. The spectre of a 'European identity kit' subjugating national identities has invariably been raised by 'Euro-sceptics'. Yet there does not seem to be a need to choose between a national identity and a European one. We can have both as a community and as individuals. As Kevin Boyle suggests.

> we can set an example for the wider Europe in how to institutional-ise pluralism and tolerance through democratic means without threat-ening the diversity of cultures that makes us up. This vision is not something to fear but something to embrace.[15]

Whilst such fears will continue, another anxiety, of a more imminent nature, arose over Germany's future role in Europe; its position, interests and goals. Will it be within or outside the EC?

POLITICAL UNION OR GERMAN UNILATERALISM?

An article in *The Economist* of 12 October 1991 starts: 'Are you afraid of Germany?' As suggested in the article this is a hidden, rather than an explicit question, but one which was the real reason for the rush behind the Maastricht agreement. In a way, it is ironic that fears about Germany should be raised when in the mid-to-late eighties there were fears that Germany was losing its national identity. By then, Germany was so geared to a policy of multinational relations designed to in-crease security and prosperity that Germans began to have doubts about their own national identity. Similarly, Germany manifested a great deal of pacifism in the Gulf conflict of 1990/91. Will a united Germany restrict use of its power more easily or delegate its own interest when in a federal Europe? After all, power, as Karl Kaiser puts it, requires the willingness to exercise it.[16]

The Economist still seems to have doubts about German intentions, stating that: 'Even if solemnly signed to do so by enthusiastic (or de-spairing) politicians, the print of a treaty does not abolish resort to 'vital interest'.[17] In support of their argument *The Economist* cites examples of German unilateral action such as the ten–point plan for German unification and decisions by the Bundesbank. *The Economist* continues:

> To be dominant in a tight European state presents temptations dangerous to all including Germany. Restraints cannot be enforced by 'locking

in' the strongest into Federal Europe. If constitutional engineers substitute economic entrepreneurs and succeed in creating a politically integrated Europe, the proceeding economic 'closer union' of the single market may be destroyed and the European House undermined without the assumed benefit from restraining the unconstrainable strongest.[18]

In view of such a scenario, it is tempting to compare the process of EC integration with the process of nation-building in the 19th century. The EC's experience is similar to the way in which Bismark first tried to establish a German state before creating a German nation. Moreover, like Prussia then, Germany now represents a large and powerful unit in the process of integration. However, in the German context, unlike in the EC one, all participants already spoke the same language with a common literature and were generally more similar. Even so, this did not prevent the occurrence of the 'Kulturkampf' between the Christian religions.

There is also a question as to whether the common will is developed to a similar degree to that which existed in the nation state movements of the 19th century. The appetite for national independence in Europe is waning, but much of the authority surrendered by national governments to the EC has gone there not out of idealism, but because the authority no longer works at home.[19] In addition, individual states are much too small to hold their own in world markets where the United States and Japan predominate. Strength therefore lies in unity.

What then can be expected from Maastricht? Will Maastricht be a departure toward a Western European federal state? In federalism the stress is upon a constitutional instrument setting out the relationship and competence of the federal and local bodies within a defined territorial area.[20] The treaty on European Union, as the Maastricht agreement is formally known, created a shift in the delicate balance between nation states and the common European institutions, giving the latter more power. Its most important achievement is to provide a blueprint, timetable and conditions for a move to one European currency and one central bank before the end of the century. But Maastricht also encountered certain objections, such as 'opt-outs' from certain obligations, and an initial rejection by Danish voters. These objections indicate once again that the pace of integration is slow and fraught with the danger of a Europe of 'various speeds'. Asking member states to go beyond the internal market and common external trade arrangements is still a difficult undertaking. Would it therefore be better to abandon notions of a federal Europe and more appropriate to let members choose the policies they want to either adhere to or not? Already there are several examples of such selectivity as witnessed in the Maastricht pillars, the Schengen accord,[21] the arrangement surrounding the social chapter of the Maastricht pact,[22] and the existence of the Franco–German military corps. The danger with such an approach lies in the overlap of policies, budgetary adjustments, and institutional arrangements, e.g. should countries who have opted out of policies have any say in such policies in either the Council of Ministers or the European Parliament? Should a majority of members prevent other member states from entering into certain policies?

In conjunction with the notion of a Europe of various speeds another concept has entered into EC decision-making. This is the principle of subsidiarity, according to which decisions should be taken at the level most appropriate (EC-wide, nationally, regionally or locally). The trouble with this principle is that different countries have different conceptions of it. For Britain it is seen as a way of stopping European law-making that is not needed to preserve the free flow across Europe of goods, services, money and people: a market-driven subsidiarity. For most other countries, especially Germany, it raises the issue of where the centre should and should not act in governing a union: a federal subsidiarity. In line with the latter perception, the German Parliament has established a commission which is to prepare a new and fundamental European article in the German constitution. This article would not only profess support for European unification but also specify the content of its goals. In return, according to Rupert Scholz, Germany expects that

> European Political Union must express its support for the principles of a democratic and social constitutional state, guaranteed by the German constitution, uphold the principle of subsidiarity, and above all, be cast in a 'federal' mould.[23]

CONCLUSION

Although there is ambivalence on the part of the general public, the Bundesbank and *Länder* authorities, this is not strong enough to outweigh German domestic support for European unification. The erosion of nationalism over the past 40 years, on the one hand, and fears of a revival of nationalism either in Germany or elsewhere, on the other, are the underlying motives for further integration. There seems little doubt that, in spite of economic problems in absorbing the five *Länder*,

German unification has reinforced German commitment towards European union. In so doing Germany has tried both to allay fears about Germany and to invite other EC partners to join in the quest for European union. This was explicit in the alternative Hans Dietrich Genscher presented to his colleagues in December 1991: 'They must either leave them [Germans] to it as they went their own sweet way for the first time, or join ranks with them'.[24]

In accord with George Kennan's earlier held view that a united Germany would be tolerable only as an integrated part of a united Europe, France has clearly seen the need for a faster and deeper integration. This was noticed again in the debate over the ratification of the Maastricht treaty in the French parliament, when Prime Minister Beregovoy warned that 'Germany could drift away from EC integration unless the Maastricht pact is ratified quickly'.[25] However, not all governments, the British being one, share France's enthusiasm for further integration and as the Danish referendum has shown, there is also public reluctance. Whilst German elites are concerned with developments in Central and Eastern Europe and pursuing economic, political and security interests in that region, there seems to be agreement among them that the Western link of a united Germany must be free of ambiguity. Accordingly, as Michael Stürmer suggests, 'Germany should neither be a bridge nor a pivot' for Eastern Europe.[26] In any case, German attempts at a 'Europeanisation' of German policy will affect Germany's links with Eastern European countries. This 'Europeanisation' is also likely to affect the relationship between Germany and the U.S. and may increasingly be transformed into Euro-American relations. Whether that relationship is based more on cooperation than on conflicts of interest remains to be seen.

There does not seem to be an alternative to the EC. It has become an economic and political necessity. As Konrad Adenauer wrote in his memoirs

> in my view the European nation state had a past, but no future. This applied in politics, the economic and the social sectors. No individual European country was able to guarantee its people a secure future on its own strength.[27]

On the contrary, there is a danger of nationalism and a danger of countries determining their policies according to national interest should integration falter. Moreover, European union eventually offers not only integration to the former communist countries but a qualitatively higher level of security.

As Germany was approaching its 45th anniversary, it clearly seemed to be prepared to dissolve itself into a federal Europe. As Helmut Kohl remarked in mid–1992 'for us in Germany the objective is to fulfill the second mandate in the tradition established by Konrad Adenauer and provided for in our Basic Law of 1949: the unification of Europe'.[28] What was less clear, however, was whether other EC countries had either enough trust in Germany or a willingness to forgo national sovereignty in favour of a federal Europe. The outcome of the intergovernmental conference planned for 1996 and the establishment of a single currency foreseen for 1999 will clearly signal which countries are prepared to move towards a federal union and which will not.

Notes

1. Svend Auken, 'A Message from Denmark', *Parliamentary Brief*, vol. 1, July 1992, no. 2 pp. 4–5.
2. The outcome of the Danish referendum on the ratification of the Maastricht agreement was: 50.7 per cent no and 49.3 per cent yes.
3. Quoted by John Eisenhamer, in 'Kohl spells out commitments to Maastricht', The *Independent*, June 17, 1992.
4. Peter R. Weilemann, 'Einstellungen zur Europäischen Union nach Maastricht', Interne Studie Nr. 30/1992, Forschungsinstitut der Konrad Adenauer Stiftung, Sankt Augustin, 22.1. 1992.
5. Horst Teltchik, 'Germany's new role in the new order', *Die Zeit*, Feb. 2, 1992.
6. This survey was based on 1483 interviews across the Community in February and March 1992, and was carried out by the Harris Research Center. It was reported by Andrew Marshall, 'Business gloom over prospects for EC union', The *Independent*, April 30, 1992.
7. Hans Tietmeyer, 'Economic and Monetary Union: A German Perspective', The Ludwig Erhard Memorial Lecture, February 18 1992, European Institute, London School of Economics and Konrad Adenauer Foundation.
8. Elizabeth Pond, 'Germany in the New Europe', *Foreign Affairs*, vol. 71, 1992, p. 115.
9. Dieter Schröder, *Süddeutsche Zeitung*, March 14, 1992.
10. These involve straightforward humanitarian aid, grants, loans, as well as activities of the European Bank for Reconstruction and Development, and the PHARE programme.
11. Hans-Dietrich Genscher, 'CSCE must create culture of coexistence between Vancouver and Vladivostok', *Der Tagesspiegel*, July 14, 1992.
12. Peter Ludlow, ed., *Setting European Community Priorities* 1991–2, (London: Brassey's, 1991), p. 101.
13. 'Excerpts from Chancellor Helmut Kohl's speech at the presentation of

the 1992 Konrad Adenauer Prizes in Munich', May 17, 1992, *Press Release* Embassy of the Federal Republic of Germany, London, May 20, 1992.

14. At Maastricht it was agreed to draw up a joint list of countries whose citizens would need visas to enter the Community. But permanent immigration and the right of asylum have been left to national governments, which will work towards common admission rules in the future.

15. Kevin Boyle, 'What Will the New Europe Mean for its Citizens?', Debate Series 'Shaping the 1990's', April 15, 1992, paper delivered at the Irish Council of the European movement, p. 4.

16. Karl Kaiser, 'Germany's Unification,' *Foreign Affairs*, vol. 70, 1991, pp. 179–205.

17. *The Economist* survey on Europe, June 13, 1992.

18. Ibid.

19. Ibid.

20. See William Olson and A. J. R. Groom, *International Relations then and now: origins and trends in interpretation*, (London: Harper Collins Academic, 1991), p. 173.

21. The Schengen Accord was signed June 14, 1985 by Belgium, Germany, France, Luxembourg and the Netherlands whereby the five states agreed to create a border-free zone among themselves. Italy signed the Agreement in November 1990 and Spain in 1991.

22. Due to British resistance in accepting the proposed social policy provisions in the Maastricht accord, the 11 other member states were forced to make a separate arrangement, the 'social charter.'

23. Rupert Scholz, 'Federal nature of the new Europe needs legal underpinning', *Die Welt*, Jul. 13, 1992.

24. See Udo Bergdoll, 'Foreign Minister Genscher: when the fixed coordinates of world affairs begin to dance', *Süddeutsche Zeitung*, Jan. 7, 1992.

25. See Paul Taylor, 'Beregovy warns against "Europhobia"', The *Independent*, May 6, 1992.

26. Michael Stürmer, 'Historical perspectives to the Cold War's fault lines', *Frankfurter Allgemeine Zeitung*, Mar. 3, 1992.

27. Quoted by Helmut Kohl 'Excerpts from Chancellor Helmut Kohl's speech at the presentation of the 1992 Konrad Adenauer Prizes in Munich', May 17, 1992, *Press Release* Embassy of the Federal Republic of Germany, London, May 20, 1992.

28. Ibid.

22 German Ostpolitik in the 1990s: Anticipating the Post-Soviet Disorder

A. James McAdams

There may be only a single, reliable clue for anticipating the Federal Republic of Germany's policy toward the morass of competing states, ethnic groups, and interests comprising the post-Soviet Union in the 1990s. This is to be found in the dramatic shift in West German relations with the USSR during the preceding decade. In the mid–1980s, the climate between the two states could not have been much worse. To all intents and purposes, contacts between the FRG and the Soviet Union had been frozen due to Bonn's 1983 decision to go ahead with the deployment on German soil of NATO intermediate-range nuclear missiles. The few exchanges that did take place between the two countries were confined to little more than slurs and invective. While the Soviet press was replete with comparisons of the policies of the German government to the militarism of the Nazi past, policy-makers in Bonn had pretty much written off the prospect of an improved relationship with Moscow anyway. At one point, the FRG's chancellor, Helmut Kohl, even likened the 'new thinking' of a rising Soviet leader and one-day president, CPSU General Secretary Mikhail Gorbachev, to the propaganda tactics of Joseph Goebbels.

How great the contrast therefore, between this period and the un-questionable high point in German-Soviet relations that was reached with the historic meeting between Kohl and Gorbachev at the Caucasus spa of Zhelezdnovodsk on July 16, 1990. On the surface, it was significant that both leaders seemed to have resolved the personal differences that had once separated them. Yet beyond this atmospheric change, the outcome of their talks had been inconceivable five years earlier. On this occasion, the FRG finally received, as Kohl himself later characterised the encounter, 'the "green light" from the Soviet government in our path to [national] unity.'[1] At once, the central issue that had frustrated the two states' relations for over four decades – the Soviet Union's responsibility for the division of the German nation – was put behind them forever. Literally, Germany's ties with Moscow could be crafted anew.

In view of this shift in the tenor of the two states' relations, it is easy to understand why the FRG's leaders should have been at a loss to know how to respond when they were presented with the stark reality of the August 1991 coup against Gorbachev. To say that they were shocked by the events that ultimately marked the end to the political career of the man who had made possible the reunification of their nation is to tell only part of the story. It is equally important to appreciate that, thanks in part to Soviet policy, German reunification came to pass under the best of all possible circumstances. In a year's time, roughly between July 1990 and August 1991, Bonn was able to realise a host of goals in its relations with the Soviet Union that had been at the heart of West German foreign policy priorities since Konrad Adenauer's time.[2] Because Germany's future leaders will undoubtedly look wistfully back on this period when ties with Moscow were at their peak, it is fitting to begin with the reasons behind this accommodation before turning to the problems that may beset German relations with the remnants of the Soviet Union in the years to come.

AN OPTIMAL ACCOMMODATION

Up to 1990, the chief dilemma facing German foreign policy-makers was *not* that a workable relationship of some kind with the Soviets was impossible. Rather, the more demanding challenge lay in assuring that the pursuit of one set of West German goals did not immediately conflict with another. Tensions among these competing priorities were as old as the FRG itself.

To satisfy those who felt that the Soviet Union could only be convinced to modify its authoritarian ways by maintaining a 'policy of strength' externally – such as the FRG's first chancellor, Adenauer – hopeful reformers of German foreign policy had often been forced to put up with the agonisingly slow pace at which their government went about opening itself to contacts with the communist bloc. By the same token, West German politicians who argued that matters of national interest should take precedence over their country's differences on political and moral questions with Moscow, frequently had to close their eyes to flagrant violations of human rights and national sovereignty by the Soviet regime. Finally, every time the West German government succeeded in making a small breakthrough toward the USSR, it also had to contend with the ever-present suspicion on the part of its Western allies, particularly the United States, of a 'new Rapallo'.[3] According to these apprehensions, the Federal Republic's commitment to the Atlantic community was supposedly so mercurial that it could easily be swayed into transferring its loyalties to the East.

The magical quality of Kohl and Gorbachev's meeting at Zhelezdnovodsk, however, was that this encounter and two directly related subsequent developments – the signing of the international treaty in Moscow on September 12, 1990 which formally ended the four-power occupation of Germany and of a comprehensive friendship treaty in Bonn on German-Soviet relations on November 9, 1990 – finally freed the FRG of having to make such hard choices. First of all, both accords acknowledged Soviet and German security interests in a manner that would never have been imaginable in the times of the Cold War. Whereas in the first half of 1990, the Soviet leadership had repeatedly balked at the idea of allowing a reunified German state to belong exclusively to NATO and insisted that some sort of relationship be maintained with the old Warsaw Pact, now the Gorbachev government agreed to let the Germans decide for themselves 'freely whether and to which alliances [they] will belong'.[4] Not surprisingly, this decision led to the FRG's full incorporation into NATO. Furthermore, Moscow also gave its consent to a formal agreement on the withdrawal of all of its troops from East German soil by the end of 1994.

Admittedly, there was little that the Soviets could have done at this late date to halt the forward march to German unity. Still, it was indicative of Bonn's eagerness to demonstrate its good will that the West German government made reciprocal concessions of its own to Moscow. In view of the staggering challenges facing the Soviet economy, for example, the Kohl administration agreed to pay nearly DM 12 billion to Gorbachev's government, both to ease the costs of providing housing for the returning Soviet troops and to cover the GDR's remaining financial obligations to the USSR. Equally salient, German negotiators also showed a notable sensitivity to Soviet security concerns, by assuring their counterparts that no NATO forces would be deployed in Eastern Germany until after the Soviet troop withdrawal had been completed and agreeing that none of these forces would be equipped with nuclear-capable delivery systems. In a similar vein, the Federal government reaffirmed a commitment, already made at the East–West talks on conventional arms reductions in Vienna, to reduce its own armed forces to a combined limit of 370 000 troops.

From Bonn's perspective, a second positive aspect of the new spirit of German–Soviet understanding was that, in reaching such accords with the Gorbachev regime, leaders like Kohl did not have to feel that they were making a deal with the devil to purchase German reunification. Very much in line with Adenauer's assumptions in the 1950s that a Western 'policy of strength' would eventually lead the USSR to turn away from communism to assure its own survival, Soviet domestic policies actually were changing in ways that could only be welcomed in the FRG. Even if Gorbachev himself was intent upon maintaining the basic elements of Soviet socialism, it was abundantly clear by the summer and autumn of 1990 that the general secretary's initial political and economic reforms had given rise to internal developments that had scarcely been conceivable only a few years earlier – the advent of a free and more critical press, the formation of rudimentary opposition parties, and major advances in the area of human rights protection.

In this regard, it was noteworthy that the November 1990 comprehensive treaty between the two governments explicitly stipulated that the nearly 2 million ethnic Germans living in diverse parts of the Soviet Union would have the right, if they so chose, to 'develop their national, linguistic, and cultural [identities]'.[5] Admittedly, it was by no means unusual for the Federal Republic to have demanded that Soviet citizens of German nationality be allowed to preserve their distinctive cultural traditions amidst a sea of Slavic culture or, failing that, to be able to exercise the option of emigrating to the West. The unique feature of this agreement, however, was that for the first time, the Soviet regime implicitly granted the FRG the right to an interest in the conduct of its own domestic politics. There can be no doubt that such a prerogative would have been peremptorily dismissed in the past as outside interference in the country's internal affairs.

The final factor that made the new German–Soviet accommodation unusual was that none of Bonn's gains had to be bought at any evident cost to the FRG's good relations with its NATO allies. Quite the contrary, the Atlantic alliance, and the United States in particular, had every reason to welcome the burgeoning ties between Bonn and Moscow. For one thing, the security-related aspects of the new relationship were largely satisfied on the West's long-standing terms. German reunification would not come at the price of the FRG's neutralisation, as Soviet leaders had ritualistically demanded in Adenauer's time, but instead under auspices with testified to a NATO victory in the Cold War. Just as consequential, for everyone who was concerned about the massive costs of maintaining stability in the East and reforming the

Soviet economy as it moved away from the extremes of state socialism, Germany's reconciliation with its former enemies seemed to provide the logical piece in the puzzle of how to construct a new European
order. With growing indications of American disengagement in the post-
Cold War era and with ominous signs from Moscow that Gorbachev's
reforms would not succeed in the absence of significant Western aid,
what power, if not Germany, was better suited to play the leading role
in facilitating the Soviet transition?

Strains in the New German-Soviet Balance

Even in the best of times, it would have been difficult to sustain such
a multi-layered accommodation between the FRG and the Soviet Union.
But in the period from the signing of the comprehensive treaty on
November 9, 1990 up to the staging of the August 19, 1991 coup
against Gorbachev, which coincided with a sudden loss of momentum
in the latter's reform course, the German *Ostpolitik* was bound to be
subject to especially acute trials. Given how much Bonn had gained
since Zhelezdnovodsk, one could not overlook the fact that the FRG
had a great deal to lose from any marked deterioration of conditions
within the Soviet Union.

It would be unfair to accuse the German government of being oblivious to the tenuous foundations on which any of its understandings
with Moscow were based. In winter and spring 1990–91, the German
press was full of stories about the extent to which the hopeful developments in the East were being jeopardised both by the behind-the-
scenes manoeuvring of conservative opponents to the reforms and
even by the ambivalent behaviour of some of the reforms' architects,
Gorbachev included. The Soviet regime's economic experiments were
slowing down as a result of rising shortages in basic goods and the
opposition of entrenched bureaucratic forces to further incursions upon
their power. More and more frequently, the government was choosing to involve itself in the affairs of its recently liberalised media.
The KGB had been granted greater powers to expose so-called economic crimes against the state. Most disconcerting, the General Secretary himself seemed tacitly to go along with military measures –
notably, those taken in January 1991 against protestors in Lithuania
and Latvia – to restore Moscow's waning authority over its dissident
republics and nationalities.

Nevertheless, while most German politicians were vocal in criticising the Soviet government for its more egregious violations of inter-

national law and human rights, it is provocative that there were a number of issues on which they were evidently just as swayed by their concern to maintain the new-found modus vivendi with Moscow. For example, authorities in Bonn were unquestionably irritated by the Soviet army's surprise decision in March 1991 to transport ex-GDR leader, Erich Honecker, to Moscow to spare their former ally the embarrassment of criminal prosecution in the Federal Republic. Similarly, they were also exasperated when the Soviet defence minister, Dimitri Yasov, made an unannounced tour of several of the new *Länder* in Eastern Germany only days before the USSR's ratification of the treaty ending four-power occupation of Germany.[6] Yet, aside from lodging a formal protest in the first instance and demanding an apology (which they later received) in the second, the FRG's representatives were still noticeably restrained in all of these critiques. Above all, Bonn was intent upon preserving Moscow's goodwill on the issue of continued progress in the withdrawal of Soviet forces from German soil. While the Kremlin had agreed in principle to pull out its troops by the end of 1994, there was little to guarantee that it would schedule the withdrawal at quite the pace, or even the cost, which the Federal Republic desired.

An even more troublesome problem for the FRG was presented by the need to devise a coherent policy on the many unanticipated expressions of discontent in the USSR that had been precipitated by the Gorbachev reforms. Of special note were the increasingly strident demands being made by national independence movements, such as those in the Baltic states. On the face of it, Bonn's approach to such challenges to Moscow's imperial rule might have seemed unequivocal. Just as the German people had been able to exercise its right to self-determination in reunifying the German nation in 1990, so too by this standard was the FRG obliged to support other nationalities in their efforts to gain a like degree of control over their destiny. In fact, this reasoning later played a major part in Bonn's successful campaign in autumn 1991 to convince fellow members of the European community to recognise the breakaway Yugoslav republics of Croatia and Slovenia.

Nevertheless, in dealing with the Soviet case, the FRG's leaders could not help being sensitive to the unpredictable implications of such stands when they were applied to the USSR's future. By itself, the dissolution of Yugoslavia was complicating matters enough for German images of stability in Europe. The prospect, however, that the Soviet Union might not survive the tumult of the collapse of communism was threatening in a much deeper sense. For, only a unified USSR, or so it seemed at the time, would be in the position to maintain the elaborate web of understandings that had been reached with Moscow in the preceding years.

Accordingly, it was suggestive that the Kohl government sought in late 1990 and 1991 – arguably, even more than its Western allies – to maintain a healthy distance from the majority of those popular movements calling for immediate steps to abandon the Soviet federal state. To be sure, in private discussions with dissident personalities, such as Lithuanian president, Vytautis Landsbergis, German officials assured their interlocutors of the Federal Republic's sympathy for the principle of self-determination. Nevertheless, they also urged their discussion partners to exercise the utmost caution in making demands of Moscow, if only to allow Gorbachev the leeway he needed to defend his reformist course. Were these signals not explicit enough, however, Bonn also strictly refused to take any action (e.g. formal recognition of the Baltic independence movements) that might have been construed as conceding the sovereignty and independence of the dissident republics.

By far the most suggestive indicator of the FRG's vested interest in the Soviet status quo, however, was the Kohl government's apparent unwillingness in 1991 even to conceive of a regime in Moscow that was not led by Mikhail Gorbachev. In a notable departure from the days when Kohl and the Soviet general secretary were trading insults, the German chancellor was practically transformed into one of Gorbachev's most forceful advocates in the West, outdone only by the enthusiasms of his rival, Foreign Minister Hans-Dietrich Genscher. No doubt, Gorbachev was not always the easiest of partners, as Kohl and his advisers discovered in the winter and early spring of 1991 when the Soviet leader temporarily seemed to throw in his fortunes with Kremlin conservatives. Yet, there was still a broad consensus within Kohl's administration that Gorbachev was deserving of every benefit of the doubt, given his role in Germany's reunification. For this reason, when the Supreme Soviet finally ratified the treaties restoring full German sovereignty in early March 1991, the general secretary's defenders felt justified in appealing for further patience and understanding in the Western world's assessment of the USSR.

It is telling that, from around the December 1990 meeting of the European Community in Rome, Bonn's support for Moscow had taken on an especially strong economic dimension. Kohl was outspoken in seeking to assure that progress toward the Community's integration did not come at the expense of the Soviet Union's reconstruction.

Predictably, he found himself at times at odds with his more sceptical British and French colleagues about how exactly Moscow was to fit into European priorities. But in the summer of 1991 in particular, Kohl made his greatest bid to aid Gorbachev, if not also to prevent his country from being saddled exclusively with the expense of financing the Soviet transition.

First, he openly campaigned among his country's Western allies to extend an invitation to the Soviet leader to take part in the upcoming world economic summit of G-7 nations in London on July 17. Then, he met with Gorbachev privately in Kiev just before the gathering in order to coordinate policy.[7] True, the Soviet general secretary was not able to obtain the 'grand economic bargain' from the West that he sought on this occasion. Nonetheless, in part thanks to Gorbachev's own salesmanship, the Kohl government was at least able to rest content when an understanding was reached among the major lending nations – many of which had previously expressed doubts about the Soviet Union's future – that some sort of concerted action should be taken to rescue the USSR, provided that its government was willing and able to implement necessary structural changes in the management of its economy. Then, too, the Soviet leader's credibility was aided by his simultaneous agreement with U.S. president, George Bush, finally to wrap up long-standing negotiations over a Strategic Arms Reduction Treaty (START), significantly reducing the number of long-range nuclear missiles held by the superpowers.

For these reasons, no matter how dire the Soviet situation may have seemed at summer's end 1991, German officials could with good reason imagine that they had preserved the best of all possible worlds. Was it not sensible to conclude that conditions in the East would continue to be manageable so long as Gorbachev remained in control in Moscow?

The Soviet Union Collapses

The German government's worst fears were confirmed on August 19, 1991 when a quasi-military council calling itself the State Committee for the State of Emergency unexpectedly emerged from among Gorbachev's own circle of appointees and summarily relieved the Soviet leader of his duties as the country's president. Bonn's reaction to the coup, however, testified to the extent to which the FRG had become wedded to the stability and predictability of the old world symbolised by Gorbachev's reign. Even more than their American or West

European allies, German officials demonstrated that, having gained so much over the previous year, they were profoundly ambivalent about making the leap into the uncertain realm of a post-Gorbachev era.

As one might have anticipated, the FRG's leaders were effusive in their praise for the fallen Soviet president, especially for his role in ushering Moscow's relations with Bonn to a new level of understanding (Helmut Kohl after the coup: 'We would never have obtained German unity now').[8] Nevertheless, everyone from Foreign Minister Genscher to Social Democratic leader, Hans-Jochen Vogel, to Kohl himself was conspicuously disinclined to take any steps that might have amounted to severing links with the new Soviet leadership. Without wanting to admit their calculations, it was almost as if they hoped that a workable understanding could somehow be reached about preserving the essentials of the recently-won German-Soviet understanding.

In this sense, it had to have been good news from Bonn's perspective that the Federal Republic did not long have to deal with Gorbachev's challengers. Almost as soon as they made their move, the plotters of the coup began to lose ground. It was only a matter of days before Gorbachev found himself, formally at least, back in power. The bad news, however, was that in the process, the coup decisively undermined those understandings that had been attained in the period after Zhelezdnovodsk. What had begun as a preemptive strike against the symbol of Soviet reform destroyed the ruling mystique of the very imperial power – the USSR – in whose name the new relationship with Bonn had been negotiated.

Recognising this single fact is more crucial than any other issue for appreciating the dilemmas the FRG will face in dealing with the post-Soviet Union in the 1990s. For in every respect in which Bonn was able to make ground in its interactions with Moscow since 1990 – in the balancing of German and Soviet security interests, in the attention to human rights questions, and in the balancing of Germany's *Ostpolitik* with the expectations of its Western allies – the Federal Republic will be hard pressed to restore the sense of harmony achieved during the period when Gorbachev was firmly in control. This is not just because of the inconvenience of losing Gorbachev himself but also because his passing coincided with the more fundamental loss in the fall of 1991 of the Soviet state itself.

Consider the most self-evident respect in which the collapse of the USSR will frustrate German policymakers, that is, by depriving them of their ability to make simple calculations about their future security interests. When the so-called Commonwealth of Independent States

(CIS) was hammered together out of a majority of the former republics of the Soviet Union on December 8, 1991, the FRG's leaders might have feigned a sigh of relief, like all of the other members of the Western alliance, that a means had been found to reunite the diverse interests that had previously comprised the USSR. Once again, there was an indisputable appeal to contending with a single negotiating partner, which would have the capability to strike deals on such sensitive international concerns as nuclear-arms proliferation and environmental protection and then of following through on these agreements. Yet, not far below the surface of diplomatic protocol, German officials could hardly disguise their deep fears that the CIS would eventually dissolve, almost as quickly as it had been formed. When that happened, they worried, Bonn would be sucked into the quagmire of national, ethnic, and economic conflicts – 'the waterfall of events [*Katarakt von Ereignissen*]', to use Helmut Schmidt's apt terminology[9] – that had been precipitated by the demise of communism.

This is not to say that, for the coming years, the Federal Republic will be unable to find sovereign states with which it can conduct serious negotiations in the place of the old USSR. There can be no doubt that the overriding focus of German diplomacy, just as in times past, will remain on Moscow. German policymakers quickly demonstrated this fact in the autumn of 1991 when they turned their energies with noteworthy agility away from the shaken Gorbachev to the hero of the anti-coup forces, Russian President Boris Yeltsin. Rather, in two distinct respects, Bonn's main torment will be in having, not too few, but instead too many quarreling contenders for its attention.

The first side of the problem has to do with the contradiction between the FRG's pro forma acceptance of the general principle of self-determination and the reality of only being able to conduct foreign relations with a limited number of states. In some ways, the failed August coup may have helped to clarify Bonn's options. Immediately after the event, for example, the Kohl government found itself in the agreeable position of being able to make up for its earlier reluctance to recognise the Baltic republics of Lithuania, Latvia, and Estonia by following Yeltsin's lead and quickly announcing the exchange of diplomatic ties with each of the newly-independent states. A high-level delegation including Bundestag President Rita Süssmuth and Hans-Dietrich Genscher was quickly dispatched to the region to assure the Baltic republics of the Federal Republic's desire to integrate them as fast as possible into the international community.[10]

Nonetheless, Bonn's future application of the ideal of self-determination to other nationalities and ethnic groupings is sure to be vastly more difficult than any of these early cases would indicate, if only because the sovereignty of the larger republics (above all, Russia) is so much at issue. What, one wonders, is the Federal government to do in response to such challenges to Russian hegemony as those represented by troublesome, but geopolitically less significant, dissident republics like Chechenya and Ingushetia, or Tataria and Dargestan? Most likely, Bonn's only recourse will be to call for the peaceful resolution of each of these conflicts – not to mention, of a hundred other potential disputes – and then hope that its counterparts in Moscow will have both the resources and good sense necessary to abide by international standards in addressing their minorities' grievances. Yet, even here, it is hard to imagine that the Federal Republic would turn to political or economic sanctions should Russia resort to less than peaceful measures to resolve such ethnic assaults upon its authority.

In addition, the related challenge for the FRG in the wake of the break-up of the USSR will be in the difficult choices it may have to make between maintaining good relations with the Russian Republic and retaining the favour of the other larger republics in the CIS. A case in point involves the growing tensions between Moscow and the Ukrainian government over the future of the Crimean peninsula, following the Crimean parliament's decision of May 1992 to secede from the Ukraine and the latter's announced determination to hold on to that strategic piece of territory that was granted to it by Nikita Khrushchev in 1954. Given Ukrainian President Leonid M. Kravchuk's warnings that his regime will not tolerate the loss of the Crimea and the equally great pressures on Boris Yeltsin to regain the peninsula – on May 21, 1992, the Russian president unilaterally declared the 1954 decision null and void – it seems almost certain that this particular dispute will not be resolved without some sort of conflict between the two republics. Should this come to pass, German authorities will undoubtedly be hard pressed to maintain a stance of disinterested neutrality on the issue.

Of even greater concern for the FRG, however, has to be how such conflicts might then spill over to more sensitive issues touching directly on German security. When in the late spring of 1992, Ukraine and the two other new members of the nuclear club, Belarus and Kazakhstan, agreed to a formula for participating in the Strategic Arms Reduction Treaty, supplementing agreements they had already reached for turning over their tactical nuclear weapons to CIS control in Moscow,

German officials could feel relieved that a mechanism had been created for holding in check the proliferation of nuclear forces less than a thousand miles from their eastern border. Yet, if there were to be a sustained altercation between Kiev and Moscow, who is to say whether the Federal Republic will have any options at all should the Ukrainian government decide to slow the timetable for its denuclearisation? Worse still, how might Bonn react should Ukraine decide to become a full-scale nuclear power in its own right?

A second arena in which Bonn is likely to find dealing with the post-Soviet Union considerably more complex than in the 1990–1 period is in the higher expectations that many Germans have acquired for domestic change in the post-communist era. Marxism–Leninism may no longer be in power in the East, but the transition to democracy and the free market is far from complete in the new republics. It is also replete with all of the paradoxical consequences of any major shift to a new set of institutions and norms. In the battle against die-hard opponents to liberal values and marketisation, even well-meaning democrats may be driven to press for short-term emergency measures – enhanced powers for the executive, tighter controls over the free press, economic austerity policies – that could jeopardise the very reforms which they espouse. In many instances, the FRG's leaders will be in much the same position as any other Western leaders as they seek to evaluate the policies of the Yeltsins or Kravchuks of the post-Soviet future. They will face the unpleasant task of having to weigh the risks of any deviation from the democratic path against the potential benefits of an eventual consolidation of post-communist authority.[11]

The FRG will confront a special challenge, however, in the question of what is to become of the millions of ethnic Germans dispersed throughout the new republics. This delicate issue seemed to be resolved to Bonn's liking with the signing of the November 1990 comprehensive treaty. Whereas at that time, however, one might have been able to settle remaining problems faced by ethnic German populations by encouraging them to emigrate to the West, this exit option may no longer be available in the 1990s. If current trends continue, average German citizens will probably be more and more concerned about, what they perceive to be, the spectre of tens of millions of refugees, Germans and non-Germans alike, descending upon their soil and adding further strains to their already overburdened social services. As a result, the Federal Republic may increasingly have no other resort than to pressure Russia and the other post-Soviet republics to make their peace with such dissident nationalities at home. The risk is that it will then open itself, much as in the period before 1990, to charges of unfairly interfering in these states' internal affairs.

Nowhere has this temptation been better illustrated than in the FRG's rather heavy-handed manipulation of a proposal in autumn 1991 by the Russian government to recreate an autonomous Volga German Republic in the area of Engels and Saratov. When the Yeltsin regime seemed to vacillate about the size and location of the new territory, German authorities made scarcely-veiled threats to withdraw promises of millions of Deutsche Marks in foreign aid should Moscow not comply with their wishes, and representatives of the Volga Germans were quick to increase their own demands of Russia.[12]

Still, even the successful creation of a Volga republic alone will hardly solve the problem of how Germany is to deal with its other extensive ethnic links to the former USSR. There are hundreds of thousands of other ethnic Germans spread throughout the region, from Ukraine to the northern Caucasus and the central Asian republics. On top of these tensions, there are undoubtedly other nascent conflicts still in the making, such as what is to become of lost German territories like the area surrounding Kaliningrad (Königsberg).[13] Even if future German governments might privately consider these issues best left dormant, one cannot be certain whether they will remain immune to domestic political pressures, from the grandchildren of post-war expellees to nationalist parties like the *Republikaner* and neo-Nazi groups, to assign them renewed vitality.

A final area in which the FRG's policy toward the East is likely to be more complicated is in the unpredictable ramifications of Bonn's stands on the region for its relations with its Western allies. If the period 1990–1 was characterised by a significant degree of unanimity on the Federal Republic's relations with the Soviet Union of Mikhail Gorbachev, the period after 1991 is certain to be more difficult to master because of the sheer number of new points of conflict caused by the USSR's fragmentation. Even in the earlier period, as evidence accumulated of the extent of the Soviet Union's economic and political problems, there were already slight hints of differences within the Atlantic alliance. Some states – generally those, such as Germany, that were closest to the USSR and bound to be most directly affected by its fate – favoured the immediate infusion of large-scale credits to stave off the imminent crisis, while others in contrast called for a policy of caution and restraint. For this reason, it was predictable that bad feelings would arise among the former group when their worst fears were realised with the Soviet Union's fall. Kohl and Genscher let it be known that the other Western powers had given much too little, much too late. Furthermore, they never tired of reminding their allies – as Kohl did in May 1992 in an explicit criticism of Japanese indifference toward the CIS[14] – that Germany alone could not be expected to spearhead the solution to the post-USSR's problems, particularly at a time when its own economy was being sorely tested by the financial costs of national reunification.[15]

What remains to be seen, however, is whether the Federal Republic's differences with its allies will be confined merely to occasional fits of pique and ill temper or manage to spill over into more sensitive questions involving the structure of Bonn's alliance commitments. The deepening conflict between Armenia and Azerbaijan over the territory of Nagorno–Karabakh is a good case in point. Although the FRG would ideally like to maintain a neutral posture in the dispute – despite manifest public sympathies for Armenia – it may one day face the uncomfortable prospect, like many of its allies, of having to choose sides. This would be an especially unpleasant choice, since it would not only be a matter of deciding between the two warring neighbours but also, by implication, amount to a choice between Baku's and Yerevan's respective allies, Russia and fellow NATO-member Turkey. Should Bonn even hint at a leaning toward Russia and Armenian, it could not help but damage its relations with Ankara, which have still not recovered from the Federal Republic's tepid support for its ally during the Gulf War of 1991. Although less likely, an even more disturbing scenario would be one in which age-old Turkish-Armenian hostilities resurfaced in the form of an outright conflict on the two states' border. Such an eventuality would necessarily lead to a serious exacerbation of tensions between the FRG and the Turkish government.

In these respects, the most striking discovery about the Cold War period may turn out to be how much the Western members of NATO depended upon the Soviet Union for their cohesion. In an era in which the North Atlantic alliance is no longer conveniently oriented toward combating a well-defined threat, all of these states' differences, some subtle and insignificant, others more deeply ingrained as a result of centuries of distrust, may resurface to generate new fissures among old allies.

EXPECTATIONS OF GERMANY

The majority of the aforementioned challenges to German foreign policy have in common the fact that they have originated outside of the Federal Republic and are driven primarily by the collapse of the Soviet Union. Would it not be wise, therefore, for the FRG's future leaders to seek to minimise the drawbacks of their involvement in the region by prudently toning down the level of German engagement and waiting for other states to make their own commitments? Given both the risks that are sure to confront any power seeking to make sense of the USSR's successor republics and the special, if irrational, apprehensions that are likely to attend an activist German presence in the East, a principled avoidance of 'foreign entanglements' might be the only sensible prescription for Bonn in the 1990s.

In fact, there is every reason to think that a policy of modest involvement would be readily welcomed by a broad spectrum of political interests in Bonn, ranging from the Social Democrats and the Free Democrats to the Greens. Nevertheless, the Federal Republic's unique dilemma may be that, like it or not, the Soviet Union's fall and Germany's reunification seem to have come at a time when international leadership is lacking. Many German leaders feel that they have no choice but to play a major role in shepherding the East out of its post-communist crisis. Certainly, this was Helmut Kohl's motivation in a major visit to Moscow in mid-December 1992 when he offered over $11 billion in debt relief as a means of propping up the shaky Yeltsin government. More provocative, though, is the fact that most of the states surrounding the FRG, allies and former enemies alike, seem to expect that Bonn will play a key part, if not *the* leading part, in reshaping the political and economic order of a region no longer governed by the brutal simplicity of Marxism–Leninism. Again, despite their own apprehensions of the FRG's economic and political might, many of the country's neighbours are tempted to ask: who, if not Germany?

Thanks to these expectations, one may justifiably wonder whether future German policy-makers will find themselves in something of a no-win position should conditions in the post-Soviet Union continue to worsen. More often than they want, they may become involved in problems from which they would instinctively prefer to keep their distance. But at the same time, paradoxically, they may also have to bear the brunt of international criticism when their efforts to carve out a semblance of order from the chaos that has descended upon the East proceed less smoothly than they or any of their neighbours desire.

Notes

1. See Kohl's press conference of July 17, 1990, in Karl Kaiser, ed., *Deutschlands Vereinigung: Die internationalen Aspekte* (Bergisch–Gladbach: Gustav Lübbe, 1991), p. 246.
2. For a provocative characterisation of this shift, see Gustav Schmidt, 'Happy Moments: Solving the Special German-Soviet Russian Conflict', *Cornell International Law Journal*, vol. 24, (Symposium 1991), no. 3, pp. 437–55.
3. For a compelling argument about why the Rapallo metaphor might not be appropriate for modern-day relations between Germany and Russia, let alone for the 1920s, see George F. Kennan, *Russia and the West under Lenin and Stalin* (Boston: Little, Brown, 1961), chapter 15.
4. See Helmut Kohl's statement of July 16, 1990, following his meeting with Gorbachev, in Renata Fritsch-Bournazel, *Europe and German Reunification* (New York: Berg, 1992), pp. 86–7.
5. See 'Treaty on good-neighborliness, partnership, and cooperation between the FRG and the USSR', November 9, 1990, in ibid., pp. 139–40.
6. Hans Jörg Sottorf, 'Genscher goes in for some Soviet stock-taking', *Handelsblatt*, March 20, 1991, in *The German Tribune*, March 31, 1991, pp. 1–2.
7. Dieter Buhl, 'Die sieben sind keine Samariter', *Die Zeit*, July 19, 1991, p. 1, and Nina Grunenberg, 'Tuchfühlung vor dem Auftritt', ibid., p. 4.
8. Cited from Frank Rafalski, 'Kohl, a close link temporarily severed', *Frankfurter Allgemeine Zeitung*, August 20, 1991, in *The German Tribune*, September 1 1991, p. 3.
9. Helmut Schmidt, 'Deutschlands Rolle im neuen Europa', *Europa Archiv*, 21 (1991), p. 614. On a similar note, see Wolfgang Wagner, 'Acht Lehren aus dem Fall Jugoslawien', *Europa Archiv*, 2 (1992), pp. 31–41.
10. Reinhard Stuth, 'Germany's new role in a changing Europe', *Aussenpolitik*, v. 43 (1992), no. 1, pp. 28–9.
11. For a hint of German uneasiness about this choice, see Helmut Schmidt's reflections on Boris Yeltsin's '*Machtinstinkt*', in Schmidt, op cit., p. 615.
12. *New York Times*, January 11, 1992, p. 4. On the Volga Germans, see Anthony Hyman, 'Refugees and citizens: the case of the Volga Germans', *The World Today*, (March 1992), pp. 41–3.
13. For an unusual suggestion about handling the Königsberg issue before it becomes a source of friction, see Marion Gräfin Dönhoff's proposal about the formation of an international condominium to develop the region that would include Russia, Poland, Lithuania, and Germany, 'Königsberg – Signal der Versöhnung?', *Die Zeit*, November 22, 1991, p. 1.
14. *New York Times*, May 6, 1992, p. 1.
15. In spring 1992, the FRG launched a public relations campaign to underscore the extent of its financial commitments to the former Soviet Union – calculated at $52.2 billion since the end of 1989 – and by implication to pressure the allies into raising the level of their own contributions. See 'German Support for the Transition to Democracy and Market Economy in the Former Soviet Union', *Focus on . . .* (New York: German Infor-

mation Center, June 1992). Typically, Germany's allies defended themselves from such criticisms by arguing that a substantial part of the FRG's contributions to the CIS had nothing to do with largess but were instead, directly or indirectly, tied to the specific problem of the withdrawal of Soviet troops from the ex-GDR.

Part VI

Conclusion

23 Are the Old Nazis Coming Back?

Peter H. Merkl

> All young males of any class or country, race or politics, want to prove themselves when their bodies become manly in adolescence. School and public sports programs . . . channel and tame what is essentially the killer instinct, the will to survive, so that the young men can then reach adulthood and meet its responsibilities. (Floyd Salas in a review of, *Always Running: La Vida Loca: Gang Days in L.A. – A Memoir. Los Angeles Times Book Review*, March 7, 1993, p. 2.)

One of the first mild Saturday afternoons in 1991, I was walking in a throng of people between the Europa Centre and the Berlin Memorial Church, and there he was, sprawled lazily over the stone steps of the great fountain, his Doc Martens splayed out provocatively. A charcoal jersey top over his battle fatigue pants, his head shaven closely except for a mini-mohawk with a splash of colour, my first East German skinhead. He might have been about 20 years old, wore no insignia of any kind, and weighed at least 250 pounds. No sign of physical exercise on this malevolent mountain of flesh except, perhaps, from the ritual lifting of glasses of beer. There were several more of his tribe about, young men of more normal dimensions, some wearing their bomber jackets, but also without political signs I could identify. He peered out from under half-closed lids, expressionless but evidently expecting admiring glances from the passing crowd, or perhaps inebriated or hung over, like a night creature lost in the glare of a bright morning.

So this is what I have been reading about in the papers, I thought, the terror of rundown urban neighbourhoods and of Vietnamese, Mozambicans, Cubans invited by the old regime, and refugee gypsies. I tried to imagine the loutish colossus in a brown stormtrooper or black SS uniform. The patent absurdity of the image broke up my composure and I ducked down behind the other passers-by so he would not think I was laughing at him. Upon later reflection, I castigated myself for jumping to conclusions. The German skinhead and youth gang scene is so varied and constantly changing that these objects of my instant revulsion could even have been Redskins (left-wing skins) or Sharpskins (anti-racist skins), the enemies of the better-known anti-foreigner skinheads. They could have been quite apolitical as many of them are.

In this essay, I shall examine critically the widespread assertions that the recent wave of skinhead and neo-Nazi attacks on foreigners and asylum-seekers denotes a German relapse into Nazism. And, to leave no doubt about my line of argument against prevailing interpretations, its main tenets will be summarised here: to liken the present trouble to the old, pre-1933 Nazi movement, for a start, is preposterous (see below). The rise and growth of the original movement took place under very different circumstances, motivations, and in a totally different form.[1] Today's hostility to foreigners and refugees which drives most of the violent acts was neither the main concern nor even a political programme point for the old Nazis – xenophobic though they were. They were a very political movement bent on capturing power to renew the war effort. The current interpretation of skinhead and neo-Nazi incidents, my second point, vastly exaggerates the political character of what we are seeing before us. To be sure, there are neo-Nazi splinter parties who would love to put the violent young skinheads and soccer hooligans in the service of their political movements. But neither are the two identical nor have the neo-Nazi parties been very successful in recruiting or controlling the young toughs. My third point is that the root problems of the violence in Germany lie in the decades-long rise of violent youth, especially of the youth gangs at the edge of big cities and in smalltown and rural areas. They belong, unlike the old Nazis, to the 'bottom third', the undereducated and underemployed underclass of Germany's 'two-thirds society'. Much like the youthful gang violence in our cities, these alienated young Germans reflect disintegrating and often violent families, the pains of immigration, violent and inadequate schools, and curtailed youth facilities and services in an era of conservative austerity, at least for them. Why are they so violent and why do they adopt some of the old Nazi symbols and salutations? Much like the gang violence in our cities, German gang members are acting out violently their despair and hostility at the society and government that deny them a future such as that of the upper two-thirds. Nazi salutes and slogans, moreover, are a surefire way to provoke and embarrass the adult establishment. The fall of communism in Eastern Europe, by letting loose an avalanche of refugees seeking asylum in Germany, has brought masses of visible foreigners to makeshift housing all over Germany, (see William Chandler, above), upsetting many people, and focusing the skinhead wrath upon rather popular victims. The manifold troubles of post-communist East Germany, more-over, have by now spread, along with the violence, a deep malaise over both East and West Germany which further focuses popular dis-satisfaction on the government and the major parties, rather than en-couraging positive and problem-solving attitudes in the populace.

PUBLIC REACTIONS TO RIGHT WING VIOLENCE

The events of the two years following this encounter of early 1991 have focused a great deal of public and media attention in this country (the U.S.) and elsewhere, but particularly in Germany, on the neo-Nazi and skinhead attacks on asylum-seekers' hostels and visible foreigners, both in small groups and as individuals, particularly in Eastern Germany. The massive influx of nearly half a million asylum-seekers in 1992 seems to have spread public apprehension and skinhead at-tacks to all of Germany (see William Chandler, above). A simultaneous rise in popular dissatisfaction with the Kohl government[2] and an in-crease in right wing party votes led to a plethora of quick conclusions about the political significance of these right wing incidents, both by well-meaning Germans and by foreign observers. Quite typical of German *bien-pensant* opinion – if historically in error – was a schoolgirl in Moelln who was quoted by a New York Times correspondent:[3] 'This is exactly the way things began the last time, in Hitler's time. First you hear speeches full of hate, then come the firebombs, and then suddenly it's out of control'. Some observers may also wonder at the awesome power with which rather small numbers of aggressive juve-niles have been able to launch hundreds of thousands of thoughtful Germans on anti-racist mass demonstrations and 'chains of lights', or how the words 'Heil Hitler' at the end of the telephone call 'claiming' the triple murder at Moelln caused public opinion inside and outside Germany to 'go ballistic' in jumping to conclusions.[4]

American opinion was difficult to pin down in that most relevant editorials and columns tended only to hint at such interpretations and conspiracies rather than to spell out their darkest suspicions. In the *Washington Post*, for example, Richard Cohen described his encoun-ters in depressed Cottbus with the neo-Nazi German Alternative (mean-while suppressed by the government) and its threatening attitudes towards a group of journalists. Their being driven away with physical threats[5] 'could happen anywhere. Germany, though, is different and that differ-ence is why the world is watching events here. In the Nazi era, the same sort of goons ruled the country. It took little imagination to see [German Alternative leader Frank] Huebner's men in police uniform. It took only memory: theirs and ours.' The writer obviously did not mean the personal memories of these young skinheads of 'quasi-punk' looks. In a column in the *Los Angeles Times*, Jeffrey Gedmin suggested that Germany must stop blaming various 'myths' for rightwing terrorism, beginning with attributing it primarily to Eastern Germany and to the wave of asylum-seekers of 1991/1992. 'Germany's leaders [though] frustrated, disgusted and remorseful . . . will never muster the political will to smash a dangerous movement if they don't explode [these] myths about the roots of the violence . . .', Gedmin wrote[6] without further details about this 'dangerous movement'. Other exhortatory *Times* editorials on the matter bore titles such as 'That Evil That Lies Within' and 'Look the Other Way No Longer' but could cite no more evidence than that the official counts of rightwing extremists and skinheads in Germany 'imply an inherent degree of organisation'.[7] 'Once Again German Nazis Are Murdering "Subhumans"' was the *Boston Globe* formula for the outrage at Moelln. The former *New York Times* editor and columnist A.M. Rosenthal, of course, has always insisted that there was no perceptible difference between neo-Nazis and the old Nazis and that both Germans and their victims were well aware of this: Nazis are Nazis and always will be.[8]

There were large demonstrations at German embassies in Athens, Tel Aviv, and, of course, in Turkey, and remonstrations at Goethe institutes and tourist agencies in many countries. The press in Poland, Italy, and in other neighbouring countries that had been under the jackboot of the Third Reich in the war, conjured up the German demons of the first half of the century and of the holocaust. In France, the press reaction from left to right was rather more differentiated with notable emphasis on the immigration angle of which the French themselves are only too aware – Jean Marie Le Pen's *Front National* has outpolled the sum of all German right radical parties by a factor of two to one on the national level throughout the eighties and early nineties.[9] Seventy per cent of French adult opinion also hoped that the concentrated onslaught of asylum-seekers on Germany might drive the Germans more towards support for 'deepening' European integration, since the lifting of internal EC border controls made this a problem that could obviously be tackled only at the EC level. The British media, while reporting the gruesome events in Germany, were also notably restrained. The *Financial Times* of London, for example, reminded its readers of the 7780 racial hate crimes reported for 1991 in England and Wales –

such references to American hate crimes were almost completely absent in the American media coverage – and *The Economist* printed a story about the British variety of racist skinheads and called 'talk of revival of Nazism . . . misleading'.[10]

We do of course have hate crimes in the United States and, while definitions may vary and national totals are missing,[11] at least some states and cities have been keeping track. New Jersey, for example, reports over a thousand hate crimes a year, mostly directed at Jews, blacks, Muslims, and Asians. Los Angeles County recorded rising levels of hate crimes in 1991, with 672 incidents and gay men, blacks, and Jews the prime victims (60 per cent of the total). Latinos and Asians, particularly recent immigrants and Koreans, bear out the rising tide of anti-immigrant violence in the United States. For 1992, the National Gay and Lesbian Task Force reported 1001 anti-gay acts of violence in five cities alone and the Anti-Defamation League counted 1730 anti-semitic acts, including 758 of harassment, assault, and threats (one assassination: Meir Kahane) and 927 acts of vandalism, including arson, bombings, cemetery desecrations etc. The French Ministry of the Interior recorded 722 'racist incidents' in 1990, a total larger than what was reported in the eleven previous years and there are probably similar statistics for much of Europe. Regarding the rising flood of youthful hate crimes in Germany, however, there is still the consensus that Germany is 'different'. The impression is hard to avoid that there is abroad in the world today, including in Germany, a new black legend haunting the young Germans of today and in the foreseeable future, the black legend of the murderous demons of the German past which are lurking underneath democratic appearances and are capable of a return to the horrors of Auschwitz and World War Two at the drop of a few symbolically pregnant words.[12]

WEST AND EAST GERMAN ANTECEDENTS

Before we examine the hard evidence of what has been going on since German unification, we need to remind ourselves of some of the basic circumstances and structures of which journalists and the general public are only dimly aware if at all. First of all, there is a history of postwar neo-Nazism in West Germany which took the form of both neo-Nazi parties and of random prejudicial actions and occurred in three waves. The first wave came in the early fifties, right after the birth of the FRG and after Allied occupation restraints had been removed from neo-Nazi (and old Nazi) mobilisation. An insecure Bonn government put an end to this challenge to its new democracy with the help of an array of legal and judicial measures which, among other actions, suppressed the Socialist Reich party (SRP) that had just garnered 11 per cent of the vote in the *Land* election in Lower Saxony.[13] A second wave came with the National Democratic party (NDP) of the mid-sixties, following the first serious economic downturn and the broad mobilisation of left wing forces – especially against the emergency laws of 1968 – and the student rebellion of those years. Neither one of these waves gained entry into the *Bundestag* for the radical right, in part because of their chronic fragmentation: too many chiefs, or would-be *Führers*, and not enough Indians. The NPD wave already included far more neo- than old Nazi elements (for generational reasons) and there were efforts to establish a more moderate, national-conservative image. All the while, authorities were also well aware of concomitant waves of right wing hate crimes ranging from smearing swastikas and slogans on walls to vandalising Jewish cemeteries and physical attacks on whoever seemed to offend rightwing individuals. Those committing the hate crimes probably included in unknown proportions neo–Nazi members and voters, but also many unruly juveniles and local drunks.

The third wave of radical right organisation – the old splinter groups, such as the NPD, continued to compete in elections but without much success – began in the mid-eighties with the Republicans (REPs) whose name emulated the American Republicans under Ronald Reagan.[14] The REP wave culminated in a number of local and *Land* triumphs just before the year of German unification, especially with the help of right wing defectors from the Bavarian CSU, and seemed to subside in the wake of the greater spectacle of unification. Once again, there was the concomitant wave of individual hate crimes, but the REPs also found it impossible to take over their competitors on the radical right, such as the NPD, the German People's Union (DVU), and a gaggle of new, militant groups such as the Free Workers party (FAP) or the Kühnen group, German Alternatives.[15] In March 1993, the REP did well in the Hessian local elections but it is not clear whether they can maintain this momentum.

The collapse of GDR communism naturally attracted West German neo-Nazi organisers and, at first, the last East German government did not permit them to come in. There were several reasons about East Germany in 1990 that promised a fertile environment for right wing extremism – in fact, the communists themselves had warned the West that there would be a resurgence of Nazism if the GDR regime was ousted. Certain legacies of communist dictatorship were one reason, especially continued authoritarian attitudes and the long years of enforced isolation from the outside world.

Why in Formerly Communist Germany?

There was a lot of official hypocrisy about anti-fascism and 'friendship among peoples' while, underneath, the crudest prejudices were tolerated against Poles, Czechs, Russians, Jews – the GDR supported Palestinian terrorists and did not recognize Israel until 1990 when the Modrow government accept co-responsibility for the holocaust – and especially the small number of visibly foreign trainees and workers from such places as Mozambique and Vietnam. The GDR population knew all along that the 'proletarian internationalism' of the communist regime was a sham and that even police misconduct towards foreigners was not unusual.[16]

A second set of reasons stems from the atmosphere of the transition which opened the floodgates of racist discrimination and violence against Poles and other foreigners – about 160 000 foreign workers had been brought in under Erich Honecker, including 60 000 Vietnamese, 14 000 Mozambicans, and 10 000 Cubans, and many were not in a position to leave the inhospitable land in 1990. There were frequent incidents of people being refused service in stores or being robbed in the street of what they had already purchased. In particular young East Germans were reported to be disoriented by the great change of authority structures and the total 'collapse of [communist] values' in their families and schools.[17] As many as 80 per cent of East German youngsters were said to be possessed by a generalised sense of *angst*, a fear of their future, and a negative self-image of being 'second-class citizens' of the new united Germany. This in turn seemed to trigger in them a virulent search for their German identity, for scapegoats, and a violent hatred of foreigners. The resulting climate of aggressiveness and violence among young East Germans even spread a fear of rape among young women and of brawls and melées among young men attending the few youth clubs that remained open.

Some 15 per cent to 20 per cent of young people in the former GDR were considered open to right wing radicalisation of a violent sort and, of course, organisers of right wing radical groups – both pre-1989 and post-1989 – were hard at work to channel the mobilised youths into their various organisations (our third set of reasons). While the neo-Nazis, of course, would love to organise the violent skinhead gangs and hooligans, the unruly temper of the latter makes lasting success unlikely. Unlike the stormtroopers of old, these alienated youngsters are not about to march or be regimented by anyone and their ostentatious nationalism is only skin-deep. One East German expert on the situation, Norbert Madlock, also pointed out that, in East Germany, the relations between skinhead groups and such parties as the NPD, the *Republikaner* and the DVU were much closer than in West Germany. The East German rightists also were far more militant and frequently mixed their violence with robbery, looting, and extortion. There is plenty of dissonance, in fact, between the pretence of championing law and order and traditional German nationalistic values and pervasive thievery and heavy alcohol abuse that characterises most of the incidents.

According to the head of the State Protection Service of the Common Criminal Police Office (GLKA) of the five new *Länder*, Bernd Wagner, the pre-1990 core of the radical right in the GDR already numbered about 1500 active neo-Nazis – a phenomenon hushed up by the communist regime – who had been active throughout the eighties and in 1987–88, organised élite cadre parties with the names National Alternative, Free Workers Party (FAP), German Alternative, and Nationalist Front some of which still organise assaults on left-wing and anarchist groups including 'alternatives' (and squatters in the abandoned houses typical of the rundown old towns of East German cities), foreigners, gays and sometimes even the police after the fall of the Wall. One step removed from this neo-Nazi hard core were the *Fascho* groups, who had absorbed much of the neo-Nazi ideology but were not yet organisationally integrated, and the skinheads whose antisocial, anarchistic demeanour was at variance with their unevenly distributed, neo-Nazi views – not all skinheads are of right-wing persuasion or likely to remain with its causes. The soccer hooligans, finally, lacked a unifying ideology other than their delight in physical confrontation although they frequently sported neo-Nazi symbols and seemed ready for recruitment.[18] Wagner also mentioned the appearance of new, hitherto unknown small groups of assailants of foreigners and left wing or anarchist groups at the margins of this social movement of the East German radical right. He described their mushrooming membership as composed of mostly fifteen to seventeen year-olds and more often found in small towns between 20 000 to 50 000 inhabitants than in larger places.[19] Wolfgang Brück of the Central Institute for Youth Research of the GDR council of Ministers reported on a pre-1989 study of a sample of 3000 youths between 14 and 25 years of whom 30 per cent expressed some understanding for the skinheads, 4 per cent 'sympa-thised', and 1 per cent 'believed' in them. The GDR police in 1987–9 examined 50 cases of criminal prosecutions of right-wingers of whom over one half were skilled workers and another one fourth apprentices to a craft. Some 82 per cent were between 18 and 25 years old and three fourths came from families of skilled workers (47 per cent) and the university-educated intelligentsia, in other words, from the com-munist social élite even before the fall of the Wall. While some of the pre-1989 neo-Nazis went to West Germany, many came back with new neo-Nazi affiliations, politicised and ready to recruit old friends for the FAP, REPs, or NPD.

In the eighties the rise of the East German right typically occurred in the larger cities and environs where alienated teenagers turned away from official socialism to the apolitical autonomy of the punk scene. Eventually, they were confronted with official anti-fascist propaganda and minor police repression, especially from about 1987 on, after a major Stasi-manipulated confrontation at a rock concert at Zion's Church in East Berlin, when the communist regime began to lash out at those 'seduced by the West'. Up until this misguided campaign, according to some of the young people themselves, their rebellion had been pri-marily for more autonomy and 'space', unfocused and unpolitical, al-though obviously in contempt of the straitjacket dogma of the SED and its youth organisation, the Free German Youth (FDJ). The auton-omous youth culture, moreover, experienced a great deal of differen-tiation into different groups, in addition to the stylish and musical punks: irrational *Grufties*, the first skinheads, and soccer hooligans, and all of them a living provocation to communist conformity which was un-able to dominate the small groups of high-school, apprenticeship, or juvenile home buddies, from which they grew. The harsh communist clampdown, along with the official bagatellisation of their group mem-bership, literally politicised the youngsters, to quote one of them: 'Since they put me in jail [for two years] I developed such an extraordinary hatred for this whole system here, a hatred for everything "red" or left-wing. This hatred really has eaten into me (*hat sich reingefressen*); it is an extremist attitude'.

Stigmatised by all-too-well-meaning communist educators and law enforcement personnel, he evidently decided in his despair to emulate the historical Nazis whom his punitive tormentors probably paraded before him as horrifying examples from the German past.[20] Social workers and parents of troubled teenagers often understand this counterproductive mechanism well whereby the rebellious youngster may pick up precisely the negative 'role model' that his or her parents most warn against. The autonomous information networks of the various small groups seized upon all the taboo subjects of the communist regime with a vengeance worthy of a better cause: foreigners, the history of the war and the Third *Reich*, the division of Germany, and the economic mismanagement and political manipulation of the communist regime. Self-taught, they turned towards crude displacement of their agonies upon scapegoats. Having been punished for taunting the communists with apolitical calls for tearing down the Berlin Wall or for German reunification in 1987–8, moreover, the actual occurrence of these events in 1989–90 must have left them at first in existential limbo. Instead of glorying in the demise of their communist enemies – or physical attacks on them – however, the skinheads, *Faschos*, and neo-Nazis of today seem to concentrate their angry violence on rather defenceless Jewish cemeteries, coloured foreigners, gays, and alternative groups.[21] The high levels of criminality among the young right radicals belie their desperate assertion of moral and cultural superiority over the allegedly dirty and criminal foreigners who are said to be 'not fit to live among Germans'.

There is a fourth set of reasons why the right radical scene in East Germany has tended to go out of control, confused law enforcement agencies. The old People's Police (Vopos), not to mention the State Security Service (Stasi), was so deeply involved with political and human repression by the communist dictatorship that the collapse of the latter left most police and court personnel quite insecure and disoriented. They felt despised and blamed for their presumed role in the repressive atmosphere of the dictatorship and in the confrontations with the popular demonstrations for democracy, in which the radical right often participated. For a while after the fall of the old regime, consequently, police were so disturbed they could not even be depended upon to intervene in street violence or to investigate simple thefts and robberies. East Germans fell into an interlude of anarchy of varying local duration which could still be felt in 1992 by such potential victims of right-wing violence as foreigners, gays, or 'alternatives'. To make matters worse, the police were ill-equipped and understaffed, entire administrative structures were being reorganised, regiments of East German administrators *abgewickelt* (phased out), or ominously asked to reapply for their own jobs, and a trickle of West German civil servants was coming in to take over in the face of East German resentment. This transitional chaos after a startling paucity of communist administrative efforts to cope with either the foreigners' need for advice or the need to supervise the young right radicals meant further anarchy, a situation made for skinheads, hooligans, and West German right-wing recruitment among them. The remaining communist loyalists, moreover, were delighted to witness the discomfiture of the new regime and to see their self-fulfilling prophecy come true: that fascism would return the moment the communist dictatorship collapsed.[22]

This description of right wing mobilisation in the former GDR can serve as the motivational fulcrum for the contemporary resurgence of the radical right throughout Germany, rather than our explaining it from the lurking demons of the Nazi past. The rebirth in the East clearly had little to do with old Nazi survivals – the 'brown sons of red fathers' were reacting to their communist and post-communist environment instead. Yet the hectic activity soon spread back to West Germany where it tended to reinvigorate both the small neo-Nazi parties and long-established skinhead subcultures. Current analyses also like to distinguish between the more conventional, electoral motivation of such 'old neo-Nazi' parties as the NPD, DVU, and REPs and the action-oriented small groups, such as FAP or Nationalist Alternative who are said to account for most of the violence. This distinction may be true and yet it is important to think of the collusion and fluidity of the boundaries among all of these organisations.[23] Given a violent disposition, or 'outgrowing' the self-restraint of the more respectable parties of the right, an individual member of one of the latter could just as easily get involved in or organise a violent attack on an asylum hostel. Many of these right-wingers, moreover, tend to be rather complex in their political motivations and quite capable of alternating between an old neo-Nazi posture of Dr Jekyll and a violent, action-oriented Mr Hyde. We also need to remind ourselves of the extraordinary mobilisation surges of the last few years in Germany: the East German mass demonstrations of 1989–90 against the communist regime, the peace movement of 1990–1, and the massive anti-racist (and pro-asylum rights) demonstrations of 1992, estimated to involve more than two million, which provide the volatile background for the recent wave of skinhead and neo-Nazi violence.

A FIRST LOOK AT THE AVAILABLE EVIDENCE

Before we proceed to a consideration of the relevant circumstances that hasty pudding journalism evidently ignored, it seems appropriate to take another look at the available evidence of the horrifying incidents and activities in question. Let us first analyse the 17 deaths resulting from right wing attacks in 1992[24] – which nearly everyone cites but apparently no one has bothered to examine in any detail. The cases are not always reported in exacting detail, but they appear to yield the following data. Of the 17 victims, the largest number were six German homeless men, generally over 50 years old and evidently victims of skinheads on 'homeless manhunts' (*Pennerfang*). Two were Germans who got involved in political arguments with skinheads or hooligans (soccer rowdies) and two more Germans appear to have died without obvious political motives.[25] These ten German casualties hardly lend credence to the popular explanations of German right-wing mayhem. Of the foreign victims, only one was a young Romanian asylum-seeker (aged 18), the main group that presumably was the target of German right-wing terror; the victim was beaten to death when about 40 right wing radicals invaded an asylum hostel near Rostock in March, 1992. Two more foreign workers, an Albanian and a Pole, appear to have had work permits. The young Polish seasonal worker (aged 24) was killed by skinheads at a discotheque. The age and sex of these young foreign victims may sometimes give a clue also to sexual jealousies on the part of the assailants, rather than just political motives. There was also a fatal knife attack on a Vietnamese man in the streets of Berlin–Marzahn, a notorious tenement suburb long haunted by violent skins. And then there were the three Turkish females, aged 10, 14, and 51 (their grandmother) who perished in the arson attack on two houses in Moelln near Hamburg where nine others suffered considerable injuries (more on this below) and which is, along with the attacks on the asylum hostels the most politically-motivated of the killings. It was certainly perceived as such by the German public which responded with anti-racist demonstrations, and by the government too which finally took some actions to suppress a few violent right-wing groups.

Any analysis of newspaper reports of violent incidents such as cases of lethal force applied by the bouncers of discos or youth clubs is subject to mere guesses about the respective importance of sexual jealousies, turf fights and anti-foreign prejudice in a particular case. As with any cursory glance at a police blotter, we can be sure of racist motivation only when there is convincing evidence of prior planning and organisation, equipment for violence, and unbiased accounts by eye witnesses. Many attacks on hostels satisfy these requirements and a few organised right-wing squads even carried communications equipment in addition to the baseball bats, gas pistols, incendiary devices, and other weapons. The difficulties of analysing the particular cases also account for the differences in the statistics of different agencies, such as the Federal Criminal Office (BKA) and Constitutional Protection Office (BfV), not to mention the views of the left-wing critics who often see racist arson attempts at work where the local police speaks of 'accident' or 'fires of undetermined origin'. Quite often, and as in some of our earlier examples, there are large roving mobs, for example of soccer hooligans on a weekend night who move from threatening the opposing soccer team and its camp followers to terrorising German motorists or restaurant personnel and patrons, and on to the nearest asylum hostel, or to groups of homeless people or foreigners in the streets. We can take for granted that all these cases had a 'right wing background', according to German police sources, but there is little evidence of political motives. One of the assailants of a homeless man in Berlin–Charlottenburg belonged to the new German branch of the Ku Klux Klan. Newspaper pictures of some neo-Nazis show a 'White Power' inscription on T-shirts and there have been other signs of connection with American and British neo-Nazi groups. Some of the neo-Nazi propaganda material comes from Lincoln, Nebraska. There are many adoptions of fanciful new names for rather temporary, though menacing new formations: One was a 'Nationalist' or 'Mobile Action Squad (*Einsatzkommando*)', another a Black Legion that promised to send arms to Croatia, several 'Citizen Vigilante' groups (*Bürgerwehr*), often with local citizenry and even mayors in support of the skinhead squads, a self-appointed 'Border Guard' against Poles and illegal immigrants, self-styled military squad groups, and a Werewolf Hunting Unit – in a country where hunting is an inaccessible sport for the average person.

It is interesting to note the weapons used and the *modus operandi* in each case: in contrast to the gun-shot mayhem among young gang-related Americans – in 1992 800 young people died in this fashion in Los Angeles alone – only one of the 17 deaths was caused by a pistol-wielding, unskilled German worker who ran amok and shot into a large group of homeless in Koblenz, killing one. Four cases involved the use of knives, two dousing with gasoline and burning, three trampling with the potentially lethal Doc Martens, and eight severe beatings usually with baseball bats – baseball is hardly a popular sport in Germany. The means of killing overlap sometimes adding up to more than 17. Thirteen of the killings involved only one or a small group of assailants (1 to 4) who, especially with the older homeless victims, often seemed to have engaged in a kind of 'wilding', or thrill-killing looking at night for relatively defenceless, lone victims. Three or four involved the kinds of larger groups of assailants, perhaps 20 to 60; who have featured prominently in the news for the last two years. Two of them appear to be less political, one an attack on an elderly homeless man and the other the massive invasion of the restaurant mentioned above – such invasions have occurred before – especially on weekends in popular resorts near metropolitan areas such as Munich and Berlin and without a discernible political motive.[26]

Of the locales of the 17 deaths, nine were in West Germany, three in various parts of Berlin, and five in the five new *Länder* which has to be compared to the population ratio of 4.2:0.22:1, respectively. In other words, the 'right wing murder' rate was highest in Berlin and more than twice as high in East Germany as in West Germany and this in spite of the possible distortion introduced by the three deaths at Moelln (more on this below). We should mention that only five of the deaths appear to have occurred in typical metropolitan areas and the other 12 in small to medium-sized towns which dramatically under-represents both the population of metropolitan areas and their much higher criminal homicide rate. Right-wing terror with fatal outcomes typically occurs in less populated, provincial, and probably under-policed areas of Germany, with the notable exception of Berlin.[27]

If this look at the 1992 fatalities falls short of explaining the media and public reactions to German rightwing terror, perhaps a look at particular, dramatic incidents and at the statistics of lower level (non-fatal) violence will help. In an earlier essay, I described four 'right wing' attacks by larger groups in April 1991 on the following targets. One was a mob of about 30 soccer hooligans and skins who had blocked a highway near Berlin with their cars, accosted other motorists, and extorted alcoholic beverages from a store. There was a second incident involving 150 hooligans from Berlin attending a soccer game in Frankfurt/Oder who attacked a bus with (German) fans of the opposing team and committed further offences against others in their path. There were also attacks by a group of Jüterbog skins on foreigners and a massive appearance and some violence by masked neo-Nazis in Frankfurt/Oder the day the Polish-German border was opened.[28] Another group of about 70 skinheads and their friends invaded a fete of homosexuals with clubs and iron bars, injuring two women severely, among other consequences. These early rampages were typical skinhead, hooligan, and neo-Nazi exploits against typical targets, if of dubious political motive, aside from many excesses by smaller groups against individuals in the street.

Major Escalation in Anti-Foreign Violence

In mid–1991, the anti-foreigner incidents underwent a drastic escalation. In January, 1991, the Federal Criminal Office (BKA) had reported only three attacks against foreign persons, four arson attacks, and 19 other offences such as property damage, insults, or spray-painting anti-foreign slogans. For October 1991, when the wave of violence reached its first peak, the BKA reported 54 attacks on persons, 167 cases of arson, and 683 other criminal offenses against foreigners. The balance between West Germany and the five East German *Länder* as crime locations was three to one, already closer than before to that between their respective populations (4.5 to one).[29] By December, 1991, the Federal Office for the Protection of the Constitution (BfV) had counted over 2000 anti-foreigner offences, including 325 arson cases – mostly against refugee or asylum-seekers' hostels – and 188 attacks on people. The police had arrested 387 persons. Chief locations among the *Länder* were Germany's largest state, North Rhine Westphalia (725 offences), Lower Saxony, Baden–Wurttemberg, Saxony, and Saxony–Anhalt.

It is not entirely clear why the extraordinary escalation in August and September, 1991, took place, except that the anticipation of mass unemployment in East Germany increased tremendously at mid year and, at the same time, the stream of asylum-seekers accelerated appreciably, bringing hundreds of asylum hostels to many a German small town or suburban location. The more conservative press went into hyperboles of concern and alarm at his 'tidal wave'. Suddenly, the polls indicated a surge in public concern about the arrival of more asylum-seekers (from 2 per cent in June to 21 per cent) and other foreigners (from 5 per cent to 6 per cent, respectively). As before, three fourths of the Ossis believed that the Bonn government was not doing enough for bringing their lives up to West German levels, while two thirds of the Wessis thought the Ossis' complaints to be unjustified.[30] But now the two had discovered a common scapegoat – the Ossis had taken a dim view of foreigners all along and now the Wessis fell in with this displacement – in the presence of foreigners in general and the surge of asylum-seekers in particular. 58 per cent of Ossis (vs. 40 per cent who disagreed) and 49 per cent of Wessis (vs 47 per cent pro-foreigners) now found the 'presence of many foreigners in Germany *not o.k.*'. 59 per cent of Ossis and 54 per cent of Wessis, moreover, wanted to restrict the number of political asylum-seekers per year that could be admitted into the country.[31] Against the background of the upheavals and civil wars of Eastern Europe, these responses show the limits of tolerance of East and West Germans for the polarising encounters to follow with the ubiquitous asylum hostels and camps and the skinhead and neo-Nazi violence against their presence. Many daily newspapers and tabloids intensified the popular fright at the 'onslaught of foreigners' with appropriate stories, filled with national stereotypes.

The concerted assault on the asylum-seekers' hostels began in early August, 1991, with such locales as Tambach/Dietharz (Thuringia) on August 2, Ueckermünde (Vorpommern) on the 9th, Zittau (Saxony) and Aschersleben (Saxony–Anhalt) on the 16th, Leising (Saxony) on the 17th, Wurzen (Leipzig) on the 24th, and Leipzig itself on the 27th, all in East Germany and some of them repeatedly. At the same time, neo-Nazis and skins continued to engage in many of their earlier, non-asylum centered acts of mayhem, such as attacking left wing squatters in occupied houses in Greifswald and Chemnitz, vandalising signs pointing to memorials of the holocaust and of the concentration camp of Sachsenhausen, clashes with Turks (including in Lower Saxony in the West), raids on restaurants, and an attack on Poles in a minivan. The widespread anti-Polish and anti-Czech prejudice generated a rising number of attacks on Czech and Polish travellers, including misbehaviour by German border and customs police and skinhead raids on Czech police stations throughout 1991–2. But in the raids on asylum hostels until mid-September, 1991, the use of Molotov cocktails and other incendiary devices was still rare, as compared to knives and baseball bats.[32] Skinheads, hooligans and 'unknown assailants' by far outnumbered recognizable neo-Nazis in police reports and the slogans reported were typical skin gang talk, such as '*Doitschland den Doitschen*' or hackneyed cries of 'Out with foreigners', as well as '*Sieg Heil*' and Nazi symbols and greetings.

In September and October, however, the attacks on asylum hostels got into high gear, outnumbering all other categories and numbering over 50 attacks a month over the next three months until winter slowed their pace. The attacks still varied a lot from rocks thrown and windows broken, or small calibre shots, to brutal invasions with attacks on people, smashing of cars and of furnishings, fires set, and, increasingly, arson attacks without invasions, i.e. by throwing incendiary devices near or through the windows or broken doors of dwellings. The continuing surge of refugees also added tremendously to the original hostels which were often refurbished or run-down multiple residential dwellings, schools, gymnasiums, temporary or trailer structures (*Wohncontainer*), and even tents. Their makeshift character and location near residential areas or in public centres often seemed intended to provoke local opposition from the start, frequently aggravated by claims of obnoxious or criminal conduct of the foreign residents.[33] Most refugees and asylum-seekers have been distinctly lower class in their personal habits, dress, and kinds of criminality which in turn fuels the German media and public stereotypes of uncleanliness, panhandling, and stealing.

In mid-August of 1991, the Interior Minister of Saxony–Anhalt, Hartmut Perschau (CDU), a 'West-import' from Hamburg, still rejected the idea of special police units to protect asylum-seekers as a 'police state kind of prior restraint, with police on location before any crimes have been committed'. There were similar official remarks from many quarters. But on September 18, the first major siege began, with some 400 right wing radicals massing in front of the hostels for, among others, 150 Vietnamese and Mozambicans in Hoyerswerda. Three days later, an assault was launched with Molotov cocktails and steel balls upon one hostel amidst a cheering mob of neighbours and towns-people. The Hoyerswerda affair ended on September 23 with the evacuation of the asylum-seekers in the midst of a pogrom-like atmosphere in the town. It takes no great expertise to see how this disgraceful – but long drawn-out and quite predictable – affair could have been changed by massive outside intervention. The skinhead and neo-Nazi mobs have long been known to run whenever they meet determined resistance or superior force. In the same week, nearly 20 such establishments were under attack elsewhere, half of them with incendiary devices and about half of them in East Germany – in other words, four times as often in East Germany as in the West (in relation to population).[34] At the same time, the bitter wrangling over the asylum reform began between the two largest parties in Bonn, with each of them accusing the other of letting the crisis get out of hand in order to get its way.[35]

In the meantime, skinhead attacks on individuals and small groups, including Germans, began to be overshadowed by the attacks on the hostels, especially in West Germany. We can conjecture that, given the greater manpower of organised neo-Nazi parties in the West and the more prominent role of skinheads and rebellious local youth in the East, the neo-Nazi parties provided the conduit for spreading the anti-foreigner violence to the West where, in the following months, the geographic share of the attacks on hostels began to catch up with the East. In the West, such attacks also featured a more specifically political message, with swastikas, SS and Nazi symbols, and stars of David painted on walls. In the 'Wild East', there were many additional attacks on such targets as Russian war monuments, soldiers, or nationals, Polish travellers, Vietnamese street merchants, even on ethnic German refugees, and on monuments of concentration camps there and the holocaust during this period. Germans who protested the attacks on foreigners also had to expect being victimised. And there were pitched battles between the extreme right and anti-fascists or 'autonomous' anarchists.

In the months from October to December 1991, there was also an ominous resurgence of attacks upon Turks, on their mosques, dwellings, restaurants, and shops, about 15 incidents in all, including several melées between skinheads and groups of young Turks. Contrary to what the American press claimed a year later regarding the deaths of three Turkish women in Moelln, there had been a lot of prejudicial incidents involving Turks all along, including fatalities at the hands of West German skinheads or neo-Nazis: one on New Year's Eve in 1981, one in June 1982 and one in 1985; and in December 1988, a neo-Nazi torched a Turkish house in Schwandorf (Bavaria), killing four and injuring another five persons severely. The post-unification incidents also included the death of a young Turk, Mete Eksi, who died of baseball bat blows to the head in November 1991, and a series of further occurrences all through 1992. Thus the outrage at Moelln was not a complete surprise even though this largest of German minorities (1.6 million) had indeed lived in the country for decades, even generations.

The Violent Face of 1992

The anti-foreign incidents of the first half of 1992 (Table 23.1) give a graphic picture of the relative share of different types of aggression and between East and West. In spite of the cold season, the arson attacks on asylum-seekers' dwellings show that the West German *Länder* now had almost three of four such events (to be proportional they would need to be ahead four to one), while in attacks on persons, the 'Wild East' was even in absolute numbers, that is to say it had four-and-a-half as many outrages per population. A look at the geographical distribution of both among particular *Länder* is also illuminating (Table 23.2): Among the arson attacks, Brandenburg, Baden–Württemberg, Hesse, Lower Saxony, Schleswig–Holstein, Saxony, and Saxony–Anhalt had a disproportionate share. Bavaria, despite its ultraconservative government – certainly on the asylum-issue – has a diminutive share of the violence, both arson and personal attacks. Of the non-lethal assaults on people, Brandenburg (nearly four times the av-

Table 23.1   Violent anti-foreigner incidents, January–June, 1992

	Location	Arson		Attacks on persons		Other offences		% of total population
Jan.	East Germany	4		22		23		
	West Germany	20		14		124		
	Berlin	1		1		3		
	Total	25		37		150		
Feb.	East Germany	1		5		23		
	West Germany	16		9		122		
	Berlin	0		0		0		
	Total	17		14		145		
March	East Germany	7		6		10		
	West Germany	13		8		97		
	Berlin	0		0		0		
	Total	20		14		107		
April	East Germany	5		15		25		
	West Germany	18		8		101		
	Berlin	0		0		1		
	Total	23		23		127		
Grand Totals	East Germany	33	26%	86	48%	221	19.4%	19.1%
	West Germany	93	73%	86	48%	885	77.9%	76.6
	Berlin	2	1%	6	4%	31	2.7%	4.3
	All	128		178		1137		100%

Source: *Bundeskriminalamt* and *Bundesdrucksache* 12/3283 of Sept. 23. 1992. Also the *Bundestagsdrucksache* 12/2440 of April 14, 1992, 12/2441, 12/2439 of the same date, and 12/2674 of May 25, 1992. There were no separate, published breakdowns for May and June, but the averages can be estimated from the available figures.

erage), Mecklenburg-Vorpommern (nearly three times), Saxony–Anhalt (nearly five times), Hamburg (nearly three times), Rhineland–Palatinate (more than twice), Schleswig–Holstein (twice), and the Saar (three times the average) provided far more than their share of the locales. The prominence of certain Eastern *Länder* in this, especially in the warmer months of May and June when both victims and assailants are spending more time outdoors, is undeniable, although the role of the Saar, Rhineland–Palatinate, and the Hamburg/Schleswig–Holstein areas is a surprise and rather different from the West German *Länder*

Table 23.2   Violent anti-foreigner incidents, January – June, 1992

Länder	Arson	Attacks on persons	Other offences	% of German population
Baden–Württemberg	19	10	90	12.2
Bavaria	4	2	51	14.2
Berlin	2	6	31	4.3
Brandenburg	9	23	83	3.3
Bremen	–	1	12	.8
Hamburg	1	5	32	2.0
Hessen	11	3	109	7.2
Mecklenburg–Vorp.	1	13	32	2.5
Lower Saxony	26	5	176	9.2
North Rhine Westphalia	18	22	295	21.6
Rhineland–Palatinate	7	19	69	4.7
Saar	–	7	6	1.4
Saxony	12	13	57	6.2
Saxony–Anhalt	8	32	34	3.7
Schleswig–Holstein	7	12	45	3.3
Thuringia	3	5	15	3.4
BKA Totals	128	178	1137	100%

For comparison:
BfV totals for
1992 (up to Nov. 22) 621   452   823

Source: See Table 23.1 and BfV.

with the most arson attacks.[36] The last category, 'other offences', consisted of robbery, threats, insults, property damage etc. and was most
evenly distributed between East and West (one to four). Here Lower
Saxony, Rhineland–Palatinate, Schleswig–Holstein, and Hesse were also
above the average and Berlin was below it.

The curve of 1992 incidents again rose prodigiously in the second
half of the year when it crested in September and was still fairly high
in November, at the time of the peak in fatalities that year. The Office
for Protection of the Constitution (BfV) counted 621 arson attacks,
including some bombings, by early December, and 452 cases of physical injury. The BfV also perceived an increasingly political emphasis
in that there were more attacks on left wing groups and 'alternatives'
who often fought back or organised counter-demonstrations or supplied guards for an asylum-hostel under siege. The resulting street battles,
the vice president of BfV reported in Los Angeles, were sometimes
reminiscent of the Nazi and communist street-fighting in the Weimar

Republic of the last two years before Hitler. He added that 38 of the violent acts had anti-semitic character, not counting 72 cases of vandalism at Jewish cemeteries or synagogues. Both categories were slightly less than in the previous year, 1991, possibly a sign that the specifically neo-Nazi actions had *not followed* the trend of the drastic explosion of skinhead activities.[37] The report by Ulla Jelpe mentioned about 22 neo-Nazi rallies and demonstrations for the year, many with substantial 'anti-fascist'[38] counter-demonstrations, and a fair number of melées between both extreme elements. The strength and ability to mobilise of the 'anti-fascists' can be seen in their claim to have fielded 10 000 to demonstrate against an appearance of revisionist historian David Irving in Berlin (May 11, 1992). Typical neo-Nazi and skinhead demonstrations and rallies, including funeral rallies for martyrs, could boast only a few hundred participants. There were also clashes with the police and some of these were deliberate and very violent confrontations.[39]

The occurrence of anti-semitic incidents is a subject of particular interest in this context. Throughout the four decades of the old FRG, polls had shown striking generational change in the levels of prejudice from the late forties when 40 per cent of German adults were considered anti-semitic to the late eighties when an EMNID study (1989) disclosed 14 per cent of that description, including 4 per cent 'hard anti-semites'.[40] Skilled observers have pointed out the linkage between one prejudice and another – comparing for example levels of 20 per cent of anti-Jewish prejudice (1987) with 33 per cent anti-Turkish and 51–52 per cent of anti-gypsy and anti-asylum-seeker sentiment in 1987 – and pointed out the small number of Jews still living in Germany today (30–45 000). They also left no doubt about the salience of Jews and Israel as symbols in the German psyche. In any case, there had been a smattering of anti-semitic incidents ranging from vandalism of Jewish cemeteries and synagogues to the smearing of swastikas and old Nazi slogans on walls throughout the years and in the face of West German government efforts to show support for Jewish survivors and the state of Israel.[41] Against the fluctuation of decades, there is little evidence of a major surge in the numbers today, but in 1992 there clearly have been efforts to provoke and threaten: 150 German volunteers, for example, had to guard the Jewish community house in West Berlin after neo-Nazi threats to mount a demonstration there against 'the Jewish influence' in the city (May 22, 1992). There were threats in Halle and also in Erfurt (July 19) where pigs' heads were thrown into the synagogue yard along with denunciations of Heinrich Galinski, the retiring head of the German-Jewish association. There were incidents involving Israelis and a number of further attacks on cemeteries and Jewish memorials in Berlin and at concentration camps (Sachsenhausen and Ravensbrück) right after an official visit of Israeli Prime Minister Itzak Rabin. A swastika, moreover, was scratched into the outside of the car of his wife, Lea.

The Cases of Rostock and Moelln

Probably the worst of the outrages of 1992 against asylum hostels took place in Rostock–Lichtenhagen in late August when several hundred right wing youths gathered, armed with Molotov cocktails, to storm the Centre for Asylum Applicants (ZAST) while a sympathetic crowd of perhaps 1000 local citizens cheered. A police force of 200 guarded the Centre and 13 suffered injuries. Two police cars were burned (Aug. 22). The following day the rebellious youths had grown to an estimated 500, many of whom came from all over Germany. This time double the number of local sympathisers cheered with cries of 'Heil Hitler' and 'Out with the foreigners' while 400 police and border police battled until the early hours. 140 right-wingers were arrested: half of them were from out of town. Seventy policemen were injured.[42] The boulevard papers of the Springer and Burda concerns played a major role in triggering the concerted assault by the many skinhead gangs that ordinarily fight each other. They not only spread their anti-asylum-seekers' panic but even set a 'deadline' by which 'something has got to be done'; the skinheads, who are usually preoccupied fighting each other, took this as their starting signal and gathered for the attack. The following night, a Sunday (August 24), the battle resumed, while the police began to evacuate the Romanian asylum-seekers in the Centre, leaving 150 Vietnamese, a television team, the official in charge of foreigners, and some antifascist defenders behind in an adjacent building. At 9.30 pm, the police unaccountably withdrew from the besieged Centre, permitting the neo-Nazis to invade the lower floors, and to set it afire, thus trapping the people mentioned above on the upper floors, including Vietnamese women and children. Fire brigades battled for two hours against neo-Nazi resistance before they could regain the protection of the police. Later investigations disclosed that the local police commanders and even the CDU *Land* Minister of the Interior had unaccountably 'gone home for the weekend' or on vacation, leaving their troops to cope with the riots which still continued for three more days, and led to 50 more injured police and a grand total of nearly 400 arrested, many only temporarily.[43] It was sheer luck that no lives were lost during this débâcle.

Let us pause for a moment to analyse the emerging pattern which appears to resemble the early race riots in the United States: the skinheads and neo-Nazis obviously made themselves the instrument of the hostility of the community against the asylum-seekers, probably glad to enjoy a smidgen of the public approval that usually eludes them. In spite of their violence, especially against the police, they proceeded rather slowly and timidly against their ultimate victims, certainly slowly enough that a determined outside intervention – for example by army or special police troops (*Bereitschaftspolizei*) – could have stopped the neo-Nazis and locals in their tracks. The crucial police failure at the top is reminiscent indeed of the failures of the (elected) sheriffs and police in Klan lynchings and early American race riots to muster sufficient force to stop the rampaging mobs. It is no coincidence that the Ku Klux Klan should have established a branch in Germany. From the perspective of African-Americans, the United States too is 'different' and any relapse into patterns of discrimination and prejudice here conjures up memories of the Klan, of Jim Crow, and of slavery and their countless victims.[44] This race riot pattern of the more spectacular attacks on asylum hostels – others resemble more the night-rider type of arson attack in past U.S. race violence – needs to be contrasted to the patterns of skinhead and neo-Nazi attacks on individuals and small groups, including gays, Poles, resident minorities (Jews, Turks), and the homeless.

The attacks on individuals and small groups, perpetrated by individuals and small autonomous groups of skinheads or neo-Nazis, also resemble the activities of youth gangs in the United States and many other countries, including attacks on recent immigrants, gays, other young ethnics, and other gangs. The German fatalities of 1992, indeed, seem to fit the latter pattern better than the former, which brings us to the nocturnal arson attack on the two private houses inhabited by Turkish families in Moelln near Hamburg. This was no asylum hostel, nor were the victims refugees or the town particularly hostile to their presence in the sense in which the locals of Hoyerswerda, Rostock–Lichtenhagen and hundreds of other German communities were towards their asylum hostels. The deadly arson was carried out as a sneak attack and the attackers immediately went into hiding. This is not to deny that, in Moelln, there were local soccer hooligans (attached to the HSV team) and skinheads who used to go to Hamburg to participate in brawls and, six or more years ago, in 'Turk-bashing' which had even led to a fatality (Ramazan Avci) in 1985. The Hamburg area Turks, however, had then formed their own self-defence squads and established a local 'balance of terror' that kept the local peace as effectively as the big balance of terror between East and West had assured international peace for decades in all of Europe. Four weeks before the Moelln outrage, however, there had been a brawl at the Moelln Autumn Fair (*Herbstmarkt*) at which a superior force of Turks and left wing militants from outside beat up and humiliated the local skinheads who had to be rescued by the police. The arson attack on the Turks of November 23, 1992, thus appears to have been bloody retribution that perhaps exceeded its mark by a country mile. The emerging pattern thus looks a lot like that of escalating drive by shootings and firebombs between the Lost Angeles Crips and Bloods or between black and Latino gangs, like retaliation among the proud *Boys'n the Hood*, rather than a political movement to bring the old Nazis back.[45]

THE VIOLENT YOUTHS

'Why are you trying to kill me', the young policeman shouted at the left wing *Autonome* squatter, who was about the same age, in the discussion circle on violence of the Berlin Academies of Art. The left wing militant spoke of a 'right to violence', a right to 'defend oneself against right wing killers'. He could see no parallel between this 'left wing readiness for self-defence' and the 'right wing will to murder and destroy'. There is a great danger that the extreme left fastens upon today's right wing violence and as in the thirties distorts our perception of it in order to legitimise itself as its chief antagonist, much as the neo-Nazis in Rostock tried to legitimise themselves as instruments of the wrath of the community against the hapless asylum-seekers. Another Berlin police officer at the discussion circle described his police role in terms many Americans will recognise: 'we are the first authority that these youths, that grow up without any restraints, ever encounter' since their parents and teachers have simply 'failed to do their jobs'. In the meantime, he said, a policeman has to let the autonomous left call him in 'fascist' while the skinheads denounce him as 'un-German'. Political polarisation a la Weimar confuses everybody and adds to the primary problem of curbing anarchy and violence.[46] And yet there is no denying that the police and judicial authorities have often moved much more harshly, even brutally, against left wing or anti-nuclear demonstrators than against the neo-Nazis. Perhaps we also need to start all over in assessing the phenomenon without recourse to the bipolar stereotypes of right and left.

The great escalation of right wing political violence in Germany in the late eighties and early nineties was preceded by an even greater level of violence on the left in the late sixties and the seventies, at least in numbers and organisation.[47] For decades now and up until 1990, the BfV has certified higher numbers and better organization to the extreme left. In the seventies and eighties, there were also the left wing terrorist organizations, the RAF, June 2 Movement, Revolutionary Cells, and others who committed a string of deliberate murders, including the assassination of the head of the Deutsche Bank, Alfred Herrhausen in late 1989, and of the *Treuhand*, Detlev Rohwedder (April 1, 1991). But even non-terrorist activists of left wing groups, especially anarchists, so-called chaotics, 'autonomous' activists, and many others have been guilty of an appalling level of violence in the streets and at demonstrations. This should not be swept under the rug now, just because we are concerned about right wing violence. In 1986, violent left wing extremist incidents were as numerous as those of the extreme right in 1992 (2003) and they were still at only about one-third (703) of that level in 1992. At one clash with a chain of policemen holding back peace demonstrators, hooded left wing assailants shot two policemen to death at point blank range – the hoods being a quaint German police concession to demonstrators then as now. It may be true that most of this mayhem has been directed at the police, at the state, or at alleged neo-Nazis and racists, but does this really excuse murder? And why should the radical left be permitted to police the right any more than the right is permitted to play border guard or morals squad (of all things!) against gays, bordellos, or illegal foreign street vendors? If we grant the extreme left a 'right to violence' in alleged self-defence – militants always pretend that they are only 'defending' someone or themselves against some kind of 'aggression' – why not the extreme right which has a reputation for venting its mayhem almost exclusively on the weak and defenceless?[48] Or should not violence remain the monopoly of the state since it is hard enough to control?

In the early seventies, a major seismic shock hit most industrial societies, the oil crisis. It was at about the time that the alienated young left wing rebels had mostly moved 'into the system' in West German metropolitan areas and at various levels of government, especially in education. It put an end to decades of economic growth and raised problems of competition, especially on the West German labour market where until then the importation of foreign labour had given the signal for upward mobility to German working and lower middle classes. In 1973, after decades of bringing in millions of workers from outside the EC (following Italians and Spaniards), particularly the Turks, the old FRG closed its recruiting offices abroad and tried to persuade foreign workers to go home. At the same time, under the SPD-FDP government of Willy Brandt, they permitted hundreds of thousands of foreign workers to bring in their families, with the result that entire urban regions became dominated by the presence of Turks, Yugoslavs, and other *de facto* immigrant populations. West Germany willy-nilly began to be an 'immigrant society' and got its first taste of the problems of cultural conflict in a multicultural setting. In big cities like West Berlin, in particular, 'multikulti' became the operative theory of ambitious programmes of cultural reconciliation under the auspices of the SPD city governments that bent over backwards to accommodate Turkish culture and ignored the increasingly flourishing Turkish and other foreign youth gangs which often reflected sharp generational and other social conflicts within the societies of the immigrants. The gangs ranged from the far left to the Grey Wolves on the right and some engaged in violence and criminal activity such as protection rackets and drug dealing. Their rule over the schools and streets, for example, of North Berlin left a marginalised remnant of German youths there many of whom eventually tended to turn to the skinheads and identified with their cultural rearguard actions of 'bashing Turks' and *Autonome*. They felt cornered because the reigning multikulti and left wing orthodoxy from the beginning characterised their complaints of being marginalised as expressions of '*fascistoid*' or 'racist' political incorrectness.[49] On a larger, more political level, the reaction to this alliance between the immigrant groups and the reigning left wing government – there was also intense frustration with the unfulfilled CDU promises to curb the flow of immigration – came out in the 1989 REP vote in the West Berlin elections (7.5 per cent): Young Berliners had a disproportionate share (one fifth) in this backlash.

Dysfunctional Families and School Milieus

Skinheads are no right wing RAF; they did not become violent criminals for political reasons but are violent criminals who are borrowing political rationalizations . . . they are dangerous because of their mass of sympathisers . . . (*Der Spiegel*, no. 50, Dec. 7, 1992, p. 36.)

Why is this question of the general level of youthful violence so important to our subject? How political is the violence? The standard explanation of political violence assumes that first there must be political attitudes and views among the persons concerned, perhaps even an ideology, and if they are strongly held, purposive violent actions will follow. If true, however, this model would explain less than half of the phenomenon before us, namely only the neo-Nazi action groups and parties – the latter rarely get into this violence, being more oriented towards elections and fearful of being outlawed or prosecuted – and the people they control. The violent neo-Nazis (1600) and particularly the skinheads (5000) of 1992 constituted less than a fifth of the radical rightists on record (41 400) and yet they committed most of the violent outrages. Over two-thirds (1400) of more than 2000 reported offences, moreover, were committed by assailants under 21, and some by very young skinheads – as young as 12 years of age. For the hooligans and skinhead gangs the violent conduct evidently comes first, and is frequently directed at other hooligan teams, police, and skin gangs battling over turf, long before and after the focus on refugees, asylum hostels, and visible foreigners emerges. The skin gangs and hoolies of Rostock and the surrounding area were deeply absorbed in their turf fights both before and after their brief period of media-inspired cooperation against the police and the asylum facilities in late August of 1992. Is the sporadic, provocative use of Nazi symbols and salutes a fad or external element of style or is it truly a sign of neo-Nazi control and fully-fledged ideological beliefs?[50] There are the recruitment efforts of the neo-Nazis, who of course would prefer to dominate the scene but little evidence of successful coordination. Perhaps, first of all we need to explain why the hooligans and skinheads have been so very violent even before they played around with Nazi symbols and slogans. Since the seventies, the levels of violence in the streets and schools of West Germany has been rising steeply year after year, much of it among youth gangs and youthful offenders and mostly hidden by embarrassed local and school authorities.[51] Just in the last ten years, the explosion of violence at German schools has been reflected in awesome collections of knives, bicycle chains, nunchakus, and gas pistols in the hands of teachers who themselves are no longer immune from attack. Juveniles as young as 14 to 15 attack, extort, threaten, rob, and seriously injure fellow students over personal slights or over objects such as fancy clothes, Walkmans, money, or, in East Germany, cigarettes and alcohol. And this violence has reached levels of brutality that are truly psychopathic: ten years ago, *Spiegel* magazine quoted a teacher saying, a typical brawl among boys would end as soon as the loser was bleeding or gave signs of surrender. Today the loser on the ground gets *eingestiefelt'*, marked with boots to the point of facial lacerations and serious injury, not to mention the psychological trauma.

Why are they so violent, we ask – as if we had not noticed the rising tide of the very same thing, including racial and anti-immigrant overtones, in the streets and schools of our own country, the U.S.? There are speculations and attempts at explanation, and many of them point to the considerable social changes that have occurred in the German family, the school, and the community since the fifties. The crime rate has more than doubled in thirty years. Social anthropologists, on the broadest level of generalisation, have suggested that, with worldwide modernisation, the growth of individual freedom is weakening the networks of social control in family and community. The internalisation of restraints that was supposed to compensate for the lessening of social control is failing, especially with marginal groups and under the battering of poverty, failed careers and future prospectives, television violence – much of what German youngsters see comes from the U.S. – and the escalating social disorganisation and violence of the schools and neighbourhoods in which many grow up. German educators and youth researchers point to the lack of individual and social values among offending youngsters, their sociopathic inability to feel remorse or compassion for their victims, their deep-seated anger which explodes in *'einfach einen umhauen'* (simply knocking down someone), regardless of why, or who the victim may be. The parents' alcohol abuse and domestic violence against spouses and children appears to be a major cause of the violent hyperactivity of youths, although there are also said to be half a million child alcoholics in Germany. A third of school age children are estimated to have experimented with drugs. Some also point to the desolation of many families and loneliness of children left alone by all-too-busy parents, the *Schlüsselkinder* (latchkey children) of a materialistic society. Two million German children only have one parent and, in a metropolis like Hamburg, half of all children have divorced or separated parents. Teachers worry about the incidence of suicidal, disoriented kids, particularly after each weekend of family stress, parental drinking, and domestic violence. Macho police attitudes that ignore the pivotal role of domestic violence in producing violent young criminals – a factor stressed also by the new U.S. Attorney General, Janet Reno, in her confirmation hearings – and instead merely call for repression and punishment increase the desperation of the young would-be offender and help turn him or her into a predatory animal. The school environment sometimes mirrors this law-and-order attitude with its punishments and relentless pressure for achievement, especially among academically weak youngsters who may respond with violence against other students when they are really rebelling against 'adult oppression'. 70 per cent of German school children reportedly suffer from headaches and stomach pains as a result of 'school stress'.

The heavy pall of social dysfunction and ignorance in action is further aggravated by the political overtones of rival interpretations. In a recent debate, for example, Beate Scheffler, a Greens *Landtag* deputy argued to the horror of her party colleagues – and under CDU applause – that the disorientation of the present youth generation (and perhaps even their right wing and anti-foreign violence) might be caused by decades of anti-authoritarian education by the 68er generation of their teachers and educational administrators. Since the seventies, she suggested, these educational formulas for the 'freedom of the child' may have stunted real education and guidance both at home and in the schools, causing the atrophy of youthful values, visions of the future, and career perspectives, and setting many young people adrift in an alienating environment. There is much evidence indeed of the anti-authoritarian teachers and parents of West Germany whose reluctance to guide and discipline (and evident lack of concern) is a boon only to the well-motivated and creative youngster while leaving the weaker students in disoriented limbo, or encouraging their pursuit of compensatory and nefarious activities, or worse.[52] On the other hand, there have been observers like Heinz Steiner of Frankfurt who see in the current wave of violence the 'militant elbows mentality' of neoconservative politics à la Thatcher, Reagan, and Kohl's German '*Wende*' (turnabout) of 1982 which promised to reward only achievement and hard work by means of ever more rugged competition. At the very least, it has starved youth social services in East and West for funds. This 'chauvinism of property (*Wohlstandschauvinismus*)' generates contempt for the poor and weak, social envy, and a fear of social decline. The 'losers' of the brutal competition, curiously, have made its hierarchy their own and are picking on people that are their 'inferiors', at least in brute, physical strength, such as asylum-seekers, the homeless, drunks, gays, the handicapped, and foreign refugees. They try to legitimise themselves by calling all these people 'un-German' or 'unfit to live in Germany', but there is of cause no reason to take such phrases seriously since they are hardly representative of mainstream or majority opinion.[53]

Skinhead and Hooligan Subcultures

This then is the violent world of family and school in which the skinheads of Germany grew up and are still growing up, among the disappointed 'losers' in the rat race for skills, jobs, and riches. To begin to understand skinhead violence, and its spurious political manifestations, we need to penetrate the youth world of the video generation, its nocturnal musical styles and scenes, and its frequently violent thrill-seeking of dubious political meanings. The skinhead subculture, like various versions of punk, was originally an import from Britain where it has flourished since the late sixties amidst Teds, Mods, Bikers, and all kinds of outlandishly garbed and coiffed young people following trends in every sphere of life. It is important to note, especially for naive political scientists, that these are not groups formed to express like-minded political opinions, but more often quasi-primary groups that are flitting from style to trendish style, including provocative political postures – anything *pour épater le bourgeois*, to provoke the straight folks. The shock value and attraction of the skinheads lay precisely in their proletarian simplicity, their shaven heads, and hints of readiness for violent thrills. It was not exactly that some of their competitors were lambs – punks had been known to terrorise whole parts of cities and the skins were not specifically right wing – some are left wing – although some of them, especially soccer hooligans, occasionally sported Nazi symbols on their leather jackets and picked up slogans like 'Out with the foreigners' from neo-Nazi parties like the NPD or the British National Front.

Soccer hooligans, or their equivalents, for example at some high-school football games in the U.S., are of course an ancient phenomenon. In the soccer-crazy countries of Western Europe and Latin America, however, they have become a major terror during halftime intermission, at their end (of the playing field), and in the streets before and after the game, beating up the camp followers of the opposing team, assaulting police and by-standers, tearing up train compartments and buses, and generally exhibiting a degree of physical violence out of all proportion with the occasion.[54] Hooligans or 'hoolies' are in it for pure lust of violence and defence of turf and not really politics, although the subculture tends towards a right wing syndrome of working-class machismo and hostility to foreigners and to the better-off, better-dressed, and better-educated. Hoolies also tend towards public inebriation and, sometimes agitated by a small minority screaming 'Sieg Heil' and 'Germany for the Germans', have engaged in massed rampages through towns, attacking shops, police, and whatever target seemed convenient. Hooliganism is a working-class sport and its chief satisfaction seems to lie in a kind of weekly dramatic self-affirmation by violent deed. The expressive violence and destruction are purposes in themselves.

In larger German cities, the skinheads have formed three 'generations' of the ever-changing alienated youth scene, along with punks, *Grufties*, heavy metal fans, and many others which since the mid-eighties again include Turkish and other foreign youth gangs. The first generation of skins was still close to the British imports wedded to reggae, ska, and oi music – the source of such language distortions as 'Doitschland' – but it did not play much of a role in West Germany until the punk style had more or less run its course, in the late seventies and early eighties (East Germany was far behind in this respect), and after the anti-nuclear and peace movement too, had died down. The second generation skins were seized by increasing political agitation by neo-Nazi action groups and nocturnal forays of bashing *Autonome* and Turks, including the 1985 slaying of Ramazan Avci in Hamburg which led to a resurgence of Turkish and other foreign gangs, as we have seen. The third generation of skins is the recent product of the explosive developments in East Germany and it threatens to overpower both the much more political left wing groups and the foreign youth gangs that used to balance skin power. Like Puerto Rican, new Latino, and Asian gangs in the U.S., the new immigrant gangs had formed largely in defence against the victimisation of young Turkish men by skinheads and others, but soon became a rallying point of identity and belonging for marginalised youth in an alien environment.[55]

The old GDR government already wrestled with the growth of punk and skinhead subcultures and its ham-handed efforts, if anything, pushed the skins into right wing postures. Older West German skinheads, by contrast, still betray shadings of the violent and alienated aestheticism of the punk and rock fan groups before any real dedication to the ethnic and political nationalism of some of their slogans. Even their hatred and violence tends to be more expressive than instrumental to any conceivable goal.[56] They express the depth of their alienation and hostility to society as do their clothes, their music, and their contempt for the social conventions of the adult world. This, of course, places particular importance on how they are treated by the establishment and also on the right wing hate and racist rock music that German authorities finally suppressed in early 1993. Long known on both sides of the British Channel, these rock and rap lyrics of groups like the Screwdriver (Britain), *Werewolf*, *Vortex*, *Böhze Onkelz*, and *Noie Werte* have probably helped to focus the violent attention of skins on foreigners and other targets and broke down the already weak self-restraint against violent 'happenings'.

The tail end of the third 'generation' of skins are the thirteen-to-sixteen-year olds who have recently been streaming into skinhead groups without much background in the subculture of music and social group life. They shave their heads and don the boots and jackets simply to provoke society. They are also the most accessible to neo-Nazi recruiters who can rent their guard services and use them for action squads. They have been easy to sign up although the neo-Nazis themselves are sceptical of the depth of their commitment. They are also more grateful than their 'elders' for the well-considered neo-Nazi efforts to make club space, weekend trips, and sports available to them. Since they are not welcome at existing youth centres – in East Germany most such centres have been shut down anyway – and organised youth activities, the political establishment seems to have abandoned them to neo-Nazi recruiters. This would appear to be another case where intelligent countervailing efforts of education and youth social work are urgently needed to halt the labelling process before it can settle in.[57] The worst strategy of well-meaning opponents or police is to brand the young toughs as incorrigible Nazi hoodlums because it will fasten the (sometimes well-deserved) label for a long time in their minds. In big cities like Berlin, the wasteland character of the youth scene is evident also from the ubiquitous graffiti, especially all over the subway cars, including the seats. It is reminiscent of the very young 'posses' of 'taggers', an estimated 30 000 in 1993 in Los Angeles, who have been decorating that city with their markings, and are beginning to imitate the gang violence of about 100 000 gang members that are already terrorising the neighbourhoods.

The younger and younger ages of violent skinheads involved in attacks on asylum hostels and other anti-foreign violence – also attacks against gays (160 attacks in 1992), the handicapped, homeless men, and Jewish cemeteries – have been noted in many quarters. Most appear to be between 14 and 20 years old and a few are even younger. This phenomenon, of course, has its equivalent in youth violence in American cities where boys as young as eleven have been packing guns at school and acting as trigger men in drive-by shootings. In both cases also, the gratuitous brutality often rose to sociopathic dimensions and this usually from the depth of the negative self-images that generated cravings for self-validation by public, violent acts, or by reducing a presumable 'enemy' to a helpless heap of flesh. German schools also have experienced a rising tide of youthful alienation and violence especially at vocational schools and at the *Hauptschule*, but of course nothing yet approaching the threats to life and limb in inner city schools in the U.S.[58] German big city schools, for example in Berlin, now have police guards – though no need yet of metal detectors – and there are discussions about whether kindergartens should have them as well. The truculent skinhead proletarians have long enjoyed bashing the *Gymnasiasten* (Latin school students) of the upper middle class and a police guard can at least secure the buildings and the approaches to a school. Their teachers, moreover, have long learned not to see a reflection of a profound ideological commitment in every neo-Nazi slogan or swastika and to understand most (not all) shouts of 'Sieg Heil' as juvenile provocations for presumably left wing teachers.

The striking parallels in the levels of youthful violence in advanced industrial societies, including in the schools, have their equivalents in the disintegrating families everywhere. The *Land* Criminal Offices (LKA) and BfV branches in West Germany have indicated that most of the right wing offenders arrested in their respective states came from dysfunctional or broken-up families characterised by domestic violence, especially by fathers against the offenders but also against mates, alcohol abuse, and egregious patterns of parental neglect. Most of them came not from successful and prosperous working-class families, but from the more marginal underclass of under-educated and less well-off workers, farmers, and small business families, a feature that bears out the thesis of the 'two-thirds society' and of the right wing youth as among the 'losers' of the modernisation process of the communications revolution of the eighties.[59] They live in grim suburban ghettos, both in the West and in the East, and see little of a future for themselves. According to the LKA Baden–Württemberg, however, most of the Western skins are by no means unemployed, but have menial jobs, work as apprentices, or still go (or should go) to school, whereas in the five new *Länder* unemployment and lack of apprenticeships probably accounts for the majority of the right wing rebels.

The family situation, on the other hand, appears to be no better in the East. On the contrary, the generation gap between parents and skinhead children is probably much worse than in the West because the collapse of the communist system destroyed parental authority at precisely the stage when teenagers are most in need of parental guidance towards adult roles.[60] The East German social discontinuity of 1990 is probably as large as it was at the ends of World Wars One and Two when German parents and children often found themselves eternities apart. Then as now, parents that grew up under the old system hardly know what to say to their children and how to keep them from following a different drummer, one that the parents may despise. The disintegration of the East German social milieus, according to Wilhelm Heitmeyer, also brought into existential question to what social group a young person belonged and thereby shifted the emphasis to such natural, ascriptive categories as ethnicity, skin colour, and language, in short national identity.[61]

If we define the meaning of 'political' in relation to winning control of government and shaping society in conformity to one's values and philosophy, how political is this phenomenon? Extreme left wing activity in this sense has obviously been political which further emphasises the contrast on the right, especially with regard to skinheads and hooligans. Skins and hoolies do exhibit a kind of primitive nationalism with emphasis on flags, symbols, and national pride – in the face of ridicule by most young Germans – but their efforts at social control are chaotic and, at best, limited to the local scene, 'our turf (*unser Revier*)', which they defend with a passion against foreigners, left wing groups, and others whose presence they insist on characterising as 'un-German'. Closer examination of the skin and hoolie scene also reveals considerable distance and resistance to the recruitment efforts of neo-Nazi action groups, such as the FAP or even the REPs. Only the youngest East German generation of skinheads seems to be an easy mark for the neo-Nazis.[62] To earlier and older skinheads and hooligans, neo-Nazis often appear to be 'too political' for comfort.

HOW DIFFERENT WERE THE OLD NAZIS?

In the face of the alarms of the well-meaning public in Germany and among its friends abroad at the riotous right wing incidents of 1991–3, there is a need to remind ourselves of the enormous differences between the old pre-Third Reich Nazi movement (not the established Third Reich)[63] and the phenomena at hand. I will concentrate, in particular, on four aspects that have no adequate parallels in the present before proceeding to a general discussion of the questions of continuity and interpretation. The old Nazi phenomenon will be examined first in its external context, then with reference to social classes, and finally with regard to its internal character and organisation, and its political environment.

When the National Socialist German Workers Party (NSDAP) first burst upon the scene in 1919–21, it was first and foremost a revanchist movement, a diehard war party bent on undoing the German defeat in World War One. The Treaty of Versailles figured prominently in most of Hitler's public addresses, as did the alleged 'stab-in-the-back' of the German army by subversives. The treaty, among other things, had declared the 'war guilt' of Germany and, more important to the professional military, insisted on limiting the armed forces to 100 000 officers and men. Hitler's political career, in fact, began as an agent of the German military who was sent out to sound out revanchist opinions among German right wing and veterans' movements of the day. The army even 'discovered' and trained him as a public speaker. A very large part of the NSDAP membership and voters from 1919 to 1933 were World War One veterans and their families who evidently shared his identification with the goals of the German war effort, the desire for European hegemony, and the quest for world power.

The organisational beginnings were similarly related to defeat in war and the military. The stormtroopers (SA) of the movement were brought under the umbrella of a Fighting Association (*Kampfbund*) of other militant veterans groups in pre-beerhall-putsch Bavaria which robbed them (and Hitler) of their autonomy to plot a seizure of power. Their organisation and officers were overwhelmingly of military derivation. The NSDAP's ultimately successful appeal to the voters – more precisely to one third of the voters in 1932–3 – was based on the promise of radically revising the Versailles Treaty, and reestablishing (and perhaps expanding) the German–Austrian imperial position in Europe. This quest had to be seen particularly in the light of the disintegration of the German and Austrian empires over what then became Polish, Czechoslovak, Hungarian, and Yugoslav successor states territories, all with substantial irredentist German minorities. German nationalists wanted to free these German minorities from the alien rule imposed upon them by the defeat in war and the peace treaties. The more ambitious pan-Germans among them went a step further and aimed at union with Austria, the re-establishment of German rule in these formerly German or Austrian areas and, perhaps even, expansion to other areas inhabited by German minorities in Eastern Europe. Hitler and the Nazi leadership in their mania set out to destroy the 'evil Soviet empire' – in their view a gigantic Jewish-Bolshevik conspiracy – and to put in its place their own restored racial empire over the allegedly inferior breeds of Eastern Europe. There were many ethnic German refugees from these areas among the early Nazi members and voters, especially along the eastern borders of the Weimar Republic. The idea of a reconquest of the German and Austrian eastern areas and the diaspora was also very popular later among the German Austrians of 1938 and the ethnic Germans who had remained behind in their respective Eastern European abodes in the twenties and thirties.[64]

It is very difficult to find any plausible parallels to this external setting of the old Nazi movement among the skinheads and hooligans today. They appear not to have any territorial or expansionist ambitions and to concentrate mostly on their immediate turf rivalries. Even in hotbeds of neo-Nazi revivalism, where no one has interfered with them, they have shown no real interest in what used to be the uppermost thought of the old Nazis. Even among neo-Nazi action groups and 'respectable' radical right parties such imperialist ambitions are rare.[65] Some of their popular ire even went for ethnic Germans (*Aussiedler*) from Eastern Europe and the former Soviet Union and, back in 1989–90, for East Germans coming to West Germany. The prejudices of young West German *Hauptschule* students today particularly focus on such fellow Germans. To be sure, there are still refugees and expellees from the Oder–Neisse area and the Sudetenland who fled or were expelled in 1944–5 and would like their old properties back but they are few in numbers (15 per cent) and can hardly expect an armed German crusade to win back these territories. Most of all, they know that their cause cannot count on majority support today, nearly half a century after the decisive defeat of the Third Reich in World War Two. The generations that served in that war, by now, are not only outnumbered one to four by younger generations but for the most part have long given up and accepted peace and the status quo. There are public opinion polls that unmistakably show the fading of the old nationalistic and imperialistic attitudes that, in the late forties, still preoccupied large numbers of Germans.[66] By the same token, the pervasive 'goose step' militarism of the old Nazi movement in its time has long faded and, at best, is represented today only by the comic opera antics of military sports groups of the far right and an occasional *Bundeswehr* draftee (not officer) of right wing leaning.

The second point is that, in its day and in retrospect, the old Nazi movement was invariably placed by observers into the context of the class struggle raging in Germany, the struggle between the rising organised labour movement and the SPD and KPD and, on the other hand, the bourgeoisie and other defenders of the pre-World War One social order. Historians and social scientists may still quibble today over the exact class composition and character of fascist movements and their electorates – the percentages of working-class versus middle class members or voters or of lower middle and independents – or over the extent to which there were conspiracies of business, industry, or other established social forces 'behind' the rise and success of any fascist interwar movement.[67] But no one can describe the old Nazi movement, or the Italian fascist movement, for that matter, without mentioning its all-out assault on labour unions and on the socialist and communist parties who had allegedly taken over the country's politics. The Nazi stormtroopers were always told by their leaders that they had to 'reconquer the streets' from the socialists and communists and, in fact, the NSDAP received much of its heavy bourgeois support for reconquering, or attempting to, the city-halls and parliaments of the nation.[68] The overwhelming majority of stormtrooper violence was directed at communists and socialists. This interpretation of the fundamental rationale of the Nazi movement was always widely accepted and, in the seventies, achieved a dominant role in the form of the popular 'theories of fascism'.

Even a casual look at today's neo-Nazis and skinheads shows us that this does not apply to them. The social context of class struggle between capital and labour has no relevance to them anymore. Most of their followers, in fact, are blue-collar workers of low skill and the rare allegations of a capitalist conspiracy behind them are implausible to anyone except perhaps the radical left. To be sure, in West Germany they frequently have done battle with left-wingers in the streets just as the stormtroopers did under the Weimar Republic, but today's left-wingers are hardly proletarian or blue collar. The *Autonome*, the left wing terrorists, or the teachers and social workers of Berlin in the SPD period have generally been well-educated scions of the middle and upper classes, which creates a curious reversal of the Weimar confrontation, that is *if* class struggle in the original sense still constituted a meaningful interpretation of today's German political reality which it does not. The modernisation theory, or seeing the skinheads and hooligans as the 'losers' of the communications revolution of the seventies and eighties supplies a far better explanation of their rise. But this interpretation in turn fails to explain the earlier phenomenon because the situation was completely different then. The old Nazis or Italian fascists did mean to protect the property of factory owners and landowners from the greedy assault of revolutionary socialists and squatters. These simply were different circumstances, different societies, and different battles than the neo-Nazis and skinheads are fighting today. It is also worth pointing out that the economic philosophy of neofascist movements – to the extent that we can ascertain it – is rather different from the statism and corporatism the old fascists favoured in the 1920s and 1930s. While there are still some statist, welfarist preferences as we would expect from people at the bottom of society, there are also elements of economic individualism that would make the old Nazis turn in their graves. This is particularly true in France, Scandinavia, and among the new leagues of Northern Italy, but also among the REPs of Germany.

The third aspect that we should compare is the internal character and organisation of the old Nazi party and movement which was utterly unified under one leader and, to speak with Maurice Duverger, characterised by its huge party militia, the stormtroopers, and by a considerable degree of internal controls on the individual member. It had a jealously guarded monopoly on the extreme right which, at the decisive moment, gave it enough leverage to get into power. The present German radical right is fragmented into over 20 separate political parties and innumerable local groups of skinheads and hooligans who are rarely under firm party control or of certain loyalty to party commands and ideology. In most cases, in fact, they have fought each other with considerable violence, for example between rival leaders, parties, and, of course, among skin gangs and hooligan teams. Their inability to form a single organisation and ideology and to agree on a single leadership figure clearly handicaps any effort to succeed at the polls or in any other way.

The fourth and last point deals with the political environment of the NSDAP before 1933 and today's extreme right. The old Nazis faced a rather chaotic political system made up of executive instability – Weimar cabinets fell at a rate comparable to the Fourth Republic of France – an extreme multiparty system in the terms of Giovanni Sartori, and unsettled civil-military relations, not to mention the latent civil war among the paramilitary armies of right and left, among whom the stormtroopers played a major role only in the last years of the republic.[69] Barely launched onto a democratic path, the Weimar Republic staggered from crisis to crisis for 14 years: the assault of left wing revolutionaries in 1918–19, the right wing Kapp putsch of 1920, the economic and political near collapse of 1923, the agrarian crisis and critical internal splits among some of the major parties in 1928–9, the onset of the Great Depression in 1929–30, and the final political collapse of 1930–3 when political violence claimed hundreds of casualties each year, and the responsible political leaders mostly made efforts to escape governmental responsibility. In 1933, the fatally weakened republic finally collapsed into the arms of Hitler and the NSDAP, having long lost the support of a popular majority for the Weimar constitution.[70] The Nazi takeover was a triumph of an authoritarian (some say totalitarian) political organisation over the disorganised Weimar political system. Contrary to what many Germans and a number of foreign journalists are claiming now, it was a well-organised party and not at all a matter of mushrooming violent prejudicial incidents and people gelling into a movement that took over the state. To be sure, there were plenty of raw prejudices around, especially anti-semitism and xenophobia, and there were waves of foreign refugees and immigrants in the early Weimar years as well as hate crimes against individuals and small groups – though nothing like today's attacks on asylum hostels – comparable to some of those in Germany in recent years, or in France, Britain, or the United States, for that matter. Prejudice and hate crimes alone, horrible as they may be, are not sufficient by themselves to cause an *apartheid* or slavery system, or a genocidal holocaust. Such horrors require organisation and the power of the state, as the history of *apartheid*, slavery, and genocide amply bears out.

The current upsurge of several parties of the German radical right is not up against anything like the tottering Weimar Republic with its fragmented popular support and anaemic democratic spirit, vitiated by the strident nationalism of an unaccepted defeat and an authoritarian political culture beneath the thin veneer of a democratic constitution. Today's gaggle of competing right wing groups faces a formidable foe in the democratic government of the FRG, with a stable party system and a well-entrenched democratic consensus that, at least in the areas of the old FRG, can look back upon four decades of reliable democratic practice. There has been a recession now but under conditions of a well-established and popular welfare state. Unlike the early 1930s, there is no major depression to endure in the absence of an adequate 'social net' – not even in East Germany where the unemployed can fall back on a well-funded unemployment insurance – and there are no establishment conspiracies against democracy, such as were present among the Weimar business, industry, and military groups.[71]

Worse yet for the right wing challengers, there is a tradition of 'militant democracy' (*streitbare Demokratie*) in West Germany – not in East Germany – that has almost instantly brought together a grand alliance of supporters of the major middle-of-the-road parties, the churches, trade unions, and business and farm organisations whenever any fundamental challenge to democracy has occurred in the past, so that the system has not needed to rely on the democratically dubious support of the far left. The massive demonstrations against xenophobia and hate crimes, which mobilised an estimated two million Germans in 1992/93, vividly show that German militant democracy is alive and well, and likely to remain so. It remains to be seen, however, whether this civic mobilisation will be channelled into anything more lasting than an anti-fascist statement by those whose democratic steadfastness was never in doubt.

CONCLUDING REMARKS

It should be obvious by now that the old Nazis are not 'coming back' and that neo-Nazis, skinheads and hooligans have very little in common with them, the ever-quotable *New York Times* notwithstanding. It would be most extraordinary, indeed, given the profound changes in external and internal conditions, not to mention the passage of generations, if they were. This is not to deny, however, that the wave of politically motivated violence of 1991–3 was horrible, whatever its causes may have been. Neither can it be denied that the Christian Democratic administrations in Bonn and in some of the state and local governments have been shockingly incompetent and laggard in rising to the occasion. Patterns of not taking seriously the danger from the right or of being much harsher in dealing with left wing protesters than with right-wingers are only now being corrected by German courts and law enforcement. Legislatures too must be faulted for being slow to recognise the problems and to take appropriate steps for their control. The opposition SPD, likewise, has failed to respond appropriately and at all levels in the states where it is in control. It has little reason to be gleeful about this embarrassment of the Kohl administration. The German media also have had a rather negative effect in two respects. One is their contribution to the level of public fear of the foreigners, especially of refugees and of asylum-seekers. The other is the failure to use their powers of persuasion to soothe public feelings about the current refugee crisis.

Why would anyone argue something as preposterous as that the old Nazis might be coming back, or that the German neo-Nazi and skinhead phenomenon is likely to turn into another Nazi movement and dictatorship? Why did they ignore the pre-existing violent youth setting and perceive only the present political overtones? One reason, especially among Germans, is partisan: such an interpretation is likely to benefit many people, in particular those who would like to pin the brown herring on the Christian Democrats (CDU/CSU) in power, thereby legitimising their own opposition to the government in office. Advocates in opposition to curbing the flow of asylum-seekers have similarly hoped to taint any reform of the current law with the Nazi label. There are striking parallels between recent American policies to slow down or halt the anticipated arrival of tens of thousands of Haitian boat people and the dilemma of Germany which had no less than 70 per cent of all asylum-seekers demanding admittance to EC countries in 1992. It is easy to call any effort at reform of the asylum law 'Nazi racism' in order to defeat it.

Aside from partisanship, sensationalising the news of course sells newspapers and magazines, or it may increase the audience of television programmes. That foreign public opinion so quickly misinterpreted the incidents as a return of the old Nazis is obviously related to memories of the distant past and to the widespread uneasiness about German unification. Besides, it is easier to go from the black legend directly into newsprint rather than to take a detour through a library. The accusation that foreign television crews at Rostock paid skinhead youths to raise their arms in the Hitler salute has a ring of plausibility. There have certainly been parallels such as interviewing an insignificant local rabble-rouser who was happy to oblige with vintage Nazi propaganda slogans for the personal attention he received, or getting skinhead youths to mug for the press cameras.

Then there is ignorance, for example, of the realities of the old pre-1933 Nazi movement, its external and internal conditions, or exactly how prejudice and organisation can produce such a movement. The occurrence of neo-fascist movements in many countries, from post-communist Russia to Louisiana, and what they may have in common also may not really be known to a person shocked by Nazi symbols and talk. Or they may not realise the similarities between Jean-Marie Le Pen of the French National Front, Franz Schönhuber of the REPs, and gubernatorial candidate David Duke. Perhaps they did not know that the REPs were named, in the mid-eighties, after the American Republican party under Ronald Reagan, or they did not reflect on what these neo-Nazis could possibly have had in mind with such a choice. Was it the social Darwinism, the carefree machismo, or what?

The most amazing kind of ignorance displayed in this connection, both by Germans and by Americans – the British press seemed to know better – has been the failure to place the German skinhead violence with its racist and anti-gay trimmings into the broader context of young urban gangs, the contemporary youth culture, and its trendy styles and music. The Nazi stormtroopers were never like this. Perhaps one can forgive the *New York Times*, which rarely ventures a glimpse at the violent youth of the greater New York area – it only reports on youth violence and racism elsewhere, like in Los Angeles. But even the *Los Angeles Times*, which conscientiously and with expressions of alarm 'covers' the extraordinary level of youth violence and racial prejudice there, never made the connection. Industrial societies today, I fear, live in a permanent state of murderous anarchy, especially when ethnic conflict and immigration stoke the fires, and parents, schools, and public authorities (including the police) appear to be rather uncaring and helpless about their violent, alienated young.

What Should the Germans Do?

What should the German authorities do, what can they do to curb their violent skinheads and neo-Nazis whenever the violence gets out of hand, as indeed it did in 1991–3? What should they not do? The most obvious mistake is to take the public relations disaster of this for Germany for the real battlefield on which they have to prove themselves. The black legend of the German past is based on realities they cannot change – two world wars and the holocaust – and there is little point in fighting the image which many Germans themselves and the outside world attach to all Germans regardless of whether they were, or could have been, involved in the horrendous crimes of the past. In a manner of speaking, the skinheads themselves have discovered how they can tweak the nose of the German establishment and rub it into the dirt of the black legend: *épater le bourgeois*, embarrass everybody, demonstrate to the world that 'we are all Nazis'. There are amazing parallels here to the thinking of the German left-wing terrorists and even the student rebels of 1968 who thought they could bring out the 'latent fascist character' of the old FRG with their violent provocations. There is little to gain from entering this game of finger pointing. This is not to say that the Kohl administration and lower level authorities should not have made more of an effort to speak out against the mounting mayhem, to 'set signals', 'view with alarm', and other gestures demanded for the public relations audience within and without. But we should be under no illusion that this would have stopped the escalating incidents, or even that it would have dissuaded people inside and outside the country from their black legend thoughts about the Germans. At best, it might have curbed the jeering citizenry of Hoyerswerda, Schwerin, or Rostock–Lichtenhagen and kept them from their public support of the anti-foreigner mobs.

The real battle for the hearts and minds should have been, and should be fought elsewhere, far from the world of public relations. First of all, there can be no doubt but that both the attacks on asylum hostels and those on individuals and small groups of victims, foreigners or not, involved major criminal acts under German law and, for that matter, any other code of law. Arson, bombs, armed robbery, physical injury, and violent death, and even the threats and physical harassment of victims all call for criminal prosecution and punishment. Germany has plenty of laws for all of this, including some making the bystanders responsible for not resisting a crime and for failing to aid a victim.[72]

The brazenness of many of the attacks – in most cases their perpetrators would run away when confronted with police authority – suggests frequent police failures and, especially in rural and small-town areas, inadequate police forces and poor logistical support. What was obviously needed was a quick riot response force and a local state of emergency and curfew – all highly controversial with Germans who fought the Emergency Laws of 1968 for ten long years in the sixties – that could have been imposed wherever mobs were gathering to menace life and limb.[73] Under such a local state of emergency, the level of sentences and punishments for riotous conduct could also be stepped up considerably from the leniency normally practised by laws and judges in Germany, especially with typical riot offences such as manslaughter, arson, and physical injury. The suppression of neo-Nazi parties and groups, also possible under German anti-totalitarian laws, promises little relief from the violence: most perpetrators neither belong to such a group nor would the dissolution of their group prevent them from acting as individuals. Prompt intervention when crimes such as the assaults on asylum hostels are about to be committed and equally swift punishment for individual perpetrators is the best prescription for a crisis at hand.

The other, long-term set of solutions is far more difficult and we can only hope that the Germans do not learn from the Americans how to ignore the root problems of violent youth, gang killings in the inner cities and violence in schools. The current skinhead and neo-Nazi violence appear to be a puzzling mix of political motives – mostly those of the recruiters of neo-Nazi parties – with the alienated and violent youth scene of skinhead gangs and soccer hooligans which is extremely volatile and, especially in East Germany, vulnerable to neo-Nazi slogans and fashions. The underlying problems, to quote the Berlin Senator for Youth and Family Affairs, Thomas Krüger (SPD), is 'the structural weakening at the centre of society' in general, and the near-collapse of the social structure, the family, and the schools in East Germany as a result of the 'earthquake of unification' and its social and economic consequences.[74] The transmission of values to the young of East Germany has been further disrupted by the fall of communism, leaving insecure parents and teachers both left without authority, and a 'naive youth prone to violence'. The centre of German society has been weakened because the mounting problems of the institutions of the family and the school interfere with their ability to acculturate its young to its mores and values. As a result, every new generation increasingly invades the established society with swords and torches (or baseball bats and Molotov cocktails) like a horde of barbarians.

The Youth and Family Senator's current programme for Berlin, *Youth with a Future*, may give us a glimpse of what some of the remedies might be, albeit under severe financial limitations. The three-year Berlin programme focuses on prevention, the social integration of youth, flexibility, and mobility, hopefully denying the right wing recruiters the receptive young audience they have found in the past. There is a lot of emphasis on vocational training for the under-educated; year-long European sojourns (outside Germany) to overcome parochialism and prejudice; an 'ecological year' of postgraduation work for jobless youth; and school class travel to foreign countries where Germans may have a bad image. For 10-to-14-year olds who are currently suffering an epidemic of stealing, joy-riding, and crashing other people's cars, there is a program *Bauen statt Klauen* (Build, Don't Steal) which teaches them to assemble sports cars and repair old cars. There are plans to offer skinhead youth sports facilities and coaching, youth clubs and rooms for rock music practice and rehearsal, youth counsellors, and special tickets for public transport and sports events.[75] Young violent offenders are to be taken to meet and talk with their victims – shades of a controversial Los Angeles programme to invite gang shooters to the autopsies of gang victims, but without the blood and gore. Berlin, in fact, planned to send 15 skinheads to meet 15 Afro-American gang members in Los Angeles.

Berlin's skinhead problems, as the Senator makes clear, are limited mostly to the urban periphery of crowded *Plattenbau* tenements in suburbs built by the old communist regime rather than found in the urban centre. The city's efforts, he hopes, could woo back up to three fourths of right wing youth by offering better vocational training, better housing, recreation, and jobs. Berlin can also emphasise its long years of intercultural experience in the schools, whereas in other East German *Länder* new youth programmes need to be introduced. Saxony and

Mecklenburg–Vorpommern (one of the more violent states) have also started promising youth programmes. The truly long-term problems of families, schools, and employment, however, require long-term dedication and more funds than are currently available.[76] Jobs continue to be scarce in East Germany for the foreseeable future and especially as long as the *Treuhand* values privatisation more than social peace and well-being (see Karl Kahrs, above). The Senator hoped that, given time and money, even the stricken society of East Germany would make its way from a 'collapsed totalitarian system' to a sound, postmodern 'information society'.

Along similar lines, an education professor at the University of Bremen, Franz-Josef Krafeld, has championed a long-range programme of '*akzeptierende Jugendarbeit*' (youth counselling on the basis of accepting), since repression and punishment alone seem to be counterproductive with the insecure young ruffians. Their extremism and provocative violence, Krafeld argued, reflect existential problems they cannot seem to master. What they need is sympathetic counselling and 'social spaces' for young groups in which they can centre their adolescent lives, among their peers. They not only need youth clubs, especially in the East, but they need to feel personally involved in building those clubs, preferably with the involvement also of adult volunteers. To quote a magazine essay by Karl-Otto Honderich, social integration in Germany has not failed in the big, political questions but at the level of 'the collective, widely shared feelings from which a sense of community and common images emerge. Here we form our ideas of good and bad ways of living together, of belonging, and of being strangers . . . These feelings are easy to excite by perverse political appeals and cannot just be commanded by political or moral fiat'.

Honderich also has a plausible theory for why the volatile mood of the populace, especially in the East, has turned upon the asylum seekers. 'Just as individuals feel deeply hurt when their persons are not recognized, there is no greater hurt for collective feelings than to ignore them which is exactly what has happened in Germany. In the former GDR, community relations have been destroyed, often all of a sudden. With the jobs, the groups at work and in housing communities, friendly clubs and vacation homes, youth organisations and youth clubs have withered away. The most affected by this have been disadvantaged, marginal groups and youth which has been abandoned at a precarious stage of their lives . . . When they advance upon an asylum hostel, the violent young gain a sense of self-confidence and belonging (to a group) which everyday life denies them . . . Together with the Western skins, they are completing German unification in their own way'. Honderich sees the West German and East German senses of identity far apart and blames this dissensus for the current spiritual trauma. East Germans in the majority, he writes, are still rooted in the national community feelings – unity, freedom, equality – of the 19th century while West Germans disdain this old-fashioned nationalism and treasure instead the welfare state, the rule of law (*Rechtsstaat*), constitutional patriotism, and their 'social market economy', values that are by and large alien to the East Germans who feel helpless and 'taken over' by this postmodern ethos. They are deeply offended that, allegedly, 'foreigners are now treated better than they are' and are venting their ire at distant Bonn by attacking the nearby asylum hostels – as a proxy and symbol of the Wessi takeover, of the *multikulti* imposition, the moral basis of distant Bonn – in order to 'force everybody into the collective [all-] German guilt and identity'.[77] He did not explain why asylum hostels have been under attack also in the West, nor distinguish between the hostility of a small minority and the community feelings of the overwhelming majority in both parts of Germany.

We are left to wonder however if, at the heart of the present German dilemma, there is not simply a dramatic gap between the promise of human freedom and the realities of a pluralistic and free society – free also to the zealots of the radical right. Since 1945, Germans have dreamt brave dreams of an open society, a democratic society in which everyone can do what they want, within reason, and where pluralistic forces in democratic competition determine what is to be done. They have been very reluctant to go back to the social, political, and police controls of the past. But their quest for individual and democratic freedom is not easily satisfied. Politics intervenes with competing sets of values and complicates everything.

After the *Wende* of 1982, when West Germans abandoned their failed social democratic experiment for a return to Christian Democratic conservatism – with overtones of Thatcherism and Reaganite social Darwinism[78] – they shifted their emphasis back to the *Leistungsprinzip* (principle of achievement), the market, and private initiative rather than the communitarian beliefs of the SPD. Little did they anticipate that the ensuing selfishness and *Wohlstandspatriotismus* (emphasis on one's own prosperity above all sharing), by 1989, would be on a collision course with the flood of poor refugees from everywhere, and with the communitarian principles of East German society with which they suddenly found themselves 'unified'. The resulting clash has left both Ossis and Wessis very unhappy in their no longer divided country, and given rise to major dislocations and dysfunctions. And while the Bonn conservatives are withholding the social support needed by East German youth, schools, and families (as they had done for a decade in the West),[79] evidently expecting Adam Smith's 'invisible hand' to take care of everything, some all too visible hands have been busy taking advantage of all that hurt and disorientation. In this period of youth unrest and fringe group mischief, Germany's salvation lies not with the market-place or with a hands-off approach by the major parties, or even less with a public relations campaign against the black legend of Germany's past. This has been the hour of the big anti-racist demonstrations and of militant democracy, the defence of the freedoms Germans hold dear against those who would destroy them.

Notes

1. Most people admit this when pressed for details. Press statements trying to deflect the alleged likeness to '1922' (New York Times) and to aggressive hordes that are said to have 'knocked down Jews and others' then – citing, of all things, Hitler's *Mein Kampf* as a source(!) – hardly help the argument out of its slough of misinformation. The issue is, in particular, whether the industrious tailors for a naked emperor can find Nazi origins in young gangs rather than among veterans of the great war.

2. According to the monthly *Politbarometer*, the number of West Germans expressing such dissatisfaction rose to 46 per cent in November 1991, while only 36 per cent were still 'satisfied' with the government's performance, *Politbarometer*, November 1992, p. 40. Satisfaction with West German democracy also had dropped from a level of 85 per cent in 1990 – the high point of pride in the Western democratic constitution then being accepted by East Germany – to a mere 61 per cent. In the East German *Länder*, an astounding 67.3 per cent declared themselves 'not satisfied' with the workings of democracy. See *Ibid.*, p. 59 and *Politbarometer Ost*, pp. 35 ff., 43 ff. and 57.

3. *New York Times*, Nov. 25, 1992, p. A4. We will explain below that 'things' did not begin this way at all 'in Hitler's time', and that they were, unfortunately, very much under the control of the Nazis. This was particularly true of the *Kristallnacht* pogrom to which many observers have compared the attacks in Rostock and elsewhere.

4. The caller was, presumably, one of the arsonists, perhaps the one who later tried to commit suicide (Lars Christiansen). West German (and now all-German) law notwithstanding, the words of the old Hitler greeting, of course, have been used a thousand times privately or publicly all throughout the decades since 1945, and not just by incorrigible old Nazis but by rebellious juveniles and drunks for their shocking effect.

5. *Washington Post National Weekly Edition*, Dec. 14–20, 1992, p. 28.
6. *Los Angeles Times*, Nov. 25, 1992, p. B7. In an article relating the story of a Romanian gypsy family deported from Cologne upon due court examination but then smuggled back and hidden by a German opposition group, foreign correspondent Tamara Jones told of a neo-Nazi vigilante group that offered a prize to recapture the mother of the gypsy family – a story reminiscent of Ku Klux Klan offers to help patrol the Mexican border. Jones, however, said the 'move recalls Gestapo roundups of Jews, Gypsies, and other non-Aryans during the Holocaust.' She neglected to point out, among other mis-statements, that the Gestapo was an arm of the state, not a vigilante group. See *Los Angeles Times*, March 9, 1993, p. A1
7. *Ibid.*, Nov. 24 and Dec. 3, 1992, editorial page. Gedmin also felt that officials' insistence that the violence was random and largely unorganised was 'unconvincing' but could only hint that current investigations of *Bundeswehr* soldiers for several murders, attacks on refugee centres, and the spread of neo-fascist propaganda might suggest otherwise.
8. One of the more intriguing shadings of American opinion management came out in the decision of *Newsweek* magazine, on the occasion of the outrage against the Turkish family of Arslan at Moelln, to use in its European edition a picture of Faruk Arslan, the sad father, while the U.S. edition of the same report showed the hateful faces of skinheads with the Hitler salute. The European caption spoke of vicious right wing terrorism sapping the self-confidence of the German nation while the American version had neo-Nazis challenging German democracy. American television coverage also tended towards suggestions of a rebirth of the Third Reich, or at least of the original Nazi movement.
9. In the first round of the presidential elections of 1988, Le Pen received 14.4 per cent of the vote. For further details, see William Safran 'The National Front in France: from Lunatic Fringe to Limited Respectability', in Merkl and Weinberg, eds., *Encounters With the Contemporary Radical Right*, Boulder, Col.: Westview Press, 1993, pp. 19 ff.
10. *The Economist*, Dec. 5, 1992, pp. 15–16, 59 f.
11. The FBI national report on hate crimes of January 1993, unfortunately, was based on less than a fifth of localities reporting. Existing state and local reports, however, indicate levels as high and higher than the British figures, with blacks, Jews, and gays the most frequent victims.
12. As we have emphasised, the black legend is very well-rooted also among Germans where it has recently been associated with 'left wing alarmism' (Klaus Hartung in *Die Zeit*, Nov. 20, 1992, no. 48) and called the 'lie (*Lebenslüge*) of German normality' (Jürgen Habermas, *ibid.*, no. 51, Dec. 11, 1992). Habermas sees the problem not in the violence itself but in the mendacity of the public discussion over political asylum and the new political assertiveness and self-regarding attitudes of moderate politicians, including the right wing of the SPD. See also *Für eine zivile Republik*, ed. by Wilhelm von Sternburg, Frankfurt: Fischer, 1992 whose contributors range from 'alarmists' like Ralph Giordano who conjures up the 'ghost of the brown renaissance' to Thomas Schmid who makes a plea against an 'anti-fascist 5-minutes-before-1933 hysteria'.

13. See also Merkl, 'Rollerball or Neo-Nazi Violence', in Merkl, ed., *Political Violence and Terror: Motifs and Motivations*, Berkeley: University of California Press, 1986, pp. 232–48 where the history of the postwar West German radical right is recapitulated.

14. To quote Floyd Salas again: 'Those boys denied this opportunity [of public sports] through race, poverty, neglect and the failure of government and the public schools to reach and train them turn this undisciplined and amoral force [a young male's survival instinct] on themselves. It is a historical fact that when American wealth is widely distributed, gangs tend to channel their youthful energy into social activism and community concerns. When public funding for social welfare is discouraged and denied, on the other hand, gangs often express this same energy in murderous rage against each other and their community. It thus may be no coincidence that crime and violence soared so dramatically in the 1980s'. In other words, the neglect of the inner cities by the Reagan administration – in fact the squandering of four and a half billion dollars by his Department of Housing and Urban Affairs that could have helped the inner cities of America – was a major cause of gangs and their violence in our cities.

15. See esp. Ekhart Zimmerman and Thomas Saalfeld, 'The Three Waves of West German Rightwing Extremism', in Merkl and Weinberg, op. cit., pp. 50–74 where the hate crimes are captured in graphs over time.

16. To quote the Head of the Foreigners Office, Almuth Berger, 'in GDR schools they thought and spoke far too little about racism, anti-Semitism and about hostility towards other nations.' There was no education in tolerance. See the interview in *Der Spiegel*, March, 1990, no. 14, pp. 106–10. Frequently observed prejudicial incidents included the treatment of foreign students from 'fraternal socialist countries' such as Hungary or the CSFR on trains. Identified from their passports, they often found themselves ordered to alight from transit trains and thereupon were arrested and prosecuted by local authorities for being in a place without a permit. The segregated workers of colour sometimes fared worse. See also *Der Spiegel*, April 2, 1990, no. 14, pp. 98–119. The racist GDR jargon for them was and still is 'Fijis.'

17. Particularly in families where the parents were officials and active members of the state communist party (SED) or its mass organisations – often currently demoted or unemployed – the teenage children have tended to be soccer hooligans or politically radicalised in the direction of the radical right, the 'brown sons of red fathers' as observers have put it in a reversal of the sixties left wing radical syndrome in ex-Nazi families of the 68ers, the 'red sons and daughters of brown fathers'. See also Walter Friedrich and Peter Förster, 'Ostdeutsche Jugend 1990' in *Deutschland Archiv*, no. 4. April, 1991, pp. 348–60, especially pp. 352–5.

18. See this writer's description of the soccer hooligan scene in Merkl, 'Rollerball . . .', pp. 229–33. Wagner believes that with the 'majority of incidents of attacks on foreigners and other such targets, there is evidence of careful preparation and planning attributable to the organised core groups, including the rallying of large hordes of assailants.'

19. See 'Gefahr von rechts wächst' in *Berliner Zeitung*, April 23, 1991. Also

Walter Friedrich, 'Mentalitätswandlungen der Jugend in der DDR,' in *Das Parlament*, no. 17 (1990), supplement B 16, and Loni Niederländer, 'Zu den Ursachen rechtsradikaler Tendenzen in der DDR' in *Neue Justiz*, no. 1 (1990). Psychologists have described the disorientation and *angst* caused by the collapse of communism, mostly among 12 to 15-year old students in the public schools, but there is probably a time lag and age group lag between the mental agonies of beginning puberty and the violent acting out by the dropouts of the next teenage stage.

20. 'Rechtsextremistische Orientierungen in der DDR-Jugend: Wie sind sie entstanden' in Magistratsverwaltung für Jugend, Familie und Sport, Jugendförderung, *Jugend und Rechtsextremismus in Berlin-Ost*, Berlin, no date (1990), pp. 9–18 which relates the 20 to 25 year old activists of 1990 to the alienated punks and hooligans of much younger age in the eighties.

21. See especially Peter Ködderitzsch and Leo A. Müller, *Rechtsextremismus in der DDR* (Göttingen: Lamuv Verlag, 1990), pp. 11–28 where the generational basis is said to be among the birth cohorts between 1965 and 1975 (p. 13) and the clash between skinheads and young people, presumably punks attending a rock concert at Zion's church is described in some detail, as well as its judicial aftermath (pp. 15–17). To the extent that today's attacks are indeed planned and directed by the neo-Nazi cadre they appear to be intended for recruitment and reinforcing small group solidarity in the movement among the new members rather than for combating a real enemy.

22. One consequence of this kind of anarchy has been the incompleteness of information about radical right organisations. There have been widely varying estimates of membership, for example, that range from partial figures of 3000 to 4000 political hard-core members and perhaps 10 000 skinheads, Faschos and hooligans – 550 skinheads in Brandenburg alone and 500 right radicals in Dresden, a hotbed – to wild exaggerations such as the 30 000 neo-Nazis claimed by an anti-fascist group to be present in the greater Leipzig area. There are far lower estimates: Bernd Wagner believes the political hard-core members not to have grown much beyond the original 1500. Some groups such as these are known to have lost half of their members in the first year of unification as compared to 1989. See also *Sachsenspiegel*, April 19, 1991.

23. The action-oriented groups also stress organisation far less than do the old neo-Nazi parties and, for that reason, have less to fear from official edicts outlawing their respective group. As long as their members are not individually caught and convicted for hate crimes, they can simply lie low for a while, individually join other action groups, or reappear under a new name.

24. The source is a listing of cases in newspapers and *Der Spiegel*, December 7, 1992, no. 49, pp. 14–15 that ends with the Turkish women in Moelln. There is some disagreement regarding additional cases.

25. One was a pensioner, aged 53, who drank copiously in a tavern with two skinheads who in the end trampled him to death and set him afire. There is some disagreement as to motive in that one view claims that his skinhead drinking companions considered the man to be gay, while another view

insists the bartender had (falsely) fingered him as Jewish. The other was a young gardener sitting in a restaurant when 60 skinheads invaded the premises and broke his skull with baseball bats. No political motive was reported for this restaurant invasion. One homeless case involved three very young skins (two of them, aged 16 and 18, were caught later) who tortured an older man in their car and then doused him with gasoline and burned him to death.

26. In the 1970s, already, groups of rowdies were occasionally reported invading restaurants and attacking patrons in the Munich area. At Berlin lake resorts and beaches in 1991, large groups of skinheads and hooligans were frequently reported terrorising other people with no particular preference of politics, nationality or race. See also Merkl. 'A New Lease on Life for the Radical Right', in Merkl and Weinberg, op. cit., pp. 220–1.

27. A final comment on the fatality list of 1992 might also draw attention to the timing of the attacks which appears not to be entirely random. The deaths came in clusters, three within one week in March, another three pairs each within periods of a few days in July and August, and six in November, similarly clustered. Seven occurred on Saturdays, traditional days of working-class carousing and rural tavern brawls. Clusters of several killings usually started with a Saturday, just as if the first excess had triggered copycat outrages.

28. The incident reported also included an attack by right wing thugs on a resort that had taken in 40 Russian children from Chernobyl. See Merkl, 'A New Lease . . .', pp. 208–10. In the meantime, there have also been reports of violence threatened against an elementary school class on an outing, threats against individual handicapped persons, and threats against an institution for young retarded students.

29. In all of 1990, according to the Federal Ministry of Youth, there had been 243 East German attacks on foreigners (128 in West Germany). In 1991 (until mid-November), there were already 1823. See *Neues Deutschland*, December 12, 1991. Eventually, the grand total of the BfV for 1991 was 2368, including 338 cases of arson and 241 attacks on people.

30. In the East German *Länder*, according to the polls of August 1991, the SPD suffered a considerable loss of support in that particular month. As before, 62 per cent of Ossis mentioned unemployment as their chief concern in August, and 51 per cent of them were not sure they would retain their job. See *Politbarometer, Aug. 1991*, pp. i, v–vii, 58–59, 106.

31. Only 23 per cent of Ossis and 16 per cent of Wessis disapproved of the right of asylum in principle while 31 per cent of Ossis and 43 per cent of Wessis believed that any political refugees should be let into the country. *Ibid.*, pp. x–xi.

32. Very few Germans play baseball but the bats have enjoyed a sales volume out of all proportion. See also *Der Spiegel*, December 7, 1992, no. 50, pp. 33–4. The data for this section are from a chronology compiled by the office of the *Bundestag* deputy Ulla Jelpe (PDS) from mostly left wing sources. Although they may at times disagree with published law enforcement reports, they are generally factual and objective. See special issue 'Rassismus und Neofaschismus in Deutschland' of *Atom* (Novem-

ber 1992), pp. 4–87.

33. Typical complaints referred to shoplifting or petty theft, but also to drug dealing and sexual matters ranging from prostitution to accosting or molesting German women. For a critical account that is sympathetic to the refugees and sceptical of their treatment by local German law enforcement (at times, local police would search these hostels and there were some reports of police misconduct in interrogations), see 'Das Märchen von der Ausländerkriminalität' in 'Rassismus und Neofas-chismus', pp. 42–5. The BKA claimed in 1991 that 'foreigners' accounted for 27 per cent of crimes while their share of the total population was only 8.5 per cent. The writer of this article felt that these statistics failed to pinpoint the offending foreigners among foreign 'occupation soldiers' and certain kinds of tourists, namely drug dealers and violent criminals, rather than the typical asylum-seekers. The racist prejudices of the tabloid press, including Springer papers such as *Die Welt*, and stereotypical perceptions among German law enforcement and bureaucracy, the article avers, spread fear among the population of small towns, especially in the provincial atmosphere of East and West German backwaters.

34. *Frankfurter Rundschau*, September 19 and 26, 1991.

35. The interpretation of 'Rassismus und Neofaschismus' is that the CDU/CSU government deliberately permitted the public reaction to the other asylum-seekers to escalate in order to browbeat the SPD and Greens into cooperating with its plans to gravely restrict the right to asylum. See 'Menschenjäger und Schreibtischtäter', ibid., pp. 6–10.

36. Some American newspaper accounts had insisted that North Rhine Westphalia was disproportionately often involved without noticing that this West German *Land* alone has more inhabitants than the entire old GDR. Only with 'other offences' was this *Land* rather above the average.

37. About 85 per cent of all right wing violence, according to the BfV, was driven by xenophobia which before 1990 was behind only about half of the right wing acts in the old FRG. The 38 anti-semitic acts (2.3 per cent of the total) were composed of nine arson or explosive attacks, four of bodily injury, and 25 of property damage. There were 39 desecration of cemeteries, half of them of proven right wing origin.

38. In the chronicle of right wing violence mentioned earlier, the references to the antifascists are usually in the female gender (*AntifaschistInnen*) and the same is the case with most mentions of the embattled foreigners (*AusländerInnen*), meaning all antifascists and all foreigners. See 'Rassismus und Neofaschismus', *passim*.

39. The BfV report listed 135 violent right wing acts against the police or other public agencies (8 per cent of total). See also the examples in 'Rassismus und Neofaschismus', pp. 32, 41, 43–5, 47, 49, 51–3. In Eberswalde–Finow (northeast of Berlin), for example, 60 rampaging skinheads attacked 40 policemen with stones and bottles after having been turned away at a disco and knocking two passers-by to the ground. 22 skins were arrested. *Ibid.*, p. 51 (June 6, 1992).

40. Unfortunately, the measurements differ considerably from the OMGUS survey of 1946 over 35 years of studies of the Institut für Demoskopie,

Allensbach, to the second half of the eighties when a near-consensus gave the level at 14–15 per cent, including 4–8 per cent 'hard anti-semites'.

41. For the pre-unification record, see esp. Alphons Silbermann, *Sind wir Anti-Semiten?*, Cologne: Wissenschaft und Politik, 1982 and, for the present, Jürgen Elsässer, *Antisemitismus in der bundesrepublikanischen Gesellschaft*, Opladen: Westdeutscher Verlag, 1991, which also supplies the social background of German anti-semites. See *ibid.*, pp. 69f., 75f., 87f., 103 and 222ff. Elsässer, who writes for the periodical *Konkret*, reflects on the possible connections between German unification and an anti-semitic revival.

42. See *Frankfurter Allgemeine Zeitung*, August 26, 1992.

43. See the report in *Der Spiegel*, November 23 and 30, 1992, nos. 48 and 49, on the Interior Minister, Lothar Kupfer. Of those arrested, two thirds were from the surrounding *Land* Mecklenburg and the rest mostly from Hamburg, Bremen, and Berlin. See 'Rassismus und Neofaschismus', pp. 64–6.

44. The *Bereitschaftspolizei* is a kind of national guard created in the fifties to counter a possible East German invasion or communist insurrection in the FRG with quasi-military force. There was no German military as yet in the early fifties and the example of the Korean War had the Allies and the West Germans worried about the armed Vopo troops that were organised by the GDR. Comparing the absence of Rostock police commanders with that of LAPD chief Daryl Gates in the early hours of the 1992 Los Angeles riots, however, is not a good parallel because the effect of Gates' absence was to permit the rioters enraged by the Rodney King verdict to get out of control only for a little while after which Gates intended to reestablish police control in an instant.

45. This plausible explanation was offered by *Spiegel*-reporter Cordt Schnibben who also offers some evidence of latent community hostility and Turkish complaints about the slowness of the voluntary (all-German) fire brigade. Moelln skins tend to support the REPs – the prime suspect worked for the NPD – and there is a DVU vote of 8 per cent.

46. This occurred at a discussion of youth violence that brought together artists and law enforcement. See *Süddeutsche Zeitung*, December 11, 1992.

47. On youthful violence, see Unabhängige Regierungskommission zur Verhinderung und Bekämpfung von Gewalt, *Ursachen, Prävention und Kontrolle von Gewalt*, 4 vols., Berlin: Duncker & Humblot, 1990 and the comments on this *Gewaltkommissionsbericht*, in Peter-Alexis Albrecht and Otto Backes, *Verdeckte Gewalt: Plädoyer für eine 'innere Abrüstung'*, Frankfurt: Suhrkamp, 1990.

48. There has also been some skinhead violence against the police as the reader will recall. On left wing violence, see also Dieter Baake, *Jugend und Jugendkulturen. Darstellung und Deutung*, Weinheim and Munich: Juventa, 1987 and *Zwischen Resignation und Gewalt. Jugendprotest in den 80er Jahren*, ed. by Th. Bock et al., Opladen: Leske and Budrich, 1989. For a report on the most recent left wing assaults on notable neo-Nazis, including some with lethal force, see *Der Spiegel*, November 30, 1992, no. 49, pp. 18–19 and the examples in December 7, 1992, no. 50, p. 34. The BfV suggested a total of 4500 left wing extremists 'ready for

violence, including the Revolutionary Cells, a well-known terrorist group.

49. Sometimes the skinheads also got blamed by both the Turkish groups and left wing opinion when in fact Turkish, Greek, Yugoslav, or *multikulti* streetgangs had fought each other or when macho Turkish gangs like the Black Panthers went on raids of gay-bashing. For details, see Klaus Farin and Eberhard Seidel-Pielen, *Krieg in den Städten: Jugendgangs in Deutschland*, Berlin: Rotbuch, 1991, pp. 19–45.

50. Skinhead and hooligan opinions, as far as they are cohesive, differ from neo-Nazi and old Nazi positions (see below) in many ways, beginning with such things as party loyalty and commitment to the neo-Nazi (and old Nazi) effort to win governmental power. Violent hostility to foreigners, the homeless, gays, and the handicapped is not quite the same as a political programme regarding these minorities. Beating up rival skin gangs or hooligans makes no sense to the political neo-Nazis who also fear political embarrassment and punishment far more than the skins and hoolies do.

51. Like the *New York Times* in the United States, the German media have been reluctant to look at these signs of German societal crisis. But see for example *Der Spiegel*, February 8, 1993, no. 6, p. 58 which reports the flight of students from the drugs and violence of public schools to the discipline and motivation of Catholic schools. Also December 7, 1992, no. 5, p. 29, October 12, 1992, no. 42, p. 36ff. and 52–79, on violence in an Essen school and the letters from teachers responding to this account on November 2, 1992, no. 45, pp. 7–8. Also no. 24, June 14, 1993. In one Frankfurt *Gymnasium*, one third of the students turned out to be armed in anticipation, they said, of having to defend themselves against attackers! There is also a boom of martial arts training among young students, for the same reason.

52. See for example, the account of a journalist's experiences with the children and PTAs in Switzerland, France, and Germany, 'Akademisch frei von klein auf', *Die Zeit*, January 15, 1993, no. 3, pp. 4–5 in which she also describes the political polarisation and stalemate between left-liberal and conservative parents in one German PTA.

53. See also *Der Spiegel*, January 11, 1993, no. 2, pp. 26, 46 and 'Wolernt man das denn?', *ibid.*, January 17, 1994, no. 3, pp. 70–74.

54. There is by now a large sociological literature in several languages. On Germany, see esp. Thomas Gehrmann, *Fussballrandale: Hooligans in Deutschland*, Essen: Klartext, 1990 and Klaus Farin and Jürgen Stark, *Das Fussball-Lesebuch*, Reinbek: Rowohlt, 1990. Also *Krieg in den Städten*, pp. 16–17, 54–6, 92, 104–7 where, among other statements, the Leipzig police is criticised for resolutely attacking out-of-town fans and hooligans and for separating opposing teams of hooligans instead of letting them fight each other *mano a mano*. Separation, the authors argue, has put a premium on lethal weapons such as stones, flare pistols, and other long distance missiles.

55. On the British youth scene and its continental derivatives, see also Diedrich Diedrichsen, Dick Hebdige, and Olaph-Dante Marx, *Schocker: Stile und Moden der Subkultur*, Reinbek: Rowohlt, 1983. By now there are skinheads in most European countries, including Eastern Europe where they tend

to be as nationalistic as those of Germany. They also exist in parts of the U.S., for example in Los Angeles. Turkish gang members often had actually grown up in Germany and felt suspended between a German society that was unfriendly and a homeland that they never knew. German attitudes ranged from suspicious law enforcement officers and a jingoistic press to the 'benign neglect' of a minority whose usefulness to the German economy has declined.

56. On East German skinheads, see esp. Frank Schumann, *Glatzen am Alex. Rechtsextremismus in der DDR*, Berlin: Fischerinsel, 1990 and Magistratsverwaltung für Jugend, Familie und Sport, Jugendförderung, *Jugend und Rechtsextremismus in Berlin-Ost. Fakten und Gegenstrategien*, Berlin: 1991, a collection of essays and reports by youth social workers who stress the 'programmatically very diffuse Nazi-skin groups' and their xenophobia and ruthless readiness for violence (p. 7). See also Peter Ködderitzsch and Leo A. Müller, *Rechtsextremismus in der DDR*, Göttingen: Lamuv, 1990.

57. The malleability of socialisation patterns at this early age has been shown on numerous examples of German youths moving from one group to another, rather different one, including from left to right and vice versa. In 1989, for example, an all-female Master Girl Crew of 14-to-16-year olds in Reineckendorf (Berlin) was turned from a career of robbery, theft, and assaults on young women in trains and stations (*S-Bahn*) by timely police intervention. See Farin and Seidel-Pielen, *Krieg in den Städten*, pp. 122–3.

58. There is a telling description of violence and destruction at a Schleswig–Holstein school (Kellinghusen) against a background of skinhead terror and the inability of the teachers to stop it in Bodo Morshäuser, *Hauptsache Deutsch*, Frankfurt: Suhrkamp, 1992, pp. 91–4n, 123–5. The fear of retaliation by violent gang youth in Germany, as in the U.S., creates a climate of intimidation that disables most efforts to 'reach' the young ruffians. The parents of the students are no help, and neither is the anti-authoritarian approach of the younger teachers (68er generation).

59. See also Ulrich Beck, *Risikogesellschaft. Auf dem Weg in eine andere Moderne*, Frankfurt: Suhrkamp, 1986, who, among other things, predicts the dawning of a 'new cluelessness (*neue Ratlosigkeit*)' in place of the cognitive and value map of the industrial revolution. There are, of course, also cases where middle-class families are involved, but the lack of communication and of parental involvement makes them just as dysfunctional as those racked by divorce, alcoholism, and physical abuse.

60. The communist social control system of the GDR youth apparently began to slacken as early as the beginning of the eighties when, in addition to spontaneous ecological and pacifistic groups, the first skinheads were observed. By the mid–eighties, soccer hooligans were a prominent feature of big games and neither right wing phenomenon was publicly acknowledged or repressed by the regime. The years 1987 and 1988 saw considerable connections and cooperation between the Eastern skins and Fascho groups and the West German action groups such as the FAP and Kühnen's ANS. See Ködderitzsch and Müller, op. cit., pp. 15–18.

61. See also Wilhelm Heitmeyer, *Rechtsextremismus Orientierungen bei*

jugendlichen: Empirische Untersuchungen und Erklärungsmuster,
Weinheim: 1989. A controversial recent movie '*Stau – jetzt geht's los*'
(freeway traffic jam – let's have a happening) depicts the psychodynamics
of spontaneous violent combustion among skinheads well. It is a kind of
group version of the American movie *Falling Down* and shares its racial
and anti-immigrant touches, as well as its absence of a specific political
consciousness. Hans-Joachim Maaz coined the provocative formula
'*Gefühlsstau*' (plugged up emotions) to describe the psychodynamics of
East German authoritarian education up to the fall of the Wall. Forced to
be free and democratic, many students and recent graduates have sought
an emotional escape in the right wing hordes, their drinking bouts, and
heroic fetishes and neo-Nazi symbols. West German 'colonisation' and
imposition of liberty aggravated the psychosocial legacy of the communist regime (see the essay by Baylis, above).

62. For example, see Farin and Seidel-Pielen, *Krieg in den Städten*, pp. 49,
53, 55, 69–75, 86–90, and 148. It should be emphasised that such initial
reluctance does not necessarily mean long-range resistance or immunity.

63. There is a consensus among historians and other specialists on German
national socialism and other European interwar fascist movements that it
is important not to confuse fascist systems in power with the pre-power
movements. Accession to power, by whatever means, tends to change
the character of the original movement with vast additions of opportun-
ists, elements of the previous establishment, and foreign supporters and
alliances. See, for example, Stanley G. Payne, *Fascism: Comparison and
Definition*, Madison, Wis.: University of Wisconsin Press, 1980, chap. 1
or Larsen et al., *Who Were the Fascists*, *passim*.

64. See also Merkl, *The Making of a Stormtrooper*, Princeton, N.J.: Princeton
University Press, 1980, pp. 131–2, Zoltan M. Szaz, *Germany's Eastern
Frontier*, Chicago: Regnery, 1960, pp. 50–2, 59, 126, and Gerhard L.
Weinberg, *The Foreign Policy of Hitler's Germany*, Bloomington, Ind.:
University of Indiana Press, 1970, pp. 87–94, 107–8, 111, and 114–17.

65. It is true that German 1950 statutes put the advocacy of war or hatred
against nations under penalty, but this does not quite explain the matter
either, because the skinheads also express strong national hostility and
have been known to attack, for example, Poles and Czechs not only in
Germany, but even the border police of both countries.

66. See Merkl, *German Unification*, pp. 404–12.

67. See, for example, A. James Gregor, *Interpretations of Fascism*, Morristown,
N.J.: General Learning Press, 1974, chap. 5 and Henry A. Turner, ed.,
Nazism and the Third Reich, New York: Quadrangle Books, 1972, chap. 4.

68. Because of the deliberate underrepresentation of working-class voters at
the state and local levels of the pre-1918 empire, the introduction of
general adult suffrage in 1919 at all levels gave the German bourgeoisie
the frightening impression that its larger towns and cities were indeed
taken over by working-class parties. See Merkl, *The Making of a
Stormtrooper*, pp. 123, 125, and 138–44, 148–59. The Italian situation
where prewar electoral laws had disenfranchised the socialist voters was
quite similar in this respect.

69. For an account of Weimar paramilitary groups and their political violence,

see Merkl, *The Making of a Stormtrooper*, chap. 2.

70. The anti-constitutional parties in addition to the NSDAP and the communists (KPD) – which together received a majority of the popular vote in July 1932 – also included the German Nationalists (DNVP) and, at times, even the German People's party (DVP). For a succinct description of the causes of the fall of the Weimar Republic, see Karl-Dietrich Bracher, *The German Dictatorship: The Origins, Structure, and Effects of National Socialism*, New York: Praeger, 1970, chapters 1–4 and other works by the same author.

71. The current recession in Germany is mostly stagnation, with economic growth having dropped to –1 per cent only in the last quarter of 1992. The Great Depression came within a few years of the introduction of German unemployment insurance and nearly destroyed the weak social net with its massive unemployment figures.

72. Some representatives of German law enforcement agencies disagree that there is a sufficient legal basis for prosecuting neo-Nazis, aside from those caught red-handed after violent crimes. See the interview with BKA director Hans-Ludwig Zachert in *Der Spiegel*, January 4, 1993, no. 1, pp. 40–6 and the discussion of modified neo-Nazi symbols and flags, *ibid.*, December 21, 1992, no. 52, pp. 41–52. Among the more sanguinary crimes of 1992 was a bomb exploded in a trash basket at the *Altstadtfest* of Hanover (August 30) which injured 16 people. The incident, presumably caused by neo-Nazis, was reminiscent of the Octoberfest bombing of 1980 in Munich which killed 17, including the perpetrator, and injured another 52. Another incident involved the discovery of enough dynamite at an asylum hostel in Baden–Württemberg to blow up the 70 people in it.

73. The problem of left wing opposition to tough emergency rules is very real precisely because the state of emergency has been abused by the right wing governments in the past and because the moderate left has always been anxious to protect left wing demonstrations and disturbances from the police and police violence.

74. Senator Krüger presented these comments in a talk at the Los Angeles Goethe Institute on January 28, 1993. He grew up under communism and was trained as a minister, in theology, before becoming one of the youngest municipal officials in a German metropolis.

75. When asked recently whether there were enough recreational facilities in town for young people, only 8 per cent of East Germans answered in the affirmative. In West Germany, it was 57 per cent. See *Der Spiegel*, January 18, 1993, no. 3, p. 56.

76. To counteract the universal breakdown of modern families in Germany, Krüger suggested, family ties need to be repaired and maintained, for example, by punishing runaway fathers. Families must be persuaded to contribute to the public life of their neighbourhood and community. East German families have suffered from the stress of unemployment and lack of housing, and women had a difficult time to adjust to life under capitalism, that is with very few jobs and childcare centres (see Joyce Mushaben, above). The schools have suffered from truancy and needed better anti-fascist instruction than the rigid and authoritarian anti-fascist line of the forties which was a kind of a 'fascist anti-fascism', pillorying all 'class

enemies' and liberal points of view. For a better way, the senator pointed to the (SPD-affiliated) *Falken* groups who have taken hundreds of youth to the site of Auschwitz, and attracted hundreds more who would like to go there, in the middle of Poland.

77. *Der Spiegel*, January 4, 1993, no. 1, pp. 29–30.
78. Fortunately, they never developed an appetite for dismantling their social welfare state, in spite of the Anglo-American rhetoric. Instead, there were only some minor cutbacks and an emphasis on private property, privatisation, and private initiative in the marketplace: possessive individualism plus the social net.
79. According to an East German *Bundestag* deputy, Kersten Wetzel, there is a 'social infrastructure' for youth services in the West but not in the East, in the aftermath of the collapse of communist youth guidance. Parliament has now passed substantial additional appropriations for non-governmental youth services (AFI), and, in particular, for an anti-violence programme addressed to radical youth. See Konrad-Adenauer- Stiftung, *German Democracy on Guard: Confronting Extremism. Neo-Nazism, and Xenophobia*, pp. 25–6.

Index

and federalism, 224–7
Kohl in, 48
women in, 87
and Yugoslavia, 51
Partnership for Peace, 367
PDS/Communist Party, 28n., 51
on anti-foreign violence, 10
assets of, 113
and East German interests, 246,
256
in local politics, 161
survival of, 118, 122, 166n.
peacekeeping missions, German,
72–4, 194, 197–8
Poehl, Karl-Otto, 391, 394
pogroms
Hoyerswerda, 443
Rostock-Lichtenhagen, 447–448
in US, 449
postindustrial, *see* postmaterialism
postmaterialism, Greens and, 307–8
Poland, 34, 46, 71, 244
and asylum policy, 12
attitudes towards Germany, 2–4,
374
in EU, 362–3, 399
and German anti-foreign violence,
430
in 1920s, 462
and Oder–Neisse line, 26–7n., 56,
221
purges in, 117–9
solidarity, 247, 284
Potsdam Agreements, 221
privatisation
of government services, 144
laissez-faire critique of, 178
socialist critique of, 177
see also chapter 9
purges, of communists, 17–18
and anti-radicals' decree, 132,
147, 256
see also chapters 6 and 7; anti-
radicals decree
purges, of East German academics
female, 92–3
GDR cultural elite, 108
at universities, 253–4, 261n.
see also chapters 5, 6, and 7

purges, of GDR officials, 114–15,
437
and civil service, 134, 139–40
high GDR officials, 246, 250
SPD and, 145–8
and unification, 118–9, 129
see also chapters 6 and 7

Rabin, Yitzhak, 10–11, 448
racism, 29n., 438
in Britain, 431
in East Germany, 433
in France, 431
in GDR, 433, 476n.
German opinion against, 11, 452
at Hoyerswerda, 443
Kohl and, 217
and the left, 292
reaction against, 351–2, 437
in US, 431
US connection of, 431, 449, 454
in 1991/1992, 213–14
radical right
and anti-foreign violence, 209, 213
in East Germany, 435–7
fragmentation of, 464
Greens and, 305
at Hoyerswerda, 443
and moderate right, 273–5
recruiters of skinheads, 470
republicans, 21
voters of, 352, 429, 432
see also neo-Nazism;
Republicans; *and chapter 23*
Reagan, Ronald
Reaganism, 468, 473
social policies of, 475n.
refugees, Eastern European, 13, 71,
345, 348
in 1920s, 428, 465
from Russia, 355
from Yugoslavia, 398–9
see also chapter 18
refugees, German, 3, 26–7n.
from East Germany, 212, 223,
347–8
expellees, 346–7, 462
numbers of, 356n.
from Russia, 419